Competition Law of Britain and the Common Market

VALENTINE KORAH, LL.M., Ph.D.
Reader in English Law, University College London

With a Foreword by The Rt Hon. Lord Diplock
Lord of Appeal in Ordinary
Formerly President of the Restrictive Practices Court

London
Paul Elek

New York
Matthew Bender

1975

First published as *Monopolies and Restrictive Practices*, Penguin,
Foundations of Law series, 1968

This revised and enlarged edition published in Great Britain 1975 by
Elek Books Limited,
54–58 Caledonian Road,
London N1 9RN.

Published in the U.S.A. by
Matthew Bender & Co. Inc. of
235 East 45th Street,
New York, New York 10017

ISBN 0 236 31031 3

Library of Congress Catalog Card No. 75–108 18

Printed in Great Britain by
Unwin Brothers Limited,
The Gresham Press, Old Woking, Surrey
A member of the Staples Printing Group

Contents

Contents

Contents

Contents

Contents

Foreword

Much water has flowed under the bridges in London and in Brussels since the first edition of this book appeared in 1968 under the title *Monopolies and Restrictive Practices*. At the time when I am writing this Foreword it is not yet certain that the flow in Brussels as it affects the United Kingdom may not be reversed. The referendum to determine whether this country is to remain within the Common Market has not yet been held. To a constitutional lawyer the adoption of this method of deciding a question so vital to the future of the nation would seem to involve an abdication of the sovereignty of parliament more fundamental than any transfer of law-making powers to the Community which opponents of the Common Market claim to be the consequence of accession to the Treaty of Rome. Nevertheless I have sufficient faith in the instinctive common sense of the British people to believe that what Mrs Korah has written about the Competition Law of the Common Market in Part Three of this work will still be directly applicable to industrial and commercial undertakings in the United Kingdom when the result of the referendum is known.

The competition law of Britain is a plant of recent growth. In the course of the nineteenth century the courts of common law resigned their claim to exercise control over agreements that were restrictive of business competition. They were content to accept that business men knew what was best for business and that what was best for business was best for the nation too. In the depression of the nineteen-twenties and thirties current economic theories in this country, in contrast to those in the United States, commended the rationalization of industry by mergers and cartels. Such limited statutory intervention as there had been in the field of competition before 1948 was designed to restrain it in the worst hit industries of agriculture and coal mining and, in the case of the latter, to promote mergers of undertakings.

The turning point came with the creation of the first Monopolies and Restrictive Practices Commission in 1948. Its early reports upon restrictive practices drew the attention of Government to how wide-spread these had become; but it was not until the year before the making of the Treaty of Rome that restrictive trade practices were made subject to effective legal control in the United Kingdom by the passing of the Restrictive Trade Practices Act 1956.

The legal control of business practices which have the effect of limiting competition in the market for goods or services confronts the legislator with a dilemma. One of the most valuable features of Mrs Korah's book is as a corrective to the view that all cartels and all concentrations of market power are *ipso facto* contrary to the public interest – a view which the decisions of the British Restrictive Practices Court may well have tended to foster. Once it is accepted that some cartels and some concentrations of market power may promote economic progress and benefit consumers of goods or users of services, the dilemma lies in the choice of the most appropriate body to undertake the task of identifying cartels and concentrations which ought to be permitted and the most appropriate procedure for carrying out the task.

There can be little dispute that the appropriate body should include, whether as members or advisers, economists and persons with practical experience of industry and commerce. In the United Kingdom persons with these qualifications are full members of the Restrictive Practices Court and of the Monopolies and Mergers Commission. Despite the initial doubts of the judiciary the composition of the Court has proved no obstacle to its adherence to the judicial procedure. The members who are not lawyers by profession enable the court to take 'judicial notice' of many facts of business life that would be beyond the ken of any judge who sits in the Restrictive Practices Court, at any rate when he was first appointed. It is not the composition of the body but the nature of the question which it has to answer that dictates the procedure best suited to its purpose: investigation and inquiry, as in the case of the Monopolies and Mergers Commission, or the adversarial judicial process as in the case of the Restrictive Practices Court.

The judicial process provides a reliable, though long and costly, means of ascertaining facts about what has happened in the past. In the adversarial system followed in the United Kingdom the facts to which the attention of the Court is directed are confined to those which the parties themselves adduce to lend support to their respective contentions. So it is not surprising that with the growing expertise of lawyers practising before the Court the assessment by the Court of the effect of what would appear to be similar restrictions in not dissimilar industries should not remain unchanged. But the ascertainment of facts about what had happened in the past is only an initial step towards a decision that depends on predictions as to what would happen in the future if on the one hand the restriction were removed, or on the other hand it were retained. It is perhaps inevitable that a court faced with the unaccustomed task of prediction should take refuge in the concept of onus of proof as the Restrictive Practices Court was encouraged to do by the terms in which the statute was drafted; and here again the way in which the evidence and the arguments are presented may be the decisive factor in the conclusion reached by the Court.

Mrs Korah's penetrating, though polite, analysis of the major judgments of the Restrictive Practices Court confirms me in my suspicion that the judicial process does not provide the most appropriate method of deciding what restrictions upon competition are justified as being in the public interest. And if this is so in the comparatively simple field of restrictive agreements between separate undertakings, it is the more so in the complex field of monopolies and mergers which the British legislator has never entrusted to a court. Nevertheless the Restrictive Practices Court has served the wider purpose of changing the attitude of British businessmen to restrictions upon competition. It was only those few agreements of which it could be plausibly argued that they could escape through one or other of the 'gateways' that came before the Court at all; and the plausibility of those arguments diminished with successive decisions of the Court. In the result there has been brought about a virtual abandonment of the type of restrictive agreement that was not exempted from registration under the Restrictive Trade Practices Act 1956. Though much of what was exempted under the Act will fall within the scope of the Community rules on competition, acceptance of the rules will not involve so great a change in business practices in the United Kingdom as it would have done if our accession to the Common Market had taken place in 1957 when the Treaty of Rome was drawn.

The authors of the Treaty laid down the rules on competition applying to undertakings in much broader terms than those used by the draftsmen of the contemporaneous British legislation. Articles 85 and 86 leave to the bodies charged with the task of determining whether the rules have been complied with in particular instances much greater latitude in making their own value judgments upon the economic consequences of concerted action by undertakings and the exercise of market power than is entrusted to the British Restrictive Practices Court. The Treaty itself by article 87 conferred upon the Council the power to lay down detailed rules for the application of the exempting provisions in article 85 and to define the respective functions of the Commission and the Court of Justice in giving effect to the rules so laid down.

By regulation 17 the Council conferred upon the Commission the primary function of determining whether what was done or proposed to be done by an undertaking was contrary to article 85 or 86. This is, according to English legal concepts, a quasi-judicial function but as an executive body the Commission was able to adopt the procedure described by Mrs Korah. This is predominantly investigatory and more akin to that adopted in this country by the Monopolies and Mergers Commission than to that followed by the Restrictive Practices Court. For my part, for the reasons already suggested, I believe that this permits of a more wide-ranging objective market analysis than is practicable under the procedures available to a court.

From decisions of the Commission there is an appeal to the European Court of Justice. Broadly speaking the grounds of such an appeal are not dissimilar to those on which the English High Court reviews decisions of administrative tribunals; but one cannot read Mrs Korah's analysis of the judgments of the European Court of Justice on the rules on competition without becoming aware that the Court exercises a much wider jurisdiction to examine the 'merits' of a decision of the Commission than an English court would think appropriate in reviewing decisions of administrative tribunals.

The reason for the difference in approach can I believe be accounted for by the fact that there is another route by which disputes about the effect of the Community rules on competition are brought before the European Court of Justice. Articles 85 and 86 were among the first provisions of the Treaty of Rome which were held to be directly applicable in the Member States. They form part of the domestic law of Member States and litigants in national courts can rely upon the invalidity of agreements made, or action taken, contrary to the prohibitions contained in these two articles. Where such reliance raises a question of interpretation of the Treaty the national court may, and if it is a court of final instance must, refer the question to the European Court of Justice under article 177. Such a reference invokes what is in the nature of an original jurisdiction of the European Court in contrast to its appellate jurisdiction under regulation 17. Whether the kind of agreement or action that is impugned falls within the prohibitions contained in the articles depends upon an assessment of its economic effect; but the reference may come from the national court to the European Court without the benefit of any prior market analysis. Although the jurisdiction of the European Court is limited to interpretation, it is inevitable that in interpreting what is expressed in such wide terms as those used in the Treaty, the Court should be driven, upon material that may not always be adequate, to form its own value judgment as to the economic consequences of particular kinds of restrictions upon competition or particular ways of exercising market power.

Some of the judgments commented upon in Part Three of this volume were given upon references by national courts under article 177, others upon appeals from decisions made by the Commission after full investigation pursuant to its own procedure under regulation 17; but there is no obvious contrast between the Court's own approach to its functions under these two disparate jurisdictions.

So in the Common Market there is no clear cut separation between the use of the investigatory procedure (by the Commission) and the judicial procedure (by the Court of Justice) for deciding whether Community rules on competition have been broken in particular instances. Sometimes these procedures follow one another; sometimes the judicial is used alone. In either case it is the value judgment of the Court upon the economic consequences of the impugned agreement or activity that ultimately prevails. My personal experience in the Restrictive Practices Court in the United Kingdom leads me to believe that the kind of market analysis that the Commission can undertake in the course of its investigatory procedure is an essential aid to any court which has to form a value judgment of this kind. It is to be hoped that the case law of the European Court of Justice in appeals from decisions of the Commission will in course of time reduce the need for references by national courts on competition law which leave the European Court to form its judgment without the help of this kind of factual analysis.

The Common Market rules on competition now interpenetrate our national legislation on restrictive trade practices and monopolies and mergers. The interpenetration is bound to grow greater if, as I assume, the United Kingdom continues to form part of the European Communities. To those concerned in the management of large scale enterprises or dealings in patents, trade marks and 'Know-how', and to the lawyers who have to advise them, the combined effect may well appear to be the creation of a legal labyrinth. The present volume charts a clearer path through it than has previously been available to English lawyers. It does not claim to answer all the questions that may arise for decision by the E.E.C. Commission or by the European Court of Justice. It does not shirk the difficulties which flow from the contrasting approaches to the problems of competition adopted by the various bodies, investigatory and judicial, charged with the task of applying the law both in the national and in the supra-national community field. What it sets out to do is to combine a scholarly analysis of the significant decisions of those bodies with practical guide lines as to what conduct is likely or unlikely to satisfy the various criteria of lawfulness. In doing this Mrs Korah will have earned the gratitude alike of businessmen and students of the law.

Diplock

Preface

In this book I have set out to describe the British and Common
Market legislation under which the acquisition and exercise of
market power is controlled, and to consider the kind of tribunal
most appropriate to assess such issues. I have attempted to do this
in such a way that the reader may be able to appreciate the circumstances in which various kinds of collaboration and restrictive
practices are likely to operate against the public interest. My hope is
that this will make the book more interesting, and that it will
also help businessmen and their advisers to defend their restrictive
agreements and practices, both formally before the three bodies that
are required to assess the public interest, and informally to the
officials concerned. Indeed it may help them to frame their agreements and policies so as not to operate in a way that is viewed by the
legislation and the bodies charged with its administration as contrary
to the public interest. It is hoped that this approach will also help
readers to understand and predict likely future developments in
policy. Throughout, I have devoted a disproportionate amount of
space to the controversial issues, omitting much detail which can be
found in larger works or derived from the regulations and cases
mentioned. I have attempted to stimulate and help understanding
rather than to produce a comprehensive treatise, which would have
been extremely costly. For those wishing to pursue the study either
of competition law in general, or of particular topics, I have, however, prepared a select bibliography, mainly of works in English. I
would have liked to set out all the relevant legislation in the Appendix,
but it would have occupied a great deal of space and added substantially to the cost of the book. I have therefore compromised and
set out only excerpts. The authentic English text of the Common
Market Treaty has been used: but that of the regulations made
thereunder has been altered to incorporate subsequent amendments.

I am also responsible for incorporating the amendments to the restrictive practices legislation.

Restrictions on competition in the U.K. are currently assessed by three quite separate bodies, each required to apply different criteria. The Monopolies and Mergers Commission and its predecessors have, since 1957, been confined mainly to deciding whether the existence of a monopoly situation, or since 1965 of a merger, may be expected to operate against the public interest. The criteria prescribed are very general and not exhaustive, so the Commission has been left to work out for itself the circumstances in which various steps taken by a dominant firm to exploit or maintain its market power are likely to harm the public, and its reports have played an important role in educating the public. The Commission habitually analyses the market in which the dominant firm operates, and describes in some detail the arguments for and against the existence of market power and the conduct of the dominant firm.

Since 1957, agreements between undertakings carrying on business in the U.K. and relating to the prices to be charged for goods and other specified matters which are particularly likely to restrict competition have been subject to registration and most were condemned by the Restrictive Practices Court within eight years. Few registrable agreements are now being made if it is thought likely that they will be referred to the Court. Although in form the U.K. legislation forbids outright only one collective restrictive practice, the chances of other restrictive agreements surviving a reference to the Court are so slim, and the consequences of failure so serious, that firms are advised not to make agreements subject to its jurisdiction. Businessmen and their advisers are now more concerned to ensure that agreements do not come within the scope of the legislation, than to defend them on their merits.

The first edition of this book, published in 1968 by Penguin Education in its *Foundations of Law* series, under the title *Monopolies and Restrictive Practices*, was concerned with the powers and experience of Commission and Court. Since then the British law has been amended by the Fair Trading Act and the U.K. has joined the Common Market. The first edition became out of date and is now out of print. In this edition, the text has been substantially revised to take into account not only the statutory changes, but also the rather different questions being asked of the Commission.

Even more important perhaps than the changes in British law is the accession of the U.K. to the European Communities. The home market is being extended by the progressive abolition of customs and other barriers to trade between member states, to cover the territories of eight other countries. Indeed, there will be no customs barriers between the Common Market and certain other countries, such as the former members of the European Free Trade Association. Consequently, there are likely to be more firms in the relevant market for all products that can be easily transported to and from the Continent. Firms are also forbidden to make agreements restricting competition within the Common Market, or to abuse a dominant position enjoyed within a substantial part of it. I have therefore added three chapters concerned with these rules and considered certain common commercial transactions in the light of both the British and Common Market law. I have, however, hardly mentioned the European Coal and Steel Community, as it affects only firms concerned in producing these products, most of them nationalized, and those who do business with them.

When I decided that it was time to prepare a new edition, I found that Penguin no longer regarded this kind of book as appropriate to the economics of paperback publishing, so with their consent and goodwill I agreed with Elek that they should publish this edition. I hope that their first venture into the field of law books encourages them to enter this market permanently. I should like to thank Mr Charles Clark, then of Penguin Education, for persuading me in 1966 to write the first edition. My relationship with Penguin has always been very pleasant and constructive and of great value to me. I should like to thank Professor Harry Street, Editor of the *Foundations of Law* series, and Penguin for arranging a release of copyright extremely rapidly when I requested it. Penguin Education has played an important role in legal education, both for those who are studying or practising the law, and for those whose interest is less technical. It continues to do so, although on a smaller scale than before.

I should also like to thank at least some of the people who in different ways have helped me with both editions of this book. I was delighted when, despite the many claims on his time, Lord Diplock, a former President of the Restrictive Practices Court, agreed to write a foreword. In relation to the rest of the book, my most fundamental debt is to Professor Yamey of the London School of Economics. Since 1964 we have collaborated in running a course for the London LL.M. on Monopoly, Competition and the Law, and I have learnt a great deal from him, as well as from our students and those invited to lead a discussion with them. Professor Yamey also read a draft of the whole of the first edition as well as of parts of the second, and made many excellent suggestions, particularly about those sections where economics are important. He made the most detailed proposals about the minimum of economics required for the introduction.

My thanks are also due to the Solicitor of the Department of Employment and Productivity, as it was called in 1969, for arranging for me to work temporarily as a civil service lawyer, mainly helping to prepare the Commission of Industry and Manpower Bill. That bill, which would have consolidated the monopolies and mergers legislation, did not reach the statute book, owing to the dissolution of Parliament in June 1970. While I was a civil servant, Mr W. C. Beckett, for whom I worked directly, stimulated my interest in the administrative law aspects of the subject and encouraged me to ponder. I learned a great deal from the experience.

I should also like to thank various experts who have read the whole or substantial parts of the second edition in draft. Mr Graham Child, who, with Mr Bellamy, wrote the successful practitioners' book *Common Market Law of Competition* in 1973, was kind enough to read the whole and made a great many well-founded and constructive criticisms of the British as well as of the Common Market chapters. Mr Peter Cottis of Lucas Industries read all the first edition and large parts of the second, and made useful suggestions on both occasions. Mrs Elizabeth Freeman of University College made several helpful suggestions about the Common Market chapters. The parts of the book where industrial property rights are involved (the end of Chapter 4 and parts of Chapters 8 and 9) were read, more than once, by Professor Cornish of the London School of Economics and are greatly improved in consequence. I sent the chapters on the Common Market law to officials of the Commission of the European Communities in Brussels. Although I gave them only two weeks in which to comment, they divided the work between Dr Benini, Mr Daltrop, M. Daoût, Madame Espion, Dr Schröter and Mr Wright, all of the Department of Competition. Each of them made most helpful suggestions. My debt to most of these officials and to their legal advisers, especially Signor Marchini-Camia, is really of longer standing. For several years I have enjoyed many discussions, received hospitality, transcripts of texts, and helpful suggestions about draft articles and notes that have since been published.

While all these people have been kind enough to devote time to the unrewarding task of improving a draft that was not their own and have been of the greatest assistance, I hasten to add that they are in no way responsible for the final draft, which none of them ever saw before publication. The remaining inaccuracies, lack of balance, infelicities of style and so forth are my sole responsibility.

My thanks are also due to Professor Clive Schmitthoff, the Editor of the *Journal of Business Law*, not only for encouraging me to develop my interest in the subject at a time when it was less important than it is now, but also for his liberal attitude towards copyright in the section editorials on restrictive trade practices, which I have been contributing for a decade. I should also like to thank Dr Neville March-Hunnings, Editor of the Common Market Law

Reports, not only for allowing me to cite from the published translations but also for letting me see some draft translations before they were finally revised for publication. I have taken advantage of this generosity, and most of the quotations from Common Market cases are taken from the C.M.L.R. I am also indebted to Miss Lise Goulding for typing most of the script, and in particular for sorting out the large number of troublesome insertions and amendments with which she has been faced. Without her loyal, constructive and intelligent help, this book could not have been prepared for publication so rapidly. Finally, I should like to thank my publishers. I contacted Paul Elek Ltd shortly before Easter 1974 and signed a contract in May of that year. I was given time to prepare the new edition and already it was published the following summer. Those who have had dealings with other publishers will envy me this speed, which has greatly reduced the amount of rewriting necessary to ensure that the book is up to date on publication. I should also like to thank Unwin Brothers for their careful handling of a complicated manuscript.

Mr John Chesshyre made many constructive suggestions for improvements in style and has reacted most flexibly and sensibly to the various problems that inevitably arise when a text is being prepared for publication. He has made it possible for me to incorporate developments in the law that occurred up till early November, and the case *Centrafarm* v. *Sterling* and *Winthrop*, decided by the Community Court in that month, has been taken into account in the section on the conflict between industrial property rights and the free movement of goods within the Common Market. Any subsequent changes will be noted only in the tables of cases and reports.

5 King's Bench Walk, Temple   Valentine Korah.

For my loves —
Angela, Hermione, Leonora,
Margaret, Alex and Richard

Glossary

AGGREGATED REBATES. Discounts to classes of customers based on the total bought by each customer in an earlier period from all members of an association and not just from the individual seller. See pp. 157–8.

ARRANGEMENT. Term used in section 6(3) of Restrictive Trade Practices Act 1956 to include forms of collusion looser than contract, such as the mutual arousing of expectations in circumstances where it would infringe a moral or legal duty not to give effect to the expectations. See pp. 94–9.

BOARD OF TRADE. Government department that was responsible for making references to the Monopolies and Mergers Commission and for making orders or taking undertakings after an adverse conclusion. In 1969, its functions were transferred to the Secretary of State; in 1974 they were being exercised by Mrs Shirley Williams (see p. 20). She also has power to extend the operation of the Restrictive Practices Act to services as well as to information agreements relative to goods or services, and to give general directions to the Director.

CARTEL. Combination of firms to restrict competition. See p. 5.

COMPANY. Concept used to enable persons and assets to be combined. See pp. 50–2.

COMPLEX MONOPOLY SITUATION. Technical expression used in Fair Trading Act to cover the situation where the one-quarter test is satisfied by a number of firms who restrict competition between themselves or others, provided that this is not done by an agreement to which Part I of the 1956 Act applies. See p. 22.

CONCERTED PRACTICES. The concept used in article 85 of

the Rome Treaty to perform much the same function as 'arrangement' in the Act of 1956 (see pp. 174–8). There seems to be no requirement that it would infringe any sort of duty to fail to give effect to the expectation.

CONSPIRACY. A civil law wrong of combining to injure by unlawful means or with malicious intent, entitling the person injured to damages and an injunction. See p. 2.

DEBENTURE. Loan made to a company, usually evidenced by writing, at a fixed rate of interest. See p. 50.

DEPRECIATION. Apportionment of capital costs over expected life of asset. See Note on Cost Concepts, p. 47.

DIRECTOR GENERAL OF FAIR TRADING. A new office established under the Fair Trading Act 1973. The Director may make references to the Monopolies and Mergers Commission, he chairs the mergers panel, and he has succeeded to the functions of the Registrar. He will normally negotiate undertakings after an adverse report from the Monopolies and Mergers Commission. He is independent of the Government in that no Minister is directly responsible for his actions. See p. 21.

DISCOVERY. Order by court to produce documents.

DOMINANT FIRM. In general usage, a firm enjoying market power. See p. 3.

In relation to the monopolies legislation of the U.K., a firm (there may be more than one) in whose favour a monopoly situation (as defined in the Fair Trading Act) exists, i.e. to, for or by whom a quarter of the products specified in the reference are supplied, either in the U.K. or any part of it. See p. 22.

Article 86 of the Rome Treaty prohibits the abuse by one or more undertakings of a dominant position in the Common Market or a substantial part of it. To tell whether a firm is dominant a market analysis is required. See pp. 199–200.

EQUITY SHARE CAPITAL. Share capital carrying the right to participate in the dividends of a company, if declared, and in net assets on liquidation. Usually carries rights to vote in general meetings. See p. 50.

EXCLUSIVE DEALING. Refers to arrangements for distributing goods whereby a supplier, usually the manufacturer, agrees to sell them to a particular franchised dealer, and not to supply anyone else within an area allocated to that dealer. The dealer usually agrees to promote the goods and not to sell competing goods and, until the U.K. joined the Common Market, a British dealer usually also agreed not to sell outside the territory allocated to him. See pp. 104–6, 230–8.

EXHAUSTION.   A concept under some national laws, according to which some industrial property rights may not be exercised in respect of goods that have been put into circulation by or with the consent of the owner of the rights. Sometimes only a sale within the country exhausts the rights. In respect of trade marks under English law, sale abroad may also do so. See p. 215.

FILLETED AGREEMENT.   Agreement from which all registrable restrictions have been removed.

HISTORIC VALUATION.   See Note on Cost Concepts, p. 47.

HORIZONTAL AGREEMENT OR MERGER.   Agreement or merger between firms at same level of trade or industry.

INFORMATION AGREEMENT.   Agreement to inform competitors of prices that will be charged, paid, etc. See also 'Post-notification agreement'.

INJUNCTION.   Order of court requiring person to do, or more often not to do, something.

'KNOWHOW'.   Drawings, formulae, skills of technicians and other aspects of information, often confidential. It may or may not be protected by patent. See p. 110.

LIQUIDATION.   Process by which company's affairs are wound up, its debts paid and any surplus assets distributed to the shareholders. See p. 51.

MONOPOLY.   Situation where market power is held by a single firm or firms. See Dominant firm.

MONOPSONY.   Situation where market power is enjoyed by a buyer. See p. 8.

OLIGOPOLY.   Market situation in which there are few sellers who react to each other's market conduct. See p. 8.

OLIGOPSONY.   Market situation in which there are few buyers who react to each other's market conduct. See pp. 8–9.

PARALLEL IMPORTS.   Mechanism relied upon to lead towards equalization of prices in the Common Market. If there are large price differentials between member states, it is likely to pay someone to buy in the low price state and sell in the high price one.

PATENT. Gives the right to prevent others from using the invention covered by the patent. 'Using the invention' includes the manufacture, sale or use of patented articles or the use of a patented process. See pp. 106–7, 215, 226.

PATENT LICENCE. Permission to use the invention.

PATENTS, MULTIPLE PARALLEL LICENCES. Phrase used by Commission of European Communities in its Christmas Message to describe licences granted to different persons under parallel patents.

PATENTS, PARALLEL. Situation where patents are obtained under the law of several member states in respect of virtually the same invention by the same person or group of companies.

PATENT, RIGHT INHERENT IN. Theory according to which it is the patent that restricts competition, so that a limited licence to make specified quantities of articles by using the invention, or to make or sell in a circumscribed area, or for a particular field of use, is not an agreement restricting competition. See pp. 242–3.

PATENTEE. Holder, or owner of patent.

PER SE ILLEGAL. Illegal in itself: wrongful without any possibility of justification.

POST-NOTIFICATION AGREEMENT. Agreement to inform about prices, turnover, and so forth, after the transactions are completed.

PRICE LEADER. Firm which initiates a price change in an oligopolistic market, either on a single occasion or frequently.

PROSECUTION ON INDICTMENT. Criminal proceedings leading to a trial by jury.

PRELIMINARY RULING. Ruling of the Community Court under jurisdiction granted by article 177 of the Treaty of Rome, enabling it to answer questions relating to the validity or interpretation of the Treaty or subordinate legislation made under it, when so asked by a national court. See pp. 171–2.

QUANTITATIVE RESTRICTION (or QUOTA). Restriction on quantity to be produced or imported. Both under section 6 of Act of 1956 and under article 30 of Rome Treaty, the term includes a nil quota, or absolute prohibition on making, supplying or importing respectively.

REGISTRAR of Restrictive Trading Agreements. Official who from 1956 to 1973 prepared the register of agreements subject to registration under Part I of the Act of 1956 and was responsible for referring them to the Restrictive Practices Court. He had similar functions under the Resale Prices Act 1964. His functions were transferred to the Director in 1973, when the only Registrar, Sir Rupert Sich, retired.

RESTRICTION. Under the Restrictive Trade Practices Act 1956, restrictions on conduct defined in sections 6–8. The prohibition in article 85 of the Treaty of Rome relates to restrictions of competition rather than on conduct.

SHARES. See 'Equity share capital'.

TENDER. Bid, or offer, to supply or acquire a commodity or service, made in response to invitation.

TRUSTEE. Owner of assets who can be compelled to use them for the benefit of someone or something else.

UNDERTAKING. Promise given to a court, breach of which is contempt of court, for which person giving the undertaking may be fined or imprisoned. If given to the Minister after a report of the Monopolies and Mergers Commission, there is no immediate sanction for its breach (pp. 29–35). Also the expression used for a firm in the Common Market legislation (see pp. 173–4).

UNIT OF ACCOUNT. Monetary unit used in Common Market legislation, defined by article 18 of the Financial Regulation of 15 November 1960, in terms of the gold value of the U.S. dollar before its devaluation in relation to gold in 1971.

VERTICAL AGREEMENT OR MERGER. Agreement or merger between a supplier and its customer.

1: Introduction

Until the beginning of the First World War, the economy of the United Kingdom was one of the most competitive in the world. Goods could be imported from abroad without customs duties being levied on them and exporters were able to sell abroad in competition with protected home industries, although they had to pay customs duties not levied on locally produced goods. Yet, by the end of the Second World War, many people of all political persuasions were deeply concerned that the economy might be riddled with practices adopted by manufacturers and traders to restrict competition and enable them to make a profit without being very efficient. Two reports published in 1946 and 1948, the first on cement and the second on building materials, showed that only those who were members of certain trade associations and who had agreed not to sell below prescribed minimum prices could obtain these products on trade terms. A builders' merchant who might have been able to reduce his costs and pass on part of this benefit to the customer by charging less than his competitors could not obtain the materials he needed at the same prices as they could. The report on radio valves in 1946 also disclosed a wide range of practices that made it difficult for new manufacturers to join the industry.

How was it that the suppliers of building materials were able to keep up the level of their prices and earn high profits without new firms entering the industry and obtaining trade by charging less? Did the law do nothing to protect the public from combinations to reduce competition?

The Common Law

Until the last quarter of the nineteenth century, the common law judges used two concepts to protect the public from sellers who

1

raised prices by agreeing to limit their trading activities. Since the
time of the labour shortage caused by the Black Death, and perhaps
since an earlier period, judges have refused to enforce a contract
that unreasonably restrains a person from exercising his trade. In
the Middle Ages it was not easy to change jobs: if a master dyer
agreed not to dye any more, he could not turn to another trade
without serving a new apprenticeship and joining the appropriate
guild; consequently, if the contract was valid, he would be unable
to contribute effectively to the skilled labour force for many years.
The judges refused to enforce such contracts, on the ground that
public policy required that workers should not be bound to give
up their calling without good reason. The disadvantage of this
method of controlling agreements that restrain trade is that, since
it is not a crime to make such agreements, the parties may legally
give effect to them even if they can not be sued for breaking them.
Methods of enforcement have been devised that are not dependent
on the assistance of the courts: people not abiding by the 'rules'
may, for instance, be deprived of their supplies.

The second weapon devised by the judges for controlling combinations against competitors was the tort of conspiracy. If you
can show that you have been injured by several persons acting in
concert, you can sue for the tort, the 'civil wrong', of conspiracy,
and not only will the court order the defendants to pay you enough
money to compensate you for the damage you can prove that they
have caused, it *may* also forbid them, on pain of being sent to gaol,
to act in a similar way in the future. In some courts in the United
States, such orders have been obtained against persons who combined to exclude people from trade. But in England the highest
court of appeal, the House of Lords, held in *Mogul S.S. Co.* v.
McGregor, Gow & Co. and others (1891) that it is a defence to show
that the combination was intended to further a legitimate trade
interest by methods that would not be illegal if adopted by a single
individual.

The defendants in the Mogul S.S. Co. case were ship-owners who
formed an association, sometimes called a conference, to secure the
tea-carrying trade from China and Japan exclusively for themselves
at profitable rates. The association regulated the ships that were to
call at each port, divided the cargoes between them, and fixed the
freight to be charged for carriage to England. The members of the
association allowed a rebate of 5 per cent to shippers who had
shipped exclusively on members' vessels during the previous six
months, and the association informed agents that they would no
longer be given work if they dealt with non-members. Mogul did
not belong to the association, and when it sent two ships to seek a
cargo of tea, the association – in accordance with an agreement

between its members – arranged that member ships were there first; these offered to carry the tea so cheaply that the Mogul ships could find cargoes only at unremunerative rates.

Mogul invoked both of the common law methods of protecting the public against combinations that restrain trade, but was unsuccessful. It is likely that the agreement between the members of the association was void as an unreasonable restraint of trade. The members had agreed with each other not to send ships to any ports unless required to do so by the association and to serve only association routes at association rates. Since, however, it was not necessary for the members to sue each other, the fact that their agreement might be void was irrelevant. It was treated merely as if it had not been made; and the members could not be sued by an outsider for making it.

The House of Lords also held that the members of the association could not be sued for conspiracy. They had not combined to injure Mogul merely because they disliked the company, but in order to protect their own profitable trade; they had not committed any crime or done anything which it would be unlawful for a single person to do. This was held to be a complete defence. The trade interests of Mogul or of any other ship-owners who might wish to operate between the U.K. and South-East Asia were not considered worthy of protection when they conflicted with those of the association's members. The short-term interest of those buying tea in England in having to pay little for the carriage of this particular cargo was considered, rather than that of later buyers who might be required to pay more. Collective discrimination to keep outsiders out of the tea-carrying trade was upheld in the name of freedom of trade!

Economics of Competition and Monopoly

Why should suppliers not be allowed to combine to exclude competitors? What do customers lose if their suppliers combine or if there is only a single supplier or a few suppliers?

Competition implies a large number of actual or potential suppliers, none of whom sells a large proportion of the total supplies of the commodity and most of whom act independently of each other. A supplier in such a market takes his prices from it: if he refrains from selling, the market price will not rise since the amount he can withhold is a negligible proportion of the total supply; he has no market power.

Monopoly implies market power. This means that a single supplier provides so much of certain goods or services that he can influence price by variations in his output.

In the real world there are few instances, if any, of 'perfect' competition, since each supplier is likely to have some degree of uniqueness as to location, service, and so on. At the other extreme, no monopolist is immune from 'competition': new competing firms may enter his industry, or substitutes for his product may be developed or already exist.

A simple, if improbable, example may illustrate the concept of market power. If one supplier of, say, fried fish, increases his prices, many of his customers will buy their fish elsewhere. Even if all the fish fryers in the neighbourhood increase their prices together, some of their customers will fry their own fish or cook eggs at home; others will buy their fried fish on their way home from work, or eat out more often, rather than pay the high local fish prices. If prices remain higher than normal, then fish fryers from elsewhere may be attracted into the neighbourhood and to encourage new custom will charge less than the established fryers, so the price will be whittled away by competition until it is not far above that charged elsewhere. Only if there are no close substitutes for the product supplied and newcomers can be prevented from eroding the monopoly, can firms increase their profits in the long run by agreeing to raise their prices together. In a small village, where the limited demand may discourage other suppliers from setting up business, one often finds prices higher than they are in the near-by town. But the extent to which a supplier can increase his prices in the long term without losing much turnover depends largely on the costs another firm would incur if it were to set up and compete with him. A sole supplier, or a group of firms that agree to keep up prices collectively, has no market power if there are close substitutes to which consumers will switch if prices are increased, or if other firms can start selling identical goods. Buying out one new entrant may only attract another.

Market power is a matter of degree. When transport was less developed than it now is, monopolies were often local. During the nineteenth century the development of the railway and canal systems eroded many local monopolies. Even now local price differences are to be expected, since travel to a lower priced market may be a nuisance and involve expense. But even a village shop in the Outer Hebrides cannot charge excessively for branded durable goods without losing trade to mail order houses, although the supply of perishable goods and of services is often localized – you cannot send your hair away to be cut or set!

In fact, the important instances of monopoly occur where entry into an industry is relatively difficult and the few firms that have become established are unlikely to lose trade to newcomers. Some of the most effective barriers to entry are legal restraints, such as a patent which makes it illegal for anyone else to make a product by using a patented invention, or to sell it; or a licensing requirement by the state. The owners or tenants of existing pubs in the locality can object to a licence being given to another firm for the consumption of alcohol on the premises, and may enjoy considerable local market power. In some industries competitive entry is forbidden altogether, as, for instance, in the case of state monopolies in the nationalized industries in the U.K. The special problems of monopoly in the *public* sector of the economy are not discussed in this book.

The need for large resources, for instance where the minimum scale of operations is very large and initial investment costly, as it is for producing some chemicals, or where considerable expenditure on sales promotion is needed to overcome established brand preferences, will prevent small firms from entering. Even large ones may be deterred when one existing plant just large enough to produce efficiently can supply a large part of the expected increase in demand for the next few years, since in such circumstances a newcomer would expect his factory to be partly idle for many years, during which it could not earn enough profits to pay for the capital invested.

In practice the problem of monopoly is complicated by the fact that it is often in the interest of a group of otherwise independent firms to concert their price policy and related matters in order to acquire market power which none of them possesses individually. Such arrangements are agreements to restrict competition; the combination is sometimes called a *cartel*. The group, however, may have difficulty in exercising its combined market power because of the need to compromise. Some members are likely to have lower costs than others, or may wish to expand more rapidly, and may want to set the group prices lower. Related to the difficulties arising from the need for compromises is the possible instability of the group; it pays each member to cheat, by charging less or giving more to customers whose orders are dependent on such behaviour, if the terms of its actual bargains can be concealed.

The exercise of market power by the restriction of supplies can be explained by means of a simple hypothetical example, which focuses on the central problem by eliminating all complicating surrounding issues.

Let us suppose that on a certain day the market supply and demand for fresh fish in a certain fishing port is as shown in the following table:

Tons on offer	Price per ton	Total receipts
10	£20.00	£200
20	£15.00	£300
40	£10.00	£400
50	£7.50	£375
60	£5.00	£300

Introduction

Suppose the total catch of all the fishermen comes to 60 tons on that day, and the fishermen compete by each selling his own catch. The fish will clear at £5 a ton. It will not be in the interests of any one fisherman to sell less than his whole catch: if he did so, he would not raise the market price, because his catch is a negligible part of the day's supply, nor would he reduce his costs; so he would simply reduce his takings. No single fisherman has market or monopoly power and he accepts the price as beyond his influence or control.

But suppose, by way of contrast, that all the fishermen have an arrangement – a cartel – by which the whole catch is pooled and is sold centrally by their monopolistic organization. As shown in the table, the organization will do best for its members if it exercises its monopoly power by offering no more than 40 tons of fish for sale, the remaining 20 tons being thrown back into the sea or sold for what it will fetch as fertilizer. The 40 tons will clear at £10 a ton, and the total receipts will come to £400 – as against £300 had the entire catch been on sale. The fishermen's income is raised by the exercise of their collective monopoly or market power, at the expense of the consumers of fish. This is what is meant when it is said that the ability to increase profits by restricting supplies is the touchstone of monopoly or market power. Consumers of the product are 'held to ransom' – a possibility which does not exist for the individual competing seller who has to take the market price as given, because it is beyond his power to control it by his own decisions.

There are limits, however, to the extent to which the public can be held to ransom monopolistically. In our example the limits of demand would have made it unprofitable for the cartel to raise the price of fish to, say, £20 a ton by putting only 10 tons on the market. The restraints on monopoly depend generally on the access, actual or potential, of consumers to substitute products and rival independent suppliers. If consumers typically regard frozen fish fillets as a perfect and complete substitute for fresh fish and if there were ample supplies of the former at low prices from independent suppliers, then the market demand table would look quite different and the fishermen collectively would have as little market power as the individual fisherman.

Objections to Restricted Supply by a Single-Firm Monopolist

The main objections to the restriction of supply by a single supplier with market power are as follows:

(1) Where a single firm has considerable market power and exercises it by restricting supplies, the monopolist will become richer than

he would have had he had no market power, and he will do so at the expense of those who consume the product.

(2) Indeed, consumers will depend on the firm's decisions, not only as regards price, but also on such matters as the amount and directions of research and development in the relevant industry, the services offered, and continuity of supply. Consumer choice may be more restricted than if the industry were competitive.

(3) The absence or weakness of competition means that there is little market pressure on the monopolist to be as efficient as possible: that is, to keep down costs. Wasteful costs can be reflected in higher prices just as much as can monopoly profits. In competitive conditions the more efficient firms are likely to sell more than their less efficient competitors, and increase their turnover at the expense of the latter, to the general benefit of the economy.

(4) The more general consideration, looking to the economy as a whole and going beyond the interests of particular consumers, is that the exercise of monopoly power causes resources to be misallocated from society's point of view. This consideration is a complex one. It is based on the economists' 'theory of welfare economics'; 'misallocation of resources' has a special, technical meaning within a highly restrictive framework of assumptions and in terms of a highly specialized criterion of 'economic efficiency'. The application of the theory to the problem of monopoly in a particular market, moreover, is greatly complicated unless in all other reasonably closely connected markets there is competition or relationships between cost and price of the kind that occur in conditions of competition. For reasons such as this, some economists doubt whether one should have recourse to this theory when considering the policy problems of monopoly and restrictive practices. However, the general implications of the theory can be stated quite simply. The monopolist restricts output because to do so is profitable. His output is 'too small'. He employs 'too little' of society's resources, and consequently 'too much' of these resources go into the production of other goods which society values less highly: in short, resources are 'misallocated'. Consumers as a whole would be better off if 'more' resources went into the production of more of the goods that are now monopolized, where the resources have more value in terms of 'consumer preferences'.

Objections to Restricted Supply by a Cartel (Sellers Acting in Concert)
The first and last of the objections given above to the exercise of market power by a single firm apply also to its exercise by a group of firms acting in concert; but the second and third need qualification.

Introduction

(2, above) A cartel may be limited in scope; members may agree only on the prices to be charged or shares of the market to be supplied, in which case consumers will not be dependent on a single set of decisions for other matters.

(3, above) Where a cartel bans competition on price, members will tend to compete for custom in other ways which raise costs, for instance by giving additional services or by spending more on sales promotion. The compromises inherent in a cartel also ensure that the total output will be produced at a higher total cost than if a single firm had equivalent market power: the latter would have an incentive to achieve that output most cheaply, for instance by closing the least efficient unit of production, whereas the former would tend to keep in being at least some high cost units of production.

Oligopoly (*a Few Sellers*)

The term monopoly is sometimes used to include the situation where there are few suppliers in an industry or trade, each or several of which may be large in relation to the market. Each will watch the market actions of every one of its handful of rivals and be ready to respond to any move; for if one of them succeeds in stealing a march and adds significantly to its sales, each of the others, being few in number, will suffer a significant drop in sales. Thus if A cuts his price, the others will be obliged to do the same – and the outcome may be that each sells much the same volume as before but at a lower and less profitable price. Since A can foresee that his initial action will provoke such retaliation, he will tend to refrain from taking it (except where he believes, for example, that both he and his rivals would be in a more profitable position if the prices of their product were lower). The result may be a situation in which the firms behave 'as if' they were operating as a collective unit or cartel. 'Conscious parallelism' – acting in the knowledge that competitors will react to market decisions – does not imply any collusion between firms. The members of an oligopolistic industry may tend to behave as if they were members of a cartel, and price competition may be weak and occasional. The fewer the firms supplying a market, however, the easier it is to organize collusion.

Buyers' Market Power

So far we have considered market power exercised by sellers; but buyers, also, may be powerful, and the same analysis applies conversely to a single buyer (monopsonist) who may restrict his purchases to obtain them more cheaply, or to several buyers who may combine to exert market power in a cartel, or to conscious parallelism between buyers who act as if they had combined without any agreement necessarily having been made (oligopsony).

Product Differentiation

In many markets the products of each individual producer are differentiated from similar products sold by competitors by branding and minor differences in design. Each producer may register a trade mark or design and be the only supplier of his own brand. The amount of power he enjoys in the circumstances depends on the degree to which other brands or designs are thought by consumers to be acceptable substitutes, and on ease of entry into the industry. The considerations peculiar to product differentiation arise from the competitive advertising and sales promotion which often accompany it. Such activities may induce buyers to treat rival brands as not being close substitutes for each other, even when there is little or no real difference between their physical qualities or performance. Where there is no price competition, there is likely to be greater expenditure on advertising and this may make it difficult for new firms to break into the market, since, unless a firm has a reputation that can readily be extended to other products, it will have to devote large sums to sales promotion before it can reach as big a turnover as the existing firms, over which to spread the costs. These aspects of the effects of advertising bear on the problems of monopoly. Other aspects, such as truth in advertising, need not be considered in this context.

A Large or Conglomerate Firm

A firm can be large in terms of assets, labour force, and turnover without having any significant market power in any of the markets in which it operates. It may be a large firm in absolute terms with a small share of a large market: a U.K. firm which sells in a relatively unified world market may have little market power even if it is big. A firm which is diversified, consisting of a number of sub-'firms', may have little market power if each is relatively small in its particular market. The latter is sometimes called a 'conglomerate firm'. This book will be confined to the problems of monopoly and market power, and will not consider whether it is undesirable for the managers of a single firm to control very large resources.

Competition or Planning?

In the United Kingdom and indeed in most Western European countries, competition is welcome mainly because it forces business-

9

men to cut prices and costs or to improve the quality of their products. In the United States and some other countries, however, there is also a political objection to economic power: it is felt that no person in a democracy should have power over the things the people want to buy or over their opportunities to work unless he has been elected and is subject to constitutional checks.

While competition is desired to lessen economic power, some economists and more businessmen believe that in some industries resources are put to better use if competition is limited. It is very much cheaper to make some products in very large plants that are in constant operation than in many separate factories. The expected demand may not be sufficient to warrant the expenditure on more than one or two plants that are big enough to achieve the full economies of scale. Few economists would wish to prevent the formation or continued existence of such 'natural monopolies'. Some businessmen and politicians are prepared to tolerate further limitations on competition: they want firms to 'rationalize' and combine in units that are larger than is necessary to achieve all the economies that are possible at the plant level, since big firms can afford to spend large sums on research and development and can borrow money more cheaply. The sole supplier of a product for which there are no close substitutes, or one of a few suppliers who act interdependently, enjoys a more secure market than firms in more competitive industries, and earns higher profits. Consequently such a supplier may be better able to invest in long-term projects such as research and development of new products, as well as of new markets, particularly overseas.

Very varied benefits are claimed to result from restrictive agreements between firms. Unfettered competition may create uncertainties for the individual firm, lead to an emphasis on short-term adjustments at the expense of long term planning, cause instability in prices to the disadvantage of consumers, or reduce profits to such an extent that firms cannot invest in research and development. Firms may not be prepared to collaborate on research or detailed methods of reducing costs, if those they help may undercut them. Many businessmen think that a suitable restraint on competition may avoid these results. Some of the arguments traditionally urged in favour of cartels will be considered in Chapters 6 and 7.

Government Intervention

To an increasing extent since the Second World War, U.K. governments have intervened directly in the market in an attempt to improve efficiency, and achieve other aims, where possible without conferring market power on private firms. The most extreme examples were the nationalization of coal and later of most steel production, the establishment of the National Health Service and the monopoly conferred on certain statutory undertakers, such as water boards.

From 1966 to 1970, the Industrial Reorganization Corporation used public money to help firms selected by it to rationalize, often through mergers. It was hoped that this would lead to economies of scale, such as longer production runs that may reduce costs dramatically. Under the Industry Act, the Conservatives invested in private firms which it was feared might otherwise have to close down, and even greater powers are being taken under the Industry Bill 1975.

Both Labour and Conservative governments have also attempted to ensure better bargains for consumers by controlling prices, or at least price increases. The Labour government did so with a minimum of compulsory powers, through the National Board for Prices and Incomes which decided whether price or wage levels were too high. Since 1972, there has been compulsory control of prices, particularly of large firms, and until the summer of 1974, also of wages. Industry complains that unless it can earn profits, and sometimes exceptionally large profits, it will increasingly be deterred from taking the risks necessary to the production of new products or the development of new markets. The distortions caused by attempts to raise prices in ways that are not forbidden, for instance by selling abroad where prices are not controlled, with the consequence that U.K. buyers have to import products at even higher prices, are becoming serious.

Whether it is desirable that government should intervene, both with public funds and other incentives as well as with price controls, is a controversial issue which will not be dealt with in this book.

Development of United Kingdom Legislation

In 1948 the Monopolies and Restrictive Practices Commission was created to investigate the supply of any goods which might be referred to it by the Board of Trade, provided that one-third of the goods specified in the reference and supplied in the U.K. came from a single firm or from a combination of firms that had made agreements restricting competition between themselves. The government was not sure that either the possession or the use of market power was necessarily antisocial. It hoped that as a result of the Commission's reports on the markets referred to it light would be thrown on the extent of practices restricting competition in the U.K. economy, while in each market the Commission would have to conclude whether or not the monopolistic or restrictive practices

11

were contrary to the public interest. The matters which it was suggested that the Commission should take into account in considering the public interest were so broad and general in scope that they did not help the Commission to reach a decision: the Commission was left to decide whether collaboration or decisions taken independently by many firms served the community better. Both the constitution of the Commission and some of its work will be considered in Chapters 2 and 3.

In 1956, the Commission's power to consider whether agreements between firms were contrary to the public interest was transferred to a new court set up under the Restrictive Trade Practices Act 1956 and called the Restrictive Practices Court. Again the government had great difficulty in framing criteria for the Court to apply in deciding whether a particular agreement restraining competition is contrary to the public interest; although there was more general agreement than in 1948 that many are. The Court is required to declare that an agreement is contrary to the public interest unless certain criteria are satisfied. These are spelled out more clearly than in the 1948 Act, but some are very difficult to apply. For instance, that the abrogation of the restriction would deprive the members of the public, as consumers, of substantial benefits enjoyed by virtue of the agreement or any arrangements or operations resulting from it. If, for instance, it is argued that collaborative research would not continue if the parties were forbidden to agree on the minimum prices each may charge, the Court must decide how far the collaboration would continue despite the possibility of price competition and, if it is likely to be reduced, whether competition would lead to better bargains for consumers. The Court must attempt to predict what will happen to the industry on the alternative assumptions that the agreement remains lawful and that it is forbidden, and then decide which eventuality is better for consumers.

When the Bill was debated in the House of Commons in 1956, the principal spokesman for the Labour Party, Mr Jay, argued that the Court was being given an impossible task. It was being asked to make political decisions which should be taken by Parliament, or at least by a minister who is responsible to Parliament and is available to answer questions in the House. The Labour Party then, and the Liberals still, wanted many restraints on competition forbidden generally. This would not only save a tribunal from having to make very difficult and dubious decisions as to whether collaboration or competition in a particular market leads to a better use of resources, but would make enforcement easier. All agreements to fix prices or boycott outsiders would be automatically illegal and the authorities would have only to detect them – not also to prove that each is against the public interest.

In the event, however, the only practice made illegal without consideration of its merits in an individual market was the collective enforcement of resale price maintenance through black lists.

In the United States, under the Sherman Act of 1890, the judges were faced with the problem of deciding what restraints on trade were unreasonable and so forbidden. As early as 1898 Judge Taft in *U.S.* v. *Addyston Pipe and Steel Co.* refused to make legality depend on the uncertain claim that the prices fixed were in fact reasonable. Not only is it impossible to tell in the absence of a competitive market whether the prices fixed are as low as they would be without the agreement, but there is also no way of ensuring that they will not be unduly raised later, or that they will not remain stationary when in a competitive industry they might have been reduced.

The definition of agreements to which the 1956 Act applies will be analysed in Chapter 4, the duty to inform an official when they are made is described in Chapter 5, and the criteria for deciding whether they are contrary to the public interest are analysed in Chapter 6 in the light of some of the cases in which they have been applied.

Until 1956, most references to the Monopolies Commission were concerned with agreements between producers, usually organized by their trade association, fixing prices and often sharing the available market. These the Commission generally condemned. Once scrutiny of such agreements was transferred to the Restrictive Practices Court, the Commission was mainly left with the more difficult type of inquiry requiring it to decide whether the fact that a single firm supplied over a third of the products specified in the reference operated contrary to the public interest and whether any conduct of the dominant firm to exploit or preserve its dominance was likely to conflict with the public interest. On such inquiries the Commission generally looked to see whether the dominant firm was trying to keep other firms out of the market, for instance by tying up existing customers for long periods. Such exclusionary tactics were usually condemned, but the Commission found it far harder to say whether the existence of market power had led to poorer performance than would be expected if the market was more competitive. It is not easy to say whether a monopolist is charging too much unless his profit rates are clearly excessive, just as it is hard to determine what would happen if the industry were more competitive.

In the Monopolies and Mergers Act 1965 the Government took power to ask the Commission about the supply of services as well as of goods and, since agreements about services could not be dealt with by the Restrictive Practices Court, it is not surprising that these references in fact related to agreed restrictions, e.g. the standard charges which suppliers of commercial services, such as estate agents and fire insurers, were recommended by their trade association to make, and the restrictions on advertising observed in certain professions. Power was also taken to ask the Commission whether a merger (i.e. the amalgamation of two firms) or contemplated merger might be expected to operate against the public interest.

An important organizational change was made under the Fair Trading Act 1973, when the office of Director General of Fair Trading was created and Mr John Methven was given power to make monopoly references to the Commission, although this may still be done by ministers also. He has taken over sole responsibility for bringing restrictive agreements before the Court. He was also given entirely new functions in relation to consumer protection, but with these last this book is not concerned. The monopoly legislation was consolidated and tightened up in detail. In particular, goods or services may be referred to the Commission if a single firm supplies or acquires a quarter of them, rather than a third.

The name of the Commission has changed from time to time, as its main functions have changed. The Monopolies and Restrictive Practices Commission became the Monopolies Commission when collective restrictive practices became the responsibility of the Court. Although it has been possible to refer mergers to the Commission since 1965, it was only under the Fair Trading Act that it became called the Monopolies and Mergers Commission.

The Common Market

Another and more fundamental change had occurred at the beginning of 1973, when the U.K. joined the Common Market. Since the Treaty of Accession provided that over the following five years tariffs should be abolished between the nine member states, the effective market for all products that can economically be supplied from a distance should be greatly extended. Many firms that have been dominant in the U.K. may be expected to face increased competition from firms in Europe. Moreover, the European Economic Community (E.E.C.) itself has competition rules, which are enforced mainly by its Commission in Brussels – not to be confused with the Monopolies and Mergers Commission. (The Commission is properly called the Commission of the European Communities, since it serves also the European Coal and Steel Community and Euratom.) The U.K. rules continue in force, but the new Common Market ones must also be obeyed. There are two sets of rules, and firms are required to comply with both.

The E.E.C. was created between the six original member states

(Belgium, France, Germany, Holland, Italy and Luxembourg) in 1958 under the Treaty of Rome, in order to achieve various economic objectives through the mechanism of a common market. According to article 2,

'The Community shall have as its task, by establishing a common market and progressively approximating the economic policies of Member States, to promote throughout the Community a harmonious development of economic activities, a continuous and balanced expansion, an increase in stability, an accelerated raising of the standard of living and closer relations between the States belonging to it.'

The market is to be integrated by making it possible for goods, services, workers, firms and capital to move freely over national frontiers. The idea is not to make it possible for the Dutch to grow lemons, but rather to make the decision where to grow lemons depend on climatic and soil conditions, the relative value of land, and agricultural wage levels in different parts of the Community, rather than on political geography. This marked a considerable change, since the economies of the original member states had been separated by various devices, including substantial tariffs charged as goods crossed any frontier. As these were to be progressively abolished, one would have expected firms in many industries, suddenly faced with increased competition, to have combined and agreed with their potential competitors in other member states that they would sell only in their home market or, at least, that if they exported they would not undercut local suppliers. Such conduct would frustrate the plans to increase wealth by integrating the market and enabling individual efficient firms to produce on a larger scale. Articles 85–90 on competition policy were therefore included in the Treaty and will be discussed in Chapters 7 to 9 of this book.

Article 85 prohibits firms from making agreements which restrict competition within the Common Market or are intended to do so. There are provisions whereby collaboration may be exempted when a fair share of the benefits are likely to be passed on to consumers. Although this provision is mainly enforced by the Commission of the European Communities, it does have an effect in English civil courts, since agreements that infringe article 85 are illegal and void, at least in respect of the restrictive clauses, and it may be that a person harmed by a prohibited agreement can sue for compensation. The abuse of a dominant position is forbidden by article 86 and the law on this topic is developing rapidly. Attempts to assess whether there is abuse of a dominant position contrary to article 86 are likely to encounter similar problems to those the Monopolies and

Introduction

Mergers Commission faces when deciding whether the conduct of a dominant firm operates or may be expected to operate against the public interest.

Some of the policy issues raised by both the U.K. and the E.E.C. legislation are shortly considered in the final chapter.

Part One

2: *Monopoly Situations*

The Creation of the Monopolies and Restrictive Practices Commission and Office of Fair Trading

During the Second World War the spur of competition was hardly needed to keep businessmen efficient: the desire to defeat the enemy was sufficient incentive to most industrialists to work effectively. When products essential to life, such as food and clothing, were scarce because of the enemy blockade, it was thought wrong that they should be allocated by price. The prices of most articles were controlled and scarce goods and materials rationed at both the consumer and production levels. During the war a managed economy was acceptable, but when hostilities were over, politicians and others wondered how far monopolies and cartels dominated our economy and whether restrictive practices adopted by those with market power were likely to operate against the public interest. The government, with the general support of all political parties, sought to find out, and in 1948 Parliament passed the Monopolies and Restrictive Practices (Inquiry and Control) Act, under which the Monopolies and Restrictive Practices Commission was created. The Act empowered the Board of Trade, the government department most closely associated with commerce and industry, to refer to the Commission the supply of any class of goods if it thought that a third or more of the goods specified were supplied or acquired in the U.K. or a substantial part of it, either by a single firm, or by several who restricted competition. Similar provisions related to the export of goods from the U.K. and to the application of a process of manufacture to goods.

The functions of the Commission have varied from time to time. In the period before jurisdiction over restrictive agreements was conferred on the Restrictive Practices Court it produced twenty-two reports, most of them relating to trade associations which controlled channels of distribution for manufactured goods, or fixed common or minimum prices which their members were required to charge. These arrangements it usually condemned, or thought should be allowed to continue only subject to some form of government scrutiny. In 1955 its report on certain kinds of collective discrimination was published. It stated that it had never come across an instance when this practice was not contrary to the public interest, although it suggested four situations in which it might be justified. This report led to the stricter and more general control of such agreements, as well as of price fixing, under the Restrictive Trade Practices Act 1956. In consequence, the Commission's functions were restricted mainly to considering whether the market power of a single firm, or any steps taken by that firm to exploit or preserve it, operated or might be expected to operate against the public interest. These enquiries were much more intractable than the earlier trade association investigations, and by 1966 it had produced only nine more reports, several of which took as long as four years to prepare.

The functions of the Commission were extended when, in 1965, the Board of Trade was empowered to refer mergers to it (Chapter 3), as well as the supply of services. Since then it has produced far more reports, taking far less time on average. Several of its dominant firm enquiries have lasted less than three years; merger investigations must be completed rapidly – usually in under five months – and the service enquiries have usually been concerned with restrictive agreements and involved less difficult problems.

In 1969 the monopoly functions were transferred from the Board of Trade to the Secretary of State. By a curious constitutional anomaly more than one minister is called the Secretary of State and in theory any could make references to the Commission. In practice, however, in 1974 Mrs Shirley Williams was responsible to the Cabinet and in the House of Commons for the monopolies functions as well as for price control and consumer protection. I shall refer to 'the Minister' or, occasionally, to 'the minister in charge of the monopoly functions'.

From its establishment until 1953, and again from 1956 until 1965, the Commission has been limited to ten members, most of whom were involved in each inquiry; but for a short period before it ceased to be able to consider restrictive agreements and again when its functions were extended in 1965, its membership was increased to a maximum of twenty-five, and it has been able to operate in groups. This it has done. Indeed, the Commission rarely meets as a whole. Recently its membership has been around twenty. In practice the Chairman acts full time, but most of the other members are appointed on a part-time basis. This enables them to continue their other occupations and keep in touch with the professional and industrial activities which make them valuable assessors of the matters referred to the Commission. These part-time appointments also enable people to become members of the Commission even if they would have been unwilling to give up interesting careers to do so. It is also said that part-time members are less likely to be always 'out for blood', condemning every possible aspect of market power. They may be less likely than full-time appointees to judge their success by the number of practices they suggest should be changed. On the other hand, busy people are not always readily available, whatever priority they may be prepared to give to the work of the Commission, and this may delay its inquiries. Usually members have included a number of professional economists, several active or newly retired businessmen, officials or former officials of trades unions, persons with experience of finance, and at least one academic lawyer. There is invariably at least one economist among the group considering a particular investigation.

A new office was created by the Fair Trading Act 1973, that of the Director General of Fair Trading, whom I shall call the Director. Although the minister responsible for the monopolies functions still has power to make references to the Commission, the Director has also been empowered to do so if he believes that a monopoly situation may exist. He is independent of the government in that there is no minister available to answer questions about his activities in the House of Commons. He must, however, have close, informal contacts with the minister in charge of the government's monopoly policy. The latter is entitled to give general directions about the criteria the Director should adopt in deciding whether to refer a monopoly situation to the Commission (s. 12). Moreover, if the Director makes a reference of which the Minister disapproves, he has power to veto it (s. 50(6)). In practice this is not as important as it might seem, since the reference will already have been announced and the Minister would have to give reasons for any veto and justify them in answer to questions in the House. Where a reference to the Commission is made by the Minister, the government is fully responsible politically. It also bears some responsibility for the references made, or not made, by the Director. Although the Director cannot answer questions in the House of Commons, the Minister could be asked why he has not used his veto or issued general directions about the considerations to which the Director should have regard in deciding whether to refer a monopoly situation.

The Commission's Task

The Commission cannot take any initiative: it may investigate only the matters referred to it by the Director or the Minister. It is required to come to definite conclusions about all the matters comprised in the reference (s. 54(2)): it may not say that it does not know or that members cannot agree.

Reference of a Monopoly Situation

Since 1965 it has been possible to ask the Commission to investigate a monopoly situation in regard to the supply of services as well as of goods if it appears to the person making the reference that a monopoly situation exists or may exist. Such a situation exists in respect of the products specified in the reference if a quarter (until 1973 a third) are supplied either within the U.K. or within any part of it (formerly a substantial part) to, for, or by either a single firm or group of companies, or a number of firms who so act as in any way to restrict competition (sections 6–11). The latter case is described in the Act as a 'complex monopoly situation'. Exports of goods have always been capable of reference to the Commission if a sufficient proportion of the trade in question was thought to be in the hands of one firm or group of companies, or subject to agreements restricting competition in exports, but here again the qualifying proportion has now been reduced from a third to a quarter. Since the one-quarter test could always be satisfied if the part of the country were defined sufficiently narrowly – the supply of books from 54–58 Caledonian Road – it is clear that not all monopoly situations will be referred. Industry must rely on the common sense of the Director and Minister to refer the supply or export of a product only if he has reason to believe that at least one supplier or customer in fact enjoys considerable market power.

The reference may direct the Commission to confine its investigation to particular agreements or practices restricting competition, or to exclude these (s. 47(2)). The reference of the supply of infant milk foods to retailers required the Commission to confine its consideration of the public interest to the practice of supplying only those who carried on certain kinds of business, in effect chemists and welfare clinics. Such a limited reference may lead to a shorter investigation. The Commission was able to investigate a single aspect of the dominant firms' distribution policies and completed its inquiry in ten months.

The Commission must be asked whether the monopoly situation exists in respect of the products specified in the reference, either in the whole of the U.K. or in any specified part of it, whether generally or as limited under s. 47(2). It must also be asked to ascertain in whose favour the situation exists and whether any steps are being taken by the dominant firm or firms for the purpose of exploiting or maintaining the monopoly situation, and what steps and what conduct of the dominant firm are attributable to the dominant position (s. 48). People who learnt the law before the Fair Trading Act was passed may refer to the monopoly situation as the 'conditions', and the steps or conduct as the 'things done', as section 6 of the 1948 Act referred to 'the conditions to which the Act applies' and to 'the things which are done by the parties concerned as a result of, or for the purpose of preserving, these conditions'. I do not think that the new formulation creates any change of substance, and I shall refer to the monopoly situation and to the steps taken by the dominant firm.

The Commission is almost invariably also asked to consider whether either the existence of the monopoly situation or the steps taken operate or may be expected to operate against the public interest. The published and reasoned conclusions of the Commission may contribute to the education of both industrialists and the wider public about the circumstances in which such conduct may be desirable or otherwise. Moreover, a finding that either the monopoly situation or one of the steps taken is harmful is required if ministers are to make an order controlling the dominant firm.

The Commission has been fairly consistent in condemning steps taken by the dominant firms to keep newcomers out of the industry, but in the last decades it has also attempted to assess whether profits are too high. (See p. 41 below.) Apart from the difficulties inherent in this task, the Commission must bear in mind that the public interest may be hurt as much by a firm which earns low profits because it is less efficient than it would have to be if it faced competition, as by a firm which sells at the same price and earns high profits. Indeed the less efficient firm, apart from wasting resources, is more anti-social, inasmuch as the firm with lower costs but higher profits contributes to the public revenue through the tax system and some of its cost-saving techniques may be copied by other firms. To decide whether prices are too high, the Commission may therefore have to decide not only whether the firm is earning high profits, but also whether it is more or less efficient than the average in industry. Since it is considering a dominant firm, there is unlikely to be any other firm comparison with whose efficiency is relevant. On page 22, one way of limiting a reference was explained. It may be framed so as to limit the investigation of the Commission to, or to exclude from it, agreements as a result of which a monopoly situation exists (s. 47(2)). Another way of limiting the investigation is to ask the Commission, after it has found that a monopoly situation does exist, to confine its investigation to those steps taken by the dominant firm that are specified in the reference (s. 49(2) and (3)). This saves it from investigating whether the monopoly situation itself operates against the public interest, as well as whether any other steps may have been taken and do the same. Sometimes the Commission is asked to investigate merely whether the price levels of a particular product may be expected to operate against the public interest, as in the case of the prices charged for breakfast cereals (p. 41 below).

When certain types of agreement relating to the supply and processing of goods were made subject to the jurisdiction of the Restrictive Practices Court in 1956, such agreements could no longer be referred to the Monopolies Commission. Section 10 of the Fair Trading Act provides that the provisions which render an agreement subject to registration shall be ignored when deciding whether a monopoly situation exists and, where one exists on other grounds, such as the market power of a dominant firm, the Commission shall not consider whether the terms of the agreement which render it subject to the jurisdiction of the Restrictive Practices Court operate against the public interest (s. 54(5)). In so far as the restrictive practices legislation is not extended to services, the jurisdiction over these given to the Commission in 1965 extends to restrictive agreements between persons who provide services. Power has, however, been taken in the Fair Trading Act to call up services for registration and, as it is exercised, the agreements called up will cease to be referrable to the Commission. The scope of the 1956 Act will be considered in Chapter 4. Now that the Director initiates procedures under both the monopolies and the restrictive practices legislation, the divided jurisdiction is less serious than it was.

Certain objectives relevant to the public interest are stated in section 84 (p. 266 below) – in rather different terms from those used in section 14 of the 1948 Act – but the Commission must still take into account any circumstances it considers relevant to the public interest in the particular case, and the objectives specified in the Acts are so broadly described that the Commission has had to develop its own criteria. It has frequently taken the interest of final consumers as the interest to be protected, in so far as possible, by the maintenance of effective competition.

General References

Under section 78 of the Fair Trading Act, the Commission may also be asked to report on the general effect on the public interest of specified kinds of practices which in the opinion of the minister in charge of the monopoly functions are commonly adopted as a result of, or for the purpose of preserving, monopoly situations, as well as on practices which prevent, restrict or distort competition. The Minister may also ask the Commission to report on the desirability of any specified kind of action for the purpose of remedying or preventing effects adverse to the public interest which result or might result from monopoly situations or from practices which restrict competition. Such a reference cannot be made by the Director, although he would, doubtless, be consulted before one were made by the Minister.

The Commission has made several reports on general references. Under the 1948 Act, it could be asked to do so only if it had already reported on particular industries, where the practices had been found to exist and had been condemned. This qualification was removed by the 1965 Act but where the Commission has been asked to report on practices which it has not already considered in an individual industry, it has not been able to be very helpful. This used to be partly because it had no power to require firms to produce evidence and, although this power has now been extended to all kinds of reference under the Act (s. 85), the Commission may hesitate to place the considerable burden of producing evidence on any individual firm or trade association when considering a practice generally, and not in relation to a particular trade or industry. Yet, without detailed evidence of how a practice actually operates, it cannot say more than that certain objections can generally be made to it, which may or may not apply in particular cases. It may also be able critically to evaluate some of the arguments commonly urged in favour of restrictions on competition, as it did in its report on professional services.

The first general report produced by the Commission, on collective discrimination in 1955, did lead to legislation controlling the practice in 1956 (it will be considered at pp. 81–2), but its later general reports have been less roundly adverse to the practices it has considered, and have rarely suggested or led to general legislation. No power has been taken to legislate by order, following on a general report of the Commission. As in monopoly references, the consideration of agreements subject to the jurisdiction of the Restrictive Practices Court is not possible.

Reference of Restrictive Labour Practices

Section 79 contains a new power for ministers, not the Director, to make a general reference of restrictive labour practices to the Commission, either in relation to commercial activities in the U.K. generally, or in relation to the supply of specified products, provided that they are not currently the subject of an industrial dispute as this was defined in the Industrial Relations Act 1971. Under earlier legislation, such as the Industrial Relations Act, restrictive labour practices could be examined only in the context of an industrial dispute, the very time when it is most difficult to reach an acceptable

25

solution. Section 79 may provide the opportunity for a long cool look, although no reference has yet been made and it is rather doubtful whether a Labour government would use this power. The Commission is required to state whether the practice exists and whether it may operate contrary to the public interest and, if so, what adverse effects it may have. It is not required to consider remedies, nor has the government taken power to make orders controlling any practices the Commission may condemn.

Procedure of the Commission

The procedure of the Commission does not follow the traditional rules of examination, cross-examination and re-examination of witnesses observed in a court of law. The Commission is empowered to determine (and has determined) its own procedure, subject to the limited requirements of section 81(1) and to any general directions which may from time to time be made by the Minister. No such directions have yet been made under this or the similar provision in the 1948 Act. Section 85 repeats the provision in the 1948 Act giving the Commission powers to require evidence on oath and the production of documents, estimates and other information. These powers are, however, rarely used, since the Commission prefers to persuade the industry concerned to co-operate voluntarily.

The previous legislation did not provide for the Commission to be told of any information or consideration that might have been in the government's mind when a reference was made, except in so far as the government had power to limit the reference to particular 'conditions' or 'things done' (see pp. 22 and 23 above). Now, however, the Director is required to give the Commission any information he has which the Commission may request or which he thinks it should have as well as any other assistance it asks for (s. 5(2)).

On receipt of a reference, the Chairman of the Commission appoints the members and chairman of the group who will conduct the inquiry and exercise the functions of the Commission. On a monopoly reference the staff take certain routine steps. Facts published about the industry are collected. The reference is advertised, and anyone interested is asked to submit written evidence. The principal firms in the industry are informed individually and are usually invited to attend an informal meeting with the group, whose chairman can then explain and discuss the procedure to be adopted and indicate the main points on which information will be sought. Often the Commission takes the initiative by circulating questionnaires and inviting firms likely to be affected, such as suppliers and customers, to give their views.

The Commission's staff examines the minutes, departmental notes and other documents produced by the dominant firm and may ask supplementary questions. The Commission is required to include in its report 'a survey of the general position with respect to the subject-matter of the reference, and of the developments that have led to the position' (s. 54(2)), and it must therefore spend some time investigating the past. Moreover, current restrictive practices may be appreciated better in their historical perspective. Minutes and some of the other documents are, however, often very succinct records of what may have been decided only after considerable discussion and the reason for the decision may not be recorded. To discover these decades later may be very time-consuming, and the Commission is unlikely to pursue its inquiry into very old decisions, although its reports usually include a short history of the industry, often from its inception.

The procedure is flexible and must vary not only with the structure of the industry involved, but also with the type of inquiry being pursued. Financial and other links between the more important firms are scrutinized, as well as the operation of any agreements restricting competition. An accounting investigation is also arranged, which may well last for a year or more. Often the figures which are readily available are not suitable. Once the Commission has found that a monopoly situation exists, it may want to know whether the charges of the dominant firm are too high and will want to see whether it is obtaining a very high return on the capital employed. Since the Commission is concerned only with the products specified in the reference, it must isolate both the profits and the capital employed on the reference products from any other products supplied. Yet the accounts prepared for shareholders and the Inland Revenue are unlikely to separate either profits or capital attributable to the different activities. They may have to be worked afresh from the original records. Quite apart from the work involved, there are basic difficulties of apportionment. Some manufacturing processes result in more than one product and other costs, such as the maintenance of the head office, are also joint, and the apportionment must be to some extent arbitrary. Sometimes 'sales' are made to another company within the group and, as it may not matter to the company at which point it takes its profit, the price at which the sale is made may not be the appropriate one for assessing the profit. If there is an outside market, then the price charged on external sales can be substituted, but there may well not be such a market for semi-manufactured products or components. The problem may be more acute if the product is sold to a related company abroad, since there is no power to require evidence from a company that is incorporated under foreign law and does not carry on business in the U.K. In trade association inquiries, which for the moment are still possible in respect of services, the different firms may have made up their accounts according to different accounting conventions and to different dates so, again, the accounts may have to be re-worked on a common basis for the purpose of comparisons. The Commission has a team of accountants on its staff who are accustomed to the kind of work involved. Recently the volume of work has been such that it has been obliged also to employ private firms of accountants, acting under the general supervision of the Accountant Adviser who heads the staff team.

While the accounting inquiry is proceeding, the Commission continues to collect evidence and to make such progress as it can with the preliminary drafting of the factual parts of the report. Complainants are heard by the group or its staff, and the Commission attempts to probe their allegations. If, for instance, discrimination is alleged, the complainant may be asked to supply copies of any letter refusing supplies or setting out the charges quoted. The Commission will endeavour to protect the anonymity of witnesses, where this is the witness's wish, insofar as this can be done consistently with the need to give the monopolist a fair opportunity of commenting on the allegations. The Commission refuses to accept evidence on the understanding that the evidence will in no circumstances be disclosed, although it is prepared to use sufficiently general language in its reports to protect trade secrets, insofar as this can be done without damage to the report. It used to be the practice to hold a clarification hearing confined to the factual issues with the main parties present, but such a hearing is not now normally considered necessary either by the Commission or by the parties.

The public interest stage starts with the public interest letter. This summarizes the facts and includes two important annexes. One lists the public interest issues as seen by the Commission and the other the complaints made to the Commission. Some industrialists say that the Commission gives them insufficient guidance as to the importance of the different issues, while others complain that further issues may emerge at an even later stage. The companies usually take several months preparing a written case in answer to the public interest letter, and then follows the public interest hearing, at which counsel usually appear. This hearing enables the Commission to question the company on its case and gives the company an opportunity to amplify it.

The difficulty that faces the dominant firms is that the Commission acts as both investigator and judge. One of the advantages claimed for the Commission's procedure is that it enables information to be obtained more rapidly and thoroughly than would be possible if an adversary procedure were adopted. The judicial procedure adopted by the Restrictive Practices Court is very laborious and it is not always easy for the judges to keep the issues in proportion. On the other hand, counsel complain that the Commission does not give them the opportunity to cross-examine the witnesses that they would have in the Restrictive Practices Court. Some dominant firms complain that the Commission asks double-edged questions, such as 'Do you think that you are devoting about the right amount of your resources to research and development?' They do not know whether the Commission fears they are devoting too much or too little. Nevertheless, it may be the right sort of question, if the Commission is interested in whether the dominant firm is making the best use of its resources.

After the formal public interest hearing, while the Commission may continue to contact the firms involved, its considerations are focused on the public interest conclusions and on any recommendations it may be minded to make. This part of the inquiry requires considerable time from the members of the group and, except only for merger inquiries, priority tends to be given to inquiries when they have reached this stage. The final chapter of the report is then written, discussed and amended in detail by the members of the Commission and the report is then signed. Some members may sign subject to a note of dissent. There is invariably an economist on every inquiry and some of the most cogent and influential notes of dissent have been written by these.

The procedure in merger inquiries (Chapter 3) is basically similar but the nature of these inquiries is such as to involve less need for close examination of past conduct, the Commission's approach is generally less detailed, and the factual and public interest stages tend to be taken together. In any case merger inquiries have to be carried out within a time limit of months. Financial results and other accountancy matters are examined in merger inquiries, but here again a broader approach is usually appropriate and less time is required.

Orders and Undertakings

Some industrialists complain that they cannot see the report before it is laid before Parliament and published by the Minister. The facts will have been put back to them during the inquiry, and they should have a fairly good idea of its main contents, but they may wish to argue that the recommendations for action are impractical. The Commission's recommendations, however, are not binding. There follows a period which may well last a year while the Minister tries to persuade the industry to give him a voluntary undertaking, not necessarily following the Commission's recommendation. The Minister may now invite the Director to carry on these negotiations (Part VIII).

Provided that the Commission has concluded that a monopoly situation exists and has specified the particular effects adverse to the public interest that either the monopoly situation or the steps taken to exploit or preserve it may have or may be expected to have, the Minister has power to make such orders as *he* considers requisite for the purpose of remedying or preventing the adverse effects specified in the report (s. 56). The order must be considered appropriate by the Minister to remedy the mischief specified by the Commission. The following conditions must be satisfied before an order can be made. First a reference must have been made to the Commission and the reference must not have been so framed as to prevent the Commission from considering the public interest; the Commission must have made a report and the report must have been laid before Parliament. If according to the Commission's report a monopoly situation exists, and either that situation or the steps taken to exploit or preserve it operate, or may be expected to operate, against the public interest, then the Minister *may* make an order exercising any of the powers set out in schedule 8 to the Fair Trading Act, even if the Commission has not recommended that they should be exercised. Identical powers arise where the Commission has concluded that a merger, concluded or anticipated, may be expected to operate against the public interest.

It is thought that the Commission's decision that a monopoly situation exists is not subject to appeal, although the decision may depend on difficult questions of law.

The order controlling the prices that Roche Products Ltd may charge for the tranquilizers it sells under the names of Librium and Valium has involved proceedings both in the House of Lords acting as a legislator and in the civil courts. The Commission recommended that its prices should be reduced to 40 and 25 per cent respectively of the prices then being charged, and the Minister made an order without consulting Roche first. Roche alleged that it had not enjoyed a fair hearing, in that it was not made very clear that the Commission was concerned that the increasing amounts spent on continuing research into other drugs, and charged against the profits of the reference drugs, might be excessive. Since the order required an affirmative resolution and affected Roche exclusively, Roche was entitled to present a petition against the order to the House of Lords. The Special Orders Committee of the House recommended that Roche should be allowed to reopen only the issue about the amount of world research expenditure to be set off against the profits of the British operations, but the House of Lords rejected the recommendation and the order was made. Roche stated that it would not comply with the order, since the Commission had infringed the rules of natural justice and consequently the report, on which the order depended, was void. The Minister therefore applied to the High Court for an injunction – an order forbidding Roche to infringe the first order. The proceedings have continued slowly. The High Court held that, like any other litigant seeking interlocutory relief, the Crown must give an undertaking that if the order was held invalid, it would compensate Roche for the loss incurred in charging the lower prices. The House of Lords reversed this decision. Proceedings must then start on the merits of the issues. Is the Commission required to abide by the rules of natural justice? If so, did it in fact do so? If Roche is successful on both these points, it is unlikely that the Minister will argue that the report is not void – he would surely revoke the order anyway. By the time the litigation is over, the patents for both drugs, which enable Roche to sell them at high prices, will have expired. The proceedings are not, however, as pointless as they seem. Anti-trust authorities all over the world have opened proceedings against Roche, which may wish to say that the validity of the British order is still subject to dispute.

Powers of the Minister

The Minister may make an order relating to conduct abroad only against a citizen of this country, a company formed under the law of the U.K. or a person carrying on business in the U.K. (s. 90). Where a British firm is party to an international cartel, it may be ordered to resign, but no order can be made against the foreigners, even if they are restricting competition within the United Kingdom. Where they are subject to Community law, it may be possible to complain to the Commission of the European Communities, and sometimes a foreign anti-trust enforcement body may be prepared to protect our economy.

Section 56 confers considerable powers on the Minister. He may make it unlawful to make or carry out specified agreements or arrangements, and may require any party to them to bring them to an end; but since the transfer of jurisdiction over agreements registrable under the 1956 Act to the Restrictive Practices Court, this power is far less important than it was formerly. He can also make it unlawful to withhold supplies or services from any specified persons, or to agree or threaten to withhold them, or procure others to do so. He may also restrain a person from refusing to supply one type of goods or services unless other goods or services

31

are bought. Any of these orders may be made conditional, or otherwise limited.

New powers were added in 1965. The Minister may make it illegal for any person specified in an order to discriminate between customers as to the prices charged, or to depart from a published price list. He can also forbid a firm to give preference to certain customers or suppliers in respect of the supply of goods or services (schedule 8, paragraphs 6–8). Sometimes a large firm is in a strong position in relation to some of its suppliers as well as to its customers. To support his use of these powers, the Minister may require a firm to publish its prices. He may also regulate a firm's prices (paragraphs 9 and 10), although it is thought that the Minister would rarely want to regulate prices in detail on a permanent basis. If a dominant firm is so powerful and uncompromising that detailed regulation of its prices day by day is needed, there is a case for nationalizing the industry; this course was recommended by a minority of the Commission in its report on gases in 1956. Price regulation in great detail might make it difficult for a firm to stay in business. The Minister might, however, wish to use the power, as he has done in the past, in order to compel a single price cut or as an ultimate sanction so as to modify the firm's own pricing indirectly. There are of course other powers to control prices under the counter-inflation legislation. Since 1973, the Minister has also had power to prohibit the recommendation of prices or of charges to be made (schedule 8, paragraph 11). This may be useful when a trade association or professional body recommends the charges to be made by its members for their services, or when a dominant firm recommends resale prices.

The Minister has had power since 1965 to order a dominant firm not to amalgamate with another firm (schedule 8, paragraph 12) and, provided it is not a nationalized industry, he can order it to dispose of some of its assets (schedule 8, paragraphs 14 and 15). Where the dominant firm produces in many plants and is not subject to much competition, such a structural remedy, intended to introduce independent competitors into the industry, may be the only effective one. On the other hand, it is often difficult to find an independent buyer, not already producing similar products, prepared to pay a fair price and there is bound to be disruption for some time. For example, sources of supply and outlets will have to be divided. Such an order has never been made in this country, probably because the costs to the dominant firm were thought to be penal. Divestiture orders still require approval by both Houses of Parliament (s. 91), and consequently the firm affected may petition in the House of Lords against the order, as Roche did against the order requiring it to lower its prices. Nevertheless, the experience of divestiture decrees in the United States has not been encouraging. When the Supreme Court was concerned that one of the two large makers of tins had acquired a firm making glass containers, it ordered it to dispose of the plants where the glass containers were made. The only purchaser to be found for most of these was one of the largest makers of glass containers – out of the frying pan into the fire! Affirmative resolutions are still required for divestiture orders, although this is no longer the case when the other powers are being exercised (s. 134(1)). Had the order reducing the prices which Roche might charge been made under the Fair Trading Act, Roche could not have presented a petition to the House of Lords. (See p. 30 above.)

In practice few orders have been made, mainly because the procedure for varying them when conditions change has proved cumbersome. The normal practice has been for the Minister to obtain an undertaking from the relevant firms, after tough negotiations, which often last over a year.

Although orders may be made only to prevent the adverse effect on the public interest of the monopoly situation or of steps taken by the dominant firm to preserve or exploit the position (s. 56), ministers have frequently required undertakings from smaller firms in the industry. It has always been doubtful whether orders could have been made against such persons, but frequently the dominant firm dislikes giving an undertaking that will tie its hands, while its competitors are free. Although the conduct of the other firms can hardly be said to be for the purpose of preserving the dominant position, they have been persuaded to give undertakings.

Since 1973, except in the case of a nationalized industry and certain agricultural products (sections 50(3) and 86(2)), the Director has been entitled to receive a copy of the Commission's report and ministers are required to take into account his advice on how to proceed (s. 86). The Minister may also ask him to carry on the negotiations with the parties to obtain undertakings as to action considered appropriate by the Minister to remedy or prevent the adverse effects specified in the Commission's report (s. 88). Where he is unsuccessful, it is still the Minister rather than the Director that makes the order. Any undertaking is given to the Minister, but it is the Director's duty to consider whether the undertaking should be modified in accordance with changes in circumstances. If it is being infringed, he should advise the Minister, who may make an order. When the undertakings are announced, they are often less onerous than the Commission's recommendations. In its report on detergents in 1966 (see p. 37 below), the Commission recommended that Unilever and Proctor and Gamble should reduce their expenditure on advertising and sales promotion by 40 per cent and

33

that some automatic sanction should be imposed, such as that the excess should not be allowed as a business expense in computing liability to corporation tax. The Board of Trade had no power to make such an order. Its President, as an important member of the Cabinet, might have been able to persuade the Chancellor of the Exchequer to insert such a power in the next Finance Bill; but in fact he accepted undertakings from the two large firms that they would introduce new brands that would be advertised only a little, and that would either be cheaper or contain more detergent for the same price. The firms were left free to spend as much as they liked on promoting their other brands. The Commission also recommended that the two large firms should reduce their wholesale prices substantially, and suggested a figure of 20 per cent; but the President was content with an undertaking that prices would not be raised for two years.

If an undertaking is infringed, the sanctions are not very strong or immediate. It is not illegal to infringe it. If the breach were clear and could not be justified, the Minister would doubtless make an order on the basis of the original report of the Commission. It is not criminal to infringe even an order, but it seems likely that an individual harmed by the breach could ask the High Court for an injunction or for compensation for breach of statutory duty (s. 93(2)), although the position is not beyond all doubt. The matter has not yet been tested because no one member of the general consuming public is likely to have a sufficient incentive to incur the costs of the action. For breach of some orders, such as one not to discriminate, a particular trader who cannot obtain supplies on trade terms may have a sufficient interest to litigate, but he may face difficulty in showing how much profit he has lost since the order was made because, if he has been unable to sell, he may not have been able to test market conditions, and it is for the plaintiff to prove the amount of his loss; although the courts are prepared to make presumptions in favour of a plaintiff who cannot quantify his damage because of the wrongful conduct of the defendant. Probably, the only effective remedy is for the Crown to ask for an injunction as it did when Roche stated it did not intend to abide by the order. The remoteness of the sanctions is in marked contrast to the position in the United States, where criminal penalties, including fines and imprisonment, may be imposed on those who have monopolized. In practice this is rarely done since it is not easy for firms to know what conduct would be considered illegal, but those who have been injured frequently sue for three times as much as they have lost. Breach of an order of the court would amount to contempt of court and be punishable by fine or imprisonment.

In the U.K., however, many people do not believe that the

evidence supports a firm line against monopolies. Certainly many of the Commission's recommendations, including those relating to detergents and petrol, have been criticized, and the undertakings given to the Board of Trade by the oil companies made the position of the small companies, which they were designed to help, more difficult, and had to be relaxed. They are now to be renegotiated.

Although a firm cannot be sued if it breaks its undertakings, it is unlikely to do so. Most businessmen make considerable efforts to keep within the law. To be accused of infringing one's undertakings is a very poor advertisement. Firms are much more likely to take pains to negotiate with the Minister before the undertakings are agreed, than to break them once they have been made. Where there has been a recommendation that pricing policies should be moderate, it is almost impossible for anyone to supervise. However, it is much easier to look into complaints about discrimination, because the traders who are boycotted may take the initiative.

Dominant Firms and the Public Interest

When assessing the public interest the Commission has rarely criticized the dominance of a firm unless it has done something to keep other firms out. If the firm has merely expanded its plant in good time to meet expected increases in demand, so that it is unprofitable for other firms to enter the industry, the Commission has not objected to its monopoly. Indeed, in its report on the supply of electrical equipment, the Commission criticized Chloride for not developing earlier the large plants which could produce batteries more cheaply, and it welcomed the policy of standardizing components adopted by Lucas, on the ground that this reduced costs, while leaving sufficient choice to consumers. Even in an industry with few independent suppliers, firms may act competitively in reducing prices if they think that their own high profits or inefficient management may encourage other firms to enter the industry and compete. Potential competition from large firms operating primarily in other markets may be as effective as actual competition in encouraging dynamic behaviour. It may later turn into actual competition. For instance, Fisons' power in part of the fertilizer market was reduced by Shell's diversification into it, and Imperial Chemical Industries meets competition from the oil companies in the supply of some chemicals.

While productivity may be increased if a firm with a small share of the market does its best to get ahead of its competitors and achieve a larger market share, a firm which already has a strong position in the market may be able to use its power to keep out others and so preserve its position. Such abuses have been condemned,

Monopoly Situations

particularly in the reports on the supply and export of matches, published in 1953, and on the supply of certain industrial and medical gases published in 1957.

Discrimination

One of the ways in which the British Match Co. acquired an almost complete monopoly of the home market was to make temporary price cuts whenever anyone attempted to enter the market. To this predatory practice the Commission objected. The British Oxygen Co., also, supplied over 90 per cent of the oxygen produced in the U.K., and discouraged competition by arranging for companies which it was not known to control to compete at very low prices in areas where other producers built their plants. The Commission recommended that the beneficial ownership by a dominant firm of other companies should be made public knowledge; and to discourage selective price cutting it recommended that the firm should publish price lists and keep to them. New firms can now build a plant, secure in the knowledge that if British Oxygen wishes to undercut them, it will have to reduce its prices nationally. Of course, discounts can be allowed to those who take large deliveries: the price list can specify these. Indeed, the Commission has several times recommended that a monopoly supplier should endeavour to make its prices to different groups of buyers reflect the difference in the cost of supplying them. This theory would require suppliers to charge for the freight of goods that are expensive to transport.

In several of its earlier reports, the Commission referred to the practice of uniform delivered pricing but, for various reasons, did not feel disposed to disturb the practice. In its report on plasterboard (1974) however, it attached weight to three factors:

'First, we are dealing with a complete monopoly. Secondly, transport costs are high in relation to total costs and vary widely between deliveries to different customers. Thirdly, the product is relatively homogenous and this eases the problem of costing and prices.' (Paragraph 139).

It had been impressed by the extent to which delivered prices were no longer uniform in other industries where transport costs are relatively high.

'A system of uniform delivered prices for plasterboard might not survive in a fully competitive situation, and there would be some advantage in loosening up the present price structure and making it more nearly resemble what would obtain under a competitive system. We have particularly in mind the possibility that a

36

newcomer setting up in an area at some distance from British Plaster Board's present installations would have the advantage of lower transport costs to merchants and users in his area and that this might more than counterbalance any additional costs (as compared with those of B.P.B.) which he would incur under other heads. At present such a potential competitor would be unable fully to deploy his cost advantage because of B.P.B.'s system of uniform prices, and might thus be deterred from entering the market. It may be that competitors would not in fact emerge, but, in our view, the possibility of their emergence would be increased if uniform delivered prices were abandoned by B.P.B.'

The Commission thought that there would not be serious regional consequences if the practice were abandoned for plasterboard, since it forms so small a part in the total costs of a building. It considered that a zoning scheme, consisting of a delivered price for each type and load of plasterboard within each zone, which would be based on the cost of production and selling plus the average transport cost for supplying that type and load to the zone, would not cause undue administrative complications.

The Commission did not conclude whether identical prices should be charged from each factory, but believed that B.P.B. might move towards the use of different ex-works figures for different factories plus the average cost of freight from the particular factory to the zone in question, and

'. . . we see advantages in this happening, provided that the ex-works prices were not employed as a means of reducing the differences between delivered prices in different zones . . . except in so far as these might be consequences of true differences in production and selling costs as reflected in selling prices.'

Advertising

The effect of advertising on the public interest is difficult to assess. On the one hand, it may enable a firm to increase its sales rapidly; the prospect of this makes it worth while building a large plant initially, thereby reducing unit costs. On the other hand, once an existing leader of industry has advertised widely, it is difficult for a firm with a smaller share of the market to compete: the same expenditure would be a larger proportion of its turnover. In 1966 in its report on detergents, over 90 per cent of which is supplied by two firms, Unilever and Proctor and Gamble, the Commission recommended that they should each reduce expenditure on sales promotion by 40 per cent. This would have two results: it would make it easier for a small firm to enter the market, since it would not be subject to any restriction on advertising and would require a smaller expenditure to compete with that of the existing giants; and it would cut the cost of the severe competition between the two existing firms and enable them to reduce their prices and so compete in a way more useful to housewives.

It would be difficult to give effect to such a recommendation. If only television advertising were prohibited, money would probably be spent on other forms of promotion that are less effective per pound spent in increasing turnover, such as sending persuasive young men round from door to door. If, on the other hand, all forms of promotion were prohibited, it would be difficult to stop the firms from granting price concessions to those supermarkets who were prepared to promote the detergents, unless complex rules to prevent price discrimination were introduced.

The firms have been unwilling to comply with the Commission's recommendation. Price competition is said not to be a real alternative to advertising. The two firms who each supply over 40 per cent of the detergents sold in the United Kingdom must match each other's prices and neither is going to be forced out of the market. Previous agreements between them to limit promotional expenditure broke down. If one firm fears that its brands, or some of them, are selling less well than those of its rival, it is under strong pressure to increase its sales promotion even if it does not think that the other is cheating. The effects of advertising in promoting efficient production and marketing are hard to assess. After the publication of the report on detergents, the Board of Trade commissioned an independent inquiry into the effects of advertising, which will be published in 1975. In the United States, too, the anti-trust authorities are concerned about the problem.

Ensuring Supplies or Markets

If a firm makes a long-term contract with its suppliers or customers, it may be able to plan future production and distribution with greater confidence, and this may reduce costs. Where it buys up its suppliers or customers, the cost savings may be even greater, as it can integrate the two activities. For instance, great economies became possible when certain steel works were integrated and the metal went through more than one process in a molten state and did not have to be reheated. If there are enough equally good suppliers and customers, no harm is done; but the Commission was critical where a market-dominating firm made an exclusive agreement with the best supplier, as when the British Match Co. agreed to buy its machinery from the Swedish Match Co., and the latter agreed to supply no one else in the United Kingdom and to refrain from supplying British

Match's competitors overseas. In theory, a firm wishing to compete with British Match could either make its own machinery or make arrangements with some other supplier. But to take advantage of economies of scale, a maker of machinery must have a larger share of the market than is needed by a match maker; consequently, a match maker would either have to make machinery on an over-expensive small scale, or find buyers for its surplus machinery. The Commission also criticized British Oxygen's deliberate attempts to control the supply of plant for producing oxygen by acquiring the companies who produced it.

Tying

The refusal to sell one product unless another product or service, too, is bought has also been condemned, and not only in the colour film report considered below at page 44. For instance, the petrol producers undertook not to require a promise from retailers to refrain from displaying on their forecourts any oil not supplied by the petrol supplier, nor to give better terms to retailers accepting such a limitation or taking a certain proportion of their oil requirements from the petrol supplier. Undertakings were also required from British Oxygen that it would be prepared to sell apparatus for storing oxygen to its customers and to those making their own oxygen; though if it supplied apparatus free, it was entitled to require an undertaking from consumers not to use it for oxygen from any other source.

Requirements Contracts

Contracts under which distributors agree to take their total requirements of a particular product from a single supplier can lead to increased costs. Wall Paper Manufacturers Ltd, which supplied over 70 per cent of the particular goods referred to the Commission, required retailers to undertake not to buy wallpaper from anyone else. As a result there were two sets of distributors: one selling Wall Paper Manufacturers' paper, and the other selling paper from other firms. Not only did this result in more retailers, each with a lower turnover, but the smaller firms, because of their weaker bargaining position, had to give their retailers higher margins. The Commission thought that requirements contracts by so powerful a firm must make it more difficult for others to compete fairly, giving value for value, and consequently condemned the practice. On the other hand, in 1965 the majority in the report on the supply of petrol to retailers though that the economies resulting from exclusive dealing agreements were sufficient to defend the practice of inducing retailers to buy only from a single firm, at any rate for up to five years. A large part of the cost of providing retailers with petrol is the cost of transporting from the nearest depot, and the concentration of a retailer's entire trade on a single supplier reduced these costs by several pence a gallon. It might have been preferable, however, as Professor Barna suggested in his note of dissent, to require an undertaking that the agreements be ended, relying on the introduction of quantity discounts to encourage retailers to buy from a single source.

In its report on metal containers in 1970, the Commission condemned not only requirements contracts by the dominant firm, but also less extreme commitments by canners, such as a promise to take 80 per cent of their requirements from Metal Box. Such agreements made it difficult for a new firm to enter the can-making market, as most of the existing canners would already be committed to Metal Box for a number of years, and often the possibility of competing for 20 per cent of the demand would not warrant investment in the necessary plant. The Commission recommended that Metal Box should bring such agreements to an end and, in so far as it should seek further orders, it should do so only for specified quantities. Nor should it make any price concessions to those who in fact bought all, or a specified proportion of, their requirements from Metal Box. It also recommended that Metal Box should modify its agreements, so that no maker of open-top cans was bound for longer than two years.

Patents

An inventor is entitled to apply for a patent to protect his invention, and if successful can sue anyone who uses the invention during the life of the patent – sixteen years from the date of the patent. It is said that this encourages firms to devote time and resources to research and development, and it probably does induce firms to publish more of their inventions. It also encourages them to grant licences to other firms, since the right to prevent others infringing the patent protects the patent holders against the danger of licensees letting any information escape. On the other hand, especially where the rate of technical innovation is slow, a dominant firm can make it difficult for others to compete if it buys up as many inventions as it can. The Commission criticized British Oxygen for buying up companies largely so as to obtain the right to use patented inventions owned by them, or which the owners had allowed them to use. In the case of food and pharmaceuticals, patents are a less serious bar to competitors, because the latter are entitled to claim a right to use the patented invention on payment of royalties. For other products it is harder to obtain a compulsory licence – the right to make use of the invention on payment of fees calculated, usually, by reference to turnover. The risk of not being successful after several years of very expensive litigation may well discourage firms from trying to obtain such a licence. It is impossible to say how many voluntary licences have been granted because of the fear that proceedings would be commenced for a compulsory one. It is doubtful how far patents do encourage innovation; it seems more likely that they encourage earlier publication and licensing. But the Commission has not dogmatically disapproved of even dominant firms enjoying patent protection. It has condemned only the deliberate collection of exclusive patent rights.

Price Levels

In most of its dominant firm reports, the Commission has attempted to assess the rate of profit earned on the capital employed (on the basis of its historic, not replacement, cost) to see whether prices are excessive. This is not entirely satisfactory, as a firm earning low profits may not be operated efficiently, in which case its prices may still be excessive; conversely, a firm may be achieving high profits because of its unusual efficiency. Yet some critics doubt whether the Commission, or indeed any outside body, can effectively assess how far a dominant firm is using its assets efficiently. (See pp. 68–9 below.) In a complex monopoly situation one can see whether the various firms involved incur very different costs, in which case one has some guide as to which are efficient, though here again different methods of operation and different accounting methods, particularly in relation to apportionments with non-reference .goods and the date at which the capital employed was last revalued, may account for the difference. In the case of a single dominant firm, there is unlikely to be any close comparison. The dominant firm has nearly always supplied a very large share of the U.K. market for a long period, and the smaller firms' costs may well be assessed on a different basis. The prices, costs and profits of firms operating abroad may be misleading, as wage levels may vary as well as the cost of power and raw materials. Moreover, accounting rules are very different and the rate of exchange between sterling and any foreign currency is subject to fluctuation.

More recently, the government has twice asked the Commission to confine its attention to the level of prices charged in investigating the public interest. Kelloggs supplied about 60 per cent of the breakfast cereals supplied in the U.K. and two other firms a further 30 per cent. Competition took the form largely of advertising and promotion, which cost about 13 per cent of turnover. The Commission concluded that:

'With so few manufacturers competing, the pricing tactics of any one of them would be bound to affect the market shares of the others. Where price reductions cannot be expected to expand the total market, it is all the more likely that any gain achieved by some reduction will be at the expense of competitors; and the breakfast cereal manufacturers, who appear to regard not price but advertising and promotion and product innovation as the effective means of encouraging total market expansion, must be assumed to have this consideration in mind. Any significant reduction (or failure to follow a general increase) in prices would therefore be seen by a manufacturer as likely to be matched by his competitors, since they would not be able to risk the consequences of having their own prices too far out of line. Thus the manufacturers would see the result of price competition as a lower general level of prices with no competitive advantage to any of them. We think that manufacturers recognise that price competition can be easily matched, whereas other forms of competition (for example a successful advertising campaign) may be less easy to match. We consider that fear of price competition, and the recognition that it is dangerous to embark on, arise from the fact that supply to so large a proportion of the market is concentrated in so small a number of manufacturers. We believe that this fear is a major factor leading manufacturers to find ways of competing otherwise than in price. We do not, therefore, accept Kellogg's assertion that the nature and extent of competition in the industry would be unaltered if there were a larger number of manufacturers.' (Paragraph 79)

The Commission went on to conclude that the reluctance to compete in price was largely responsible for competition taking the form of sales promotion and for the substantial profits earned. Kelloggs acknowledged that it was the price leader, but also stated that it could not charge as much as it liked without encouraging new firms to start making breakfast cereals at the expense of Kelloggs' share of the market.

In the Commission's eyes, therefore, the level of prices set was a step taken by Kelloggs both to exploit and to preserve the monopoly situation. It was therefore required to consider the public interest. The rate of profit made on the capital employed had been as high as 70 per cent between 1962 and 1966, but had fallen since then, partly as a result of a serious fire and labour unrest. From 1967 to 1971 it had averaged about 46 per cent and was running at 36.8 per cent in the last of these years. Kelloggs argued that this high rate was a result of its efficiency in using its capital intensively on a three-shift basis and in reducing labour costs. Even so, there was a marked difference between the profits of Kelloggs and the 25.8 per cent average return on capital for the firms in the upper quartile of manufacturing industry. This is calculated as the average percentage return on capital employed of the first quarter of a list of all the manufacturing firms, arranged in order of profitability. For the food industry, the upper quartile earned only 22·2 per cent. The Commission did not use these figures to indicate a limit on profits, but as a general yardstick. It concluded that in view of Kelloggs' efficiency, the current prices, yielding a lower level of profits than in the past, were not contrary to the public interest, but that prices and profits might well in time return to levels which were excessive. It therefore concluded that the level of prices 'may be expected to operate against the public interest' and should be reviewed by the government.

Since that report was published, the profitability of the major manufacturing firms in the country has been controlled under the counter-inflation legislation, so there may be less room for this sort of argument in the near future. Prices are controlled so that they may not be increased proportionately more than costs have increased, nor may they yield a higher proportional profit on turnover. The Price Commission however, which assesses these matters, is not required to determine whether the original profit level was excessive, only whether it has been raised unduly. Indeed, the firms that were originally efficient may have less chance than others to improve their profitability. While the comparatively simple criteria for price control are laid down by the Treasury for the Price Commission to apply, one wonders whether it is sensible for the Monopolies Commission to be required to attempt a more difficult and complicated task in the same field. We will see (p. 206) that the Council of Ministers of the European Communities has also asked the Commission of the European Communities to try to control prices through the provisions for controlling dominant firms.

Conclusion

Generally, the Commission has not said that dominance by a single firm has operated, or may be expected to operate, against the public interest. In a few industries it is so much cheaper to produce a product in a large plant that can be continuously used than in many smaller ones, that one or two plants of the minimum efficient size can supply the expected demand and there is room for only one or two suppliers. In its report on the supply and processing of colour film, the Commission was not surprised to find that only two firms had plants in the United Kingdom.

On the other hand, it has been able to point to certain tactics adopted either to spread the power from one market to another, or to inhibit competition by making it more costly for newcomers to enter the market; these it has condemned as steps taken for the purpose of preserving the monopoly situation.

But throughout it has adopted a very flexible approach: it has rarely made general pronouncements that certain practices are undesirable. Its conclusions on the public interest have been very closely related to the facts of each particular industry, and so vary from one report to the next. This doubtless conforms with the intentions of those who created the Commission. It was intended primarily to investigate the facts, and the criteria of the public interest were so general as to preclude any presumption against certain practices.

REPORT ON THE SUPPLY AND PROCESSING OF COLOUR FILM, 1966

Often a report is concerned with the effect of more than one practice on the public interest and the description of the final chapter of a single report may give the reader a better impression of the sort of work performed by the Commission.

The Commission found that from 1962 to 1964 Kodak supplied over 70 per cent of the colour film in the U.K., whether measured by its selling price or by the square foot. Obviously, there was a monopoly situation in relation to its supply. It was not clear that any one firm applied a process called the negative–positive process to a third of the films so processed; consequently, a monopoly situation did not exist in respect of that process, and the public interest inquiry could not be extended to it. In each year, however, more than 60 per cent of the substantive reversal film was sold at a price that covered processing; so more than a third of such film processed in the U.K. was processed by or on behalf of persons who operated this practice. The Commission considered that the practice restricted competition in the processing of this type of film, and recommended that both manufacturers and importers should charge separately for processing, if required, and that they should give technological help to firms who wanted to process colour films.

In more than one report, the Commission has disapproved of the tying of one product or service to another by a firm with a substantial market share. If all sellers of film sell only on the basis that processing is paid for when the film is bought, then no independent processor can enter the market, unless he is acting for an existing supplier of film, or unless he can sell as much film as he wishes to process. In the United States, tying by a firm with substantial market power is almost always illegal: it enables a strong position in one market, such as the sale of colour film, to be extended to another, such as the processing of the film.

The Commission considered the factors that had led to Kodak's predominance: the patent rights which prevented others from copying its research successes too closely and quickly; the ability of Kodak's parent company in the United States to continue providing films for amateurs during the war when, in the United Kingdom, film was reserved for military use; and the customs duty, equal to over 7 per cent of the retail value of film if the value of the processing is excluded. Only Kodak and Ilford had factories in the United Kingdom, and all imports had to pay this duty. As a result Kodak and Ilford had a margin of 7 per cent plus the small cost of carriage from abroad within which they could reap higher than average profits, or could afford to let costs rise, or could keep prices down to exclude competitors. That only two firms should manufacture in the United Kingdom was not surprising, since it is very much cheaper to make films in large plants, but the tariff did reduce foreign competitors' freedom of manoeuvre. Some might otherwise have charged that much more and made greater profits in the short term; others might have been prepared to reduce prices or to spend more in sales promotion and so compete more effectively with Kodak.

None of these reasons for Kodak's predominance in the market amounted to a criticism of its conduct. In deciding whether it had abused its dominant position, the Commission looked to its policy in relation to prices and profits. The Commission made comparisons with other industries, and examined tables setting out the profits made by the Kodak company as a whole expressed as a proportion of the capital employed, as well as the profits that Kodak had made on colour film in proportion to the capital used in that business. This test of fair pricing was somewhat arbitrary. Some of the machinery must have been built long ago, when costs were lower; and since, according to accountants' conventions, the value would have been written down each year in proportion to its expected life, its capital value may well have been very much more than the figure in the accounts. Moreover, some of the plant that was built years ago may have been obsolescent, so that nowadays one would build very different machinery, and then even the written-down value may have greatly exceeded its real value in terms of its capacity to make or process film. (The treatment of costs is considered in the Note on Cost Concepts at the end of this chapter.)

The Commission was in a dilemma here: it could probably have obtained a reasonably accurate current valuation of Kodak's plant and so a more accurate idea of the profits being made using it, but this would have been of little use for purposes of comparison, unless the Commission could also have obtained recent valuations of investments in other, more competitive, industries. These were not available. But other figures are available for the various branches

45

of industry, showing the percentage profits earned on capital as they appear in companies' balance sheets, which are based on historical costs. It is, therefore, to historical costs that the Commission normally looks. But the comparison is a very rough one. In the colour film investigation, the Commission found that Kodak's profits on capital employed from 1958 to 1964 on the colour film business had increased from 27·5 per cent to 55·6 per cent, while on its other business it had increased from 14·2 per cent to 22·8 per cent. In almost all these years the percentage for colour film was over twice that on its other business.

Despite the difficulties of comparing the figures, the Commission thought it was fair to say that Kodak had earned profits on its whole business rather above those of industry in general; its colour film business was very much more profitable. Amongst other arguments, Kodak pointed out that its film had to compete for consumers' leisure money with materials for other hobbies; that the public was prepared to pay more for Kodak's products than for similar films supplied by other manufacturers, so must prefer its quality or service; that its prices had been kept stable for seven years – during which time the index for miscellaneous retail prices had risen by 40 per cent – and that its increasing profits were due to continuous improvement in its efficiency; and that Kodak was a growing company and so expected better profits than those earned by industry as a whole.

The Commission pointed out that colour films were likely to become more popular and that the industry did not face a particularly high risk of a decline in demand. Since the industry was growing, Kodak might invest part of its profits in plant; but the Commission thought that the requirements for financing future growth should not determine current prices: today's buyers should not be forced to pay for the benefit of tomorrow's. It pointed out that a fall of a fifth in the prices at which Kodak sold would still leave the company with a higher than average profit on the capital employed; it was not trying to say what was the highest desirable rate of profit, but to demonstrate Kodak's room for manoeuvre. The Commission added, however, that Kodak's pricing policy was a 'thing done' as a result of its monopoly position and was contrary to the public interest. It recommended that the company should lower its selling prices and that tariffs on colour film should be abolished. It also thought that Kodak allowed retailers too large a profit margin.

Despite the Commission's recommendations, the Board of Trade decided that it would not be in the public interest to change the tariff. This is understandable: not only was the country's balance of payments so weak in late 1966 that customs duties had been generally increased by 10 per cent, but it is at least arguable that had the German firm Agfa–Gevaert been able to export more film to

England, Ilford, the only firm apart from Kodak manufacturing in the U.K., would not have been able to stay in business. It may be that if a firm is inefficient it should not be protected, but Ilford is the only sizeable U.K. firm that can offer competition to Kodak. Furthermore, the U.K. was then engaged in hard international tariff bargaining under the 'Kennedy round', and a unilateral cut in customs duty without obtaining a compensating cut in the duty imposed on some commodity in an export market was hardly to be expected. On the other hand, the Commission's suggestion that tariffs should be abolished would have provided an automatic sanction to prevent overcharging. As soon as British prices became too high, Agfa and other firms would have been able to increase their sales in the U.K., and there would have been a substantial incentive for Kodak and Ilford to watch their costs constantly and charge prices which would discourage Agfa from making a determined onslaught on the U.K. market. As it was, how could the Board of Trade decide whether Kodak's prices were too high? Only if it could put in a team of efficiency experts could it tell whether the firm was being run efficiently. Merely to know what profit Kodak was earning on such part of its capital as was devoted to colour film making and processing did not enable the Board to decide whether prices were reasonable, since inefficiency may swell costs. This may be twice as harmful as monopoly profits, in that costs can be deducted from profits in assessing liability to tax, and so reduce the government's receipts. Kodak did, in fact, reduce its charges to retailers by $12\frac{1}{2}$ per cent and recommend that the prices charged to the public by retailers should be reduced by 20 per cent, almost as much as the figure suggested by the Commission. This, however, provided no security for the future. Kodak also started to sell its colour film exclusive of the processing cost, although at any one shop, consumers might not be able to choose whether to pay for processing when buying a film.

Note on Cost Concepts

Depreciation; Historical and Replacement Valuations of Capital

A manufacturing firm incurs various types of costs. First it must usually build or buy a factory and install machinery. This is usually treated as a capital cost by accountants. If the factory cost £100,000 and is expected to last for fifty years, then they may assign £2,000 a year of the revenues to depreciation. That is to say the cost of the factory is apportioned to the various processes carried on inside it over its expected life. Some twenty-five years later, the factory will stand in the firm's accounts as being worth only £50,000: that is called its 'written-down value'. Its market value, however, will probably be higher, because the prices of most things will have risen during the twenty-five years and, further, the factory may be built in an area where land values have risen even more. The entry in the accounts will then not reflect the actual value of the capital – it will be based on historical costs (what the factory cost, less the depreciation) and not on a replacement basis (the cost of a building that would perform the same function today). Machinery is usually treated in the same way and the written-down value at any time may be greater or less than the replacement value. In an industry where technology is developing rapidly it may be that, although a machine is not worn out, no one would think of replacing it as it is. Its value to the firm is what it would cost to buy a machine that would produce the same products, after allowances have been made for the different costs of doing so. It may be that a new machine would need less maintenance, could be worked by an elderly woman instead of a strong young man, would run on cheaper fuel, and so on. An examination of a firm's books will usually disclose capital on a historical basis: few of even the most up-to-date firms have revalued their capital more than twice since the war, and the longer it is since the last valuation, the less accurately the accounts reflect the true worth of the capital employed.

Inflation Accounting

With recent accelerating inflation, the discrepancy between market values and the figures at which a firm's assets are entered in the accounts has become so great that a committee representing the main professional accounting bodies has published a 'provisional statement' for inflation accounting. It would be too expensive for every large firm to revalue everything each year, so the proposed standard does not suggest that this should be done. Instead, it states that a general price index should be used to adjust accounts. For instance, if this index has increased by 50 per cent since the acquisition of an asset, then historical cost should be multiplied by one-and-a-half. The main results will be to make balance sheet figures somewhat more realistic (though an adjusted historical cost will not necessarily be near the current value of a particular firm's assets), and to raise costs in the income statement and thereby deflate profits which were artificially swollen in accounts based on unadjusted historical costs.

Average and Marginal Costs

The average cost of making most products includes overheads, such as the cost of building the plant, inventing the product or ways of making it, salaries to be paid to staff whom it would not be possible, or sensible, to dismiss when demand is weak. In manufacturing industries, the average costs will be lower if demand is sufficient to keep the plant and personnel fully occupied, since the receipts for the product, or its turnover, will be larger, and each item will bear a smaller part of these overheads. Other costs are proportional to turnover: fuel, materials and so on usually vary almost arithmetically with the amount produced. Maintenance falls in between: some maintenance is needed even for idle plant, more is needed if the plant is fully used. The marginal cost of a product is what it costs to make one extra unit. If the plant already exists and is not fully utilized, this will consist of the components or raw material needed, and the additional fuel and labour; nothing need be allowed for the capital, since it could not be used in any other way. If the plant is already fully used on a normal working basis, then the marginal costs may be higher: overtime will have to be paid, a shift system introduced, or, in the longer term, a new plant acquired. In deciding whether production should be increased, it is largely marginal costs that should be considered. In deciding whether to build a plant, the management must hope to make sufficient profits to cover depreciation, but once the factory is built, a manufacturer who maximizes his profits makes his decisions on the basis of marginal costs. One cannot say, however, that a monopolist is acting contrary to the public interest because his profit is very much larger than his marginal costs, provided it is not much larger than his average costs. If he could not usually earn enough to cover depreciation and interest on his capital, he would have little incentive to invest. He is not holding the public to ransom if he charges enough to cover these costs.

3: Mergers

Company Law

The company is a concept used to facilitate the coming together of money, labour and management for a common purpose. Companies do not exist in the physical world; most are just entries in the register of companies. Suppose that you want to start a business and will need £10,000 capital, you can fill in certain forms and thereby create a company for a £50 fee, though further costs will be incurred in keeping it alive. It can then create shares and debentures, and if you manage to sell 5,000 shares at £1 each on its behalf, it will have half the capital needed. This is sometimes called the 'equity share capital'. The owner, or 'holder', of each share will be entitled to a one five-thousandth share of such of the profits of the company, if any, as its directors decide to devote to paying dividends. If you can then persuade someone to lend the company £5,000, it can issue debentures to that amount. The terms of debentures can vary considerably, but by definition they are loans made to a company and acknowledged in writing. They usually carry a fixed rate of interest. Whether or not profits are earned, the debenture holders may be entitled to interest. Ordinarily they have little control over the management, except in relation to transactions which directly affect the value of their holdings, such as the issue of new debentures having priority over or ranking equally with their own. Normally, debenture holders undertake little risk; they will be paid in priority to shareholders, and consequently will lose their capital and rights to interest only if the company fails badly.

Shares are likely to alter in value far more than debentures bearing a fixed rate of interest; if the company is very successful it will pay no more interest to the debenture holders than if it is only moderately successful, and all the additional profits may be paid in dividends to the shareholders or spent on assets which are expected to increase the profits in later years – again for the benefit mainly of the shareholders. In a sense the shareholders together own the company, inasmuch as by acting together they can replace the board of directors and, where appropriate, appoint a liquidator to realize the company's assets, pay its debts out of the proceeds, and divide anything that remains between the shareholders.

An individual shareholder, however, can rarely force the liquidation of a large company quoted on a stock exchange, unless its business has failed badly. Usually there are so many shareholders, each owning only a small proportion of the shares, that it is difficult to persuade shareholders owning a majority of the shares to appoint a liquidator and so, in effect, oust the existing directors from control of the company. Directors are usually employees of the company they control, but since they are likely to have negotiated their own contracts on its behalf, they may well be entitled to large sums of money if they are dismissed. The directors manage the company, and the shareholders can use their power to control them only in a general meeting, which, except in special circumstances, is held only once a year. Few shareholders attend the meetings or have a detailed knowledge of the company's business, so it is rare for directors to be challenged, provided that they declare a dividend no smaller than that paid during the previous year. If, however, someone who wishes to obtain control of a company is successful in acquiring sufficient shares – probably by buying a large number by agreement with holders of substantial blocks of shares and then making an offer to the remaining shareholders to buy their shares – he can vote the existing directors out of office and appoint a new board.

There are many ways in which one company, let us call it A Ltd, can merge with another, which we will call B Ltd. The simplest is for A Ltd to buy all the shares in B Ltd. This may, however, be too expensive. Moreover, B Ltd's shareholders may want to retain an interest in the combined enterprise. This can be done in various ways. A Ltd may issue shares and exchange these for the shares in B Ltd. B Ltd may retain a separate existence and business, or its assets may be transferred to A Ltd and then it can be wound up and cease to exist. Alternatively, a holding company, which we will call 'H Ltd', may be created, to which the shareholders in A and B Ltd transfer their shares in exchange for shares in H Ltd. The number of shares received by the respective shareholders will be proportional to the agreed worth of each share, though not necessarily to its market value immediately before the merger. The directors negotiating the transaction will have more knowledge about the companies' prospects than the buyers and sellers on the stock exchange. Share prices are related to the expected flow of future dividends, which in turn depends on the future profits of the company and its policy towards the distribution of profits. They depend as much on the quality of the management as on the assets owned. The debentures of the old companies can be left outstanding, or can be paid off or, with the consent of the debenture holders, exchanged for debentures in H Ltd. The device of creating a holding company is very flexible.

Sometimes a merger is only partial: for instance, A Ltd may buy only some of the shares in B Ltd. If no one person holds very many shares in B Ltd, quite a small proportion of its shares may give A Ltd control over B Ltd's activities, at least as long as B Ltd is prosperous. A Ltd may need as little as a third or a quarter. Since few shareholders attend and vote at meetings, A Ltd's block will usually decide any issue. If B Ltd holds a similar proportion of shares in C Ltd and C Ltd in D Ltd, and so on, a very small investment in A Ltd may give control over a very large company at the end of the chain. A more obvious device for obtaining control without investing a large amount of capital is to create two classes of shares: 'A' ordinary shares which have no votes, or only one apiece, and others retained by the controller having more than one vote apiece, but carrying the same right to dividends as the 'A' ordinary shares.

In order to prevent control being acquired to the detriment of other shareholders, the City Code provides that where one person, or several acting in concert, without the consent of the Takeover Panel acquires 30 per cent or more of the voting rights in a company quoted on a stock exchange in the U.K., he must offer to buy the rest of the shares of the same class. Although the code cannot be enforced in the courts, there are substantial sanctions, such as the possible loss of a stock exchange quotation. This book, however, is not concerned with the protection of shareholders.

Mergers are usually effected by the acquisition of all the shares in the target company, but the flexible concepts of company law could be used to avoid control measures unless they define 'merger' in terms that cover all the ways in which one person or group of people may be able to exercise considerable influence over more than one enterprise. The definition must be very wide if all mergers likely to inhibit competition are to be controlled.

Economics

On the other hand, most mergers have little effect on competition. If one small company buys another operating in a different market, it is unlikely that competition will be reduced. There may be many good commercial reasons for mergers. A company with good managers but few assets may merge with one with ill-used assets and poor managers in order to find an outlet for its managerial talent. A large firm wishing to diversify may find it cheaper to buy and expand the activities of an existing firm than to acquire the necessary technical information. In some industries, the minimum size of plant that can produce the product cheaply may be so large that a small company with few assets may be able to raise the money to build a larger plant only by merging with another company, and scrapping the the existing plants when the new one is ready. Sometimes if a supplier or customer can be acquired, operations can be integrated and economies achieved. It is important not to discourage mergers that increase productivity, unless competition is likely to be substantially reduced. Most mergers take place with the consent of the existing directors, who either receive payment for the loss of their jobs, or continue to work for the enlarged company. But sometimes A Ltd will buy as many shares as possible in B Ltd without the agreement of B Ltd's directors, probably by making a general offer to buy all the shares; and if it succeeds in buying enough to gain control, it may then dismiss B Ltd's directors and take over the company. The fear of a possible takeover bid is one of the most effective inducements to the managers of a small firm continually to make the best use of its resources. A contested bid is likely to increase efficiency whether or not it is successful. A Ltd is likely to make a bid only if its managers think it can make more profit from B Ltd's assets than B Ltd's managers will do, and if the bid is successful they will have an opportunity to try. If it is unsuccessful, it is likely to be because B Ltd's existing directors have convinced the shareholders that their shares are worth more than A Ltd is offering, and they would do this by proving that they can produce even greater profits from B Ltd. It is said that I.C.I.'s unsuccessful takeover bid was the making of Courtaulds.

For many years economists have attempted to isolate the relevant factors for distinguishing mergers that should be controlled in the interest of preserving competition; but they have not achieved much success. Since 1914, section 7 of the Clayton Act in the United States has forbidden mergers 'that may substantially lessen competition', although it had little effect until the Celler–Kefauver Anti-Merger Act 1950 widened the definition of a merger. Since then, the Supreme Court has held many mergers to be illegal; but it has not been able to evolve rules which will help businessmen to know in advance what types of merger should be avoided. In 1968 the Department of Justice published 'guidelines' setting out the criteria it would apply in deciding whether to contest a merger in the courts, but they have not proved very helpful in practice.

If a company that dominates a substantial market merges with its competitors, especially if it buys those who have most frequently gained customers from it, or if it merges with the best customers or sources of supply, dangers to competition seem substantial. The greatest difficulty has been experienced when there are comparatively few firms in the market. If the firms in a very competitive market start to merge until only four or five are left, it may well become oligopolistic: each firm is more likely to take its competitors' reactions into account when it makes its business decisions. Even with the advantage of hindsight it may be difficult to say which of a series of mergers resulted in this interdependence. There have been competitive industries with four firms, and oligopolistic ones with a dozen or more. As the number decreases, consideration of competitors' reactions to price cuts is more likely to inhibit manufacturers from overt competition in price, particularly if they each sell an identical product. If another industry makes a product which is a close substitute, then it may be that competition from it is more important to those making pricing decisions than competition from those making the same product. But even in an industry with few producers and no close substitutes, Professor Galbraith argued in his 1966 Reith Lectures, there would not necessarily be a tendency to keep up prices and produce less. The decisions of large companies are taken by its managers, who may own few shares, and their objective may not be to make the greatest possible profits. Their position in society is largely dependent on the size of the firm's turnover, rather than on the extent of its profits. This personal interest in expanding production may be reinforced by the social consciences of directors who have become pillars of the establishment and feel that it is more worthwhile to provide employment and reduce prices than to swell the profits to be distributed to shareholders. If this is so, then there may be substantial price competition even where there are very few firms.

The Commission's Attitude to Mergers in Monopoly References

The Commission criticized British Oxygen for its persistent policy of buying rival producers of oxygen and acetylene, even though it admitted that this had been done partly to achieve economies of scale. It even criticized the Imperial Tobacco Company's ownership of a minority share in Gallaher Ltd, its most important competitor. Imperial had purchased a majority of Gallaher's shares in 1932, but by the time of the reference its interest was only 42 per cent, and the Commission accepted that Imperial had not attempted to use its shares to influence Gallaher's policy. Nevertheless, Imperial then supplied over 60 per cent of the cigarettes in the United Kingdom and Gallaher about 30 per cent. Gallaher was not only Imperial's most substantial rival, it was at that time the cigarette manufacturer that was most rapidly expanding its share of the market. The Commission feared that Imperial's not very aggressive trading policy might have been partly a consequence of the realization that it would recoup 40 per cent of the trade it lost to Gallaher either in the form of higher dividends or in capital appreciation, as its Gallaher shares increased in value. Although the Commission recognized that there was some rivalry between the factories making the different Imperial brands, this was not such a strong spur to efficiency as the fear of losing profits to an outsider would be. The Commission went so far as to recommend that Imperial should be required to dispose of its Gallaher shares; but at that time the Board of Trade had no powers to give effect to this, and the Conservative government refused to take legislative action. Earlier, in 1953, the Commission had criticized the British Match Co. for buying independent producers until there was virtually no competition from the home market. It was not prepared, however, to recommend that the various factories operated by that company should be transferred to different independent companies; it feared that the resulting disturbance might outweigh the benefits to be expected by increasing competition, despite the fact that some of the factories had far higher costs than others, and were probably wasting the resources.

In 1963, however, the Commission accepted the policy adopted by Lucas and Chloride in acquiring their rivals so as to expand capacity quickly when demand was rising. This conclusion is perhaps surprising, since the exclusion of rivals was not entirely absent from Lucas's calculations, and it was only at the beginning that Lucas acquired companies that would have been likely to fail if they had remained independent. But the Commission explained that in protecting its markets by acquiring competitors, Lucas was laying the basis for economies of scale. Presumably these economies were thought to outweigh the effect of competition in encouraging productivity, even though they could be achieved only when new plant was installed.

More recently, in its report on the supply of asbestos (1973), the Commission condemned the practice of the leading firm, Turner and Newall Ltd, of acquiring competing manufacturing businesses, or customers. Nevertheless, it did not recommend that it should dispose of those acquired some six years before, since that might involve disruption of what had become an integrated business. It did, however, recommend that Turner and Newall should not acquire any more competitors in specified lines of business, without the prior consent of the Department of Trade and Industry.

How Should Mergers be Controlled to Preserve Competition?

The refusal of the President of the Board of Trade to initiate legislation to give effect to the recommendation that Imperial should dispose of its shares in Gallaher aroused considerable criticism. It is, however, difficult to decide just what form of control should be imposed. The remedy in the case of Imperial's shareholding would have been simple: it had only a minority holding, and to require it to sell that on the market, or distribute the shares to its own shareholders, would have been easy. But where complete ownership has been obtained, and the assets of the two companies mixed – new assets acquired and old ones sold by the new company – then it may be impossible to unscramble the egg. At the most, one could break up the company into new constituents, some factories being sold if a buyer could be found or else allotted to a new company. The shares in the new companies could either be sold on the stock exchange or distributed to the shareholders of the old company. In the short term, this might be expected to increase costs: central services such as development and research would have to be duplicated. Fear of the possible effects of disturbance dissuaded the Commission from recommending that British Match should be required to dispose of some of its factories.

Would a better solution be to require prior ministerial consent to a merger or to empower the Minister to forbid certain mergers? This approach avoids the disadvantages of breaking up a going concern, but has two drawbacks. Before a merger has been consummated it is very difficult to estimate the economies likely to result. Usually these depend on reorganizing the separate firms into a new unit, cutting out certain duplications of effort, and possibly sacking some of the former management. This is likely to take many months, or even years. Yet the main public benefit derived from mergers is the economies that they make possible. If prior consent is required or if a report is required before the merger has been consummated, it will be difficult to estimate the extent of these economies. Furthermore, if a merger is held up long enough to allow a full investigation to be made, the delicate balance of interests usually achieved in agreeing the terms of the merger is likely to alter, and it may be difficult to maintain the secrecy usually kept while such negotiations are proceeding.

Part V of the Fair Trading Act 1973

In the event, the Labour government adopted all three solutions in the Act of 1965. Under similar provisions in the Fair Trading Act most newspaper mergers require prior clearance by the Commission; other mergers may be referred to the Commission by the Minister, but if this is not done within six months of the merger, then it is too late (now sections 55, 64 and 75). In fact, most substantial mergers are notified to the Minister and clearance is almost always granted within three weeks. Not all mergers that come within the statutory definition are referred – indeed until the autumn of 1972, only about 2 per cent of them were, though the proportion is rather higher now. If a reference is made, the Minister may forbid the consummation of a merger while the Commission is making its investigation. If a prospective merger is condemned by the Commission, the Minister has power to forbid its consummation (s. 73 and schedule 8, paragraph 12) and, where the merger condemned by the Commission has already taken place, he may order divestiture (s. 73 and schedule 8, paragraphs 14 and 15). Such orders are subject to the affirmative resolution procedure, which enables the firm to petition the House of Lords not to affirm the draft order. (See p. 30 above.) This may be important, as the Special Orders Committee does not consider only whether the Minister has power to make the order, but also whether it is proper for him to exercise his powers.

Definition of 'a Merger Situation Qualifying for Investigation'

The first problem in framing an anti-merger provision is how to define a merger. Section 64 provides that the Minister may refer a merger situation to the Commission for investigation and report, where it appears to him that (a) it is or may be the fact that two or more enterprises, one of them carried on in the U.K., have 'ceased to be distinct enterprises'; and (b) either the value of the assets taken over exceeds £5 million or a monopoly situation relating to the supply of goods or services is created or intensified as a result or the merger.

The following provisions defining the various terms used can be fully understood only after a close analysis of seven pages of the statute. An 'enterprise' is defined in section 63(2) as 'the activities, or any part of the activities, of a trade or business.' When B.P. bought Distillers' chemical interests, it bought an enterprise, although it did not buy the whole Distillers' company, which continued to produce and supply spirits independently of B.P.

Section 65(1) provides that

'. . . any two enterprises shall be regarded as ceasing to be distinct enterprises if either –

(a) they are brought under common ownership or common control (whether or not the business to which either of them formerly belonged continues to be carried on under the same or different ownership or control), or

57

(b) either of the enterprises ceases to be carried on at all and does so in consequence of any arrangements or transactions entered into to prevent competition between the enterprises.'

This definition includes an arrangement by which one firm buys a competitor's assets and persuades it to leave the industry, and so is able to expand its own capacity without worrying about its ability to sell its products. Such arrangements may not be against the public interest: the economies of production on a large scale may outweigh any dangers to competition, as the Commission decided in the case of Lucas, but their probable effects may require investigation and if, in the Commission's view, there are insufficient benefits to balance the reduction in competition the transaction can be forbidden.

The draftsman gives a wide definition to 'common control'. This covers not only a complete merger under company law, as when A Ltd buys all the shares in B Ltd, or where A Ltd's and B Ltd's shares are exchanged for shares in H Ltd, as was discussed above: under section 65(2)

'enterprises shall . . . be regarded as being under common control if they are –

(a) enterprises of interconnected bodies corporate, or

(b) enterprises carried on by two or more bodies corporate of which one and the same person or group of persons has control, or

(c) an enterprise carried on by a body corporate and an enterprise carried on by a person or group of persons having control of that body corporate.'

In section 137(5) 'interconnected bodies corporate' is defined by reference to section 154 of the Companies Act 1948 as a company and all its subsidiaries. One company is a subsidiary of another if

'(a) that other either –
(i) is a member of it and controls the composition of its board of directors; or
(ii) holds more than half in nominal value of its equity share capital; or

(b) the first-mentioned company is a subsidiary of any company which is that other's subsidiary.'

If one company is a subsidiary of the other, or both are subsidiaries of a common parent company, then they are inter-connected bodies corporate. So if A Ltd and B Ltd are distinct businesses, and A Ltd starts to buy shares in B Ltd, then the enterprises cease to be distinct when A Ltd has acquired enough for it to own half the equity share capital in B Ltd or is able to control the composition of its board.

If one person can control two companies, he may well have a personal interest in their profits, so it is not very likely that they will compete against each other very strongly. Paragraph (c) of section 65(2) covers the control of the enterprises where one is a company and the other is not; enterprises cease to be distinct when, for instance, Mr A, who already carries on one business, acquires half the shares in a company that carries on another.

These definitions do not cover all the ways in which competition may be restrained between companies without a cartel agreement being made. One may be able to control the policy of a company without owning half the equity share capital: some companies have separate classes of shares, like the 'A' ordinary shares described at p. 52, entitling their holders to the same dividends, but one class carrying no right to vote, a second class carrying one vote each, and a third ten votes each. The owner of half the votes would normally be able to control the composition of the board of directors by exercising his votes in general meeting, but it would be possible to make some of the votes ineffective for this purpose. In section 65, therefore, the draftsman extended the idea of common control:

'(3) A person or group of persons able, directly or indirectly, to control or materially to influence the policy of a body corporate, or the policy of any person in carrying on an enterprise, but without having a controlling interest in that body corporate or that enterprise, may . . . be treated as having control of it.

(4) . . . a person or group of persons may be treated as bringing an enterprise under his or their control if –

(a) being already able to control or materially to influence the policy of the person carrying on the enterprise, that person or group of persons acquires a controlling interest in the enterprise or, in the case of an enterprise carried on by a body corporate, acquires a controlling interest in that body corporate, or
(b) being already able materially to influence the policy of the person carrying on the enterprise, that person or group of persons becomes able to control the policy.'

These provisions take us beyond the control exercised under company law. Where the managing director of A Ltd becomes the managing director of B Ltd too, then clearly a person becomes able to control or materially to influence both enterprises, even if he owns no shares in either. A person who makes a loan to a company may be able to influence company policy by threatening to take proceedings to recover his money. A large customer or supplier, also, may be able to influence policy. But where a creditor or customer has never attempted to influence an enterprise, it may be difficult to tell whether the power to do so really exists. In such a case it is far from clear when or even whether a merger has taken place.

Where a person who has control over one enterprise becomes able materially to influence the policy of another company or human being running a business, then the enterprises cease to be distinct, and the Minister has six months during which he may refer the merger. Where the merger was not generally known, this period may be extended under section 64(4) to six months after the Minister should have known of it. A further merger occurs when the person who was previously only able to influence the enterprise's policy either acquires a controlling interest (by obtaining half the shares, or otherwise) or obtains de facto control.

If this were all, it might be possible to avoid establishing common control by arranging for a man to control one company, while his wife or relatives owned another. So it is provided in section 77(1) that

'associated persons, and any bodies corporate which they or any of them control, shall (subject to the next following subsection) be treated as one person.'

Subsection (4) defines what persons are 'associated':

'the following persons shall be deemed to be associated with one another, that is to say –

(a) any individual and that individual's husband or wife and any relative, or husband or wife of a relative, of that individual or of that individual's husband or wife;

(b) any person in his capacity of trustee of a settlement and the settlor or grantor and any person associated with the settlor or grantor;

(c) persons carrying on business in partnership and the husband or wife and relatives of any of them;

(d) any two or more persons acting together to secure or exercise control of a body corporate or other association, or to secure control of any enterprise or assets.'

Subsection (6) states that

'In this section "relative" means a brother, sister, uncle, aunt, nephew, niece, lineal ancestor or descendant. . . .'

Some experience in drafting this sort of definition had been obtained under tax law, and this particular definition is very similar to that defining a 'close' or family company for the purpose of corporation tax. If Mr A and Mr B are partners and Mrs A's uncle controls U Ltd and Mr B's nephew acquires control over N Ltd, then the partnership is treated as being in common control with each company separately, but it is thought that U Ltd and N Ltd are not under common control. The merger between N Ltd and the partnership can be referred to the Commission, if it fulfils the other requirements of section 64, and in that inquiry the relationship with U Ltd might be a relevant circumstance. But if the merger with the partnership did not satisfy the other conditions of section 64, then the fact that a merger between U Ltd and N Ltd would satisfy them would be irrelevant.

The provisions of the section cannot be avoided by Mr B's nephew arranging for the shares in N Ltd to be held by someone else for the benefit of his family, since under section 77(4)(b) the trustees would be treated as associated with Mr B. It is thought that the draftsman was justified in introducing the idea of associated persons, since where there is a close personal relationship the policies of the enterprises may not be managed independently.

The definition of common control is certainly very wide: some 'associated persons' may not even know each other, still less collaborate to stifle competition. But this is hardly crucial, since the Minister has to exercise his discretion before referring a merger situation to the Commission, except in the case of newspapers, which will be considered later.

In practice, moreover, all the merger situations actually referred to date have consisted of complete amalgamations. Since the statute is drafted so widely that it is impossible to obtain control without creating a merger situation, businessmen have not attempted to avoid its provisions.

What Mergers Can be Referred to the Commission?

Before the Minister can refer a merger situation to the Commission, not only must two enterprises have ceased to be distinct, but the

61

other conditions of section 64 must be fulfilled: not only must it appear to the Minister that two or more enterprises have come under common control within the previous six months, it must also appear to him that, as a result, either (a) the conditions specified in subsections (2) or (3) prevail or do so to a greater extent, or (b) the value of the assets taken over exceeds £5 million.

In language rather difficult to grasp at first reading, subsections (2) and (3) apply to mergers the one-quarter rule adopted for the reference of a monopoly situation: that a quarter of the goods or services are supplied by one person in the U.K., or a substantial part of it, by, to or for a single person. There is one difference from the definition of a monopoly situation: where the reference specifies only part of the U.K., it must be 'a substantial part' of it and not merely 'any part'. Provided, however, that the monopoly situation arises or is intensified in a substantial part of the U.K. or that the assets taken over exceed £5 million, the Minister may ask the Commission to limit its consideration to any part of the country (s. 69(3)).

Most of the complexities of deciding whether two or more enterprises have ceased to be distinct have already been considered; but it is noteworthy that only one of the enterprises need have any connection with the U.K. If a U.K. company acquires a foreign company, the merger may be referred; but it is perhaps more likely that a reference will be made if a foreign company acquires control over a U.K. one. The bid made by the Dentists' Supply Co. of New York for the Amalgamated Dental Company was referred to the Commission, and though the majority did not condemn the merger, the delay did enable the U.K. company to fight off the bid. If a United States company, which has less than half the shares in a U.K. company but already influences its policy, decides to buy the outstanding shares – as happened with Ford some years ago – then its acquisition of shares bringing its holding of the equity share capital up to 50 per cent, or giving it power to control the composition of the board of directors, amounts to a merger within section 64.

It is surprising that a reference can be made when the only connection with the U.K. is that one company was created under the law of England, Scotland or Northern Ireland, a connection with the U.K. that does not seem relevant to economic policy. True, two foreign companies may merge and, if both might have started to compete in the U.K., their merger may directly affect competition in the area; but this could be so whether or not one of the companies was formed under U.K. law.

Normally the Minister must refer the merger within six months of its taking place (s. 64(4)), but under section 75 he may refer the matter to the Commission before the merger is consummated, and meanwhile may make an order forbidding or restricting anyone from acquiring control over a second enterprise (s. 74(1)). When Imperial Tobacco was about to merge with Smith's Potato Crisps, the Board threatened to use these powers and the merger was not completed. Where, in consequence of a transaction or of a series of transactions between the same parties, any enterprises successively ceased to be distinct, then under section 66 all the mergers completed within two years may be treated as taking place together on the latest date when any occurred. So if A Ltd acquired one part of B Ltd's business in January 1974, another part in the following January, and yet another in December 1975, then all three mergers can be treated as if they took place in December 1975 and can be referred to the Commission up to June 1976. For this provision to apply, however, the transaction must be between the same parties or interests; so if A Ltd absorbs first B Ltd, then C Ltd, and so on, the provision does not apply.

Section 64(1)(a) provides a sensible criterion of mergers that may lessen competition: those which result in a single firm enjoying a quarter of the market in the U.K. or a substantial part of it. It may be objected that competitors may consider each other's reactions to the market decisions long before any of them has reached a quarter share of the market, but the test is stricter than that before 1973 when a one-third share was required, and may cover looser oligopolies. Another weakness of the provision is that vertical mergers – those between a supplier and his customer – are not covered. If A Ltd mergers with its suppliers or customers, and thereby weakens the position of its competitors, it may eventually increase its share of the market: but even if the increase takes it beyond a one-quarter share, this will not result directly from the merger; and it is not clear how far indirect results can be considered. In fact, the first merger that was condemned by the Commission, that between Ross Group Ltd and Associated Fisheries Ltd on 18 May 1966, was criticized partly because of the vertical consequences.

Where the enterprise taken over is large, then the weaknesses in paragraph (a) of subsection 64(1) are taken care of by paragraph (b), permitting a reference where the assets taken over exceed £5 million in value. The figure of £5 million can be increased by the Minister (s. 64(7)). The value of the assets taken over is determined by taking the assets as they stand in the enterprises' books of account (s. 67). As was mentioned in the Note on Cost Concepts at p. 47, this may be very much less than the cost of replacing them.

Section 67 also defines which assets should be valued. Where one or more of the enterprises remains under the same control, then it is the value of the assets of the other enterprise that count. Even where no assets are actually taken over, because a customer or creditor merely gains the power materially to influence the policy of another enterprise, it seems that there may be a merger qualifying for reference owing to the unusually wide definitions of 'ceasing to be distinct enterprises' in section 65 and of 'the value of the assets taken over' in section 67. Where no enterprise remains under the same ownership and control then the assets to be valued are those of all the enterprises except the one that has the assets with the highest value. It may seem a little strange that if a company with assets valued at £10 million acquires all the shares of another worth £4 million in return for its own shares, no reference can be made, unless the one-quarter test is satisfied, but that in the reverse case it can.

References by the Minister

Merger references can still be made only by the minister responsible for the monopoly functions. It is impossible to define the criteria for reference clearly enough to entrust the selection of mergers to an official who is constitutionally not available to answer parliamentary questions, and the responsibility remains ministerial. Nevertheless the Director is required by section 76 to take steps to keep himself informed about actual and prospective merger situations and to recommend what action should be taken by the Minister. It has been announced that the Director will chair the mergers panel, a group of senior civil servants with fluctuating membership. While clearly those most closely concerned with making a reference and their legal advisers would regularly be members of the panel, those with particular knowledge of the industry would join the panel on an ad hoc basis, in relation only to a particular merger situation. The proceedings of the panel remain secret, since confidential information must be discussed – indeed, when the Minister is first informed of a possible merger, it may be vital to keep the possibility of the merger secret, or stock exchange valuations might alter violently at a time when it is far from certain whether the merger will be pursued on commercial grounds. The criteria of the public interest to be considered by the Commission are now the same as those set out in section 84 for monopoly references. But as the list is not exclusive and no weighting is given to the various economic and social factors, many of which are likely to conflict, this is not very helpful. To some extent the relevant considerations have been developed by the Commission in its reports on mergers. In 1968, when there was not very much experience, the Board of Trade published a handbook called *Mergers: a Guide to Board of Trade Practice*, in which it set out some of the considerations it took into account when considering whether to refer a merger. This mentioned the obvious considerations, but did not greatly help an outsider to decide whether a merger was likely to be referred. The most important factor in the case of mergers with horizontal elements (between firms which produced the same or similar products) or with vertical elements (those where one firm bought the sort of products sold by the other) was the possible diminution of competition. What factors would minimize this detriment to the public – did large buyers have countervailing power, were the firms prepared to give assurances about the way they would exercise their increased market power? Were there other benefits to be expected from the merger such as production in a larger plant or one accomplishing two or more processes, leading to large cost savings?

It is not easy for financial and industrial journalists to tell why a particular merger has or has not been referred, but comment in the financial press has improved recently. A new edition of the handbook is also expected and it should be able to indicate developments in the practice since 1968 and particularly since the Director came to organize the vetting process. In particular, it may be possible to give rather better guidance about conglomerate mergers – those with no important horizontal or vertical elements, where competition is not likely to be greatly affected and where the main problem may be whether the new management is as likely as the old to use the firm's assets effectively.

Not much time can be spent on this preliminary investigation – it seldom exceeds three weeks – since it may not be possible to keep the merger 'on ice' once it is known, and it is not easy to keep such an important matter secret. Information is usually supplied by both firms, and some critics have complained that mergers are unlikely to be referred unless someone, whether rival bidder, competitor, customer, supplier, or the firm which is being taken over against its will, provides the mergers panel with reasons for objecting to the merger. Nevertheless, the panel will also have access to published information about the merger and there is a great deal of information about most industries easily accessible in the relevant civil service production department. The Office of Fair Trading also employs economists in senior positions, who should be capable of putting up an independent case against a merger which is likely to be harmful. An outsider is not in a position to judge the validity of the criticism and the need for secrecy must prevent the Office from divulging the information.

There was a time when the Industrial Reorganization Corporation, created by the government, used to encourage mergers which it thought would further industrial rationalization. It was, however, allowed to die in 1970, and the government seems no longer as convinced as it was in 1968 that most mergers are desirable. Already the proportion of qualifying merger situations where the reference is announced is increasing, although frequently the merger is called off after being referred, so that the Commission does not actually have to investigate the matter.

The Commission's Task

The Commission's task is very similar to that involved in a monopoly investigation. Section 72 requires that the Commission shall come to definite conclusions and give reasons therefor. Usually the reference will require the Commission to consider whether a merger situation qualifying for investigation has been created and if so, whether it operates or may be expected to operate against the public interest (s. 69(1)). As before, however, the reference may direct the Commission to consider only the £5 million asset test, or only whether a monopoly situation has been created or intensified (s. 69(2)). Moreover, the public interest issues may now be limited to such elements in, or possible consequences of, the merger as are specified in the reference (s. 69(4)). Where the Commission concludes that the merger, or any of the specified elements or consequences of it, operate or may be expected to operate against the public interest, it is required to consider whether to recommend that certain steps be taken either by any minister, or by any of the persons controlling any of the enterprises which have ceased to be distinct, to remedy or prevent any adverse effects on the public interest (s. 72(2)).

The principal problems arising in many merger references, particularly those made in the early years, related to restriction of competition. Often there were substantial horizontal or vertical elements involved so the most important issue was whether there were any checks available for minimizing the effect on the public. One merger was allowed between makers of car components G.K.N. and Birfield (1967), on the ground that the vehicle makers were then sufficiently powerful to look after themselves and, if necessary, could start making their own components or persuade some other firm to do so. In B.M.C./Pressed Steel (1966) and BICC/Pyrotenax (1967), when the Commission received assurances that buyers from the firm acquired would continue to receive supplies on the same terms as the acquiring firm, it found that the mergers would not operate against the public interest. The value of taking such assurances is, however, dubious. First, the terms on which one company buys from another within the same group may not be negotiated at arm's length – the 'price' is only a book-keeping entry. Secondly, there is no way of enforcing assurances given to the Commission, unless it has concluded that the merger may be expected to operate against the public interest. An adverse finding is required to trigger the government's order-making power.

Even if the reduction in competition were substantial and could not be minimized, the merger might be conceivably be approved if it would lead to very substantial cost saving. A vertical merger might be a way of arranging that the existing plant should be scrapped and a new plant built in which several manufacturing processes could be carried out in a single operation. As we saw earlier, in steel making there may be considerable savings if the final product can be made without cooling the metal. For the production of some chemicals, huge economies can be achieved by building large plants, and in some cases a single plant of optimal size can produce enough to supply the whole of the U.K. and perhaps much of Europe too. The vital but difficult question is whether a merger is required to eliminate the existing plants. If there are such savings, any firm which invests in a large plant would be able to cut prices until those using the old plants were driven out of existence. Although the merging firms are usually asked to analyse and quantify the expected cost savings, neither normally knows enough about the detailed operation of the other to be able to quantify them at all accurately. All one can say from the Commission's reports is that it has usually adopted a fairly sceptical attitude. Indeed, in no investigation where it has found that the merger may be expected to reduce competition has it concluded on such grounds that it may not be expected to operate against the public interest.

More recently, rather different questions have arisen on merger references. In 1969, two mergers were referred although there were no very significant vertical or horizontal aspects, and the Commission appended to its reports on these some general observations on mergers. In the United States, some courts have been concerned about the anti-competitive effects even of conglomerate mergers, but the Commission did not think that these were very important. It was more concerned that the efficiency of a large company, with many different activities, could not be judged easily – if the activities acquired were run less efficiently than before, this might not appear from accounts that relate to the company as a whole. It therefore suggested tentatively that the law should be changed so as to require companies to include in their reports to shareholders separate turnover and profit figures for each class of business that might be prescribed by the Board of Trade, and that, after an acquisition, separate figures for the acquired enterprise should be made available for at least three years.

The Commission condemned Rank's proposed acquisition of De La Rue (1969) on the ground that it was satisfied that, if De La Rue were taken over, there would be a real risk that some of its key personnel would leave the company, with adverse effects on the return and effectiveness of the company's business. For example, since countries arranging for the production of bank notes depend to quite an exceptional extent on the care and honesty of their supplier, the loss of personal contacts might disrupt this important side of the business. Considerable adverse criticism was directed at this attempt by the Commission to evaluate directly the likely effects of a merger on the efficiency of the business. In its monopoly reports, the Commission has frequently stated that it had no reason to doubt the efficiency of the firm and, indeed, this is a necessary step in deciding whether profit levels are excessive. Yet it is very difficult for an outsider or outside body to judge the efficiency of a firm directly, and even more difficult to say whether a merger, which will alter the structure of management, is likely to lead to improvement or deterioration. This was doubtless the reason why, in the early days, only mergers likely to reduce the spur to efficiency provided by competition were referred.

In 1973, the Commission did not condemn B.M.C.'s bid for Wilkinson Sword. Again, it dismissed most of the arguments used in America to show that conglomerate mergers reduce competition as insignificant in effect, and concentrated its attention on the likely effect of the merger on efficiency, particularly on management. It concluded that

'although the success of the new corporate management could not, in the nature of things, be regarded as a certainty, it was nevertheless a reasonable probability.'

In Boots/Glaxco/Beecham (1972) and in Davy International/British Rollmakers Corporation Ltd (1974), the Commission was concerned with efficiency indirectly, through the loss of the spur of competitive research, and in the last case, although classical monopoly considerations were present, the Commission was also concerned about the danger of entrusting the whole U.K. roll-making effort to a company mainly concerned with international contracting. This is reminiscent of the fears expressed in its 'General Observations' that the new management might be less efficient than the old in running the company acquired. In Eagle Star/Sunley/Grovewood (1974) the effect of the mergers on the protection available to Eagle Star's policyholders was given considerable prominence, as was the effect on management efficiency. At the time of writing, the Boots/Frazer (1974) report is not available, owing to the strike at the government printers, but the government have announced that the Commission found that the merger would be likely to operate against the public interest, because it would probably reduce efficiency. Evidently, the

Commission also expressed general concern about mergers of large retail chains.

From the references now being made, it seems that the government is concerned not only that mergers may reduce the spur to efficiency provided by competition, but also that, even when competition is unlikely to be greatly affected, the new managers may run the target company less well than it would have been run, had it remained independent. Similarly, the Commission does not confine its investigation to competition, but also attempts to consider whether the new management is as competent as the old, and whether sufficient attention would be devoted to the affairs of the target enterprise. This is usually a more difficult task, and inevitably provokes criticism. Outsiders are not in a position to assess the validity of the general impressions on which the conclusions may to some extent be based. Nevertheless, as the Commission argued in its 'General Observations', there are various reasons why the Commission may sometimes have more information than the stock market or the acquiring company. This counteracts the argument that, in the absence of anti-competitive effects, the commercial wisdom of a merger should be left to the assessment of managements and investors.

It is usually clear very early what the main objections to a merger are likely to be. This is important since, in accordance with section 70, the commission may be given only six months or less in which to make its report, although the Minister may extend the period by three months when there are special reasons. In fact the Commission has nearly always managed to complete its reports well within the time limits set, although it may take rather longer to publish the report.

REPORT ON THE MERGER BETWEEN GUEST KEEN & NETTLEFOLDS LTD AND BIRFIELD LTD

In this inquiry, the Commission received most of its information from the parties to the merger, but also heard some of their customers and competitors. It found that the two companies were virtually the only suppliers of vehicle propeller shafts and that Birfield was virtually the only supplier of constant velocity joints in the U.K. and that, although they met independent competition for other motor car components, the merger would increase Guest Keen's share of the drop forgings market to about 40 per cent. There was, therefore, no difficulty in finding that in respect of these there was a merger situation qualifying for investigation. The reference, however, specified many other components of which a far smaller share was produced by the merging enterprises, so the merger situation did not qualify in relation to the reference products considered as a whole under the one-third test then used (now one-quarter – s. 64(2)). Since, however, the £5 million test was satisfied and the merger had been completed during the Commission's investigations, it was able to consider whether the merger might be expected to operate against the public interest.

Until 1959, Birfield's subsidiary had been the only maker of propeller shafts in the United Kingdom, and its customers complained that until then there had been difficulty in obtaining adequate and uninterrupted supplies. Birfield answered that this had happened only when the forecasts made by the car industry had proved inadequate. Some motor manufacturers persuaded Guest Keen to start making propeller shafts, and since 1959 supplies had been more regular and adequate. Clearly the motor manufacturers preferred to be able to buy their shafts from more than one supplier; but the shaft-makers' profits had been low and they feared that Birfield might be acquired by another firm, possibly American. Their evidence was that they would prefer it to be acquired by Guest Keen than by any other company.

Even if Guest Keen became a monopoly supplier there was a ceiling on its power to restrict production and raise prices. Firstly, propeller shafts accounted for less than 3 per cent of the combined firms' turnover; if enough were not made, fewer cars would be produced, and stocks of other components provided by the firms would accumulate. Secondly, the larger car manufacturers were technically in a position to start making their own shafts, or to persuade some other manufacturer to do so. Smaller firms might import them. Since, however, it would take nearly two years to build the necessary plant, this potential competition would not impose an immediate and narrow limit on the prices that Guest Keen could obtain.

The Commission decided that common ownership of separate plants did not increase the risk of stoppage through fire, accident, or industrial disputes, but was unable to decide whether the spur of competition would be more effective in promoting efficient research and development than collaboration between the former research teams would be.

Certain major issues could not be resolved: whether Birfield would continue to be independent if the merger were forbidden; the extent of the expected economies of scale; the efficiency of research and development; and the extent of customers' power to keep prices down. To some extent, the economies of scale were dependent on customers' agreement that plants should become more specialized, despite the increased risk of a stoppage at a single plant disrupting the whole industry. Guest Keen did not even attempt to estimate them. The Commission could not possibly obtain information on these matters so soon after the merger. Yet it was required to come to a decision. It could only make a guess, and it decided that the merger was not expected to operate against the public interest as regards propeller shafts. The position as regards constant velocity joints was not greatly affected by the merger, since Birfield was already the only supplier of these in the United Kingdom. The Commission hardly considered the relationship between constant velocity joints and propeller shafts, although each performs much the same function: the shafts being for cars with rear wheel drive, and the joints for those with front wheel drive. The competition between these components cannot, however, be very intense, since only by changing the whole design of a car could a manufacturer switch his demand from one to the other. In a rapid inquiry, which could not hope to be profound, the Commission was probably right not to bother about such a slight effect on the market.

As regards other components, the merger increased concentration only slightly; but Guest Keen would be able to use its position of power in the supply of propeller shafts and constant velocity joints either as a lever to obtain higher prices for its other components, or to sell more of them. It is thought that the first possibility is just a disguised way of saying that it could raise the prices for its propeller shafts to some extent: the tying problem is more serious. If a firm has to buy its drop forgings from someone, it may have little objection to buying them from the sole supplier of other components it needs; consequently efficient suppliers of drop forgings may be unable to compete. Guest Keen's answer was that in the past it had made package deals, at slightly lower prices than where the components were bought singly, only at the request of customers. If this was so, then it seems that the Commission was right not to object. The danger is most serious where the monopolist refuses to supply shafts on normal terms to those who are not also customers for other components. The Commission thought, though it did not say that it had been proved, that the lower prices charged for 'package deals' might merely reflect the lower costs of delivering a full 'package'. To object to such differentiation would be contrary to the principle the Commission has several times supported: that a monopolist's charges should, as far as practicable, reflect the differences in the cost of supplying different customers.

The Commission's conclusion that it did not consider that the merger was likely to operate against the public interest may well have been right, but it certainly could not be proved. In the Commission's inquiries, no onus of proof is placed on the parties; and much of what the Commission decides must be based largely on conjecture since, until a merger has been cleared, the firms dare not integrate and the results of the merger cannot be assessed. Even later assessment may be difficult, since companies alter all the time in response not only to internal pressures, but also to the state of the various parts of the economy; and one cannot say what would have happened if the firms had remained independent of each other. Had Guest Keen decided to increase its export activities without having taken over Birfield, it might well have been successful when tariffs become lower as a result of the international agreement made in 1967 called the 'Kennedy round'.

Orders

If, and only if, the Commission concludes that a merger operates or may be expected to operate against the public interest can the Minister make an order exercising any of the powers set out in schedule 8 (see pp. 31–5). The usual remedy is the prohibition of the proposed merger under schedule 8, paragraph 12, as in the case of Ross Group and Associated Fisheries: the Minister can forbid the merger unless an undertaking is given, although there is no direct way of enforcing the undertaking after the merger is complete. Or the Minister can decide not to bar the merger, but instead require the new company to dispose of one or more of its activities or factories under paragraph 14. This has been the practice of the High Authority of the European Coal and Steel Community; where a merger will make it difficult for a customer to be sure of continuing supplies, its authorization may depend on the new firm selling the capacity to make those products either to the customer or to an independent firm. In the U.K. prior authorization is not required, but the Minister can direct that certain assets be 'hived off'. He has considerable flexibility in framing safeguards for the public. He can exercise some of the powers listed in schedule 8 or he can negotiate undertakings or actual actions by threatening to use the powers or to initiate legislation giving additional powers. Nevertheless, unless a whole plant can be disposed of, it is doubtful, when a customer merges with its suppliers, whether any safeguards can be devised adequate to ensure that the customer will continue to take supplies from independents should demand fall, or that the supplier will continue to sell to its former customers should a shortage develop.

Newspaper Mergers

Newspapers – sufficient newspapers to represent most of the widely held political approaches – are so important in a democracy that it has been made illegal to transfer a paper to the owner of others without the prior consent of the Minister. This can usually be given only after the transfer has been considered by the Monopolies Commission. Newspapers have become heavily dependent on advertising revenue, because the price paid by purchasers is far below the cost of production. Once a paper begins to lose readers, advertisers begin to buy space elsewhere, and the revenue from advertisements drops off very rapidly. Advertising revenue became particularly low after mid-1966 owing to the credit squeeze, and many people feared that there might be more newspaper failures, and that some political parties, particularly on the left, would be left with no organ to express their views.

Where a newspaper cannot survive, a merger with another paper may be the kindest way of ending its life: some of the staff may be found jobs, and some of the editorial staff may even have an opportunity to express their views. But where a paper might have continued, the concentration by merger of the organs for influencing public opinion is damaging. Consequently the requirements for a press merger are more stringent than for others. Unless the Minister is satisfied both that the paper to be transferred is not economic as a going concern and as a separate newspaper, and also that it is not intended to continue publication, or unless the matter is urgent or the paper transferred has an average circulation on the day of publication of not more than 25,000 copies, the merger must first be referred to the Commission.

Section 58(1) provides:

'A transfer of a newspaper or of newspaper assets to a newspaper proprietor whose newspapers have an average circulation per day of publication amounting, together with that of the newspaper concerned in the transfer, to 500,000 or more copies shall be unlawful and void, unless the transfer is made with the written consent given (conditionally or unconditionally) by the [Minister].'

Except in the cases mentioned above, this may be given only after the Minister has received a report on the matter from the Commission. The Minister is empowered to make his consent conditional. In the Commission's report on *The Times*, Mr Davidson, in his note of dissent, recommended that the consent given to the transfer of the paper to the Thomson organization should be made conditional on certain formal undertakings being given to the Minister. In fact, however, the Minister's consent was not made conditional, although the majority recommendation that the transfer was not likely to operate against the public interest was influenced by assurances that had been given by Lord Thomson. In the unlikely event of these assurances to the Commission being broken, nothing could be done.

Where, however, a merger takes place without the Minister's consent, or in breach of any condition imposed by him, then any person convicted of being privy to the transfer or to a breach of condition, as the case may be, is liable to imprisonment for two years, or a fine, or both. Proceedings can be commenced only with the consent of the Director of Public Prosecutions (s. 62).

Transfer to a Newspaper Proprietor

The definition of 'a merger' for newspapers is far simpler to apply than that for other activities. Where there is no punishment for merging without consent, the definition of 'control' can be very wide and include a relative's spouse becoming able materially to influence another enterprise's policy; but where a person can be sent to prison for being privy to a merger, then the definition must be clear and simple to apply. It is illegal to transfer a newspaper to someone who already controls at least one, and who will, as a result of the transfer, control papers with a combined average circulation on the day of publication of half a million. If A controls one daily paper with a circulation of a quarter of a million and two locals with circulations of 100,000 each, and a third local paper with the same circulation is transferred to him, the four papers combined have an average circulation on the day of publication of over half a million even if they are published on different days; in this circumstance, prior consent is required. The period for which an average is taken according to section 57(3) is six months, ending either six weeks before an application for consent or, if consent was not applied for, six weeks before the transfer.

The definitions of 'newspaper' and 'newspaper proprietor' are wide:

'57. – (1) In this Part of this Act –
(a) "newspaper" means a daily, Sunday or local (other than daily or Sunday) newspaper circulating wholly or mainly in the United Kingdom or in a part of the United Kingdom;
(b) "newspaper proprietor" includes (in addition to an actual proprietor of a newspaper) any person having a controlling interest in a body corporate which is a newspaper proprietor, and any body corporate in which a newspaper proprietor has a controlling interest;
and any reference to the newspapers of a newspaper proprietor includes all newspapers in relation to which he is a newspaper proprietor and, in the case of a body corporate, all newspapers in relation to which a person having a controlling interest in that body corporate is a newspaper proprietor.

(4) For the purposes of this section a person has a controlling

interest in a body corporate if (but only if) he can, directly or indirectly, determine the manner in which one-quarter of the votes which could be cast at a general meeting of the body corporate are to be cast on matters, and in circumstances, not of such a description as to bring into play any special voting rights or restrictions on voting rights.'

A person can 'indirectly determine' how votes shall be cast where he controls a company which in turn is entitled to a quarter of the votes; but it is not clear whether a person able to influence the person with the legal right to make a decision is included. However, under section 77(1) 'associated persons', as defined in relation to section 65 as well as section 57(1) (pp. 60–1 above), are to be treated as one. So if Mr A can determine how a fifth of the votes shall be cast and his wife's cousin owns another 5 per cent, together they form a single newspaper proprietor. A person with only a quarter of the votes may not be able to control the policy of the papers concerned, but that would be a matter for the Commission to take into account when considering whether one body will be able to exercise too much influence over public opinion; it would not be a factor affecting the definition of a transfer of a paper to a newspaper proprietor. Similarly if Mr A controls papers with a circulation of 300,000 and his wife's nephew controls others with a circulation of 250,000, section 58(1) is satisfied, although the concentration of control may be less serious, especially if A is not on speaking terms with his wife's nephew.

The definition of a 'newspaper proprietor' is also used in section 57(2) to explain a 'transfer of a newspaper'. This includes any transaction by virtue of which someone would become or be entitled to become a newspaper proprietor, and any transfer of assets necessary to the continuation of a newspaper as a separate newspaper (including goodwill or the right to use the name of a newspaper). It is thought that this is important. In the United States, the Clayton Act, section 7, as originally drafted, referred only to the acquisition of shares, and it became very easy to avoid its application. It was eventually held that even if A Inc. bought all the shares in B Inc., but managed to transfer all B Inc.'s assets to itself before the Federal Trade Commission intervened, there was nothing the Commission could do, however severely competition was lessened by the merger. It was only in 1950 that this loophole was plugged, and there was a spate of anti-merger cases thereafter. In the U.K., transfer of a newspaper includes any transfer of plant or premises used in the publication of a newspaper, other than a transfer made without a view to a change in the ownership or control of the newspaper or to its ceasing publication.

Mergers

Many newspapers are printed on plant belonging to the proprietors of other newspapers, for instance the *Guardian* and the *Observer* were printed on presses owned by the Thomson organization, which owns their main competitors, *The Times* and the *Sunday Times*. If a paper sells its press to a competitor while making alternative arrangements for printing, it may continue to be fully independent. On the other hand, where a newspaper buys its rival's press and the rival makes no alternative arrangements, this could amount to buying up the rival and seeing that the competition it offers is brought to an end. A transfer of the name and goodwill of a paper may be effective to transfer it, since it may have hardly any other assets except the benefit of contracts with its staff, and these can be renegotiated after the transfer.

This definition of a transfer is far less elaborate and inclusive than that of a merger situation qualifying for investigation. But since other mergers are referred to the Commission only if the Minister thinks fit, it does not matter if the definition is too broad, and there is no reason for not attempting to prevent persons from avoiding its provisions. Press mergers must be referred, however, if the paper has a sufficient circulation and is not failing, so the definition should not cover too many transactions that are unlikely to reduce the number of independent organs for expressing opinion. Further, as was said earlier, to transfer a newspaper to a newspaper proprietor may be a crime, so it is important that the definition should be relatively simple and easy to apply. The consequences of not informing the Minister about mergers of other activities are only that the Minister has six months after he ought to have known to consider the matter. If a remote relative marries the relative of someone able materially to influence the policy of a competitor, the Minister is unlikely to want to act. It does not matter if the definition includes unexpected transactions, because nothing need be done in consequence.

The Commission's Task

According to section 59, when the Minister receives an application for consent to a transfer, he must within one month refer the matter to the Commission for investigation. The Commission must report within three months from the reference or, in exceptional circumstances, six, as to whether

'. . . the transfer may be expected to operate against the public interest, taking into account all matters which appear in the circumstances to be relevant and, in particular, the need for accurate presentation of news and free expression of opinion.'

REPORT ON 'THE TIMES'

The first reference of a newspaper transfer related to the transfer of *The Times* to the Thomson organization, which already owned the *Sunday Times*, many weekly newspapers, magazines, some book-publishing companies, two television companies, and various other interests in the U.K. as well as many papers abroad. The reference was made to the Commission the very day that the application for consent was received by the Board of Trade.

After reporting the facts, the Commission first dismissed as extravagant fears that *The Times* might not be able to carry on independently. The paper had been making losses, and might continue to do so, but its circulation had expanded, and doubtless its advertisement revenue would soon increase in consequence. What the paper mainly needed was good management and marketing, and this the Thomson organization was well able to provide. There would be some economies: it would not be necessary to send separate journalists to all countries, and *The Times* could be printed on Thomson presses, enabling its new building to be sold. It is thought that this second economy could have been achieved by a long-term contract, without a concentration of the control over the editorial policy. But it is strange that the Commission first considered the reasons in favour of the transfer: it might have been expected to consider the reasons against it, and only if these were substantial should those requesting consent have had to show that advantages to the public would be likely to outweigh them. The Commission went on to point out that *The Times* was no longer unique although the wide range of its news reporting, its accuracy, and its freedom from bias were very valuable, as was the freedom of its editors to express opinions on the great issues of the day, even when those views were unpopular. The acquisition of *The Times* would add to the power of the Thomson organization, but the organization would control only 7 per cent of the national and provincial daily papers, although a higher proportion of the quality papers. In practice the Thomson organization allowed its editors considerable freedom, and although its successors might not always abide by this policy, the Commission thought there was little risk in allowing the transfer of *The Times* to such an organization.

The *Observer* and the *Guardian* were at the moment printed on Thomson presses, and when they both competed with Thomson papers, they might be worried about the continuity of this arrangement. The Commission, however, thought that they should safeguard their own interests. It could not make the Minister's consent conditional on an undertaking to continue printing without stating how the charges were to be fixed; and merely to say that outside

77

papers should be charged on the same basis as controlled ones would not suffice, since any 'charge' made by the Thomson organization to its own papers would not be negotiated at arm's length – it would not matter whether profits were made by *The Times* or by the printing press, since both would swell the profits of the organization as a whole (contrast page 66 above).

If *The Times* survives under Thomson ownership, this will make life somewhat more difficult for its competitors, but so would any way of saving *The Times*. Perhaps the major objection to the transfer is that *The Times* and *Sunday Times* may speak with one voice, but it is difficult to frame conditions to prevent this. The Commission hoped that the two editors would be independent, but to place some national figures on the board of directors, when they would remain in a minority, would be of little help. The Commission therefore concluded that consent should be given to the transfer, although *The Times* might well have survived on its own; the Minister announced his unconditional consent.

This reference does underline some of the difficulties with which the Commission is faced. It has only three months to complete its inquiry. Whether *The Times* and the *Sunday Times* remain independent will depend on the individuals appointed as editors in the future, and the extent to which they are allowed to remain independent. While the consent can be made conditional on an undertaking being given first, it is difficult to see what would happen if the undertaking was later broken, except that other papers might comment adversely. It is impossible to plan for an independent press; if papers are compelled to continue in production when they are making losses, the government money needed would itself reduce independence.

All the subsequent newspaper references have been takeovers of local newspapers. All have been approved, although the Commission has expressed anxiety about the possible consequences if the tendency for local newspapers to be bought by national groups should continue.

Part Two

4: *Agreements Subject to Registration*

The Collective Discrimination Report

In the first report it made on a general reference (see pp. 24–5), that on collective discrimination in 1955, the Commission found that the practices referred to it 'in some degree restrict competition' and the majority concluded

> 'that the general effect of each of these practices is against the public interest though we recognize that there may be special circumstances . . . when the use of some of them at any rate may be justified in the public interest.'

In the particular industries it had investigated, however, it had not come across a single instance where the restrictions had not in its opinion been contrary to the public interest, and it thought that they must be rare. It therefore recommended that the practices – collective exclusive dealing, collective boycotts, aggregated discounts, and collective resale price maintenance – should be prohibited in general, although provision might be made for exempting certain agreements *after* individual scrutiny. The majority considered it would not be sufficient merely to require the registration of the agreements and provide for the prohibition of some of them, since that would require an individual review of all agreements, the great majority of which would be contrary to the public interest. The review would take many years, during which time many injurious agreements would remain legal, while the parties to those first examined would not be allowed to give effect to agreements similar to, or perhaps less harmful to the public than, those which were lawfully being observed in other trades.

An influential minority, however, was not convinced that all the practices referred to the Commission were generally injurious to the public, and it was not prepared to condemn them until the particular parties had been given an opportunity to defend them. It therefore recommended that agreements to discriminate should be registered, and that an official should be required to bring them one by one before a tribunal to decide whether each was contrary to the public interest. The minority claimed two desirable results of this procedure: the publicity provided by registration might persuade the parties to abandon many of the most obnoxious practices voluntarily; and the register would provide information for whoever was charged with the duty of bringing individual restrictions before a tribunal empowered to forbid them.

Outline of the Restrictive Trade Practices Act 1956

Soon after the publication of the report, the Conservative government, with considerable support from the Labour and Liberal parties, introduced the Restrictive Trade Practices Bill. Contrary to the policy advocated by the Labour and Liberal parties, however, it was the minority's solution that was adopted.

Part I of the Act

In section 6(1) various types of agreement that are likely to restrict competition are listed; not only the agreements to discriminate which had been the subject of the general reference, but also those fixing prices, limiting production, or sharing markets. Subject to certain exceptions set out in sections 7 and 8, particulars of agreements under which restrictions in respect of any of these matters are accepted by at least two persons were to be furnished to the Registrar of Restrictive Trading Agreements. The Registrar's office was created by the Act and was held by a former senior civil servant appointed by the Crown. His functions have now been transferred to the Director General of Fair Trading (s. 94). The Director is required to compile and maintain a register of these agreements and he, or the parties to an agreement, can ask a new court, set up by the Act and called the Restrictive Practices Court, whether a particular agreement is registrable. The Director is required to refer each of the agreements, particulars of which have been furnished to him, to that Court. In some ways this Court resembles an administrative tribunal, although it is expressly stated to be a superior court of record and its members include High Court judges, as well as lay members qualified by their knowledge of or experience in industry, commerce, or public affairs. A High Court judge or member of the Court of Session in Scotland always presides and any decision on a point of law is made by the judges, although on questions of fact – and most of the difficult questions are factual –

the Court decides by a simple majority. Even if he disagrees with it, the judge delivers the Court's judgment and no dissenting opinions can be given.

The Court has been given a most difficult task. Under section 20 it must decide whether any restrictions as defined in sections 6 to 8 are contrary to the public interest. If they are, then the agreement automatically becomes void in respect of those restrictions, and the Court may order the parties not to give effect to it or make any other agreement to the like effect. Since its power to make orders is limited to registrable restrictions, the Court may have to decide whether a particular restriction is registrable. Parliament tried to help the Court to decide whether restrictions are likely to harm the public by setting out the criteria in section 21. Any registrable restriction is deemed to be contrary to the public interest unless it can be shown first that it passes through one of eight 'gateways', for instance, under paragraph (a) that it is reasonably necessary to protect the public from injury to person or premises, and secondly that it satisfies the 'tailpiece' to section 21(1): that the restriction is reasonable having regard to the balance of the circumstances enabling it to pass through a gateway and any detriment to the public resulting or likely to result from the operation of the restriction. To defend a restriction, the parties must show that one of these specified justifications applies and that it is not outweighed by detriments of any kind to the public. These criteria and the Court's decisions applying them will be considered in Chapter 6.

In practice very few agreements have been upheld by the Court. The cases require considerable preparation and the hearing of some of the most recent ones has lasted over forty days. The trade witnesses, often pillars of the establishment, frequently find that being cross-examined for several consecutive days is a considerable strain and the costs, both in lawyers' fees and in time that might be better spent managing the business, are high. Consequently, apart from three lengthy hearings under the Resale Prices Act 1964 (see p. 84 below), there have been since 1965 only two contested hearings as to whether an agreement is contrary to the public interest. Attention has turned from justifying agreements under the criteria of section 21 to avoiding the requirement of registration, or persuading the Director to seek directions not to refer an agreement to the Court under section 9(2) of the 1968 Act (considered on p. 116 below).

Part III of the Act: Reduction in the Functions of the Commission

Since agreements restricting competition in the ways defined in sections 6 to 8 were to be assessed by the Restrictive Practices Court, section 29 of the Act of 1956 (now Sections 10(2), 54(5) and 78(3) of the Fair Trading Act) provided that the Monopolies Commission should no longer have jurisdiction over any provisions of an agreement by virtue of which it is subject to registration.

Part II of the Act: Resale Price Maintenance

Part II of the Act is concerned with arrangements whereby suppliers, usually either manufacturers or the owners of brands who place their mark on goods produced by others, ensure that the goods supplied are sold retail at uniform prices everywhere. Section 24 makes it unlawful for manufacturers or other suppliers collectively to enforce provisions for maintaining resale prices by refusing to supply dealers who have cut them. Section 25, however, enabled individual suppliers to obtain an injunction, that is an order from a civil court, restraining a dealer who acquired goods with notice that their resale price was maintained from selling at any other price. This section was often invoked by trade associations which sent round private detectives to discover whether dealers were undercutting and took defaulters to court in the name of the person whose goods had been sold at cut prices.

Dr Pickering analysed the effects of this legislation in his book *Resale Price Maintenance in Practice*. It delayed the advent of mail order discount houses and may have retarded the development of self service cash and carry shops. If I must pay as much for goods I carry home and pay for in cash as for those delivered on credit, the incentive to shop in low cost stores is slight. Of course, not all goods were subject to resale price maintenance, and the practice broke down in groceries without any legislative action. Nevertheless, there were increasing objections to the practice published during the fifties and early sixties. In 1964 the Resale Prices Act was passed under which, as the result of decisions of the Restrictive Practices Court, it has become unlawful to attempt to maintain minimum or fixed resale prices for any goods other than books and pharmaceutical products. Dr Pickering has also analysed the effects of this Act in an article published in 1974 in *Oxford Economic Papers*, p. 120. Since the practice is now confined to some 2 per cent of consumer expenditure, it does not seem worth while analysing the provisions of the 1964 Act, as I did in the first edition of this book. The most convenient and accurate analysis of the legal provisions is to be found in the chapter edited by Mr Jeremy Lever, Q.C., in *Chitty on Contracts*.

Subsequent Legislation

The 1956 Act was amended in detail by the Restrictive Trade Practices Act 1968 and again by Parts IX and X of the Fair Trading

Act 1973. The restrictive practices legislation has not been consolidated as the monopolies legislation has been, so I shall refer
to the three Acts by reference to their dates. The basic pattern of
the 1956 Act remains, but it has been tightened up in various ways
and power has been taken to extend its scope to cover services as
well as the supply and acquisition of goods or the application of a
process of manufacture to them.

Registration

Section 6 defines the agreements to which Part I of the Act applies:
those under which restrictions are accepted in relation to the supply
or acquisition of goods or to the application of a process of manufacture to them. Agreements between hairdressers even about
minimum charges are not covered by the Act of 1956, unless they
relate to the prices to be charged for lacquers, lipstick or other
goods. Power has, however, been taken to extend the legislation by
order to bring under control such services as may be specified
(Part X of the Act of 1973, pp. 118–23 below). In August 1974, the
Minister issued a notice stating her intention of exercising this power
across the board, extending control to all services, subject to only
a few specified exceptions. Particulars of agreements to which the
1956 Act applies should be furnished to the Director before the
date on which any restriction is to take effect (s. 10 of the 1956
Act and sections 6 and 7 of the 1968 Act) so that in due course he
can refer them to the Restrictive Practices Court.

Section 6 is set out in the Appendix (p. 257) and the reader is
advised to refer frequently to it if the following analysis is to be
understood.

'Two or More Persons Carrying on Business within the U.K.'

To be registrable the agreement must be made between at least two
persons carrying on business in the production, supply, or processing
of goods in the U.K. If a monopolist in the U.K. adheres to an
international cartel which ensures that the foreign members will not
sell in the U.K. in return for his promise not to export to their
home markets, the 1956 Act does not apply to it, provided that
none of the other parties carries on business in the U.K. The cartel
would amount to a complex monopoly situation, capable of reference
to the Commission; but very few such references have been made.
For the agreement to be registrable, not only must there be two
parties carrying on business in the U.K., they must also do so 'in
the production or supply of goods, or in the application to goods of
any process of manufacture'. Suppliers of services, who do not carry

on such business, may agree about the prices they shall pay for the articles they use in their business without making a registrable agreement, although of course the supply of such goods could also be referred to the Monopolies and Mergers Commission.

'*An Agreement under which Restrictions are Accepted by Two or More Parties in Respect of the Following Matters*'

The Liberal M.P. Mr Wade proposed an amendment to make an agreement registrable even if restrictions were accepted by one party only, but it was rejected by the government on the ground that it would render exclusive dealing agreements, which are common commercial transactions, subject to registration. Suppose that Shell refuses to supply a filling station with petrol on favourable terms unless the retailer agrees not to sell any other brand. Shell accepts no restriction – it just refuses to supply the retailer unless he accepts restrictions – so the restriction accepted by the retailer is not registrable. At the Report stage in the Bill's passage through Parliament, an express exemption was inserted in what is now section 8(3) to provide for exclusive dealing agreements; but by then the Liberal amendment had been lost and, although the reason for its rejection had ceased to be valid, it could not be reintroduced at such a late stage.

The persons who accept restrictions need not be carrying on business in the U.K. If, for instance, an agreement is made between a foreign manufacturer exporting to the U.K., an English manufacturer exporting to the foreigner's home market, and an English merchant, the two English firms satisfy the conditions about carrying on business in the supply of goods in the U.K.; and if the manufacturers each agree not to export to the other's home market, even though the distributor accepts no restrictions, the agreement is registrable. Such an agreement, however, would probably not be made with the Act in force.

The key term 'restriction' is not defined, except that it must be in respect of one of the matters listed in heads (a) to (e), and under section 6(3) it 'includes any negative obligation.' Is the restriction one on conduct, or one on competition? The former construction seems to be correct, and even if the restriction is unlikely to have any effect on competition it may be registrable. Many trade associations, for instance, charge their members a small equal fee, plus an amount that varies with their turnover. Such agreements were registrable until the position was altered by section 96 of the 1973 Act. In form, they cannot be distinguished from market sharing schemes, under which those who exceed their quota pay compensation to those who do not reach theirs, and which are made registrable under section 6(5). These will be discussed later (see p. 91). It is thought that it is right that even unimportant agreements should be registered initially, so that they can be scrutinized to see whether their effect is anti-competitive; although the procedure for dealing with those that do not restrict competition has had to be made less cumbersome (p. 116 below).

In two early cases, *Waste Paper*, decided in April 1963, and *Telephone Apparatus Manufacturers*, in 1962, the Restrictive Practices Court suggested that the restriction must be one that goes farther than the general law. If parties are already bound by some other contract that is not registrable, then the acceptance of a restriction that is not more extensive does not count. Where, however, several separate contracts were negotiated at the same time and signed on the same day, it was held in *Schweppes (No. 2)* (1971) that the earlier agreement would not have been made except in the expectation of the later ones, so they formed part of the same 'arrangement'. Consequently, by virtue of section 6(3) which is discussed at p. 94 below, the restrictions were accepted under a single agreement.

'Dead' Agreements

When the various types of restriction were first made registrable by orders of the Board of Trade, there was a three month period during which agreements could be varied or terminated; it is thought that considerable use was made of this period to abandon many collective boycotts and other particularly obnoxious agreements, so that they were not required to be registered. But new agreements containing registrable restrictions were required to be registered within three months after they were made, even if meanwhile they had been brought to an end, or altered so that no registrable restrictions remained. The latter are called 'filleted agreements' by the Director's department. Since 1968, the Registrar (now the Director) has been under no duty to refer 'dead' or 'filleted' agreements to the Court, as section 9(1) of the Act of 1968 gives him a discretion to do so or not, as he thinks fit.

Restrictions in Respect of the Prices to be Charged

The first kinds of restrictions listed in section 6(1) are those in respect of the prices to be charged:

> '(a) the prices to be charged, quoted or paid for goods supplied, offered or acquired, or for the application of any process of manufacture to goods';

87

We will see (p. 94 below) that an agreement may be registrable if one party accepts a restriction of this kind and another accepts a restriction listed under one of the other paragraphs.

The restrictions accepted by two or more parties must be 'in respect of' the matters set out in paragraphs (a) to (e). Each of these contains the words '*to be*' charged, supplied, etc. Does '*to be*' mean 'which are required to be' charged, etc., connoting that the parties have agreed to charge such prices? Or, is the tense future, or future perfect – the prices which shall have been charged? It is thought that the draftsman's choice of the passive infinitive was unfortunate. The Registrar was advised that the phrase does not cover agreements by parties to inform each other about the prices that shall have been charged, quoted, or paid for goods. Such information agreements, under which the parties agree to disseminate information about prices after they have been charged, etc., may restrict competition. Where there is a duty by one manufacturer with a substantial share of the market to inform a competitor who also has a substantial share about bargains at special prices within minutes after they have been made, the first knows that if he were to capture an important order by making a price concession, the competitor would not be able to afford to see the demand for his own products tumble and would have to react by making at least similar reductions in his price. The two firms would end up with perhaps the same shares of the market, but with lower receipts and, probably lower profits, unless demand for their turnover were sufficiently elastic, and their plant sufficiently idle, to enable them to benefit from the increase in demand. As a result, neither firm would 'start the rot' and even powerful buyers would not be able to win price concessions (see p. 8).

But although agreements for exchanges of information about prices after the event may make price competition less likely, it was thought by the Registrar that such information agreements were not 'in respect of the prices *to be* charged'. He may well have been right. The law was not clear. Consequently, the Board of Trade may also have hesitated to refer the supply of products subject to an information agreement to the Commission, since by virtue of section 29 (now s. 10(2) of the 1973 Act) there would be a monopoly situation only if such agreements are not subject to Part I of the Act.

In 1964 the Conservative government declared in its white paper on Monopolies, Mergers and Restrictive Practices (Cmnd 2299) that although information agreements may increase productivity, they may also be made with the purpose and effect of limiting competition. It therefore proposed to empower the Board of Trade to make them, or some of them, subject to Part I of the 1956 Act. When he was

President of the Board of Trade in the Labour Government in May 1967, Mr Jay also announced that legislation would be introduced bringing information agreements within the scope of the 1956 Act. The Registrar had in several of his reports noted the anti-competitive effects of some information agreements; and in his fourth report he also recommended that they should be made registrable, although he suggested, as did the Conservative proposals, that they might be defended when they do not restrict or deter competition.

Provision was made by section 5 of the 1968 Act for the Board of Trade (now it is the Minister) to call up information agreements for registration. An 'information agreement' is defined as 'an agreement between two or more persons carrying on within the U.K. any such business as is mentioned in [section 6(1)] of the Act of 1956, . . . being an agreement under which provision is made for or in relation to the furnishing by two or more parties to each other or' a third party, of information relating to the prices charged, and other matters listed in paragraphs (a) to (e) of section 6(1) of the earlier Act, or to costs. Before the Minister may make an order, he is required to publish a notice describing the classes of agreements to which the proposed order would apply and specifying a period of at least twenty-eight days, during which representations may be made to him about it. Only one order has so far been made (S.I. 1969 No. 1842). The notice was published in the *Board of Trade Journal* and covered a far wider class of agreements than those affected by the final order. One may infer that the Minister received some sensible representations which persuaded him that there would be undesirable consequences if the order was drawn as widely as originally envisaged. The actual order relates to information about the prices which have been charged for goods. The drafting is complex and will not be analysed here.

The other suggestion of the Registrar was also adopted in section 10 of the 1968 Act. A new gateway was introduced, in relation to all agreements and not only to information agreements called up under section 5: that the restriction does not restrict or discourage competition. This will be considered below, not only at p. 158 when the other gateways are analysed, but also at p. 116 when we consider when the Director may seek directions from the Minister not to refer an agreement to the Court.

Other post-contractual restraints are excluded by the phrase 'to be'. In *Blankets*, decided by the Court of Appeal in 1959, there was an agreement between suppliers which fixed a minimum price and quality for certain types of blankets. These restrictions were condemned by the Court. The agreement also contained a clause that forbade members of the association concerned to renegotiate the prices of blankets when a purchaser had already agreed to buy them. The price of blankets varies to some extent with the fluctuating world price of wool, and if prices are negotiated in advance and wool prices fall, the purchaser may be faced with a substantial loss. In the long term, it may pay the seller not to insist on the full price: since he is paying less for his wool he can afford to take a reduction, and to insist on the full price may mean that the buyer goes out of business. Without such a clause, members of the trade association were under no duty to renegotiate prices in such a situation, but for the trade association to forbid them to do so is within its narrower sphere of application just as rigid as to require members to charge a minimum price. Yet the Court of Appeal held that this was not a restriction in respect of the 'prices *to be* charged, quoted or paid' within subsection (1)(a); consequently it had no power to condemn the restraint under section 20. Similar arguments can probably be used to show that post-contractual restrictions in respect of the matters in the other paragraphs are also not registrable.

Lord Cameron decided in *Scottish Monumental Sculptors* (1965) that a restriction that relates to any element in the price is 'in respect of' it, so that an agreement about the charges to be made for executing the lettering on a tombstone was in respect of the price to be charged for it. In this way a certain number of services related to goods are brought within the ambit of the statute.

Restrictions in Respect of the Prices to be Recommended

'(aa) the prices to be recommended or suggested as the prices to be charged or quoted in respect of the resale of goods supplied;' (added by section 95 of the 1973 Act)

When it was made illegal for a supplier to maintain the resale price of goods, it was made clear that an individual supplier might recommend resale prices, provided that he took no steps to boycott dealers who sold below that price. Nevertheless, it has now been made clear that an agreement between suppliers that they will all recommend particular prices, or a recommendation by a trade association that, for instance, its members should not recommend a price that does not allow small dealers a margin of at least x per cent, is subject to registration.

Restrictions in Respect of Terms or Conditions

'(b) the terms or conditions on or subject to which goods are to be supplied or acquired or any such process is to be applied to goods;'

This paragraph includes terms and conditions as to credit, time for delivery and so forth. Often, a restriction may come within the scope of more than one paragraph. An agreement not to grant certain credit terms to traders not on a list would relate both to the terms on which goods are supplied within this paragraph, and to the persons to be supplied within paragraph (e).

Restrictions in Respect of Production, Supply, Acquisition or Processing

'(c) the quantities or description of goods to be produced, supplied or acquired:

(d) the process of manufacture to be applied to any goods, or the quantities or descriptions of goods to which any such process is to be applied; –'

During the depression of the 'thirties, agreements to restrict production when demand was weak were actively encouraged by the government. Supply might be restricted either by limiting the amount of goods to be produced, or by permitting one supplier to produce some products and another to produce others. More often it was agreed that no firm should produce more than a certain proportion of the product supplied by the whole industry, based on the proportion supplied in earlier years. Such a scheme was adopted for instance by the calico printers. Each firm was originally allotted a quantum based on the amounts supplied earlier. If it exceeded its quantum, it had to pay certain sums, calculated to equal the profit on the excess, into a compensation pool which was used to compensate those who supplied less than their quanta. A firm cannot estimate the absolute amount of its quantum until the period to which the quantum applied is past, so most quantum schemes provide for compensation. The calico printers also re-assessed the quanta each year, allowing an increase of part of the excess, or a decrease of part of the deficit, processed. This enabled firms slowly to increase their quanta by processing more, and made the scheme less rigid than it would otherwise have been. Strictly such schemes do not come within paragraph (d), since the quantum may be exceeded by paying compensation, but they are caught by subsection (5).

Subsection (5) was drafted sufficiently widely to include the method by which many trade associations charge their members – a small fee, plus a tiny percentage of their turnover. In this way, the large firms, which can afford a larger fee and may use the association's services more, can be charged more than the smaller firms. This used to cause trouble, as every change of membership had to be notified to the Registrar, though it sufficed to notify him of the current membership every three months. This is, however, no longer necessary (p. 116 below). Moreover, by virtue of section 96 of the Fair Trading Act a proviso has been added to subsection (5) to exclude bona fide subscriptions to trade associations.

Quantum compensation schemes are often also caught by paragraph (a), because if firms are to be allowed to increase their quanta slowly, they might do so by competing in price; this may therefore be forbidden by the cartel agreement. When some firms agree to supply only certain amounts of a product, then it is not necessary to fix prices, though this is often done to lessen the incentive to cheat.

The 'descriptions' of goods within paragraph (c) was held in *Waste Paper* (1963) to refer to the kinds of goods rather than to the way in which they are defined, so that a definition of the many grades of waste paper to be acquired by members did not come within the paragraph, since there was not the slightest restriction preventing the parties from supplying any other grade. It is thought that this was a sensible resolution of the ambiguity and should also be applied to paragraph (d). The case might be differently decided now, however, since an 'arrangement' to make no other grades might be inferred from the parties' conduct (see pp. 94–9).

In *Scottish Monumental Sculptors* it was held that 'the application of any process of manufacture to goods' within paragraph (a) included the carving of tombstones provided by the monumental sculptors themselves. If this construction is used to interpret the phrase 'the processes of manufacture to be applied to any goods' within paragraph (d) as well, a possible loophole has been closed. Lord Cameron's decision is also wider than it might have been, in that it might have been argued that carving a stone was more a craft than a process of manufacture.

Indeed, as construed by the courts, it is thought that these two paragraphs cover most of the cases where production is restricted in order to raise prices, or acquisitions restricted to lower them. There are a few ways in which such objects may be achieved indirectly, for instance by limiting the number of staff to be employed, but even these may be caught by subsection (3).

Market Sharing and Collective Boycotts

'(e) the persons or classes of persons to, for or from whom, or the areas or places in or from which, goods are to be supplied or acquired, or any such process applied.'

Market sharing agreements can take more than one form. Paragraphs (c) and (d) cover those by which specific orders are not parcelled out, but each party is given preference over part of the market on accounting principles, each being entitled either to a certain turn-over or to a proportion of the cartel's turnover, or by which each party is given the exclusive right to make or process particular products. Paragraph (e) covers another way of dividing markets, a firm being allocated the customers on a list, or those belonging to a certain body, or those doing business in a certain area. Again the converse case is covered of manufacturers or traders making similar types of agreement about those from whom they may buy.

But paragraph (e) includes more than agreements to divide the market: certain persons may be excluded altogether as suppliers or customers. It used not to be unusual for manufacturers to form an association and dealers to form another association. The members of the manufacturing association would then agree to deal on trade terms only with members of the dealers' association. In return for manufacturers' forgoing contacts with 'illegitimate traders', the dealers would agree to press the wares of manufacturers who were members of the association. Such an agreement can injure the public. The dealers will probably control entry to their association, and may do so on grounds convenient to themselves rather than to the public. The newspaper retailers' association used to have a rule that a new entrant to the retail trade would be considered only if there was no other retailer with a shop within two miles. Sometimes the conditions may be at least partially appropriate to the public interest: dealers may be required to maintain adequate stocks and display them, and so help to advertise the manufacturers' produce. In a remote area, however, the trade may be inadequate to warrant such overheads, while it would be convenient for inhabitants to be able to order on the basis of either a smaller selection, or with the help of catalogues and patterns of items which could be ordered for individual customers. Consumers might benefit if such minimum standards were imposed by individual manufacturers who could relax them when the circumstances warranted it. Retailers have an interest in restricting the number of retailers who can compete with them, while the manufacturers' interest may be closer to the public's since they benefit from an increase in the number of outlets for their goods.

Many restrictions that came within paragraph (e) are not only collective boycotts, but also relate to prices within paragraph (a). (See *Electrical Installations at Exeter Hospital* (1970).) Usually the manufacturers agree to give trade discounts only to members of the retailers' association. This would also come within either paragraph (a) or (b). But the manufacturers might have altered their agreements to exclude dealings with non-members altogether, so paragraph (e) was needed to cover such agreements.

'Classes of persons' has been given a sensible meaning by the Restrictive Practices Court in *Birmingham Builders* (1963). Builders agreed not to tender for contracts over a certain value unless a bill of quantities was supplied: a bill of quantities is a detailed list setting out the materials and work required. It was held that those wishing to order such work without providing the bills first were a 'class of persons', since they could be ascertained at the time the rule became applicable; the restriction was therefore registrable.

Subsection (2)

This subsection provides that to come within subsection (1) it is sufficient if two people accept restrictions described in the same or in different paragraphs. Manufacturers may agree together about the prices each may charge, all accepting restrictions within paragraph (a) of subsection (1); or a single manufacturer may agree with his dealer that he will not sell to anyone else within the dealer's territory – a restriction within paragraph (e) – and the dealer may agree that he will not sell competing goods – a restriction within paragraph (c). Each of these agreements comes within the definition of section 6(1), although we will see that if there are no other restrictions, the second may be exempt from registration by virtue of section 8(3).

Subsection (3): 'Arrangements'

Subsection (3) is vital to this section:

> 'In this Part of this Act "agreement" includes any agreement or arrangement, whether or not it is or is intended to be enforceable (apart from any provision of this Act) by legal proceedings, and references in this Part of this Act to restrictions accepted under an agreement shall be construed accordingly; and "restriction" includes any negative obligation, whether express or implied and whether absolute or not.'

Most of the restrictions listed in subsection (1) restrain trade, and would be unenforceable at common law unless they are reasonable. Yet such agreements are not unlawful. It has been suggested that the agreement in the *Mogul* case (discussed on pp. 2–3) would have been unenforceable at common law as an unreasonable restraint, but since it was not actionable as a conspiracy and the parties wished to keep it in operation, the association was able to retain the tea-carrying trade from the conference ports for its own members. Clearly agreements should be subject to control even if they are not enforceable. Often the parties to restrictive agreements restrain trade without ever having to enforce the contracts in the courts. Indeed, they seldom trouble to provide for liquidated damages – the sum to be paid for breach of contract which, if reasonably related to the likely loss, will save the plaintiff the difficult task of proving to the court how much profit has been lost because of the breach. Many agreements restricting competition are never intended to be sued upon.

Even more important is the inclusion of the word 'arrangement'. This is not a well-defined term; indeed the flexibility of the concept is one good reason for employing it. Businessmen may show great ingenuity in devising ways of restricting competition between themselves without falling within the terms of a well-known definition. A flexible definition which can be extended to include any particular agreement that restricts competition may make this more difficult.

In *Austin*, however, the first case, decided in 1957, on the construction of this word, Upjohn, J. gave it a limited ambit. Before the Act came into force, Austin had made multilateral contracts with the various types of dealers buying Austin cars – the distributors, dealers, and retailers. Since the distributors and dealers were permitted to sell only a few cars directly to the public, they accepted restrictions in respect of the classes of persons to whom goods were to be supplied within paragraph (e); all the trade buyers accepted restrictions as to the persons from whom they might acquire cars within paragraph (e) and as to the price at which they might resell them within paragraph (a); so this agreement would clearly have been registrable had it not been altered before the time that the Act came into force. By that time, however, new bilateral agreements had been made on very similar terms between Austin and each of its dealers. These were so drafted that the Registrar accepted that they came, on their face, within the exceptions of sections 7(2) and 8(3), which are considered later. He argued, however, that there was also a tacit multilateral 'arrangement' between the dealers. None of them would accept such restrictions unless he were sure that these would bind other dealers.

In rejecting this argument, Upjohn, J. said:

'. . . to escape the alleviation afforded to the subject by section 8(3), some arrangement binding three or more parties must be spelt out of the facts. . . . Whether enforceable at law or not, it seems to me that an arrangement must at least connote an arrangement whereby the parties to it accept mutual rights and obligations.'

He then held that there were no rights and obligations undertaken by each dealer towards the others and, consequently, that Austin's system of orderly marketing was not subject to registration.

By early 1959, it had become clear that few registrable restrictions, if any, would survive a reference to the Restrictive Practices Court; attention was turned from justifying agreements to substituting for those that were clearly subject to Part I of the Act, others that had similar effects on competition but were thought to avoid the requirement of registration. In *Austin* the judge had refused to infer a tacit arrangement from the similarity between the terms accepted by each dealer from Austin and those under the earlier multilateral agreement. Encouraged by this precedent, many businessmen entered into new agreements that did not appear to be registrable. For some time it remained entirely safe to attempt to avoid registration. We will see (p. 124 below) that until 1968 the duty to register was probably not placed on anyone in particular so, even if the new agreement was eventually held to be registrable, the unpleasant consequences of wrongly assuming an agreement was not subject to registration were minimal, unless an undertaking had already been given to the Restrictive Practices Court not to make any other agreement to the like effect to one already condemned. Now that a considerable number of agreements, including ones that were dead or filleted, have been taken to the Court and the 1968 Act has tightened up the duty to notify, it is crucial to know whether an 'arrangement' has been made.

The second case in which the ambit of the term 'arrangement' was in issue was *Basic Slag*, decided by the Court of Appeal in May 1963. Several steel makers argued that an agreement made in 1954 was exempted by section 8(3). Basic slag is a by-product of steel manufacture and, when it is ground, can be used as a fertilizer. For some years the steel makers had disposed of their entire output of slag to a company called British Basic Slag Ltd (hereafter called 'Basic'), in which each of them owned shares, and to the board of which each nominated a director. When the contracts under which this was arranged came up for renewal in 1954, their terms were considered at several of Basic's board meetings. One of the questions the Court had to decide was whether, on the assumption that the agreements between each firm and Basic were exempt under section 8(3), there was a horizontal arrangement between the steel makers, under which each accepted a restriction not to sell any slag except to Basic. The Court decided that there was. At first instance Cross, J. said

'. . . all that is required to constitute an arrangement not enforceable in law is that the parties to it shall have communicated with one another in some way, and that as a result of the communication each has intentionally aroused in the other an expectation that he will act in a certain way.'

This definition went far farther than was required to decide the case. The directors nominated to Basic's board had discussed the detailed terms of the agreement with each other.

> '. . . when the point was reached at which the agreements were sent out to the . . . eight members [of Basic] for execution, everyone concerned expected that all would execute theirs.' (p. 196)

In the Court of Appeal, Willmer, L. J. pointed out that this was not inconsistent with Upjohn, J.'s earlier decision in *Austin* (p. 146).

> 'For when each of two or more parties intentionally arouses in the others an expectation that he will act in a certain way, it seems to me that he incurs at least a moral obligation to do so.'

The decisions of the Court of Appeal are accepted as defining the law in all the courts in England, except the House of Lords; and the Court of Appeal has accepted that to arouse mutual expectations about the matters listed in section 6(1), if not exempted by sections 7 and 8, amounts to an 'arrangement' to which Part I of the Act applies. It has not been necessary to decide whether obligations binding at least in honour must also have been accepted, though each of the judges has added such a qualification. All the judges' formulations, however, have been prefaced by statements that they should not be taken to be definitive. The ways of arranging to restrict competition are so diverse that the judges probably wished to retain room for manoeuvre if businessmen or their advisers should devise a new method. The word 'arrangement' has also been given a wide ambit under the Income Tax Act 1952, section 411, and in *Crossland* v. *Hawkins* it was held to cover the case where an actor merely left his solicitor and accountant to work out a way of minimizing his family's liability to tax. This precedent has not yet been followed in interpreting the 1956 Act.

In two cases decided late in 1965, *Schweppes* and *Telephones*, the Court of Appeal held that since an arrangement is made when mutual expectations are aroused and mutual obligations accepted, the Registrar is entitled to obtain documents relating to the circumstances in which an agreement that appears on its face to come within one of the exceptions set out in section 7 or 8 was entered into, because that might show that a non-exempt arrangement had been made. In *Tyre Mileage* (1966), the Restrictive Practices Court accepted that the reciprocal representations about future conduct need not be made verbally, but may be inferred from conduct. The parties had expressly agreed to disseminate information only about the level at which bids *had been* made to firms hiring tyres, but in fact the machinery set up was also used to inform each other about the levels at which each was minded to bid. The Restrictive Practices Court held that when a firm is given such information on the assumption that it will reciprocate by disclosing its proposed bids, then a moral obligation binding at least in honour arises from its conduct. Since the parties had made an arrangement 'to which Part I of the Act applied' – an arrangement similar in 'effect' to an agreement that had been condemned – they had broken their undertakings, and were punished for contempt of court.

This wide ambit given to the term 'arrangement' has enabled the Registrar to catch some agreements that restrict competition; but it is very important that it should not be given so wide a meaning that rational ways in which a firm can individually increase its profits are included, especially when firms have already given an undertaking to the Court. In *Basic Slag*, Sir Lionel Heald, Q.C., arguing against the Registrar, pointed out that the formulation of 'arrangement' adopted by Cross, J. at first instance and based on the mutual arousing of expectations is wide enough to cover the announcement of a price rise by a supplier with only a few competitors (see p. 8). If the firms normally follow any price changes announced by one of them, even without having expressly agreed to do so, it could be argued that each has aroused expectations that it is likely to follow any new changes. The firm that first announces a rise to its customers also arouses expectations in his competitors that it will charge the new prices, provided that the others all announce similar increases. But if this amounts to an 'arrangement'; any firm which has given an undertaking to the Court not to make any agreement to which Part I of the Act applies to the like effect to a price fixing agreement will be guilty of contempt of court. Where the firms have agreed to charge similar prices, and even decided which of them shall announce the new prices, they have clearly made a registrable agreement, but where there has been no collusion it would be ludicrous to forbid any of them to announce new prices or to follow another's price changes.

Where the market is concentrated, it is rational for those responsible for setting a firm's prices at a level that will yield the greatest profit to consider the probable reactions of its competitors. To forbid any firm in such an industry to raise prices would merely result in its business becoming so unprofitable that it might cease to produce something for which buyers would be prepared to pay more than it costs to supply. The only sensible ways of controlling oligopoly are either to increase the number of competing firms by breaking up firms that are larger than is necessary to operate efficiently and forbid them to acquire competitors by merger, or to forbid such practices as post-information agreements which enable a firm to react to the decisions of more of its competitors than it could if it had to discover them for itself. It is thought that, provided that some form of moral duty must be accepted for an 'arrangement' to exist under which restrictions are accepted, price leadership can be excluded. Unless there is prior agreement, other firms have no duty to follow the leader, and if one firm decides that the additional turnover will compensate it for the lower unit prices, it breaches no moral obligation by setting an independent price.

Price leadership probably does not amount to an 'arrangement' unless the firms have communicated with each other, in words or conduct, before publishing a price change, and have not only led each other to expect certain action, but have also done something encouraging the others to rely on it occurring. In *Schweppes* (*No. 2*) (1971) Stamp, J. made it clear that one could not avoid registration by splitting the restrictions into several contracts since, where one is made only in expectation of the other, there will be an underlying 'arrangement' incorporating both contracts under which restrictions are accepted. On the other hand, when businessmen are negotiating a commercial transaction which they intend should develop into a contract, then until the contract is made, Stamp, J. said in the same case, no restrictions will be accepted. If, however, the formal contract is never concluded, but the parties' conduct changes in accordance with the general objectives that were being negotiated, the Director may well suspect that rather more had taken place than the mere negotiation 'subject to contract' of a transaction that proved abortive.

Other Provisions Supporting Section 6(1)

Subsection (4) extends the idea of a restriction by providing that, if an agreement confers benefits on those who comply with conditions as to the matters listed in subsection (1), it shall be treated as an agreement under which restrictions are accepted. This provision was more important in the days before the courts had developed the concept of 'arrangement' so widely.

Subsection (5) has already been mentioned (p. 91) in relation to the old market sharing compensation scheme adopted by the calico printers. It is needed to complete the application of paragraphs (c) and (d).

The next two subsections are very important and extend subsection (1) to agreements or recommendations made by trade associations. According to subsection (8), a trade association is a body of persons formed for the purpose of furthering the trade interests of its members. Under subsection (6), an agreement made by a trade association is treated as if it were made between all its members or persons represented by members. So where a manufacturers' trade association agrees with a dealers' association that its members should supply only the members of that association, then it is treated as if the members of the manufacturers' association have accepted restrictions in respect of the classes of persons to whom goods are to be supplied within subsection (1) (e). Reciprocal restrictions would also normally be accepted by members of the dealers' association to give preference to the products of the manufacturers' association.

Subsection (7) goes even further:

'Where specific recommendations (whether express or implied) are made by or on behalf of a trade association to its members or to any class of its members, as to the action to be taken or not taken by them in relation to any particular class of goods or process of manufacture in respect of any matter described in the said subsection (1), this Part of this Act shall apply as if the constitution of the association . . .'

required its members to comply with the recommendations. According to this statutory fiction, even when members are entirely free to ignore the recommendations made by their association, they are treated, for the purposes both of registration and of reference to the Restrictive Practices Court, as if they were bound by them. The provision used to give rise to conflict between the effect of this Act and the increasing incidence of government planning. Suppose that the 'little Neddy' for a particular industry recommended that manufacturers should not raise their prices more than 2 per cent during the next twelve months. If the industry's trade association issued a statement to this effect, there would probably be an 'implied specific recommendation' that its members should comply with the recommendation. Power was therefore taken in section 2 of the 1968 Act for any one of a large number of ministers to exempt from registration agreements and arrangements relating exclusively to the prices to be charged and designed to prevent or lessen an increase therein or to secure a reduction. At one time a very large number of such agreements were in operation, but prices are currently being controlled under the counter-inflation legislation rather than through voluntary restraint negotiated by the government with trade associations.

Exemptions from Registration

Even if an agreement comes within the definition of section 6, it may not be subject to registration: sections 7 and 8 provide certain automatic exemptions. The restrictions noted in section 7 must be disregarded in deciding whether an agreement is registrable, while under section 8 certain agreements under which only certain limited types of restriction are accepted are not registrable; and, according to section 8(9), in deciding whether an agreement comes within the exemptions of section 8, one may disregard the restrictions described in section 7. If two persons each accept a restriction, one of which comes within section 7, the agreement is not registrable since one restriction can be disregarded, and that leaves only one party who has accepted a restriction. But if one restriction comes within section 8, and the other is not exempt, then the agreement would be registrable, because the restrictions would not be exclusively of the kind described in one paragraph of section 8.

Agreements between Coal and Steel Suppliers

Since 1973, control of agreements restricting competition between the producers and most distributors of coal and steel has been exercised by the Commission of the European Communities. The Commission claims that its competence is exclusive and ousts that of national courts under their own restrictive practices law. It is not clear that this assertion is correct but, in any event, section 99 of the Fair Trading Act provides that in agreements between undertakings subject to the Treaty of Paris, under which the European Coal and Steel Community was created, restrictions relating to coal and steel accepted by two or more such undertakings shall be disregarded in deciding whether the agreement is subject to registration (see p. 229 below). This important limitation makes the old exemption under section 7(1) comparatively unimportant. Section 7(1) relates to agreements between iron and steel producers to make collective exclusive dealing agreements with the suppliers of the raw materials they require.

Section 7(2): Restrictions Relating to the Goods Supplied

This subsection is of more general application. In deciding whether Part I of the Act applies to an agreement for the supply of goods, or the application of a process of manufacture to them, no account shall be taken of any term which relates exclusively to the goods supplied, or which the process is applied to, in pursuance of the agreement. But where restrictions of the kinds listed in section 6(1) are accepted by more than one person at the same level of trade, section 7(2) applies only if the restrictions were accepted in pursuance of an agreement that has already been registered. This exemption used to enable an individual supplier to maintain the resale price of his goods, even if he himself accepted some other restriction. Now that resale price maintenance is unlawful except for books and medicaments, the exemption is more important in enabling one to disregard a restriction preventing a dealer from selling goods outside his area, or to specific customers. If all the dealers collectively agree on their respective areas or groups of customers or products, the agreement is registrable, but if each dealer agrees with the manufacturer or wholesaler separately, subsection (2) enables one to disregard the restriction. Care must be taken, however, over agreements that have been exempt under this provision, as 'no poaching' clauses are severely treated by the Community Court and the Commission of the European Communities (see pp. 179–80). We will return to section 7(2) when section 8(3) is considered (at p. 104), since the two subsections often affect the same agreements.

Section 7(3): British Standards Institution Standards

The British Standards Institution is a government-financed body which defines standards for different types of merchandise, and the makers of goods complying with the standards may affix the Institute's mark to them. There is no further incentive to comply with the standards. Makers may agree with each other to conform to them without making a registrable agreement, but they cannot go farther and agree to abide by the standards defined by any other body and avoid doing so. Such an agreement would restrain them from making goods of a lower or different quality, and if poorer but cheaper goods would still serve some purpose this might limit the choice available to consumers. The British Standards Institution is required to consider consumers' interests, so is unlikely to set too high a standard; a standards committee set up by manufacturers in their own interest might do so. Since 1968, however, the exemption of restrictions to comply with standards has been extended to those prescribed or adopted by trade associations, provided that the standard (not merely the association) has been approved by the Board of Trade (now the Minister). The Minister may be expected to protect the interest of consumers as carefully as does the B.S.I.

Section 7(4): Workmen

'(4) In determining whether an agreement is an agreement to which this Part of this Act applies, no account shall be taken of any restriction which affects or otherwise relates to the workmen to be employed or not employed by any person, or as to the remuneration, conditions of employment, hours of work or working conditions of such workmen. . . .'

'Workman' is defined as 'any person who has entered into or works under a contract with an employer, whether the contract be by way of manual labour, clerical work or otherwise.' This could be used as an indirect way to limit production; though if it was, the Court might find that an arrangement to do so by means of the exempted restriction had been made. Moreover, the exemption was narrowly construed in *Scottish Daily Newspapers* (1971). Journalists employed by the *Glasgow Herald* tried to increase their remuneration by striking. The publishers of the other Scottish daily papers therefore agreed that they would not publish until the *Glasgow Herald's* journalists resumed normal working. Despite the wide terms in subsection (4) 'affects or otherwise relates' – the Restrictive Practices Court held that the restriction on publication did not relate directly to the workmen to be employed, nor directly to the remuneration of the journalists on strike, so the exemption did not apply. Since, however, the restriction was not expected to last more than a few days, the Restrictive Practices Court eventually held that it did not 'directly or indirectly restrict or discourage competition to any material degree in any relevant trade or industry' within paragraph (h) of section 21, so the agreement was not condemned.

Section 8(1) and (2): Agreements Expressly Authorized by Statute and Rationalization Schemes

Section 8(1) exempts agreements expressly authorized by statute. The most important examples used to be the marketing schemes for certain agricultural products. There are now some dozen exemptions under various statutes. The most general exemption is that under section 2 of the European Communities Act 1972, which makes U.K. law subject to any directly applicable provision of European Community law, and section 10, which gives the Court and the Director a discretion to refrain from exercising their respective functions in view of Community law. This will be considered in Chapter 9 below. Nevertheless, there are not very many statutory exemptions. Subsection (2) provides a narrow exemption for schemes certified by the Board of Trade under Part XXIII of the Income Tax Act 1952 (now Part XIV of the Income and Corporation Taxes Act 1970). Such schemes were occasionally promoted by the government under earlier legislation which was consolidated by the Taxes Act of 1970, to encourage industry to rationalize production so as to avoid excess supplies during the depression. Firms were acquired so that their plant could be destroyed and the market divided between the firms that remained.

Section 8(3): Exclusive Dealing

Much greater use can be made of this exemption, so it is worth setting it out in full:

'This Part of this Act does not apply to any agreement for the supply of goods between two persons, neither of whom is a trade association within the meaning of section six of this Act, being an agreement to which no other person is party and under which no such restrictions as are described in subsection (1) of section six of this Act are accepted other than restrictions accepted –

(a) by the party supplying the goods, in respect of the supply of goods of the same description to other persons; or

(b) by the party acquiring the goods, in respect of the sale or acquisition for sale, of other goods of the same description.'

When the exemption was added to the Bill on the Report stage, it was claimed that exclusive dealing agreements were normal commercial contracts and should be permitted. Such agreements usually contain restrictions by the manufacturer or brand owner that he will not supply any other dealer within the territory allotted to the concessionaire; and by the dealer that he will not sell any competing products and that he will not sell the manufacturer's goods outside his allotted territory in that of any other exclusive dealer. Dealers used frequently to agree also that they would not sell below the retail prices for the time being maintained by the manufacturer, although such an agreement is now illegal under the Resale Prices Act 1964, except in relation to books or medicaments. According to sections 7(2) and 8(9), no account is taken of the last two restrictions, since this is a vertical agreement between only two persons and the restrictions relate exclusively to the goods supplied. This leaves only the first two restrictions, and as these are of the type permitted under section 8(3), paragraphs (a) and (b), Part I of the Act does not apply.

The policy of permitting such agreements to be made may be questioned. We will see that the Commission of the European Communities has been consistent in not allowing the type of restriction covered by section 7(2) to go unscrutinized: dealers in the Common Market are not normally protected from competition by other dealers selling outside their primary territory; although there may be exceptional circumstances in which an absolute territorial protection might be permitted temporarily for a new product. Unless an exclusive dealer knows that no one else can sell the product in his territory, he might not be prepared to take the risk of investing in stocks of a new, untried product and in the necessary advertising. In the United States, exclusive dealing agreements are illegal if the supplier has a substantial share of the market and, where most outlets are tied, as little as 7 per cent is substantial. If the supplier has any substantial market power, an exclusive dealer may be substantially protected from competition. If the dealers have market power because of the need to obtain some form of licence – a licence to sell alcohol for consumption on the premises, or planning permission to adapt a site for use as a petrol filling station – then suppliers may find it worth their while to pay considerable sums to tie dealers to them for substantial periods of time. If such a policy is widely adopted, it may make it difficult for new firms to obtain sufficient retail outlets quickly enough to make large-scale production possible, and the existing suppliers may be protected from competition. If they are important enough, the product they make may be referred to the Monopolies Commission; but the Commission's inquiry into the supply of petrol to retailers took nearly five years, and for a year afterwards no undertakings were given; so for six years the existing suppliers were able to carry on tying new outlets. Today such an inquiry would probably be faster.

Requirements Contracts. Even if the supplier does not agree not to supply other dealers within the buyer's territory, and the buyer does not agree not to poach outside his area, but merely to buy all his supplies for resale from a single supplier, the agreement is subject to the common law doctrine of restraint of trade. Such 'requirements contracts' are frequently made by those who sell petrol by retail. Since the petrol is supplied from a tank in the dealer's station it is almost impossible to poach. In fact the oil companies do not often supply more than one station in one district, thus protecting the dealer's territory. Although such agreements are not registrable, the House of Lords held in *Esso* v. *Harper's Garage* (1967) that they do restrain trade, and will not be enforced unless the restriction not to buy from other oil companies is reasonably necessary to protect the parties' trade. The refusal to enforce such contracts is an effective sanction, since a retailer who has agreed to buy only from Esso can be induced by another supplier to change his loyalty. But the public interest protected by the common law is very narrowly conceived. It does not attempt to ensure that suppliers of petrol should compete with each other so as to provide better bargains for motorists; it merely enables a particular retailer who has agreed to buy all his petrol from one company to go back on his bargain. Since the retailer probably acquired his premises cheaply, or obtained a loan on favourable terms as the 'price' of the tie, he deserves little sympathy – he made a bargain at arm's length.

The doctrine may have served a useful purpose in the Middle Ages, when the shortage of labour was acute after the Black Death and it was difficult to change trades. A master dyer who agreed not to dye could not become a clothworker without first becoming an apprentice and joining a new guild. But in these days, if a garage owner by his own agreement limits the ways in which he can sell petrol, there are many other useful occupations open to him and many others who may perform the function he has given up; so the public interest in his continuing to work is not in jeopardy. The common law control seems to look at one of the least important aspects of requirements contracts.

Section 8(4): Patent Licences

A person who has made a new invention may apply for a patent. This gives an exclusive right, for a period of sixteen years in the U.K., to produce goods by use of the invention or to make and sell goods which embody the invention. If the patent is granted, the patentee can sue for patent infringement anyone who, without his consent, 'makes, uses, exercises or vends' the invention or goods made by use of it. In the short term, this exclusive right is anti-competitive. A monopoly protected by law often cannot be eroded. On the other hand, the arguments that are used to justify the patent monopoly include the assertion that without it there might be fewer inventions, or more might be kept secret, for there is an obligation on those applying for a patent to give a sufficient description of the invention to enable others to perform it. To the extent that this encourages investment in research and development, it may increase competition in the long run and, even in the short term, publication of the patent specification enables competitors to use the idea for their own research purposes, although they cannot exploit the invention commercially without the patentee's consent until the patent has expired. There are some further provisions to limit the reduction of competition contained in the Patents Act 1949. If the patent is not being adequately exploited, or after an adverse report by the Monopolies and Mergers Commission, the Comptroller-General of Patents, a public official, may require the patentee to grant licences on terms to be fixed by the Comptroller. There is an additional provision regarding food and drug patents under which compulsory licences are much more readily obtainable.

Few inventions which result in patents today are the result of individual research or inspiration. Far more come from the activities of industrial enterprises which employ research and development personnel. An important invention needs to be separately patented in every country which may become an important market for the product, so sometimes a dozen or more separate applications to patent offices throughout the world may be required. A single firm may not itself be able to exploit all its patents, so it may license another firm, or several firms, to supply some markets, while it concentrates on others. A patent licence may be granted under only the U.S. patent, or for part of the U.K. Or it may relate to a single field of use: if the application of a novel drug for veterinary purposes were licensed, this would leave the patentee free of competition in the market for human consumption. A patenteè may also license another firm to make and sell the product provided it charges a minimum price, or does not produce or sell more than a specified number of goods. Other restrictions are possible: the patentee may promise not to license anyone else at all, or for certain areas, fields of use etc., and usually there is a 'grantback' clause under which the licensee is required to tell the patentee about any improvements it makes in the methods of production and to grant a licence to the holder of the basic patent under any improvement patents that the first licensee may acquire, exclusively or otherwise. Sometimes, the owner of a master patent – one protecting a major breakthrough – may license many firms, each of which is required by the 'grantback' clause to inform the master patentee of improvements, grant him a licence royalty free under any improvement patents, inform other licensees of improved techniques and grant them licences under improvement patents in return for a reasonable royalty.

How far are such agreements subject to registration? A bare licence imposes no restrictions, so does not come within section 6(1). It merely permits the licensee to do what would otherwise be illegal. Since the licensee is usually required to pay a lump sum, or a royalty for each unit produced, the patentee will still have some competitive advantage, a margin within which he can earn a monopoly profit, if there are no close substitutes for the products made by the invention. Even a bare licence with no restrictions may reduce the licensee's incentive to develop a competing process, and may thus have some anti-competitive effect. Nevertheless, unless licences are permitted, small firms might not be able to exploit their inventions and the incentive to them to invest in the original research would disappear, or be diminished. A restriction on licensing other firms or a duty to grant cross-licences is also not caught by section 6(1), so P, the holder of a patent, may license L(i) and L(ii) under his patent, require each of them to pay him a royalty for each unit produced, to license him royalty free under any improvement patents he may obtain, to grant licences to each other subject to royalties and not to license anyone else. If L(i) and (ii) are his only serious competitors, P may have stifled all competition in research and development. Neither licensee is likely to invest in innovation when the main beneficiary for a substantial period will be P. P will also have the competitive edge in not having to pay any royalties. Provided that he can find another important patent before the first expires, he may be able to prolong a dominant position in the industry.

It is not clear whether there is a registrable agreement when P relies on his patent rights rather than on any agreement to restrict his licensees. If he grants a licence to L(i) to manufacture and sell not more than 1,000 units in Scotland and to L(ii) to manufacture and sell for veterinary purposes in England, he can rely on his patent to prevent them producing or selling outside the limits of the licences. It is argued that since the licence has made it possible for the licensees to compete to a limited extent, it has not taken away any freedom they previously enjoyed. On the other hand, to permit P to grant such limited licences increases the value and extent of his exclusive rights under patent law, and those concerned with policy may doubt whether this additional power is necessary in order to encourage P to grant a licence, or to undertake the original research and development (see pp. 242–3 below). Some lawyers advise that such an agreement is not within section 6(1), since it is the patent privilege rather than the agreement that restricts the licensees (*Telephone Apparatus Manufacturers*). On this argument, P may also accept restrictions, as restrictions must be accepted by two or more persons before Part I of the Act applies to an agreement.

The Court has never had to determine the validity of this argument because of the very wide exemption originally provided in section 8(4) for restrictions contained in licences granted under a patent or registered design, or in an agreement to grant such a licence, even if the patent has not yet been granted. These escaped registration provided that all the restrictions of the kind listed in section 6(1) accepted by licensor or licensees were in respect of

'(a) the invention to which the patent or application for a patent relates, or articles made by the use of that invention; or

(b) articles in respect of which the design is or is proposed to be registered and to which it is applied, as the case may be.'

This enabled both the patentee and each licensee to accept restrictions as to the quantity of products that may be produced, their price, the areas in which they may be sold, the markets in, or fields of use for which, they may be sold, etc. Until 1973, it was possible for a whole industry to take advantage of this provision and organize a

108

patent pool. Sometimes all patents were assigned to the trade association and each member was licensed under all the patents. Sometimes royalties were paid to the inventor, sometimes to the trade association, sometimes no royalties were payable but research was financed in some other way. Such pools made it easier for members to compete with each other in production – no one was inhibited by fears that he might be infringing a patent – but they may have reduced the incentive to innovate individually. It often made it very difficult, however, for a newcomer to enter the industry. If the patent pool was exclusive, he might find that all avenues of development were blocked.

Under the Fair Trading Act, the exemption of section 8(4) was therefore removed from the pooling of patents and registered design pools (s. 101). As first introduced in the House of Commons, the definition of patent pool was so wide as to include almost all bilateral licences. Provided that two persons had some interest in any patent (even one used in a different factory in a different industry from that affected by the agreement, or even under foreign law) and each agreed to grant to the other a licence under any existing or future patents, there was a patent pool. Since the licensee is almost invariably required to grant a cross-licence under improvement patents, most bilateral licences would have been registrable, if both parties accepted restrictions as to price, quantity, area or field of use etc. As a result of representations from industry, the definition was narrowed to require at least three parties to be members of the pool. But if P owns an English patent, L(i) a Japanese patent and L(ii) a United States one, licences from P including the usual 'grantback' clause amount to a patent pool, even if the licences are non-exclusive and competition between the three firms would have been impossible without the agreement. If then at least two of them accept restrictions of the sort described in section 6(1) the agreement is registrable. More frequently, however, the three manufacturers would have patent protection in each of the relevant countries, in which case, if such restrictions were accepted, it would not be unreasonable to call the arrangement a patent pool and require its registration.

Some people argued that the main result of this would be to deter licensing and reduce the use made of inventions. If the government was worried about patent pools it might have been better to require their notification to the Director and arrange for them to appear on a secret register, as do export agreements under section 8(8) (pp. 113–14 below). If there were then found to be many such agreements, some of the products affected could be referred to the Monopolies Commission which could develop precedents about the circumstances in which various sorts of clauses are contrary to the public interest. Eventually it might be asked to make a general report, as a result of which the law could be changed. The concern behind this criticism is that it is so expensive to defend an agreement before the Restrictive Practices Court, and the outcome so uncertain, that a licence to which more than two persons are party is unlikely to be granted. (Moreover, if one licence is made only in expectation of another, there is an underlying 'arrangement' under which restrictions accepted in both are accepted.) Patentees are therefore able to make highly restrictive arrangements with a single licensee, but have a justification for not allowing a second licensee to join in. The result may be to lessen, rather than increase, competition.

In Chapter 9, we will see that the Common Market rules about patent licences, and on the sale in one member state of goods which have already been sold in another with the patentee's consent, have been developing. It is because patent licences are so important in practice under both U.K. and E.E.C. law, that I have devoted a somewhat disproportionate amount of space to them. Both systems have had to compromise between the need for exclusive industrial property rights given to encourage kinds of innovation that are thought desirable and the policy of encouraging free competition. In the short term at least, and possibly in the longer, these conflict. The 1956 Act did provide for some exemptions in the case of licences under patents and registered designs. The exemption for knowhow licences is narrower, while that for trademark licences is minimal, and there are no exemptions at all in respect of copyright, appellations of origin or any other forms of industrial property.

Section 8(5): 'Knowhow' Agreements

Many incidental items of knowledge about the operation of industrial processes are not capable of being protected under the Patents Act. Whether or not a patent affects a machine or process, the firms using it may find various better ways of exploiting it that are not sufficiently original to be protected by an improvement patent. Sometimes a firm decides not to apply for a patent, even when an invention is capable of patent protection, in order to avoid expense or because it prefers to keep its invention secret rather than publish it in the patent specification. These unpatented results of research and development, consisting of drawings, formulae, skills of technicians and many other aspects of information, much of it confidential, are loosely called 'knowhow'. A firm established in a field may grant a 'knowhow' licence to another. This may involve not only the imparting of information, but also arrangements to train staff etc. There may well be a reciprocal obligation for the recipient to divulge improvements and even existing information.

Even exclusive 'knowhow' cross-licences cannot keep newcomers out of the industry in the same way as patent pools, since if a new firm can develop the processes for itself without breach of confidence, it will not be precluded from using them. On the other hand, the exchange of 'knowhow' will not lead to publication, so it may be less influential than a patent in spreading interest in the results of innovation.

Subsection (5) provides that Part I of the Act shall not apply to an agreement for the exchange of 'knowhow' made between only two parties, if the only restrictions accepted are in respect of the descriptions of goods to be produced by those processes or to which those processes are to be applied. It seems that to qualify for this exemption it is not enough for A to agree to inform B, unless B also agrees to inform A about existing processes – it is doubtful whether an obligation merely to give particulars of improvements amounts to an agreement for 'the exchange of "knowhow"'. Moreover, the restrictions accepted must relate exclusively to the kinds of goods to be produced or processed and it is thought that restrictions as to the price at which they may be sold etc. would prevent the application of the exemption.

The exemption for agreements relating to the exchange of information is far narrower than that for patent licences. Since one cannot rely on more than one of the subsections of section 8, where a patent licence is accompanied by an agreement to exchange 'knowhow' it is customary to attach any restrictions to the patent licence and rely on subsection (4) rather than subsection (5). The only restriction commonly accepted in relation to the knowhow, in such a situation, is not to divulge it. This is not one of the kinds of restriction listed in section 6(1).

Section 8(7): Trade Mark Licences

Goods are often sold under a brand name or trade mark. The exclusive right to apply a mark to goods may be acquired by usage, but it is more usual to register the mark under the Trade Marks Act 1938, as it is then easier to prove the exclusive right to use the mark. The purpose of marking goods in this way is to build up the goodwill of customers, who will treat the mark as indicating the trade origin of the goods. By permitting the first user or registered proprietor of the mark to stop others from using it on similar goods, the law protects both the consumer from being misled and the mark owner from losing the benefit of his advertising and other promotional expenditure. Often the proprietor of a well-known brand may make a more or less identical product, to which the retailer's house-mark is applied, and which is sold on the same shelf at a

111

considerably lower price. Nevertheless, many shoppers may buy the more expensive and highly advertised goods. It is not clear that this should be prevented. If consumers choose to pay more for the advertised brand, which may have different characteristics, why should they be deprived of the opportunity?

A trade mark is said to indicate to the buyer the 'origin' of goods to which it is applied. This does not mean that all goods to which the mark is applied remain identical. Not only may they be developed over time, but they may need to vary from one area to another: the kind of detergent, for instance, suitable in a soft water area would be very inefficient if used where the water is hard. Nor does it mean that the proprietor has necessarily made them himself, but only that he can control the way they are produced. There are 'registered user' provisions in section 28 of the Trade Marks Act which aim to ensure that, if a mark is not assigned outright to a new proprietor, the original proprietor remains responsible for the specification of the goods to which it is applied by a registered user. One business system which makes extensive use of registered user agreements of this kind is franchising: a franchisor who has already built up the goodwill in a trade mark permits independent franchisees in different areas to offer goods or services using the trade mark but subject to controls over their quality or variety. Widely different kinds of goods may be offered under a single mark in such a scheme.

To enable the proprietor of a mark to make the declaration required by section 28(4) of the Trade Marks Act, which requires a statement of any conditions or restrictions proposed with respect to the characteristics of the goods, or the mode or place of permitted use, section 8(7) of the 1956 Act exempts an agreement between the registered proprietor of a trade mark and a person or persons authorized to use the mark, provided that no restrictions are accepted

'except in respect of the descriptions of goods bearing the mark which are to be produced or supplied or the processes of manufacture to be applied to such goods or to goods to which the mark is to be applied.'

The exception is far narrower than that for patent licences. It does not allow the proprietor of the mark to set the prices etc. of goods to which it is to be applied. Although where the proprietor supplies the goods for processing to the registered user he may be able to divide the market by virtue of a restriction to be disregarded under section 7(2), he cannot accept a restriction not to license anyone else in the vicinity. At first sight such a restriction does not seem to be of the kinds described in section 6(1), but its acceptance by the franchisor might arouse an expectation by his licensee about the kind of goods to be supplied there which might amount to a restriction within paragraphs (c) and (e).

Section 8(6): Certification Trade Marks

Section 37 of the Trade Marks Act 1938 provides for certification trade marks. These must be

'adapted in relation to any goods to distinguish in the course of trade goods certified by a person in respect of origin, material, mode of manufacture, quality, accuracy or other characteristic, from goods not so certified'.

The proprietor may not himself trade in the goods certified, but may be an association of those who do. An obvious example of a certification mark is the wool sign so often advertised.

Subsection (6) of the 1956 Act exempts from registration agreements authorizing their use, where the only restrictions accepted are those permitted by the minister who makes regulations about the use of such marks. At first sight, this seems an innocuous exemption: the Minister has an interest in promoting rather than restricting forms of competition likely to help consumers and it would be deceptive to allow the use of the wool sign in connection with artificial fibres, when its function is to show that the fibre used is exclusively wool.

Nevertheless, certification marks may restrict competition. In *Stilton Trade Mark* (1966), it was held that a certification mark might be granted for cheese of a certain kind made from the full cream milk of English dairy herds by a producer resident in the counties of Leicester, Derby or Nottingham. The village of Stilton is in fact outside these, so if cheese came to be made there in the way prescribed, the certification mark could not be used. If a Canadian cheese maker, using the traditional method of producing 'Stilton', were to sell it in England as 'Canadian Stilton', an injunction could be obtained to restrain him, although consumers would presumably not be deceived.

Section 8(8): Exports

Where all the restrictions accepted relate exclusively to exports, the agreement is not subject to Part I of the Act. For this purpose, 'exports' is widely defined to include not only the supply of goods by export from the U.K., but also the production or processing of goods outside the U.K. and the acquisition of goods to be delivered

113

outside the U.K. and not imported to the U.K. for home use, as well as the supply of goods to be delivered outside the U.K. otherwise than by export. Nevertheless, particulars of such agreements as include restrictions about the supply of goods by export from the U.K. in the narrow sense should be furnished to the Director (s. 102 of the 1973 Act), who may use the information to help him decide whether to make a reference to the Monopolies and Mergers Commission. These agreements, not being subject to Part I of the Act, do not appear on the public register, and cannot be referred to the Restrictive Practices Court. It is a crime for the Director or his staff to disclose the existence of such agreements, except for the purpose of facilitating the performance of the functions of the Director, Commission and Ministers (s. 133 of the 1973 Act), or in pursuance of a Community obligation. We will see (p. 213 below) that the Director may be required to give information in certain circumstances to the Commission of the E.E.C.

The exclusion of export agreements, in this wide sense, from control under the 1956 Act reflects the national rather than the international interest. The U.K. has no interest in protecting consumers abroad, and where U.K. exporters enjoy tariff preferences, cartels may help improve the U.K. balance of payments. To come within the exemption, there must be no restrictions affecting the home market, so at an early stage export cartels were separated by their members from any that might apply to the home market, and have been separately treated. Nevertheless, the need to meet and discuss prices, capacity etc. in relation to the export cartel may reduce competition in the home market too.

Although agreements containing restrictions about the delivery or production of goods in the Common Market (other than the U.K.) are not subject to Part I of the 1956 Act, care must be taken to comply with Community law.

Restrictions Coming within Two Paragraphs of Section 8

Although restrictions of the kind listed in section 7 can be disregarded entirely in deciding whether Part I of the Act applies to an agreement, this is not the case in relation to section 8. In *Schweppes* (*No. 2*) (1971) there were some restrictions of the kind listed in section 8(3) and others relating to the specification of goods to which a trade mark might be affixed of the kind mentioned in section 8(7). Stamp, J., following the wording of this paragraph – 'being an agreement under which no such restrictions as are described in subsection (1) of section 6 of this Act are accepted other than restrictions' of the kind listed in a particular paragraph – held that the trade mark restrictions prevented section 8(3) from applying and vice versa.

Section 8(9): Inter-Connected Bodies Corporate

A single group of companies is treated as a single person, even if one company has only just over half the shares in the other, or is only able to control who can sit on its board of directors (see p. 58). One can hardly expect competition between the different companies in a single group, yet many economic activities could not take place without large corporate groups to bring together sufficient capital, skill, and labour, so this is probably justified. Similarly, individuals in partnership need not register an agreement not to compete with their partnership. Since no partner would be prepared to devote his efforts to the partnership and share the profits from them with his partners unless they agreed not to compete with it, agreements between partners, like those between related companies, are likely to increase rather than diminish effort. The provision, however, does not extend to companies carrying on a business in partnership.

Although for the purposes of deciding whether Part I of the Act applies to an agreement, inter-connected bodies are to be treated as a single person, they need not be treated as the same person. In *Schweppes* (*No. 2*) (1971), it was argued that a contract whereby a parent company was to supply goods to its subsidiary was not exempt under section 8(3), as it was not an agreement for the supply of goods, since a person cannot supply himself. Stamp, J. observed, however, that in sections concerned with the counting of heads, it was not necessary to treat the two companies as being the same. Since a similar definition is used in sections 6 and 7, it seems that for all purposes of deciding whether Part I applies to an agreement, they should be treated as different persons. Consequently a parent company that does not itself carry on business in the U.K. can make an agreement with a person who does, without it being subject to Part I of the Act. Any subsidiary that carries on business in the U.K. will be treated as a different person, although care must be taken to ensure there is no underlying 'arrangement' to which it is party.

Discretionary Exemptions from Part I of the Act

As it became more expensive to defend an agreement before the Restrictive Practices Court and more clear that few agreements would survive a reference, it was feared that some desirable forms of co-operation would not take place. So in 1968 the Board of Trade took power in section 1 to exempt from registration proposed agreements to promote the carrying out of an industrial or commercial project or scheme of substantial importance to the national economy. There are various limiting conditions, drafted in rather vague terms. In practice the power has been exercised only once. In deciding whether the Minister should exempt an agreement, it is customary to look at the statements made by the minister sponsoring the Bill in 1968. Ministerial discretion is frequently exercised in accordance with statements made when the discretion was granted, even though courts of law do not look to Parliamentary debates.

To obtain exemption, it is necessary to prepare a case carefully. The official with whom the firms may carry on the preliminary discussions is unlikely to advise the expenditure of time by a panel of senior civil servants advising the Minister and their assistants unless the firms have made out a prima facie case. The panel is not unlike the mergers panel (described on p. 64 above). The official will try to help the firms to establish their case by stating what points have not been adequately covered in their supporting statement.

In Section 2, power was also taken to exempt from Part I of the Act agreements to hold down prices made on the request of a minister. During the voluntary stage of the prices and incomes policy this exemption was widely used for short periods, but is not currently being invoked.

Directions Discharging the Director from the Duty to Refer Agreements to the Restrictive Practices Court

Under section 9(2) of the 1968 Act, the Minister may, upon representations made by the Director, discharge him from the duty of referring a particular agreement to the Court. This replaces the rather cumbersome provisions contained in section 12 of the earlier Act and has become most important in practice. On no occasion has the Minister refused to give directions sought by the Registrar (now the Director). The power exists only in relation to restrictions which are 'not of such significance as to call for investigation by the Restrictive Practices Court.' The Registrar has judged significance, not by reference to the importance of the agreement, but to the likelihood of it being approved by the Restrictive Practices Court. In this connection gateway (h) added to section 21(1) by section 10 of the 1968 Act is most important:

'that the restriction does not directly or indirectly restrict or discourage competition to any material degree in any relevant trade or industry and is not likely to do so.'

In his report for the three years ending in June 1972, the Registrar stated:

'I have not found it necessary during the period under review to modify the criteria described in my last Report which we apply in deciding whether a representation can be made. We would not make one if the agreement appeared capable of causing detriment of which the [Restrictive Practices] Court would be likely to take account if the agreement came before them. Thus the primary consideration is whether the agreement is likely to reduce competition between those affected in any respect in which it would be to the advantage of customers or consumers, whether by affording them a useful choice or by acting as a spur to the efficiency of those engaged in the trade or industry. We of course also consider whether the agreement is likely to produce discriminatory or other unfair results. In applying these principles we regard ourselves as watchdogs especially for the smaller trade customers and the consuming public who have little individual bargaining power, and I hope the future will show that their interests have been reasonably protected in the cases to which the Acts apply. . . .

We have been able to make representations in respect of several "voluntary groups". Generally these involve the recommendation of resale prices in relation to promotions and sometimes to "own brand" goods. There are also sometimes provisions restricting wholesale members from dealing with retailers outside their allotted area. . . .' (pp. 7 and 8)

A single firm acting both as wholesaler and retailer can adopt an integrated trading policy, producing promotional material stating that prices will temporarily be reduced to a certain sum, for use in one branch after another. Similar action by the Co-ops and voluntary groups, however, amounted to a recommendation by their trade association as to resale prices which was subject to Part I of the Act. Directions by the Minister not to refer these are more likely to increase than to restrain competition. Although the Co-op is now to be treated as a single person (Fair Trading Act, sections 97 and 98) directions will doubtless continue to be sought for the voluntary groups.

The terms of agreements in respect of which directions have been given are available for public inspection on the register, but why directions have been given is not stated. Whether an agreement increases or reduces competition often depends on a market analysis. Suppose that two firms have been importing a component that is not made in the U.K. If they enter a joint venture, under which they will collaborate to make the component, they will increase competition, at least in the short term: there will be one firm making it in the U.K. On the other hand, the joint venture makes it unlikely that either firm will make that component on its own. If either firm would have been likely to enter the market on its own, with the spur to efficiency provided by the possibility that the other might do

117

so if its prices were high, the supply would be more competitive; if both might have entered separately, then the joint venture will clearly reduce competition. The effect on competition depends not so much on the terms of the agreement – the firms may not agree expressly not to compete with the joint venture – as on the likelihood that each parent would have started production individually.

One useful feature of the Registrar's practice that is now being adopted by the Director has been his willingness to discuss with firms in advance whether a proposed agreement would be subject to registration and whether he would be minded to seek directions not to refer it to the Court. He is even prepared to discuss ways in which the agreement might be altered so as to enable him to seek directions. This is almost the only provision under which the Director has been able to adopt a flexible attitude. The exceptions from Part I set out in sections 7 and 8 are automatic in their nature. The exemptions under sections 1–3 of the 1968 Act are ministerial: the first section has been applied only once, and the second was of limited application. Since section 9(2) enabled the Director to seek directions not to refer particular agreements to the Court, he has been able administratively to discharge the task previously performed by the Court, though presumably he would not seek directions except when he was satisfied that the Court would not declare the agreement contrary to the public interest. This has opened the gateways of section 21 (discussed in Chapter 6 below) to small trade associations and firms who have not got the resources to defend a reference, but it has also removed the assessment of the public interest from public scrutiny. Most of the judgments in which an agreement was not declared to be against the public interest have been subject to cogent criticism. When the Director seeks directions, sufficient facts about the industry are not disclosed for criticism to be possible.

Application of Part I of the 1956 Act to Services

The 1956 Act has been successful inasmuch as few firms of any size now make the sort of cartel agreements that were common before 1956. When it became possible to refer the supply of services to the Monopolies Commission, the Commission admitted that the economics of manufacturing industry and service industries might be different, but still acted on the assumption that agreements restricting charges etc. were likely to have undesirable effects. In its report on fire insurance (1972), for instance, it stated (paragraph 317) that:

'We accept that the distinction [between manufacturing and

service industries] exists and that we have to form a judgment on the effects of a particular collective restrictive system in the circumstances of a particular service industry. Nevertheless, in forming this judgment we think it right to take into account the fact that such restrictions have, when examined, generally been found to have some undesirable effects, though there may be cases where these effects are outweighed by advantages arising from the restrictions. It is to be expected that a collective arrangement, such as that adopted by the [Fire Offices Committee], which significantly limits the freedom of the parties in the conduct of their businesses, will tend to have some or all of the following effects – higher prices, less efficient use of resources, discouragement of new developments and rigidity in the structure and trading methods of the businesses. What we have to consider is whether there are, nevertheless, special features in this industry which should lead us to conclude that in this case removal of the restrictions would be likely, on balance, to produce effects more disadvantageous, or less advantageous, than those which may be found to result from the restrictions.'

This amounts to a presumption against the fixing of charges and restrictions on the kind of business that may be undertaken by the parties, which can be rebutted only by showing countervailing benefits to the public. It may be that where the public is not in a position to judge the quality of technical services until it is too late, there should be restrictions on the people who may offer them. Certainly, qualifying exams are needed to enter certain professions and sometimes this requirement is supported by statute. But the need for any such limitation, unless prescribed by statute, will have to be demonstrated.

On this view, there is something to be said for the decision to confer jurisdiction over agreements restricting competition in the supply of services on the Restrictive Practices Court. It may be expected that, as in 1959 and 1960, it will soon become apparent that few agreements will survive a reference and that the disciplinary and other bodies formed to protect the interest of service industries will cease to recommend standard charges or limited competition in other ways.

The provisions conferring jurisdiction on the Restrictive Practices Court, contained in Part X of the Fair Trading Act, are complex. Most of the provisions contained in sections 6–8 had to be modified in their application to services. The exemption, for example, of the export of services under section 115(6) relates to the supply of services outside the U.K. or the supply of services to persons or in relation to property outside the U.K., since passing from a U.K.

119

port is not a feasible test save in relation to goods. It might have been easier to provide that, when restrictions relating to goods or services are accepted by more than one person in respect of the charges etc. for either goods or services, the agreement should be subject to control under Part I of the Act of 1956, but it would have been difficult to decide what exemptions should be permitted under section 8 in a case where one party accepted restrictions in respect of goods and the other in respect of services. In the event, it was decided to keep the treatment of goods and services distinct. Moreover, a decision was not made in 1973 to bring all services under control. It was provided that the minister in charge of the monopoly functions should have power to call up services for registration by order, either individually, in groups, or across the board. Particular additional exceptions and exemptions may also be provided in such an order.

To facilitate consultation with those using or providing the services likely to be affected by the order, provision was made in section 111 for the Minister first to publish a description of the classes of services to be affected, indicating the scope of the intended order and that of any exemptions. The public must then be given at least twenty-eight days in which to make representations. Although the Minister is required to take these into account, he is not bound to follow the advice proffered. Indeed, much of it may be ill-informed. The procedure does, however, enable those likely to be affected by an order to draw officials' attention to the less obvious probable effects. Certainly (as stated on p. 89 above), experience of the procedure in relation to information agreements leads one to think that it may be a useful aid to co-operation between business and government in the legislative process and enable the Minister and his advisers to avoid some difficulties.

'Services Brought under Control by Order'

The class of services to be brought under control must be specified in the order (s. 107, reproduced at p. 266 below). For the agreement to be one to which Part I of the Act of 1956 is extended, there must be two parties to it who carry on business in the U.K. in the supply of services brought under control. It is not necessary that they should both supply services brought under control by the same order unless it is so limited (s. 110(3)). Moreover, there must also be restrictions in respect of matters specified in the order accepted by at least two persons. An agreement between two persons who carry on a business of supplying a service brought under control, one of whom also carries on a business in the supply of goods, will be subject to registration as a result of Part X of the 1973 Act, but only restrictions relating to the supply of services will be relevant. If there were a third party to the contract who carried on business in the supply of goods, then the agreement would be subject to Part I of the Act in relation to both services and goods, provided that at least two persons accept restrictions relating to goods and at least two accept restrictions relating to services.

In August 1974 the Minister, Mrs Shirley Williams, announced her intention of bringing under control all services across the board, subject only to specified exceptions. In view of this, it does not seem worth analysing the complex provisions of the Act whereby she could have called up a smaller class of agreements. The Act provides that certain services, described in schedule 4, cannot be designated in the order. These include certain skilled professions, including certain medical and quasi-medical professions and the law. Consequently, recommendations as to the charges to be made for such services, even if made by professional bodies, are not subject to control, although recommendations about the charges their members may make for other services will become subject to registration if the order follows the terms of the Minister's notice.

The Schedule to the notice also lists six kinds of agreement to which it is not intended to extend Part I of the 1956 Act. Some of these are the subject of international agreement. The first three relate to transport, the fourth to agreements between building societies relating to interest charges, the fifth to agreements with the Bank of England about monetary or credit policy, and the sixth to certain agreements between insurance companies. Of course, when the actual order is drawn up, the list may be extended in the light of any representations that may be made to the Minister. The agreements now excepted may be brought under control at a later time. Equally, subsequent orders may revoke or vary any order that is made so as to exclude certain services from its scope.

Section 108 provides on similar lines for orders bringing information agreements in service industries under control. Part I of the 1956 Act shall apply to agreements which

'(a) are agreements between two or more persons carrying on business within the U.K. in the supply of services brought under control by the order, or between two or more such persons together with one or more other parties, and

(b) are agreements under which provision is made for or in relation to the furnishing by two or more parties to each other or to other persons (whether parties or not) of information with respect to matters specified in the order for the purposes of this paragraph.'

The matters that may be specified are defined on the lines of section 5 of the 1968 Act to include '(a) the charges, made, quoted or paid or to be made, quoted or paid for designated services which have been or are to be supplied, offered or obtained;' and the other matters in respect of which information agreements about goods may be made subject to control.

The Minister's announcement in 1974 that she would extend Part I of the 1956 Act to services did not extend to information agreements. If, however, it is found that associations abrogating recommendations about the charges their members should make start to disseminate information about those in fact made and so forth, information agreements may later be brought under control, as they were in relation to goods.

Orders may be drafted in a great many different ways. The Minister may aggregate services brought under control in a single order with other services already brought under control, so that agreements between two or more persons carrying on the business of supplying any of the services may be caught, if at least two accept restrictions in respect of any of the relevant matters. On the other hand, the Minister may isolate a particular group of services, so that only if two parties accept restrictions in respect of those is an agreement brought under control (s. 110).

There follow complex provisions along the lines of sections 6–8 of the 1956 Act, supporting sections 107 and 108. The modifications to section 6(6) and (7), which enable Co-ops and other industrial and provident societies to compete with the chain stores, apply also to agreements relating to services. All the exceptions of sections 7 and 8 have been modified to apply to services (sections 114 and 115), and the definition of public interest has also been modified by section 116.

If the order is made in accordance with the Minister's announcement, the Director's restrictive practices staff will first be concerned to enter agreements notified to him on the register. A few agreements will doubtless be defended when referred to the Restrictive Practices Court. If the Court is as strict in considering the public interest as it was in relation to goods and the Commission has been in relation to services, few will be justified. There would therefore be much to be said for using the three month period after any order is made and before notification is required to consider whether to abandon agreements about fees and the customers to be served. This would avoid the worry caused to those who have been required to give an undertaking to the Restrictive Practices Court not to make any agreement (or arrangement) to the like effect to the one condemned. Now that the Director's office has accumulated experience over eighteen years, registration is likely to buy far less time for operating restrictions than it did in 1957 and 1958. Minimum standards of entry to a profession are found in most of the professions which cannot be designated. There may be others, in which case such restrictions might be worth an attempt at justification. After the initial activity of registering and referring the first agreements, the Director is likely to return to his policing role, ensuring that agreements and recommendations are not being made without particulars being duly furnished to him. At that point, information agreements may also be brought under control by a subsequent order.

5: Registration

Duty to Furnish Particulars

By December 1957, all the agreements to which Part I of the 1956 Act applies had been called up for registration. From 1970, agreements to furnish information about prices charged or to be charged, quoted or to be quoted, have also been registrable, but until orders are made under the Fair Trading Act there is no duty to notify agreements relating to services. Particulars are required to be furnished to the Director General of Fair Trading of all agreements to which Part I of the Act applies, as well as of export agreements. Until 1968, there was some doubt whether a duty to furnish particulars was imposed upon anyone, but the provision has been substantially tightened up. Under section 6 of the 1968 Act, particulars are required to be furnished before the agreement comes into operation and, in any case, within three months after it is made. When a new class of agreements is called up for registration, there must be a three month period during which the parties can consider whether to abrogate the agreement or to register (s. 6(1) (c) and (h) of the Act of 1968). A three month period was also allowed under the 1956 Act and it is thought that many of the least defensible agreements, including many collective boycotts, were abandoned during that time without any administrative action by the Registrar being required.

The Director is required by section 1 of the 1956 Act to maintain a register of agreements to which Part I of the Act applies, and sections 11 and 19 empower him to make regulations as to how the register is to be kept. It can be inspected in Chancery Lane, London, and also in Edinburgh and Belfast; but one special section is not open to the public because the agreements in it contain information the publication of which would in the opinion of the Minister be contrary to the public interest, or because they contain trade secrets.

It is the whole agreement that should be registered and not just those clauses that contain restrictions. Indeed, where an agreement is clearly registrable on account of restrictions accepted by at least two parties, no one may trouble to analyse it to isolate all the other restrictions until it is referred to the Restrictive Practices Court, when the Director does so in the pleadings – the documents which define the issues in dispute.

The Director should be furnished with particulars not only of new agreements, but also of their variation or termination. This used to cause trouble to trade associations, since any change in membership amounted to a variation which was required to be notified. Subscriptions that vary with the member's turnover (previously subject to registration by virtue of section 6(5)), are now exempt, as are the Co-ops' promotions. The problem would remain for other trade association agreements and recommendations about the matters listed in section 6(1), had the Registrar not taken advantage of the power conferred in 1968 to make regulations (S.I. 1968, no. 1755) requiring the notification of only certain classes of variation.

The Director's Powers of Investigation

The Director's powers under sections 14 and 15 of the Act of 1956 to obtain information about agreements that have not been registered voluntarily have been criticized for their weakness. Of course, much can be discovered from commercial and trade journals, and his office has encouraged complaints. Many business managers will take care to answer informal questions truthfully. Under section 14(1), if the Director has reasonable cause to believe that any person who carries on business in the U.K. in the production or supply of goods is or may be a party to a registrable agreement, he may give notice to him requiring him

'to notify the [Director] whether he is party to any agreement relating to any such matters as are described in [section 6(1)], and if so to furnish to the [Director] such particulars as may be so specified of that agreement.'

If the Director has been given some particulars of an agreement, then, under section 14(2), he can ask the person who furnished them, or any party to the agreement, to furnish further documents or information in his possession or control. The object of serving such notices is that when this has been done, the Director may apply to the Restrictive Practices Court under section 15 for an order that the person so served shall attend and be examined under oath. The Director takes part in such examination and may be represented by a solicitor or barrister. The person examined must answer all the questions which the Court may put or permit to be put to him. He is entitled to be represented at his own expense by a solicitor or a barrister, who may put to him such questions as the Court may think just, for the purpose of enabling him to explain or qualify any answers given by him. Notes are required to be taken of the examination and may be used in evidence against the person examined. By virtue of section 15(2) (d), the Court may also require the person examined to produce any such particulars, documents or information in his possession or control as may be specified in the notice given under section 14. This process is called 'discovery'.

In *Schweppes* v. *Registrar* (1965), Diplock, L. J. (as he then was), a former President of the Restrictive Practices Court, suggested that there might be a loophole in the provision for discovery when, in answer to a notice under section 14(1), the supplier states that he is not party to a registrable agreement. Section 15(2) (d) limits discovery to the documents specified in a notice given under section 14. Some particulars may be specified under section 14(1), but unless some particulars have been furnished to the Director, he cannot serve a notice under section 14(2) requiring further documents or information to be furnished, so it would seem that discovery would be limited to those particulars specified in the original section 14(1) notice.

A notice under section 14 can be given only to a person who carries on business in the U.K. It cannot be given to an employee, who manages someone else's business. In the case of a company, however, there is provision for examining on oath not only its central managers (s. 15(3) of the Act of 1956), but also any other employee who appears to the Court to be likely to have particular knowledge of any of the matters in respect of which the notice was given (s. 103 of the 1973 Act). This provision may be useful in obtaining information from sales or branch managers, as well as from salesmen.

During the Parliamentary debates on the 1956 Bill, these provisions were criticized as inadequate by Labour and Liberal Members. Even after the Acts of 1968 and 1973, the Director has no powers of search. He cannot arrive unexpectedly with a search warrant and look through a firm's files, as the authorities in the United States and Canada can do and, to a considerable extent, officials of the Common Market Commission. Only if he has reasonable cause to believe that a registrable agreement has, or may have been, made can he exercise the powers under sections 14 and 15, and the Master of the Rolls has criticized the Registrar for serving a notice when he did not have reasonable cause to believe that an agreement had been made, though there were some grounds for suspicion (*Registrar* v. *W. H.*

Smith Ltd (1969)). He did not mention that section 14(1) refers to reasonable cause to believe not only that the person given notice is, but also that he '*may be*', party to a registrable arrangement. Where the Director's staff know what they are looking for, sections 14 and 15 are said to be useful, but cannot be used to confirm a mere suspicion that there may be an agreement.

In his latest report, for the three years ending on 30 June, 1972, the Registrar stated that an appreciable number of registrations had resulted from enforcement procedures. He had been particularly successful in discovering many arrangements to rig tenders in the building and contracting trades.

Where an agreement has been made, but it is doubtful whether Part I of the Act applies to it, then under section 13(2) any party to it, or the Director if particulars have been furnished to him, may apply to the Restrictive Practices Court, to decide whether Part I does apply to it. This, however, does not enable the Director to take the initiative: any party to the agreement may apply, but the Director can do so only if some particulars have been furnished to him. Where an agreement has actually been inaccurately entered in the register, then any person aggrieved may apply to the Restrictive Practices Court under section 13(1) for an order that the entry on the register be rectified. It is not clear whether the person who furnished the Director with inaccurate particulars is 'aggrieved', and it is thought that persons against whom the agreement discriminates are not. But after the first *Schweppes* case (1964), the section 13 procedure was not used until *Schweppes* (*No. 3*), heard at the end of 1974. In the first case the Registrar obtained discovery of documents relating to the circumstances in which a contract was made in order to see whether there was an underlying registrable arrangement. Since Diplock, L. J. suggested that discovery could not have been obtained under sections 14 and 15, had some particulars not been furnished to the Registrar, some legal advisers are chary of furnishing anything. Those who are more cautious advise businessmen to furnish the Director with particulars while stating that there is no agreement to which Part I of the Act applies. If the Director agrees, he will not enter it on his register, but the parties have fulfilled their duty to furnish particulars, while if the Director does register it, they can apply to the Restrictive Practices Court for rectification.

Few new agreements are now being registered voluntarily. In his fourth report the Registrar stated that when the Act first came into force, most businessmen did furnish him with the appropriate particulars. During the period covered by his first report only 10 per cent of the registrations arose out of inquiries made by his office, but in the three years from July 1963 three-quarters of the 145 new agreements registered were the result of enforcement. Some of these were agreements of only local application and others related to less obvious applications of the Act. But the Registrar believed

> 'that this failure to comply with the law is too often due to the wider realization that no ill befalls parties who do not register, and that once registered their agreement's chances of survival are thin.'

In his more recent reports he suggests that the stricter sanctions imposed in 1968 have discouraged the operation of unregistered registrable agreements, though even in his latest report he states that an appreciable number of those registered have resulted from enforcement procedures.

Sanctions

Until 1968, the sanctions for failure to register were minimal. Where there was wilful default, the High Court, which used then to deal with matters relating to registration, was empowered to make an order forbidding the parties to give effect to the agreement or to make any other to the like effect, without considering any merits (s. 18). The provision has now been repealed, but more effective sanctions are provided for in section 7 of the 1968 Act. Under subsection (1) the agreement is automatically void in respect of the restrictions, and it is unlawful to give effect to or attempt to enforce the agreement in respect of them. Suppose that a patent pool is formed, but particulars are not duly furnished. The patent licences are not restrictions of the kind described in section 6(1) of the Act of 1956; nor are any restrictions not to license outsiders. These provisions can, therefore, be enforced, but any restrictions on prices or markets are probably void.

It is not a crime to attempt to enforce such restrictions, but anyone harmed, for instance by a collective boycott, can sue to recover damages for any loss he has suffered (s. 7(2) of the Act of 1968). Such civil actions, however, are not frequently brought as the plaintiff must show (i) that there was an agreement or arrangement, (ii) that effect was given to it and (iii) the amount of damage he incurred thereby. He may be able to show that several suppliers refused to supply him, but it is more difficult to show that this was collusive. He would also find it difficult to show what loss he has suffered, if he has not been able to test the market.

The most effective sanction is probably the power of the Restrictive Practices Court, which now deals with registration issues (s. 13 of the 1968 Act), to make an order under section 7(3), where it is satisfied by the Director that particulars were not duly furnished. In its discretion, it may restrain any party to the agreement, who carries on business within the U.K.

'(a) from giving effect to, or enforcing or purporting to enforce the agreement in respect of any relevant restrictions;

(b) from giving effect to, or enforcing or purporting to enforce, other agreements in contravention of subsection (1) of this section:'

The first restriction is normally imposed on the parties to an agreement which is not justified to the satisfaction of the Restrictive Practices Court, but the second is far wider. Parties to an unregistered agreement who, having given an undertaking in the terms of section 7(3) (b), discuss any of the matters mentioned in section 6(1) of the 1956 Act, even if they relate to a completely different product, without furnishing particulars in due time are guilty of contempt of court. Breach of any order of a superior court of record, such as the Restrictive Practices Court, is a serious matter and is discussed at p. 132 below.

An order in the terms of section 7(3) (b) was made against the trade association of the makers of *Flushing Cisterns* (1973), on the ground that failure to register an agreement which was clearly outside the exemption provided in section 8(4)

'constitutes a grave and persistent dereliction of the duty of responsible company officers so to direct and manage the company affairs as to comply with the restrictive practices legislation. . . . But, in the view of this court, an injunction is required under s. 7(3) (b) in order to bring home to all these respondents that their standards in respect of this legislation simply have not been high enough, and that unless they radically revise their standards of efficiency in respect of their obligations under the Acts, sanctions will be applied by this court.'

Most of the sanctions under the monopolies and restrictive practices legislation are civil, but a person can be prosecuted under section 16 of the 1956 Act, if he should fail to comply with a notice given to him under section 14, and has no reasonable excuse. If he should be convicted, he may be fined up to £100. Wilful or reckless deceit in supplying information or documents is also a crime for which a person convicted may be imprisoned for three months, or fined £100, or both. If the prosecution is on indictment, then the person convicted may be imprisoned for up to two years, and the possible fine is unlimited. Provision is also made for continuing default in complying with a notice, and where the offences are committed by a company, certain managing officers of it may be convicted if they have consented to or connived at the offence. No prosecution can be brought, however, except with the consent of either the Director General or, in England and Wales, the Director of Public Prosecutions, or in Northern Ireland, the Attorney General for that country.

6: Investigation by the Restrictive Practices Court

Jurisdiction

Not only is the Director charged with the duty of preparing, compiling, and maintaining the register, he is also required by sections 1 and 20(1) to refer to the Restrictive Practices Court any agreement of which particulars are for the time being registered, to see 'whether or not any restrictions by virtue of which this Part of this Act applies to the agreement . . . are contrary to the public interest.' As we saw earlier (p. 87) particulars remain registered even if an agreement has been varied so as to bring all the registrable restrictions to an end; and the Court's jurisdiction continues even if no restrictions are still in operation.

Under section 20(3),

'Where any such restrictions are found by the Court to be contrary to the public interest, the agreement shall be void in respect of those restrictions; and without prejudice to the foregoing provision the Court may, upon the application of the Registrar, make such order as appears to the Court to be proper for restraining all or any of the persons party to the agreement who carry on business in the United Kingdom –

(a) from giving effect to, or enforcing or purporting to enforce, the agreement in respect of those restrictions;

(b) from making any other agreement (whether with the same parties or with other parties) to the like effect.'

This section is the heart of the Act: it provides the sanction against continuing to give effect to condemned restrictions. The

131

whole agreement may not become void: the Court declares that specified restrictions are contrary to the public interest, and the automatic result is that the contract, if any, becomes void in respect of those restrictions. Whether the rest of the contract remains valid will depend on the agreement looked at as a whole. Some agreements could not be enforced in the courts anyway: the dead or filleted agreements were already void in respect of the restrictions and others were never intended to be legally binding.

Often competition cannot be effectively protected by merely making a restrictive contract void. The agreement between the members of the association in the *Mogul* case (see p. 2) was probably void as an unreasonable restraint of trade, yet, since the parties were all willing to give effect to it, enforcement in the courts was not needed to keep non-members out of the tea-carrying trade. The Court therefore normally requires an undertaking that the parties will not give effect to the old agreement, or make any other to the like effect to which Part I of the Act applies. These undertakings usually follow the wording of paragraphs (a) and (b) of subsection (3), except for the insertion in paragraph (b) of the qualification 'to which Part I of the Act applies'. Orders are made only if the respondents have behaved improperly or if some of them cannot be found to give the undertaking. Whether an undertaking has been given, or an order made, makes little difference: if either is broken deliberately, the Director can apply to the Court to punish for contempt of court the person who has broken it, and the Court can then imprison the person in contempt for an indefinite period, or impose a civil fine. So far it has been content to impose fines and, as the persons in contempt have been companies, this has not caused substantial hardship to the individuals responsible. The Court, however, has given warning that those who play with fire by using nice devices that they believe may restrict competition without amounting to registrable agreements must expect to find their fingers burnt if they are wrong. This is generally interpreted as a warning that, in future, higher managers may be sent to prison if they fail to take sufficient steps to prevent the infringement of an order or undertaking.

One of the weaknesses of the Act is the narrow meaning that has been given to 'to the like effect'. In *Black Bolts (No. 2)* the Court did not look to the effect on competition, but to the way the parties intended the agreement to operate. In the first case the Court held that a restriction about supplies to large users of black bolts could not be defended, and the usual undertaking was given. Under the restriction condemned in the first case the parties agreed to exchange information about the prices they *had* quoted to large users and, in practice, the final offers were almost invariably based on the list of prices which were charged to other customers. It was held that a subsequent agreement to charge the list prices to large users was not 'to the like effect', since the new agreement was not intended to operate in substantially the same way as the earlier agreement. The new agreement was therefore valid until it was, in turn, considered by the Restrictive Practices Court in 1966 and eventually upheld.

In 1966, however, in *Tyre Mileage*, the Court did not look merely at the terms of the contract in deciding whether it was 'to the like effect' to a condemned agreement to rig tenders, but also at its effect on pricing. The Court pointed out that the new agreement had the same purpose as the old, although the machinery used to achieve it was different. In *Tyre Mileage* the conduct that was held to infringe the undertaking was merely an 'arrangement' arising from the conduct of the parties in informing each other of the prices at which they intended to bid; so it would have been of little use to look at its effect in creating legally enforceable rights and duties. It was thought that the Court of Appeal's decision in *Basic Slag* has marked a new approach to Part I of the Act, and that the Court may now look to the effect on pricing, production, and the other matters listed in section 6, not only in considering whether an implied 'arrangement' is 'to the like effect', but also whether an express contract is.

In *Transformers* (*No. 2*) (1970), however, Stamp, J. refused to look at the likely economic effects of the two agreements. Following the judgments in *Black Bolts* (*No. 2*) he decided that, in comparing the effects of the two agreements, he was entitled to look only to their terms and to the findings and reasons for the judgment in the earlier case. Since the preponderant buyer of large transformers would be present at the meeting when the prices were to be fixed, the proposed new agreement would be a bargain struck between both sides, whereas the original agreement had resulted in prices being dictated by the suppliers, so he held that the new agreement would not be to the like effect as that condemned in 1961. On almost any test, this decision must be right; prices agreed with the customer are likely to be lower than the prices fixed in his absence. But in following the reasoning in *Black Bolts* (*No. 2*) so closely, the judgment may enable suppliers who are well advised to find new formulae that will have a similar effect in raising prices, without being held to infringe the undertaking given. The willingness of the Court to grant a declaration that the proposed new agreement would not be to the like effect before it was entered into protects the companies from the risk of committing contempt of court. Where the agreement is intended to take effect shortly, the Registrar or Director may not be able to obtain an order forbidding the parties to enter into the new agreement, which has not been considered on its merits, before its expiry.

This may matter rather less now, since under section 105 of the Fair Trading Act the Director may ask the Court for an interim order in the terms of section 20(3). This may be granted only in respect of specified restrictions which could not reasonably be expected to fall within any of the gateways provided by section 21(1), and where the operation of the restrictions while the proceedings last is likely to cause material detriment to the public or a section of the public or to an individual not party to the agreement. It is not clear yet how this will operate in practice. We will see that it is difficult to predict whether an agreement will be successfully defended before the Restrictive Practices Court, particularly under paragraph (b), as the arguments both ways are often incapable of proof. Detriments under the 'tailpiece' are irrelevant to an application for an interim order.

Under section 20(5) the Court may also make such an order in respect of any variation made after the agreement has been referred to it; but it has refused to exercise this power in respect of an amendment made at the end of the hearing, and has said that, while it might do so if the variation was raised in the pleadings, it would be loath to do so if it was made later, as the Court would need to consider the effect of the variation fully. This left a weakness in the Act: if the parties, expecting to lose their case, made a new agreement after the hearing but before the judgment was delivered or an order made, and duly furnished the Registrar with particulars, it was not contempt to give effect to it. This weakness was remedied by section 104 of the Fair Trading Act, which added a third paragraph to section 20(3):

'or

(c) where such an agreement as is mentioned in paragraph (b) of this subsection has already been made, from giving effect to that agreement or enforcing or purporting to enforce it:'

Section 21: Definition of the Public Interest

Since jurisdiction over agreements was being transferred to a court from the Commission, it was thought that Parliament should attempt to frame criteria on the basis of which it could decide whether particular restrictions were contrary to the public interest. Throughout their history, the common law judges have altered the law, and made important decisions on public policy in doing so. When a court has to decide whether an injured pedestrian should obtain damages from the motorist who hit him, it considers whether both sides have acted reasonably in the circumstances. In other words, it has to decide how motorists and pedestrians should behave in modern times. To drive a car without someone carrying a red flag in front might have been dangerous seventy years ago; clearly the answer would be different today. In applying the criterion of what is reasonable, the judges look to what people are in fact doing, but they also affect people's conduct in as much as they decide what is reasonable today, and thereby develop rules.

Yet it is frequently said that the courts' job is to apply the existing law, not to make decisions on policy. These should be made by the people's elected representatives, or at least by the Cabinet or a minister who is responsible to Parliament and to whom questions can be addressed in the House. Yet the distinction between applying flexible standards, such as reasonableness, and making decisions on policy is not clear cut. If the application of the law were always clear, it would be necessary to go to court only when the facts are disputed. But the open texture of the English language and the use of what some Americans call 'india rubber definitions', leave the courts with considerable discretion, which they attempt to exercise in the interests of the community as a whole.

The Restrictive Practices Court – which consists not only of High Court judges but also of lay members qualified by their knowledge of or experience in commerce, industry, or public affairs – may be in a better position than most courts to assess the effect of restrictive practices on an industry. But it was felt wrong to ask it to decide whether they operate contrary to the public interest without prescribing standards. These are provided in section 21 which is set out in the Appendix (pp. 263–4). A restriction is deemed to be contrary to the public interest unless the respondents can prove, first, that it can pass through one or more of the eight 'gateways' and, secondly, that the restriction is not unreasonable having regard to the balance between the circumstances enabling it to do so and any detriments to the public. But although the respondents must produce an argument in defence of the restriction, the standard of proof is the usual civil law one – the balance of probabilities – and the Court has several times accepted conjectural arguments. It is required to predict what will happen to a particular industry on two alternative assumptions: first, that the restriction is allowed to continue and, secondly, that it is abrogated. The prediction is complicated by the fact that sometimes the Court has to predict changes in the external environment in which the industry will be operating. The issues under the first and last two gateways are no more difficult than many others with which the courts are accustomed to deal, but as each is analysed I shall argue that the others are indeterminable.

135

Protection of the Public against Injury to Persons or Premises

'(a) that the restriction is reasonably necessary, having regard to the character of the goods to which it applies, to protect the public against injury (whether to persons or to premises) in connection with the consumption, installation or use of those goods; . . .'

This gateway, derived from the Monopolies Commission's report on collective discrimination, should not give rise to much difficulty. The *Chemists' Federation* attempted to pass through it in the first case decided by the Court, in 1958. An association of manufacturers of the dealers in proprietary medicines agreed to supply these only to those retailers who employed a registered pharmacist on the premises. The list of medicines included many that were not very dangerous, such as cod liver oil, and other products, such as barrier creams, that were hardly even medicines. Legislation which prohibits the sale of most dangerous drugs unless they have been prescribed by a doctor protects the public from the most dangerous forms of self medication. The Court therefore found that the risk of injury was negligible; and, since there was no requirement that the persons buying the listed preparations should in fact be served by the pharmacist, the restriction was not appropriate to protect the public had it needed any protection. Devlin, J. (now Lord Devlin) framed this test:

'We have to ask ourselves whether a reasonable and prudent man who is concerned to protect the public against injury would enforce this restriction if he could. He would not do so unless he was satisfied, first, that the restriction afforded an adequate protection and, secondly, that the risk of injury was sufficiently great to warrant it.'

There can be few restrictions that can pass such a test, since the government usually makes regulations when there is a substantial risk of injury.

The General Gateway

'(b) that the removal of the restriction would deny to the public as purchasers, consumers or users of any goods other specific and substantial benefits or advantages enjoyed or likely to be enjoyed by them as such, whether by virtue of the restriction itself or of any arrangements or operations resulting therefrom. . . .'

This 'gateway', which has been pleaded in almost every case, and through which most businessmen would like their restrictions to pass, is far more difficult to apply. The only criterion of the public interest is the substantial benefit to consumers; that of the parties to the agreement does not count.

Yarn Spinners, the second case decided by the Restrictive Practices Court, early in 1959, came as a shock to the business community. It had been thought that the traditional arguments in defence of restrictive agreements could be used to save many under the general gateway; but the Court read a presumption in favour of competition into the Act, and refused to accept them. The yarn spinners had agreed on a formula for fixing the minimum prices they would charge to the doublers and weavers, based on the current cost of raw cotton and a somewhat hypothetical average cost of converting it.

Maintenance of Price Stability. It was said that since prices could not fall below the minimum price when demand was slack, prices were more stable than they would have been without the restriction. It was also said that spinners would be encouraged to spin for stock, since they knew that they would always be able to clear these stocks at at least the minimum price when demand revived. This argument was roundly condemned by Devlin, J. (now Lord Devlin) when he delivered the Court's judgment:

'Any form of price control will probably make prices more stable than they would be in a free market. If price stability could be obtained without the sacrifice of a free market, it would undoubtedly be a benefit; . . . But we do not think that the proper way of considering this point is to admit price stabilization as a benefit to the purchasing public, and defer for subsequent consideration the question whether the loss of a free market is a detriment to the public generally. We have to look at both sides of the medal. A question, for example, as to whether a contract for the sale of goods is beneficial is not divisible into two parts; it could not be argued that the acquisition of goods was of itself always a benefit, and that the fact that they had been acquired at double the market price, while it might be a detrimental corollary, did not prevent the acquisition from being beneficial. What we have to consider is whether price stabilization as an alternative to a free market is a benefit to the purchasing public in the circumstances of this particular case. We cannot think that as a general rule it is a benefit; if we were to hold that, we would be going contrary to the general presumption embodied in the Act that price restrictions are contrary to the public interest. There may be particular cases where price stabilization confers a peculiar benefit sufficiently great to outweigh the loss of a free market, but this is not one of them.' (p. 189)

It is difficult to see where the general presumption in favour of competition is enacted. According to its long title, the Act is:

'An Act to provide for the registration and judicial investigation of certain restrictive trading agreements, and for the prohibition of such agreements when found contrary to the public interest. . . .'

This does not seem to favour competition over collaboration. It is true that section 21 enacts that the agreement is deemed contrary to the public interest unless it comes within one of the gateways; but the question was whether under paragraph (b) the purchasers of any goods, either the trade buyers of yarn, or consumers buying shirts, dresses, and so on, benefited from the price agreement.

Devlin, J.'s statement was followed in several early cases. Lord Cameron, another judge who favours competition, said in *Scottish Bakers* (1959) that it is only stabilization at the right price that benefits the public; and he demonstrated some of the difficulties of deciding whether the price agreed is as low as that which would prevail without the restriction. Price stabilization has been argued in many cases and condemned with a citation from Devlin, J.'s judgment. It was not successful until *Distant Water Vessels* was decided in 1966, and was successful then only because the Court held that in the long run prices would be lower than they would be without the restriction, even though temporarily increased by the minimum price scheme.

In *Yarn Spinners*, the Court was also unsympathetic to the argument that the minimum price agreement encouraged spinners to maintain sufficient capacity during recessions. Demand was declining, so there was scope for reducing capacity; the fluctuations in demand were not so severe as to call for exceptional measures, and sufficient capacity would be retained to allow any boom demanded to be met, at least if more double-shift working was introduced.

Improvement in Quality. In *Yarn Spinners*, it was also argued that since the spinners could not compete in price, they had a greater incentive to compete in other ways: by improving the quality of their product or by giving additional or better service. The Court held that the ending of the scheme would enable the spinners to choose how they would compete, whether in price or other ways. The benefit of channelling competition into quality and service was, at most, negligible. The Monopolies Commission had rejected a similar argument by the calico printers on the ground that it curtailed consumer choice.

138

In *Lino* (1961), Russell, J. added that the addition of a new, cheaper grade of lino was not a debasement in quality nor a detriment to buyers: if the old qualities were maintained, it would increase consumer choice.

Collaboration to Improve Quality or Reduce Costs and Prices. In many of the cases, the parties to a minimum or fixed price agreement alleged that there was considerable technical and other co-operation between the firms, and that this would cease if the firms started to compete in price. In *Black Bolts* (*No. 1*) (1960), Diplock, J. (now Lord Diplock) referred to the exchange of technical information and joint research, and mentioned that this had enabled the smaller firms, in particular, to improve their efficiency; he added

> 'We think that it is right to say that co-operation of this kind has been fostered by the absence of price competition, since it is only human nature to be more reluctant to impart "knowhow" to a competitor who may use it to undercut one's own prices and take away one's own customers than to a competitor who can only use it to benefit himself and his product.'

One might argue, however, that if co-operation has helped the parties in the past, they would continue to collaborate to the extent that it is likely to pay, even if they are permitted to compete in price: particularly if they compete against outsiders abroad. It may be human nature not to impart 'knowhow' to a competitor who may use it to undercut one's own prices; but it is equally human nature to endeavour to stay in business. Alternatively, it may be argued that it is impossible to say whether collaboration or individual research and development would give better results. One can usually point to specific developments that have resulted from co-operative research, but it is impossible to say what developments might have resulted from each firm conducting its own research in the fear of being put out of business by its competitors achieving a technical lead.

In the early cases, the collaboration argument was not successful. In *Black Bolts* (*No. 1*), Diplock, J. concluded:

> 'We do not think that the rate of investment in the industry as a whole would be reduced if the price restrictions were removed, and although the high degree of co-operation between members, which now exists, might well be reduced, it is, in our view, a matter of speculation only as to what effect any reduction of this kind of co-operation would have in the efficiency of the industry as a whole if price competition replaced the present system.'

139

In *Transformers* (1961), Russell, J., another judge in favour of competition, thought that to the extent that it paid manufacturers to collaborate, they would continue to do so.

More recently, however, the argument, so cogently stated by Diplock, J., that if the price restrictions were abrogated, collaboration would decrease, to the substantial detriment of the public as purchasers of goods made by the cartel, has been accepted by Mocatta, J. in *Magnets* (1962) and by Buckley and Megaw, JJ. in *Standard Metal Windows* (1962). In the early days many arguments were rejected as speculative. More recently the Court has accepted arguments in favour of restrictions, even when the result could not be strictly proven or quantified.

Buying Costs of Purchasers Reduced. The argument that prices would be higher if the restriction were abrogated was also rejected in the earlier cases, but accepted later. In *Scottish Bakers* (1959), Lord Cameron criticized the formula used to fix bread prices. He objected to it because it was based on the average costs of production, and not on those of the baker able to produce most cheaply. If price competition were allowed, the producers whose costs were lower might be able to cut their prices, drive some of those with higher costs out of business, and expand their scale of operations. This in turn might enable them to produce even more cheaply, and they might sell at lower prices to discourage other firms from entering the baking industry.

Further objections were made by Pearson, J. in the *English Bakers* case (1959). What level of profit should be allowed? Should one compare the bakers' profits, divided by the value of the capital used for baking, with similar figures for other industries which are published in the *Economist*, as the Registrar suggested? There are three objections to this measure: first, the *Economist*'s figures are based on the capital as it appears in the companies' balance sheets – that is, computed according to the usual accountants' conventions at cost less depreciation, and not on replacement valuations (see pp. 47–8); secondly, some of these industries may not be competitive in price; and thirdly, it is difficult to tell whether the producers whose agreement is being investigated are more or less efficient than average, or whether they are incurring costs in producing services etc. for which buyers would prefer not to pay.

One further difficulty was illustrated in *Phenol* (1960). Phenol is mainly made by fractional distillation from tar acids, and many other by-products result from the process. How should the costs be apportioned between the different tar acids? Within wide limits, any cost apportionment is arbitrary.

While all these objections to the ways of discovering what prices would prevail if price competition were permitted are valid, economists would add that if firms are not permitted to compete in price, some, especially those with low costs, or those with unused capacity who wish to expand, may compete by providing services which cost more than they are worth to customers. If no charge is made for delivery, why should a shopper with a car parked outside the shop bother to carry the goods home? The proliferation of costly and unnecessary services may be the result of intense competition when prices are fixed.

Although most of the objections made in the earlier cases could have been urged against the way that prices for *Black Bolts* were fixed, the Court in 1960 said that prices were not unreasonable, by which it meant that they were no higher than they would have been without the price restriction. As Diplock, J. said,

'It is incapable of proof either way whether, as the registrar claims, there would have been greater efficiency and progress if there had been no price-fixing, or, as the association claim, there would have been less.'

Yet the Court had accepted on the previous page that overall prices would not have been lower had there been free competition in price; nor, if they continued to be fixed in future in the same way as in the past, would they be higher than they would be under free competition.

This case, decided late in 1960, seems to mark a watershed. Until then, apart from a very low minimum quality restriction in *Blankets*, no case had succeeded under the general gateway, largely because it was impossible to tell whether prices were as low as they would have been without the restriction. The early cases had read a presumption in favour of competition into the Act. Yet the civil law standard of proof is only on the balance of probabilities, and arguments that had been dismissed as 'nebulous', 'speculative', or 'indeterminate and indeterminable' in earlier cases were sometimes successful after 1960. It is admitted that the finding that prices were no higher than they would have been in the absence of the restriction was only one half of the argument accepted by the Court in *Black Bolts*. The Court also accepted the more positive proposition that the uniformity of prices saved the buyers of black bolts from the expense of 'going shopping' for the cheapest source of supply. The respondents made several thousand types or sizes of nuts and bolts, and some of their customers said it would cost 10 per cent of the purchase price if they had to 'go shopping'. The saving in administrative costs was a benefit to them; not only did they have to pay no more, but the cost of acquisition was actually less. Yet it is difficult

141

to refute the Registrar's argument that if it is not worth while to shop around, buyers will not waste their time; and that if it is, they will welcome the opportunity to do so, at least occasionally. It became standard practice to plead this argument; and though it has never been accepted since that case, it has never been judicially refuted.

After this decision, several price restrictions passed through the general gateway wholly or partly on the ground that they resulted in better bargains for buyers. In *Magnets* (1962), the Court found that the joint research and collaboration which might not have survived the abrogation of the price agreement had resulted in magnets that were either cheaper or else more powerful and no more expensive than they would have been had there been no restrictions. In *Tiles* (1964), the Court found that a price restriction that encouraged buyers to concentrate their orders on certain sizes had reduced costs to the benefit of buyers, and would continue to do so, although the restriction was more rigid than was required for the purpose and although different manufacturers had very different levels of profit. The measurement of profit in terms of the return on the capital employed is not entirely satisfactory, but there is no better test of 'reasonable prices' in industries in which capital costs are a large proportion of turnover; and where the profits earned by the different manufacturers vary widely, there is at least a prima facie case that some could have expanded their share of the market more quickly had they been allowed to compete in price and so have been able to take advantage of any economies of scale.

In *Cement* (1961), the Court accepted that prices had been kept down by a common price agreement, although no subsidiary argument, such as the encouragement of technical collaboration, supported its conclusion. Such a startling decision deserves analysis. Cement is made in factories with complex plant which require very few workers, so capital costs constitute a large part of the total cost. The demand for cement is expected to go on rising. The Cement Makers' Federation argued that the price restriction made the industry less risky, since makers knew that prices could not fall and as a result could borrow money at a lower rate of interest than could many firms of comparable size in other industries. The cheaper capital available to the industry enabled it to keep its prices lower than if there was no agreement on common prices. The Court accepted this line of reasoning. It has, however, been criticized. The National Board for Prices and Incomes in its report on Portland Cement Prices (1967, Cmnd 3381) observed that there were cheaper ways of financing cement works than those considered by the Court. The Court found that the demand for cement would continue to expand, with only occasional short-term setbacks. Thus, even without the price agreement, the firms could have looked forward to favourable long-term conditions. Moreover, the Court observed that the structure of the industry would ensure that price cuts were unlikely even during the temporary setbacks in demand. Thus it is difficult to see why there would have been serious instability in prices and profits in the absence of the agreement. It may be noted in passing that if the Court's assumption that the demand for cement would rise steadily should prove to be incorrect, the Director could make a second reference to the Court under section 22, on the ground that there is 'prima facie evidence of a material change in the relevant circumstances.' Consequently, the protection of the price restriction might be removed at the very time that price competition was likely to occur.

Conclusion on the Economic Issues. In the early cases, when either Devlin, J., Lord Cameron, or Pearson, J. presided, the presumption in favour of competition which was read into the Act seems to have influenced the lay members – who had had no judicial experience to give them the confidence to take an independent line – to such an extent that early in 1960 it was argued that no price agreement would ever survive a reference. Either the agreement kept the level of prices higher than it would be without the restriction, which would cancel any other benefits to the public as purchasers, or, as in the very low minimum prices adopted by the *Blanket* makers (1959), it would have little effect on price levels, in which case its beneficial effects would not be substantial. In *Black Bolts*, Diplock, J. stated that whether the price restrictions had led to a more efficient industry could not be proved either way; but nevertheless the Court found as a fact that the prices on an average were no higher than they would have been without the restriction. The presumption in favour of competition was whittled down. There followed a period when if Russell, J. was presiding, no agreement got through the gateway, but if Diplock or Buckley, JJ. sat, some did, and it was difficult to forecast their decisions. This may well have been what was intended when Parliament created a Court to decide the public interest on such imprecise criteria. Later, the results seem to have depended less on which judge presided, although the Scottish Court has condemned every agreement referred to it except for one which was held not to restrict competition to any material degree (p. 159 below.) Many judges who have sat in the English Restrictive Practices Court have been rapidly promoted, while the lay members of the Court have served far longer, and may have more confidence in their own powers of prediction than they had in 1959 and 1960. The arguments in favour of the restrictions are better presented now and very occasionally an agreement survives a contested reference. Neverthe-

143

less, few industries do contest the reference of a price fixing agreement; so the weaker cases are unlikely to be defended before the Court. The new gateway (h), added in 1968 – that the agreement does not 'restrict or discourage competition to any material degree – is now likely to be urged in preference to the general gateway whenever possible, as the arguments are probably simpler. Professor Stevens has argued that the addition of a new gateway based on competition will dissuade the Court from adopting the early pro-competitive approach to gateway (b) and so enlarge its ambit. If there is a special defence that competition is not inhibited, it must be assumed that the other gateways are now intended to enable the respondents to defend restrictions that are likely to restrict or discourage competition. It can however, be argued that the new gateway was introduced primarily for the justification of information agreements, the registration of which was provided for by the same Act of Parliament.

Why should the result of references under the general gateway be so difficult to predict? It is thought that whether a price restriction is expected to benefit consumers substantially depends on one's basic economic and political assumptions. Some think that central planning by the industry as a whole is likely to be more efficient than competition: others fear to leave substantial power to decide what is produced in the hands of a cartel and prefer to refer to the more impersonal test of the market, which they think may be more sensitive to those consumer demands that are supported by a willingness to pay. Most fixed or minimum price schemes adopted by industrialists can be supported on the ground that they encourage joint research, or technical co-operation; most of those adopted by dealers promote orderly marketing. One element of risk is removed from future planning. The obverse side of this is that such restrictions prevent the lowest-cost firms from expanding their market share through price reductions, and that thus they lessen the incentive to prune costs: indeed, competition may take the form of proliferating services that cost more than they are worth. Unless more guidance is given to the Court about the desiderata under this general gateway, it is thought that it cannot be expected to take a rational and consistent line. It has not been told how far competition is in the public interest, nor what sorts are desirable. This is in no way a criticism of the judges who have been required to make very dubious predictions about the future effect of a restriction on an industry, and decide whether the restriction is desirable, but rather a criticism of Parliament for leaving such policy questions to the Court.

Questions of Construction. What benefits are 'specific' or 'substantial'? In the early cases counsel for the Registrar argued that a benefit is 'specific' only if it applies to very few industries; a benefit which could merely be specified or defined, and is common to many industries, was treated as not counting when Parliament enacted the general presumption in favour of competition. This is implied by Devlin, J.'s treatment of price stability in *Yarn Spinners* (see pp. 137–8). Since all price restrictions make prices more stable, the benefit does not count except in exceptional cases. In *Net Books* (1962), however, Buckley, J. expressly decided that it suffices that the benefit can be specified.

Similarly, 'speculative' and 'nebulous' evidence of probable benefits was sometimes rejected in the early cases, but in *Net Books* Buckley, J. said that the word 'substantial' does not demand a strictly quantitative or proportional assessment and is probably not susceptible of more precise definition. As has already been mentioned in considering how far the various arguments have appealed to the Court, the burden of proof placed on the parties to the restrictions seems to be easier to overcome now than it was in 1959. The word 'other' does not seem to be very important; it merely excludes the benefit spelt out in paragraph (a).

The alleged benefit to the public as purchasers, consumers, and users need not be a direct result of the restriction, if without the restriction the parties would act so differently that the benefit would not continue. If technical collaboration and joint research would not continue without the price restriction, that is enough, because the benefits ensuing from the collaboration are enjoyed, if not 'by virtue of the restriction itself', then by virtue of 'any arrangements or operations resulting therefrom'.

It was held in *Black Bolts* that 'the public as purchasers, consumers or users of any goods' means the public looked at collectively in any one of these categories; so if most of the buyers of the goods in the category selected by the respondents benefit substantially from the restriction, the gateway can be passed, though it is not clear whether a simple majority by number or turnover would suffice. It is not only buyers of such goods for their own use that count: in *Net Books*, Buckley, J. said that public libraries and retail sellers were part of the public as purchasers of books. Indeed, if the restriction affects components, the only buyers may be manufacturers. In *Black Bolts* the makers selected as the relevant goods the bolts and nuts they made, not the cars, bridges, and so on in which these components are incorporated before being used by the consumer. The 'public as purchasers' included very few people buying for their personal use.

Counteracting a Monopolist

'(c) that the restriction is reasonably necessary to counteract measures taken by any one person not party to the agreement with a view to preventing or restricting competition in or in relation to the trade or business in which the persons party thereto are engaged; . . .'

The Court has never delivered a judgment on this defence, although it was pleaded and argued in *Sulphur* (1963) (see pp. 149–51). Until 1968, it was the only provision in the Act in which the promotion of competition is specifically indicated as an objective, and the only gateway in which the subjective intention of another firm is relevant as well as the expected effects of the cartel. It is thought that the single firm's measures must in fact restrain competition; otherwise it would not be 'reasonably necessary' to combine to counteract them. According to Mr Thorneycroft's speech during the passage of the Bill through the Commons, the defence was inserted to give effect to the suggestion of the majority of the Monopolies Commission in its report on collective discrimination, but the Commission recommended that the defence be limited to the activities of a single very large firm at the same level of trade. The paragraph does not refer to the size of the single person, but unless it were in relation to the market it would probably not be able to indulge in predatory practices.

According to section 21(2), the 'one person' may be a group of companies or a partnership; but one cartel is not allowed to counteract the power of another, or many industries could be divided into two cartels, each necessary to counteract the measures of the other. It seems that the cartel cannot be defended under paragraph (c) unless the monopolist has already taken measures to prevent or restrict competition. But it is not simple to distinguish 'competing' from 'taking measures to restrict competition'. It is thought that an efficient firm which anticipates demand and sells at such low prices that it is very difficult for new firms to enter the market in competition with it is not taking measures with a view to preventing or restricting competition: it is merely competing successfully. Even if it deliberately promotes one cheap brand in order to discourage new entrants generally, it is merely competing. But if, when ever a new supplier begins business, the monopolist introduces a fighting brand which is sold cheaply just where the newcomer can most easily sell, then that is a predatory practice against which other suppliers may be allowed to combine. But although both British Oxygen and British Match, the two single-firm monopolists examined by the Monopolies Commission before 1956, did engage in such practices, it is thought that one of the achievements of the Commission has been to discourage such measures throughout industry; and it is not surprising that the defence has been pleaded only once, and then against a foreign company. If, however, predatory practices are adopted by a firm supplying, etc., a quarter of the market, then the products affected can be referred to the Commission. Fear of the publicity given to the Commission's reports, the resulting criticism, and any action that may be taken by the Minister, as well as the trouble of dealing with a reference ot the Commission, may deter monopolists from conduct that might result in a reference being made.

As was argued in *Sulphur*, the paragraph can also apply where the monopolist is active at a different level of trade. Suppose that a powerful supplier of product A requires his customers also to buy all they require of product B from him, and refuses to sell A to them otherwise. It is thought that not only the suppliers of product B but also the buyers of A could combine to defeat the extension of the supplier's market power from A to B. But as Upjohn, J. decided in *Boilermakers* under paragraph (d), the cartel will not be 'reasonably necessary' if restrictions are accepted that are much wider than are required to counteract the measures taken by the monopolist (see p. 150).

Counteracting a Preponderant Buyer or Seller

'(d) that the restriction is reasonably necessary to enable the persons party to the agreement to negotiate fair terms for the supply of goods to, or the acquisition of goods from, any one person not party thereto who controls a preponderant part of the trade or business of acquiring or supplying such goods, or for the supply of goods to any person not party to the agreement and not carrying on such a trade or business who, either alone or in combination with any other such person, controls a preponderant part of the market for such goods.'

'*Any One Person*'. As in paragraph (c), a person includes a partnership or group of companies. It was feared that if the paragraph could avail against several persons in collusion, then again there could be a cartel at both levels of trade, each defended on the ground that it is necessary to obtain fair terms from the other. The second part of the paragraph, however, does allow combinations to obtain fair terms from a cartel to which Part I of the Act does not apply because the agreement was not made between persons carrying on business in the production, supply, or processing of goods, as is required by section 6(1). Probably through an oversight, this leniency was not extended to cartels to obtain fair terms from a foreign cartel, which is also not subject to registration on the ground that there are not two persons carrying on such a business in the U.K.

One further problem remains: need the combination actually buy its supplies from the preponderant seller or sell to the preponderant buyer? Suppose that the preponderant seller acts as a price leader, but that a buying pool obtains its supplies from smaller firms who are not willing to undercut it. The pool might argue that unless it can obtain 'fair terms' for a small quantity from the price leader, it will not be able to get them from the other firms, and that it is therefore 'reasonably necessary' to combine 'to negotiate fair terms' from the leader, even if only minimal quantities are obtained from that person.

'*Controls a Preponderant Part of the Trade or Business*'. Before deciding whether a buyer or seller controls a preponderant part of the trade, one must consider the market in which he exercises power. In *Wire Ropes* (1964), the National Coal Board bought 82 per cent of class I mining ropes. Such a large proportion would almost certainly make it a preponderant buyer if the respondents were allowed to classify such mining ropes separately from other stranded wire ropes. Indeed, it was conceded that the Coal Board was a preponderant buyer of locked coil ropes, a different kind of rope of which the Board bought 95 per cent. Megaw, J. said, however, that if challenged the respondents must show that 'any division or fragmentation or selection of goods which he may make is commercially sensible', if their argument that the Coal Board was a preponderant buyer was to be upheld. He added:

'within the area of stranded wire ropes, we are satisfied that there are no sufficient differences, whether of size, appearance, manner of production, general nature of machinery used, conditions of composition of the sellers' side of the market or the buyers' side of the market, or any other factor, so as to have the effect, whether individually or collectively, of making the association's division into class I and class II mining ropes a sensible commercial division.'

To test the Coal Board's market power it is necessary to consider two questions; firstly to whom can the ropemakers sell their ropes? and secondly where else could the Coal Board buy them? If the same machinery can be used to make engineering ropes, then if the Coal Board withholds its orders, the ropemakers could quickly switch to making engineering ropes, and the Board's market power depends, in anything but the very short run, on its power over the total market for stranded wire ropes.

Since the respondents alleged that if the price restriction in respect of class I mining ropes could be defended, then it would also be necessary to retain the restriction on class II mining ropes – as otherwise the Coal Board might buy these – it seems that not only was the machinery used to make the two types of rope of the same kind, but that one rope could do the work of the other; in which case the Court was correct in refusing to separate the market.

In two of the earlier cases, *Transformers* (1961) and *Sulphur* (1963), the Court had held that the relevant territorial market was the United Kingdom, and that consequently the Central Electricity Generating Board was a preponderant buyer of large transformers, although it probably had little power in world markets. On the other hand, in both cases it was said that in deciding the extent of the control, the world market might well be relevant. It does not matter if when considering whether a firm is preponderant, the Court ignores matters which reduce its market power, provided that they are taken into account in assessing whether it *controls* a preponderant part of the relevant trade or business. Where, however, the Court ignores a consideration which increases the power of the firm alleged to be preponderant, it may prevent the application of the gateway in circumstances in which it was intended by Parliament to apply.

The Court mentioned that the Coal Board bought 38 per cent of the stranded wire ropes sold in the U.K., but, although it gave the basic figures, it does not appear to have noticed that the Board bought only a quarter of that produced by the respondents, who exported 30 per cent by value. It held that the Board did not control a preponderant part of the trade. It is thought that many firms which control as much as 38 per cent of the trade may well be preponderant, although the share of the market enjoyed by the important firm is only one of many factors to be considered in assessing its market power. In *Sulphur*, Sulexco supplied less than half of the sulphur used in the U.K., and Megaw, J. considered many other factors which demonstrated its market power.

In *Daily Mirror Newspapers Ltd* v. *Gardner* (1968) the Court of Appeal granted an interim injunction to restrain the newsagents' trade association from recommending a boycott of the *Daily Mirror*. Such preliminary applications are heard and decided very rapidly and the judgments cannot be carefully prepared, so the Court of Appeal is not bound to follow them in later cases involving similar issues. Both Lord Denning, M.R., and Russell, L.J. held that paragraph (d) does not apply unless goods are bought directly from the person who controls a preponderant part of the trade or business. If they are right, then a preponderant seller could always prevent the formation of a buying pool, by insisting on dealing through inter-mediaries. When the boycott of the *Daily Mirror* was defended

149

under section 21, it was argued that the retailers had to negotiate with the newspaper proprietor if they were to obtain fair terms, although they bought through wholesalers. Their defence failed on other grounds, so the point was not decided, but it is thought that the argument was correct.

'Reasonably Necessary'. Although the paragraph says 'controls' in the present tense, it was held in *Sulphur* that the Court must also look to the future, since it is not 'reasonably necessary' to combine to obtain fair terms if the market power is likely to be transitory.

If the restriction is considerably wider than is necessary, then the paragraph will not save it. In *Boilermakers* (1959), although the Central Electricity Generating Board controlled a preponderant part of the business of acquiring large water-tube boilers, the restriction was held to be too wide in that it covered also the far smaller industrial boilers; so it failed to pass this gateway. In *Sulphur*, however, various minor objections to the restriction were made, but nevertheless the gateway was passed. The unnecessary width of the restriction is a matter of degree, and only if it is substantially too wide will the defence fail.

'Fair Terms'. The criterion of 'fair terms' is far more difficult to apply, and the Court has vacillated. With the benefit of hindsight, Professor Yamey lists four possible interpretations: where the parties to the agreement are sellers faced by a preponderant buyer, the object of the agreement may be (1) to enable the sellers to earn 'fair' profits (2) to secure equality of treatment as between the preponderant buyer and other buyers (3) to prevent the preponderant buyer from making unfair profits, and (4) to sell at prices approximating to those which would prevail if there were no agreement and no preponderant buyer. A similar set of objectives can be listed for the converse case where the buyers combine against a preponderant seller.

In *Boilermakers*, Upjohn, J. adopted the first test: 'fair terms' were defined as 'terms upon which the efficient manufacturer can make and sell his goods at a reasonable, but no more than a reasonable, profit.' In *Transformers*, Russell, J. appeared to accept this test, but went on to say that it was not of universal application and mentioned the second test:

'It may be that the paragraph is limited to such a restriction as would prevent the preponderant buyer obtaining more favourable or more unfair terms than the generality of buyers: and this view might be supported either by regarding the word "fair" in the section as not absolute but relative to the market generally, or by regarding the words "reasonable profit" in the judicial definition as relative to the level of profit obtainable from other purchasers.'

During a recession, when prices to other buyers were low, the earlier test might have resulted in the preponderant buyer having to pay more than other buyers, unless a reasonable profit is to be understood as not allowing any deduction for the use of plant that would otherwise be idle. Russell, J. also observed in *Transformers* that the gateway could seldom apply when the disposition of the powerful buyer was such that he would not deliberately exploit his market power.

Sulphur, the third case in which this paragraph was considered by the Court, involved the converse circumstance of a combination of buyers in the U.K. to counteract a preponderant seller abroad. The Court first found that the test used in *Boilermakers* could not apply, since there was no way of finding what profits Sulexco, the American seller of sulphur, was earning. One might have thought that the application of Upjohn, J.'s test would have required a consideration of the profits of the buying pool, not of the foreign seller. But as Professor Yamey has observed, it is clear that the Court did not adopt the first objective he listed, that of safeguarding the profits of the parties to the agreement. The Court referred to the third objective, that of preventing the powerful firm from earning unduly large profits. As, however, there was no evidence about these, Megaw, J. adopted the fourth aim:

'Again we do not propose to attempt a definition of "fair terms" in a case such as this. But we think that a suitable initial approach, in the present case, is to apply the test: Are prices which the buyers would have to pay, in the absence of the restriction, likely to be substantially higher than the prices which they would have had to pay in market conditions which are similar, except that there is no one supplier controlling a preponderant part of the trade or business?'

The difficulty of applying this 'initial approach', which was not followed by any more definitive statement, is that it is impossible to say what the market conditions would have been had no one supplier controlled a preponderant part of the trade. Is one to assume that he is replaced by several smaller suppliers whose total turnover equals his? Would such suppliers compete in price?

Megaw, J. spelled out this test rather more fully in *Wire Ropes*, and reconciled it with Russell, J.'s test in *Transformers* by saying:

'we are unable to accept that, at any rate in the absence of some

151

exceptional circumstances, restrictions are reasonably necessary to enable the negotiation of fair terms if the result of the restrictions is that buyers would be paying higher prices than they would pay in conditions or workable competition.'

Had class I mining ropes been a distinct market (see pp. 148–9), so that the Coal Board was a preponderant buyer, the association would still lose,

'because, in our judgment, prices for such ropes would probably be lower in conditions of workable competition (that is, including the hypothesis of no preponderant buyer and no price-fixing by the sellers) than in the conditions which would prevail with the price restrictions maintained and the N.C.B. a preponderant buyer.'

In that case this finding was fairly clearly right, since there was excess capacity in the industry. It was therefore likely that had there been five or six independent buyers instead of the Coal Board, and no collusion by the respondents, prices would have been lower. The Court said that the position might change if the excess capacity were eliminated; but if it were, it is thought that it would be impossible to apply the test adopted.

The Court's basic difficulty is that there is no test of 'fair terms' in the absence of a competitive market. One cannot tell whether an industry is efficient. In the United States, where many utilities are owned by private persons but cannot increase their charges without permission, a great many tests of a fair profit, and, consequently, of a fair charge, have been adopted by the different regulatory bodies. None of them is wholly satisfactory, though some are less bad for one industry than for another.

'Negotiate'. 'Negotiate' was given a loose and common-sense meaning in *Transformers*. The large transformers, the price of which was fixed under the agreement, are bought as a result of tenders: the Central Electricity Generating Board asks the different firms how much each would charge, each firm makes an offer, and the Board then has to choose which offer to accept. The parties may never meet to haggle over the terms; nevertheless, Russell, J. was prepared to classify this procedure as negotiation.

Unemployment

'(e) that, having regard to the conditions actually obtaining or reasonably foreseen at the time of the application, the removal of the restriction would be likely to have a serious and persistent adverse effect on the general level of unemployment in an area, or in areas taken together, in which a substantial proportion of the trade or industry to which the agreement relates is situated;'

The policy giving rise to this gateway, which was not suggested in the collective discrimination report, has been criticized on several grounds. First, if the local unemployment is expected to be persistent, would it not be better to encourage other industries to enter the area than to permit the existing firms to raise their prices? How can a cartel which raises profits by restricting production employ more workers? Perhaps, in the absence of price competition, old firms with obsolescent plant will stay in business, with the result that the others will not be able to afford to buy modern labour-saving plant and use it intensively, because they will not be able to find sufficient buyers without cutting prices.

The only cartel to pass through this gateway was the *Yarn Spinners'*, in 1959. There was considerable difficulty in estimating the amount of unemployment in the areas of Lancashire at the date of the hearing. Many of the workers were married women; if they were out of work they might not be entitled to unemployment benefit, in which case they would not appear in the statistics. Further, many mills worked only four days a week, and were closed on Mondays, the day the statistics were taken. It was even more difficult to know how many mills would close if the minimum price restriction were abrogated. Despite the inadequacy in the statistics showing the present level of unemployment and the conjecture over the future level, Devlin, J. said

'we ought not to disregard these other factors because they are unquantifiable but should make the best estimate we can of their effect.'

This was in marked contrast to his earlier dismissal as 'speculative' and 'nebulous' of the *Chemists'* claim that if the restriction requiring manufacturers to supply only retailers who employed a registered pharmacist were abrogated, enough such chemists would not remain to support the National Health Service. But the Court is required to make predictions about the level of employment in the future, on the two assumptions that the restriction remains in force and that it is abrogated. Even the government, with the aid of economists and computers, has been unable to forecast levels of unemployment accurately. The Court has no access to these, or to government information about probable tax changes, alterations in hire purchase regulations, projected government expenditure or other matters likely to affect the general level of unemployment. Nor would it have

153

confidential information about matters likely to affect the level locally, such as whether the Minister was likely to approve an application for planning permission for a large factory or intended to designate the area as one to benefit from incentives to investment given to firms who build plants therein.

In 1954 the Monopolies Commission was sceptical about a similar argument urged by the calico printers, another branch of the same industry. It thought that the price scheme would increase the unemployment rather than reduce it. The price rigidity throughout the cotton industry 'must result in a loss of orders for cloth to overseas competitors, and so in a smaller volume of business being done than could have been secured if printing prices were lower'.

Although the *Yarn Spinners'* agreement passed through this gateway, it was finally condemned under the 'tailpiece' which is considered below.

Exports

'(f) that, having regard to the conditions actually obtaining or reasonably foreseen at the time of the application, the removal of the restriction would be likely to cause a reduction in the volume or earnings of the export business which is substantial either in relation to the whole export business of the United Kingdom or in relation to the whole business (including export business) of the said trade or industry; . . .'

From the debates, it appears that this gateway, again not derived from the collective discrimination report, was included to help the balance of payments. But it is worded more narrowly. It is only export boosters that are encouraged, not import savers. In *Lino* (1961), it was even held that imported materials should not be deducted from the export receipts in deciding whether the reduction in export earnings would be substantial. It would be very difficult to work out the exact effect on the balance of payments of many activities: U.K. agriculture is sometimes defended on the ground that it saves imports, and the needs of the hotel business are often pressed on the ground that they encourage foreign tourists and that some of their receipts are equivalent to exports. It is impossible to assess the size of these effects on the balance of payments. The test of paragraph (f) is rather simpler, though it might have been drafted to take account of other fairly direct effects on the balance of payments.

It is the reduction in the turnover of the export business, in comparison with either the whole business of the industry, or with the whole export business of the U.K., that must be substantial. The second test seems to assume that the whole export business of the United Kingdom is smaller than the whole business of the trade or industry; but this is so unlikely that it can be ignored. It *may* be, however, that a different test of substantiality would be adopted when the comparison is made with the whole United Kingdom export business: a lower proportion, perhaps less than one per cent, would be substantial; whereas nothing below, say, two per cent would be treated as substantial when the comparison is made with the earnings of the particular industry. Under paragraph (b), 'substantial benefit' does not require a quantitative or proportional assessment, as Buckley, J. decided in *Net Books* (see p. 145). But paragraph (f), by providing the comparisons, does seem to indicate a proportional assessment. Yet there seems to be no sensible economic policy which is likely to depend on the proportionality with the trade of the particular industry. If the car industry were to lose a small proportion of its export business, the effect on the U.K. balance of payments could be serious, while a large proportional reduction in the exports of a small industry might be comparatively trifling. This alternative comparison was defended in Parliament on the ground that many small industries export, and between them make a substantial contribution to the United Kingdom export trade. They should not be treated more strictly than larger industries. It might be thought that if the turnover of the parties to the agreement is small, then the harmful effects of the agreement may be less; but this does not follow. The small industry may be a key one, so that customers will have to pay substantially more for the goods they need; and anyway, the extent of the detriments can be taken into account under the 'tailpiece' to section 21(1) (see pp. 159–61).

In practice the Court has wavered on the question of how substantial the reduction in export earnings must be shown to be. In *Boilermakers*, Upjohn, J. said:

> 'It is not possible to express any quantitative views . . . [but] the loss in any one year of even one overseas contract may represent a substantial reduction in the export figures of the industry. . . .'

The ground for this statement was that the price of water-tube boilers was large and increasing. They then cost between £6 million and a few hundred thousands, although the total turnover of the United Kingdom manufacturers over the previous seven years had averaged £96 million a year, of which £14 million was earned by exports. The judgment did not demonstrate that the agreement, which provided for level tenders and enabled higher prices to be charged, would result in a single extra export order being earned.

155

Yet in *Magnets* and *Net Books*, Buckley, J. seemed to require a much heavier burden of proof to be overcome. In the former case, he accepted that the end of the restrictions would have an adverse effect on the association's exports, but added:

> 'we are not in possession of sufficient information as regards overseas markets to be able to find that such adverse effect, within the reasonably foreseeable future, would be likely to cause a reduction in the exports of the association which would be substantial [on either comparison]. . . .'

Since it is never easy to estimate the effect of the restrictions on demand abroad, this stricter approach makes the defence of an agreement under this gateway very difficult.

In *Transformers*, Russell, J. decided some of the difficult questions involved in the construction of this provision. The paragraph refers to a 'reduction in the volume or earnings of the export business.' If volume is a test of amount, measured by yards, gallons, or tons, should earnings be given a different meaning: the profits made by the exporting industry – what it charges for its exports less the cost of materials and labour? Russell, J. said:

> 'Although the paragraph is not easy to construe in all its parts on any basis, we consider this construction is wrong. 'Earnings', in our view, means turnover. That is what concerns the public interest in relation to the export trade, and not the rate of profit earned by individual exporters.'

The gateway was passed in *Boilermakers*; but it has not been since, although it has frequently been argued. Since, however, export agreements are often separated from those affecting the home market, and are not subject to judicial review, the arguments in favour of exports have usually been indirect. In several cases, it was argued that the confidence engendered by the lack of price competition in the home market encouraged members to invest in research and equipment, and so make a more reliable and cheaper product to export. This argument failed, for instance in *Transformers*, on the ground that the Court did not think that such investment would be reduced if it paid members to invest.

In *Lino*, the respondents were also members of an international price fixing cartel, and they argued that if prices fell in the United Kingdom then the international cartel might break down, to the detriment of United Kingdom exports of lino, as foreign dealers might be able to buy lino cheaply in the U.K. and sell it abroad below the cartel prices. If the U.K. manufacturers benefited as much as they claimed from the restrictions abroad, then this argument could be sound, but it has not yet been accepted by the Restrictive Practices Court. Since 1973 it has become less likely that it will be raised, as such a cartel would probably infringe the E.E.C. competition rules.

Ancillary Restrictions

'(g) that the restriction is reasonably required for purposes connected with the maintenance of any other restriction accepted by the parties, whether under the same agreement or under any other agreement between them, being a restriction which is found by the Court not to be contrary to the public interest upon grounds other than those specified in this paragraph, or has been so found in previous proceedings before the Court.'

When a restriction has passed through one of the gateways, some of the minor restrictions necessary to support it may get through the same gateway or may pass through paragraph (g). For instance, when the price restriction in *Black Bolts* was successfully defended under the general gateway because it saved customers from 'going shopping', the standard conditions of sale were saved under paragraph (g) on the ground that unless such conditions remained common, buyers would still have to 'shop' for longer credit, and so forth. This is rather surprising: one might have thought that the defence should have succeeded under paragraph (b). Nevertheless, in later cases, too, standard conditions of sale have been defended under paragraph (g).

Various other restrictions have also been supported under paragraph (g). For instance, in *Cement*, a pricing scheme was successfully defended under paragraph (b), and the rule that if orders were placed long in advance they must be made for the prices ruling on the day of dispatch was defended under paragraph (g), because otherwise the makers could 'cheat': they could conclude contracts long in advance at fixed prices, and rely on inflation to make these cheap when the cement was actually delivered years later.

It is rather surprising that aggregated discounts have not been successfully defended on the ground that they are needed to keep the cartel together. In *Cement* the basic price scheme was justified under paragraph (b) on the ground that it reduced the risk and, consequently, enabled members to raise capital more cheaply and so reduce costs and prices. Yet the scheme whereby buyers were entitled to discounts based on the quantities they had bought, not from an individual supplier but from all members of the Federation in an earlier period, was condemned on the ground that it did not reflect cost savings for the individual supplier. Individual quantity discounts, however, were permitted. Consequently, one would expect large construction firms, with projects all over the country, to concentrate their orders on those cement makers who had plants in many areas and from whom they could buy sufficiently large quantities to maximize their discount. Small cement firms with only one plant would not then receive many orders from the large buyers, and might leave the cartel. Where, on the other hand, individually based quantity discounts are not allowed, it may be difficult to keep the large firms in the cartel: they may be able to offer better terms outside it, since the big regular orders would enable them to plan their production well. Yet aggregated discounts have always been condemned without any consideration whether they may be necessary to keep together the cartel approved by the Court.

Competition

'(h) that the restriction does not directly or indirectly restrict or discourage competition to any material degree in any relevant trade or industry and is not likely to do so.' (Added by s. 10 of the 1968 Act.)

The 1956 Act was criticized for making various cost saving and other desirable arrangements difficult to organize. Restrictions on the supply free of expensive kinds of promotion for *Blankets*, such as transparent wrapping and large samples, were condemned in 1959 on the ground that they did not provide a substantial benefit to buyers, although they were of some use in reducing costs. The effect of the new gateway has been most noticeable in encouraging the Registrar – it will in future, no doubt, also encourage the Director – to seek directions under section 9(2) of the 1968 Act discharging him from the duty to refer agreements to the Court. The agreements subject to such directions are appended to the Registrar's two latest reports. For the last three years, over half have related to the terms and conditions on which goods are supplied, although the Registrar has sought to ensure that members were entitled to depart from them to meet special circumstances, except on the large commodity markets, where identical terms are necessary to enable the market to function efficiently. The more important agreements concerning voluntary groups of grocers and others were discussed earlier on p. 117.

The only agreement actually defended before the Restrictive Practices Court under this gateway was the one where members of the *Scottish Daily Newspaper* Society (1972) agreed to stop publication until normal working was resumed by the journalists on the *Glasgow Herald* (described on p. 103, in relation to section 7(4) of the 1956 Act). The next day, before the strike was settled, the other four daily newspapers resumed publication. The Society argued that competition was restricted when the *Herald* was unable to publish and that the agreement, by helping to end the strike, increased rather than restricted competition – indeed, by helping the *Herald* to remain financially viable, it contributed to its continued publication. The Court did not accept that the agreement not to publish during the strike helped to settle it. In the Court's view, it ended because of concessions made by the managers of the *Herald*. Even when the agreement was made, however, it was clear that it would not continue for long. In the circumstances, the agreement came within the paragraph. Although the public suffered the detriment of not having daily newspapers for a day, this was balanced by the importance of the *Glasgow Herald* continuing to be available, so the agreement was upheld.

Severance of Restrictions

Often an agreement may contain different restrictions, and some of them may be defended under one gateway, and others under another. For instance, in *Transformers*, the parties wanted to defend a restriction to the prices for large 'category C' transformers under the preponderant buyer gateway; and since they had drafted this as a separate restriction, the Court said that this was permissible. They attempted to defend restrictions relating to a wide range of transformers under the export gateway, and this too was allowed. But to take advantage of this precedent, the parties must draft their agreements so that the restrictions are separated. If a single restriction is considerably too wide, then, according to *Boilermakers*, the Court will not sever it. Consequently it will not pass through gateways (a), (c), or (d) under which the restriction must be 'reasonably necessary' to achieve the result promoted by the paragraphs. Nor is it likely to pass through paragraph (g), according to which the restriction must be 'reasonably required'. It might, however, pass through the general, unemployment, export and competition gateways, which are not so limited.

The 'Tailpiece'

'and is further satisfied (in any such case) that the restriction is not unreasonable having regard to the balance between those circumstances and any detriment to the public or to persons not parties to the agreement (being purchasers, consumers or users of goods produced or sold by such parties, or persons engaged or seeking to become engaged in the trade or business of selling such goods or of producing or selling similar goods) resulting or likely to result from the operation of the restriction.'

Although in *Black Bolts* (*No. 1*) Diplock, J. said that the onus of proof under this paragraph is also on the respondents, it seems likely that the Director must argue that there are some detriments; if he does not, then the Court will merely mention that there are no detriments to be balanced.

The main problem of construction is whether the second phrase in brackets – '(being purchasers, consumers or users of goods produced or sold by such parties, or persons engaged or seeking to become engaged in the trade or business of selling such goods or of producing or selling similar goods)' – restricts the ambit of the 'public' or only of 'persons not party to the agreement'. The question has not been considered by the Court, but one of the Court's conclusions depends on the first construction and two on the other.

In *Boilermakers*, Upjohn, J. held that electricity is not included in the term 'goods', and so the disadvantage to consumers of having to pay more for their electricity was not relevant under the tailpiece. Yet unless the phrase in brackets qualifies 'the public' in its capacity as buyers of the 'non-goods', electricity, it is difficult to follow this argument, as increased charges for electricity must be a detriment to 'the public'.

On the other hand, in *Scrap Iron* (1964), the detriment to the scrap creators was held to be relevant. They were suppliers to the parties to the restrictive agreement, so did not come within the words in brackets, which mention only buyers from the cartel and those who would like to compete with it. They must therefore have qualified as being part of 'the public'.

In *Yarn Spinners*, too, after deciding that the unemployment gateway had been passed, the Court considered that it was outweighed by three detriments: slight increases in the eventual price of goods made from cotton, the loss of a few export orders, and, mainly, the waste of national resources caused by excess capacity. The final detriment is not within the qualification of the phrase in brackets, which must therefore have been assumed to qualify only 'persons not party to the agreement' and not 'the public'. It is thought that this is the better construction, as otherwise detriments to suppliers of the cartel would be irrelevant: indeed the words 'the public or' would be meaningless. On the other hand, it is very doubtful whether the Court should attempt to consider what the effect of increasing prices in one industry will be on the economy as a whole, as the Court attempted to do in *Yarn Spinners*. The waste of resources in that industry was the relatively small number of strong young men who might have migrated to other regions to take jobs, the old men and married women (most of whom would have left the labour market), and the mills themselves – which did not seem at that time to have any other use, though they have since been used to breed broiler chickens. The value of these 'wasted resources' to the economy in their 'next best use' does not seem very great. In no case except *Yarn Spinners* has the Court attempted to assess the effects of a restriction on parts of the economy not directly related to the industry in respect of which the restriction was accepted.

Even if that case is not followed, the Court has a difficult task when the agreement has passed under the 'unemployment', 'preponderant buyer', or 'export' gateways. If the restriction results in higher prices for purchasers, how is the detriment to them to be weighted against the interests of a different class of people under a gateway? This has rarely occurred, except in *Yarn Spinners* and *Boilermakers*; and in the second case the higher prices charged for electricity did not count, either because electricity is not included in the term 'goods' or, alternatively, because the higher prices were so thinly spread over a large number of households that they were dismissed as 'infinitesimal'. It is, however, not clear why a small detriment to many people should be less important than a large detriment to a few.

Where, on the other hand, the restriction has passed under gateway (b) on the ground that it leads to prices lower overall than they would be without the restriction, then any detriments to anyone who pays more have either already been balanced under the general gateway, as was suggested in *Black Bolts* (*No. 1*), or outweighed by the benefit to buyers as a whole under the tailpiece, as in *Tiles*.

Conclusion

The safety gateway provided by paragraph (a), and paragraph (h), which enables an agreement to be justified on the ground that it does not reduce competition, are probably more important, in that they are borne in mind by the Director in deciding whether to seek directions not to refer an agreement to the Court, rather than in proceedings before the Court itself. All the other substantial gateways require decisions that are not easily made. The general gateway requires the Court to decide whether collaboration or competition is likely to lead to better bargains for buyers; under paragraph (c) the Court must distinguish between competition and measures taken with a view to restricting it; the preponderant buyer or seller gateway requires the Court to decide what terms are fair in the absence of a competitive market; and the export gateway, while drafted so narrowly that it is not squarely based on the criterion of the effect on the balance of payments, creates very difficult balancing problems when the 'tailpiece' is considered. The same objection can be brought against the unemployment gateway; and one may ask whether permitting a cartel to continue is an appropriate way of curing persistent regional unemployment. Paragraph (g) is merely ancillary. The new gateway, based on competition, is probably easier to apply than the general gateway under paragraph (b), but the kind of competition to be encouraged is not spelled out. The treatment of the 'tailpiece' is particularly unsatisfactory when the interests protected under a gateway are not comparable with the detriments alleged; but even where they are comparable, the Court has appeared to overlook simple logical points. By the time the 'tailpiece' is considered, it sometimes seems as if the Court has already decided to save the agreement; and after a long trial of complex issues, it is difficult to remain clear-headed.

Some cases have been argued for forty days or more and even the earlier ones lasted for three or four weeks. Since the Court must also read through lengthy proofs of evidence before the trial starts, it is extremely difficult for it, or indeed for counsel and witnesses, to dwell on the salient issues without being distracted by a host of disputed and interesting but peripheral details. Only one part-time member, who has sat only in Scotland, is a professional economist, trained to consider the sort of issues involved. Most of the judgments that have upheld agreements have been subjected to devastating criticism showing logical inconsistencies or complex and unlikely assumptions that are not mentioned in the judgments. This does not mean that the conclusions are wrong; merely that they are not supported by the detailed analysis of certain facts described in the judgments. The inconsistencies may reflect differences of opinion between the members of the Court, who are not permitted to write dissenting judgments. Where the agreement has been struck down, it is usually not possible to find a logical fault: the Court merely states that it is not satisfied that particular results would follow as a result of the abrogation of the agreement. Sometimes the Court's conclusions have not been fully borne out by later events. In *Bottles*, Russell, J. did not think that a war would ensue if the price agreements were ended: but acute price competition did develop. It is a matter of opinion whether it was severe enough to be called a 'price war', but even if it was, the Court's finding was not due to any logical inconsistency; and the prediction that the abrogation of the price agreement would not lead to a deterioration in standards was in fact borne out.

It is harder to demonstrate logical faults in the Commission's reports: usually the logic is not spelled out as fully as it is when the Court upholds an agreement. The reports are therefore more difficult to criticize. One of the strongest arguments in favour of the judicial procedure is the Court's care to ascertain the true facts. Most human beings believe a great many myths, even about their own business. Yet if they remain on oath on the witness stand for a considerable period of time and have their myths questioned by lawyers skilled in so doing, they may find that managers of parts of their business are not in fact doing what they had thought they were doing.

This care about established facts, however, is difficult to project into predictions about what is likely to happen in very different trading conditions when a restriction is ended. Whatever tribunal is entrusted with the task is confronted by complex and intractable problems.

The defence of a restrictive agreement before the Restrictive Practices Court is a very substantial undertaking. Apart from three contested hearings under the Resale Prices Act, the only cases defended since *Distant Water Vessels* (1965) have been the *Scottish Daily Newspapers* case, which did not involve the more difficult gateways, and the *National Federation of Retail Newsagents*. Since 1968, firms interested in making agreements that may restrict competition are likely first to consider ways of doing so that are not registrable, for instance by confining the restrictions to a single party. If this cannot be done, they may talk to the Director, to see whether he would be prepared to seek directions not to refer the agreement under section 9(2) of the 1968 Act. He may give an indication that he would seek directions if certain clauses were modified. This has built a useful degree of flexibility and common sense into rather formalistic legislation. Where, however, it seems that a reference to the Restrictive Practices Court will follow, few agreements are being made and notified to the Director. If an agreement is not defended before the Court, the firms will be required to give undertakings not to make any other agreement to the like effect, and even an accidental breach of that undertaking by a subordinate salesman would amount to contempt of court.

Although it is said that the U.K. legislation deals with abuse rather than providing rules of automatic application, this is true only at a formal level. In practice, unless the Director indicates willingness to seek directions not to refer, or it is thought likely that he will do so, agreements are not made and notified. In practice there are very great disincentives to making an agreement to which Part I of the Act applies and most legal advisers discourage it.

Although the law is strict in that respect, it may be that the

163

Director has inadequate powers to police it. As was seen earlier, he cannot enter a firm's premises and take copies of any documents he thinks may disclose unnotified agreements to which the legislation applies, and according to Lord Denning, M.R., he cannot even serve a notice under section 14 on suspicion. Moreover, once an agreement has been condemned, the narrow, formalistic interpretation by the Court of 'agreement to the like effect' has resulted in restrictions being abrogated only after lengthy proceedings, or indeed, in their not being abrogated at all. (See pp. 131–4.)

Part Three

The Common Market

7: ·Restrictive Agreements and Impediments to Trade between Member States

The Concept of the Common Market

As we saw in the introduction, the main objective of the Common Market is to improve economic performance by eliminating barriers to all kinds of economic activity between member states. Article 2 of the Treaty of Rome, under which the European Economic Community was established, states that:

'The Community shall have as its task, by establishing a common market and progressively approximating the economic policies of Member States, to promote throughout the Community a harmonious development of economic activities, a continuous and balanced expansion, an increase in stability, an accelerated raising of the standard of living and closer relations between the States belonging to it.'

These objectives may seem rather dated now – there is no mention of the improvements in the quality of life to be derived from international control of pollution – but read in the light of the preamble, which affirms

'as the essential objective of their efforts the constant improvement of the living and working conditions of their peoples',

the Treaty has been used to further other aims. We will see that these introductory principles are vital in the construction and application of Community law. The more specific provisions of the Treaty are construed in the light of the objectives of the Community more than by a literal interpretation of the language used.

The Free Movement of Goods

The integration of the market is to be achieved through the various freedoms provided for in the Treaty. According to article 3, the activities of the Community shall include

'(a) the elimination, as between Member States, of customs duties and of quantitative restrictions on the import and export of goods, and of all other measures having equivalent effect;

(b) the establishment of a common customs tariff and of a common commercial policy towards third countries; . . .'

The free movement of goods within a single customs area is the most obvious of the freedoms and was largely attained by the abolition of import duties (articles 12 and 13) between member states by mid-1968, even sooner than was anticipated in the transitional provisions for the Community. There is a common external tariff to be charged at uniform rates on goods entering the Common Market, but thereafter, like goods produced within the Common Market, they are free to pass over national frontiers inside it without any further payments. Already customs duties in the three states that joined the Community in 1973 are beginning to be aligned on the common external tariff but, unless the transitional period is shortened, the rates will not become identical until January 1978 and, meanwhile, customs formalities will be necessary as goods pass between the U.K. other member states.

Ad valorem customs duties are not the only way of insulating national markets; most countries also had quota arrangements, according to which import licences were required, and these were granted for 'sensitive' products only up to a specified quantity. Quotas, too, and measures of equivalent effect between member states were therefore prohibited by article 30.

These provisions, ensuring the free movement of goods between member states, are so fundamental that the Community Court has construed them very widely. Quantitative restrictions include a nil quota, or absolute prohibition on all imports, while a charge of equivalent effect includes

'the imposition of any pecuniary charge on goods circulating within the Community by virtue of the fact that they cross a national frontier.' (The *Social Funds* case (1969))

Although the Treaty expressly protects the existence of industrial and commercial property rights (article 222), the Community Court has held that their exercise to prevent imports may be forbidden by article 30 (see Chapter 8 below). Even slight obstacles to the free circulation of goods, such as the requirement of a particular kind of evidence to show that goods genuinely comply with the description of them, is a measure of equivalent effect to a quantitative restriction (*Scotch Whisky* (1974)).

When we come to consider what may or may not be achieved in a patent licence, we cannot ignore these vital rules on the free movement of goods. This book is far less concerned with the other freedoms, although in the long term they are also vital to the integration of the market.

Free Movement for Persons, Services and Capital

The rules ensuring the free movement of workers have already had a perceptible effect. At the beginning of 1973, there were 6·2 million migrant workers in the Common Market, of whom a fifth came from one member state to another. Large numbers of Italians are to be found working in Germany. Arrangements have been made to advertise jobs in other member states and citizens of one are entitled to go to another to seek work. There are provisions ensuring not only that they should be allowed to reside there with their families, but also that a worker who moves around the Common Market does not thereby prejudice his pension and social security rights.

Chapters 2 and 3 of the Treaty, which provide for the right to set up business, known as the right of establishment, and freedom to provide services have been more difficult to implement. An English lawyer, who has not studied French law, cannot be admitted to the French bar, but he may set up an office in Paris, describe himself as a legal adviser and give advice on English or Community law. Moreover, since no qualification is required in France, he is permitted to advise on French law, although he may not appear before a French court. The Community Court has recently held that a Belgian provision allowing only Belgian citizens to become lawyers is contrary to the Rome Treaty, which prohibits discrimination on grounds of nationality. A Dutch citizen, who had taken the courses and passed the exams which would have led to a Belgian being entitled to practise, was entitled to be admitted to do so (*Reyners* v. *Belgian State* (1974)). But that case involved a simple discrimination; it is far more difficult to say whether a doctor who qualified in one state should be permitted to practise in another – his training may have been shorter, or he may have done more academic study and spent less time on clinical work, or vice versa. The Council of Ministers has been considering forty directives which would require member states mutually to recognize equivalent qualifications for twelve professions. It has not yet been able to agree on any, although some of the directives are no longer needed in view of the *Reyners* decision.

The right to transfer capital from one member state to another is also established in principle but, as in the case of the other freedoms, there are safeguard clauses and any country with an acute balance of payments problem is unlikely to allow its residents to invest large capital sums abroad. Nevertheless, unless money can flow throughout the Common Market, the commercial services of the financial centres of Europe will be inhibited, and firms who want to raise capital for investment will have to consider national regulation, which would impede the integration of the Common Market.

When the Common Market was being established, its founding fathers thought that it was insufficient to require governments to eliminate barriers to trade and other commercial activities, if individual firms were free to agree to keep out of each other's markets. So agreements, the object or effect of which is to restrict competition are subject to control under article 85. These rules apply to public as well as private undertakings (article 90) and the various subsidies or aids which may be granted by national governments are controlled under articles 91–94.

The Constitution of the E.E.C.

The constitution of the European Economic Community (E.E.C.) derives from the Treaty of Rome made by the six original member states in 1957: Belgium, France, Germany, Italy, Luxembourg and the Netherlands. In 1973, Denmark, Ireland and the U.K. also joined the E.E.C. The Treaty of Rome contains many provisions which require subordinate legislation. Most of these provide that the Commission of the European Communities shall propose draft legislation to the Council of Ministers. Usually this draft must also be debated in the European Parliament and sometimes in the Economic and Social Committee, but these bodies have no formal power to amend or veto the measures before them, though their opinions may influence the final version. The decisions are made in the Council of Ministers, a Community institution, consisting of representatives of member states. In practice, even where the Treaty enables legislation to be passed by a qualified majority, each member state is allowed to impose a veto on any measure that affects its very important interests, so measures are passed often as a result of political package deals, under which one state may refrain from opposing a provision it dislikes, in order to obtain some other advantage. The legislation is negotiated rather like an international treaty, as well as being considered on its merits by technical and political working parties. Often disagreement is resolved by the Commission amending its proposal, since the Council may amend it only if all states agree. The Commission first sounds out the national representatives in order to find an acceptable compromise.

There are various forms of legislation that may be enacted by the Council on the proposal of the Commission. In the field of competition, the most important is the regulation. According to article 189,

'A regulation shall have general application. It shall be binding in its entirety and directly applicable in all Member States.'

Once a regulation is duly passed, it becomes part of the law of the U.K., and if it is inconsistent with an earlier Act of the U.K. Parliament, it overrides it (s. 2 of the European Communities Act 1972). Some Council regulations provide for the Commission to make implementing regulations. For instance, Council regulation 17 of 1962 (regulation 17/62) provides the main procedural rules for implementing the competition rules, but also provides for the Commission to make regulations prescribing the forms to be used by undertakings notifying agreements to it. This power was exercised in regulation 27/62.

When we examine regulation 17/62, we will see that it is mainly the Commission that decides whether and how far agreements restrict competition and whether they should be allowed to continue in operation.

The other important institution in the field of competition is the Court of the European Communities (sometimes called 'the European Court of Justice', but which I prefer to call the Community Court). An appeal lies to it from any decision of the Commission about the application of the competition rules on four grounds, of which the most important are that the Commission has violated the Treaty or that it has used its powers for a wrong purpose (article 173). In practice this requires the Court to interpret the articles in the Treaty or subordinate legislation, and to reverse a decision if the Commission has not complied with them or has failed to set out adequate reasons for coming to its decision (article 190 and *Noordwijks Cement Accoord* (1967)). The other way in which the Court may be asked to construe the rules arises under article 177. We will see that agreements that infringe article 85 are automatically void, so if one English undertaking sues another in England, the defendant may allege that the contract is void. If the construction of the Treaty or any of the regulations is necessary for the judge's decision, an ultimate court of appeal must, and a lower court may, ask the Community Court for what is called a preliminary ruling at any time before giving judgment, either before or after the relevant facts have been proved. In theory the Community Court is confined to answering the abstract question of law posed by the national court, but in practice it has been far more helpful, frequently reformulating the questions so as to be more specific and providing answers that are more easily applied by the national court.

Before the Community Court delivers its judgment, one of its members, called an 'Advocate General', gives his opinion on the issues. Usually, this is fuller than the Court's judgment: he should consider all the issues, even if one would dispose of the case, since he may not be followed on that point. Moreover, his opinion may influence the Court and does not bind it later, so it is the practice to give fuller reasons, and cite the earlier cases. He performs some of the functions of a judge of first instance, providing a reasoned opinion, on which the final court can base its decision, even if it does not follow it. The parties, however, cannot reopen the argument before the Court after the Advocate General has given his opinion.

Prohibition of Restrictive Agreements (Article 85(1))

Article 85(1) provides that:

> 'The following shall be prohibited as incompatible with the common market: all agreements between undertakings, decisions by associations of undertakings and concerted practices which may affect trade between Member States and which have as their object or effect the prevention, restriction or distortion of competition within the common market, and in particular those which:...'

There follows a list of the sorts of agreement most likely to restrict competition. The article is set out in full in the Appendix at page 268 below. The generality of this prohibition is in marked contrast with the U.K. legislation. We are told the purpose of the provision – the integration of the Common Market – but the details are not specified in the meticulous and literal manner adopted in the 1956 Act. The prohibition relates to agreements having the purpose or effect of restricting competition, which may depend on the state of the market, more than on the nature of conduct that may be restrained. The Commission of the European Communities has been able to condemn agreements to disseminate information about prices, or about projected investments, under this wide statement of principle, without the need felt in the U.K. to make a special provision calling them up for registration by order.

Paragraph 2 of the article provides that:

'Any agreements or decisions prohibited pursuant to this Article shall be automatically void',

and paragraph 3 provides for exemptions from the prohibition.

In this chapter, the various elements of article 85 will be analysed in the light of the decided cases, from a policy viewpoint as well as literally, disproportionate space being devoted to the more controversial issues. It is hoped that this will be more interesting than simply stating the conclusions which the author may feel are justified, and it should help the reader to understand the approach adopted to the interpretation and application of Community law, which is so different from that used in the U.K. The procedure for control established by virtue of regulation 17/62 will then be described, as well as the exemptions granted by the Commission and the consequences of invalidity in national courts.

Collusion between Undertakings

'*Undertaking*' has no established technical meaning. It clearly includes a company as well as an individual trader, a public undertaking (article 90) as well as one privately owned. A company, together with any subsidiaries over which it can and does exercise control, is treated as a single undertaking (*Commercial Solvents Corp.* v. *E.C. Commission* (1974)), at least where any agreement merely allocates the task between them. It also appears to include a partnership, whether or not the partnership is treated under national law as separate from the partners (*Prym/Beka* (1973), where the Commission exempted an agreement between a German limited partnership and a Belgian company, without stating whether under German law a partnership is treated as a separate legal person). There used to be some doubt whether a society should be treated as an 'undertaking' in its relationships with its members, but in *Belgische Radio en Televisie* v. *S.A.B.A.M. and Fonior* (*No. 2*) (1974) the Community Court followed the Commission's earlier decision in *GEMA* (1970) (p. 201 below) and decided that S.A.B.A.M., the only performing rights society operating in Belgium, was an undertaking within the competition articles when it was exploiting its members' commercial rights for its own benefit as well as theirs. It did not decide whether the artists who were its members were also 'undertakings' and there has long been doubt whether the word includes the liberal professions. In my opinion, both are included in so far as they are arranging for the exploitation of their services. Article 85 applies broadly over all economic activities that are subject to the Treaty of Rome and it would be very difficult to draw the line between artistic and professional services on the one hand and commercial and technical ones on the other.

Coal and steel, however, are subject not to the E.E.C. but to the European Coal and Steel Community (E.C.S.C.) established in 1948 under the Treaty of Paris. That Treaty contains its own competition rules which apply to agreements between undertakings that are subject to that Treaty – producers and distributors of coal and steel. The Commission of the European Communities functions under both treaties and may have to apply the relevant articles of each to different aspects of the same agreement. At present there are less than 300 undertakings subject to the Treaty of Paris, and it is not intended to deal with it in this elementary book. Although much of the wording in article 65 resembles article 85 of the Treaty of Rome, the coal and steel industries have been integrated in complex ways for so long, and there are so few competitors, that decisions under the Treaty of Paris as to whether competition is restricted, particularly in respect of coal, are of little value when considering the application of the Rome Treaty.

Special regulations also modify the application of the competition rules to agriculture (regulations 26/62 and 49/62) and transport (regulations 141/62 and 1017/68 as amended). With these too this book is not concerned.

Agreements. For article 85 to apply, there must be some element of agreement. 'Agreements' include 'gentlemen's agreements' that are not intended to be enforced in the courts (the *Quinine Cartel* (1969)). A particular contract may be only part of an underlying agreement – one may appoint franchised dealers only for a year at a time under a contract which expires annually, but the underlying agreement may continue. We shall return to this when we come to the problems of provisional validity. The exact scope of the concept of an agreement is unimportant, as 'concerted practices' (below) includes slighter elements of agreement.

'*Decisions of associations of undertakings*' has been held to include recommendations by trade associations to their members, even when there is no obligation to comply with them (*Vereeniging van Cement-handelaren* (1972)). It is only those recommendations that restrict competition and affect trade between member states that are controlled, although the effect on competition will be judged in the light of the share of the market supplied by or to its members.

'*Concerted practices*' is a concept of uncertain scope and may well include conduct that would not amount to an 'arrangement' under the U.K. law. Although in the *Dyestuffs* case (1972) the Community Court has said that it does not include price leadership in the absence of any further element, it may be that the announcement of price rises some weeks before they are to come into effect provides that element, since it removes some of the risk inherent in announcing a price increase without knowing whether the other suppliers will follow it.

On three occasions, nine or ten of the most important producers of dyestuffs in the Common Market, who between them produced 80 per cent of the dyes sold there, individually announced price rises. On 7 January 1964, CIBA announced a rise of 15 per cent for most aniline dyes in Italy to take effect immediately. I.C.I. made a similar announcement on the 9th to apply in Holland and Bayer on the 10th for Belgium. In each case the other producers followed suit within two or three days. The following October, B.A.S.F. announced that the increase would be applied in Germany from January 1965 and that a 10 per cent increase would be applied there to other products. Increases of 10 per cent for these products were announced by the leading firms in all the other Common Market countries except France, where the government had imposed a price freeze, and Italy. The Italian firm A.C.N.A. decided not to increase prices in Italy or Germany because of the recession in Italy, and the other firms decided to renounce the increase in Italy. It is not clear whether they revoked an increase already announced for that country, though the Commission says that one was intended. An increase in 1967 of 8 per cent was announced to its competitors in August by Geigy, to take effect in October. Francolor, the main producer in France, decided to raise prices there by 12 per cent and again all the producers except A.C.N.A. followed these rises.

The Commission decided that these increases were concerted and fined all the firms. There was considerable evidence of actual collusion, and the Commission did not trouble to find whether there was an 'agreement'. The Commission states that the parties met and discussed prices at London and Basle. On the first occasion, four of the parent companies sent instructions by telex to their subsidiaries abroad within an hour of each other and two more within the next two hours. It seems unlikely that this could happen in the absence of an agreement. Moreover, the wording of these instructions to the subsidiaries in each country was said to be surprisingly similar. The Commission also pointed to other factors which do not seem to me to indicate collusion very strongly.

The dyestuff producers argued that in a market with only a handful of important sellers, no one could raise prices unless the others did so too. Profits in the industry were low and prices continually eroded by the individual contracts negotiated by most of the larger buyers. As soon as one of the main suppliers raised his prices, each of the others knew that, unless they each followed, he would have to rescind the rise. No one therefore would increase his share of the market by refraining from following the increase and, with low profits and increasing, though different, costs, there was a large incentive to follow the price leader.

Where it is unlawful to agree to raise prices together, an enforcement authority is unlikely to find direct evidence of an agreement – even if there has been collusion it is unlikely to be recorded. Whether it is right to infer agreement from circumstantial evidence is rarely clear, but there were substantial grounds for the Commission's finding.

It is thought, however, that the Community Court, in upholding the Commission's decision that there was a concerted practice, extended the concept to include methods of co-ordination that did not involve any prior assurances in words or by conduct. In its decision, the Commission said:

> 'It is not conceivable that without detailed prior agreement the principal producers supplying the Common Market should several times increase by identical percentages the prices of the same major series of products, practically at the same time, and should have done so in various countries in which the market conditions in dyestuffs differ.'

Before the Court its submission went further:

> 'In order that there should be a concerting, it is not necessary that the parties should draw up a plan in common with a view to adopting a certain behaviour. It suffices that they should mutually inform each other in advance of the attitudes they intend to adopt, in such a way that each can regulate its action in reliance on its competitors behaving in a parallel manner.'

Does this cover the announcement by B.A.S.F. in 1965 of a price increase which was not to come into effect for nearly three months? Within a few days the other firms could announce whether they would follow, and when A.C.N.A. did not do so for Italy and Germany, the others had time to decide to refrain from price rises in Italy, but to face the competition in Germany. Was B.A.S.F. informing the other suppliers, when the information went directly to customers, in the knowledge that the other producers would soon discover it?

The Court did not mention the circumstantial evidence of collusion which formed the basis of the Commission's decision. Its judgment was more general. It said:

> 'If article 85 distinguishes the concept of "concerted practices" from that of "agreements between enterprises" . . ., this is done

with the object of bringing under the prohibition of this article a form of co-ordination between undertakings which, without going so far as to amount to an agreement properly so called, *knowingly substitutes a practical co-operation between them for the risks of competition.*' (My italics)

It added that the co-ordination might appear from conduct and that

'Although a parallelism of behaviour cannot by itself be identified with a concerted practice, it is nevertheless liable to constitute a strong indication of such a practice when it leads to conditions of competition which do not correspond to the normal conditions of the market, . . . especially where the parallel behaviour is such as to permit the parties to seek price equilibrium at a different level from that which would have resulted from competition. . . .'

This last paragraph is difficult to apply in a market with few producers, where each must take into account his rival's market decisions. One does not know at what level prices would have reached equilibrium had the market been more competitive. If there were more producers, each might have had shorter production runs and higher costs. The reference is to the unknowable.

After considering various features of the dyestuffs industry, the Court pointed out that the announcements in 1965 and 1967, made in advance and to competitors, gave time for the producers to eliminate all uncertainty as to their future behaviour, and hence a large part of the normal risk involved in any autonomous change in behaviour on one or more markets. It is difficult to reconcile the Court's statement that parallel behaviour by itself is not a concerted practice, coupled with a reference to unknowable conditions of the market and price levels, with its later inference of concert from the interval between the announcement of the later price rises, and their coming into effect. There would have been no difficulty in accepting the Court's judgment had it relied on the circumstantial evidence that swayed the Commission, but it did not mention it, and its formulations seem to go further than those of the U.K. courts on the ambit of 'arrangement', in that there does not seem to have been even the slightest obligation accepted by each producer not to change its mind individually after announcing a price rise. The judgment has given rise to considerable concern, because it would be silly to restrict an oligopolist from raising his prices individually when costs rise, and in such markets, prices are likely to be raised by similar proportions by each supplier, even if there is no prior agreement (see p. 8 above).

I have possibly overstressed the difficulty for producers in concentrated markets by omitting some of the Court's rather unsatisfactory market analysis. But the Court's judgments, which upheld substantial fines (though reducing that imposed on A.C.N.A.), points a warning to those attempting to reduce the risks of competition.

Restrictions on Competition

Although the Treaty refers first to the effect of an agreement on trade between member states, the Commission habitually deals with restrictions on competition first. I shall do the same, as it is only when one understands the intended or actual effects of an agreement on the market that one can assess its effect on trade between member states. Moreover, the importance of the condition that the agreement may affect trade between member states is being rapidly diminished.

When the Treaty was first agreed, there was considerable disagreement about the scope of the abstract phraseology:

'and which have as their object or effect the prevention, restriction or distortion of competition within the common market, and in particular those which:
(a) directly or indirectly fix purchase or selling prices or any other trading conditions;

(b) limit or control production, markets, technical development, or investment;

(c) share markets or sources of supply;

(d) apply dissimilar conditions to equivalent transactions with other trading parties, thereby placing them at a competitive disadvantage;

(e) make the conclusion of contracts subject to acceptance by the other parties of supplementary obligations which, by their nature or according to commercial usage, have no connection with the subject of such contracts.'

Not until 1964 did the Commission begin to publish formal decisions whether individual agreements came within the prohibition and, if they did, whether they should be excepted by virtue of article 85(3) because of favourable economic effects. The first decision against which an appeal was taken to the Community Court related to the exclusive dealing agreements made by *Grundig* (1964) for the distribution of its tape recorders and other apparatus. Grundig itself supplied dealers in Germany, but in the other Common Market countries it sold to a single franchised dealer. In 1957, it gave Consten the franchise for the whole of France. Consten undertook to sell Grundig products and no competing goods in France; to advertise, install a repair workshop and keep adequate stocks of spare parts. It agreed to undertake the guaranteed after-sales service. Grundig promised not to deliver directly *or indirectly* to anyone else in France, and in pursuance of this obligation and similar obligations undertaken towards other exclusive dealers, it required each of its dealers to refrain from selling outside his territory. As an additional method of ensuring that Grundig products should not enter France indirectly, Consten was allowed to register the trade mark Gint (Grundig international), which was applied in a not very obvious place to every Grundig machine, not just those destined for France.

The price of the various Grundig machines was considerably higher in France than in Germany – at the end of 1962, by as much as 23–44 per cent, net of customs duty and turnover tax. Only part of this differential was accounted for by the fact that Grundig undertook considerable advertising in Germany, but left its franchised dealers to incur this expense abroad. The substantial price differentials made it profitable for traders to buy Grundig products wholesale in Germany and sell them to French retailers at prices lower than those charged by Consten. From 1961, U.N.E.F. did so, and even in that year supplied some 10 per cent of the Grundig products sold in France. By 1964, the price differentials between Germany and France had narrowed to an average of some 20 per cent, presumably under pressure from these indirect sales, the very outcome the Common Market was established to achieve. In 1961, however, Consten sued U.N.E.F. and other parallel importers for the tort of unfair competition, for inducing the German wholesalers to infringe their obligation not to sell to French traders. It also sued for infringement of the trade mark Gint. It succeeded on both counts in the Paris Commercial Court, although U.N.E.F. argued that the franchise agreements infringed article 85 and were therefore void by virtue of article 85(2) that neither cause of action could be based upon it. The Paris Court of Appeal adjourned its proceedings to allow the Commission to decide whether the agreement did in fact infringe article 85.

The Commission analysed the territorial protection from competition guaranteed to Consten. Not only did Grundig undertake not to export to anyone else in France directly or indirectly, thereby enabling Consten to sue parallel importers under French law for unfair competition, it also made an ancillary agreement under which Consten had become entitled to the exclusive right to import or sell in France goods bearing the Gint mark. The mark was not required to indicate the goods' origin, as it was intended to be applied only to

179

goods already bearing the Grundig mark. The protection from competition was not absolute, in as much as Consten competed with the sellers of other brands, but the Commission observed that such products were not identical and that it was difficult for consumers to assess their relative value. The Commission concluded that the agreements were designed to restrict or distort competition within the Common Market. It was not prepared to exempt the agreement, since it granted absolute territorial protection, a restriction not essential to obtain the benefits in distribution which, it was claimed, resulted from the agreement. It therefore decided that both the franchise agreement and the ancillary one relating to the Gint mark infringed article 85(1), and ordered the parties to cease making it difficult for third parties to obtain the franchised products from other dealers in the Common Market.

Grundig and Consten appealed to the Community Court against the Commission's decision under article 173. They alleged that article 85(1) does not apply to an agreement between those carrying on business at different levels of trade, but only to horizontal agreements between manufacturers, or between wholesalers and so on. Exclusive dealing agreements do not appear in the list at the end of article 85(1). They supported this argument by alleging that since the parties to such an agreement are not on an equal footing, the agreement was not made between 'undertakings'. They argued that such agreements should be controlled only if they amounted to an abuse of a dominant position contrary to article 86. The Court first adopted a literal argument – no distinction is made in the Treaty between vertical and horizontal agreements. Indeed the last two items on the list, discrimination and tying, presuppose more than one level of trade. It added that competition could be distorted not only by agreements which restrict competition between the parties, but also by agreements which restrict competition between one of the parties and others. Finally, it stressed the importance under the Treaty of not restoring national divisions to trade between member states.

More cogently, the firms argued that the Commission was wrong in looking only at Grundig products. To see whether competition was restricted, a market analysis was necessary. The applicants also argued that vertical agreements should receive more favourable treatment, since they are less likely than horizontal ones to restrict competition. The Court, however, stated that article 85 was concerned with competition between dealers in the same brand as well as between the producers of different brands. An analysis of the concrete effects of an agreement is not required when it appears that its object is to restrict competition. It examined the Commission's finding that the appellants intended to eliminate any possibility of competition in Grundig products at the wholesale level through the restriction accepted by Grundig not to deliver its products even indirectly to third parties in the dealer's area, and the arrangement about the Gint mark. The Commission had rightly considered Grundig's whole network of agreements and not only the particular one with Consten. As the Court has frequently stated since, the agreement should be considered in its economic and legal context. If valid, it would result in the complete insulation of the French market and it was not necessary to consider the price differences between France and Germany for each product.

The Court did, however, uphold one objection to the decision. The Commission had condemned the whole agreement, but it should have condemned only those features of it that restricted competition. Presumably, the contracts of sale were valid as well as the obligation accepted by Consten to advertise, maintain stocks, forecast probable demand, provide the after-sales service, and so forth. It seems likely that the obligation accepted by Grundig not to export directly to France and Consten's duty not to deal in competing products would have been exempted had the agreement not also attempted to confer absolute territorial protection. It was only the clauses preventing each dealer from selling outside his territory, particularly when that was the whole of a member state, and the arrangements about the Gint mark, that should have been condemned.

The applicants also objected that the Commission had violated the Treaty in declaring that the agreement under which the Gint mark was registered in France was illegal, and that Consten should not rely on the mark to exclude indirect imports. Article 222 of the Treaty provides that

'This Treaty [including the competition rules] shall in no way prejudice the rules in Member States governing the system of property ownership.'

The Court stated that Consten had been able to register the Gint mark in France and so become owner of that mark only because of its agreement with Grundig. It would be pointless to prohibit the agreement, if the parties were free to take advantage of its result – the Gint mark. Article 222 may protect the existence of industrial and commercial property, but not all exercise thereof.

This has proved to be the beginning of a most important development, to which we must return (p. 215). It is difficult to distinguish the existence of a right from all the ways in which it may be exercised. If it cannot be exercised at all, it can hardly be said to exist. Nevertheless, an important difference, based on an unclear distinction, is a powerful weapon for judicial law reform. We will see that the

Court has been able to prevent the use of national industrial property rights to insulate national markets, saying that it is their exercise that is restrained by the Treaty, not their existence which is denied.

The *Grundig* case settled many doubts. It established that the list of examples in article 85(1) is merely illustrative and neither sufficient nor exhaustive – it is the general words which precede it that govern; that the prohibition applies to vertical as well as to horizontal restraints; that a particular agreement should be assessed in the light of ancillary agreements between the parties and, indeed, of the whole network of agreements entered into by one of them. It also established that only those clauses or aspects of the agreement that restrict competition and affect trade between member states are prohibited. The particular agreement might be condemned by the Commission without a full market analysis of its actual effects since, in the *Grundig* case, the Commission found, on substantial grounds, that its object was to restrict competition by insulating the French market for Grundig products.

At much the same time, the Court gave a preliminary ruling under article 177 on the interpretation of article 85(1), on the request of the Paris Court of Appeal. In *La Technique Minière* v. *Maschinenbau Ulm* (1966), it was settled that, when the object of the agreement is not in issue but its effect on competition, then a full market analysis is required. In *Volk* v. *Vervaeke* (1969) the Court ruled that an agreement restricting the dealer from selling outside his national territory and intended to assure absolute territorial protection might not be prohibited when the market shares of both manufacturer and dealer were insignificant. Without giving such protection, the manufacturer might not be able to persuade a dealer to invest in the advertising, stocks etc. required to sell in a new market.

Since it is impossible to tell whether an agreement not to do something will restrict competition significantly without making a full market analysis, the Commission tried to assist businessmen and their advisers by issuing a notice in May 1970 stating that, in its opinion, collaboration between undertakings whose aggregate turnover does not exceed 15 million units of account, and whose share of the market within that part of the Common Market where the agreement is effective does not exceed 5 per cent, does not restrict competition significantly. In assessing both turnover and market shares, companies within the same group should be taken into account. This notice has no legal effect: it merely represents the view of the Commission. Neither the Community Court, nor the Commission nor national civil courts are bound by its terms. Nevertheless, it seems to be safer to rely on this notice than is the case with certain others issued by the Commission.

Whether it is the object or the effect of the agreement that is alleged to restrict competition, some market analysis is required. There must be some significant possibility of competition, actual or potential, to restrict. Nevertheless, in few of its decisions has the Commission followed this view. In *SOCEMAS* (1968), it did grant negative clearance (see p. 186 below) to an agreement under which 77 chain stores, representing some 20,000 shops throughout France, collaborated in buying from abroad products for resale, and thereupon ceased to buy from abroad individually. These combined purchases were not a significant part of any of the relevant markets and the demand for such purchases had been static for some years before the agreement. Its market analysis was rather fuller in two later negative clearances: the *Limeburners'* decision (1969) and *S.A.F.C.O.* (1971). Usually, however, it has found that an agreement not to do something does restrict competition significantly, within article 85(1), even when it then exempts the agreement under article 85(3) on the ground that without such a restriction, certain products would not have been made available within the Common Market (e.g. *Davidson Rubber* (1972)). If that was the case, it is difficult to see how the agreement restricted any significant competition contrary to article 85(1). The difference between a negative clearance and an exemption is important in as much as agreements must normally be notified to the Commission if an exemption is required.

Effect on Trade between Member States

To come within the prohibition of article 85(1) the agreement must also be one which

'may affect trade between Member States'.

Until the Court's judgment in the *Grundig* case, there was considerable dispute about the meaning of 'affect'. Any effects seem relevant according to the French authentic text, '*affecter*' though there is a faint nuance of an unfavourable effect. The Italian text, '*pregiudicare*', clearly connotes unfavourable effects and the other two authentic texts come between these extremes. Yet although literal arguments were raised before the Community Court in the *Grundig* case, it looked not so much to the wording, as to the basic objective of article 85(1) – the integration of the market. In its view,

'it is necessary in particular to know whether the agreement is capable of endangering, either directly or indirectly, in fact or potentially, freedom of trade between Member States in a direction which could harm the attainment of the object of a single market between States. So the fact that an agreement favours an increase, even a large one, in the volume of trade between States is not sufficient to exclude the ability of the agreement to "affect" the trade in the above mentioned direction.'

More recently, it has not been necessary to show an adverse effect on imports and exports between member states. In *Vereeniging van Cementhandelaren* (1972) the Community Court confirmed the decision of the Commission condemning optional recommendations made by the trade associated of Dutch cement dealers about the prices at which its members were advised to resell throughout Holland. It stated that an agreement operating throughout a member state 'by its very nature may affect trade between Member States'. This was a strong precedent, in that control over the supply of foreign cement to Holland was exercised through a different cartel, not the subject of those proceedings. One might have thought that if a Dutch dealer would lose orders by following the advice of its trade association, it would not do so. It is difficult to know how far to apply the general statements of the Court to other agreements, where the surrounding facts differ. In the case of cement, most important dealers were members of the association; Holland imports a third of the cement it uses from other member states and, until shortly before the Court's hearing, the prices recommended had been obligatory for small deliveries.

The Commission has since decided that an export subsidy, which was intended to increase exports of cement from Belgium to other member states, infringed article 85(1) (*Cimbel* (1973)). Contrary to its usual practice, it did not consider the effect on trade between member states under a separate heading. Nevertheless, in refusing to grant an exemption, it stated that this subsidy was at the expense of consumers in Belgium and competitors abroad, so it must have jeopardized the unity of the market and distorted the flow of cement.

In *Commercial Solvents Corp.* v. *Commission* (1974) (see p. 206), the Community Court went further in minimizing a similar condition in article 86. An abuse of a dominant position is prohibited only in so far as it may affect trade between member states. Commercial Solvents and its subsidiary had cut off supplies of raw materials from Zoja, a former customer. This was likely to eliminate Zoja as a principal competitor to the subsidiary in the production of the drug ethambutol. The appellants alleged that this was unlikely to affect trade between member states perceptibly, since Zoja sold 90 per cent of the ethambutol it produced outside the Common Market, and much of the rest in Italy, where it was produced. Indeed, it would have difficulty selling in other Common Market countries without infringing the patents of the third large producer of ethambutol in the Common Market. The Commission decided that Zoja already exported to France and Germany and that its exports to other member states would increase. Consequently, its elimination would affect both the actual and potential trade in ethambutol between member states. The Court has gone further in stating that

'When an undertaking in a dominant position within the Common Market abusively exploits its position in such a way that a competitor in the Common Market is likely to be eliminated, it does not matter whether the conduct relates to the latter's exports or its trade within the Common Market, once it has been established that this elimination will have repercussions on the competitive structure within the Common Market.'

This very general proposition seems to imply that there is no need to show that the abusive practice by the dominant firm affects exports from one member state to another, although the Court went on to point out that Zoja had begun to export to France and Germany.

In the United States the requirement that interstate trade be affected was gradually read out of the Sherman Act, and it seems that a similar process has been in operation in the E.E.C. By 1974 it seems to have been established that any agreement with the object or effect of significantly restricting competition within the Common Market will be treated as likely to affect trade between member states, even if the effects on imports and exports between them are neither obvious nor immediate. The Court has not yet condemned an agreement which has identical effects throughout the Common Market. The Commission has announced its intention of giving a favourable decision in respect of a franchise agreement to cover the whole of the Common Market (*Duro-Dyne/Europair* (1974)), but has not yet said whether it comes outside article 85(1) or will be exempted. The distributor, Europair, itself uses different franchised dealers for each member state, so there will be competition at the next level of distribution. Certainly, it is no longer safe to rely on the earlier decisions of the Commission in which it granted negative clearance to fertilizer cartels that were confined to trade in the home market or outside the Common Market.

Invalidity of Contracts under Article 85(2)

With deceptive simplicity, article 85(2) provides that

'Any agreements or decisions prohibited pursuant to this Article shall be automatically void.'

The difficulties experienced by national civil courts asked to enforce a contract which is capable of exemption from the prohibition of article 85(1) can be understood only in the light of the first nine articles of the first regulation implementing the competition rules of the Treaty.

Regulation 17/62

Under article 87, the Council may, on the proposal of the Commission, issue regulations or directives to give effect to the principles set out in articles 85 and 86. It has not yet issued any directives, but the first implementing regulation, No. 17/62, has been of the utmost importance in developing a uniform system of control, protecting possibilities of competition throught the Common Market.

Article 1 reaffirms the principle that agreements of the kind described in article 85(1) and the abuse of a dominant position within the meaning of article 86 shall be prohibited, no prior decision to that effect being required in any particular case. This basic provision is, however, made subject to the powers of the Commission to grant exemptions from the application of article 85(1), by virtue of article 85(3) of the Treaty and of articles 6 and 7 of the regulation, and to certain transitional provisions about agreements that had already been exempted by national authorities under article 85(3).

Under article 2, the Commission may certify that on the basis of the facts in its possession, there are no grounds under article 85 or 86 for action on its part. Such a certificate is known as a negative clearance.

Article 3 enables the Commission, by a formal decision, to order an undertaking to bring to an end any infringement of article 85 or 86 found by the Commission (see p. 207 below).

Notification. Articles 4 and 5 provide for agreements to be notified to the Commission. There is no duty to do so, but there are incentives. The regulation distinguishes new from old agreements. Old agreements were originally those made before regulation 17 came into force. To these, the Treaty of Accession whereby the U.K. joined the European Communities added agreements made before 1973, which became subject to Community control only because of their enlargement. These I shall call 'accession agreements'. An agreement between manufacturers in England and Denmark, having no significant effect on competition within the area of the 'six', and which was made before accession, is to be treated as an old agreement under the regulation. An agreement between a French and an English manufacturer, under which each agreed before 1973 to keep out of the other's market, would probably have been subject to

Community law in the view of the E.E.C. authorities, in which case it is not an accession agreement. If it had significant competitive effects within the Common Market of the Six, it would probably have 'affected trade between Member States' (pp. 183–5 above).

Article 4(1) of the regulation provides that new agreements must be notified to the Commission if the parties seek exemption, and article 6 states that no exemption may be retrospective to a period earlier than notification. A list of agreements which are dispensed from notification follows in article 4(2) (set out in the Appendix at p. 271 below), and in respect of these, exemptions may be retrospective to the time when the agreement was made. The concept of agreement is less precise than that of contract. Contracts between the same parties that are annually renewed form part of the same underlying agreement, possibly even if there are minor changes in their terms. But all the agreements made over a period of time on a single standard form, if identical in terms with an old standard agreement notified in due time, are treated as old (*Parfums Marcel Rochas* (1971)).

Article 5 contains almost identical provisions for old agreements. There are two important differences between new and old agreements stated in the regulation. There were transitional periods for notifying old agreements – originally, before November 1962 and February 1963 – and accession agreements – before July 1973. Article 7 provides that where the Commission considers that an old agreement does not qualify for exemption, but the parties are prepared to abrogate it or amend it so that it qualifies in the future or no longer infringes article 85(1), then the Commission may, in its discretion, exempt it retrospectively. This is sometimes called 'sweeping the dirty past under the carpet'. The application of this article is, however, limited. The agreement must be an old one, it must have been sufficiently notified to the Commission in due time and, even if it is of the kind dispensed from notification under article 5(2), a decision applying article 7 cannot be invoked against a party who did not expressly consent to the notification. Where the article does apply, however, it is very important. Under article 6, the Commission can exempt an agreement only as it stands, so if there are some restrictions which are not necessary to obtain the alleged benefits, then the agreement can be exempted only from the time when they are abrogated (*Prym/Beka* (1973)). This may preclude the parties from enforcing the restrictions which are eventually exempted, for the period before the other restrictions were abrogated, although clauses that do not restrict competition significantly may remain valid. Where article 7 applies, however, the whole agreement may be exempted from the beginning, the unnecessary as well as the indispensable restrictions.

187

Article 8 provides that when the Commission does grant an exemption, it shall be limited in time, though it may be renewed. It may also be granted subject to conditions and obligations. An exemption may be revoked or amended only if circumstances have changed, or the parties have behaved in specified improper ways.

Competence. Article 9(1) provides that the Commission shall have exclusive power to exempt an agreement from the prohibition of article 85(1). The next paragraph provides that it may also apply the prohibitions of articles 85(1) and 86 of the Treaty, but this power is not exclusive, since, until it has initiated such proceedings, the cartel authorities in member states may do so. Before returning to article 9(1), I should like to deal with the other substantive provisions of the regulation. Articles 10 – 14 deal with investigations, which will be considered in Chapter 8, when the substantive law has been described. Article 15 is important, since it enables the Commission to impose very substantial fines on undertakings that have infringed article 85(1) or 86 – up to a million units of account (one unit of account being equal to the gold value of the U.S. \$ in 1958) or 10 per cent of the turnover of the offending undertaking for the previous year, whichever is larger. There are also provisions for periodic penalties. The remaining provisions relate to procedure and will be described at the end of Chapter 8.

Provisional Validity

Article 9 of regulation 17 provides that only the Commission may exempt an agreement under article 85(3) of the Treaty. Yet, as the Community Court confirmed in *Belgische Radio en Televisie* v. *S.A.B.A.M. and Fonior* (1974), the competition rules of the Treaty are directly applicable in the courts of member states. Consequently, a civil court should not enforce a contract, if it contravenes article 85. As the Community Court observed in the *Bosch* case (1962), article 85(2) avoids only such agreements as infringe the article as a whole. The national court needs to know whether an agreement is exempt from the prohibition, but is precluded from making the decision itself. The matter may cause prolonged hardship, since even when the Commission has initiated proceedings, it is unlikely to grant an exemption in less than two years and often takes far longer. Proceedings in relation to agreements that do not obviously jeopardize the objectives of the Treaty may not be opened for many years, or even for decades, although the Commission states that it gives priority to agreements that are subject to litigation in member states.

In the *Bosch* case (1962), the Hague Court of Appeal sought a preliminary ruling as to whether the clauses restricting Bosch dealers from exporting to other member states were void by virtue of article 85(2). The Treaty contains no transitional provisions to protect agreements made before it came into force, or before the ambit of the abstract phrases in article 85 was worked out. The Community Court took into consideration the uncertainty then prevailing and ruled that old agreements notified in due time should not be treated as void from the date the regulation came into force. There was considerable doubt as to the extent of this provisional validity. German and Dutch courts treated properly notified agreements as fully valid, but the Belgian Cour de Cassation, the highest court in the country, held that 'the precariousness of this validity limits the power of the courts when the parties refuse to abide by their contract voluntarily.'

In *Portelange* (1969), the Community Court stated quite generally that 'agreements within article 85(1) of the Treaty, which were properly notified . . . are fully valid as long as the Commission has not issued a decision pursuant to article 85(3) and the provisions of regulation 17.' The question asked of the Court under article 177 related to an old agreement, but the ruling was not expressly so limited. In *Bilger* v. *Jehle* (1970), the Court went further in ruling that agreements dispensed from notification could not be retrospectively treated as void if they were eventually condemned by the Commission. This was an extreme result, and probably inconsistent with the wording of the Treaty.

By the 'seventies, many people were concerned that the doctrine of provisional validity developed by the Community Court, coupled with the Commission's delay in dealing with the agreements notified to it, were reducing the impact of article 85 in preventing the isolation of national markets. In *Parfums Marcel Rochas* (1971), the Commission argued that even if an agreement had been duly notified, a restriction on exports was so likely to jeopardize the integration of the market that it should not enjoy provisional validity, but the Court ruled otherwise. It even ruled in that case that a contract made after the regulation came into force, but in identical terms with an old standard contract notified in due time, should be treated as an old agreement.

In *Brasserie de Haecht* v. *Wilkin* (*No. 2*) (1973) the Community Court, which is not bound by its earlier decisions, was given an opportunity to reconsider the matter. The brewery had lent furnishings and money to the owners of a small café, in return for a promise that no beer or soft drinks other than those supplied by de Haecht would be sold there. When other products started to be sold at the café, de Haecht sued to recover its money and furnishings and for damages. Before dealing with the specific questions asked of it, the Court made some general observations. It pointed out the difficulties that existed when regulation 17 came into force and stressed the provision in article 7, allowing the Commission to ensure juridical certainty. The Court therefore made a clear distinction between new and old agreements for the first time:

'8. As far as old agreements are concerned, certainty of law as regards contracts requires that a court cannot, particularly when an agreement has been notified in accordance with Regulation 17, establish nullity until after the Commission has made a decision under this regulation.'

The Court did not consider the effects of a subsequent condemnation of the agreement by the Commission – for instance, how far money paid thereunder could be recovered. It continued:

'10. As far as new agreements are concerned, it follows from the regulation, on the assumption that so long as the Commission has made no pronouncement the agreement can only be operated at the risk of the parties, that notifications under Article 4(1) of the regulation are without suspensory effect.'

It added that a new agreement of the kind dispensed from notification was void as a matter of law if it infringed article 85, and that the nullity provided for by article 85(2) does have retrospective effect.

The Court also ruled that the notification in 1969 of a standard form of contract did not suspend the invalidity of a contract made earlier, even if it were old and dispensed from notification. The Court implied that such an agreement does not enjoy provisional validity, so it is now less important to ascertain whether an agreement is dispensed from notification under article 4(2). The Court also reversed the statement it made in *Bilger* v. *Jehle*, that agreements dispensed from notification could not become invalid, even if they were not eventually exempted. If they were in fact not notified within the time limits prescribed for article 7, exemption could not be retrospective to a time when clauses incapable of exemption were in operation.

Businessmen who ask their legal advisers about the consequences of entering into a proposed contract often cannot be given firm answers, unless the agreement can be brought within one of the group exemptions (pp. 233 and 240). It is generally thought that old agreements that were notified in due time enjoy provisional validity, although it is not clear what happens if the Commission fails to exempt them under article 7. Often one cannot advise firmly whether an agreement restricts competition within the meaning of article 85(1), since a complete market analysis is necessary, and, as will be seen, the standards for granting an individual exemption under article 85(3) are so flexible that the result often cannot be foretold with certainty.

Nevertheless, in the light of the Court's judgments in *Brasserie de Haecht* v. *Wilkin* (*No. 2*) and in *Belgische Radio en Televisie* v. *S.A.B.A.M. and Fonior* (1974), the position in a U.K. court is far clearer than it was. A national court asked to enforce a contract must, if asked, consider whether it infringes article 85(1), even if the Commission has already initiated proceedings. To do this, it must make a market analysis, which is far from easy, often involving an inquiry into the whole industry, such as is made in the U.K. by the Monopolies Commission. If the court considers that it is clear that article 85(1) is not infringed, it can enforce the contract. It is unfortunate that the English rules of court provide no procedure whereby, if the Commission does later condemn the agreement, the defendant could return to the court to reopen the matter, and perhaps recover the damages he was required to pay. If the agreement clearly infringes article 85(1) and there is no possibility of exemption, because the agreement was not notified, or perhaps because the agreement so clearly jeopardizes the objects of the Common Market, the court should probably treat the agreement as void, in respect of the restrictions. In the intermediate case, where it is not clear whether the agreement restricts competition or, if it does, whether it would be exempted, the national court is required by Community law to adjourn its proceedings. Unfortunately, such an adjournment is likely to last over a year, so it becomes very important to consider what interlocutory relief may be granted. Where it is likely that the contract will eventually be upheld, an English court may well grant an interlocutory injunction, but it will require from the person seeking it an undertaking to compensate the other party, if the agreement is eventually condemned (*Löwenbräu München* v. *Grunhalle Lager International Ltd* (1973)). There do not seem to be any powers for the English courts to make an interlocutory order for damages, except in personal injury cases, although this seems to be one of the appropriate remedies in the case of a patent licence, when the validity of the patent may be outstanding for some years.

One important doubt remains for English businessmen. Do accession agreements, duly notified, count as old or new agreements for the purpose of provisional validity? The Commission considers that they should be treated as provisionally valid by way of analogy to old agreements (*Third Report on Competition Policy*, paragraph 5(a)). The question, however, would not be decided by the Commission, but by national courts, subject to the possibility of inviting the Community Court to give a preliminary ruling under article 177. Article 7 clearly applied to accession agreements, and this provision was stressed by the Court in the second *Brasserie de Haecht* case. On the other hand, the Court made it clear that provisional validity was a judicial creation intended to overcome the great uncertainty prevailing in 1962 about the application of article 85. Now that there is a considerable case law and some group exemptions have been granted, this is far less serious than it was. The answer is not known.

Exemption from the Prohibition of Article 85(1) (Article 85(3))

Article 85(3) provides that:

> 'The provisions of paragraph 1 may, however, be declared inapplicable in the case of:
>
> – any agreement or category of agreements between undertakings;
>
> – any decision or category of decisions by associations of undertakings;
>
> – any concerted practice or category of concerted practices; which contributes to improving the production or distribution of goods or to promoting technical or economic progress, while allowing consumers a fair share of the resulting benefit, and which does not:
>
> (a) impose on the undertakings concerned restrictions which are not indispensable to the attainment of these objectives;
>
> (b) afford such undertakings the possibility of eliminating competition in respect of a substantial part of the products in question.'

After the Treaty was signed, there was a dispute between the French and Germans as to whether this provision automatically excepted those agreements to which it applied, or whether it provided a discretionary power to exempt in such circumstances. Regulation 17 managed to avoid this problem by providing in article 9(1) that:

> 'Subject to review of its decisions by the Court of Justice, the Commission shall have sole power to declare Article 85(1) of the Treaty inapplicable pursuant to Article 85(3) of the Treaty.'

The criteria for exemption are so flexible that if the Commission should wish to refuse exemption, it would be able to find that one of the conditions is not fulfilled. The Community Court has recognized that the exercise of the Commission's powers under article 85(3) necessarily implies complex economic judgments, and that judicial control of its decisions should respect that character by limiting itself to an examination of the materiality of the facts and legal descriptions which the Commission deduces therefrom.

The Treaty envisages both individual and category, or group, exemptions, but in 1962, when the Commission announced that it would grant a group exemption, the member states questioned whether it had power to do so under article 9(1) of regulation 17. In an attempt to reduce the flow of notifications it expected, it announced on 24 December that sole agency agreements and certain clauses in patent licences did not, in its opinion, infringe article 85(1). We will see later that these notices, which were never intended to have legal effect, but merely to give an indication to the public about the Commission's view of the law, do not validate agreements within their scope and, in particular, that the notice about patent licences is now highly suspect, since the Commission's policy for them has changed meanwhile. The issue of the notices did, however, reduce the uncertainty prevailing when regulation 17 came into force.

In 1964, the Commission began to grant exemptions in individual cases, mainly to exclusive dealing agreements. In the following year, the Council acted on a proposal of the Commission and, in regulation 19/65, empowered the Commission to issue regulations exempting categories of exclusive dealing agreements and those relating to industrial property licences. The Commission's regulations are required to define the categories of agreement to which they apply and to define the clauses which may or may not be included in exempted agreements. We will look at particular group exemptions in more detail in Chapter 9 where specific kinds of contract are considered.

Economic Benefits

Since most of the early cases concerned exclusive dealing agreements, the benefits claimed were mainly the improved distribution to be obtained thereby, for a manufacturer who wished to take advantage of the Common Market by starting to export to another member state. He needed the support and advice of a dealer familiar with local commercial practices to promote his products and advise him on any adaptations desirable. The dealer would also have to provide forecasts of likely demand and provide a pre- and after-sales service. This would involve an investment in stocks. To ensure his individual attention, the dealer would be required to promise not to deal in competing goods. To provide an incentive, the manufacturer would often promise not to supply anyone else directly in the country.

Where there were no features preventing the goods from entering the dealer's territory from intermediate dealers in other countries, or the dealer from selling on request outside his area of primary responsibility, the Commission exempted such agreements on the ground that they improved distribution. Consumers shared in the benefits, in that they enjoyed the local supply of a wider choice of products and so forth.

The Commission later came to exempt various specialization agreements, particularly between manufacturers in different member states. One of the earlier exemptions related to the agreement between *Clima Chappée* and *Buderus* (1969). Clima Chappée was a French subsidiary company which had perfected air-conditioning apparatus, while Buderus was a German undertaking which had only just started to make hot-air generators. Each agreed to refrain from making a range of products until the other had reached a specified turnover, and to buy its requirements of these for sale in its home market from the other. The agreement was not very restrictive. There were many competing manufacturers in the Common Market. Neither party was precluded from making apparatus it had already started to make. Each sold under its own trade mark, so when the specified turnover was achieved, it would have developed a market for its own manufactures. Each was free to sell competing products in third countries. The Commission held, nevertheless, that the agreement had the object of restricting competition within article 85(1), as each undertaking agreed for an indefinite period not to make certain equipment, not to supply other equipment in its partner's country to anyone else, and to give preference to its partner for products not reserved to either. Both undertakings had sufficient financial backing and technical potential individually to develop and manufacture competing equipment. The agreement therefore eliminated potential competition between the firms. The parties were in different member states, so the agreement would influence the flow of trade between France and Germany and between each of these and other member states.

Nevertheless, the Commission granted an exemption for ten years. The agreement enabled each party to eliminate duplication of surveys, research and investment for perfecting and making the articles to be bought from the other. The parties would be able to pass to series production and improve their use of manufacturing facilities. This would lead to cost savings and enable them to compete in the market, where large firms were already established. They would be able to offer customers the complete range of products. The agreement was intended to lead to the rationalization of production and distribution. This rationalization depended on the reciprocal exclusive distribution in the two countries. The preference to be given to each partner in respect of other products was an accessory and closely linked clause, so was apparently considered indispensable.

Since then, for similar reasons, the Commission has exempted many specialization agreements, most of them made between undertakings in different member states. At times the policy of so doing has been more dubious. In its decision on *Fine Papers* (1972), the Commission did little more than certify the matters about which it must be satisfied if it is to grant an exemption. The parties to the agreement, each of which agreed not to make certain types of paper, were the principal French producers of fine papers. Between them, they produced over half the cigarette paper made in the Common Market, although some 60 per cent was exported outside, and until 1939 they had dominated the world supply. Their market position for other thin papers was far weaker. Cigarette paper was being made in Germany and Italy, but parties to the French agreement supplied 80 per cent of that used in France and 70 per cent in Benelux. The Commission accepted that the agreement did restrict competition and affect trade between member states, but exempted the agreement. It observed that it had enabled the parties to enjoy longer production runs and instal larger production units, but did not say whether its continuation was necessary to encourage yet larger units, nor whether there were further substantial economies of scale to be achieved. It referred to strong competitive pressures wherever the parties sold and to the large size of their customers, to show that economies would be passed on to customers.

Under the Restrictive Trade Practices Act, the Court must be satisfied that the abrogation of the agreement would lead to certain detriments; it is less clear that this is the appropriate criterion under article 85(3), which refers to agreements 'which contribute' to certain benefits. It is thought, however, that the difference in wording is not significant. In *Transocean Marine Paints* (1967) the Commission granted an exemption for a limited period on the grounds that the firms were small and could invade a market supplied by larger firms only in collaboration. When this expired, another exemption was granted subject to more restrictive conditions, presumably because the firms were now better established and needed less protection. Although in 1974 the Community Court reversed the second decision for procedural reasons, it has told the Commission to reconsider the matter, thereby implying that it is the circumstances at the time of the decision to renew exemption that are relevant rather than those at the time the agreement was made.

It is difficult for an outsider to criticize the Commission's decisions. Fewer facts are given than in the U.K. and the arguments are more formally reported. One may ask whether, if there were still substantial economies of scale to be reaped, it would not have paid one producer of fine papers to have increased its capacity for some ranges and then slashed prices to increase its turnover. Although this might have driven the firms to specialize, each would know that the others might re-enter the market if it raised prices. Specialization often yields dramatic cost savings, by leading to automatic production, but agreements may be the second best way of achieving them.

The Commission has only recently relied distinctly on the ground that an agreement promotes technical or economic progress (*Davidson* (1972), *Henkel/Colgate* (1971)) although it had previously exempted collaboration in research and development on the ground that production and sometimes distribution would be improved. In *A.C.E.C./Berliet* (1968) it found that A.C.E.C. had invented a low-weight, high-yield electrical transmission for commercial vehicles, and in particular for buses. It applied for a patent and then sought the collaboration of a firm experienced in designing, making and selling buses to develop the system. A.C.E.C. agreed with the French firm Berliet that it would sell the system, if and when developed, only to Berliet in France and to one manufacturer in each of Germany, Italy, Holland and Luxembourg. Berliet was to buy electric transmissions from no one but A.C.E.C. Despite these exclusive clauses, which were to last for ten years and could be tacitly renewed thereafter, exemption was granted, since the agreement aimed at enabling both parties to achieve long production runs. The agreement provided for collaboration between firms that were already specialized and the intended outcome was a new and desirable type of bus. It was hard to predict in detail how consumers would benefit, but there was sufficient likelihood that results would be obtained more rapidly as a result of the joint research, and that consumers, especially bus operators, would benefit from the new product. Competition from traditional buses would ensure that consumers would benefit. Exemption was granted only until 1973, in order to enable the Commission to reconsider the agreement in the light of subsequent events. Exemption was granted retrospectively under article 6 of regulation 17, although there had been an amendment since the agreement was first made to increase the number of countries in which A.C.E.C. might sell to one manufacturer (but see *Prym/Beka* (1973), p. 187 above).

Benefits to Consumers

These cases show how the Commission is likely to ensure that a fair share of the benefits is passed on to consumers. There were competing manufacturers, so the cost savings would be passed on or the new product sold on favourable terms. The franchise cases demonstrate that the benefit to consumers need not be pecuniary. Ready availability of an increased range of products suffices. There seems to be no requirement of proportionality in the concept of 'a fair share'. It seems that the Commission treats as consumers the immediate buyers of the product. The French text refers to '*utilisateurs*' – users, rather than final consumers. The Commission referred to bus operators rather than tourists or commuters in the *A.C.E.C./Berliet* decision. It seems likely, however, that when these immediate customers themselves meet competition, they will also be forced to pass on some of the benefits. Whereas the U.K. Monopolies Commission has clearly referred to the interests of the final consumer as the criterion of the public interest, the Commission of the European Communities refers expressly to the interests of those who buy from the undertakings collaborating in production, although in the exclusive dealing cases it did mention the interest of consumers in a wider choice of products adapted to the local market.

No Indispensable Restrictions

There must be no restrictions not indispensable to benefits to be achieved. The prohibition on exports was an unnecessary restriction that prevented the exemption of the *Grundig* agreement. Often the Commission informs the parties that it is not prepared to exempt an agreement as it stands, and that it will do so only if certain clauses are abrogated. Even if this is done, the eventual exemption may be restrospective only to the time when they were abrogated (*Prym/Beka* (1973)) although, in the case of old agreements that were notified in due time, the exemption may be made restrospective under article 7 of regulation 17, as it was in *Fine Papers*.

Competition not Eliminated

Usually, before it considers this test, the Commission has either pointed out that consumers will benefit from the agreement through the pressure of competition, or that the agreement restrains competition unnecessarily.

8: Abuse of a Dominant Position, Enforcement of the Competition Rules, and the Conflict between Industrial Property Rights and the Free Movement of Goods

Article 86

Article 86 provides that:

> 'Any abuse by one or more undertakings of a dominant position within the common market or in a substantial part of it shall be prohibited as incompatible with the common market in so far as it may affect trade between Member States.'

There follows an illustrative list of the possible types of abuse.

In several cases dealing with industrial property rights, the Community Court has been asked to rule on the construction of article 86. In *Sirena* v. *Eda* (1971), speaking of a trade mark protected by Italian law, the Community Court ruled that:

> 'According to the words of [the article] the situation prohibited must fulfil three requirements: the existence of a dominant position, the improper exploitation of that position and the possibility that this may be prejudicial to trade between Member States.'

'One or More Undertakings'

We have already considered the meaning of the word 'undertaking' (p. 173 above). It includes any sole trader or any body of people carrying on economic activities independently. It probably does not include the activities of employees – their employers are the undertakings and are responsible for their actions. The dominant position may be enjoyed by a single firm, but in its decision on the *Sugar Cartel* (1973) the acts of two important firms acting in concert were condemned under article 86 rather than 85. Where concert cannot be proved, but only interdependent behaviour such as parallel pricing, the conduct may not be subject to article 85, but it may be subject to control under article 86. This has not yet been decided in any individual case, but it is understood that proceedings have been commenced by the Commission against several oil companies in Holland, which each refused to supply an independent undertaking with refined oil. It may well be argued that in the absence of collusion between them, no one or more is dominant, since each must take into account the reactions of the others to his market behaviour.

'*A Dominant Position*'

Dominance can be determined only by assessing the market power of the undertaking concerned. As the Commission stated in its decision on *Continental Can* (1971),

> 'Undertakings are in a dominant position when they have the power to behave independently, which puts them in a position to act without taking into account their competitors, purchasers or suppliers.'

Such absolute dominance must be rare; but the Commission continued to state that 'dominance' may be relative. As we saw when discussing the judgment of the Restrictive Practices Court in *Wire Ropes* (p. 148 above), in assessing a firm's market power one must consider to whom its customers could turn if it should raise its prices. This depends on whether the other suppliers could expand production quickly and whether new suppliers could enter the market, and on the possibility of expanding the supply of substitute products to which at least some customers could turn. Converse criteria apply to assessing the market power of a dominant buyer. To see whether an undertaking is dominant in a substantial part of the Common Market, one must make a market analysis.

In *Continental Can* (1971), the Commission attributed to the American parent company the dominance of its subsidiary Schmalbach in parts of Germany over three products: light containers for preserved fish and meat and metal closures for glass jars. The Court pointed out that the market for these products should not be arbitrarily separated from the general market for light metal containers. It objected that the Commission had not specified the ways in which these markets were separate from those for cans used for fruit and vegetables, condensed milk, fruit juice, and so forth. It referred also to production characteristics, presumably in order to tell whether the makers of fruit and vegetable cans could turn to making preserved meat or fish cans, if Continental Can should

199

charge more. It also wished to know why the large canners could not start making their own cans.

A market is rarely capable of exact definition: one shades imperceptibly into another. To some extent tube or rail tickets are substitutes for cars and petrol, but the price of one has to rise considerably more than the price of the other for commuters to change their habits. For practical purposes, only fairly immediate substitutes are treated by most competition authorities as being in the same market. The Community Court has been criticized for its quashing of the Commission's decision on the ground that the Commission did not consider the production flexibility of the makers of vegetable cans, or the ability of large canners to start making cans. These would be relevant only in the long term, so Continental Can knew that for several years most of its customers would be bound to accept its prices and would be likely to take their custom elsewhere only if they thought that prices would continue to be considerably higher than would be charged by someone else.

To be subject to control under article 86, the undertaking must enjoy a dominant position in a substantial part of the Common Market. Small areas are probably not relevant for goods which are fairly valuable in proportion to the cost of transporting them. In *Continental Can*, the Advocate General doubted whether Germany was a separate geographic market for metal closures for glass jars, which could economically be imported from as far away as Dorset. For empty cans, which could not economically be carried far, however, the Commission did treat parts of Germany as a substantial part of the Common Market, and for sugar, the Commission treated Holland on its own, and Belgium and Luxembourg combined, as substantial parts of the Common Market. It is not known whether the accession of three additional states has altered this position, nor whether the Commission's decision on the *Sugar Cartel* (1973) will be upheld on appeal.

Abuse

After the general words of article 86, there is an illustrative list of conduct which may be treated as abusive:

'Such abuse may, in particular, consist in:

(a) directly or indirectly imposing unfair purchase or selling prices or other unfair trading conditions;

(b) limiting production, markets or technical development to the prejudice of consumers;

(c) applying dissimilar conditions to equivalent transactions with other trading parties, thereby placing them at a competitive disadvantage;

(d) making the conclusion of contracts subject to acceptance by the other parties of supplementary obligations which, by their nature or according to commercial usage, have no connection with the subject of such contracts.'

It is clear from the wording of the examples of abuse that the prohibition applies to the abuse of buying as well as selling power. In *GEMA* (1971) (pp. 203 ff. below), the Commission condemned the society's dealing with authors and composers from whom it obtained copyright, as well as its dealing with those exploiting these rights. More recently, in *Eurofima* (1973), the Commission objected to one of the conditions for tendering imposed by a preponderant buyer of railway stock, although when the condition was abandoned, it did not proceed to a formal decision.

Until the judgment of the Community Court in *Continental Can* (1973), there was considerable controversy about the extent to which conduct likely to affect the structure of the market was subject to control under this article. The Commission, however, has acted against deliberate conduct that would foreseeably and substantially reduce competition. If it were confined to regulating prices once dominance were obtained, the Commission would have to decide what prices were fair in the absence of a competitive market. If the dominant firm were allowed to charge on a cost plus basis, the spur to efficiency and innovation would be blunted and, without duplicating many of the dominant firm's decisions, a regulatory agency can hardly tell how far the firms it controls are efficient. In the United States there are many privately-owned natural monopolies, such as railways, gas and electricity or telephone suppliers, that are subject to control and require permission before they raise their prices. Different tests have been prescribed for different kinds of utility, but all suffer from at least one fundamental objection. Where the nature of the market is such that only one firm can operate efficiently, regulation or nationalization may be a better solution than uncontrolled market power, but the Treaty confers no power to nationalize and, where there is no natural monopoly, the Commission, which has always been kept short of staff, prefers to prevent the consolidation or extension of market power.

Since 1973, it has been supported by the Court in its view that conduct by a dominant firm leading to a substantial reduction in competition is an abuse prohibited by article 86. A dominant firm

201

may increase its share of the market by internal growth – by investing in new plant without buying a competitor – but such growth does not directly remove a competitor from the market and the Commission has not suggested that this would infringe article 86.

The Community's Court's judgment in *Continental Can* (1973) is of vital importance to the construction not only of article 86, but also of the Treaty as a whole. As was mentioned earlier, the American firm, through its German subsidiary company, Schmalbach, was found by the Commission to be in a dominant position over the supply of light metal containers for preserved meat and fish, as well as for metal closures for jars. It announced a bid for the Dutch company, Thomassen, which made all the cans used for preserving fish and meat products in Holland. The market for empty cans was considered fairly local, for reasons already discussed. The Commission mentioned barriers to entry, such as the patents and know-how required to make cans. Consequently, if meat and fish cans really were a separate market, the merger, by eliminating competition between the firms, must have been likely to reduce competition substantially. The Commission's decision clearly put forward its construction of article 86:

> 'For an undertaking in a dominant position to reinforce that position by means of merger with another undertaking with the consequence that the competition which would have existed actually or potentially in spite of the existence of the initial dominant position is in practice eliminated for the products in question in a substantial part of the Common Market constitutes behaviour which is incompatible with Article 86 of the Treaty.'

The Commission was in a dilemma. There had been little competition between the parties to the merger, but this may have been a result of agreements between them and other suppliers of metal containers. The Commission was still investigating this under article 85 and could not come to a conclusion before having to decide whether to prevent the merger being completed. Consequently, it had difficulty in showing that competition was actually likely to be reduced by the merger, and referred to a reduction in potential competition.

The Commission's more general statement about abuse was much disputed at the time. Some scholars observed that, unlike article 66 of the treaty governing the E.C.S.C., article 86 makes no provision for controlling mergers. The Community Court, however, supported the Commission. Rather than looking to the wording of the article and the contrast with that in the earlier treaty, it looked to the system and aims of the Treaty of Rome. The purpose of the competition rules, in its view, is to preserve the principles of article 2, which states that certain economic aims are to be achieved by the establishment of a common market, and article 3, paragraph (f) of which provides for the 'institution of a system ensuring that competition in the common market is not distorted'. It stated that articles 85 and 86 are intended to achieve the same aim – the maintenance of effective competition in the Common Market. Previously this had not been universally accepted. It was thought by some lawyers and scholars that article 86 was intended to protect consumers, by regulating the prices of dominant firms, or at least providing the mechanism for regulation if required. The Court's next few statements were even more important:

> 'The restriction of competition, which is prohibited if it is the result of behaviour coming within article 85, cannot be allowed by virtue of the fact that this behaviour is successful under the influence of a dominant undertaking and results in a merger of the undertakings concerned. In the absence of express provisions, it cannot be supposed that the Treaty, which in article 85 prohibits certain decisions of normal associations of undertakings restricting but not eliminating competition, intended in article 86 to permit undertakings, by merging into an organic unit, to obtain such a dominant position that any serious possibility of competition is almost eliminated.'

Articles 85 and 86 then, are to be read together, in the light of articles 2 and 3(f), to form a seamless web, through which no gap may be opened up by those wishing to restrict competition without being subject to control. This was a wide interpretation of the competition rules, but the Court is the final arbiter of the construction of the Treaty. It has approached its task in the dynamic manner, sometimes adopted by courts interpreting a constitution made decades before, when circumstances have changed meanwhile. Some wonder whether circumstances have changed sufficiently for such an approach to be justified after only fifteen years, but it has proved very difficult to pursue the integration of the market through the legislative means provided for in the Treaty: the Council of Ministers, which now acts unanimously when important interests of one or more members of the Council are at stake.

The Commission had adopted the view that the consolidation of a dominant position was an abuse capable of control under article 86 before this. In *GEMA* (1970), it objected to some of the rules of the only performing rights society in Germany. To become members of the society, copyright owners were required to assign all their rights, present and future, throughout the world, until five years after they left the society. This enabled GEMA to grant a licence to anyone who wished to play, reproduce or broadcast any works subject to copyright. Through agreements with similar societies outside Germany, it could also license those reproducing in Germany under the copyright of members of foreign performing rights societies. Only those resident in Germany could become ordinary members, and foreign residents were deterred by being excluded from certain valuable rights.

Although it is arguable that the exploitation of performing rights is a natural monopoly better organized through a single society which can give those wishing to reproduce works in public a universal licence, the Commission decided to introduce some possibility of competition between the various national societies. First it objected to the exclusion of non-residents from ordinary membership, a rule which presumably was intended to consolidate the market power of the other national societies, rather than GEMA's. It also objected to the universality of the assignment required of members. It thought that composers, authors etc. should be able to assign their rights for some kinds of exploitation only, and remain free to exploit other rights individually, or through some other performing rights society.

In effect the Commission seems to have considered it an abuse for GEMA to increase the market power of the performing rights societies in other member states and not only its own, although it does not seem to have considered whether article 86 forbids the consolidation by one dominant firm of the market power of another. The Commission also seems to have assumed that article 86 enables it to provide for charges to be controlled indirectly through competition, rather than directly, and to have concluded that more competition was desirable in this field without investigating its likely effects on members and those paying for the use of their compositions and performances. The Court has impliedly confirmed these views in its ruling in *Belgische Radio en Televisie* v. *S.A.B.A.M. and Fonior (No. 2)* (1974).

Another decision of the Commission, extending the concept of abuse beyond the examples listed in article 86, related to *Commercial Solvents Corp.* (1972). This company was the only producer in the world on an industrial scale of the chemical aminobutanol. During the 'sixties it was discovered that this could be used to make the drug ethambutol. In 1962, Commercial Solvents had acquired 51 per cent of the voting shares in an Italian company, Istituto Chemioterapico, which until 1970 acted as a re-seller of the aminobutanol made by Commercial Solvents in America. In 1966, Zoja, an Italian company, started to buy the chemical from Istituto for the production of the drug and specialities based on it. In 1968, Istituto also started to make ethambutol. Between 1968 and 1969 there were abortive negotiations for a merger between Istituto and Zoja. In

1970, Zoja discovered that it could buy the chemical more cheaply from intermediate dealers in the Common Market, who were selling it for other end uses, and was released from part of its contractual obligation to buy from Istituto. During 1970, however, supplies dried up, and when Zoja sought further supplies from Istituto, it was eventually told that Commercial Solvents no longer had amino-butanol available for resale.

On Zoja's complaint, the Commission decided that (1) Commercial Solvents and Istituto should be treated as a single undertaking, since Commercial Solvents had the power to control Istituto and had exercised it; (2) the group had a world monopoly of the supply of aminobutanol, an essential raw material for the manufacture of ethambutol on an industrial scale; (3) the group had abused its dominant position in ceasing to supply raw materials to one of the principal producers of ethambutol in the E.E.C., conduct which would lead to the elimination of Zoja as a producer of the drug, and (4) this affected trade in ethambutol between member states in that Zoja exported to France and Italy.

As mentioned at p. 199 above, the Community Court confirmed the Commission's holding that the parent and subsidiary company it controlled should be treated as a single enterprise. This overcame two difficulties: it enabled the Commission to make orders against the parent, which had itself done nothing in the Common Market except supply its subsidiary with limited quantities of the raw material, and it enabled it to link the market power of the parent with the refusal to supply by the subsidiary. The Court neither affirmed nor denied the very sweeping view of its Advocate General that the test for treating two companies as one was control, and that this would be assumed to exist over a subsidiary company.

The Advocate General considered that the refusal of the group to supply Zoja at all was discriminatory, in which case it might come within paragraph (c) of article 86. He also pointed out that under some national laws, refusals to supply were sometimes illegal, though he did not add that these prohibitions applied even if the person supplying had no market power, and so served different interests. He did not say how patients in need of the drug would suffer if Zoja was eliminated. The Court too failed to spell out the theory on which it held that

'an undertaking being in a dominant position as regards the production of raw material and therefore able to control the supply to manufacturers of derivatives cannot, just because it decides to start manufacturing these derivatives (in competition with its former customers), act in such a way as to eliminate their competition which, in the case in question, would have amounted to eliminating one of the principal manufacturers of ethambutol in the Common Market. Since such conduct is contrary to the objectives expressed in Article 3(f) of the Treaty. . . .'

What interests was the Court protecting? Only that of Zoja in continuing to be able to use the equipment it had installed and the skills it had developed in the expectation that supplies of the raw material would continue to be available after the expiry of its contract, in which case there is no duty for a dominant firm to supply new customers or to increase supplies beyond what was expected by old ones. Or was the Court also concerned with the protection of those paying for the drug? If so, then there may be a duty on a dominant firm to supply anyone on reasonable terms unless a refusal can be justified.

When considering whether the elimination of Zoja would affect trade between member states (in the passage cited at p. 185 above), the Court did seem to be concerned with the maintenance of such competition as existed in a not very competitive market, but it is not clear whether it would also be concerned to introduce further competition. If the Court had spelled out more clearly the interests it was protecting, it would be easier to advise businessmen on the legality of refusing supplies to new customers.

'*May Affect Trade between Member States*'

This too was considered in relation to the similar condition for the applicability of article 85(1) at p. 184, where the judgment in *Commercial Solvents* which has limited the scope of this condition in both articles 85 and 86 was discussed.

The Future

In December 1973, the Council of Ministers adopted a resolution on measures to be taken at both Community and national level against rising prices, and invited member states and the Commission to organize regular exchanges of necessary and specific information about price movements and price comparisons in member countries. In particular, it desired member states to aid the Commission in the economic and commercial research required for the systematic application of article 86. So we may expect greater use to be made of the article even if it is some time before proceedings reach the stage where formal decisions are issued. Monopolization cases are inherently difficult, and, in my view investigations should not be unduly hurried.

206

Merger Control

Not much can be said on this topic at a practical level. The judgment of the Community Court in *Continental Can* established that, provided the Commission makes a proper market analysis, it has power to control mergers under article 86. Where a firm that is already dominant in one market reduces competition substantially by merging with an actual or potential competitor, the Commission has power to make an order under article 3 of regulation 17 ordering it to terminate the infringement. In the light of the Court's judgment in *Commercial Solvents*, the Commission may be more specific, and it is thought that it has power to order the firms either to become separate, or to dispose of certain elements in their business. Of course there are major practical difficulties in re-introducing competition once it has been eliminated by a merger and after the managers of one firm have seen the confidential information of the other. Moreover, it may be difficult to find an independent buyer for the assets, and there are considerable difficulties involved in arranging for their disposal to the shareholders of the merged companies, as suggested at pp. 32 and 72 above. The Commission probably also has power to control vertical mergers, since the possible foreclosure to customers or suppliers, if one of the firms is already dominant, may have significant repercussions on competition within the Common Market.

The limitations to control under article 86 are, however, substantial. Almost certainly the Commission cannot restrain a merger unless one of the firms is already dominant – the merger that leads to the original dominance can hardly be said to be an abuse of it, although in practice as time passes lesser degrees of market power may be taken to fulfil the requirement of dominance. The Commission cannot hold up a merger while it is deciding whether to intervene. Nor has it the power to control a merger with no horizontal or vertical aspects. Such a merger may lead to a single set of managers controlling many people's possibilities of employment, and may be thought to reduce efficiency, but is unlikely to have a significant effect on competition. On the other hand, it is doubtful whether the Commission has power to exempt from article 86 a merger which is likely to restrict competition substantially, but also to lead to countervailing benefits, such as important economies of scale or integration, or desirable effects on regional unemployment and so forth. There is no express provision for exemption in article 86, but in *Continental Can* the Court condemned only 'a substantial reduction of competition *to the detriment of consumers*'. It may be that where a merger is likely to lead to sufficient benefits, in which consumers may share, it is not abusive. There are some signs that justifications may be relevant under article 86: that the Commission may achieve by limitation what cannot be exempted.

Ministerial control of mergers under British law faces none of these limitations. To overcome them, the Commission has proposed to the Council of Ministers of the Communities a draft regulation that would extend its powers. Very large firms, which together have a turnover exceeding a thousand million units of account, would not be permitted to proceed with a merger unless three months' prior notification was given. If by then the Commission should decide to initiate formal proceedings, the merger may be held up for up to another nine months. Businessmen have complained that these periods are far too long. In the U.K. it rarely takes more than three weeks to decide whether to refer a merger to the Monopolies and Mergers Commission, and the Commission has seldom failed to meet its deadlines – rarely over four or five months. Doubtless there will be a struggle on these points in the Council, unless the Commission decides that it can operate more rapidly and amends its proposal. The comparison with the U.K. is not entirely fair, however, since it is easier for national civil servants to know whom to consult to obtain information rapidly. If the firms operate in the U.K. or in Germany, advantage may be taken of assistance from national competition authorities, but there is no control of mergers in the interest of competition in the other member states. According to the current proposal, smaller firms may proceed without notifying mergers, but if together their turnover exceeds 200 million units of account, their merger may later be held illegal without limit of time. If, however, the merger is in fact notified, proceedings can be initiated only within three months.

The proposal is extremely controversial. The definition of a merger, based on control, is as wide as that in the U.K. Unlike the U.K. position, however, it is illegal to proceed with a merger whereby the undertakings 'acquire or enhance the power to hinder effective competition in the common market or in a substantial part thereof'. Consequently, uncertainty as to whether a transaction amounts to a merger or has such an effect is more serious. Since, however, the draft regulation may be amended before it is passed, it is not proposed to discuss it in detail here.

Enforcement of the Competition Rules

In order to explain the doctrine of the provisional validity of contracts, the first nine articles of regulation 17/62 were described at pages 186–8 above. The system of notification established for new and old agreements provides the Commission with information about many agreements that may infringe article 85(1), although there is no duty to notify.

The Commission's principal power is contained in article 3, which enables it to order an undertaking to put an end to an infringement of article 85 or 86 of the Treaty. Such an order is required to be made by decision, since it changes the legal position of the parties and must therefore be made subject to the possibility of an appeal to the Community Court. (See p. 171 above.)

Frequently, the Commission has merely ordered an undertaking, quite generally, to terminate the infringement. Sometimes, such an order may not be very helpful, and in *Continental Can* the Commission ordered the parties to present proposals for terminating the infringement within a time limit. It was thought that the Commission might have been willing to permit the merger, if the parties agreed to dispose of certain plants. In *Commercial Solvents* (1974) the order was far more specific – to supply Zoja with specified quantities of the raw material. This was upheld by the Court. It seems that not only may specific orders be made, they also may be renewed from time to time. Had Zoja not made a long-term contract with Istituto, it would have had to come back whenever an order for supply ran out.

The other important power, also exercisable by decision, is to impose fines and periodic penalties. Under article 15(1), the Commission can impose fines of up to 5,000 units of account for supplying false or misleading information when seeking an exemption or negative clearance. More important is article 15(2), which as mentioned enables the Commission to impose a fine of up to a million units of account, or 10 per cent of the firm's turnover for the previous year, whichever is the greater, for intentionally or negligently infringing articles 85 or 86 of the Treaty. By virtue of paragraph (5), however, fines do not run for the period during which an agreement is notified. Nevertheless, paragraph (5) does not apply when the Commission has intimated to the undertaking that, after a preliminary examination, it considers that an agreement infringes article 85.

For a time the Commission ceased to invoke this procedure after the Court held in the *Noordwijks Cement Accoord* (1967) (p. 171 above) that such an intimation amounts to a decision, owing to the internal steps necessary if the Commission is to make one. Nevertheless, some of the formalities required before a decision is taken on the substantive application of article 85 or 86 are not required here, and the producers of polyester fibres were given such an intimation in 1972, and thereupon cancelled the agreement they had notified. The Commission appears to believe that such a decision cannot lead to fines for the period after notification and before the intimation is communicated, even if the agreement restricts competition seriously, but I would not advise businessmen to rely on this. Fines are required to be related to the gravity and duration of the offence. It seems that the Commission divides the fines between the participating enterprises roughly in accordance with their turnover. Nevertheless, it did impose a smaller fine on A.C.N.A., the Italian firm that had refrained from following the two later price rises, than on the other dyestuff producers, although 40,000 units, instead of the 50,000 imposed on the others, does not seem to be a very substantial difference in view of the fact that A.C.N.A. prevented two increases in Italy. The earlier Commission decisions do not spell out very clearly the reason for the particular fines imposed, although in its decision on the *Sugar Cartel* (1973) the Commission looked to the turnover of each participant, its market power and the gravity of its participation.

At first the fines imposed by the Commission were fairly mild, although fines amounting to 500,000 units of account were imposed on the producers of quinine, and fines are far lower than those currently imposed by the Bundeskartellamt in Germany. Nevertheless, after condemning the *Sugar Cartel* (1972), the Commission imposed total fines of over 9 million units of account, one-and-a-half million units on a single undertaking. For several years, officials of the Commission have been saying that businessmen should now have a fair idea of what is prohibited by the competition rules, thereby implying that they may expect heavier fines for infringement.

Article 16 of the regulation imposes periodic penalties of up to 1,000 units of account per day to compel undertakings to put an end to an infringement of the Treaty in accordance with a decision taken under article 3 of the regulation; to comply with a decision revoking or amending an exemption under article 8(3) of the regulation; to supply information or submit to an investigation ordered under the regulation (considered at p. 211 below). These daily penalties appear to be the normal mechanism for enforcing the Commission's decisions. They may be recovered as a judgment debt in the U.K., once registered in the High Court or Court of Session (article 192 of the Treaty and The European Communities (Enforcement of Community Judgments) Order, 1972, S.I. 1590). The maximum daily penalty of 1,000 units of account, however, is so small that it might be less inconvenient for an undertaking to pay than to comply, with, for instance, a divestiture order. If this should happen, the Commission might apply for an injunction to restrain infringements of the competition rules as being in breach of the European Communities Act 1972, although there are no express provisions for an injunction as there were in the statute, under which the order controlling the prices to be charged by

Roche was made (pp. 30–1 above). The Commission might ask the Attorney General to lend his name to what is called 'a relator action'. As the law enforcement officer of the Crown, the Attorney General might petition the High Court to restrain a continuing or reported infringement, but the Commission, as relator, would be responsible for costs. The position, however, is far from clear. It has never yet been necessary to enforce in the U.K. an order made by the Commission under regulation 17, still less to enforce one where the defendant prefers paying the daily penalties to compliance with an order under article 3.

Investigation by the Commission

Much of the Commission's information about agreements that may restrict competition comes from the notifications it receives. Even when the notifications arrived from the three new member states in July 1973, the Commission was able to make a quick preliminary examination of these on the day they were received, although it was a year before large firms of English solicitors were asked to deal with many requests for further particulars. The information to be derived from notifications is likely to relate mainly to the kinds of agreement which may possibly be exempted from the prohibition of article 85, although occasionally an important firm may ask for a negative clearance in relation to conduct that might conceivably infringe article 86.

Complaints may be a useful source of information about the more serious infringements. They may be made formally in accordance with article 3(2) of regulation 27/62, but there is no need to use the Commission's form for this. The advantages of making a formal complaint are that the Commission must inform the complainant if it does not intend to take it up, giving reasons and enabling the complainant to submit further written comments (regulation 99/63, article 6).

By virtue of articles 11, 12 and 14 of regulation 17, the Commission may take the initiative in investigating. For the purpose of carrying out its functions under article 89 of the Treaty, which include the investigation of suspected infringements of the competition rules,

'the Commission may obtain all necessary information from the Governments and competent authorities of the Member States and from undertakings and associations of undertakings.'

If the Commission were to ask the Director General of Fair Trading, who is probably a 'competent authority', whether a certain undertaking is a party to an agreement prohibited by article 85, he would

211

probably be under a statutory duty to reply helpfully, although in article 11 this duty is spelled out more fully in respect of undertakings. Section 2 of the European Communities Act 1972 has made Community law part of U.K. law, and Community law includes regulation 17. This could cause difficulty if the particulars of export agreements notified to the Board of Trade under the 1956 Act have been retained by the government or passed on to the Director General. The tradition of compliance by business with statutory obligations is stricter in the U.K. than in some of the Common Market countries, and U.K. firms may have notified the authorities here, relying on the secrecy provided for by section 33 of the 1956 Act. If their Common Market collaborators did not notify the Commission of the European Communities, the provision of information under article 11 of the regulation by the U.K. government or Director General might be thought unfair.

Article 11 is supplemented by article 14, which enables Commission officials to undertake investigations necessary for the same purpose. They act under a Community, not a national, warrant. They have power to enter premises, examine books and business records, take copies or extracts from them and ask for oral explanations on the spot. Taking copies and extracts may be a laborious process as officials do not take copying machines with them, and the undertaking being investigated may not be prepared to make its copier available. The more serious weakness in the procedure under both articles 11 and 14 is that, unless the undertaking being investigated complies voluntarily, a formal decision is required. If this is made, the competent authority in the state where the undertaking being investigated has its seat must be informed and no one knows whether those in certain member states may drop a hint to the undertaking to be investigated. It is, however, exceedingly difficult to destroy evidence once it has been filed without leaving a trace, and any attempt to do so may attract daily penalties for failing to supply complete and correct information requested by a decision made under article 11, or to submit to an investigation under article 14. The other disadvantage of having to make a formal decision is that it normally takes at least three months to complete the necessary formalities.

The Commission may, by virtue of article 13, request the competent authorities in member states to make an investigation under article 14, in which case the Commission officials may assist.

The powers conferred by articles 11 and 14 may also be used when the Commission is making an inquiry into a sector of the economy under article 12, and not only when it is investigating the existence of a particular restrictive agreement or abuse of a dominant position.

Enforcement by Authorities in Member States

By virtue of article 88 of the Treaty and article 9(3) of regulation 17, competent authorities in member states may apply articles 85(1) and 86 if the Commission has not already initiated proceedings. It is thought that this is unlikely to be greatly used nowadays. Before regulation 17 was issued, the German Bundeskartellamt did enforce article 85 quite extensively. The judicial system employed in the U.K. for controlling agreements would probably not be very suitable to the application of article 85, under which far more flexible criteria are used and economic appraisal is required. It may be that even agreements to which Part I of the Restrictive Trade Practices Act 1956 applies can be referred to the Monopolies and Mergers Commission under article 88 of the Treaty, despite the exceptions written into the Fair Trading Act, which must take effect subject to Community law (European Communities Act 1972, s. 2(4)); but it is thought that neither the Director General nor the government is very likely to wish to enforce the Community provisions, when the Commission of the Communities is available for the purpose. As regards monopoly situations not based on agreements, the Director probably has all the powers he is likely to want under the U.K. provisions. The definition of the public interest is open-ended so, under U.K. law, the Monopolies and Mergers Commission could take into account the desire to prevent partitioning of the Common Market.

The Commission's Procedure

The Commission encourages businessmen to consult it informally. On one occasion (*Henkel/Colgate* (1971)) an agreement was made to come into effect only if cleared or exempted by the Commission. It is unlikely, however, to issue a formal decision before the agreement comes into operation, and it is not always possible to obtain firm guidance before completing the negotiations for a contract. Before proceedings have been formally started, but when the Commission has made its views known to the parties, they may suggest amendments to their agreements and discuss these informally with officials. The agreement may then never be the subject of a formal decision. This saves officials' time, and enables them to deal with more agreements, but results in less guidance being available to those wishing to know what will be approved in future, or those wishing to tell how uniform the decisions are.

Formal proceedings start with the communication of objections to the parties by the Commission. Article 19 of regulation 17 requires that they be heard before decisions are made whether to grant negative clearance under article 2, whether to exempt an agreement under articles 6 or 7, or revoke or amend an exemption under article 8, whether to order the termination of an infringement under article 3, or whether to impose fines or daily penalties under articles 15 and 16. Interested persons are also entitled to be heard. If a negative clearance or exemption is to be given the Commission is required to publish a summary of the notification and give interested parties at least a month in which to make observations. Often these notices, which appear in the *Communications Series* of the *Official Journal*, are so short that it is impossible to tell just what clauses are contained in the agreement. Article 20 imposes a duty on officials not to disclose information, subject only to the Commission's duty to publish the main contents of decisions, and to give interested parties an opportunity to object. The detailed terms of agreements are not open to public inspection as they are in the U.K.

Although the communication of objections must be sufficiently precise to enable the parties to defend their position (*Transocean Marine Paints* (1974)), the proceedings are administrative rather than judicial, and the parties are not entitled to examine the file, nor to cross-examine the witnesses against them (*Grundig* (1966)). The answers to the points of objection are normally written. Documentary evidence may be appended, and the names of persons who may corroborate facts may be suggested. The Commission must provide an oral hearing in answer to a request in the written comments, if the person requesting it shows a sufficient interest, or if it is intended to impose a fine or daily penalty. Notice of the oral hearing must be sent to the competent authorities of all the member states, who may send an official to attend and take part. The parties are entitled to be represented by a permanent employee or by a lawyer entitled to appear before the Community Court.

Before a final decision is made to grant or refuse negative clearance or an exemption, to revoke or amend an exemption, to order the termination of an infringement, or to impose fines or daily penalties, the Commission is required by article 10 to consult its Advisory Committee on Restrictive Practices and Monopolies. This consists of officials from the competition authorities of member states. Normally the Commission likes to consult it more than once – informally the first time in order to collect views, and formally later. This is time-consuming and is one of the reasons why the Commission takes so long to reach a decision. So far, the fastest of which I know took eight months and ended in a fine being imposed (*W.E.A.-Filipacchi Music S.A.* (1972)). Often an exemption is granted, sometimes retrospectively, only after the agreement has been in operation for four years or more.

Industrial Property Rights, Considered as an Obstacle to the Free Movement of Goods

At the beginning of Chapter 7, the provisions ensuring the free circulation of goods were described. By virtue of article 30, quantitative restrictions on imports and measures having equivalent effect are prohibited between member states, but by virtue of article 36, this does not preclude

'restrictions . . . justified on grounds of . . . the protection of industrial and commercial property, provided that such prohibitions or restrictions do not constitute a means of arbitrary discrimination or a disguised restriction on trade between Member States.'

In its judgment in the *Grundig* case (1966) (p. 180 above), the Court ruled that articles 36 and 222 preserve the existence of national industrial and commercial property rights, but that their exercise may be subject to other provisions in the Treaty. Before the judgment in that case, it was widely thought that, as long as patent and industrial property rights were territorially limited under national law, a firm with valuable exclusive rights could segregate the national markets and sell products protected by such rights at a different price in each. Territorial restrictions in a patent licence might infringe article 85, but if an injunction could be obtained under the national patent law to prevent sales in one country of goods sold more cheaply in another, no territorial restrictions in the agreement were needed.

Under the law of some member states, a patentee is considered as sufficiently rewarded for his innovation if he can extract a monopoly profit at one link of the chain of trade. If he uses the invention to produce the goods himself, then he is recompensed by the high price he charges as he sells them. If on the other hand a licensee sells them, the patentee can obtain his reward from the royalty or other charge he makes for granting a licence, and the licensee can recoup the charge when he sells each item. Consequently, it is said that a sale of the goods made by the patentee or with his consent exhausts his rights in respect of those articles, which might otherwise have enabled him to control where or to whom or under what conditions they might be resold. Under the law of some countries, and in relation to some kinds of industrial property rights, it is only a sale within the country that exhausts the right.

A monopolist may be able to increase his profits by selling at different prices in each country. In *Centrafarm* v. *Sterling* (1974) (considered at p. 220 below), the price of a drug was twice as high in the Netherlands as it was in the U.K. This was largely due to changes in the rate of exchange, and partly to the buying power of the Department of Health in the U.K., which was deliberately used to lower the prices charged for drugs. If the rules for the free circulation of goods were to prevent him from invoking his Dutch patent to keep the drug out of the Netherlands, he might decide that it would pay him better not to sell in Britain, where he would obtain only a modest contribution to his research and promotional costs and to profits, since his highly profitable monopoly in Holland, and indeed in other Common Market countries, would be undermined. If this is the case, then to permit him to obtain an injunction under Dutch law to restrain seepage from the low priced market to the high would have the effect, which some think desirable, of encouraging him to supply both markets. It would also reduce his incentive to hold out against the British monopsonist for a high price. If, however, he would have supplied both markets anyway, it would have the undesirable effect of enabling him to keep up the price in Holland. The ability to keep the markets separate when the prices obtainable therein differ, for any one of a large number of reasons, may increase the value of the patent, although there is some doubt whether such additional profits are sufficiently certain to be taken into account by a firm deciding whether to invest in the initial research and developments (see p. 242 below) and whether, in consequence, the possibility of earning them in this way should be permitted.

There is under discussion a draft convention for the introduction of a Community patent which, if granted, could be enforced in the courts of all member states. It is envisaged that national patents may continue to be granted, but there is a provision in article 97 of the draft convention according to which even national patent rights will be exhausted once goods made by use of the invention have been put into circulation in any member state by or with the consent of the patentee. According to the current draft, this is to apply only after a transitional period of five to ten years, but the Commission argues that a transitional period is not necessary and should be deleted from the draft. Plans for a Community trade mark are still embryonic and I know of none for the introduction of other industrial and commercial property rights at a Community level. The problem of ensuring that the exercise of national rights does not interfere with the free movement of goods may be a transitional one, which will be partially solved if the proposed Convention for the Community patent comes into operation, but it has generated considerable controversy ever since the *Grundig* case in 1966, when the Court adopted the distinction between the existence of the rights, which is not affected by the Treaty, and their exercise, which may be (p. 181 above).

The next case concerning restriction of imports to reach the

Community Court was *Parke Davis* v. *Probel* (1968). Parke Davis had valid patents for the drug chloramphenicol in five Common Market countries, but in Italy patents cannot be obtained for drugs. At the request of the firm it had licensed under its Dutch patent, Parke Davis sought an injunction there to restrain the import of the drug from Italy. The Dutch court requested a preliminary ruling on various aspects of articles 85 and 86, together with articles 36 and 222. The Community Court held that the exercise of patent rights does not infringe article 85(1) unless there is an agreement prohibited by the article, and did not suggest that the original licence might amount to such an agreement. It added that a patent action is not necessarily contrary to article 86. It went on to consider articles 30 and 36, and decided that the exercise of national patent rights is not in itself a means of arbitrary discrimination or a disguised restriction on trade between member states within the proviso to article 36, and might be justifiable. If Parke Davis could not recoup the costs of its research and development in Italy, where drugs could not be patented, any other decision would have deprived it of most of the value of its industrial property right. The Court, however, did not consider whether the answer would have been different if the drug were imported from a country where Parke Davis enjoyed patent protection or could have done so, nor did it mention that the drug had in fact been made under a knowhow licence in Italy, so that Parke Davis had recouped some of its research expenditure, though perhaps not as much as it could have obtained had it enjoyed a valid patent there, although it returned to these issues in *Centrafarm* v. *Sterling* (1974) (p. 220 below). Although drug prices are said to be higher in Italy than in countries where they enjoy patent protection, it does not follow that the additional profit goes to the inventor rather than the producer.

In *Sirena* v. *Eda* (1971) an American firm, Mark Allen, had assigned an Italian trade mark to Sirena before the war. Many years later, it licensed someone else to use the same mark in Germany. When shaving cream to which the mark had lawfully been applied in Germany was sold in Italy, Sirena sued for trade mark infringement under Italian law. The Italian court referred certain questions about articles 85 and 86 to the Court, but the Advocate General also discussed article 36. The Court ruled that an agreement made before the Common Market was established might infringe article 85 if it is still producing the prohibited effects. There was evidence that Mark Allen had recently asked its licensee in Germany to prevent the import of goods bearing the mark assigned to it to Italy, so there may well have been a continuing prohibited agreement.

The Advocate General demonstrated little sympathy for trade mark protection, and observed that such rights were of less value to mankind than the drug penicillin – an unfortunate reference since in its first form penicillin was never patented. Moreover, it seems to presuppose that all patents are for valuable inventions, and that trade marks never produce substantial public benefits. He concluded that the existence of trade mark protection might be an obstacle to imports prohibited by article 30 and, though it might be justified in the same way as patent protections under article 36, this was less likely in view of the lesser social value of the interest protected. The Commission had argued before the Court that there was no evidence that the Italian and German shaving creams were identical, and certainly their composition had been under separate control for thirty years. Italians used to the Sirena product may have been deceived into buying the German preparation. Trade mark protection is a less serious obstacle to imports than patent law – the goods can be repacked under a different label, so that the exporting firm does not damage or reap the benefit of the reputation of the firm owning the mark in the country where the product is sold. The Court has never suggested, however, that the seriousness of the obstacle to trade between states should be taken into account in deciding whether it is justified under article 36. The Court's judgment was based almost entirely on articles 85 and 86, so the case was mainly important for the controversy it aroused.

The important development in the construction of articles 30–36 came in *Deutsche Grammophon* v. *Metro* (1971). Records pressed by Deutsche Grammophon were sold in France by its subsidiary. Metro bought these at a price which enabled it to sell them in Hamburg for several marks less than the retail price maintained by Deutsche Grammophon in Germany. By German law Deutsche Grammophon was entitled to a sound recording right (akin to copyright) in the performance reproduced on the record, and sued Metro for infringing it. Under German law, the owner of such a right is entitled to recoup the reward for organizing the performance only once, so it is a defence to an action for infringement to show that the right has been exhausted by a sale made in Germany by the owner or with his consent, but there was controversy as to whether a sale abroad exhausted the right.

The Community Court, after referring to the aims of the Treaty of Rome and, in particular, to the realization of a uniform market among member states, to be established by the rules for the free movement of goods and the establishment of undistorted competition throughout the Common Market, mentioned in article 3(f), stated that article 36 permits restrictions on imports

'only to the extent that they are justified for the protection of the rights that form the specific object of this prohibition.'

If the German law enabled Deutsche Grammophon to prevent the import of records sold by it or with its consent in another member state, that would maintain the isolation of the national markets and conflict with the essential aim of the Treaty: the integration of the national markets into one uniform market.

The Court did not attempt to reconcile this decision with the *Parke Davis* case. Under French law, there is no sound recording right, although to sell records produced from someone else's without licence would probably amount to the tort of unfair competition. It may be that only where there is no right at all in the country where the goods were first put into circulation, may their import to another member state be restrained. Alternatively, it may be that the Community rules relating to patents are more lenient than those for sound recording rights.

The Community Court's judgment in *Van Zuylen Frères* v. *Hag A.G.* (1974) has further developed the *Sirena* precedent. The defendant made coffee under various marks, including the letters HAG. In 1934 it assigned its Luxembourg marks to its subsidiary, Hag S.A., which carried on business there. After the war, the shares in Hag S.A. were sequestered as enemy property and sold to the Van Oevelen family. In 1971 Hag S.A. sold the Hag mark to the partnership Van Zuylen Frères, and the assignment was registered the following year. Van Zuylen Frères applied the mark to coffee made by Hag S.A., which did not itself market coffee. Meanwhile Hag A.G. continued to make decaffeinated coffee, which it sold under the Hag mark in Germany and as Decofa in Belgium and Luxembourg. When coffee bearing the Hag mark and stated on the label to be made in Germany was sold in Luxembourg, Van Zuylen Frères sought from a Luxembourg court an order to restrain infringement of its trade mark. In answer to its questions, the Community Court was able to affirm that where there is 'no legal, financial, technical or economic link between the two present holders of the mark', there can be no question of an infringement of article 85. It ruled, however, that:

'the fact of prohibiting the trading in a Member State, in a product lawfully bearing a trade mark in another Member State, for the sole reason that an identical mark, sharing the same origin, exists in the first state, is incompatible with the provisions laying down the free circulation of goods within the Common Market.'

It added that it does not matter whether the product was sold in the first state, here Luxembourg, by the owner of the mark in the second state or by a trader who had bought the goods from him. Since article 36 provides an exception to one of the fundamental

219

principles of the Common Market, it can derogate from it only insofar as is justified by the protection of rights which constitute the specific object of such property. In repeating what it had said in *Deutsche Grammophon* the Court confirmed that the application of article 36 to different forms of industrial and commercial property may not be identical. It observed that partitioning the Common Market through the exercise of national trade mark law is particularly serious, since such rights are not limited in time, but again failed to mention that the obstacle to import was less serious than a patent in that, once relabelled, the goods can be lawfully sold in another member state. The Court showed more concern for consumers than had the Advocate General in *Sirena*:

> 'While in a single market the indication of the origin of a trade-marked product is useful, consumers can be informed by means other than those which would affect the free circulation of goods.'

Yet I doubt whether the statement 'made in Germany' is a sufficient indication of origin. Consumers are interested not so much in where the goods were made as in who controlled their composition. They might have been interested to be told, in large clear type, that the composition of the German Hag coffee was not necessarily the same as that previously sold in Luxembourg under that name by a different and independent organization. Consumers of decaffeinated coffee may well be particularly anxious about control of its composition.

In *Centrafarm* v. *Sterling* and *Winthrop* (1974), the Community Court was given a further opportunity to rule on the extent to which patent and trade mark rights may be used to exclude imports from another member state. An American company, Sterling, held parallel patents in several member states for methods of producing the drug acidum nalidixicum. It granted licences under each of these – sometimes merely to sell and sometimes also to manufacture – to different wholly-owned subsidiaries. An independent firm, Centrafarm, found that there was a sufficient price difference to make it profitable to buy the drug in Germany and the U.K., where it was sold under the trade mark Negram, and sell it in Holland. The drug was not produced there, but imported and sold under a patent licence by a Sterling subsidiary, Winthrop B.V., which owned the Dutch Negram mark. Sterling and Winthrop sued for patent and trade mark infringement respectively and petitioned a Dutch court for orders restraining Centrafarm from selling the drug in Holland. Apart from the impact of the Treaty of Rome, each would have been successful since the Dutch supreme court assumed that a sale abroad, even with consent, does not exhaust patent or trade mark rights. The Hoge Raad carefully framed questions relating both to the free movement of goods and article 85 on which it asked the Community Court for a preliminary ruling.

The Court stated that the Dutch law under which a patent is not exhausted by the marketing of a protected product in another member state, even by or with the consent of the holder, may constitute an obstacle to imports prohibited by article 30, and that where the marketing abroad had taken place with the patentee's consent, exercise of patent rights could not be justified under article 36. Nevertheless, it reserved its position on the situation that had arisen earlier in *Parke Davis* (p. 217 above).

'[11]. While such an obstacle to free movement may be justifiable for reasons of protection of industrial property when the protection is invoked against a product coming from a Member State in which it is not patentable and has been manufactured by third parties without the consent of the patent holder or where the original patent holders are legally and economically independent of each other, the derogation to the principle of free movement of goods is not justified when the product has been lawfully put by the patentee himself or with his consent on the market of the Member State from which it is being imported, e.g. in the case of a holder of parallel patents.'

The Court's reservation is narrowly limited. It appears that the product must not be capable of patent protection in a third member state; it is not enough that it is not in fact patented. Should firms, therefore, apply for patents when it is doubtful whether they would be granted, merely so as to be able to show from the rejection of the application a right to an injunction to restrain sales in a different member state? What of patents that have been issued in the exporting country which are of doubtful validity, or which have expired? What of firms that wish to obtain some reward for their research where the product cannot be patented by granting a 'knowhow' licence on terms more favourable than might have been demanded for a patent licence, or which markets the product itself at a competitive price in a country where the invention cannot be patented? Although some of these difficulties were raised in argument, they were not mentioned by the Court. The law is not yet settled: it is hoped that the Court was not drawing a line, but merely taking a decision about two points on different sides of it.

'[12]. If the holder of a patent could forbid the import of protected products which had been marketed in another Member State by him or with his consent he would be enabled to partition the national markets and thus to maintain a restriction on the trade between the Member States without such a restriction being necessary for him to enjoy the substance of the exclusive rights deriving from the parallel patents.'

Sterling had argued that patents are rarely truly identical or parallel because of the variations between national laws and practices; but the Court replied:

'[14]. . . . that despite variations in national rules on industrial property . . . , the essential element for the judge to decide in the notion of parallel patents is the identity of the protected invention.'

The Court made it quite clear that its ruling was not based on the fact that all the patent licensees were subsidiaries of the owner of the parallel patents. It applies wherever the goods were put into circulation in another member state by or with the consent of the patentee. The ruling therefore applies also where the holder of parallel patents has granted a licence to make or sell in the other member state, to an independent undertaking.

'[20]. Thus the grant of a sales licence in a Member State has the result that the holder can no longer oppose the marketing of the protected product throughout the Common Market.'

This statement has important implications for patent licences. We will see that in theory there are circumstances in which an exemption might be given under article 85(3) to a territorial restriction in a patent licence. Neither the Advocate General, Signor Trabucchi, nor the Court seemed concerned that the effect of such a ruling might be that drug companies would no longer supply drugs in the U.K. at prices far lower than those obtainable in Europe (compare pp. 215–16 above). The Court stated that the fact that public authorities in the exporting state were acting to depress prices did not justify measures in another member state that were incompatible with the free movement of goods. Indeed it pointed out that

'[23]. The Community authorities have among their tasks that of eliminating factors which could be likely to distort competition between Member States, e.g. by the harmonisation of national measures for the control of prices and by the prohibition of aids incompatible with the Common Market, as well as by the exercise of their powers in competition matters.'

Yet some people think that a licence limited to sales in the U.K. might preserve the supply of cheap drugs there and provide part of the recompense for the original innovation, without doing any harm in other member states. True, since the patent rights could not be relied upon on the Continent, a very wide price difference could not be maintained without making it profitable for a dealer to buy in the U.K. for sale on the Continent, but it is hoped that the Court's judgment has not precluded the possibility of territorial restraints in patent licences where this is likely to increase sales.

In relation to article 85, the Court stated that agreements to allocate functions between a parent and its subsidiary, where the subsidiary enjoys no real autonomy in making its market decisions, do not restrict competition. In the Advocate General's opinion, agreements between members of the same corporate group which restrict the conduct of third parties may infringe article 85. This is difficult to reconcile with the Court's view earlier in the same year in *Commercial Solvents* v. *Commission* (p. 177 above) that for the purposes of article 85 as well as 86, companies within the same group are not separate undertakings, between whom an agreement may be made.

Its judgment about trade marks was very similar and adds little to the earlier cases. In relation both to patents and trade marks, the Court based its decision on the lawful marketing of the drug abroad by or with the consent of the owner. In *Van Zuylen Frères* v. *Hag*, however, the coffee had been lawfully marketed in Germany without the plaintiff's consent, as all links between Hag A.G. and Hag S.A. had been severed by the sequestration. It may be that the Hag decision was based on the common origin of the mark: this was expressly stated by the Court and the Commission had argued – dubiously in my view – that the sequestrator could not confer a greater right than existed before the sequestration. In relation to patents, it expressly reserved its position on the issues that would arise where an independent undertaking owns the right abroad. Consequently it no longer seems as important as it did previously to ensure that no one should become entitled to use abroad trade marks relied upon in one or more member states. Some firms, already concerned that they might not be able to obtain relief to prevent goods lawfully bearing a mark in another member state from being marketed in the U.K., to the detriment of their own reputation, have been registering their marks in other member states. This is, however, not always possible in the U.K. or the Republic of Ireland, where registration cannot be obtained unless a reputation has already been won there, or is intended to be. Some firms, especially smaller ones, may not wish to market goods bearing the mark in every state immediately, and so may not be able to protect the home market from exports from those countries. Several member states, including the U.K., have already signed the Vienna Trade Mark Registration Treaty of 1973. Whether it comes into operation depends largely on whether the United States is prepared to recognize registration in the absence of a reputation in the mark. If it is ratified by a sufficient number of states, it will become possible by a single registration to claim a mark in all the states which have done so.

As long as any partitioning of the market by use of industrial property rights was controlled through articles 30–36, the Commission could take no initiative. National courts should not grant injunctions to prevent the import of goods from other member states, but judges and counsel may not be familiar with this aspect of Community law, and the Commission has no competence under articles 30–36. As guardian of the Treaty, it might require states to refrain from impeding imports, but it might not always be politically desirable to invoke the procedures of article 169 of the Treaty, taking member states to the Community Court.

Shortly after the *Hag* ruling, the Commission attacked the division of national markets by a decision in pursuance of article 85. In view of its first phrase, 'as incompatible with the common market', that article has long been applied so as to prevent the market being partitioned. In *Advocaat Zwarte Kip* (1974), the Commission stated that,

> 'So long as undertakings act in accordance with principles which do not conform to the E.E.C. Treaty in the field of trade mark rights, article 85 of the Treaty will be applicable, provided the circumstances are such as to constitute an infringement of the article and that, in particular, there exist links of a legal, financial, technical or economic nature between the two groups.'

It therefore held that the assignment before the war of a trade mark in Belgium and Luxembourg, by an undertaking which continued to apply it to Advocaat put into circulation in Holland, infringed article 85, since it was then intended to partition countries that later joined the Common Market, and continued to have that effect. This goes further than the Court's ruling in *Sirena*, as little continuing collaboration to restrict competition was mentioned.

Since the product marketed under the Zwarte Kip mark in Holland had a lower alcoholic content than that bearing the mark in Belgium and Luxembourg, the facts directly raised the question of consumer protection. The Commission decided that

> 'the consumer is in danger of being misled only if the supplier omits to state either the composition or the origin of the goods.'

The Dutch product did state the alcoholic content, but as the other did not do so, consumers were in no position to compare.

Where an area which used to be divided territorially, through separate trade mark laws in each state, becomes in effect a single trade mark area by virtue of the interpretation now placed on article 30 of the Treaty, there are real difficulties for those undertakings which enjoyed trade mark protection in one area against imports from another, where an 'independent' producer, connected only by a licensing arrangement with a third party, applies the same mark to goods of possibly different composition. Consumers may wish to be informed either that the composition of the imported product is different from that to which they are accustomed, or that it is subject to control by an independent undertaking. It has been suggested that member states might legislate to require this information to be affixed to imported goods, but if the legislation does not also apply to goods produced or marketed within the country, would that not also be an obstacle to the free circulation of goods prohibited by the Treaty? The Court has not yet considered the extent of the obstacle to imports in deciding whether it is justified under article 36, although it did refer to other means of protecting consumers in its judgment in *Van Zuylen* v. *Hag*.

The days are long over when advice was given that the Common Market could be partitioned by taking advantage of the territorial limitations to national industrial property rights. I do not regret the extension of the doctrine of exhaustion to prevent the owner of such a right in one state from restraining imports of goods which were put into circulation in another by him or with his consent, except possibly in the field of patents. An inability to segregate markets, where the patent laws differ, may conceivably lessen the original incentive to innovate and grant licences and so limit the number of countries in which some products are sold. Where this is judged by the Commission under article 85, territorial restrictions can be permitted by virtue of paragraph (3) though, unless the exemption extends to a class of agreements, probably too late to encourage the original investment and probably the licence! It is difficult to see how exemptions could be permitted under article 36, now that it is being so narrowly construed by the Community Court.

Until the judgment in *Centrafarm* v. *Winthrop* (1974), I was more concerned that the owner of a mark in one country might not be able to prevent the sale there of products bearing the mark, which had been marketed in another member state by an independent firm which owned the mark there. Often the existence of identical marks in different states would be due to some form of plagiarism, in which case an action for passing off or, on the Continent, for some form of unfair competition, might lie. This would, however, be difficult to prove and might not even exist. Some owners of marks in one or more member states have been trying to obtain defensive registrations in all the others, but unless the system to be established under the Vienna Treaty comes into operation, this may require multiple applications, and is not possible in some countries, in the absence of an existing or potential reputation there. The Court's judgment in *Centrafarm*, however, reserves the position where 'the original patentees are legally and economically independent of each other', and says nothing to the contrary about marks, so it may be that the Hag judgment will be limited to cases of common origin. The Court has begun to take a less unfavourable view of trade marks than it adopted in *Sirena* and has shown concern for preventing confusion among consumers, although it has not yet acknowledged that by attaching the holder's reputation to goods, trade marks may encourage them to improve their products.

9: Some Kinds of Common Commercial Contracts Considered under the Law of Both the U.K. and the E.E.C.

The Double Barrier Theory

Until now, I have assumed that businessmen should comply with both the U.K. and the E.E.C. rules. This is largely true, but it is time to look at both the judgment of the Community Court in *Wilhelm* v. *Bundeskartellamt* (1969) and section 10 of the European Communities Act 1972.

In November 1967, the Bundeskartellamt imposed fines on the four firms which produced dyestuffs in Germany, in relation to the price increase in 1967, which we have already considered (p. 174 above). After the German competition authority had started proceedings under the German cartel law, but before it imposed the fine, the Commission of the European Communities commenced proceedings under article 85, challenging the 1967 price increase as well as those made earlier, in Germany as well as in other member states. The four firms appealed to the Berlin Court of Appeal, alleging, amongst other matters, that the German authorities should not have proceeded at the same time as the European Commission. The Berlin Court referred various questions under article 177 to the Community Court. This confirmed the double barrier theory, according to which agreements are legal only if they comply with both Community and national law, but added a qualification. After observing that, according to article 9(3) of regulation 17, the initiation of proceedings by the Commission prevented national authorities from enforcing article 85, it added that

'One and the same agreement may, in principle, be the object of two sets of parallel proceedings, one before the Community authorities under Article 85 of the E.E.C. Treaty, the other before the national authorities in application of internal law. . . . How-

227

ever . . . , such parallel application of the national system should
only be allowed in so far as it does not impinge upon the uniform
application, throughout the Common Market, of the Community
rules on restrictive business agreements and of the full effect of the
acts decreed in application of those rules. . . . Conflicts between
the Community rule and the national rules on competition should
be resolved by the application of the principle of the primacy of
the Community rule.'

Clearly, firms must comply with the Community rules in their
entirety, but how much of the U.K. law survives its accession to the
Treaty? An exemption under the restrictive practices legislation may
exempt from the application of that legislation but clearly does not
have any effect on the application of Community law. May a
restrictive agreement be condemned under U.K. law, when it is not
under Community law? Where negative clearance is given by the
Commission on the ground that the agreement is unlikely to affect
trade between member states, it would clearly not be improper to
forbid the parties in the U.K. to give effect to it. In my view, the same
answer applies if the Commission considers that it does not restrict
competition, while under U.K. law it is an agreement to which Part I
of the Act of 1956 applies. Whether or not the Restrictive Practices
Court (exercising its jurisdiction under section 20 of the 1956 Act),
or the Director (considering whether to seek directions not to refer
an agreement to the Court, by virtue of section 9(2) of the 1968 Act),
thought that the agreement did not materially restrict competition
within the meaning of the new 'gateway', there might be detriments
to the public that outweigh that consideration. The difficulty arises
when exemptions are given under Community law. Where this is
done individually, because of the economic benefits to be expected, it
is widely thought that national bodies should not put obstacles in the
way of the parties, but where the exemption is of a group of agreements, the position is not clear. Article 85(3) appears to apply only if
the agreement would bring economic benefits to be shared by
consumers, but it may well be that some of the agreements that come
within the group exemption granted to specialization agreements
may on balance restrict more competition than the immediate
benefits would warrant. Dr Markert, when he was legal adviser to
the Bundeskartellamt, wrote in 14 *Antitrust Bulletin* 869:

'The present article has given a rather narrow interpretation to the
"prejudice" proviso developed by the Court. Application of
national antitrust law can be excluded only where it would prevent
an agreement . . . from being put into effect when that agreement . . .
has already been authorised by the E.C. Commission under

Article 85(3) and where, in addition the Commission has clearly indicated that in the particular case it considers this authorisation a part of its economic policy. This narrow interpretation of the judgment is necessary because under the present circumstances in the Common Market any further limitation of national antitrust law would seriously weaken free competition in the E.E.C.'

He pointed to the delay with which the Commission acts. One might add that, since he wrote, the Commission has granted a group exemption for specialization agreements that may well restrict competition in ways that would be forbidden under U.K. and German law.

The European Communities Act 1972, after providing in section 2(4) that any existing or future Act of Parliament should be 'construed and have effect' subject to Community law, provided in section 10 that both the Registrar (now the Director) and the Restrictive Practices Court might, in their discretion, decide not to exercise their respective functions

> 'if and in so far as it appears . . . to be right . . . having regard to the operation of any [directly applicable provision of Community law] or to the purpose and effect of any authorisation or exemption granted in relation thereto.'

It seems likely that where an agreement has received an individual exemption, the Director would be unlikely to refer it to the Court. If such an agreement had already been condemned by the Restrictive Practices Court, the parties may apply under section 22 of the 1956 Act, to have the order discharged, even though the agreement does not come within any of the U.K. gateways. It has not yet been stated on what principles the Director will exercise his discretion to refer agreements subject to a group exemption. The Commission asserted in its second *Competition Policy Report* (1972, paragraph 27), that it has exclusive Competence over agreements, mergers, or the abuse of a dominant position contrary to the Treaty of Paris, under which the E.C.S.C. was created. If it is correct, and there is no very clear authority for that proposition, such agreements and so forth cannot be referred either to the Monopolies and Mergers Commission or to the Restrictive Practices Court. Parliament, however, seems to have taken a more narrow view of the Commission's exclusive jurisdiction, as there are more limited exemptions in section 7(1A) of the Act of 1956 (added by s. 99 of the Fair Trading Act) and section 10(2) of the European Communities Act, although after consultation with Commission officials, the Director General and Minister might so exercise their respective discretions as not to make references.

Public conflict is unlikely to arise between the Community and U.K. monopolies legislation, since the latter is discretionary. Both the Director and ministers who might make a reference to the Monopolies and Mergers Commission are likely to maintain contact with officials of the Commission and are unlikely to use resources in duplicating investigations. Through the Advisory Committee on Restrictive Practices and Monopolies of the Commission, U.K. officials will also have a chance to consider decisions before they are made by that body. Any disagreements as to policy or fact are likely to be resolved through consultation, rather than appear in rival investigations.

The remainder of this chapter is technical and more detailed than the earlier ones. The reader is required to bear in mind the rules described in Chapters 4 and 7, as well as of the group exemptions, which are discussed here for the first time. It would be helpful to read this chapter with a text of these regulations, some of which are to be found in the Appendix, pp. 270–8. They can be found in full in *Volume IV: Competition* in the series of *Secondary Legislation of the European Communities* (H.M.S.O.), and in the practitioners' books on competition. For those with practical business problems, or for those making a serious study of this branch of law, it is hoped that the chapter will help to bring together the various parts of the book. Those whose interest is broader may prefer to skip to Chapter 10.

Exclusive Dealing Agreements

As has been said earlier, the U.K. law is far more formalistic than that of the E.E.C. Unless restrictions are accepted by at least two persons, the agreement does not come within section 6(1) of the Act of 1956 (see p. 86). Even if the dealer agrees not to deal in competing products or sell outside his territory and the manufacturer agrees to supply no one else within the dealer's territory, the agreement can be drafted so as to escape control under that Act, however substantially competition may be restricted. Competition between manufacturers is likely to be restricted by requirements contracts, when dealers who enjoy market power agree not to deal in competing products. This is likely to be the case only when there are serious barriers to entry, such as those caused by licensing requirements. To develop a fore-court for the sale of petrol in the U.K., planning permission is required and is granted on very restrictive criteria, and as over 90 per cent of the petrol sold in the U.K. is sold through outlets tied to the supplier, it is difficult for an oil company entering the U.K. market to increase its turnover sufficiently quickly to justify the necessary investment in refining capacity. The Italian company Agip gave this as the reason for abandoning its efforts to enter the U.K. market. Competition between dealers in products for which there are no close substitutes is likely to be restricted when each agrees not to sell outside his territory, or it is difficult for him to do so. A dealer may also achieve considerable market power if he is franchised by the maker of a leading brand, for a large area, particularly if the goods are expensive to transport far.

The U.K. Law

The effects on competition may be difficult to consider without the sort of inquiry that the Monopolies Commission made in relation to the retail supply of petrol (1966) and of beer (1969). Exclusive dealing has long been accepted as a normal commercial transaction, so as we saw (pp. 104–6) such agreements are not controlled under the Act of 1956. By virtue of section 7(2) (set out in the Appendix at p. 259 below), restrictions as to where or to whom the goods may be resold, or as to their price, may be disregarded on the ground that they relate exclusively to the goods supplied, provided that there is no horizontal agreement between the dealers, or between suppliers. By virtue of section 8(3), if the only restrictions accepted by the supplier are in respect of the supply of goods of the same kind to other persons, and the only restrictions accepted by the person acquiring the goods are in respect of 'the sale or acquisition for sale of other goods' of the kind described in section 6(1), the agreement is not subject to control under the Act. There is no need to analyse the market to see whether any of the restrictions in fact restrict competition substantially, although in the two trades where the dealers enjoy local market power, references were made to the Monopolies Commission. It is fairly easy to tell whether an agreement is exempt.

Nevertheless there are limitations to the ways in which competition may be restricted. It is not always easy to ensure that the dealers do not make a horizontal arrangement between each other (pp. 94–9 above), unless the initiative comes entirely from the supplier, nor can manufacturers take advantage of these exemptions to limit competition between themselves, by sale to a common dealer, without almost inevitably making a horizontal arrangement preventing the application of the exemptions (*British Basic Slag* (1962) (p. 96 above). Both sections 7(2) and 8(3) apply only where goods are supplied, so do not cover the sort of franchising agreement (described at pp. 112–13 above) under which the owner of a trade mark licenses someone to apply it to goods produced by the licensee. Section 8(3)(b) enables the dealer to accept restrictions only in respect of 'the sale or acquisition for sale of other goods of the same description'. 'Sale' is narrower

231

than supply and excludes hire, or hire purchase. Nor does the subsection allow the dealer to accept restrictions as to the acquisition of goods which he will substantially alter before sale. If he buys pigs to sell pork by the pound or in his restaurant, are the pigs bought for sale? Some parts will never be sold, and those that are will be considerably changed. Where processing by the dealer changes the nature of the goods less, for instance when the dealer is merely required to charge a battery, or perhaps to dilute and bottle concentrated fruit juice, the subsection probably does apply.

The E.E.C. Law

To be prohibited by article 85(1), the agreement must be intended to restrict competition significantly, or in fact do so. This depends less on the terms of the agreement than on the situation of the market. Even when a civil court is merely attempting to decide whether an agreement is void by virtue of article 85(2), it is required to make a market analysis. In *Brasserie de Haecht (No. 1)* (1968), Advocate General Roemer listed as relevant many of the factors which would be so considered by an economist, or by the U.K. Monopolies Commission, but with which our civil courts were not troubled before 1973.

'Regard should be had to the number of restrictions accepted, their duration, the quantities of marketed goods to which they apply, the ratio between those quantities and the amounts which are marketed by producers, the volume of obligations undertaken towards foreign producers, the density of the obligations undertaken in given geographical areas, a comparison with the sales made independently of the cafés and the tendency of such sales together with the possibility of opening other cafés or creating whole chains of points of sale. Account must finally be taken of the importance of the breweries which cause the obligations to be undertaken and the volume of sales which are the subject of individual contracts. . . .'

If one is concerned with the restriction of competition these are, surely, the relevant factors. On the other hand, it makes it very difficult for civil courts to decide whether an agreement is void under article 85(2). Indeed, the Commission was so concerned by the task left to the tribunal in Liège that it started a sector inquiry itself into the supply of beer in Belgium. In fact, as the Advocate General pointed out, only about 50 per cent of the cafés were tied and, as was not stated, it is very easy to open a new café in Belgium – there is no need to obtain a licence – so it was fairly clear, as Dr Roemer indicated, that this requirements contract made with one of the smaller breweries did not restrict competition significantly.

The law of the E.E.C. does not differ greatly from the U.K. as regards the exclusivity permitted by section 8(3) of the Act of 1956, but those restrictions relating exclusively to the goods supplied, which are to be disregarded under section 7(2), include some of those to which most objection is taken under article 85. A 'no poaching' clause, whereby the dealer agrees not to sell outside his territory, may be disregarded under section 7(2), but is considered particularly likely to jeopardize the integration of the Common Market (*Grundig*), probably even if the dealer's territory does not cover the whole of a member state. (See *Commercial Solvents*, p. 185 above.) It may be that such a clause would be allowed for a time when a new, small producer is trying to enter the market and may need to give a stronger incentive than usual to persuade his dealer to make the necessary and risky investments in stocks and promotion. Even clauses imposing maximum rather than minimum resale prices or recommending fixed ones, which may be disregarded according to section 7(2) and are not controlled under the Resale Prices Act 1964, remove the dealer's incentive to export to other member states where prices are higher. Consequently, they discourage parallel exports, the mechanism relied upon to reduce differences in price between member states. Positive obligations, for instance to store the goods in a dry place or at prescribed temperatures and so forth, probably do not come within section 6(1) or article 85(1), but if they do they can be disregarded under U.K. law by virtue of section 7(2) and, if sensible, would be exempted under article 85(3).

The Group Exemption

In the light of both the decisions of the Commission and the judgments of the Court in *Grundig* and other cases, it became clear in the mid-sixties that exclusive dealing agreements were acceptable, since the Commission considered that they might be required to attract sufficient investment by the dealer to enable a manufacturer in one member state to start selling in another. There were some doubts whether article 9(1) of regulation 17 permitted the Commission to grant exemption to categories of agreement, so, as already mentioned, the Commission proposed and the Council passed regulation 19/65, empowering the Commission to grant group exemptions for exclusive dealing and patent licensing agreements. Where an agreement can be drawn so as to fall within such a group exemption, the need to make a market analysis to see whether competition is, or is intended to be, restricted significantly is avoided; nor is there any need to notify the agreement to the Commission, since even if it falls within the prohibition of article 85(1), it is automatically exempt under article 85(3) and, consequently, is not rendered void by virtue of article 85(2).

The Commission has still not exercised its power to exempt categories of patent licences, but in regulation 67/67 (reproduced in the Appendix at p. 275) it has exempted certain exclusive dealing agreements. The application of this regulation requires rather a formal approach reminiscent of that to which British lawyers are accustomed, since the regulation defines the clauses which may or may not be included, without any consideration of the likely effect on competition being required. Nevertheless, it is probably to be read in a less literal manner than the U.K. statute, in the light of its recitals, which refer to the benefits in distribution, rather than in production, to be obtained from exclusive dealing agreements. Originally the exemption was for five years only, but it has been extended until the end of 1982.

It is rather surprising that some of the difficulties that had arisen were not dealt with when the exemption was prolonged. Article 1(1) is very similar to section 8(3) of the Act of 1956. It exempts agreements to which only two persons are party and whereby

'(a) one party agrees with the other to supply only to that other certain goods for resale within a defined area of the common market; or

(b) one party agrees with the other to purchase only from that other certain goods for resale; or

(c) the two undertakings have entered into obligations, as in (a) and (b) above, with each other in respect of exclusive supply and purchase for resale.

Paragraph 2 states that:

'Paragraph 1 shall not apply to agreements to which undertakings from one Member State only are party and which concern the resale of goods within that Member State.'

The second paragraph was said to have been inserted on the advice of the Advisory Committee on Restrictive Practices and Monopolies, which wished it made clear that such agreements did not need exemption, since they were unlikely to 'affect trade between Member States' and so were not within the prohibition of article 85(1). In view of the subsequent judgments of the Community Court in *Vereening van Cementhandelaren* (1972) and *Commercial Solvents*

(1974) (p. 185 above), many businessmen regret this exclusion. In theory a requirements contract may make it difficult for producers in other member states to sell in the U.K., if there are high barriers to entry at the retail level, as in the case of beer or petrol (see p. 231 above). The supply of these products, however, has already been investigated by the Monopolies Commission, and high entry barriers at the retail level are unusual, so it seems that little advantage and much uncertainty has resulted from so limiting the group exemption. Certainly such agreements are less likely to jeopardize the objectives of the Common Market than those between enterprises in different member states, which may be exempt.

Although agreements between undertakings in the same member state are not automatically exempt under the regulation, the parties can probably rely on an individual exemption being granted on analogy to the group exemption. Provided that the agreement is notified to the Commission by the time it comes into operation, and there are no clauses that cannot be exempted, such as the allocation of certain customers to each party, the exemption is likely to be fully retrospective. In *Prym/Beka* (1973) an agreement did not come within the group exemption given to specialization agreements, but led to benefits similar to those recited in that regulation, and was granted an individual exemption by analogy to the group exemption, although only from the date when certain clauses to which the Commission took exception were abrogated. If one of the oil companies should find it necessary to sue one of its solus dealers and an English judge should come to the conclusion that the agreement does come within article 85(1) – and he might well not – the court would probably be prepared to grant an interlocutory injunction, provided that the normal undertaking was given to compensate the dealer in the unlikely event of the agreement eventually being condemned by the Commission (p. 191 above).

'*To Which Only Two Persons Are Party*'. As under sections 7(2) and 8(3) of the English statute, it is important to ensure that the agreement is bilateral. Where two leading suppliers sell to the same exclusive dealers or through the same agent, there will almost always be some sort of agreement or concerted practice between the manufacturers, which prevents the application of the group exemption. Care must also be taken to ensure that one dealer does not try to make it difficult for his customers to sell in another member state or there may be a prohibited concerted practice between the dealers (*Scotch Whisky* (1974)). In the next section, we will see that a feature of specialization agreements, which may fall within another group exemption, is that each manufacturer sells the full range of products, often acting as exclusive dealer or as one of a limited number of dealers for goods produced by the others. Since such agreements may be made between more than two parties the agreement under which each agrees to sell only to the other parties may be made between more than two persons. But such agreements are automatically exempt only when the parties' combined market shares and turnover do not exceed certain limits. Where the market shares are high, such agreements are very likely to be condemned (*Kali und Salz/Kali Chemie* (1973)) (aliter *Fine Papers* (1972)).

'*Defined Area of the Common Market*'. It was early assumed that the area might be as large as the whole of a member state and in *Beguelin* (1971), the Community Court did not rule that an area including both Belgium and France could not come within the group exemption, although the existence of a single dealer for several member states may reduce the benefits to be obtained from parallel imports. In that case, the Court merely stated that the exemption does not apply where the agreement makes it difficult to obtain the franchised goods from other dealers within the Common Market. It has always been doubted whether the regulation applies where the dealer is franchised for the whole of the Common Market. In 1974, the Commission announced its intention of giving a favourable decision to the agreement whereby *Duro-Dyne* appointed *Europair* as its exclusive general distributor for the whole of the Common Market. Europair itself sells to different exclusive dealers in each member state, so competition would remain at that level. Until the formal decision is published, the grounds of the decision are unknown – it may be that Duro-Dyne is too small to be able to support an independent network, and that an individual exemption would enable it to maintain the scale of its operations.

Resale. The other problems that arise on the application of this article are similar to the problems experienced in Britain. Under paragraph 1(a) the supplier may agree to supply the dealer exclusively 'for resale'. This may be even narrower than 'acquisition for sale' under section 8(3)(b). Does the dealer 'resell' a soft drink concentrate, which he places in a bottle, together with water and carbon dioxide? Does he resell a concentrated form of drug, which he places in capsules before sale? Some officials in the Commission say that the dealer who merely packs, for instance by bottling, does resell the goods supplied, but not if he adds anything, even items of small value, such as water and gas; others say that he 'resells', provided that what he does was what was expected when the original goods were sold to him. This might cover even the dealer who makes a hut or a boat out of planks supplied, and seems too wide. In such a case, what benefit results to users from the exclusivity in which consumers can share? Where on the other hand the dealer merely charges a battery or adds bulk to a concentrate, the agreement seems to come within the recitals to the regulation, which refer to improvements in distribution, so that the agreement should receive an individual exemption if it is held not to come within the group one. Where there is any doubt whether the dealer 'resells', it would be safer to notify the Commission. Where a single manufacturer uses a standard form of contract for his dealers, it suffices to notify just the form (regulation 27/62, article 4, incorporating form A/B prescribed by regulation 1133/68 and Part II 1(b) of that form). Notification should be made in a Community language and seven copies are required.

Permitted Restrictions. Article 2 of regulation 67/67 lists certain other restrictions which the dealer may accept: not to distribute competing goods until a year after the agreement ends, and not to seek customers outside his territory, or establish a branch or maintain a distribution depot outside. Although he may not be prevented from selling outside his area, he can be required not to solicit sales outside. Large customers may seek him, when there are sufficient price differences between member states. Paragraph 2 makes it clear that he may be required to stock complete ranges or minimum quantities, to use particular trade marks, to advertise, to provide after-sales and guarantee services and to employ staff with specialized training.

Limitations on Exemption. Article 3 is most important. The exemption does not apply to reciprocal agreements whereby two manufacturers appoint each other as exclusive dealers. Such clauses may be contained in specialization agreements, for which there is a separate group exemption. But if the only competing manufacturers were each to agree only to supply the other, they could eliminate competition between each other, and this is not permitted under regulation 67/67, which applies irrespective of the parties' market power. The other limitation was to be expected in the light of the *Grundig* case (1966). The parties must not make it difficult for intermediaries or customers to obtain the goods to which the contract relates from other dealers within the Common Market.

Even if an agreement comes within the group exemption, article 6 provides that the Commission may withdraw the exemption after individual scrutiny. Presumably, it would receive no notification if the agreement was clearly within the regulation, but it might receive complaints.

When contemplating the negotiation of an agreement coming within the terms of the articles of this, and indeed of the other, regulations granting group exemption, care must be taken to ensure that it also comes within the recitals, which in this case refer to improvements in distribution, rather than production. I can see no reason why the agreement which eventually received an individual exemption in *Prym/Beka* (1973) (p. 241 below) after the restriction allocating customers between the firms was abrogated, did not come within regulation 67/67. Prym agreed to stop producing sewing machine needles and to take its requirements from Beka. An obligation accepted by a dealer not to manufacture is permitted under article 2. A British lawyer would expect this to include an obligation to cease production. Such an argument, however, ignores the recitals to the regulation. Anyone concerned to ensure that agreements come within the group exemption must take care to read it as a whole and in the light of the objectives recited. The literal interpretation of the operative articles so often adopted by British courts may not be appropriate.

Transitional provisions enabled accession agreements to come within the group exemption, if they were modified to do so before July 1973. If so modified only later, they enjoy the benefits of exemption only from that later date.

Agency Agreements

If a manufacturer chooses to distribute not through an independent dealer, but through an employee, the agreement between them will not be caught by sections 6(1) of the Act of 1956, as there will be only one party carrying on business. Where he appoints an agent, who is remunerated by commission or otherwise, again the agreement will be outside section 6(1) since the agent's business will not be in the production or supply of goods. The manufacturer retains the ownership in the goods, until the agent sells them on his behalf, so it is the manufacturer who supplies them to the customer.

The position is similar under E.E.C. law. In the famous 'Christmas Message', a notice issued by the Commission on Christmas Eve 1962, it stated that, in its opinion, agency agreements were not caught by article 85(1), on the ground that an agent's functions are merely auxiliary. Nevertheless, the position under the two legal systems is not identical. The notice makes it clear that the distinction between an independent dealer and an agent does not depend on the legalistic distinction between a dealer, who buys and owns the goods until he sells them, and an agent, who merely retains possession of them on behalf of his principal. According to the notice, the distinction is based on the nature of the distributor's functions. In particular, for the relationship to be treated as agency, the producer must bear the risk of unsold stocks. In *Pittsburg Corning Europe*

(1972) the Commission imposed a fine on an American firm which distributed in Belgium through an agent and in Holland through a dealer. The reason why Formica Belgium was appointed as an agent for an initial period was to avoid the double payment of the cascade turnover tax then in force there. Invoices were sent out in the name of the manufacturer and the distributor was paid by commission, but the matters normally regulated in a contract with an independent dealer were covered in a similar way, although we are not expressly told who bore the risk of unsold stock. The dealer was of sufficient standing to act independently. The Commission therefore decided that the distributor was an agent only in form, but carried on the functions of an independent dealer, and the agreement did therefore restrict competition contrary to article 85(1).

Specialization Agreements

Where one manufacturer agrees to make only one range of products, leaving another range to the other party to the contract and vice versa, cost savings are often dramatic. Each may be able to plan for long production runs on specialized plant and still be able to sell the full range of products. The disadvantage to the public is that competition between the firms is eliminated. Where they meet competition from many others, the restriction on competition may be negligible. Indeed, by enabling the parties to cut costs and prices, it may introduce a viable competitor on to the market. Where the firms were already viable and met little competition, such agreements may restrict competition substantially.

There is little to be said about such agreements under the U.K. law. Clearly each party accepts a restriction within section 6(1)(c) of the Act of 1956 in respect of the descriptions of goods to be produced or supplied. None of the exemptions provided for in section 7 or 8 apply. The only exemption granted under section 1 of the Act of 1968 was in fact for a specialization agreement between the two main producers of certain types of coated papers that are used for glossy magazines. Nowadays, where the agreement increases competition, it is more likely that the Director would seek directions under section 9(2) of the Act of 1968 not to refer the agreement to the Restrictive Practices Court. It might well be difficult, however, for large manufacturers to convince him that the agreement increases, rather than diminishes, competition.

Under the law of the E.E.C. such agreements have received favourable treatment. At pp. 194–5 above, we considered the decisions in *Clima Chappée* and the more dubious one in *Fine Papers* (1972) where competition seems to have been severely restricted. Meanwhile in 1970 the Commission issued a notice, not confined to

239

specialization agreements, stating that in its view an agreement would not restrict competition significantly, contrary to article 85(1),

' – when the products involved in the agreement represent, in the part of the common market where the agreement is effective, not more than 5 per cent of the volume of business affected with identical products or products considered by consumers to be similar on account of their properties, price or use and

– when the aggregate annual turnover of the undertakings participating in the agreement does not exceed 15 million units of account or, in the case of agreements between commercial undertakings, 20 million units of account. . . .'

For this purpose, the parties include a company and anyone holding 25 per cent of its capital directly or indirectly, as well as affiliates in which it holds 25 per cent of the capital. When the parties are near these margins it may be difficult to apply this notice. They may not know which products count as substitutes for working out the 5 per cent share, and they may not know their competitors' turnover very precisely. Moreover, it is always dubious policy to rely on a Commission notice, since it merely amounts to a statement of the Commission's view; it is not an exemption, which must be recognized by national civil courts. In my view, it is often worth notifying the Commission, if it may become necessary to sue on the agreement. By making retrospective individual exemptions possible, notification increases the likelihood that a national court would grant interlocutory relief. Moreover, where there is any doubt whether an agreement comes within article 85(1), the notification is a form of insurance against the imposition of fines.

Regulation 2779/72 was passed by the Commission under the powers granted by regulation 2821/71 of the Council. Since specialization agreements may lead to improvements in both production and distribution, article 1 of the regulation exempts agreements under which manufacturers agree mutually to leave the production of certain products to the other or others. Again certain ancillary clauses are permitted by article 2. The limitations of size and market shares appear to be based on the earlier notice concerning minor agreements.

'Article 3

(1) Article 1 shall apply only:
(a) if the products which are the subject of the specialization represent in any member country not more than 10 per cent

of the volume of business done in identical products or in products considered by consumers to be similar by reason of their characteristics, price or use; and

(b) if the aggregate annual turnover of the participating undertakings does not exceed 150 million units of account.'

There follow similar provisions about affiliated and parent companies holding 25 per cent of the voting share capital. As in regulation 67/67 there are provisions for bringing the exemption to an end in particular cases, particularly if consumers are not in fact sharing the benefits. When in doubt as to whether the exemption applies, for instance because it is not clear what substitutes sohould be considered within article 3(1)(a), the safest course is to notify the Commission as a precaution.

The individual exemption granted to the agreement between *Prym/Beka* (1973) is important for various reasons. First, an agreement whereby one firm was to cease production and take its requirements of sewing machine needles from the other was exempted on analogy to this group exemption, although the specialization was not reciprocal. Secondly, the exemption was granted, although the firm ceasing to produce transferred its plant to the other, and thereby made it difficult to restart production. In effect the agreement amounted to a merger of the firms' interests in sewing machine needles, and once it had been carried out, there was little the Commission could do to re-introduce competition. Thirdly, the exemption was not made retrospective beyond the period when the parties abrogated a clause whereby they agreed which outlets should be served by each. Whether intending to take advantage of the exemption automatically or hoping for individual exemption by analogy, insertion of clauses unlikely to be permitted may prevent one party from suing the other for the period before they are abrogated.

Specialization agreements appear to be treated more favourably under Community than under U.K. law. The Director General is likely, therefore, to have to decide whether to refer to the Restrictive Practices Court agreements that come within the group exemption (see p. 229 above).

Patent Licences and Agreements

Although the Commission has had power to issue a group exemption for patent licences since 1965, it has not yet done so. It has not found it easy to decide what restrictions should in general be permitted and which forbidden. Before the new states joined the Community in 1973, it had dealt with most of the agreements notified to it under regulation 17, but was still left with some 3,500 agreements about licensing industrial property rights. To these were added another 1,200 or 1,300 from Denmark, Ireland and the U.K., most of them also relating to industrial property rights. The bare grant of a non-exclusive licence in return for royalties or a lump sum is unlikely to restrict competition. Certainly, in the short term it increases it by allowing one additional producer. Problems arise in relation to the restrictions either party may accept.

The 'Christmas Message'

The notice issued by the Commission on Christmas Eve 1962 applied not only to exclusive dealing agreements, but also to agreements for patent licences. Although for many years it provided the only guidance available about the Commission's thinking on the subject, it is dangerous to rely on it. In 1962, the Commission was greatly influenced by the theory expressly incorporated in the German cartel law of the inherent right of the patent. According to this theory, since the patentee is entitled to prevent anyone else exploiting the invention, a limited licence, by permitting competition that would not otherwise be legal, increases rather than restricts competition. Consequently, the notice stated that limitations on exploitation by the licensee by reference to time, space, quantity, field of use and so forth do not come within the prohibition of article 85(1). This opinion is now suspect. Officials of the Commission refer to the article by Professor Buxbaum (cited in the Bibliography at p. 283) in which the public interest issues were viewed quite differently. The objectives sought by the patent law are to reward and encourage investment in innovation, and to enable use of the resulting ideas to spread. While the exclusive right restricts competition for the duration of the patent, there may be greater use of invention in a country the law of which protects the inventor, than in one that does not. The important question is how much protection is necessary to encourage invention, or rather at which point should the public interest in encouraging innovation and its use be balanced against the restrictions on competition during the life of the patent.

Professor Turner of Harvard (in a paper discussed in Tokyo, see p. 283 below) has suggested that although greater profits may be obtained by a monopolist who can partition the market, this additional revenue is too uncertain at the time that the decision to invest in research and development is made, for the firm to take it into account. If he is right, then whether territorial restrictions should be permitted should depend on whether a firm that has already perfected the invention and obtained a patent would licence at all if he were not allowed to grant a limited licence. If he is wrong, and firms' budgets for research and development are affected by the possibility of granting limited licences, then the public interest would require the advantage of increased innovation, as well as increased numbers of licences, to be balanced against the advantages of wider licences when granted. This is no easy task. In either case, it is important that firms should know how restrictive licences may be at the appropriate time: when the agreement is made if Professor Turner is right, and when the budget for research and development is approved if he is not.

It is clear from the Court's judgment in *Centrafarm* v. *Sterling* (1974) (p. 220 above) that territorial restraints cannot be imposed by granting a licence under the law of only one or more member states, relying on separate patent rights to prevent sales in others. But where prices are considerably lower in one state as a result of government pressure or otherwise, so that without a territorial restriction it would not pay to supply there, could an agreement for a Patent licence containing such a restriction be exempted from article 85(1)? In *Centrafarm* the Court stated that the specific object of the exclusivity conferred by patent law is, *inter alia*, to enable the holder to obtain a reward for his creative effort, but it did not exclude other objectives, such as the encouragement of licensing when otherwise a low price area would not be supplied. Moreover, its formulation made in relation to article 36 may not apply without modification to article 85, which provides for exemptions in certain circumstances. Nevertheless, even if territorial restraints might sometimes be permitted, very large price differentials might be difficult to maintain, in view of the the judgment in *Centrafarm*, since such a restraint would bind only the licensee and it would pay someone to buy from him in the low price area for export to other member states.

Whether or not an exemption may be given to a territorial restraint accepted under a patent licence, it is dangerous to rely on the statement in the Christmas Message, that limited licences do not infringe article 85(1). The notice was based on the inherent rights theory which is no longer accepted by the Commission and the licensor cannot rely on patent rights in other member states to prevent the import or sale of goods originally put into circulation with his consent.

In 1962, the Commission also stated that provisions for the non-exclusive grant of licences under improvement patents and of know-how by the licensor, or by both parties, do not restrict competition, since the parties remain free to licence other firms. In 1974, officials were considering whether such clauses might not unduly reduce the incentive to innovate and so lessen competition in research and development. If one can rely on obtaining the benefits of others' research, why should one invest in innovation oneself? It did, however, announce its intention to give a favourable decision to one agreement containing such a clause – *Kabelmetal* (1974). The third statement that is now suspect is that sole or exclusive licences do not, as such, affect trade between member states. We will see that the individual decisions of the Commission in 1971 and 1972 are difficult to reconcile with the view that a restriction accepted by the licensor not to exploit the patent himself, nor to licence anyone else, is outside the prohibition of article 85(1).

One other statement in the Christmas Message is supported by the *Burroughs* decision (1971) (see below): the Commission thought that an obligation on the licensee to mark the product with an indication of the patent preserves the legitimate interest of the patentee, provided that the licensee is not prevented from adding his own mark. It also stated that quality standards, and the duty to obtain supplies from a specified source, are permissible in 'so far as they are indispensable for the technically perfect exploitation of the patent'. This may still be true, but in the light of the American experience, parties to an agreement should be prepared to show that it is not sufficient to specify the characteristics of the supplies required.

The notice ended with a note of caution, reserving the Commission's position in relation to reciprocal licences and patent pools and to multiple parallel licences – the grant by the owner of patents relating to a similar invention in several states of licences to different undertakings under each patent.

Individual Decisions

Burroughs (1971) was the first decision granting negative clearance to two patent licences. Burroughs is an American undertaking which granted licences for the manufacture of plasticized carbon paper to two firms, Geha in Germany and Delplanque in France. The licensee had the exclusive right to manufacture in the respective countries, but all three undertakings were entitled to sell throughout the Common Market. Since such carbon papers are valuable in relation to their bulk, freight would be no barrier to such sales. The Commission considered each licence in the light of the other. It stated that an exclusivity clause, such as that under which Burroughs agreed not to license anyone but Delplanque in France, might, in theory, infringe article 85(1), but that in this case the restriction of competition was not significant, owing to the small share of the French market for multi-use carbon paper supplied by Delplanque, and to the freedom of Geha and Burroughs to sell there. This was the first clear indication that the Christmas Message might no longer be a reliable guide. One might argue that licences to two undertakings amounted to 'multiple parallel licences', to which the 'Message' did not extend, but the Commission did not make this point and its reasoning was quite general. Why was the existing market share of Delplanque relevant? When a patent represents a breakthrough, the initial market share of both licensor and licensee may well be nil, yet the patent may enable one of them to supply the whole market. The Commission did not consider the extent of the advantage of plasticized carbon papers over other multi-use ones, but merely selected the wider market without comment. A product enjoying patent protection frequently differs to some extent from its substitutes. The Commission stated that certain other clauses do not restrict competition:

(a) the non-exclusive right to use the Burroughs trade mark, when the licensee was entitled also to affix his own as well:

(b) the licensee's duty to produce sufficient quantities and comply with technical instructions;

(c) the duty after the end of the licence, not to use the 'knowhow' or to communicate it to anyone else during the period of the licence and for ten years afterwards, since secrecy is the essence of 'knowhow', which is not protected by any statutory monopoly right;

(d) the prohibition on sub-licences, since the patentee must be able to decide who may use his invention, and otherwise the secrecy of the 'knowhow' might be at risk;

(e) the arbitration clause.

The decision in *Davidson Rubber* (1972) was made six months later. Davidson, an American company, held patents in most member states for a process for producing padded seamless objects, such as elbow rests and seat cushions for motor vehicles, and also patents for the machinery for carrying out the process. As early as 1959 it granted three parallel exclusive licences, and later a fourth, for various member states. The parties agreed to exchange all relevant information and keep it secret and to grant licences to each other under any improvement patents. The licensees were allowed to sub-license only with Davidson's consent, which was given on one occasion.

The Commission decided that the exclusivity given to each licensee within its territory did infringe article 85(1), since the Davidson process was the most important one for cars. Inconsistently, in my opinion, it granted exemption to the agreement, including the restriction on granting further licences, on the ground that but for such protection the Davidson process could not have been made available within the Common Market. Moreover, since the agreements had been amended so as to permit each of the licensees to sell throughout the Common Market, all competition was not eliminated. Had the Commission taken seriously the ruling of the Community Court in *La Technique Minière* v. *Maschinenbau Ulm* (1966) and *Brasserie de Haecht (No. 1)* (1968), it should surely have given a negative clearance on the ground that the agreement did not in fact eliminate any significant competition that was possible.

Before the decision was made, the parties abrogated a clause whereby the licensees agreed not to challenge the validity of Davidson's patents. The Commission stated that, had they not done so, the agreement would not have received exemption. Such a clause, by restricting the person with the most obvious interest in challenging a patent from doing so, may ensure that the patentee enjoys the benefits of monopoly, when the invention should be open to everyone. The Commission did not think that such a clause was indispensable to obtain the benefits of the agreement. There has been some concern that if this view stated in the context of a particular case is generalized, firms may hesitate to grant patent licences to firms over whom they have no control. The objection to restrictions on challenging the validity of the patent was first upheld in the United States, and there the licensee has the best of both worlds. He may call upon the patentee to prevent others from infringing, and then later he may use the invention but withhold the royalties while challenging the validity of the patent. If at the end of the patent litigation, the patent is upheld, then they may be recovered by the patentee, but he may be out of his money for many years, since patent litigation is lengthy as well as expensive and, in the U.S.A., the outcome is very uncertain. The Commission has not yet stated whether a clause that royalties should continue to be payable while the licensee is challenging the patent is valid. Such a clause would reduce the incentive to challenge by affecting the liquidity of the challenger meanwhile. On the other hand, the inability to insert it might reduce the incentive originally to grant a licence. If such a clause is held to be invalid, need a clause be inserted if the law under which the patent is granted enables the patentee to recover royalties while the patent is being challenged, in the absence of an express clause to the contrary? (See *Scotch Whisky* (1974).)

More individual decisions are expected in the near future. These will probably decide how far territorial restrictions may be imposed on the licensee. There is discussion whether the patentee may protect his own territory, though it seems to be less likely that he will be generally allowed to protect the territory of other licensees. Yet in the case of a firm which engaged in research and development for sale, rather than for its own use, the protection of each licensee against the others may increase its revenue, and the incentive to invest in the research originally. The other question is whether the Commission should take advantage of the distinction between the existence and the exercise of a patent to reach this result, or whether it should grant a group exemption to licences which are no more restrictive territorially than the Commission thinks desirable. Personally, I hope that the group exemption method is used. It gives security to businessmen who may well not license if there is any doubt about the enforceability of the restrictions under article 85(2). Moreover, it enables the Commission to think again in the light of experience, by refusing to renew the exemption when it expires without amendment.

Contrast with the U.K. Law

We saw (p. 107 above) that restrictions on licensing other parties do not come within section 6(1) of the Act of 1956, and are therefore not subject to control. Many people believe that limited licences are not registrable, as it is the patent rather than the agreement which restricts the licensee from selling or producing outside the scope of his licence (see *Telephone Apparatus Manufacturers' Application* (1963)). Until 1973, even if such restrictions came within section 6(1), they were exempt by virtue of section 8(4), provided that there were no other restrictions that did not relate to articles made by use of the patented invention. By virtue of section 101 of the Fair Trading Act, however, section 8(4) no longer applies to patent pools to which there are more than two parties. Where each licensee would not have taken a restrictive licence unless assured that any others would be subject to converse restrictions, then the patentee and both licensees may well be party to a multipartite arrangement (*Schweppes* (*No. 2*) (1971)), and it may now be necessary to decide whether restrictions within the scope of the patent are restrictions accepted under an agreement within section 6(1).

There is doubt under U.K. law whether a duty not to challenge the patent is implied, but such a restriction is commonly expressed in agreements for a patent licence, and is not a restriction of the kind described in section 6(1). Where restrictions are accepted by only one person, or where only one person party to the agreement carries on business in the U.K., Part I of the Act of 1956 does not apply. Where restrictions within the scope of the patent are accepted by a licensee and none by the licensor, provided that the licence was in no way dependent on the terms of other licences, then the agreement is not subject to Part I of the Act. In this area too, the U.K. law is more formalistic than that of the E.E.C. Where, however, a patent licence is not subject to control under the Act of 1956, the supply of goods or services affected by the patent may, of course, be referred to the Monopolies and Mergers Commission, which is then not precluded from considering whether the agreement is contrary to the public interest.

In both the U.K. and Germany, the authorities with power to control dominant firms have been concerned with the amount of profit that may be extracted from the patent of a particularly valuable invention. In December 1973, the Council of Ministers passed resolutions suggesting that various measures within the province of national states and of the Commission should be taken to mitigate the pressures towards excessive prices, and in particular that the Commission should consider how far article 86 might be invoked for this purpose. It is believed that the Commission is also considering whether to regulate the prices charged for certain patented drugs. Such action does not, however, depend on whether the patentee has granted a licence – indeed, competition from his licensee may somewhat reduce the need for control. The law of several member states provides that the patentee should grant a licence when the controlling authorities consider that the patent is not being sufficiently exploited.

Ancillary Restrictions Relating to Industrial Property Rights

Little can be said under E.E.C. law about licences under any rights other than patents, as the Commission has not yet made any decisions. It seems to be clear that an obligation accepted by the recipient of knowhow to keep it secret will be held by the Commission not to restrict competition, and the Commission may even support restrictions on the grant of sub-licences. Where the right which is the subject of the licence will eventually expire, as in the case of a patent, the Commission may approve an agreement whereby the licensor's mark be placed on the goods, only if the licensee is permitted to establish his own reputation by placing his own mark on the article as well. This may also apply to specialization agreements (*Clima Chappée* (1969)) where the distributor as well as the maker of each product may place his mark on it.

The *Advocaat Zwarte Kip* decision described at p. 224 above shows that, through article 85, the Commission intends to take the initiative in preventing the exercise of industrial property rights from dividing the Common Market; and, despite the contrary assumption by the Court in *Parke Davis*, it may hold that the mere assignment of rights, and presumably a licence granted under one or some of the laws of member states, may be forbidden in so far as it may be intended to partition the market or has that effect. This may continue to be important as long as the conventions creating a Community patent and trade mark are not in operation.

Part Four

10: Contrast between the Approaches Adopted by the Various Bodies Described in this Book

The reader who has persevered this far may be struck by the different approaches adopted by the Monopolies and Mergers Commission, the Restrictive Practices Court and the Community institutions. The legislation governing references to the Monopolies and Mergers Commission has always given the referring authority a wide field within which to choose sectors of industry for reference, and under the Fair Trading Act this field has been made even wider. With so much scope for selection, the referring authorities are unlikely to choose for a monopoly reference sectors where the Monopolies and Mergers Commission could not find that there was a monopoly situation within the meaning of the Act, especially as the criterion for the existence of a monopoly situation is the proportion of the referred goods or services supplied by the monopolist and not anything so open to discussion as the extent of his 'market power'. Nevertheless, it may be assumed that the referring authorities would not in practice wish to refer sectors where the monopolist was not thought to have some significant degree of market power, and the Commission certainly concerns itself with the extent of market power when considering the effect of a monopoly situation on the public interest. In its reports the Commission habitually describes the main features of the market, including the extent to which substitutes for the referred goods may limit the ability of the dominant firm to raise prices. Since monopoly investigations normally last for several years and facts can be ascertained informally, the Commission is able to obtain evidence relating to the supply and demand situation throughout the market and, with the aid of the professional economists on its staff, as well as among its members, is in an excellent position to assess the competitive forces at work.

This informal system is possible only because it is in no way illegal to enjoy market power, or even abuse it. Firms are required to

253

take no initiative in adjusting their exercise of market power to any general rules. It is only conduct after the investigation is complete and an order made that can be illegal. The disadvantage of this ad hoc approach is that the impact of a particular report of the Commission on the conduct of other firms is mainly indirect, although it may, of course, deter those who wish to avoid the trouble, expense and possible adverse publicity of a reference. The existence of the Commission for a quarter of a century and the long series of reports it has produced has undoubtedly introduced some caution into the exercise of market power by many firms in prominent positions.

The approach of the restrictive practices legislation is quite different. Citizens are required to take the initiative in furnishing particulars to the Director, so they must be able to find out what agreements are subject to registration. Moreover, although once an agreement is notified there is probably no duty not to give effect to it, unless and until it has been condemned by the Court, the costs of defending a reference to the Court are so high, and it is so difficult subsequently to ensure that any undertaking required to be given to the Court is not infringed, that most firms are advised not to enter into agreements subject to control. The legislation is drafted in a formalistic manner, so that businessmen may know clearly what agreements are subject to control. Most of the restrictions of the kind defined in section 6(1) usually reduce competition, but firms are not required to make a market analysis in order to decide whether they are under a duty to notify. This used to result in the discouragement of some forms of collaboration that probably increased competition, but since 1968 the Registrar and Director have been able to seek directions not to refer such agreements to the Restrictive Practices Court, and have sometimes even been prepared to inform businessmen before the conclusion of contracts between them whether they were minded to do so. Flexibility was introduced to enable promotions by 'voluntary groups' and others to be organized. Apart from the concept of 'arrangement', however, there is still no flexibility to extend the application of the legislation to agreements that may restrict competition without coming within the ambit of the legislation. Nevertheless, these do not entirely escape control, since such collaboration may amount to a complex monopoly situation referable to the Monopolies and Mergers Commission. Now that the Director may make references to both the Restrictive Practices Court and the Commission, conduct which cannot be dealt with by one can more easily be referred to the other. Nevertheless, I regret that jurisdiction is divided. It is unlikely to be easy to refer to one body conduct that the other has stated is outside its competence – not only might this appear oppressive, but the powers to obtain the information needed to decide whether to make a reference under the monopolies legislation are separate from those under the Act of 1956, although information properly obtained for one purpose can, no doubt, be used for the other.

When an agreement is considered on its merits, either by the Director when considering whether to seek directions not to refer, or by the Restrictive Practices Court, actual and probable effects on competition are relevant, rather than the form of the agreement, and a market analysis must be made.

The definition of the conduct prohibited under the Rome Treaty depends on criteria that are economically appropriate, but difficult to apply. The uncertainty caused by the need for a market analysis is made more acute by article 85(2) which renders void agreements prohibited by article 85. Consequently not only the Commission, which is served by professionally qualified economists, but also civil courts in national states, must assess the actual, probable, or intended effects of the agreement upon the market. Not only is it unlikely that the evidence necessary to assess the competitive situation of a whole market is available: there is also no reason why judges should be skilled in economic appraisal. From the point of view of businessmen, it is very difficult to obtain firm advice as to whether proposed action is legal, until many years after the event, unless an agreement can be framed to benefit from a group exemption. The additional risk inherent in making commercial decisions may increase competition, but it also may deter firms from forms of collaboration that many think desirable.

In an attempt to provide clearer precedents for businessmen, the Commission is wont to examine agreements clause by clause, to isolate restrictions on conduct, rather than on competition, particularly when applying article 85(1). We are told in *Davidson* (1972) (p. 245 above) that an exclusive licence under an important patent restricts competition because it prevents the holder from granting licences to others. Yet a page or two later, it is stated that without such a clause the technology concerned could not have been introduced to the Common Market, presumably because no manufacturer would have been prepared to undertake the necessary investment without the protection of an exclusive licence. The result of this practice may be that the Commission, which should have the resources and expertise to make a proper market analysis, rarely does so, except under article 85(3); yet national civil courts required to decide whether a contract is void by virtue of article 85(2) must either make a decision for which they have neither the training nor the appropriate information, or adjourn, possibly for over a year.

It is not easy to say what sort of control over market power is desirable. All three systems have their drawbacks as well as their

255

advantages. In the U.K. it is often possible to advise a businessman whether a proposed agreement would be subject to the restrictive practices legislation. There are areas of considerable doubt, such as agreements licensing industrial property rights other than patents, and now patent pools, but the Director's staff try to be helpful. It is difficult to ensure that salesmen do not make registrable agreements without informing general management, so considerable pains are taken to avoid making an agreement that would lead to having to give an undertaking to the Court. It is far more difficult to advise a firm whether proposed conduct would attract a reference to the Monopolies and Mergers Commission, although the criteria adopted by the Director General may become clearer. Any sanctions, however, will relate only to conduct after the investigation by the Commission is complete and an order made. The U.K. legislation gives a high priority to the liberty of the subject to do anything, unless it is clearly unlawful. The Community legislation has given a higher priority to preventing the division of the Common Market and the restriction of competition within it, even though the Commission has insufficient staff to examine agreements quickly and in depth. The introduction of the two group exemptions has made it easier to advise businessmen in certain common situations, but the group exemption for patent licences has long been awaited. There are many areas where it is not possible to give firm advice whether a contract will be enforceable, and informal discussions with the Commission's staff do not bind civil courts later asked to enforce the contract, nor even the Commission itself; although fines have been imposed for conduct that was not clearly illegal at the time only in one or two cases.

Restrictive Trade Practices Act 1956

Agreements to which Part I applies

6.—(1) Subject to the provisions of the two next following sections, this Part of this Act applies to any agreement between two or more persons carrying on business within the United Kingdom in the production or supply of goods, or in the application to goods of any process of manufacture, whether with or without other parties, being an agreement under which restrictions are accepted by two or more parties in respect of the following matters, that is to say:—

(*a*) the prices to be charged, quoted or paid for goods supplied, offered or acquired, or for the application of any process of manufacture to goods;

[(*aa*) the prices to be recommended or suggested as the prices to be charged or quoted in respect of the resale of goods supplied] (added by Fair Trading Act 1973, section 95)

(*b*) the terms or conditions on or subject to which goods are to be supplied or acquired or any such process is to be applied to goods;

(*c*) the quantities or descriptions of goods to be produced, supplied or acquired;

(*d*) the processes of manufacture to be applied to any goods, or the quantities or descriptions of goods to which any such process is to be applied; or

(*e*) the persons or classes of persons to, for or from whom, or the areas or places in or from which, goods are to be supplied or acquired, or any such process applied.

(2) For the purposes of the foregoing subsection it is immaterial whether any restrictions accepted by parties to an agreement relate to the same or different matters specified in that subsection, or have the

same or different effect in relation to any matter so specified, and whether the parties accepting any restrictions carry on the same class or different classes of business.

(3) In this Part of this Act "agreement" includes any agreement or arrangement, whether or not it is or is intended to be enforceable, (apart from any provision of this Act) by legal proceedings, and references in this Part of this Act to restrictions accepted under an agreement shall be construed accordingly; and "restriction" includes any negative obligation, whether express or implied and whether absolute or not.

(4) For the purposes of this Part of this Act an agreement which confers privileges or benefits only upon such parties as comply with conditions as to any such matters as are described in paragraphs (*a*) to (*e*) of subsection (1) of this section, or imposes obligations upon parties who do not comply with such conditions, shall be treated as an agreement under which restrictions are accepted by each of the parties in respect of those matters.

(5) Without prejudice to the last foregoing subsection, an obligation on the part of any party to an agreement to make payments calculated by reference—

(*a*) to the quantity of goods produced or supplied by him, or to which any process of manufacture is applied by him; or

(*b*) to the quantity of materials acquired or used by him for the purpose of or in the production of any goods or the application of any such process to goods,

being payments calculated, or calculated at an increased rate, in respect of quantities of goods or materials exceeding any quantity specified in or ascertained in accordance with the agreement, shall be treated for the purposes of this Part of this Act as a restriction in respect of the quantities of those goods to be produced or supplied, or to which that process is to be applied. [Provided that this subsection does not apply to any obligation on the part of any person to make payments to a trade association of which he is a member, if the payments are to consist only of bona fide subscriptions for membership of the association.] (Added by Fair Trading Act, section 96.)

(6) This Part of this Act shall apply in relation to any agreement made by a trade association as if the agreement were made between all persons who are members of the association or are represented

thereon by such members and, where any restriction is accepted thereunder on the part of the association, as if the like restriction were accepted by each of those persons.

(7) Where specific recommendations (whether express or implied) are made by or on behalf of a trade association to its members or to any class of its members, as to the action to be taken or not taken by them in relation to any particular class of goods or process of manufacture in respect of any matter described in the said subsection (1), this Part of this Act shall apply in relation to the agreement for the constitution of the association notwithstanding any provision to the contrary therein, as if it contained a term by which each such member, and any person represented on the association by any such member, agreed to comply with those recommendations and any subsequent recommendations made to them by or on behalf of the association as to the action to be taken by them in relation to the same class of goods or process of manufacture and in respect of the same matter.

(8) In this section, "trade association" means a body of persons (whether incorporated or not) which is formed for the purpose of furthering the trade interests of its members, or of persons represented by its members; and for the purposes of this section, two or more persons being inter-connected bodies corporate or individuals carrying on business in partnership with each other shall be treated as a single person. (Limited in relation to subsection (6) by section 11 of the Act of 1968, and, in relation to subsection (7), by Fair Trading Act, sections 97 and 98.)

Restrictions to be disregarded

7.—(1) In determining whether an agreement to which iron and steel producers as defined by the Iron and Steel Act, 1953, are party, whether with or without other parties, is an agreement to which this part of this Act applies, no account shall be taken of any term whether express or implied which has been approved by the Iron and Steel Board and by the Board of Trade—

(*a*) by which those producers agree to acquire raw materials or other iron and steel products as so defined exclusively from a person who undertakes as a common service for the iron and steel industry the importation of those materials or products, or the distribution of those materials or products when imported, or from any person nominated by such a person; or

(*b*) by which any such person agrees to supply such materials or products exclusively to those producers.

[(1A) In determining whether an agreement is an agreement to which this Part of this Act applies, where–

> (*a*) the parties to the agreement are or include two or more bodies [subject to the E.C.S.C. Treaty]
> (*b*) restrictions to coal or steel, or relating to both coal and steel, are accepted under the agreement by two or more such bodies, whether the restrictions so accepted by those bodies are the same restrictions or different restrictions,

no account shall be taken of any such restriction which is accepted under the agreement by a body to which this subsection applies, whether that restriction is also accepted by any other party to the agreement or not . . . .] (Added by section 99 of the Fair Trading Act.)

(2) In determining whether an agreement for the supply of goods or for the application of any process of manufacture to goods is an agreement to which this Part of this Act applies, no account shall be taken of any term which relates exclusively to the goods supplied, or to which the process is applied, in pursuance of the agreement:

Provided that where any such restrictions as are described in subsection (1) of section six of this Act are accepted as between two or more persons by whom, or two or more persons to or for whom, goods are to be supplied, or the process applied, in pursuance of the agreement, this subsection shall not apply to those restrictions unless accepted in pursuance of a previous agreement in respect of which particulars have been registered under this Part of this Act.

[(3) In determining whether an agreement is an agreement to which this Part of this Act applies, no account shall be taken of any term by which the parties or any of them agree to comply with or apply, in respect of the production supply or acquisition of any goods or the application to goods of any process of manufacture—

> (*a*) standards of dimension, design quality or performance; or
> (*b*) arrangements as to the provision of information or advice to purchasers, consumers or users,

being either standards or arrangements for the time being approved by the British Standards Institution or standards or arrangements prescribed or adopted by any trade association or other body and for the time being approved by order of the Board of Trade.] (Substituted by section 4 of the 1968 Act, as amended by section 100 of the Fair Trading Act.)

(4) In determining whether an agreement is an agreement to which

this Part of this Act applies, no account shall be taken of any restriction which affects or otherwise relates to the workmen to be employed or not employed by any person, or as to the remuneration, conditions of employment, hours of work or working conditions of such workmen, and for the purposes of this subsection "workmen" has the same meaning as in the Industrial Courts Act. 1919.

Excepted agreements

8.—(1) This Part of this Act does not apply to any agreement which is expressly authorised by any enactment, or by any scheme, order or other instrument made under any enactment.

(2) This Part of this Act does not apply to any agreement which constitutes or forms part of a scheme certified by the Board of Trade under Part XXIII of the Income Tax Act, 1952 (which relates to contributions and payments under schemes for rationalising industry).

(3) This Part of this Act does not apply to any agreement for the supply of goods between two persons, neither of whom is a trade association within the meaning of section six of this Act, being an agreement to which no other person is party and under which no such restrictions as are described in subsection (1) of section six of this Act are accepted other than restrictions accepted—

(a) by the party supplying the goods, in respect of the supply of goods of the same description to other persons; or
(b) by the party acquiring the goods, in respect of the sale, or acquisition for sale, of other goods of the same description.

(4) This Part of this Act does not apply to any licence granted by the proprietor or any licensee of a patent or registered design, or by a person who has applied for a patent or for the registration of a design, to any assignment of a patent or registered design, or of the right to apply for a patent or for the registration of a design, or to any agreement for such a licence or assignment, being a licence, assignment or agreement under which no such restrictions as are described in subsection (1) of section six of this Act are accepted except in respect of—

(a) the invention to which the patent or application for a patent relates, or articles made by the use of that invention; or
(b) articles in respect of which the design is or is proposed to be registered and to which it is applied,

as the case may be. (Limited by Fair Trading Act, section 101.)

(5) This Part of this Act does not apply to any agreement between two persons, neither of whom is a trade association within the meaning of section six of this Act, for the exchange of information relating to the operation of processes of manufacture (whether patented or not), being an agreement to which no other person is party and under which no such restrictions as are described in subsection (1) of section six of this Act are accepted except in respect of the descriptions of goods to be produced by those processes or to which those processes are to be applied.

(6) This Part of this Act does not apply to any agreement made in accordance with regulations approved by the Board of Trade under section thirty-seven of the Trade Marks Act, 1938 (which makes provision as to certification trade marks) authorising the use of such a trade mark, being an agreement under which no such restrictions as are described in subsection (1) of section six of this Act are accepted, other than restrictions permitted by the said regulations.

(7) This Part of this Act does not apply to any agreement between the registered proprietor of a trade mark (other than a certification trade mark) and a person authorised by the agreement to use the mark subject to registration as a registered user under section twenty-eight of the said Act of 1938 (which makes provision as to registered users), being an agreement under which no such restrictions as aforesaid are accepted except in respect of the descriptions of goods bearing the mark which are to be produced or supplied or the processes of manufacture to be applied to such goods or to goods to which the mark is to be applied.

(8) This Part of this Act does not apply to an agreement in the case of which all such restrictions as are described in subsection (1) of section six of this Act relate exclusively—

(*a*) to the supply of goods by export from the United Kingdom;
(*b*) to the production of goods, or the application of any process of manufacture to goods, outside the United Kingdom;
(*c*) to the acquisition of goods to be delivered outside the United Kingdom and not imported into the United Kingdom for entry for home use; or
(*d*) to the supply of goods to be delivered outside the United Kingdom otherwise than by export from the United Kingdom;

and subsection (7) of section six of this Act shall not apply in relation to recommendations relating exclusively to such matters as aforesaid.

(9) For the purposes of this and the last foregoing section two or

more persons being inter-connected bodies corporate or individuals carrying on business in partnership with each other shall be treated as a single person; and any reference in this section to such restrictions as are described in subsection (1) of section six of this Act shall be construed, in relation to any agreement, as not including references to restrictions of which, by virtue of any provision of section seven of this Act, account cannot be taken in determining whether the agreement is an agreement to which this Part of this Act applies, or of restrictions accepted by any term of which account cannot be so taken.

Presumption as to the public interest

21.—(1) For the purposes of any proceedings before the Court under the last foregoing section, a restriction accepted in pursuance of any agreement shall be deemed to be contrary to the public interest unless the Court is satisfied of any one or more of the following circumstances, that is to say—

(*a*) that the restriction is reasonably necessary, having regard to the character of the goods to which it applies, to protect the public against injury (whether to persons or to premises) in connection with the consumption, installation or use of those goods;

(*b*) that the removal of the restriction would deny to the public as purchasers, consumers or users of any goods other specific and substantial benefits or advantages enjoyed or likely to be enjoyed by them as such, whether by virtue of the restriction itself or of any arrangements or operations resulting therefrom;

(*c*) that the restriction is reasonably necessary to counteract measures taken by any one person not party to the agreement with a view to preventing or restricting competition in or in relation to the trade or business in which the persons party thereto are engaged;

(*d*) that the restriction is reasonably necessary to enable the persons party to the agreement to negotiate fair terms for the supply of goods to, or the acquisition of goods from, any one person not party thereto who controls a preponderant part of the trade or business of acquiring or supplying such goods, or for the supply of goods to any person not party to the agreement and not carrying on such a trade or business who, either alone or in combination with any other such person, controls a preponderant part of the market for such goods;

(*e*) that, having regard to the conditions actually obtaining or reasonably foreseen at the time of the application, the removal of the restriction would be likely to have a serious and persistent adverse effect on the general level of unemployment in an area, or in areas taken together, in which a substantial proportion of the trade or industry to which the agreement relates is situated;

(*f*) that, having regard to the conditions actually obtaining or reasonably foreseen at the time of the application, the removal of the restriction would be likely to cause a reduction in the volume or earnings of the export business which is substantial either in relation to the whole export business of the United Kingdom or in relation to the whole business (including export business) of the said trade or industry; or

(*g*) that the restriction is reasonably required for purposes connected with the maintenance of any other restriction accepted by the parties, whether under the same agreement or under any other agreement between them, being a restriction which is found by the Court not to be contrary to the public interest upon grounds other than those specified in this paragraph, or has been so found in previous proceedings before the Court,

[(*h*) that the restriction does not directly or indirectly restrict or discourage competition to any material degree in any relevant trade or industry and is not likely to do so.] (Added by Act of 1968, s. 10.)

and is further satisfied (in any such case) that the restriction is not unreasonable having regard to the balance between those circumstances and any detriment to the public or to persons not parties to the agreement (being purchasers, consumers or users of goods produced or sold by such parties, or persons engaged or seeking to become engaged in the trade or business of selling such goods or of producing or selling similar goods) resulting or likely to result from the operation of the restriction.

(2) In this section "purchasers", "consumers" and "users" include persons purchasing, consuming or using for the purpose or in course of trade or business or for public purposes; and references in this section to any one person include references to any two or more persons being inter-connected bodies corporate or individuals carrying on business in partnership with each other.

Fair Trading Act 1973

Definition of monopoly situation in relation to the supply of goods

6.—(1) For the purposes of this Act a monopoly situation shall be taken to exist in relation to the supply of goods of any description in the following cases, that is to say, if—

(*a*) at least one-quarter of all the goods of that description which are supplied in the United Kingdom are supplied by one and the same person, or are supplied to one and the same person, or

(*b*) at least one-quarter of all the goods of that description which are supplied in the United Kingdom are supplied by members of one and the same group of interconnected bodies corporate, or are supplied to members of one and the same group of inter-connected bodies corporate, or

(*c*) at least one-quarter of all the goods of that description which are supplied in the United Kingdom are supplied by members of one and the same group consisting of two or more such persons as are mentioned in subsection (2) of this section, or are supplied to members of one and the same group consisting of two or more such persons, or

(*d*) one or more agreements are in operation, the result or collective result of which is that goods of that description are not supplied in the United Kingdom at all.

(2) The two or more persons referred to in subsection (1)(*c*) of this section, in relation to goods of any description, are any two or more persons (not being a group of interconnected bodies corporate) who whether voluntarily or not, and whether by agreement or not, so conduct their respective affairs as in any way to prevent, restrict or distort competition in connection with the production or supply of goods of that description, whether or not they themselves are affected

by the competition and whether the competition is between persons interested as producers or suppliers or between persons interested as customers of producers or suppliers.

Definition of the public interest

84.—(1) In determining for any purposes to which this section applies whether any particular matter operates, or may be expected to operate, against the public interest, the Commission shall take into account all matters which appear to them in the particular circumstances to be relevant and, among other things, shall have regard to the desirability—

(*a*) of maintaining and promoting effective competition between persons supplying goods and services in the United Kingdom;

(*b*) of promoting the interests of consumers, purchasers and other users of goods and services in the United Kingdom in respect of the prices charged for them and in respect of their quality and the variety of goods and services supplied;

(*c*) of promoting, through competition, the reduction of costs and the development and use of new techniques and new products, and of facilitating the entry of new competitors into existing markets;

(*d*) of maintaining and promoting the balanced distribution of industry and employment in the United Kingdom; and

(*e*) of maintaining and promoting competitive activity in markets outside the United Kingdom on the part of producers of goods, and of suppliers of goods and services, in the United Kingdom.

(2) This section applies to the purposes of any functions of the Commission under this Act other than functions to which section 59(3) of this Act applies.

Order bringing under control restrictive agreements relating to services

107.—(1) The Secretary of State may by statutory instrument make an order in respect of a class of services described in the order (in this Act referred to, in relation to an order under this section, as "services brought under control by the order") and direct by the order that, subject to the following provisions of this Part of this Act, the agreements to which Part I of the Act of 1956 applies shall include agreements, whether made before or after the passing of this Act and whether before or after the making of the order, which—

(*a*) are agreements between two or more persons carrying on business within the United Kingdom in the supply of services brought under control by the order; or between two or more such persons together with one or more other parties, and

(*b*) are agreements under which restrictions, in respect of matters specified in the order for the purposes of this paragraph, are accepted by two or more parties.

(2) A class of services described in an order under this section, as being the services brought under control by the order, may consist—

(*a*) of services of one or more descriptions specified in that behalf in the order, or

(*b*) of all services except services of one or more descriptions so specified, or

(*c*) of all services without exception.

(3) The matters which may be specified in such an order for the purposes of subsection (1)(*b*) of this section are any of the following, that is to say—

(*a*) the charges to be made, quoted or paid for designated services supplied, offered or obtained;

(*b*) the terms or conditions on or subject to which designated services are to be supplied or obtained;

(*c*) the extent (if any) to which, or the scale (if any) on which, designated services are to be made available, supplied or obtained;

(*d*) the form or manner in which designated services are to be made available, supplied or obtained;

(*e*) the persons or classes of persons for whom or from whom, or the areas or places in or from which, designated services are to be made available or supplied or are to be obtained.

Articles 85 and 86 of the Rome Treaty

Article 85

1. The following shall be prohibited as incompatible with the common market: all agreements between undertakings, decisions by associations of undertakings and concerted practices which may affect trade between Member States and which have as their object or effect the prevention, restriction or distortion of competition within the common market, and in particular those which:

(a) directly or indirectly fix purchase or selling prices or any other trading conditions;
(b) limit or control production, markets, technical development, or investment;
(c) share markets or sources of supply;
(d) apply dissimilar conditions to equivalent transactions with other trading parties, thereby placing them at a competitive disadvantage;
(e) make the conclusion of contracts subject to acceptance by the other parties of supplementary obligations which, by their nature or according to commercial usage, have no connection with the subject of such contracts.

2. Any agreements or decisions prohibited pursuant to this Article shall be automatically void.

3. The provisions of paragraph 1 may, however, be declared inapplicable in the case of:

– any agreement or category of agreements between undertakings;

– any decision or category of decisions by associations of undertakings;
– any concerted practice or category of concerted practices;
which contributes to improving the production or distribution of goods or to promoting technical or economic progress, while allowing consumers a fair share of the resulting benefit, and which does not:

(a) impose on the undertakings concerned restrictions which are not indispensable to the attainment of these objectives;
(b) afford such undertakings the possibility of eliminating competition in respect of a substantial part of the products in question.

Article 86

Any abuse by one or more undertakings of a dominant position within the common market or in a substantial part of it shall be prohibited as incompatible with the common market in so far as it may affect trade between Member States. Such abuse may, in particular, consist in:

(a) directly or indirectly imposing unfair purchase or selling prices or other unfair trading conditions;
(b) limiting production, markets or technical development to the prejudice of consumers;
(c) applying dissimilar conditions to equivalent transactions with other trading parties, thereby placing them at a competitive disadvantage;
(d) making the conclusion of contracts subject to acceptance by the other parties of supplementary obligations which, by their nature or according to commercial usage, have no connection with the subject of such contracts.

Regulation 17 of the Council

First Regulation implementing Articles 85 and 86 of the Treaty

Article 1

Basic provision

Without prejudice to Articles 6, 7 and 23 of this Regulation, agreements, decisions and concerted practices of the kind described in Article 85 (1) of the Treaty and the abuse of a dominant position in the market, within the meaning of Article 86 of the Treaty, shall be prohibited, no prior decision to that effect being required.

Article 2

Negative clearance

Upon application by the undertakings or associations of undertakings concerned, the Commission may certify that, on the basis of the facts in its possession, there are no grounds under Article 85 (1) or Article 86 of the Treaty for action on its part in respect of an agreement, decision or practice.

Article 3

Termination of infringements

1. Where the Commission, upon application or upon its own initiative, finds that there is infringement of Article 85 or Article 86 of the Treaty, it may by decision require the undertakings or associations of undertakings concerned to bring such infringement to an end.

2. Those entitled to make application are:

(*a*) Member States;
(*b*) natural or legal persons who claim a legitimate interest.

3. Without prejudice to the other provisions of this Regulation, the Commission may, before taking a decision under paragraph (1), address to the undertakings or associations of undertakings concerned recommendations for termination of the infringement.

Article 4

Notification of new agreements, decisions and practices

1. Agreements, decisions and concerted practices of the kind described in Article 85 (1) of the Treaty which come into existence after the entry into force of this Regulation and in respect of which the parties seek application of Article 85 (3) must be notified to the Commission. Until they have been notified, no decision in application of Article 85 (3) may be taken.

2. Paragraph (1) shall not apply to agreements, decisions or concerted practices where:

(1) the only parties thereto are undertakings from one Member State and the agreements, decisions or practices do not relate either to imports or to exports between Member States;
(2) not more than two undertakings are party thereto, and the agreements only:
(*a*) restrict the freedom of one party to the contract in determining the prices or conditions of business upon which the goods which he has obtained from the other party to the contract may be resold; or
(*b*) impose restrictions on the exercise of the rights of the assignee or user of industrial property rights—in particular patents, utility models, designs or trade marks—or of the person entitled under a contract to the assignment, or grant, of the right to use a method of manufacture or knowledge relating to the use and to the application of industrial processes;
(3) they have as their sole object:
(*a*) the development or uniform application of standards or types; or
[(*b*) joint research and development;
(*c*) specialisation in the manufacture of products, including agreements necessary for achieving this,

Regulation 17 of the Council

—where the products which are the subject of specialisation do not, in a substantial part of the common market, represent more than 15% of the volume of business done in identical products or those considered by consumers to be similar by reason of their characteristics, price and use, and

—where the total annual turnover of the participating undertakings does not exceed 200 million units of account.

These agreements, decisions and practices may be notified to the Commission]. (Amended by Regulation 2822/71 of the Council.)

Article 5

Notification of existing agreements, decisions and practices

1. Agreements, decisions and concerted practices of the kind described in Article 85 (1) of the Treaty which are in existence at the date of entry into force of this Regulation and in respect of which the parties seek application of Article 85 (3) shall be notified to the Commission [before 1 November 1962]. (Substituted by Regulation 59, Article 1 (1).) [However, notwithstanding the foregoing provisions, any agreements, decisions and concerted practices to which not more than two undertakings are party shall be notified before 1 February 1963.] (Added by Regulation 59, Article 1.)

2. Paragraph (1) shall not apply to agreements, decisions or concerted practices falling within Article 4 (2); these may be notified to the Commission.

Article 6

Decisions pursuant to Article 85 (3)

1. Whenever the Commission takes a decision pursuant to Article 85 (3) of the Treaty, it shall specify therein the date from which the decision shall take effect. Such date shall not be earlier than the date of notification.

2. The second sentence of paragraph (1) shall not apply to agreements, decisions or concerted practices falling within Article 4 (2) and Article 5 (2), nor to those falling within Article 5 (1) which have been notified within the time limit specified in Article 5 (1).

272

Article 7

Special provisions for existing agreements, decisions and practices

1. Where agreements, decisions and concerted practices in existence at the date of entry into force of this Regulation and notified [within the time limits specified in Article 5 (1)] (substituted by Regulation 59, Article 1) do not satisfy the requirements of Article 85 (3) of the Treaty and the undertakings or associations of undertakings concerned cease to give effect to them or modify them in such manner that they no longer fall within the prohibition contained in Article 85 (1) or that they satisfy the requirements of Article 85 (3), the prohibition contained in Article 85 (1) shall apply only for a period fixed by the Commission. A decision by the Commission pursuant to the foregoing sentence shall not apply as against undertakings and associations of undertakings which did not expressly consent to the notification.

2. Paragraph (1) shall apply to agreements, decisions and concerted practices falling within Article 4 (2) which are in existence at the date of entry into force of this Regulation if they are notified [before 1 January 1967]. (Substituted by Regulation 118/63, Article 1; and see Article 25.)

Article 8

Duration and revocation of decisions under Article 85 (3)

1. A decision in application of Article 85 (3) of the Treaty shall be issued for a specified period and conditions and obligations may be attached thereto.

2. A decision may on application be renewed if the requirements of Article 85 (3) of the Treaty continue to be satisfied.

3. The Commission may revoke or amend its decision or prohibit specified acts by the parties:

(*a*) where there has been a change in any of the facts which were basic to the making of the decision;
(*b*) where the parties commit a breach of any obligation attached to the decision;
(*c*) where the decision is based on incorrect information or was induced by deceit;
(*d*) where the parties abuse the exemption from the provisions of Article 85 (1) of the Treaty granted to them by the decision.

In cases to which subparagraphs (*b*), (*c*) or (*d*) apply, the decision may be revoked with retroactive effect.

Article 9

Powers

1. Subject to review of its decision by the Court of Justice, the Commission shall have sole power to declare Article 85 (1) inapplicable pursuant to Article 85 (3) of the Treaty.

2. The Commission shall have power to apply Article 85 (1) and Article 86 of the Treaty; this power may be exercised notwithstanding that the time limits specified in Article 5 (1) and in Article 7 (2) relating to notification have not expired.

3. As long as the Commission has not initiated any procedure under Articles 2, 3 or 6, the authorities of the Member States shall remain competent to apply Article 85 (1) and Article 86 in accordance with Article 88 of the Treaty; they shall remain competent in this respect notwithstanding that the time limits specified in Article 5 (1) and in Article 7 (2) relating to notification have not expired.

[**Article 25** (added by Treaty of Accession, Annex 1, V. Competition)

1. As regards agreements, decisions and concerted practices to which Article 85 of the Treaty applies by virtue of accession, the date of accession shall be substituted for the date of entry into force of this regulation in every place where reference is made in this Regulation to this latter date.

2. Agreements, decisions and concerted practices existing at the date of accession to which Article 85 of the Treaty applies by virtue of accession shall be notified pursuant to Article 5(1) or Article 7(1) and (2) within six months from the date of accession.

3. Fines under Article 15(2)(a) shall not be imposed in respect of any act prior to notification of the agreements, decisions and practices to which paragraph 2 applies and which have been notified within the period therein specified.

4. New Member States shall take the measures referred to in Article 14(6) within six months from the date of accession after consulting the Commission.]

Regulation 67/67 of the Commission

on the application of Article 85(3) of the Treaty to certain categories of exclusive dealing agreements

Article 1

1. Pursuant to Article 85 (3) of the Treaty and subject to the provisions of this Regulation it is hereby declared that until [31 December 1982] (substituted by Regulation 2591/72) Article 85 (1) of theTreaty shall not apply to agreements to which only two undertakings are party and whereby:

(*a*) one party agrees with the other to supply only to that other certain goods for resale within a defined area of the common market; or

(*b*) one party agrees with the other to purchase only from that other certain goods for resale; or

(*c*) the two undertakings have entered into obligations, as in (*a*) and (*b*) above, with each other in respect of exclusive supply and purchase for resale.

2. Paragraph (1) shall not apply to agreements to which undertakings from one Member State only are party and which concern the resale of goods within that Member State.

Article 2

1. Apart from an obligation falling within Article 1, no restriction on competition shall be imposed on the exclusive dealer other than:

(*a*) the obligation not to manufacture or distribute, during the

275

duration of the contract or until one year after its expiration, goods which compete with the goods to which the contract relates;

(*b*) the obligation to refrain, outside the territory covered by the contract, from seeking customers for the goods to which the contract relates, from establishing any branch, or from maintaining any distribution depot.

2. Article 1 (1) shall apply notwithstanding that the exclusive dealer undertakes all or any of the following obligations:

(*a*) to purchase complete ranges of goods or minimum quantities;
(*b*) to sell the goods to which the contract relates under trade marks or packed and presented as specified by the manufacturer;
(*c*) to take measures for promotion of sales, in particular:
 – to advertise;
 – to maintain a sales network or stock of goods;
 – to provide after-sale and guarantee services;
 – to employ staff having specialised or technical training.

Article 3

Article 1 (1) of this Regulation shall not apply where:

(*a*) manufacturers of competing goods entrust each other with exclusive dealing in those goods;
(*b*) the contracting parties make it difficult for intermediaries or consumers to obtain the goods to which the contract relates from other dealers within the common market, in particular where the contracting parties:

(1) exercise industrial property rights to prevent dealers or consumers from obtaining from other parts of the common market or from selling in the territory covered by the contract goods to which the contract relates which are properly marked or otherwise properly placed on the market;
(2) exercise other rights or take other measures to prevent dealers or consumers from obtaining from elsewhere goods to which the contract relates or from selling them in the territory covered by the contract.

Article 4

1. As regards agreements which were in existence on 13 March 1962 and were notified before 1 February 1963, the declaration contained in Article 1 (1) of inapplicability of Article 85 (1) of the

Treaty shall have retroactive effect from the time when the conditions of application of this Regulation were fulfilled.

2. As regards all other agreements notified before the entry into force of this Regulation, the declaration contained in Article 1 (1) of inapplicability of Article 85 (1) of the Treaty shall have retroactive effect from the time when the conditions of application of this Regulation were fulfilled, but not earlier than the day of notification.

Article 5

As regards agreements which were in existence on 13 March 1962, notified before 1 February 1963 and amended before 2 August 1967 so as to fulfil the conditions of application of this Regulation, the prohibition in Article 85 (1) of the Treaty shall not apply in respect of the period prior to the amendment, where such amendment is notified to the Commission before 3 October 1967. [As regards agreements, decisions or concerted practices for exclusive dealing already in existence at the date of accession to which Article 85 (1) applies by virtue of accession, the prohibition in Article 85 (1) of the Treaty shall not apply where they are modified within six months from the date of accession so as to fulfil the conditions contained in this Regulation.] (Added by the Act concerning the conditions of Accession and Adjustments to the Treaties, Annex 1, V. Competition.) The notification shall take effect from the time of receipt thereof by the Commission. Where the notification is sent by registered post, it shall take effect from the date on the postmark of the place of dispatch.

Article 6

The Commission shall examine whether Article 7 of Regulation No 19/65/EEC applies in individual cases, in particular when there are grounds for believing that:

(a) the goods to which the contract relates are not subject, in the territory covered by the contract, to competition from goods considered by the consumer as similar goods in view of their properties, price and intended use;

(b) it is not possible for other manufacturers to sell, in the territory covered by the contract, similar goods at the same stage of distribution as that of the exclusive dealer;

(c) the exclusive dealer has abused the exemption:

(1) by refusing, without objectively valid reasons, to supply in the territory covered by the contract categories of purchasers

who cannot obtain supplies elsewhere, on suitable terms, of the goods to which the contract relates;

(2) by selling the goods to which the contract relates at excessive prices.

Article 7

1. Article 4 (2) (*a*) of Regulation No 27 of 3 May 1962, as amended by Regulation No 153, is hereby repealed.

2. Notification, on Form B1, of an exclusive dealing agreement which does not fulfil the conditions contained in Articles 1 to 3 of this Regulation shall, if such agreement is not amended so as to satisfy those conditions, be effected before 3 October 1967, by submission of Form B, with annexes, in accordance with the provisions of Regulation No 27.

Article 8

Articles 1 to 7 of this Regulation shall apply by analogy to the category of concerted practices defined in Article 1 (1).

Article 9

This Regulation shall enter into force on 1 May 1967.

This Regulation shall be binding in its entirety and directly applicable in all Member States.

Done at Brussels, 16 June 1967.

Select Bibliography

Part I. Monopolies and Mergers

J. P. Cunningham, *The Fair Trading Act 1973: Consumer Protection and Competition Law*. London, Sweet & Maxwell, 1974.
(Clear, accurate analysis of both the monopolies and mergers and restrictive practices law by a perceptive lawyer, accustomed to advising a large industrial group of companies, written in terms easy for a layman to understand.)

V. Korah, 'The Control of Mergers in the U.K.' (1969) 5 *Texas International Law Forum* 71.

T. S. Ellis III, 'A Survey of the Government Control of Mergers in the U.K.' (1971) *Northern Ireland Legal Quarterly* 251 and 451.

B. Hindley, *Industrial Merger and Public Policy*. Hobart Paper 50, London, Institute of Economic Affairs, 1970.

A. Sutherland, 'The Management of Mergers Policy', Chapter 7, in A. Cairncross (ed.), *The Managed Economy*. Oxford, Blackwell, 1970.

A. Sutherland, *The Monopolies Commission in Action*. Cambridge, C.U.P., 1969.
(A critical analysis of the then recent reports of the Monopolies Commission on dominant firms and mergers.)

Annual reports of the Board of Trade and Secretary of State under the Monopolies and Mergers Acts.
The Director is required to produce annual reports on his activities after the end of 1974 and subsequent years. These are expected to be more general than those of the Board of Trade and Minister.

Bibliography

Part II. Restrictive Practices

Books for Lawyers

J. Lever, Chapter 11 in Vol. II of *Chitty on Contracts*. London,
Sweet & Maxwell, 1968. This is a revised version of his book,
The Law of Restrictive Practices and Resale Price Maintenance.
London, Sweet & Maxwell, 1964.
(A carefully prepared book for lawyers, succinct, clear, accurate
and brought up to date as needed by supplements. The book is
too expensive for many individuals to own, but to be found in
most law libraries. There is little reference to works by
economists.)

J. P. Cunningham, *The Fair Trading Act 1973* (See Part I).

Books and articles of more general interest, largely on economics

R. B. Stevens and B. S. Yamey. *The Restrictive Practices Court:
A Study of the Judicial Process and Economic Policy*. London,
Weidenfeld and Nicolson, 1965.
(A classic analysis of the work of the Restrictive Practices
Court in its early and active years, and of the problems with
which it is confronted, both legal and economic, now out of
print. The authors consider how far the court has access to the
relevant evidence and whether the orders it is permitted to make
are appropriate for furthering the public interest.)

D. Swan, D. P. O'Brien, W. P. J. Maunder, W. S. Howe, *Competition
in British Industry*. London, Unwin University Books, 1974.
(Survey of effects of restrictive practices legislation on British
industry.)

Lord Wilberforce, *Law and Economics*. Holdsworth Club, 1966.

W. J. Kenneth Diplock, *The Role of the Judicial Process in the
Regulation of Competition*. Lionel Cohen Lectures, Hebrew
University of Jerusalem, London, Oxford University Press, 1967.

G. C. Allen, *Monopoly and Restrictive Practices*. London, Unwin
University Books, 1968.

B. S. Yamey (ed.), *Economics of Industrial Structure*. Harmonds-
worth, Penguin, 1973.

B. S. Yamey (ed.), *Resale Price Maintenance: Studies*. London,
Weidenfeld and Nicolson, 1966.
(Studies of the effect of resale price maintenance in seven
countries, and of its abolition where this has occurred. The
Editor describes the main economic issues in an introduction.)

B. S. Yamey, *Resale Price Maintenance and Shoppers' Choice*.

Hobart Paper No. 1, London, Institute of Economic Affairs, 4th ed. 1964.

(An influential attack on the practice, in more polemical terms than the more academic book he had written earlier, which has long been out of print and so is not listed here.)

J. F. Pickering, *Resale Price Maintenance in Practice.* London, Allen & Unwin, 1966.

(An empirical study of the way in which resale price maintenance worked in the U.K. and its extent, rather than a theoretical case for or against the practice.)

J. F. Pickering, 'The Abolition of Resale Price Maintenance in Great Britain.' (1974) 26 *Oxford Economic Papers*, 120.

(An empirical study of the consequences of abolishing the practice as it became illegal for one class of goods after another under the Resale Prices Act 1964.)

Law Reports. The official reports of the judgments of the Restrictive Practices Court, including summarized versions of counsel's submissions, were published by the Incorporated Council of Law Reporting in seven volumes of *Restrictive Practices Cases*, cited as e.g. (1960) L.R. 2 R.P. (p. –). These were amalgamated in 1972 in the *Industrial Court Reports*, but only a couple of cases were reported there. The Council has decided to continue that series under the name *Industrial Cases Reports*, and it will continue to include any restrictive practices cases.

Before being so published, the cases are reported without counsel's arguments in the *Weekly Law Reports*, cited as e.g. [1962] 1 W.L.R. (p. –). Butterworths also publish the *All England Reports*, cited as, e.g. [1960] 2 All E.R. (p. –). All these reports are reliable, and references to each are given in the table of cases.

The *Reports of the Registrar* have described the Registrar's work over the years, the state of register, and sometimes his views about amendments he would like to make in the law. These are obtainable from Her Majesty's Stationery Office, Cmnd Nos. 1273, 1603, 2246, 3188, 4303, 5195. It seems likely that in future they will be replaced by a chapter in the annual report the Director is required to make.

Part III. Common Market

Willy Alexander, *The E.E.C. Rules of Competition.* London, Kluwer Harrap, 1973.

(Short, perceptive legal practitioners' guide.)

C. Bellamy and G. Child, *Common Market Law of Competition.* London, Sweet & Maxwell, 1973.

(Good legal practitioner's work, perceptive, thorough, more footnotes.)

J. P. Cunningham, *The Competition Law of the E.E.C. – a Practical Guide*. London. Kogan Page, 1973.

(A clear and accurate guide for businessmen and their advisers by a perceptive legal adviser to a large group of companies.)

A. Deringer and others, *The Competition Law of the E.E.C.* New York, Commerce Clearing House, 1968.

(Commentary for practitioners – excellent, particularly on regulations. Refers to national competition law, not only in Germany but also in France and the Netherlands, but out of date.)

R. Joliet, *Monopolization and Abuse of Dominant Position: a Comparative Study of the American and European Approaches to the Control of Economic Power*. The Hague, Nijhoff, 1970.

(Classic, clear analysis of crucial issues: in English, by a Belgian lawyer with a clear grasp of economic issues.)

R. Joliet, *The Rule of Reason in Antitrust Law. American, German and Common Market Laws in Comparative Perspective*. The Hague, Nijhoff, 1967. (As above.)

C. W. Oberdorfer, A. Gleiss and M. Hirsch, *Common Market Cartel Law*. New York, Commerce Clearing House, 2nd ed. 1971.

(Commentary based largely on German sources and adapted to the U.S. market.)

M. Waelbroeck, *Le droit de la communauté économique européenne. Vol. 4, Concurrence*. Brussels, Université libre de Bruxelles institut d'études européennes, éditions de l'université de Bruxelles, 1972.

(Most reliable, detailed, scholarly and practical commentary.)

Commission of European Communities, *Reports on Competition Policy* – annual from 1971, published in April.

European Court Reports (E.C.R.), the official reports of the Community Court, useful since 1973, and English translations of earlier cases are being made.

Official Journal – gazette of the Communities. The L volumes contain the decisions of the Commission. Before 1973 *Journal Officiel* in French.

Common Market Reporter (C.M.R.), Commerce Clearing House.

(An expensive but useful series of loose-leaf volumes including reports of the decisions of the Commission and Judgments of the Court, together with a comment on the Treaty – not confined to competition.)

Common Market Law Reports (C.M.L.R.).

(Law reports, from which most of the quotations in this book have been taken. Omits Court's summary of the arguments presented to it, includes cases in courts of member states.)

In General, Not Limited to One Part of the Book

A. D. Neale, *The Antitrust Laws of the U.S.A.: A Study of Competition Enforced by Law*. Cambridge, C.U.P., 2nd ed. 1970.

Koch and Froschmaier, 'The Doctrine of Territoriality in Patent Law and the European Common Market'. Appeared in English in (1965) 9 *Idea: The Patent, Trademark & Copyright Journal of Research and Education* 343.

(The German version was instrumental in leading to the challenge under Community law of the right to an injunction in *Deutsche Grammophon*.)

R. M. Buxbaum, 'Restrictions inherent in the Patent Monopoly: a Comparative Critique' (1965) 113 *University of Pa. Law Review* 633.

(Thought by officials of the Commission E.C. to destroy the validity of the inherent rights doctrine in those systems of law in which it is not expressly incorporated by the cartel legislation.)

The O.E.C.D. has been holding international conferences and many interesting papers have been published in the proceedings. The conference at Frankfurt in 1961 was reported in *Cartel and Monopoly in Modern Law*; another as *International Conference on monopolies, mergers and restrictive practices: papers and reports*, Cambridge, 1969; and the papers circulated before the conference in Tokyo in 1973 will probably be published before this book. Two papers from the Tokyo conference are of particular interest in relation to E.E.C. developments: D. F. Turner, 'Territorial Restrictions in the International Transfer of Technology'; and 'Trans-national Mergers as a Source of Production Scale Economies', in which Professor E. M. Scherer raises the question whether the economies of scale being obtained by specialization agreements might not be achieved without the loss of one or more competitors.

The author contributes quarterly comments on recent developments in the U.K. and E.E.C. to the *Journal of Business Law*. Notes and articles are frequently published in the *International and Comparative Law Quarterly, Common Market Law Review, Cahiers de Droit Européen, Revue Trimestrielle de Droit Européen, Europarecht, Wettbewerb in Recht und Praxis mit Kartellrecht und Werberecht, Antitrust Bulletin, Law Quarterly Review, Modern Law Review, Law Society Gazette* and many other journals.

Tables of Cases

British and American Cases

Cases are listed alphabetically by the description used in the book; the fuller citation follows. The following abbreviations have been used: H.L., House of Lords; C.A., Court of Appeal; Ch.D., Chancery Division of the High Court of England and Wales; R.P.C., Restrictive Practices Court. Restrictive practices cases are referred to as L.R. (law reports) [volume number], R.P. [page number]. The other reports cited where available are the *All England Reports* (All E.R.) and *Weekly Law Reports* (W.L.R.) For cases not reported there, I have occasionally inserted a different citation, such as to the *All England Reports Reprint* (All E.R. Rep.) or to the old *Law Journal Reports*. Other citations are to journals– J.B.L., *Journal of Business Law*; M.L.R., *Modern Law Review*; O.E.P., *Oxford Economic Papers*. Page numbers in italics indicate the more important references.

Austin, re Austin Motor Co. Ltd's Agreements (1957) L.R. 1 R.P. 6; [1958] Ch. 61; [1957] 3 All E.R. 62; [1957] 3 W.L.R. 450 (Ch. D.) *95-6*, 97

Basic Slag, re British Basic Slag Ltd's Application: British Basic Slag Ltd v. Registrar of Restrictive Trading Agreements (1962) L.R. 3 R.P. 178; [1962] 3 All E.R. 247; [1962] 1 W.L.R. 986 (Ch. D.);   *96-7* (1963) L.R. 4 R.P. 116; [1963] 2 All E.R. 807; [1963] 1 W.L.R. 727 (C.A.) *96-9*, 133, 231

Birmingham Builders, re Birmingham Association of Building Trades Employers' Agreement (1963) L.R. 4 R.P. 54; [1963] 2 All E.R. 361; [1963] 1 W.L.R. 484 (R.P.C.)   *94*

Black Bolts (*No. 1*), re Black Bolt and Nut Association's Agreement (1960) L.R. 2 R.P. 50; [1960] 3 All E.R. 122; [1960] 1 W.L.R. 884 (R.P.C) *Comment* Yamey (1961) 24 M.L.R. 488   *132*, 139, 141, 143, 145, 157, 160, 161

British and American Cases

Löwenbräu München v. *Grunhalle Lager* International Ltd [1974] *Fleet St Reports*, 1; [1974] 1 C.M.L.R. 1   191

Magnets, re Permanent Magnet Association's Agreement (1962) L.R. 3 R.P. 119; [1962] 2 All E.R. 775; [1962] 1 W.L.R. 781 (R.P.C.)   *Comment* Yamey (1963) 26 M.L.R. 185   140, 142, 156

Mogul S.S. Co. Ltd v. *McGregor, Gow & Co. and Others* [1892] A.C. 25; [1891–1894] All E.R. Rep. 263; 61 L.J. Q.B. 295 (H.L.)   2–3, 94, 132

National Federation of Retail Newsagents', Booksellers' & Stationers' Agreement (No. 3) (1969) L.R. 7 R.P. 27; [1969] 3 All E.R. 97; [1969] 1 W.L.R. 875 (R.P.C.)   163

Net Books, re Net Book Agreement, 1957 (1962) L.R. 3 R.P. 246; [1962] 3 All E.R. 751; [1962] 1 W.L.R. 1347 (R.P.C.)   *Comment* Yamey (1963) 26 M.L.R. 691   145, 155, 156

Phenol, re Phenol Producers' Agreement (1960) L.R. 2 R.P. 1; [1960] 2 All E.R. 128; [1960] 1 W.L.R. 464 (R.P.C.)   140

Registrar of Restrictive Trading Agreements v. *W. H. Smith & Son* (1969) L.R. 7 R.P. 122; [1969] 3 All E.R. 1065; [1969] 1 W.L.R. 1460 (C.A.) 127

Schweppes Ltd v. Registrar of Restrictive Trading Agreements (1964) L.R. 5 R.P. 103; [1965] 1 All E.R. 195; [1965] 1 W.L.R. 157 (C.A.)   97, 126–7

Schweppes (*No. 2*) (1971) L.R. 7 R.P. 336; [1971] 2 All E.R. 1473; [1971] 1 W.L.R. 1148 (Ch.D.)   87, 99, 114, 115, 247

Schweppes (*No. 3*) Judgment of Cumming-Bruce, J. delivered 21 February 1975, *The Times* 24 February 1975   *Comment* [1975] J.B.L. (to be published July)   127

Scrap Iron, re British Iron and Steel Federation's Agreement; re National Federation of Scrap Iron, Steel and Metal Merchants' Agreements (1964) L.R. 4 R.P. 299   160

Scottish Bakers, re Wholesale and Retail Bakers of Scotland Association's Agreement; re Scottish Association of Master Bakers' Agreement (1959) L.R. 1 R.P. 347; [1959] 3 All E.R. 98; [1959] 1 W.L.R. 1094 (R.P.C.) 138, 140

Scottish Daily Newspapers, re Scottish Daily Newspaper Society's Agreement (No. 1) (1971) L.R. 7 R.P. 379; re Scottish Daily Newspaper Society's Agreement (No. 2) (1972) L.R. 7 R.P. 401   103, 143, 159, 163

Scottish Monumental Sculptors, re Scottish Master Monumental Sculptors' Association's Agreement (1965) L.R. 5 R.P. 437 (R.P.C.)   90, 92

Standard Metal Windows, re Standard Metal Window Group's Agreement (1962) L.R. 3 R.P. 198; [1962] 3 All E.R. 210; [1962] 1 W.L.R. 1020 (R.P.C.) *Comment* Yamey (1963) 26 M.L.R. 185; Hope (1965) 17 O.E.P. 376   140

Stilton Trade Mark 1966 [1967] Reports of Patent Cases 173 (Ch.D.)   113

Sulphur, re National Sulphuric Acid Association's Agreement (1963) L.R. 4 R.P. 169; [1963] 3 All E.R. 73; [1963] 1 W.L.R. 848 (R.P.C.) *Comment* Korah [1964] J.B.L., 65   146, 147, 149, 150, 151

re *Telephone Apparatus Manufacturers' Application* (1963) L.R. 3 R.P. 462; [1963] 2 All E.R. 302; [1963] 1 W.L.R. 463 (C.A.)   87, 108, 247

Telephones or *Traffic Lights*, Automatic Telephone and Electric Co. Ltd v. Registrar of Restrictive Trading Agreements (1964) L.R. 5 R.P. 135; [1965] 1 All E.R. 206; [1965] 1 W.L.R. 174 (C.A.)   97

Tiles, re Glazed and Floor Tile Home Trade Association's Agreement (1964) L.R. 4 R.P. 239 (R.P.C.) *Comment* Korah (1964) 3 *The Solicitor Quarterly* 318; Sutherland (1965) 17 O.E.P 385, 400   142, 161

Transformers, re Associated Transformer Manufacturers' Agreement (1961) L.R. 2 R.P. 295; [1961] 2 All E.R. 233; [1961] 1 W.L.R. 660 (R.P.C.)   140, 149, *150–1*, 152, 156, 159

Transformers (No. 2), re Associated Transformer Manufacturers' Agreement (1970) L.R. 7 R.P. 202; [1971] 1 All E.R. 409; [1970] 1 W.L.R. 1589   133

Tyre Mileage, re Mileage Conference Group of the Tyre Manufacturers' Conference Ltd's Agreement (1966) L.R. 6 R.P. 49; [1966] 2 All E.R. 849; [1966] 1 W.L.R. 1137 (R.P.C.)   97–8, 133.

U.S. v. *Addyston Pipe and Steel Co.* (1898) 85 Fed 271 (U.S. Federal, 6th circuit, affirmed (1899) 175 U.S. 211) L.B. Schwarz *Free Enterprise and Economic Organisation* 4th ed. 421; Areeda *Antitrust Analysis* 2nd ed. 263   13

Waste Paper, re British Waste Paper Association's Agreement (1963) L.R. 4 R.P. 29; [1963] 2 All E.R. 424; [1963] 1 W.L.R. 540 (R.P.C.)   87, 92

Wire Ropes, re Locked Coil Ropemakers' Association's Agreement; re Mining Rope Association's Agreement; re Wire Rope Manufacturers' Association's Agreement (1964) L.R. 5 R.P. 146; [1965] 1 All E.R. 382; [1965] 1 W.L.R. 121 (R.P.C.)   148, 151–2, 199

Yarn Spinners, re Yarn Spinners' Agreement (1959) L.R. 1 R.P. 118; [1959] 1 All E.R. 299; [1959] 1 W.L.R. 154   *137–8*, 145, 153–4, 160–1

287

British Reports

The reports of the Monopolies and Mergers Commission (and its predecessors) have been divided into Monopoly situations, Mergers and General. As the titles are long, I have listed those on monopoly situations by reference to the short description of the products referred. Where I have also referred to the dominant firm, that appears in brackets thereafter. Page numbers in italics indicate the more important references.

Board of Trade

Report on Radio Valves, 1946   1

Ministry of Works

Committee of Enquiry into the Distribution of Building Materials and Components, 1948   1

Committee on Cement Costs, 1946   1

Monopolies and Mergers Commission, Reports on Monopoly Situations

Asbestos
Report on the Supply of Asbestos and certain Asbestos Products, 1973, H.C.P. 3   55

Beer
Report on the Supply of Beer, 1969 H.C.P. 216   231, 235

Breakfast Cereals (Kelloggs)
Report on the Supply of Ready Cooked Breakfast Cereal Foods, 1973, H.C.P. 2.   24, 41

Calico Printing
Report on the Process of Calico Printing, 1954 H.C.P. 140   *91*, 99, 138, 154

British Reports

Monopolies and Mergers Commission, General Reports

Judgments of the Community Court

The first reference in each case is to the *European Court Reports*, the official English versions published by the Court. For judgments delivered before the accession of the U.K., the French version, *le Recueil de la Jurisprudence de la Court* (Rec.), is cited. The second citation is to the *Common Market Law Reports* (C.M.L.R.) and the third to the *Common Market Reporter* (C.M.R.) published by Commerce Clearing House. The following abbreviations for journals are used: C.M.L. Rev, *Common Market Law Review;* I.C.L.Q., *International and Comparative Law Quarterly;* I.I.C., *International Review of Industrial Property and Copyright Law;* J.B.L., *Journal of Business Law.* Page numbers in italics indicate the more important references.

Beguelin Import Co. v. S.A.G.L. Import-Export, case 22/71, (1971) 17 Rec. 949; [1972] C.M.L.R. 81; C.M.R. para. 8149.   *Comment* Joliet [1972] *Revue trimestrielle de droit européen* 427   236

Belgian Radio and Television, or *Belgische Radio en Televisie* v. *Fonior and S.A.B.A.M.*, case 127/73, [1974] E.C.R. 51 and 313; [1974] 2 C.M.L.R. 238; C.M.R. paras 8268 and 8269   *For comment see Brasserie de Haecht* v. *Wilkin* (No. 2)   173, 188, 191, 204

Braurie Bilger v. *Jehle*, case 43/69, (1970) 16 Rec. 127; [1974] C.M.L.R. 382; C.M.R. para. 8076   189, 190

Bosch v. De Geus, case 13/61, (1962) 8 Rec. 89; [1962] C.M.L.R. 1; C.M.R. para. 8003   188–9

Brasserie de Haecht v. *Wilkin Janssen* (*No. 1*), case 23/67, (1967) 13 Rec. 525; [1968] C.M.L.R. 26; C.M.R. para. 8053   232, 246

Brasserie de Haecht v. *Wilkin Janssen* (*No. 2*), case 48/72, [1973] E.C.R. 77; [1973] C.M.L.R. 287; C.M.R. para. 8170   *Comment* Vogelaar and Guy (1973) 22 I.C.L.Q. 648; Wertheimer (1973) 10 C.M.L.Rev. 386; Wael-

291

Judgments of the Community Courts

broeck [1974] *Cahiers de droit européen* 165; Gijlstra and Murphy [1974] *Legal issues of European integration* 79   189–92

Centrafarm v. *Sterling* and *Winthrop*, cases 15 and 16/74, [1974] E.C.R. ; [1974] 2 C.M.L.R. 480; C.M.R. para. 8246   *Comment* Joliet (1975) 28 *Current Legal Proglems* (not yet published); Cornish, [1975] J.B.L. 50; on exhaustion, see F. K. Beier, 'Territoriality of Trademark Law' (1970) 1 I.I.C. 48   xxi, 215, 217, *220–4*, 225, 226, 243

Commercial Solvents, Istituto Chemioterapico Italiano SpA and Commercial Solvents v. Commission E.C., cases 6 and 7/73, [1974] E.C.R. 223; [1974] 1 C.M.L.R. 309; C.M.R. para. 8209   *Comment* Korah [1974] J.B.L. 253; Korah [1974] 11 C.M.L.Rev. 248   173, 184–5, *204–6*, 207, 209, 223, 233, 234

Continental Can, Europemballage and Continental Can v. Commission E.C., case 6/72, [1973] E.C.R. 215; [1973] C.M.L.R. 199; C.M.R. para. 8171   *Comment* Joliet [1973] *Europarecht* 97; Korah (1973) 26 *Current Legal Problems* 82; Mestmacher (1972) 6 *World Trade Law* 615 and (1973) 7 *Ibid.* 36   200, *201–3*, 207

Deutsche Grammophon Gesellschaft v. Metro- SB- Grössmarkte, case 78/70, (1971) 17 Rec. 487; [1971] C.M.L.R. 631; C.M.R. para. 8106 *Comment* Korah (1972) 35 M.L.R. 634; W. Alexander (1971) *Cahiers de droit européen* 594   218, 220

Dyestuffs, I.C.I. and others v. Commission E.C., cases 48–69/72, (1972) 18 Rec. 619; [1972] C.M.L.R. 557; C.M.R. para. 8161   *Comment* Joliet [1974] *Cahiers de droit européen* 251; Korah (1973) 36 M.L.R. 220 174–8

Grundig, Consten and Grundig v. Commission E.C., cases 56 and 58/64, (1966) 12 Rec. 429; [1966] C.M.L.R. 418; C.M.R. para. 8046   *Comment* Joliet *The Rule of Reason* (see bibliography, p. 282), p. 156   *180–2*, 183–4, 214, 215, 216, 233, 237

S.A. *La Technique Minière* v. Maschinenbau Ulm G.m.b.H., case 56/65, (1966) 12 Rec. 337; [1966] C.M.L.R. 357; C.M.R. para. 8047   *Comment* Joliet, *Ibid* p. 166   182, 246

re *Noordwijks Cement Accoord*, S A. Cimenteries C.B.R. Cementsbedrijven N.V. v. Commission E.C., cases 8–11/66, (1967) 13 Rec. 93; [1967] C.M.L.R. 77   171, 209

Parfums Marcel Rochas Vertriebs-G.m.b.H. v. Bitsch, case 1/70, (1970) 16 Rec. 515; [1971] C.M.L.R. 104; C.M.R. para. 8102   187, 189

Parke, Davis & Co. v. *Probel*, case 24/67, (1968) 14 Rec. 81; [1968] C.M.L.R. 47; C.M.R. para. 8054   *217*, 219, 221, 248

Decisions of the Commission of the European Communities

The names by which the case is referred to in the text are italicised. The first reference in each case is to the *Journal Officiel* (*Official Journal* since accession of the U.K. to the Communities), the second is to the Common Market Law Reports—from 1966, the Commission's decisions have been included separately in the blue pages, the page numbers of which start with D. The final reference is to the *Common Market Reporter*. Page numbers in italics indicate the more important references.

Advocaat Zwarte Kip, Soenen-Bouckaert v. Cinoca S.A. and Van Olffen VB [1974] O.J. L237/12; [1974] 2 C.M.L.R. D79; C.M.R. paras 9669 and 9728   *Comment* Cornish [1975] J.B.L. 50, 54   *224–5*, 248

A.C.E.C./Berliet, re Ateliers de 'Constructions Electriques de Charleroi and Berliet [1968] J.O. L201/7; [1968] C.M.L.R. D35   *196–7*

Burroughs/Delplanque and *Burroughs/Geha* [1972] J.O. L13/50 and 53; [1972] C.M.L.R. D67 and D72; C.M.R. paras 9485 and 9486; 3 I.I.C. 259   *For comment see Davidson Rubber*   244

re *Cimbel* [1972] J.O. L303/24; [1973] C.M.L.R. D167; C.M.R. para. 9544   184

re *Clima Chappée*/Buderus [1969] J.O. 195/1; [1970] C.M.L.R. D7   194, 239, 248

Commercial Solvents. See Zoja

re *Continental Can* [1972] J.O. L7/25; [1972] C.M.L.R. D11; C.M.R. para. 9481   199–200, 202, 209

re *Davidson Rubber* [1972] J.O. L143/31; [1972] C.M.L.R. D52; C.M.R. para. 9512; 3 I.I.C. 528   *Comment* Korah [1972] J.B.L. 324; W. Alexander

[1973] *Cahiers de droit européen* 3; W. Alexander (1967/8) 5 C.M.L. Rev. 465   183, 196, 245-6, 255

Duro-Dyne/Europair [1974] O.J. C73/2; C.M.R. para. 9661; decision now published [1975] O.J. L29/11; [1975] 1 C.M.L.R. D62; C.M.R. para. 9708A. (The group exemption does not apply where a single distributor is allocated the whole of the Common Market.) *Comment* Korah [1975] J.B.L. (to be published April 1975)   185, 236

Dyestuffs [1969] J.O. L195/11; [1969] C.M.L.R. D23   *Comment* Korah [1972] J.B.L. 319   174-6, 210, 227

re *Eurofima* [1973] C.M.L.R. D217; C.M.R. para. 9654; press release from Commission, No. I.P. (73) 67, 16 April 1973   201

Fertilizer Cartels, Cobelaz and Others (No. 1) [1968] J.O. L276/13; [1968] C.M.L.R. D45; re Comptoir Français de l'Azote [1968] J.O. L276/29; [1968] C.M.L.R. D57; Kali und Salz/Kali Chemie, *see below*. Other decisions on fertilizer cartels in other parts of the Common Market are cited in *1st Report on Competition Policy*, para. 12.   185

Fine Papers, Papeteries Boilloré and Braunstein Frères S.A. [1972] J.O. 182/24; [1972] C.M.L.R. D94: C.M.R. para. 9523   195, 197, 236, 239

re *GEMA* [1971] J.O. L134/15; [1971] C.M.L.R. D35; C.M.R. para. 9438   *Comment* Joliet [1973] *Europarecht* 97   201, 203-4

Grundig/Consten [1964] J.O. 2545/64; [1964] C.M.L.R. 489   *Comment* Joliet *Rule of Reason* (see bibliography) 143   178-82, 197, 233

Henkel/*Colgate* [1971] J.O. L14/14; previously announced in re Research and Development [1971] C.M.L.R. D31; C.M.R. para. 9491   196, 213

re *Kabelmetal* [1974] O.J.C. 157/2; C.M.R. para. 9700   244

Kali und Salz/*Kali Chemie* [1973] O.J. L19/22; [1974] 1 C.M.L.R. D1; C.M.R. para. 9627   Appeal to be heard 1975   *Noted, Third Report on Competition Policy*, para. 49   236

Limeburners' Convention [1969] J.O. L122/8; [1969] C.M.L.R. D15; C.M.R. para. 9303   183

Pittsburg Corning Europe, Formica Belgium/Hertel [1972] J.O. L272/35; [1973] C.M.L.R. D2: C.M.R. para. 9539   238-9

Polyester Fibres (1972) *Second Report on Competition Policy* para. 31   209

Statutes and Statutory Instruments, United Kingdom and United States

Statutes are listed chronologically. Page numbers in italics indicate the more important references.

297

Treaties and Subordinate Legislation Made Thereunder

Page numbers in italics indicate the more important references.

302

Treaties and Subordinate Legislation Made Thereunder

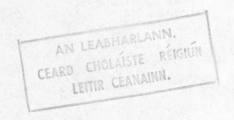

Index

Page numbers in italics indicate the more important references.

Absolute territorial protection 179, 182. *And see* Restriction, territorial
Accession agreement 186–7, 191, 238
Accounts 27–8, 67. And *see* Inflation accounting
Advertising 8, 9, 33–4, 42, 72–3, 105, 112, 179, 220, 224–5. *And see* Dominant position
Advisory Committee of Commission of the European Communities 214, 230, 234
Advocate General 172
Affirmative resolution of both Houses of Parliament 30, 33, 57
Agency 193, *238–9*
Aggregated discounts 81–2, 157–8
Agreement
  Dead or filleted *87*, 96, 131–2
  Common Market law 172–96
    accession 186–7, 191
    distinction between new and old 186–92
    made before establishment of Common Market, but continuing to have effects 189, 217, 224
    object or effect of restricting competition 178–83, 194, 232
    prohibited pro tanto 181
    single, may underlie a series of contracts 187
    And see Market analysis, need for, Provisional validity, Trade between Member States, affect
  horizontal
    aggregated discounts 81–2, 157–8
    boycott and discrimination 2–3, 20, 71, 81–2, 92–3, 124, 128, 136, 149
    exclusive dealing 20, 81–2, *93*, 100, 194, 203–4
    price fixing 1, 3–6, 7–8, 13, 20, 82, 87–90, 184

    price recommendation 90, 184, 233. *And see* Trade association, recommendation
    production limiting 5–6, 82, 91–102, 103
    joint ventures 96, 115–16, 117–18
    market sharing 2, 13, 82, 86, 91–4, 99, 103
    quotas 86, 91, 99
    rationalization 103, 115
    resale price maintenance 13, 81–2, 84, 90
    specialization *194–6*, 228, 229, 235–6, 237, *239–41*, 248, 283
    tender rigging 127, 155
    And see Horizontal combination
  vertical
    exclusive dealing 38–40, 86, 93, *104–6*, 178–82, 189–91, *193–4*, 196–7, *230–8*
    resale price maintenance 83, 84, 90, *101–2*, 104, 233
    tying 39, 44
    And see Vertical combinations
  And see Monopolies and Mergers Commission, functions, complex monopoly situation, Patent licence, Restriction, Restrictive Practices Court *and* Trade association
Agreements, made void 2–3, 15, 83, 94, 128, 131–2, 171, 174, 185–6, *188–92*, 232–3, 234, 241, 255, *268*
  interlocutory relief 191, 235, 240
Agreements to which Part I of the 1956 Act applies 82–3, 85–123
  directions not to refer to Court *116–18*, 158, 161, 163, 228, 239, 254
  exceptions 100–15, 118, 122
  exemption 115–16
  And see Goods, Restrictions and Services

Department of Prices and Consumer Affairs, *ctd*
  vise, after adverse report of Commission 25, 26, *29–35*
  reference to Commission 20, 21, 24, 25, 64–6
  registration, power to call up agreements for 85, 89, 120–3
Depreciation 47–8
Devlin, Lord 136, 137, 138, 143, 145, 153
Diplock, Lord xi–xvi, 127, 139, 141, 143, 160
Director General of Fair Trading
  functions for consumer protection 14
  functions under 1956 Act 14, 82, 124–34, 229, 256
    maintain register 82, 122, 124–30
    refer agreements to Court 82–3, 122, 131, 229
  general directions from Minister, subject to 21
  monopoly functions 21
  mergers panel, chairman of 64–6
  office of 14, 21
  power to negotiate undertakings from dominant firm, or after merger report 30, 33, 72
  power to refer supply or export of goods where monopoly situation exists 14, 21
Discovery of documents 97, 125–7
Discrimination 28, *36–7*, 38, 71, 205, 216, 222–3
  collective, *see* Agreements
Dominant position 253–6
  abuse 186, 200–8
    justification 206, 207–8
  definition of *3–6, 148–9, 199–200*
    barriers to entry 1, 4–5, 35, 45–6, 202, 230
      advertising and sales promotion 9, 33, 37–8, 105, 112
      exclusivity conferred by law 4–5, 105, 230–1
      minimum scale large in relation to market 5, 43, 45
      patents 4, 31, 40–1, 106, 184, 202, 242
      tariffs xviii, 14–15, 45, 46–7, 168
    countervailing power 66–7, 70, 145–52
    potential competition 3, 35, 70, 199–200, 202
    prices, limits to power to raise 5–6, 70
    substitute products 4, 6, 9, 46, 54, 71, 148–9, 199–200, 253
  public interest 6–7, 35–47, 253–6.
    And see Dominant position, abuse *and* Public interest

steps taken to preserve 1, 13, 35–44, 146, 201–2
  advertising 37–8, 41–2
  conglomerate mergers 65, 67
  discrimination 2–3, 36–7, 40, 71, 205–6
  foreclosing customers or suppliers 2–3, 38–40, 66, 71, 72, 78, 207, 230
  horizontal mergers 55, 66, 69, 202, 207–8
  long term exclusive dealing agreements 38–40, 203–4, 230–1, 232
  loyalty discounts 2, 40
  patents, use of 40–1, 45, 106
  predatory pricing 3, 36–7, 146
  prices, uniform delivered 36–7
  refusal to supply 205–6
  tying 39, 44, 71
  vertical mergers 38, 66, 207
Double barrier theory 14–15, 101, *227–30*
Drugs 136, 216, 217, 222

Enforcement 12
  Community law, of 186, 208–14
  monopolies legislation, orders and undertakings 29–35, 67, 72, 105
  And see Orders and undertakings, Notification *and* Registration
Equity share capital, *see* Shares in a company
European Coal and Steel Community xix, 101, 174
European Economic Community xviii, 167–72
  constitution 170–2
European Free Trade Area xix
Evidence 25, *26–9*, 69, 83, 97, 125–30, 153–4, 162–3, 176, 177, 211–14. *And see* Restrictive Practices Court, standard of proof
Exceptions from Part I of 1956 Act 100–15, 118, 122
  subject to Community law 228
Exclusive dealing 86, 104–6, 193, 230–8. *And see* Agreement
Exemptions from article 85(1) *192–7*, 228–9, 233–41
  benefits to consumers 196–7
  economic benefits 193–6, 228, 234
  exclusive competence of Commission 188, 192
  group 228, 229, *233–8, 240–1*, 247, 255, 256
  individual 192–7, 228, 239–40
Exemptions from restrictive practices legislation 115–18, 228
Export agreements 109, 113–14, 119–20, 159, 212

Nationalized industries 5, 11, 32, 33, 201
Negative clearance 57, 183, *186*, 228
Newspaper transfers 72–8
    definition 74–6
Notices issued by Commission of the European Communities 182, 238, 239–40, 242–5
Notification 186–7, 211. *And see* Registration (*for U.K.*) *and* Provisional validity (*for E.E.C.*)

Oligopoly *8*, 42, 54, 63, 88, 98–9, 143, 175–8, 199. *And see* Arrangement *and* Concerted practices
Orders and undertakings
    after adverse report of Monopolies and Mergers Commission 23, *29–35*, 46–7, 57, 67, *72*, 105
    calling up agreements for registration 85, 89, 120–3, 124
    civil courts, by 2–3, 34, 84. *And see* Civil law remedy
    by Commission of the European Communities to terminate infringement 186, 207, 209, 210–11, 214
        negative clearance 186
    divestiture 32–3, 55–6, 57, 72, 98, 207, 210
    Restrictive Practices Court, by 83, 96, 98, 131–4, 163–4
Parallel imports 168–9, 179, 215–26, 233, 237. *And see* Restriction, territorial
Parallel pricing 199. *And see* Oligopoly
Parliamentary questions 21, 135
Partnership 115, 146, 147, 173
Passing off action 225
Patent 31, 40–1, 106, 184, 215–7, 220–3
    compulsory licence 40–1, *106*
    exhaustion 215, 216
    function of 106, 242
        specific object of 218, 220, 243
    public interest 40–1, 106, 248
    And see Industrial property rights
Patent, Draft Convention for Community 216, 249
Patent licence *106–110*, 169, 234, *241–9*
    arbitration 245
    compulsory 40–1, *106*,
    cross, *see* Patent pool
    exclusive 107, 244, 245–6, 255
    grantback clause 107, 109, 243–5
    'knowhow', confidentiality of 245, 248
    limited 107–9, 215, 222–3, 225, 242–3, 247
    multiple parallel 243, 244–6
    'no challenge' clause *246*, 247

public interest 109–10, 242–9 *passim*
quality standards 244, 245
territorial restriction 242–3, 246–7
theory of inherent right of patent 107, 108, *242–3*
Patent pool 107–10, 244, 247, 256
Patents, multiple parallel 107, 244–6
Pearson, J. 140, 143
Pickering, Dr 84
Planning, more desirable than competition? 9–11
Post–contractual restraints 88–90
Potential competition 202
Preliminary rulings 171–2
Preponderant buyer or seller 133, 147–52, 159, 201, 216
Price agreements, difficult to maintain 5, 157–8
Price and wage control 11, 19, 43, 100, 116, 175, 201, 215, 222
Price leadership 98–9, 148, 174–8. *And see* Oligopoly
Prices, *see* Dominant position *and* Public interest
    recommended 90, 174
    uniform delivered 36–7
Product differentiation 9. *And see* Advertising *and* Trade mark
Provisional validity 185–6, 188–92
Public interest *35–47*, *66–72*, *76–78*, 105–6, *134–64*, 167
    alleged benefits of collaboration or dominance 10, 52–3
    buyers need not 'go shopping' 141–2, 157
    capacity maintained 138, 142
    consumers, to 136–45, 196–7, 205–6, 207, 220, 224–5, 226
    cost savings 10, 35, 38, 43, 45, 67, 77, 141, 158, 194, 235, 239
    counteract dominant firm 145–52, 195
    counteract local unemployment 152–4
    distribution to 39, 144, 193–4, 196, 234–8
    duplication eliminated 77, 194
    economies of scale 70, 77. *And see* cost savings *and* large plants
    economic and technical progress promoted 196
    efficiency increased 35, 38, 67, 68, 194, 239
    exports encouraged 114, 154–7
    final consumers, to 197, 205–6
    investment, reduced risk to 10, 139, *142*, 144, 156
    large plants *10*, 35, 37, 43, 45, 53, 55, 67, 195
    natural monopoly 10, 67, 201, 204, 205
    orderly marketing 114

309

Index

Public Interest, *ctd.*

    prices lower than they would otherwise be 43, 138, 140–4, 239–41

    price stability 10, 47, *137–8*, 142–3, 162

    production runs longer 43, 47, 194, 195, 196, 239

    production, to 10, 38, 45, 67, 194, 196, 235

    quality higher than otherwise 46, 138–9, 162

    rationalization 10, 55, 70, 103, 194, 196, 239–41

    research and development encouraged 10, 106, 144, 156

    research and development, collaboration in, productive 10, 70, 139–40, 142, 144, 145, 194–6

    safety 136

    service better than otherwise 46

    standardization 35, 142

    technical and economic progress 196

    unemployment reduced 152–4, 162

alleged detriments to public of market power and restrictive agreements 6–8, *159–61*

    capacity reduced 5–8, 70

    common market partitioned 172, 180, 183, 213, 215–26, 256

    exports lost 160, 197

    foreclose suppliers or customers, ability to 38–40, 66, 77

    prices higher than in competitive market 4, 6, 7, 13, 23, 27–8, 41–3, 119, 152, 160, 248

    rigidity of prices 154

    rigidity of structure 84, 119, 144

    rigidity of trading methods 84, 119

    resources misallocated 7, 119, 160–1

    services proliferated 8, 84, 141, 144

    single set of decisions 7

    spur to efficiency reduced 7, 68, 117, 144

    spur to new developments reduced 70, 84, 107, 119, 144

    undemocratic 10

issues that are hard to judge (*and see* Restrictive Practices Court, whether issues justiciable)

    efficiency 23, 41–3, 46–7, *67–9*, 70, 201

    level of prices *13*, 23, 27–8, 30–1, 41–3, 45–7, 133, 140–4, 201, 248

    level of profits 23, 27–8, 41–3, 45–7, 138, 248

    And see Cartels, Dominant position *and* Mergers

Quantitative restrictions by governments 168, 215

Refusal to supply 71, 93, 184, 205–6. *And see* Discrimination

Register, 124–5

Registrar of Restrictive Trading Agreements 88, 89, 95, 97

    functions transferred to Director General 82

Registration (*for E.E.C.*, *see* Notification) 81–2, 124–30

    duty to furnish particulars 124–5

    Director's powers of investigation 97, 125–30, 163, 164, 255

    sanctions for failure 96, 128–30

    time for 124

    And see Agreements to which Part I of the 1956 Act applies

Regulation 171

Relator action 211

Resale price maintenance

    collective 13, 81–2, 84, 90

    individual 83, *84*, 101–2, 233

Research and development, *see* Patent *and* Public interest

Restraint of trade at common law 2–3, 94, *105–6*

Restriction of supplies, to increase price 5–6

Restrictions 83, 85, 86, 94

    accepted by two or more persons 86, 120, 230

    advertising, on 14

    ancillary 157–8

    coal and steel producers, between 101, 229

    defined 86, 94, 99

    exports, on 179–80, 188–9

    found contrary to the public interest 83. *And see* Orders and undertakings

    goods, relating to, *see* Goods, supply of

    indispensable 159, 197

    insignificant 116–18

    licensing, on 107, 112

    market sharing 2, 13, 82, 86, 91–4, 99, 103

    patent licence, in, *see* Patent licence

    post-contractual 88–90

    prices, in respect of 1, 13, 20, 82, 87–90, 107, 112

    quotas 91, 99

    relating exclusively to the goods supplied 101–2

    secrecy of knowhow 245, 248

    services, relating to, *see* Services, supply of

    severance of 156, *159*, 181, 182

    terms or conditions, in respect of 90–1, 157, 158

310

Restrictions, *ctd.*
  territorial 102, 104–5, 107, *179–80,*
    181, 182, 215–23, 225, 233, 237,
    242–3, 246–7
  tying 39, 44
  workmen, accepted by 25–6
  workmen, in respect of 102–3
  And see Agreement
Restrictive Practices Court xviii
  composition of 82–3, *135,* 162
  functions of, whether issues justi-
    ciable 12, 83, 134–5, 137–9, 141,
    143–4, 153–4, 161–5
  orders by and undertakings to 83,
    96, 98, *131–4,* 163–4, 254
  procedure of 29, 83, 162–3
    time and cost 115, 254
  public interest 12, 83, *134–64*
  standard of proof 135, 141, 143–4,
    145, 155, 160
Restrictive Trade Practices Bill 12, 82,
86, 104, 126, 146, 155
Russell, J. 139, 140, 143, 149, 150, 151,
152, 156, 162

Sanctions, *see* Agreements made void,
Civil law remedy, *and* Orders and
Registration
Secretary of State, *see* Department of
Prices and Consumer Affairs
Secrets 110, 124, 207, 212, 245, 248.
And see Confidentiality
Sector enquiry 212, 232
Services, supply of, subject to control
13–14, 22, 24, 85, 90, *118–23,* 124,
160
Shares in a company, 50, 64, 75.
And see Corporate group
Stamp, J. 99, 114, 115, 133
State aids 170
Statistics, available often inappro-
priate 27, 45
'Steps taken', *see* Dominant position
and Monopolies and Mergers Com-
mission, functions of

Stevens, Professor R. 144
Substitute products, customers or
suppliers, *see* Dominant position *and*
Market, definition of

Tariffs xviii, 1, 14, 15, 45, 46–7, 168
Thorneycroft, Mr Peter 146
Tort 2, 34, 128
Trade associations 1, 2–3, 13, 14,
19–20, 28, 84, 86, 90, 91–2, 93, 99–100,
102, 109, 113, 118, 122, 125, 174
  recommendations 90, 99–100, 117,
    122, 125, 149, 174, 184
Trade between Member States, affect
183–5, 187, 206, 228, 233, 234, 244
Trade marks 9, 84, 111–13, *179–82,*
216, 217–18, 219–20, 223–6, 245, 248
  function 111–12, 218, 220, 224
Trade secrets, *see* Confidentiality *and*
Secrets
Traders' lists, *see* Agreements, hori-
zontal, exclusive dealing
Transport 174
Turner, Professor Donald 242
Tying 39, 44

Undertaking
  (promise), *see* Orders and under-
    takings
  (firm) 173–4, 180, 198–9, 205, 223
Unfair competition 179, 225
Upjohn, J. 95, 97, 150, 151, 155, 160

Vertical combinations 38–40, 63,
65–7, 77, 101–15, 180, 182, 230–41
Voluntary groups 117, 125, 158, 254

Wade Mr 86
Williams, Mrs Shirley 20, 121. *And
see* Department of Prices and Consu-
mer Affairs
Willmer, J. 97
Witnesses, trade 83, 163
Workers' restrictive practices 25–6

Yamey, Professor B. 150

Strategies for Survival

Carter G. Woodson Institute Series

Deborah E. McDowell, *Editor*

STRATEGIES
FOR SURVIVAL

Recollections of Bondage

in Antebellum Virginia

William Dusinberre

University of Virginia Press   *Charlottesville & London*

University of Virginia Press

© 2009 by the Rector and Visitors of the University of Virginia
Printed in the United States of America on acid-free paper

First published 2009

9 8 7 6 5 4 3 2 1

Library of Congress Cataloging-in-Publication Data

Dusinberre, William, 1930–
Strategies for survival : recollections of bondage in Antebellum
Virginia / William Dusinberre.
    p.   cm. — (Carter G. Woodson Institute series)
  Includes bibliographical references and index.
  ISBN 978-0-8139-2822-7 (cloth : alk. paper)
    1. Slaves—Virginia—Social conditions—19th century.
2. Slaves—Virginia—Biography. 3. African Americans—
Virginia—Interviews. 4. Agent (Philosophy)—Case studies.
5. Slavery—Virginia—History—19th century. 6. Virginia—Race
relations—History—19th century. I. Title.
  E445.V8D87 2009
  326´.0975509034—dc22   2008054102

To Juliet
with love

Contents

Acknowledgments

My greatest obligation is to Roscoe Lewis, the Hampton Institute professor who in 1936 and 1937 organized the interviewing of elderly former slaves in Virginia that lies at the heart of the present book. Lewis recruited as interviewers mainly African Americans, to whom the former slaves spoke remarkably candidly. Many of their interviews might nevertheless have remained unpublished had it not been for the editorial work, some forty years later, of Charles L. Perdue Jr., Thomas E. Barden, and Robert K. Phillips, all of whose activity has been indispensable to me.

Dr. John A. Thompson and Dr. Michael Tadman very good-heartedly postponed their own work in order to read early versions of my manuscript. The text has benefited hugely from their criticisms, and I am most grateful to them for their interest in the project. Errors and infelicities of expression that remain are of course my own responsibility. I owe a special debt to Professor Charles Joyner, a staunch ally, whose expert scholarly advice and generous friendship have been for many years vital to my work.

My sister, Nancy Blake—an early reader of the manuscript—observed that it focused on how people managed to survive even the most dreadful of conditions. That comment led to the book's title. Afterward I realized that in my subconscious had lain the memory of a first-rate article by Jim Roark and Michael Johnson, "Strategies of Survival," and I apologize to them for having lifted, and adapted, their words.

I have had the good fortune to spend most of my working life in the splendid history department of the University of Warwick, which has had an incalculable influence on my approach to history. The writing of this book is intended, in some degree, as a small payback to colleagues there whose intellectual vigor has been so important in shaping my own interests. I have also benefited enormously from the stimulating meetings of the University of Cambridge's American history research seminar and from the extraordinary kindness and support over many years of John Thompson, Betty Wood, Tony Badger, Michael O'Brien, and William Brock. Similarly, I have derived huge benefit from the stimulus and support of generous colleagues in the association of British American Nineteenth Century Historians. I am grateful to the staff of the Cambridge University Library for their many instances of quiet, efficient professional assistance. I am particularly grateful to Ian Agnew of the University of Cambridge geography department, who yet again has expertly made my maps, and to Andrew Leader, Girton College's computing officer, who extricated me from many technological quagmires. For personal favors I am indebted to, among others, Larry O'Brien, Tim Lockley, Mary S. Clark, and William Link.

I owe a vast amount to other scholars of antebellum Virginia. These include especially Brenda Stevenson, Philip Schwarz, Lynda Morgan, Joshua Rothman, Peter Wallenstein, Midori Takagi, Ronald Lewis, and William Link, as well as a host of other experts named in the book's endnotes. The enthusiasm and encouragement of the staff of the University of Virginia Press, and particularly of Richard Holway, have been very much appreciated. I owe a great deal to Carol Sickman-Garner for her meticulous copy-editing, especially for her skill in clarifying many of my convoluted sentences and for the phenomenal accuracy of her work. Ruth Steinberg has been a most excellent and judicious project editor

My family has been wonderfully supportive. My mother, Charlotte Snelson, was still at 106 my strongest backer. Martin Dusinberre's astute advice has been invaluable, and Asuka Dusinberre's interest has been inspiriting. Edward and Beth Dusinberre have generously encouraged the project and shared their expertise with me. Juliet Dusinberre has, in every way, done the most of all.

Strategies for Survival

Introduction

This book presents a view of antebellum North American slavery as experienced by the slaves themselves. Although it focuses on the state of Virginia, I believe most of its conclusions are suggestive for nearly all of the "Middle South" and for most of the "Deep South."[1] The book discusses how far slaves' experiences varied depending on whether they had a "good" master or not; whether they lived in a city or not; and whether they were members of a privileged "third caste" or not. It attempts to define the nature and the extent of the slaves' oppression, and to convey what that oppression meant to the lives of individual people. It assesses bondpeoples' responses to their oppression—the nature of the slaves' dissidence, the character of their religion, the effect of slavery upon their family lives, and the means by which some bondpeople sought to develop their individual talents. At the heart of the present book lies the question, What was the balance between the master's power and the agency of the slaves?[2]

Modern writers, when dealing with this question of the slaves' "agency," have sharply reversed direction. They once treated slaves as the nearly defenseless victims of an oppressive system, but bondpeople later came to be seen as heroically resisting the constraints of a system that offered surprisingly many ways for the oppressed to create for themselves rich and vibrant lives. More recently, a compromise has emerged between these two approaches. But we still need a comprehensive assessment of where the balance lay between oppression and self-determination.

One difficulty arises from the sources used by each school of historians. Those stressing oppression (e.g., Kenneth Stampp, *The Peculiar Institution*) have depended largely on plantation records

1

kept by white people, and on accounts published by white travelers—
sources that offer only limited insight into the ways slaves responded
to their oppression.[3] Historians stressing the slaves' self-determination
(e.g., John Blassingame, *The Slave Community*) have sometimes relied
substantially on memoirs published before 1861 by fugitive slaves—a heroic but unrepresentative group of former bondpeople who often wrote
with abolitionist purpose.[4] Other historians (e.g., Eugene Genovese, *Roll,
Jordan, Roll*) have depended heavily on interviews conducted in the 1930s
by mainly white interviewers with aged black survivors. The racial "etiquette" of the time probably impelled many of these interviewees to dis-
semble. They flattered their white interlocutors that masters had often
been kindly, and the slaves happy. This tendency aided the perpetuation
of the view that American slavery was an essentially paternalist system.[5]
Reliance on interviews conducted by black interviewers might help to
modify this view.

In Virginia there has been preserved an extraordinarily rich set of interviews conducted by black Works Progress Administration (WPA) interviewers, in 1937.[6] Elsewhere in the South the great majority of the WPA
interviewers were white. But nearly all of the 159 Virginia interviews were
conducted by black people.[7] The Virginia interviewees appear to have spo-
ken much more frankly than they would have done to white interviewers.
Their interviews can be supplemented by a variety of other sources. These
include the testimony of eighteen Virginia slaves who escaped to Canada
and were interviewed there by a sympathetic white interviewer in 1855.[8]
Several former Virginia slaves were interviewed in the years immediately
after the Civil War; and a handful of former Virginia slaves published accounts of their bondage. By relying on these sources and others, one may
be able to apprehend the slaves' experience of bondage more successfully
in Virginia than in any other state.

To focus on Virginia may nevertheless seem a doubtful strategy. The
principal cash crops in Virginia were tobacco and wheat, not the cotton
that dominated the Deep South. It must indeed be acknowledged that
Virginia's system of slavery was marked by distinctive features. Slave
plantations had been longer established in Virginia than elsewhere, and
malaria did not drive rich Virginia planters away from their homes for
six months each year (as it did Low Country South Carolina planters).
Consequently, a regime developed that should have been more paternal-

ist than anywhere else in America. The relative proximity of free states (in contrast, say, to the situation in Mississippi) made the possibility of a slave's escaping permanently to the North substantially greater than in the Deep South; and anxiety not to goad slaves into permanent flight might be expected to have fostered a less harsh regime in Virginia than in the Deep South. On the other hand, Virginia's financial dependence on exporting thousands of slaves annually to the Cotton Kingdom was likely to have made the slaves' family attachments less secure than may have been the case in the Deep South. Thus, Virginia, like every other region in the South, was in some respects sui generis; and the variety of conditions encountered by slaves in Virginia was as great as it was anywhere else in the South. The experience of slaves in Virginia may nevertheless offer general insight into the world of Southern slaves.

The central justification for focusing here on Virginia is my conviction that in certain important respects slavery was virtually the same system in all of those major regions of the South where slaves comprised more than about 15 percent of the total population. Despite the exportation of hundreds of thousands of slaves, more bondpeople still lived in Virginia in 1860 than in any other state; and thousands of other slaves—by then resident in the Cotton Kingdom—had been raised and acculturated in Virginia before being exported. Thus, Virginia's slaves formed a crucial element in the whole slave system. No doubt the border slave states— Delaware, Maryland, Kentucky, and Missouri—were different, as were the mountainous areas of some other Southern states (principally eastern Tennessee, and those counties of western Virginia that by 1863 had seceded from the rest of the state in order to create the Unionist state of West Virginia). But elsewhere slavery, in certain of its fundamentals, was a single system. The society of each major Southern region was dominated by an entrepreneurial class of slavemasters. Furthermore, the laws of slavery were virtually uniform throughout the South: slaves were property, they could not testify in court against a white man, their family lives were legally unprotected. In each of those major Southern regions where slaves comprised more than about 15 percent of the population, there resided large classes of politically enfranchised white yeoman farmers, and of relatively poor whites, whose racial anxieties and economic and social aspirations impelled them to support the slave system. Although there were of course significant differences between the South's major regions, in many respects the slave systems of the Cotton Kingdom, and even of the Rice Kingdom and the Sugar Kingdom, resembled that of the Tobacco (and Wheat) Kingdom. Consequently, the experiences of slaves in Mississippi, in South Carolina, in Louisiana, and in Virginia were comparable. To apprehend the tenor of slave life in Virginia is to apprehend it— in broad outline—nearly everywhere in the Middle South and in the Deep South.

It may be worth glancing briefly at the history of slavery in Virginia, identifying the four principal slaveholding regions of the state. Since the seventeenth century, when slavery was established in North America, there had been more slaves in Virginia than anywhere else on the continent. This remained true even in 1860, when the number of the state's bondpeople had grown to half a million. When the frontier moved westward between 1790 and 1860, half a million more Virginia slaves had been forcibly removed from the state to labor in Kentucky, Tennessee, and, especially, the Southwestern cotton belt.[9] Considering that the total number of American bondpeople in 1860 was about four million, it is clear that the state's slaves had always played a central role in the whole Southern economy.

At first Virginia's slaves grew tobacco. The voracious European demand for that weed made the fortunes of many Virginia planters, including those who played a dominant role in the American Revolution. Then, during nearly the whole thirty-six-year period from 1789 until 1825, the American presidency was held by a series of Virginia slavemasters—George Washington, Thomas Jefferson, James Madison, and James Monroe. The profits from growing tobacco were so great—and tobacco's exhaustion of the soil so speedy—that its cultivation had spread remarkably early (well before 1775) from the older eastern counties of Virginia into the newer Piedmont region. But agricultural depression, and soil exhaustion in the east, had there impelled (again remarkably early) a shift from tobacco to grain cultivation.[10]

By 1860, then, the state of Virginia comprised four markedly different regions (see map 1). First, in Eastern Virginia (and in the northern Piedmont), tobacco cultivation had long since been abandoned, but some proprietors still made large profits by using slave labor to raise wheat and corn. Second, in Virginia's Tobacco Belt (in the central and south-

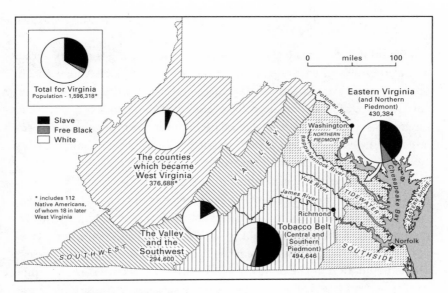

Map 1. Four regions of Virginia, 1860

Table 1. Population by Groups in Four Virginia Regions (1860)

Region	Total	Slave	Free black	White
Eastern Virginia and Northern Piedmont	430,384 (100%)	174,950 (40.6%)	32,475 (7.5%)	222,959 (51.8%)
Tobacco Belt (central and southern Piedmont)	494,646 (100%)	254,447 (51.4%)	16,004 (3.2%)	224,195 (45.3%)
Valley and the Southwest	294,600 (100%)	44,306 (15.0%)	5,675 (1.9%)	244,619 (83.0%)
Counties That Became West Virginia	376,688 (100%)	17,162 (4.6%)	4,000 (1.1%)	355,526 (94.4%)
Total Virginia (1860 boundaries)	1,596,318 (100%)	490,865 (30.7%)	58,154[a] (3.6%)	1,047,299 (65.6%)

Sources: U.S. Bureau of Census, Population (1860), 516-18; Susan Carter et al., Historical Statistics of the United States, 1: 359, 368, 2: 376. The names of the counties included in each of my four regions are listed in my appendix. In my "Tobacco Belt" I include—in addition to the twenty-four counties discussed in Lynda Morgan's *Emancipation in Virginia's Tobacco Belt, 1850-1870*—seven other counties (Caroline, Chesterfield, Dinwiddie, Greene, Hanover, Orange, and Spottsylvania). These all, except Greene, produced over 1,000,000 pounds of tobacco in 1859.

Note: Because of rounding, percentages do not add exactly to 100.0 percent.

[a] Includes 112 Native Americans, of whom 18 were later in West Virginia.

ern Piedmont), tobacco production was booming during the 1850s; grain
was also grown in this region. Third, in the Shenandoah Valley and in
Southwestern Virginia, mixed farming—grain, livestock, and some tobacco—often still depended on slave labor, but to much less extent than
farther east. Finally, slavery was relatively unimportant in most of the
large northwestern region, which seceded from Virginia during the Civil
War and formed the Unionist state of West Virginia.[11]

Virginia's slaves were concentrated in the first two regions. In the east
(and in the northern Piedmont) over 40 percent of the total population
were slaves. In the Tobacco Belt the proportion was even higher: this region resembled the states of South Carolina and Mississippi, where slaves
outnumbered free people. By contrast, slaves made up just 15 percent
of the population of the Shenandoah Valley and Southwestern Virginia.
And, except in one or two isolated areas, slaves never comprised a large
proportion of the people living in the future state of West Virginia.[12]

By 1860 a little more than one-third of the state's slaves (175,000 of
them) still lived in Eastern Virginia, or in those northern Piedmont counties where wheat was the main crop.[13] In the competition between raising
wheat with slave labor in Virginia, and raising it with free labor in the
Northern states, Virginia planters were surprisingly successful. While it
is true that the very largest planters of the antebellum South were concentrated in the Deep South—where they raised cotton, rice, or sugar—
eight of Virginia's ten largest planters actually grew wheat. These included
Richard Baylor, Virginia's largest grain producer, who owned 520 slaves;
William Allen, with 446 slaves; Williams Carter, with 427 slaves; and two
other Virginia wheat planters who each owned over 250 slaves. Another
great East Virginia wheat planter was William Tayloe, who, in addition
to 169 Virginia slaves, owned 325 out-of-state bondpeople, mainly on
his Alabama cotton plantations. Philip St. George Cocke was a Virginia
wheat planter who owned 283 slaves in the state, as well as 375 more on his
Mississippi cotton plantations. And James Galt was the last of these great
Virginia wheat planters; he owned 251 slaves in the central Piedmont.[14]

The income from a big wheat plantation could be huge, rivaling that of
a Deep South cotton plantation. Thus, in 1853 William Allen grossed over
$40,000 from his grain sales—this at a time when a plantation overseer
was likely to earn less than $500 a year, and even the governor of Virginia
was paid only a $5,000 annual salary.[15] In Eastern Virginia wheat was gen-

erally raised on the richer river-bottom lands, while corn to feed the slaves and the livestock (and to sell) was grown on the uplands. Of course, most of Virginia's wheat producers owned many fewer slaves than did these grandees; but the fact that an established slavemaster like Richard Baylor bought another huge (4,500-acre) East Virginia wheat plantation in 1852 suggests that the shift from tobacco to wheat production had not ruined every member of the Virginia gentry.[16] The typical East Virginia slave seems to have worked on a plantation of between 20 and 25 slaves.[17]

In 1860 over half of Virginia's slaves (more than 250,000 of them) lived in the central and southern Piedmont region, where the great bulk of the state's tobacco was now grown.[18] Although, even in the Piedmont, low prices had led to a slight shift away from tobacco growing during the 1840s, higher prices in the 1850s had elicited a doubling of the state's tobacco harvest. Two of Virginia's great slaveholders—Ruth Hairston and her first cousin Samuel Hairston—lived in the southern Piedmont, where together they owned nearly 500 slaves (and Ruth owned almost 500 more across the border in North Carolina). Their slaves produced corn and cotton, as well as tobacco.[19] Most tobacco farmers of course owned many fewer slaves than did the Hairstons. But the average Piedmont tobacco farmer seems to have owned as many slaves as—or even more than—the typical East Virginia wheat planter; and the proportion of Tobacco Belt farmers who owned slaves was greater than elsewhere in Virginia.[20]

In 1860 less than one-tenth of Virginia's slaves (some 45,000 of them) lived in the Shenandoah Valley, or were scattered in the hilly counties of Southwest Virginia, where the average slaveholding farmer owned considerably fewer bondpeople than did Piedmont farmers.[21] And less than 4 percent of Virginia's slaves (about 17,000 of them) lived in the region that became West Virginia.[22]

Although conditions of life for slaves varied somewhat from one region of Virginia to another, one factor was constant: slaves born in Virginia stood a substantial chance of being uprooted from their native soil and forcibly moved out of the state. Between 1790 and 1810 most of the enslaved émigrés had been taken to Kentucky or Tennessee by masters who were themselves migrating to those western states.[23] But after 1810 most of the slaves deported from Virginia were sent to the Southwest—especially to Alabama, Mississippi, and farther west—and more than half of them were sold to slave traders rather than accompanying emigrating masters. Sale to traders massively disrupted slave families. Young men and women were often sold away from their partners, and young children were frequently sold away from their parents. The stream of Virginia slaves sent away from the state was already large during the decade of the 1810s, and it became even greater in subsequent years (averaging nearly 90,000 slaves each decade from 1810 to 1860). The stream rose to flood proportions during the cotton boom of the 1830s, but subsided surprisingly little even during the 1840s.[24] Some of the most vivid memories of the old people interviewed in 1937 focused on the heartbreaking impact that slave sales had upon family life.

It is important to discuss the value of the Virginia interviews. They were conducted under the auspices of the WPA's Virginia Writers' Project and were published some forty years later as edited by Charles Perdue and his associates.[25] The supervisor of most of the Virginia interviews was Roscoe Lewis, a black man who taught at the Hampton Institute in Virginia. Lewis understood the value of recruiting African Americans to interview former slaves. Most of the interview material in Perdue's volume (68 percent) is taken from typescripts preserved from the Virginia Writers' Project, supplemented by manuscripts (17 percent) or typescripts (2 percent) from Roscoe Lewis's personal papers, or occasionally by material prepared for a 1940 volume, *The Negro in Virginia* (12 percent).[26] From these sources the Perdue editors collated the fullest possible version of each interview, and they scrupulously identified the source of each paragraph of every interview.

It seems likely that black interviewers elicited more candor than white interviewers would have done (especially because of the "Southern etiquette" that still prevailed in Virginia in 1937, which probably would often have deterred blacks from saying much that might offend a white interlocutor). A ninety-one-year-old woman, for example, told her (obviously African American) interviewer in 1937 that—so angry was she that a white man had sold her sister in 1860—she never allowed white people into her house.[27] The historian Paul Escott, whose statistical analysis of WPA interviews throughout the South seldom distinguishes interviews with black interviewers from those with white interviewers, nevertheless calculates that interviewees were more than three times as likely to express a very unfavorable attitude to their former master when speaking to a black interviewer than when talking to a white one. Historians, for example, have discovered records of two WPA interviews of the same South Carolina woman, one evidently conducted by a black interviewer, the other (three months later) by a white interviewer. The interviews are wholly different from each other in content and in tone.[28]

I hope the following chapters demonstrate that the Perdue collection of Virginia interviews, nearly all conducted by African American interviewers, is a splendid resource for the study of slavery. Yet even the best possible sources have limitations, and those of the Virginia interviews must be acknowledged.

First, a substantial number of the interviews actually proved to be of little value for the study of slavery. Some are very brief—only five or six lines long. Some of the interviewees were born so late (in 1864 or later) that they could have had no firsthand memories of slavery, and some of these interviewees failed to report what their parents, or other older family members, had told them about slavery. Furthermore, some of the reports are obviously unreliable, as when the interviewee claimed to have been an eyewitness to an event that he or she evidently could not have seen.

Anthropologists have warned historians about "the social construction of oral history"—that is, that what a narrator tells her or his audience is shaped, to some degree, by the customs and traditions of the local community.[29] Of course, the distortion is likely to be smaller (as in most of the Virginia interviews) when the interviewee is old enough to have witnessed an event—or to have heard a reliable report from an older person—than when several generations have ensued between event and narration (as has sometimes occurred in oral narrations analyzed by anthropologists). Yet even firsthand accounts are somewhat shaped by social customs (e.g., in 1937 neither interviewers nor interviewees felt free to say much about the Virginia slaves' sexual lives).

Material from the Virginia interviews falls roughly into three categories: (1) firsthand or secondhand reports, (2) tradition, and (3) folklore. Distinguishing "tradition" from first- or secondhand reports is sometimes difficult. I think that by the 1930s it had become a tradition among African Americans that slaves often retaliated against the hated patrollers (the white nightriders licensed to require black people to show passes authorizing their absence from their home plantations) by placing vines in their paths or in some other way leading them into trouble. This surely happened sometimes, but I judge that the frequency of such events was exaggerated in oral tradition. Yet such tradition cannot be ignored; and sometimes tradition is very accurate indeed. Thus, if an interviewee born in 1864 claimed to have seen slaves whipped until blood ran down their backs—after which brine was rubbed into the wounds—the claim to have been an eyewitness is unbelievable, yet the tradition that this is what was done to slaves is wholly credible.

"Folklore" is even more difficult to handle, for it is not always clear when a believable "tradition" has slipped into becoming an incredible piece of folklore. Fugitive slaves often hid successfully in the local woods for weeks or even months at a time; but can one believe that a fugitive named Pattin hid for fifteen years with his wife and their fifteen children (one produced annually) in an underground den "'bout size of a big room, 'cause dat big family washed, ironed, slept and done ev'ythin' down dar, dat you do in yo' house"?[30]

Furthermore, a question sometimes arises whether an interviewee is projecting backward—from 1937 to the 1850s—convictions that were actually different in the 1850s. Perhaps interviewees projected their rather conventional Southern evangelical Christian beliefs of 1937 back onto the 1850s, when African religious influences may have been less attenuated than they later became. Here, as elsewhere, I have done my best to weigh the evidence.

There is a further problem with using the Virginia interviews: the interviewees did not comprise an entirely representative sample of antebellum Virginia slaves. It is true that the interviewees had been held in bondage in various parts of the present state of Virginia (*roughly* in proportion to the distribution of slaves throughout the state in 1860).[31] But 60 percent of the Perdue interviewees were women, contributing to the over-representation of female house slaves among those interviewees, and to the underrepresentation of male field slaves.[32] Even more significant, those interviewees who survived until 1937—and who then became known to the interviewers as potential interviewees—cannot have been wholly typical. On average they probably had been better nourished than the average Virginia slave; they, or their parents, are more likely to have been house or yard servants than was common; their masters are less likely than average to have treated them brutally; they are more likely than average to

Current Check-Outs summary for McManus,
        Wed Oct 30 12:06:51 GMT 2013

BARCODE: 30114012367176
TITLE: Slavery and freedom : an interpre
DUE DATE: 06 Nov 2013

BARCODE: 30114014862448
TITLE: Strategies for survival : recolle
DUE DATE: 06 Nov 2013

have lived in an urban area like Norfolk/Portsmouth or Petersburg; they are more likely than average to have lived relatively prosperously into the early twentieth century; and there is a more than average possibility that they were of mixed-race background.[33] To the limited extent that I have depended on "tradition" rather than upon firsthand accounts, this tends to correct the bias inherent in the Perdue interviews. And privileged slaves (like Virginia Shepherd) sometimes provided the most graphic accounts of brutality experienced by other slaves whom they knew. Thus, despite the limitations of Virginia's WPA sample, I do not believe the picture I have drawn of slavery is romanticized. But if I have erred, the probability is that—because the Virginia interviewees were not wholly typical—the situation of most Virginia slaves was even grimmer than here depicted.

In 1937 the Virginia interviews were recorded in dialect, but somewhat inconsistently. Although the quotation of dialect is not now universally accepted, I think it would be a mistake for me to try to translate dialect into standard English, and I have reproduced quotations exactly as they are printed in the Perdue volume. Perdue discusses the issue, and supports his discussion with a six-page appendix.[34]

I have of course supplemented the Perdue interviews with other records of former Virginia slaves' memories of bondage—especially those in John Blassingame's *Slave Testimony*, Benjamin Drew's *The Refugee*, George Teamoh's *God Made Man, Man Made the Slave*, and (for comparative purposes) Harriet Jacobs's *Incidents in the Life of a Slave Girl*.[35] My debt to the dozens of specialized studies of antebellum slavery in Virginia is evident in my endnotes.

The following pages seek to convey a sense of the slaves' experiences of bondage, as felt by the slaves themselves. Part I, however, focuses on alleviations that reduced the harshness of the lives of certain groups of slaves. I begin with these alleviations, *not* because most slaves benefited from them—most slaves certainly did not—but because in two previous books I stressed the harshness of the regime, and I need to acknowledge here that some slaves escaped the worst rigors of the system.[36] It has become a truism that conditions of life now are very different for middle-class African Americans than for those blacks who are economically the worst off. But even during slavery times, conditions of life for the "better-off" bondpeople were substantially different from those experienced by the worst-off slaves. The differences were smaller in slavery times than they are now, and the proportion of slaves who were "better off" was much smaller than the proportion today of middle-class blacks. But the two different eras nevertheless resemble each other in this respect. The Virginia interviews underscore how differently slavery was experienced by certain "privileged" slaves than it was by the vast majority of bondpeople.

Part II attempts to analyze the aspects of slavery that most strongly offended the slaves' sense of justice. How far, for example, were material deprivations (e.g., inadequate food rations) at the center of bondpeoples' consciousness? And how far were immaterial factors—such as the contempt to which slaves were normally subjected—most prominent in their minds?

Part III discusses the bondpeople's responses to their enslavement, seeking to establish—for example—which forms of dissidence were most significant in the slaves' lives. It examines the slaves' religion and their family institutions. It considers not only the bondpeoples' community life, but also the efforts made by individual slaves to develop their own skills and talents.

The concluding chapter seeks to assess the balance between the masters' oppression (as delineated in part II) and the slaves' responses (as discussed in part III). I hope in this way to contribute to a growing movement among recent historians who seek to give full weight both to the slaves' substantial achievements and to the power of the masters, which inevitably limited the scope of those achievements.[37]

This is a heartening story of the human capacity to survive, and to make the best of circumstances even under conditions of extreme oppression. But it is also an account of the heavy price paid by many African American subjects of that oppression.

Part I

ALLEVIATIONS

1

Good Mistresses and Masters

Before the Civil War, and for more than a century thereafter, apologists for the slave regime of the Old South claimed that the typical slavemaster was a benevolent figure who treated his "servants" indulgently and was loved by them. Although Eugene Genovese strongly dissented from that view, his brilliant and groundbreaking *Roll, Jordan, Roll* (1974), which placed paternalism at the center of its analysis, may have exerted an unintended influence toward perpetuating a rose-colored view of plantation slavery. Descendants of slaves, some critics of Genovese's work, and so-called neo-abolitionist historians have naturally been tempted to dismiss talk of slavemaster benevolence and to reject myths about the geniality of the ancien régime.

But there is evidence from the lips of former slaves that an appreciable number of slavemasters were indeed seen by their bondpeople as in some sense "good" masters. It may be appropriate to investigate what African Americans meant by this term. Most of the following chapters discuss the offenses committed by white people against enslaved blacks, and the ways in which the slaves tried to cope. But evidently, not all slavemasters were regarded as "mean"; nor was the situation of all bondpeople unrelievedly abysmal. The wrongs of slavery might be alleviated to some extent if a slave had a "good" mistress or master, if the bondperson were of mixed-race origin, or if the slave lived in a city and/or worked in industry. We shall examine these possible sources of alleviation before focusing on the darker side of the lives of most slaves.

Some Virginia mistresses and masters won the genuine esteem of blacks who had been enslaved to them. Among the best regarded of such whites were those few who had enabled their bondpeople to become free. In Winchester, Virginia, for example, lived a family of "Dutchmen" who had raised a slave girl (an orphan?) almost as though she were their own child. The girl became their house servant, and may have been the wet nurse for some of her mistress's children. "I was living very well," the black woman (later named Mrs. Joseph Wilkinson) testified in 1863, "—same as if I was free, although they hadn't given me my free papers. I had no hardships." Mrs. Wilkinson's husband, however, had been owned by a master who treated him badly, and Joseph Wilkinson had managed to flee to Canada. Soon thereafter (in about 1836) the black woman's kindly mistress freed her and her young child so that they could follow her husband to Canada. Many years later, in 1857, Mrs. Wilkinson made a trip from Canada back to Virginia "to see the old place & my friends. . . . I saw my master's family. I wanted to see them—indeed I did, for I nursed them." This interview was conducted in Canada in 1863. Showing her interviewer a daguerreotype of a son of her old master, Mrs. Wilkinson continued: "I nursed that man when he was a child. . . . I nursed his brother, too. They thought a good deal of me. . . . I was just raised up like one of the family. I used to call my master 'father,' & the old lady 'mother.'" Mrs. Wilkinson was talking to a white man, but her testimony is credible because the interviewer was an abolitionist whose predisposition would have been to doubt a story of slavemaster benevolence.[1]

Although a substantial number of Virginia slaves had been emancipated by their masters during the twenty years before 1806, the passage of a restrictive law that year reduced the stream to a trickle. During antebellum years the majority of manumissions (liberations of a slave) were effected not through the gift of the owner—as had fortunately happened to Mrs. Wilkinson—but through the slave's purchasing his or her own freedom. This depended upon a master's willingness to let a slave earn considerable sums of money while still enslaved and the master's willingness to let the slave use accumulated savings to buy his or her freedom. One such master was Thomas Gilmer, who became governor of Virginia in 1840. In 1829 Gilmer had attended the auction of Thomas Jefferson's slaves and had bought, for $500, Israel Jefferson, a privileged servant of Thomas Jefferson. Gilmer let Israel Jefferson earn money, and by 1841 the former slave had saved $300. When that year Gilmer was elected to Congress, he wanted to take Jefferson with him to Washington as a servant, but Jefferson demurred. He did not wish to be separated from his wife, a free mixed-race woman; and in any case he wanted to be free. He proposed that Gilmer let him buy his freedom at the same purchase price he had paid a dozen years earlier—$300 down and the rest to be paid within a couple of years—and Gilmer assented. The transaction was completed as agreed, and soon thereafter Jefferson, his wife, and their children moved to Cincinnati, Ohio, where Jefferson was, and felt, genuinely free. He worked there for good wages as a waiter, and later (for even better wages) on a steamboat. When Israel Jefferson was interviewed in 1873 by an Ohio journalist, he spoke of "my good master, Governor Gilmer"—so good that Gilmer was willing to authorize a privileged house servant to buy his own freedom, on favorable terms.[2]

During the 1850s the average annual number of Virginia slaves manumitted was less than 250, and most of these—like Israel Jefferson—were obliged to buy their own freedom. Freedom was such a boon, however, that every mistress or master who freed a slave, or let a slave buy his or her freedom, deservedly ranked as "good."[3]

Another type of "good mistress" was the white woman who might turn a blind eye to a slave's escape, or might even encourage the slave to flee. One such woman was the daughter of a tobacco farmer named Sowers, who (according to the escaped bondman David Holmes) "was a churchman, and wouldn't allow us slaves to be whipped." When Sowers died, he sought to free all his slaves by will, but his son broke the will. Sowers's daughter, however, sympathized with her father's purpose. She told the slaves about the will, and later, when she learned that David Holmes was to be sold, she warned him and said "[I'd] better make off, or else I should be sent down South." The black man, of course, was the person who undertook the great dangers of his long wintertime flight to the North (for the Sowers farm was in Mecklenburg County, adjacent to North Carolina and hundreds of miles from Pennsylvania); but Holmes owed something to the sympathy and encouragement of his kindly "young *missus*."[4]

A few planters were extraordinarily generous to all, or most, of their slaves. George Follkes, for example, "was a real [i.e., a beneficent] marser," who after the Civil War bequeathed to his freedpeople about 1,550 of his 1,700 acres. To achieve this goal, Follkes enlisted the support of several

respected white men in Chatham, Virginia; after his death they thwarted
the efforts of other whites to break the will. During slavery times Follkes
usually had let his bondpeople work at their own pace, unsupervised.
When he once hired an overseer, he soon fired him because he had been
about to whip a slave woman. This intended whipping of the interviewee's
aunt "made ole marse so angry dat he run de overseer off de plantation jes'
lak he was a dog" (*Interviews*, 297–98).[5]

Another exceptional planter was Powhatan Mitchell, the master of a
slave boy named Byrl Anderson. Mitchell was, according to Anderson, "a
Whig who owned slaves but was against slavery." Mitchell—if Anderson
is to be believed—preached the little slave boy an egalitarian message:
"'Never call no white man master. For all are brothers and all are equal.
Black is good as white. So always keep courage and never back off from
a white man.'" Anderson (who later became a trade union official in the
Tennessee coal fields) declared that he had followed the principles inculcated by his master when he was a little boy: "I followed his instruction:
I have always . . . contended for what was rightfully mine. I have never
feared no man, white nor black." Apparently, Anderson derived his ambition from his enslaved father, and his sense of probity partly from his
grandmother's religious instruction; but he also owed much to the pre-
cepts of his white master, Powhatan Mitchell (*Interviews*, 9).

Masters not so openhanded as Follkes, or so egalitarian as Mitchell,
might nevertheless gain credit with their slaves because of the contrast
between the conditions on their plantations and those prevailing elsewhere. As a child Mariah Hines—who was orphaned very young—directed much of her emotional energy toward her master and mistress. She
accepted her inferior status and counted her blessings. "My white folks
treated us good," she reported. "There was plenty of 'em that didn't fare as
we did. Some of the poor folks almost starved to death. . . . [By contrast]
we always had plenty of food, never knowed what it was to want food bad
enough to have to steal it like a whole lot of 'em. . . . Plenty [of clothing]
to keep us comfortable, course it warn't silk nor satin, no ways the best
there was, but 'twas plenty good 'nough for us, and we was plenty glad to
git it. When we would look and see how the slaves on the 'jining farm was
fareing . . . , it made us feel like we was gittin' 'long most fine." Hines's
master—probably John A. Persons—was exceptional. He didn't make his
slaves start work so early in the morning as did neighboring farmers, and

although he was a large planter (with about 56 slaves), he let his bond-people work relatively unsupervised, using neither a white overseer nor an enslaved driver to push them on. When he himself walked around the field, he "always had a smile and a joke wid you. He allu's tell us we was doing fine, even sometimes when we wan't." This master and mistress won their slaves' affection. "We loved, 'spected master, ['cause] he was so good to us," recounted Hines. The slaves, she declared, loved their mistress so well that they did all the chores for her: "Missus didn't have to do nothing, hardly. Dare was always some of us round the house." Had this story been told to a white interviewer, it would excite disbelief, but told to a black interviewer—who editorialized at length about how rare such a planter was—it carries conviction (*Interviews*, 139–41).[6]

Yet another exceptional master was Thomas Hatcher. According to Hatcher's mixed-race granddaughter, he "was very kind to his slaves an' didn't 'low dem to be too severely punished." Indeed, Hatcher gained the reputation among the neighboring slaves that, if they fled temporarily from a cruel master, they could find shelter at his place and he would "protect dem 'til he foun' out where dey came f'om an' de circumstances o' de leavin'." Then apparently Hatcher would intercede for slaves whom he felt had been unfairly treated. In Hatcher's white family, however, beneficence and sex became intertwined. His son entered a sexual relation with a slave woman, which led to the birth of a mixed-race child, Patience Avery, in 1863. Patience Avery's mother told the child that a buzzard had laid her. But one day the mother introduced her little girl to her white father, which suggests that the black woman had some positive feeling for the white man. One may perhaps infer that there had at one time been a loving relationship between Thomas Hatcher's son and Patience Avery's mother, but that he had failed to sustain that fragile tie after the birth of their child (*Interviews*, 15–16).[7]

Although a few masters—such as John Persons, Powhatan Mitchell, George Follkes, and David Holmes's master Sowers—extended their beneficence to most or all of their slaves, kindliness was generally confined to privileged house servants like Israel Jefferson and Mrs. Joseph Wilkinson, or to skilled artisans. Thus, Anna Crawford, whose grandmother was a mammy (children's nurse), and whose mother was a maid (and whose father had probably already learned as a slave the crafts that enabled him to become a cabinetmaker after the war), said that "our master[s] was good and kind to their slaves. Neither one were cruel to us." A remarkable story was told by Allen Wilson, who at age seventeen had been given to his (younger) master as a body servant, accompanying him to Petersburg, where the white youth attended an academy. The slave was hired out to work in a tobacco factory during the day, while in the evenings, Wilson reports, "I went to our quarters which was his [the young master's] room and stayed dar to look after him—soughter companion like." Here—as so often for slaves—relatively good memories of some whites ("soughter companion like") were mixed with bitter ones. Back on the plantation Wilson's mother had been whipped so cruelly by the overseer that Wilson thought he would one day have killed the overseer, if freedom had not intervened (*Interviews*, 77, 328, 330, 327).

Cordial relations developed most frequently between certain female house servants and some of the white mistresses with whom they were thrown into close contact. Mary Jones's mother, born in 1837, a mammy in the natal family of the novelist Thomas Nelson Page, told her daughter Mary about the Page household: "Mother claimed that she rather be a slave than to be free, because of her nice treatment by her master and mistress." She (the mammy) had been named, presumably by the master and mistress, for one of the Page daughters, and she was later given to that young white woman as a bridal gift. Besides caring for this woman's children, the slave became a midwife, and she was the wet nurse for at least one white child. Religious principle helped to shape the white women's conduct. The Pages—Episcopalians—"had a special pew for their slaves every Sunday." They taught their slaves to memorize the Episcopal catechism and parts of the Bible, but banned them from looking at other books. Only once did the white mistress ever slap her slave woman (for alleged impudence in not correctly answering a simple question). When the Northern army arrived at the plantation during the Civil War, the enslaved mammy successfully hid the white family's silver in the chicken house. This may sound like the stereotypical picture—cherished by many Southern white people—of a faithful servant loyally doing her duty to genteel, beneficent masters; but because the story was told to a reliable black interviewer (who recorded many stories of a very different ilk from other elderly African Americans), it is credible (*Interviews*, 187–88).[8]

The relatively good treatment another mistress accorded an eighteen-year-old slave woman, Julia Jordan, paid dividends when the Northern army approached the plantation (near Petersburg, Virginia) in 1865. "Missus came runnin' into de cabin one mornin'," Jordan said, "wid all her silver an' Marsa's money bundled up in her apron." She asked the slave woman to hide them from the approaching Yankees. Jordan secreted them under the mattress where her baby was sitting, and the soldiers—beguiled by the baby—never found the silver or the money. "When freedom come de Missus gimme a silver mug for savin' all de valuables," Jordan reported with satisfaction. "My daughter in Clarkesville has still got it, I reckon. I give it to her cause she was de baby that saved it from de Yankees dat day" (*Interviews*, 188–89).[9]

Religious principle impelled another white family to substantial—if limited—beneficence. Apparently, either Mr. or Mrs. Joe Crews of Richmond, Virginia, had been a Quaker before their wedding, but they had abandoned that antislavery faith at marriage in order to become slavemasters. The couple retained enough antislavery conviction, however, that they freed the children of their slaves at age twenty-one. And when they hired out adult slaves, or their teenage children, they appear to have let them keep a larger fraction of the hiring fee than was customary. "My mother was de cook . . . ," recalled Hannah Johnson. "Dey [Mr. and Mrs. Crews] was crazy 'bout her. I [born ca. 1850] come up as one of de white chillun—didn' know no difference. We et together at de same table. I slept in de same bed wid de white folks and I played wid de chillun. I didn' go to school wid dem, but went ev'y place else most, 'cept to church and parties. Dey would always tell me what dey learned in school so I knowed as much as dey did, near 'bout. When I got 'round ten, I was a nurse [i.e., a nanny to the smaller white children] an' den I had to stop playin' so much. I always call de ole misses 'grandma,' like de other chillun." Thus, although easy sociability between white children and the enslaved child of a trusted domestic servant might wither away after the age of about ten, it could sometimes occur before then (*Interviews*, 158).

John Brown—who was only five years old when freedom came in 1865—had played happily with white children when he was very young. Brown's mother, a housekeeper, seems to have been the only adult slave owned by Mrs. Sarah Prince. The two women got on well. Mrs. Prince, Brown recalls, "had seven gals, yeah I was raised up wid dem gals jes' like a brother. . . . When dese gals come from school we git our dinner—we all eat together. Dem gals would say, 'John, come on in de back yard we gwine git lessons.' . . . I had a time wid dem gals out dar an' to tell de truth ain' nary one of us done any studyin'. You see dey got deirs de next day in de school house. . . . Mistress was very, very good. . . . I ain' nebber seen dem white folks whip mother nor me." When these white children learned in 1865 that the slaves had been emancipated, they seemed delighted for the sake of their five-year-old black comrade: "John, John, you is free! You's free John." The little black boy was confused, however, "an' I made out like I was cryin' . . . a hollorin' I didn' want to leave my mistress." John made little mention of his father, who lived across the river from his own home. Here—as in some other cases where the black woman worked all day— the white woman shared the slave woman's maternal role to a consider- able extent, and the child probably was reluctant to lose his white mistress (*Interviews*, 61–62).[10]

The mistress of "Sister" Harrison took over a maternal role toward slave children to an even greater extent. This mistress owned only Harrison's mother, her two children, and an old man. "Mistress," Harrison reports, "was always kind, she was never mean nor cruel an' didn't like to see any- one treated cruelly." There was pain, however, for the enslaved mother, pushed into a subordinate maternal role, whose child nearly died from an accident that occurred when the child was under the white woman's care. Sister Harrison's mistress "rented my mother out an' she [the white woman] stayed at home an' took care of me an' my sistuh. Once while Mother wuz at work, I fell in the grate an' burnt myself somethin' terrible. Mistress most had a fit. The doctor said he didn't think I could live long, but the mistress took as good keer of me as my mother an' I lived." The relation that had developed between the white woman and the black child continued for years after Emancipation. "I lived with my mistress after the war," Harrison reports, "an' stayed with her until she died" (*Interviews*, 134–35).[11]

Thus, some mistresses and masters earned the genuine regard of at least some of their slaves—either by enabling them to become free, by treating all of their slaves in a kindly way, or (much more often) by de- veloping a kind of intimacy with a handful of privileged slaves, especially female house servants. Occasionally, the children of privileged house ser- vants grew up in close association with the children of the mistress's fam- ily. Cordial relations, then, did indeed subsist between some mistresses/

masters and some of their slaves; and these slaves sometimes expressed affection for their mistresses and masters.

Often, however, the slaves of "good" masters felt that their masters were only relatively good, in comparison to the low standard on most nearby plantations. Thus, the wedding of Martha Robinson's grandparents stood out in contrast to the unceremonious character of most slave weddings, and the relatively lengthy leave granted her grandfather on that occasion contrasted with what most enslaved bridegrooms could expect. Martha Robinson's grandmother "belonged to . . . good Christian people. They had the wedding [of Robinson's grandparents] in the front parlor with a preacher in charge. Gramma wore a silk gown of Mrs. Miller's, and Mr. Cox [the grandfather's master] let grampa wear an old suit of his." The limited extent of these kindly masters' generosity, however, quickly becomes apparent. Robinson's grandfather lived twelve miles away from his bride and was allowed to visit her only on Saturday nights. For the wedding his master gave him a three-day pass (*Interviews*, 240).

Normally—even in the case of "good" masters—the slaves' tone was not warm. When an interviewer asked Allen Crawford whether he had a good master, Crawford replied cynically, "My fust marsus was so ole and paralyzed he bound to have been good fer he couldn't do nuthing else." The interviewee Beverly Jones perceived that self-interest lay behind his master's having provided his slaves with enough food. "Simple fare, it was," Jones observed, "but they was always plenty of it. Master believed in givin' his niggers a good meal. Niggers work better on a full stomach" (*Interviews*, 74, 181).

Most "good" masters were felt to be only relatively so—that is, they were "good" because they did not authorize in their domain the excessive brutalities often inflicted on slaves elsewhere. Virginia Shepherd's master, for example—who had inherited some 250 slaves, and who (being a bachelor) had no family of his own for whom to provide—stood out from his neighbors. "He was a pretty good master," Shepherd recalled, "never worked his slaves very hard. He allowed them to hire themselves out and when they come home he got what he could out of them. No, he never bothered to collect their wages himself. In fact, our master allowed his slaves so much freedom that we were called free niggers by slaves on other plantations." The overseers on this plantation "weren't particularly mean. If some slave was defiant, he got a whipping and that ended [it]" (*Interviews*, 255). By this low standard, a master who *did* authorize the whipping of recalcitrant slaves, or the sale of a persistent fugitive, might nevertheless be felt to be a "good" master.

Similarly, Philip Coleman, the slave of a tobacco planter who owned twenty-seven bondpeople, took for granted that his good master would nevertheless whip a foot-dragging or disobedient slave. "We had a very kind and generally considerate master . . . ," Coleman acknowledged, "and there were none of us on the place who were really badly treated. Of course, when one of the boys [i.e., enslaved men] went wrong he got what was coming to him, but so long as we did what we were told was expected of us there was never any trouble."[12]

Richard Slaughter was another bondman who didn't "know much about the meanness of slavery. . . . I belonged to a very nice man. He never sold but one man, fur's I can remember, and that was cousin Ben. Sold him South." Presumably, Ben had been caught after fleeing the plantation, or had engaged in some act of overt resistance. Slaves had to live with the fact that even "very nice" masters would sell disruptive slaves (*Interviews*, 269).

"We were worked hard—," William Johnson, a privileged butler, testified, "but we got plenty of good food, nice quarters in which to stay and our master was not mean—he seldom ever had any of his slaves whipped." Because Johnson's master had more slaves than he could work on his own plantation, he hired out the surplus ones on annual contracts, preferring to do this rather than selling them. He did, however, sell his literate coachman to Mississippi, when the bondman was discovered to have forged documents enabling four slaves from a neighboring plantation to escape to the free states. Slaves realized that such punishments were standard, and in William Johnson's eyes this master nevertheless qualified as "not mean" (*Interviews*, 165–67).

Frank Bell understood that even an exceptionally good master would sometimes whip a slave, or sell a persistent fugitive: "Ole Marser Fallons was the best slave owner in thum parts"—a wheat-farming area of northern Virginia. Fallons "would hire out his slaves [on short-term contract] in slack times to cut timber an' build barns or fences, but he never let no one whip his slaves. He allus told the white man who hired his slaves dat if dey didn't do right he was to bring them back an' he would handle them, but not to hit any of his property. When he had to whip a slave he would always cut hisself a cherry sapling, cause a cherry sapling don't make no soar [scar?] on a slave's back."

Unlike most big Virginia planters, Fallons did not hire a white man to oversee his 150 slaves; he depended instead on an enslaved foreman. Unusually, this black driver permitted Fallons's slaves to work in family groups, a concession that slowed down the pace, because stronger workers helped weaker members of the family to keep up. But (as Frederick Douglass put it), while the slave of a bad master wanted a good master, the slave of a good master wanted to be his own master. Fallons's black driver tried repeatedly to escape to the free states. Eventually, Fallons—"the best slave owner in thum parts"—sold his valiant subaltern to the Deep South. "Goodness" in masters was relative (*Interviews*, 26–27).

Mildred Graves, a midwife, said that her master and mistress "was good to me. Cose at time things was purty bad, but on a whole dey was decent peoples." Graves felt it unfair that, when her master hired her out to act as midwife for another white family, he paid her only a small portion of the fee he charged for her services. But she compared her master to his neighbors. "He would give me only a few cents [of the fee]," she complained, "but dat was kinda good o' him to do dat. Plenty niggers was hired out an' didn't get nothin'" (*Interviews*, 120–21).

A good master might feel obliged to sell slaves in order to pay a debt. That Edward Hicks's master was a good man was indicated by an incident narrated by Hicks. Although the master employed a tough overseer, he stood up for his slave when Hicks disobeyed an unreasonable order from this overseer. The overseer had demanded that three slaves eat tobacco worms that they had missed when removing worms from the tobacco leaves. Hicks had refused and fled into the local woods. The master told "the overseer, that he shall pay a dollar a day for every day that I was gone, for he had no business to make that disturbance among the people." Hicks returned voluntarily after three weeks, and his master prevented him from being flogged. At the end of the year, the master deducted Hicks's lost time (presumably about $18) from the overseer's pay, and the overseer left. Yet the sons of this good master were gamblers, for whose debts the master felt responsible, and to pay their debts, he auctioned some slaves, including Hicks, who then fell into the hands of a bad master. Thus, even a good master might put the financial interests of his (worthless?) sons over the welfare of a bondman.[13]

The slave of a good master was likely to have been owned—or subsequently to become owned—by a bad master, because of the frequency with which ownership changed. An estate might be divided among heirs, or a slave might be given to another member of a white family, or a master might simply decide to sell someone. Thus, Henrietta King's second master and mistress "was good; all I had to do was mind de chillun" (i.e., she no longer had to dust, sweep, or empty the slops). After freedom King, recognizing that these were good masters, stayed with them until she married. But when King was only eight or nine years old, she had had a terrible experience with her first mistress. This woman, trying to hold the struggling girl in place—so that a whipping could be administered—had inflicted a serious, permanent injury on the girl. King's later good treatment by her second mistress scarcely compensated for the lasting damage done her by her first mistress—"a she-debbil what's burnin' an' twistin' in hell" (*Interviews*, 191–92).[14]

Levi Douglass and James Wright were Shenandoah Valley slaves who experienced first a good mistress, then a harsh master named Simmons. Their young mistress treated them well up until the moment she married Simmons; but then they became the property of her husband. So mild had her rule been that these two young slaves had dared to offer her advice about whom she should marry—an extraordinary breach of Southern etiquette. They "had ventured [according to the white abolitionist who interviewed them in 1853] to ask their mistress not to marry this Simmons, for they feared his cruel treatment. This fact came to his knowledge, and, to punish their audacity, he determined to sell them to the far south." (This story, however, had a happy ending, because the two young men succeeded in escaping from the slave trader and finally reached a secure freedom in Canada.)[15]

Even when slaves had a comparatively good master, the picture of their lives that emerges is usually somber. Thus, Beverly Jones testified that his master was a "purty good ole codger" who fed his slaves adequately, who "never would have no overseer," and who treated privileged slaves with forbearance. For example, "Uncle Jackson was a favored nigger even though he was always fixin' fo' to run away." Apparently, the master banned the local patrollers from whipping Jackson, even though he authorized them to whip his other slaves if they were caught away from the plantation without a pass. And the master tolerated a bitter outburst from Jones's Aunt Crissy, without whipping her for insubordination. But what provoked Crissy to her outburst against this "purty good ole codger"? The master had sold two of Aunt Crissy's seven children, in order to enrich himself. Crissy "went to him an' tole him he was a mean dirty slave-trader."

Even for the slaves of this "purty good" slaveowner, the religion preached to them by the local white minister was a stale message of obedience to their masters. And when male slaves from this plantation would creep off at night to a "hush-harbor" to listen to a black man preach a different version of Christianity at an unauthorized religious meeting, their wives and children would be terrified that the men, if caught, would be savagely whipped by the local patrollers (*Interviews,* 181–84).[16]

Thus, there was great diversity among slavemasters and mistresses. A handful treated most of their slaves with genuine kindliness; an appreciable number of others were kind to a few privileged bondpeople; and a substantial number were, at least, less harsh than was common, therefore earning recognition as "good," or "purty good," or "not mean." It made a great difference to a slave's life if she or he had a kindly—or even a relatively good—master and mistress, rather than a mean one. But the slaves of kindly masters were still slaves; and those who had relatively good masters counted their blessings only in contrast to their less fortunate fellows in bondage.

2

Mixed-Race Ancestry and
Long-Term Relationships

Just as there was great diversity among slavemasters, so was there vast diversity among African Americans. In New Orleans and in seaports in the Deep South like Charleston and Mobile, there existed a three-caste system resembling that of Brazil or the West Indies, where free people of mixed-race ancestry occupied a status somewhere between that of a free white person and an enslaved black. A species of three-caste system may also have functioned in the Middle South, possibly mitigating the harshness of slavery for some enslaved people of mixed-race background.

The best-known account of such a system appears in Harriet Jacobs's *Incidents in the Life of a Slave Girl*. Jacobs depicts life in Edenton, North Carolina, a small seaport just a few miles south of the Virginia border; but interviews with Virginia ex-slaves suggest that Jacobs's memoir can throw light on the lives of certain mixed-race slaves even in rural Virginia.

Since the publication in the 1980s of research that copiously demonstrated the authenticity of Jacobs's 1861 memoir, Jacobs's experiences as a slave have become almost as well-known as those of that other famous mixed-race slave, Frederick Douglass. Jacobs wrote that "slavery is terrible for men; but it is far more terrible for women" because of the sexual harassment endured by so many enslaved women. Jacobs vividly detailed the relentless harassment to which she herself was subjected by her master, Dr. James Norcom—a 1797 graduate of the University of Pennsylvania medical school who was thirty-five years her senior.[1] Jacobs wrote surprisingly candidly (in view of Victorian constraints upon public discussion of sexual matters) about the ethical quandaries that Norcom's conduct imposed on her, and she argued convincingly that ethical standards for enslaved women must necessarily differ from those for free women. Hers is one of the most gripping and illuminating accounts of slave life ever published.

Jacobs's book records the privileges that might be accorded in the Middle South to light-skinned slaves, treated almost as members of a third caste, neither black nor white. Yet Dr. Norcom's sexual tastes may have been such that it was precisely Jacobs's light color that made her particularly attractive to him. Nevertheless, Jacobs lived in a town where the pressure of public opinion curtailed Dr. Norcom's freedom to enact all of his fantasies.

Jacobs's privileges arose directly from her status as a light-skinned person of mixed-race ancestry, living in a family that was partially sheltered by white protectors—one that was regarded by both blacks and whites as almost free. Jacobs's father, "a light shade of brownish yellow," was a skilled carpenter and master builder, who for several years had been permitted to earn money in order to buy his freedom (although this purpose was thwarted when his master died). Because Jacobs's mother—also of mixed-race ancestry, and so privileged that she wore a wedding ring—died when the child was only six years old, the role of surrogate mother was embraced by Jacobs's maternal grandmother. This woman, Molly Horniblow, exercised the most important formative influence on Jacobs's life.[2]

Molly was the daughter of a Carolina planter and presumably a mixed-race slave woman. In 1828 she was purchased and quickly emancipated with funds supplied by Albert Gatlin, a man of such prominence in Edenton that he was the U. S. congressman from that district. In Edenton Molly had been operating a bake shop patronized by white people, and apparently she had saved more than enough money to pay her purchase price; thus, Congressman Gatlin's role—indispensable though it was—was that of intermediary, not financier. Molly Horniblow soon bought the house from which she ran her bake shop, in the middle of town among white neighbors, one or two of whom were devoted friends. Harriet Jacobs's own position in town derived largely from that of her grandmother. She was finally able to escape from slavery at the age of twenty-nine because she was sufficiently light-skinned to pass as a free white woman on the vessel transporting her from Edenton to Philadelphia.

Molly Horniblow, Jacobs's grandmother, had by no means led an untroubled life. Although we do not know all of her troubles, they must have included the failure of Molly's Carolina father to effect his wish to free his enslaved mistress (Molly's mother) and her three children. Much later, an executor tried to frustrate the purpose of Elizabeth Horniblow (Molly Horniblow's second owner) that she be emancipated. But Molly found relief in 1828 when, put on the block for sale in Edenton, she was bought for the derisory sum of $50 by the elderly spinster sister of her deceased mistress, and the old white woman almost immediately emancipated her. This transaction was made possible by the forbearance of potential bidders who, sympathizing with the plight of the slave woman, permitted the sole bidder to win the auction for this low bid. The transaction was also made possible by help from Congressman Gatlin, who lent not only the $50 with which Molly Horniblow was bought, but also the substantial sum of $400 for the purchase of Molly's son Mark, which Molly seems to have repaid to Gatlin in 1830. Mark led the life of a virtually free man (nominally owned by his mother, Molly) until he became legally free in 1843.[3]

The affection between Molly Horniblow and Hannah Pritchard—the old white woman who bought her in 1828 and immediately freed her—was strong and genuine. The two women had lived in the same household for forty years when Molly was owned by Hannah's sister, and the feelings then nurtured survived when Molly later was living in her own house. Hannah Pritchard, who owned no slaves, was illiterate and apparently impecunious, but when she came to Molly's house, she was entertained with bourgeois propriety. "My grandmother," Harriet Jacobs avers, "loved this old lady. . . . She often came to take tea with us [at Grandmother's house]. On such occasions the table was spread with a snow-white cloth, and the china cups and silver spoons were taken from the old-fashioned buffet. There were hot muffins, tea rusks, and delicious sweetmeats. My grandmother kept two cows, and the fresh cream was Miss [Hannah's] delight. . . . The old ladies had cosey [sic] times together. They would work and chat, and sometimes, while talking over old times, their spectacles would get dim with tears. . . . When Miss [Hannah] bade us good by, her bag was filled with grandmother's best cakes, and she was urged to come again soon."[4]

With a grandmother like this, and a father who was saving money with the promise of purchasing his own freedom, Harriet Jacobs grew up (until the age of twelve) feeling that she was virtually free herself. Her father, "on condition of paying his mistress two hundred dollars a year, and supporting himself . . . , was allowed to work at his trade [as a master builder], and manage his own affairs. . . . [We lived in Edenton] in a comfortable home," Jacobs continued, "and, though we were all slaves, I was so fondly shielded that I never dreamed I was a piece of merchandise." Slave children belonged to their mother's owner. Because Jacobs's father and mother had different owners, Jacobs became the possession of a young white woman who treated her extraordinarily kindly. From the age of six, when Jacobs's mother died, until nearly twelve, the little slave girl was constantly in the company of this young mistress, who taught her to read and to spell. The mistress "was so kind to me," Jacobs wrote, "that I was always glad to do her bidding. . . . I would sit by her side for hours, sewing diligently, with a heart as free from care as that of any free-born white child."[5] When this young mistress sickened and died in 1825, Harriet Jacobs and her friends believed the young white woman would emancipate Jacobs in her will, but their hopes were crushed.

Instead of freeing Harriet, the young mistress bequeathed the child to an older sister, Mrs. James Norcom, who proved to be of very different temperament.[6] Mrs. Norcom seems to have felt that Harriet Jacobs— "a light mulatto" with hair "which can be easily combed straight," who dressed above her station and regarded herself as of a different caste from enslaved blacks—must be put in her place. "I have a vivid recollection of the linsey-woolsey dress given me every winter by Mrs. [Norcom]," Jacobs exclaimed. "How I hated it! It was one of the badges of slavery." Jacobs's presence soon became a source of marital discord within the Norcom household. Dr. Norcom eyed the twelve-year-old girl with interest, and by the time she was fourteen, he was whispering suggestive things into her ear and devising various schemes to be alone with her. Never beating her himself (until later), and never letting anyone else punish her, he tried to persuade Jacobs that her life could be transformed for the better if she were kind to him; and he drove his wife into fits of unfounded suspicion that Jacobs had accepted his advances.[7]

Harriet Jacobs instead fell in love with a freeborn "colored" man, a carpenter who wanted to buy Jacobs so that she would be free from the Norcoms' dominion. She asked Norcom's permission to marry this young man (who was probably darker-skinned than she). Norcom utilized the three-caste presumption—that a light mixed-race woman would think herself above the attentions of a dark-skinned man—to further his own aims. "I supposed . . . that you felt above the insults of such puppies," Dr. Norcom remarked. Jacobs's father, a high-tempered man, had bred a spirited daughter, and she had the temerity to reply to her master: "The man you call a puppy never insulted me, sir." Correctly understanding this response as an insult to himself, Norcom for the first time administered a stunning blow to Jacobs; but if she had been a male, she would not have escaped so lightly for this proud assertion of her own status. Jacobs knew a well-disposed white woman (probably a friend of her grandmother's) who was a good friend of Dr. Norcom's, and she persuaded this woman to petition Norcom to sell Jacobs to her carpenter beloved. But Norcom would not relent. He banned Jacobs from seeing the young man and pursued his own plans to wear down her opposition.[8]

When a slave woman entered sexual relations with a white man, historians often, and justly, term such relations "rape" or "forced sex," while acknowledging that sometimes there were "consensual unions." But none of these terms precisely matches Jacobs's experiences. Not long after being banned from marrying her black sweetheart, the sixteen-year-old slave girl entered what *might* be termed a consensual union with Samuel Sawyer, an unmarried white man thirteen years older than she, whose standing in Edenton was such that he was later elected U.S. congressman from that district. Jacobs hoped that Sawyer would be able to buy her from Norcom, and she believed Sawyer would then free her and their children. Sawyer fathered two children by Jacobs, and much later he did find opportunities to buy them (and also to buy Jacobs's younger brother); all three of these mixed-race slaves eventually became free. Although Sawyer never succeeded in getting Norcom to sell him Jacobs herself, he tried hard to do so. Jacobs's faith in Sawyer was moderately well placed.[9]

But was it a "consensual union"? Jacobs was candid in acknowledging that one of her motives in accepting Sawyer as a lover was her desire to revenge herself against Norcom by driving him into a frenzy of jealousy. Much more significant, however, was the need of this young woman to secure protection against her master's determination to have sex with her. Although Jacobs lived in town, where she was not so isolated as she would have been on a lonely plantation, and although her color, culture, and acquaintance marked her as a member of a caste substantially distinguished from that of most plantation slaves, she had no supporters. Her parents were dead. Neither her free grandmother, nor her grandmother's circle of white female friends, nor well-disposed white men in town had the power, or the constant concern, to protect her against her master. Mrs. Norcom's angry shouting matches with her husband were equally ineffectual in deterring him from his plans. Harriet may have calculated that the only thing that could permanently thwart Norcom was perhaps the sexual possessiveness of an honorable white man. "To be an object of interest to a man who is not married, and who is not her master," she explained,

> is agreeable to the pride and feelings of a slave, if her miserable situation has left her any pride or sentiment. It seems less degrading to give one's self, than to submit to compulsion. There is something akin to freedom in having a lover who has no control over you, except that which he gains by kindness and attachment. . . .
>
> When I found that my master had actually begun to build the lonely cottage [where he intended to domicile Jacobs], other feelings mixed with those I have described. Revenge, and calculations of interest, were added to flattered vanity and sincere gratitude for kindness. I knew nothing would enrage Dr. [Norcom] so much as to know that I favored another. . . . I thought he would revenge himself by selling me [to a slave trader], and I was sure my friend, Mr. [Sawyer], would buy me. . . . I thought my freedom could be easily obtained from him. . . . [I] felt quite sure that [my children] would be made free. . . . I feel that the slave woman ought not to be judged by the same standard as others.[10]

Harriet's hopes that Sawyer would buy her freedom were disappointed, but her analysis of the complexities of her situation highlights the inadequacy of the concept of consent.[11]

The clearest indication of the privileges accorded in Edenton to some members of a light-skinned mixed-race caste, and the limits within which those privileges were confined, came two or three years later, in 1831, in the aftermath of the Nat Turner insurrection. Southampton County, Virginia, the seat of the insurrection, lay only a few miles north of Edenton, and panic quickly struck the North Carolina town. After two local blacks were intimidated into making false accusations, nineteen local blacks were then arrested, of whom eight were indicted (though all were eventually released); and a rural mob, organized as the militia, stormed into town and searched the house of every black or mixed-race person, slave or free.[12]

This crisis was extremely dangerous for most of the town's blacks, but Harriet Jacobs, staying at her grandmother's house, was relatively free from fear; indeed, she took some trouble to annoy the poor rural militiamen, under their planter captain, by displaying the possessions her grandmother had accumulated, and the good order in which they were kept. When the militia arrived to search her grandmother's house, Jacobs summoned "a white gentleman who was friendly to us" to observe the conduct of the militiamen. "I entertained no positive fears about our household," Jacobs averred, "because we were in the midst of white families who would protect us."[13]

Jacobs's account of these events demonstrates the class prejudice of a literate mixed-race slave, protected by a genteel white townsman, against rampaging "country bullies and the poor whites." She pictures a cross-class alliance between these illiterate whites and the wealthy slavemaster who was their militia captain, but who "felt above soiling his hands with the search. He merely gave orders; and if a bit of writing was discovered, it was carried to him by his ignorant followers, who were unable to read." Well-to-do whites had mustered the militia because of their fear of insurrection, but the militia got out of hand. In Jacobs's view, this served as a license to powerless poor whites: "It was a grand opportunity for the low whites, who had no negroes of their own to scourge. They exulted in such a chance to exercise a little brief authority." Jacobs reported that

> the dwellings of the colored people, unless they happened to be protected by some influential white person, who was nigh at hand, were robbed of clothing and every thing else the marauders thought worth carrying away. All day long these unfeeling wretches went round, like a troop of demons, terrifying and tormenting the helpless. At night they formed themselves into patrol bands, and went wherever they chose among the colored people, acting out their brutal will. Many women hid themselves in woods and swamps, to keep out of their way. If any of the husbands or fathers told of

these outrages, they were tied up to the public whipping post, and cruelly scourged for telling lies about white men.[14]

Miscalculating the strength of the approaching tornado, the eighteen-year-old Jacobs had deliberately provoked the militiamen's hostility: "Nothing annoyed them so much as to see colored people living in comfort and respectability, so I made arrangements for them with especial care. I arranged everything in my grandmother's house as neatly as possible. I put white quilts on the beds, and decorated some of the rooms with flowers." As the militiamen routed around the house, seeking evidence of a conspiracy, there were repeated cries of irritation. "My grandmother had a large trunk of bedding and table cloths," Jacobs reports with satisfaction, contrasting the accents of the poor whites with the standard English enunciated by her grandmother. "When [the trunk] was opened, there was a great shout of surprise; and one [militiaman] exclaimed, 'Where'd the damned niggers git all dis sheet an' table clarf?' My grandmother, emboldened by the presence of our white protector, said, 'You may be sure we didn't pilfer 'em from *your* houses.'" The militiamen then brought to their captain, for his interpretation, a piece of paper they had discovered, on which was suspicious writing. This proved to be verses written to Jacobs by a friend. Having showed—to the captain's surprise—that she knew how to read, Jacobs said, "Most of my letters are from white people." This boast (and the quiet hint that her white friends could protect her) enraged the militia captain as much as the trunk full of bedding had annoyed the militiamen, and the captain "swore, and raved, and tore the paper into bits." The conversation was interrupted by another "exclamation of surprise from some of the company. . . . Some silver spoons which ornamented an old-fashioned buffet had just been discovered. My grandmother was in the habit of preserving fruit for many ladies in the town, of preparing suppers for parties; consequently she had many jars of preserves." The rich planter who commanded these militiamen regarded the inhabitants of Molly Horniblow's dwelling as a group of "half free niggers," and as the militiamen left, he "turned back, and pronounced a malediction on the house. He said it ought to be burned to the ground, and each of its inmates receive thirty-nine lashes."[15]

Jacobs's memoir was published nearly thirty years after this event, and she may have exaggerated her and her grandmother's defiance of the militiamen. But, wherever it is possible to do so, the details of the memoir have been exhaustively authenticated. The events of that extraordinary day would have been indelibly engraved in the memory of the eighteen-year-old woman, and Jacobs's account has the ring of authenticity. It is a vivid portrayal of the lives of a mixed-race enslaved elite, partially protected by association with well-disposed, "respectable" white people, and partly by the self-respect bred into them by members of their own family and by their own struggles to make decent lives for themselves.

Yet Dr. Norcom would not sell Jacobs to Samuel Sawyer, the father of her two children, and eventually he deported her from Edenton to a plantation several miles away, run by Norcom's adult son. When she learned that her children were about to be taken away from the relative security of her grandmother's house, the twenty-two-year-old Jacobs resolved to flee. The story of her successful flight is almost incredible, yet enough details can be authenticated that the story seems to be true. Even here, as everywhere else in her life as a slave, Harriet Jacobs depended upon help both from resourceful African Americans and from a handful of well-disposed white people. She hid for a week at the house of a black woman in Edenton, then for two months was hidden by a well-to-do white woman (probably Martha Blount, the widow of a substantial slaveholder; Mrs. Blount's brother was a prominent merchant in Edenton, and Clerk of the County Court). This woman "had known [Jacobs's grandmother] from childhood and always been very friendly to her," and her succor was indispensable during the many weeks when Jacobs's grandmother's house, and the houses of other black and mixed-race relatives and friends, were being searched. Jacobs then returned to her grandmother's house, where Jacobs's uncle, a skilled carpenter, had built a trapdoor to a tiny garret; here Jacobs was sequestered for seven years. A Southern-born ship captain was eventually found who, for a substantial fee (paid by members of Jacobs's free or nearly free family), was willing to undertake the considerable risk of taking Harriet, and another mixed-race slave who could also be represented as a free woman on her way to meet her husband, on his vessel from Edenton to Philadelphia.[16] Although Harriet Jacobs's membership in a privileged caste of people of mixed-race ancestry only partially protected her from Dr. Norcom's sexual harassment, and although her life and struggles were in many ways devastatingly harsh, her membership in that caste enabled her to escape some of the rigors of slavery.

As in Edenton, North Carolina, so too in Virginia something like a three-caste system existed. Its origins lay in the power of white men to demand sex from slave women. The Virginia interviews are most valuable on this point, because the elderly interviewees were less reluctant to talk about such matters with black interviewers than they would have been with white people. The frequency with which white men took slave women was striking. "My mama said that in [slavery] times a nigger 'oman couldn't help herself," reported May Satterfield, "fo' she had to do what de marster say. Ef he come to de field whar de women workin' an' tell gal to come on, she had to go. He would take one down in de woods an' use her all de time he wanted to, den send her on back to work. [Some] times nigger 'omen had chillun for de marster an' his sons and some times it was fo' de ovah seer. Dat's whar ha'f white niggers come from den" (*Interviews,* 245).

One interviewee after another recalled the sexual abuse of African American enslaved women. Ethel Mae, "a yaller girl . . . , couldn't help herself," one informant indignantly recalled. "She told me 'bout [her] Marsa bringing his son . . . down to the cabin. They both took her—the father showing the son what it was all about—and she couldn't do noth-ing 'bout it." This same informant had a mixed-race half-brother, the child of a white man who apparently had forced himself upon the informant's mother (*Interviews,* 300–301).

Some slave women successfully resisted attempted rapes. Minnie Folkes's mother told her that the overseer had whipped her for refusing to have sex with him, and that this happened a dozen times. She hadn't told her master because "ef slave would tell, why dem overseers would kill 'em [i.e., whip them particularly brutally]." Fannie Berry's report was the same. She herself had successfully resisted a rapist, but she sympathized with those women who submitted to compulsion. "Oh, honey," she ad-dressed her female interviewer, "some slaves would be beat up so, when dey resisted, an' sometimes if you'll [re]belled de overseer would kill yo'. Us colored women had to go through a plenty, I tell you" (*Interviews,* 93, 36).

Virginia Shepherd was the child of an apparently consensual union be-tween an unmarried house servant and an unmarried medical doctor who had just migrated to Virginia from the North. But Shepherd knew of the repeated rapes of another house servant, Diana Gaskins, by her master, a married man. Gaskins, Virginia Shepherd declared, "was dignity personified, the prettiest black woman I ever saw":

> Old master Gaskins . . . had his wife and children, but he just wanted his Diana in every sense of the [word]. He was really master of all he surveyed. He made demands on Diana just the same as if she had been his wife. Of course she fought him, but he wanted her and he had her. He use to send Diana to the barn to shell corn. Soon he would follow. He tried to cage her in the barn so she couldn't get out. Once she got away from him, went to the house and told her mistress how Gaskins treated her. The mistress sympathized with the girl, but couldn't help her, because she was afraid of her own husband. He would beat her if she tried to meddle. Indeed he would pull her hair out. Once when Diana was successful in fighting him off, he bundled her up, put her in a cart, and took her to Norfolk and put her on the auction block. (*Interviews*, 255, 257)

It was a matter for proud family recollection if an enslaved male ancestor had been able successfully to protect his daughter, or his wife, from rape. "In those days if you was a slave and had a good looking daughter," Robert Ellett averred, "she was taken from you. They would put her in the big house where the young masters could have the run of her." Ellett's father, however, was a valuable, strong, and fearless man who, Ellett said, had successfully protected his daughter from attempted rape, and Ellett was immensely proud of his father for having done so.[17] The Reverend Ishrael Massie was far less sanguine: "Marsters an' overseers use to make [married slave women] . . . do as dey say. Send husbands out on de farm, milkin' cows or cuttin' wood. Den he gits in bed wid slave himself. Some women would fight an tussel. Others would be 'umble—feard of dat beatin'. . . . My blood is bilin' now [at the] thoughts of dem times. Ef dey told dey husbands he wuz powerless. . . . When babies came [the white fathers] ain't exknowledge 'em. Treat dat baby like 'tothers—nuthing to him. Mother feard to tell 'cause she know'd what she'd git" (*Interviews*, 84, 207).

Not only were slave women subject to sexual abuse from white males, but they were likely to incur the wrath of jealous white females. This could happen even when a slave woman was *not* sexually involved with a white man. For example, a nearly white slave named Mary, who may have been a blood relation of her young mistress, Josephine, innocently provoked the jealousy of both Josephine and Josephine's mother. Mary had a seemingly privileged job as a house servant and probably was assimilated to the white people's genteel culture. "Mary was what de slaves called a 'clabber-colored' gal," reported the interviewee,

> wid long black [presumably straight] hair. Neither Josephine nor Missus Octavia liked her 'cause she was better lookin' dan either of dem. One day when Miss Josephine was in her room a-primpin' an' tryin' to make herself look purty, her feller come, so she sent Mary down to light a candle in de front room. Mary took de taper in to light de candle an' dis young spark of Miss Josephine's thought it was some white gal.
>
> "Won't you set down," he said to Mary, gettin' to his feet. Mary ain't said nothin', only light de candle an' hurry back upstairs. But Miss Josephine had heard it, an' she got so furious she wouldn't come down stairs at all. De nex' day she made Marsa take Mary to Richmond, an' dey say he hired her out or sol[d] her. (*Interviews*, 190)

Indignant and jealous white women often suspected their husbands of sleeping with slave women. The famous South Carolina memoir, *Mary Chesnut's Civil War*, expresses its author's loathing of African American women. "Those beastly negress beauties," Chesnut exclaimed passionately. "Animals—tout et simple." Although the aristocratic Mary Chesnut expressed hatred for the way white men of her class carried on with these women, her passion was directed most powerfully against the enslaved women themselves: "We live surrounded by prostitutes. . . . Alas for the [white] men! No worse than men everywhere, but the lower their mistresses, the more degraded they must be. . . . [We Southern white women are] surrounded by another race who are the social evil!"[18] The responsibility for adultery was that of the white men who betrayed their wives; yet the Southern social system impelled the white female victims of this treachery to direct their anger principally against other women.

Passions like those of Mary Chesnut stirred many Virginian white women who, betrayed by their husbands, turned their usually well-justified anger against other women. Often a plantation mistress would pretend to ignore the situation, but eventually might be goaded to assert herself. Jim, for example, was the favored child of a slave named Martha. "Ole Marse John ain't never had no chillun by his wife," an interviewee recalled. "His wife was pow'ful jealous of Martha an' never let her come near de big house, but she didn't need to 'cause Marsa was always goin' down to the shacks where she lived. Marse John used to treat Martha's boy, Jim, jus' like his own son, which he was. Jim used to run all over de big house, an' Missus didn't like it, but she didn't dare put him out." However, the wronged wife did finally revolt: "Never would let dat boy in de house no mo'" (*Interviews*, 91).

Mary Wood's great-aunt Fannie had not just one, but three "white chillun" by her master, and he favored her by banning the overseer from whipping her. He also tolerated her failure, sometimes, to obey his wife's orders. But one time Fannie's disobedience reached such a pitch that "ole misus got mad . . . and tole marse Ben dat he jes had to whip Fannie." Marse Ben's wife then discovered that, instead of whipping Fannie in the barn, he was having sex with her, confirming his wife's suspicions that the three mixed-race children were his. The "ole lady rared and charged so [that] the next week they sold Fannie . . . somewhere down South." In Harriet Jacobs's phrase Fannie had perhaps "submitted to compulsion," and this had earned her privileges for a time, but eventually she was forcibly separated from her children and her home (*Interviews*, 332).[19]

The same fate befell a slave woman named Aunt Charlotte. She had a "white baby by her young master," but she was sold to Georgia—never to see child or home again—when the child was only three months old. The master of another slave woman waited much longer before he punished his enslaved mistress (this time by deporting her children). After the master had produced six mixed-race children by the slave woman, there was finally "a fuss between him and his wife, and he sold all the children but the oldest slave daughter. Afterward [William Thompson testified], he had a child by this daughter, and sold mother and child before the birth."[20] Subject as white women were to their husbands' dominion, the Southern social system constrained the wronged white women to act, not against their male betrayers, but against their weaker female rivals.[21]

These were the circumstances under which a large number of mixed-race children came into the world. But although the sexual oppression of enslaved women is the most important part of this story, it is not the whole story. A substantial number of slave women tried, with varying degrees of success or failure, to turn white men's sexual desires, or their affection, to their own, and their children's, advantage. Light-skinned women were disproportionately successful in this effort. For example, Alice Marshall reported that her mother

> was de house maid an' de seamstress on de place. She ain' never got beat; she kinda favorite wid de white folks. . . . She a very light 'oman. My father? . . . It ain' my shame. 'Twas ole massa Jack Nightingale, mistiss' husband. . . . Chile, dat was ev'y day happenin's in dem days. Why on de 'jinin' plantation ole massa had a brother [Oliver Nightingale] what had a grea' big fat colored 'oman for his house maid. She light too. 'Deed dem two lived together jes' same's dey's married. And ole fat Sophie had chillun right and left. 'Twas more'n seven of 'em. I know. Sophie was treated very kind too. 'Pears lak dey got 'long better when dey's havin' dem babies. . . . [Ole marse Oliver] give Sophie all she need an' dem passel o' chillun of hern always look good. . . . One of [marse Oliver's mixed-race] sons is a smart doctor in Notoway County now (*Interviews*, 202).

The best-known illustration of this slave-woman's strategy was provided by Sally Hemings, President Thomas Jefferson's longtime mistress. Although we do not know Hemings's motives, we know the results of her gamble. She was a member of Virginia's third caste, not white, but not black either. She was the daughter of Jefferson's father-in-law, John Wayles, by a mixed-race slave woman, and was so light-skinned that she could almost pass for white (as two of her children by Jefferson later did). As the half-sister of Jefferson's wife, Martha Wayles, Sally Hemings so much resembled Martha physically—and perhaps to some degree culturally—that there need be no surprise that Jefferson was sexually attracted to her after Martha died. Jefferson probably promised Sally to free their children if she would become his mistress; and if there was a commitment, Jefferson honored it. By 1826, the year of Jefferson's death, all four of Sally's living children by Jefferson were free, and Sally herself was living in Charlottesville as though she too were free.[22] Perhaps Sally had calculated—as Harriet Jacobs later did in Edenton, North Carolina—that, in the constricted world of slavery, to become the mistress of a trustworthy white man might offer some slave women the best chance they could find of decent lives for themselves and their children.[23]

The historian Joshua Rothman suggests that it was precisely because Thomas Jefferson "could tell himself that Sally Hemings was somehow not really black" that Jefferson, with a sense of intellectual consistency, could maintain a long-term relationship with her, even though publicly and privately he expressed repulsion at the idea of sex between whites and blacks. Sally Hemings, to Jefferson, was not "black"; she belonged instead to a privileged intermediate group and "was technically considered a 'mulatto.'" Indeed, her children by Jefferson might become "white." From Sally Hemings's point of view, entering a risk-laden liaison with Jefferson finally paid off. "Every one of Sally Hemings's children," Rothman concludes, "[lived] their entire adult lives in freedom. No other enslaved woman at Monticello ever accomplished so much."[24]

Sally Hemings's son Madison Hemings benefited from interracial liaisons not only because he gained his own freedom (by Jefferson's will) but also because of the circumstances of his wife. Her name was Mary McCoy, and she married Madison Hemings in 1834. She was the granddaughter of a slave woman who (in Madison Hemings's words) had "lived with her master, Stephen Hughes, near Charlottesville, as his wife. She [Mary McCoy's grandmother] was manumitted by him, which made their children free born." Thus, Mary McCoy—as the daughter of a free black woman—was herself free, and consequently she was able to emigrate to Ohio with Madison Hemings (two years after their marriage). The couple thus profited hugely from the fact that Mary's grandmother had entered a liaison with a white man who had proved to be trustworthy.[25]

The advantages that might accrue to the slave mistress of a white man in Virginia are well documented, as in the case of Lucy Langston, a "very light" slave owned by a well-to-do bachelor, Captain Ralph Quarles. In 1806, after the birth of Lucy's first child by Quarles, the white man freed both Lucy and this child. Lucy had three more children by Quarles, and when he died in 1834 he bequeathed to these children the bulk of his considerable estate. One of them, John Mercer Langston—a graduate of Oberlin College—became the first African American congressman from Virginia. The well-known twentieth-century African American poet, Langston Hughes, was Lucy Langston's great-grandson. Although Lucy Langston's union with Ralph Quarles—which for want of a better term might be called a "long-term relationship"—was unorthodox, Quarles's influential white friends enforced the provisions of his will, and Lucy Langston was buried beside Captain Quarles, as that will specified. Lucy Langston secured for herself and her children lives that would scarcely have been open to them without Ralph Quarles's aid.[26]

In Virginia at least half a dozen other enslaved—or formerly enslaved—partners in similar long-term relationships are known to have been granted substantial legacies by plantation owners. In 1821 Frederick Ivey willed to his "wife" Priscilla (a dark-skinned woman) 1,300 acres, making her the biggest free black landowner in the state. Nathaniel Harrison willed to his common-law wife, Frankey Miles, an estate of 1,100 acres, along with ownership of nineteen slaves. In 1849 Henry Anderson left to Martha Farley (probably his long-term partner), and her sons, land totaling 1,550 acres, as well as twenty slaves. James Jackson freed his slave woman Patty in 1819, and in 1850 bequeathed to her and her children 950 acres. In 1821 Walter Gilliam willed thirty slaves and "large amounts of land" to Easter Tinsley and her two daughters. (When one of these daughters, Rebecca Tinsley, died in 1849, her estate was valued at the huge sum, for a free black, of $10,000.) In 1825 Henry Lipscomb's will granted twenty-seven slaves and substantial amounts of land to the African American Nancy Lipscomb and ten other members of Nancy's family. These grants are remarkable not only for the size of the bequests, but because of the rarity after 1806 with which rural slavemasters made a gift of freedom to any of their other slaves. (The great majority of slaves manumitted after 1806 bought their own freedom, and most often they did it with money they had earned in Richmond, Petersburg, or other Virginia cities.)[27]

Among Virginia's many WPA interviewees of mixed race, Robert Ellett best illustrates the advantages that might accrue to a child of mixed background. "I am a mixture of Negro-Indian-French and white blood . . . ," Ellett asserted, "so you can see why I was so proud, fearless, and full of the devil." Ellett alleged that his father's grandfather had been governor of Virginia, and this claim to ancestry in the state's ruling elite had probably contributed to Ellett's father's independence of spirit. "Father was French, Indian, and African," Ellett declared. "Such a mixture, you know, hated any walking white man [by which perhaps Ellett meant, any white man who did not behave respectfully]. Paw was very mean and always said just what he wanted. He met you half way and expected you to meet him the same." Ellett's mother was also of mixed race, her father having been a white preacher and her mother part Indian. "We was favored slaves," Ellett recalled. "My parents was the two best slaves on the plantation. They was valued high."

Ellett's maternal grandfather (the white preacher) bequeathed his mixed-race daughter and her children to a white woman, on condition that the enslaved family could not be sold out of the legatee's family. "I grew up with the young masters," Ellett remembered proudly. "I played with them, ate with them and sometimes slept with them. We were pals. Because of my unusual strength and spirit I would let none of them beat me at any game or in any wrestle." Ellett's refusal to call his young masters, "masters," got him into trouble with their father, who wanted to sell the stubborn child. But Ellett's special status as a mixed-race child—protected by his white grandfather's will from being sold out of the white family—averted the threatened sale. "That's all that saved me," Ellett acknowledged (*Interviews*, 84–85).

Of course, white ancestry did not always protect a mixed-race child. Ellett's cousin Rosena Lipscombe was the daughter of a white man (not her master) who, as her guardian, surreptitiously sold her South in violation of her master's instructions. Yet even in this case Rosena's being of mixed-race ancestry eventually accrued to her advantage. The man who bought her "said that she was too pretty and fine a girl to be sold." Rosena became the mistress of her new owner, and after the war he (on behalf of Rosena and himself) successfully sued Rosena's father for the property that should have been hers (*Interviews*, 86).

One reason that white ancestry might benefit a mixed-race child was that a white man who started by simply using a slave woman for sex might end up, to his surprise, caring for the children of this union. "Ole Marse [Tom] Greene" was one such person: "he buy a nigger 'oman name Betsy f'om some whar," an interviewee reported matter-of-factly, "an' use her. He was a bachluh you know an' he need a 'oman. . . . I useto play wid de kids. Dat 'oman had three chillun. . . . An' I clare if ole man Greene didn't think much o' dem chillun o' Betsy's as if dey was by a white 'oman" (*Interviews*, 250).

Rarely, a white man might even become so possessive of his mixed-race child that he would openly treat that child as a member of a third caste, separated from ordinary slaves. Thus, Matilda Perry's maternal grandfather, a rich planter who was the brother-in-law of a man named Tom Harris, separated his mixed-race daughter from the other bondpeople. "My mother was belonging to Tom Harris," Perry explained with some embarrassment. Harris's brother-in-law—the father of Perry's mother— "took [Perry's mother] away from her mother . . . and raised [her] up wid de white folks—didn't let her stay wid nigguhs. They was rich folks, you see. Didn't let 'em stay." Although Perry's white ancestry did not exempt her from sexual insults when she herself was a young girl, in later life she employed her connection with the white family to protect herself from these insults. Many slave women were afraid to protest against being sexually abused by white men, but Matilda Perry had the courage to do so: "I went and told [my mistress] because I was kin, don't you see?" Then—and here Perry became impatient with her male interviewer—"she objected him from, uh, you know, suffering me. . . . No more insults did I get from 'im 'cause she objected it. If I hadn't been kin, you understand, I would not come through like dat. 'Cause it was slavery times . . . , and you had to do what the white man said or the white woman said. . . . Don't care what dat was you had do what he said. Now what mo you want?" (*Interviews*, 224–25).

The "light complexioned" Hannah Bailey attributed the close social relations between her mother's family and the Montgomery family (who had owned her mother) to their kinship. "My mother . . . ," Bailey explained, "was a slave until she was about eighteen years old, but she was freed before the war. Her owner was ole Montgomery. He was a bachelor. He freed her before the war, left her money an' land an' some livestock, but she didn't get any of it." Apparently, Montgomery's white relatives successfully claimed that the war, and the abolition of slavery, made it impossible for them to honor the bequest Montgomery had made to his mixed-race daughter. Perhaps Bailey's mother felt there was some truth to this allegation, for she seems to have maintained a somewhat egalitarian relation with the white family, even after the bequest was nullified. "Mother used to mingle freely with the Montgomerys," Bailey recalled. "The families always have helped each other" (*Interviews*, 18–19).

Another Virginia master, named Munford, willed a very large sum to an African American family. The interviewee did not specify that Munford was the father of a mixed-race child, but this is the probable explanation for his generosity. "Old man Munford was very fond of this colored man's family," Virginia Shepherd explained, "and when he died recently, left young Munford $15000." Shepherd added, however, that Munford's white relatives had challenged the will, and she believed the young African American would not get a penny: "Of course the court backs the whites" (*Interviews*, 262).

Although the situation of a mixed-race child was always precarious, benefits often arose from the child's intermediate status. Candis
Goodwin, for example, smarted as a child from the taunts of children, at
the neighboring Williams plantation, that their master was her father.
"I knowd dat since when I's a lil thing," she recalled. "I uster go over to
Massa William's plantation. Dey tell me 'bout myself. De folks over dah
dey uster say to me, 'Who's yo' pappy? Who's yo' pappy?' I jes' say 'Tuckey
buzzard lay me an' de sun hatch me,' an' gwan 'bout my business. Cose all
de time dey knows an' I knows, too, dat Massa Williams was my pappy."
But although her mixed ancestry subjected Goodwin to derision at the
Williams homestead, her light skin may have won her favor at the home
plantation, where her mother was the cook. "My white people dey good
to me," Goodwin testified. "Cose dey gits mad wid you but dey don' beat
non o' us; jes' ack lak it. Why, I was jes' lak dey's chullun; I played wid 'em,
et wid 'em an' eb'n slep' wid 'em." Candis Goodwin's white half-brother
(the legitimate son of master Williams) became a dentist in Cape Charles,
Virginia, and although in public he kept quiet about his mixed-race half-
sister, he "uster go to see my son an' his wife lots o' times. Yes, dey's good
frien's" (Interviews, 107–8).

Other mixed-race interviewees felt they had derived benefit from their
white ancestry. Archibald Milteer's father was "a white 'free issue,'" whose
parents had also been free, and Milteer himself was born free to a free
African American mother. Another interviewee—Dr. Carter, a "light-col-
ored Caucasian featured mulatto"—was the child of a white father who
freed him and, according to Carter, trained him in root and herb doctor-
ing (Interviews, 213–14, 67). The Northern traveler Frederick Olmsted
witnessed (on a train approaching Fredericksburg, Virginia) the special
treatment accorded to a very light-skinned young slave woman who accompanied her middle-aged mistress, an older dark-skinned mammy, and
a youthful white girl. "There was a young white girl, probably [the white
woman's] daughter," Olmsted surmised, "and a bright and very pretty,
nearly white, mulatto girl of about the same age; the latter was dressed
as expensively, and appeared every way as well as the former, and they
talked and laughed together, as if on terms of entire equality and perfect
familiarity."[28] It was as though the mixed-race slave girl were a member of
a third caste.

"Lots o' white men had cullud wives," said another WPA informant

(*Interviews*, 250). It is clear that most such "wives" had submitted to compulsion; even a slave woman who "consensually" had sex with a white man undertook a grave risk that he, if untrustworthy, would betray her. One such untrustworthy white man was the rich Virginia planter whose slave Rachel (in about 1816) bore twins—a boy and a girl— whose father was the planter. The planter soon sold Rachel and the twins to his brother, who later resold Rachel and her daughter. When Rachel's son (later known as Thomas Hughes) grew up, he managed to find his father and "begged him to purchase and manumit me." Hughes also asked what had become of his mother, Rachel, and of his twin sister. "To all my entreaties he turned a deaf ear," Hughes lamented, "and in public would not speak to me as he passed. . . . So indifferent was he to [the fate of Rachel and her daughter], he had not taken the name of their purchaser, or the destination of the drove of which they formed a part."[29] Yet some slave women—especially some of those in the privileged intermediate caste—found in long-term relationships with a white man their best gamble that they might secure permanent advantage for themselves and their children.

As Harriet Jacobs said, different ethical standards were appropriate to slave women: their marriages did not have the sanction of law, and they were vulnerable to sexual exploitation unless they could find a trustworthy man to protect them. No doubt some of these slave women were opportunists, but others, like Harriet Jacobs, were honorable people doing their best under unimaginable circumstances.[30] It would scarcely behoove a later generation to be censorious of them.[31]

The contours of a three-caste system in Virginia were blurred by the presence of people who prided themselves on Indian ancestry. Some of these were slaves, others free. As previously indicated, the slave Robert Ellett attributed his father's pride partly to white ancestry (the father's grandfather was supposed to have been governor of Virginia); but Ellett was also proud of his mother, "part Red Indian." Similarly, the privileged position of Lizzie Hobbs as a slave child—"I stay' in de house with my mistiss. . . . I had sheets an' pillows to sleep on"—may have derived from her mother's being part Indian. And the same was perhaps true of Della Harris, whose mother—the cook—was also Indian (*Interviews*, 84, 142, 130–31).

Moble Hopson, however, experienced a very different version of a three-caste system. Born free, Hopson identified himself with the descendants of

Indians and whites, with no intermixture (he wanted to believe) of blacks. Although Hopson had white skin, "ah ain't white an' ah ain't black," he asserted, "leastwise not so fur as ah know." Hopson's mother seems to have been a free Indian, and his father was free too, though "sorta dark-skinned." "My people," Hopson said—adopting the explanation his father had offered—were produced by unions of white men with Indian women, after the whites had killed the Indian men. Hopson's father and an Indian uncle apparently had been landowners before the Civil War. The uncle, who owned slaves as well as land, fought on the Confederate side dur-ing the war, and resented the fact that black soldiers in the Union Army had taken Richmond. Before the war Hopson had sat on the benches in the church school beside his uncle's children, but sometime after the war the white people imposed a *two*-caste system: "First dey say dat all whut ain't white is black. And den dey tell de Injuns yuh kain't marry no more de whites. An' den dey tell usen dat we kain't cum no more tuh church school." Hopson's father's caste pride now wrecked the youth's chance to get an education: "My dad wouldn't let us go to school wid de Negroes, so we didn't git no schoolin'." Banned from marrying a white woman, and loath to marry one of his first cousins, the white-skinned Hopson ended up marrying a black woman. "An' dat make me black, ah 'spose 'cause ah ben livin' black ev'y sence" (*Interviews*, 146, 143, 144, 146, 148, 146).

Thus, Virginia's social system—prior to the imposition of a two-caste system after the Civil War—seems to have comprised four different ele-ments: white, black, mixed black/white, and Indian/white. Some Indians, like Moble Hopson's father and uncle, distinguished themselves from people of mixed black/white ancestry, but probably most people of part Indian descent (like Ellett, Lizzie Hobbs, and Della Harris) already re-garded themselves as part of the mixed black/white caste before 1861.

Appreciable numbers of Virginia slaves were granted privileged posi-tions within the plantation's occupational hierarchy (see chapter 13). Disproportionate numbers of these privileged slaves were probably of mixed-race ancestry.[32] These occupational privileges tended to reinforce the status distinctions accorded by masters to certain mixed-race slaves.

But very-dark-skinned slaves also sometimes held occupational posi-tions of great privilege. A notable instance—in South Carolina—was that of the valiant Stephen Gallant, an extraordinarily privileged body servant to Carolina's Governor Robert Allston, who quietly bided his time until the week in 1864 when he daringly executed the escape—to a Union vessel patrolling the seacoast—of almost his entire family.[33] This example suggests that the concept of a "third caste" must not be pushed too far. We may nevertheless conclude that a three-caste system operated, not only in seaport cities like New Orleans and Charleston, but also—to some degree—even in rural Virginia. Not only did it provide benefits to some free African Americans of mixed-race ancestry, but occasionally it offered substantial alleviations to the oppression of a few mixed-race bondpeople.

3

Cities and Industry

The harshness of a slave's existence might be mitigated by a good mistress/master, or if the enslaved person chanced to have mixed-race ancestry. A further factor might also lessen slavery's rigors: urban life. Just over 5 percent of Virginia's bondpeople lived in small cities where they could experience, by associating with substantial numbers of free blacks, a wider world than that of the plantation. Slavery has sometimes been seen as incompatible with urban life; but Virginia's urban tobacco factories depended on slave labor, and the growth of the state's tobacco-manufacturing towns (even during the 1850s, when slave labor was in heavy demand for the booming Cotton Kingdom) suggests that there was no inherent contradiction between slavery and urbanization. Factory owners were glad to hire enslaved workers on annual contracts, and many rural slave owners were happy to send their surplus slaves to work in town. Urban life offered these slaves more autonomy than they found on the plantation, without seeming substantially to undermine the solidity of the slave system.[1]

Virginia's antebellum cities were quite different from modern metropolises. They were towns whose population comprised between 6,500 and about 40,000 inhabitants, of which Richmond, with a population of just over 40,000, was the largest. In fact, by 1860 within the future Confederate states, Richmond was (except for the cotton-exporting seaport of New Orleans) the largest of all Southern cities, having just assumed this preeminence from Charleston, South Carolina.[2] Richmond's industrial prominence arose largely from its numerous tobacco-manufacturing firms, whose 3,500 workers were nearly all blacks, and mainly slaves. Petersburg (twenty miles south of Richmond) and Lynchburg—

(one hundred miles to the west)—were the two other Virginia cities whose industrial labor force consisted primarily of tobacco-manufacturing slaves.

Apart from these industrial towns, Virginia's urban life was concentrated in old seaports. Norfolk and the adjacent town of Portsmouth had a combined population of 24,000, while Alexandria (far up the Potomac River but still a destination for oceangoing vessels) ranked, with nearly 13,000 inhabitants, as Virginia's fourth-largest town.

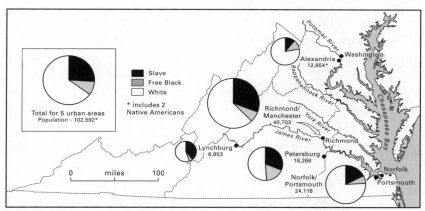

Map 2. Urban areas of "residual Virginia" (excluding later West Virginia), 1860

Table 2. Population of Five Virginia Urban Areas (1860)

Urban Areas	Total	Slave	Free black	White
Richmond/Manchester	40,703	12,442	2,798	25,463
Norfolk/Portsmouth	24,116	4,218	1,589	18,309
Petersburg	18,266	5,680	3,244	9,342
Alexandria	12,654[a]	1,386	1,415	9,851
Lynchburg	6,853	2,694	357	3,802
Total (5 urban areas)	102,592[a]	26,420	9,403	66,767
Percentage of the Total Population of These Five Urban Areas	100%	26%	9%	65%

Source: U.S. Census of Population, 1860

[a] Includes 2 Native Americans

Each of these urban areas had a black population of over 2,700 people. African Americans comprised 35 percent of Virginia's total urban population, 26 percent of them slaves and 9 percent free. Virginia's 26,000 urban slaves, living cheek by jowl with hundreds or even thousands of free blacks, and residing in cities where they might hope to evade the close supervision characteristic of plantation life, would have experienced slavery in a different form from that encountered by the great rural majority of slaves.

The distinctive character of urban life is demonstrated by the experiences of George Teamoh, a Portsmouth slave who later—during Reconstruction in 1869, only four years after the end of the Civil War—rose to local eminence when he was elected from Portsmouth as a member of the Virginia state senate. Teamoh was by no means a typical urban slave, for his mistress was extraordinarily beneficent, and he may well have had mixed-race ancestry. Teamoh's autobiography, begun in 1871, nevertheless indicates how urban life could widen the prospects of an enslaved African American.

Born in 1818 near Hampton, Virginia, Teamoh—together with his mother, a privileged house servant—was taken as a young child to Portsmouth when his mistress, Jane Thomas, married a man who lived in that city. Teamoh records that Jane Thomas was a most "generous, virtuous, and fair minded Christian lady," who promised Teamoh's mother that in due course she would emancipate George. His mother was the wet nurse for Jane Thomas's children, and when Teamoh was a child, he was dressed in a house boy's outfit and put to work in "parlor service and the [white children's] nursery." His consciousness of the differences between urban and rural slavery was sharpened when, at about age twelve, he was sent for a few months of labor on a Tidewater wheat plantation. The overseer regarded him as of a different breed—"a city nigger," a "spiled [sic] nigger," dressed in tights as though he were going to a ball. Teamoh compared the plantation's uncomfortable sleeping arrangements with what he had been accustomed to in the city, contrasting the smoke-filled quarters over a February night with his smoke-free urban dwelling, the dull food (and the chore of grinding corn at night after other labors were finished) with the fare and work pattern at Jane Thomas's.[3]

Outdoor political rallies took place in cities like Portsmouth and adjacent Norfolk, and a black person might sometimes manage to attend them in a servile role. The boy George Teamoh did so and claimed that before he learned his alphabet (at the age of fourteen), he had learned how to pronounce polysyllabic words, like "constitutionality," by listening carefully to public speakers. Apparently, as an adult he continued this form of urban education: "Though often driven from political meetings, I would as often shoulder my broom or be seen [as a servant], bearing a pitcher of water." In the early 1840s Teamoh worked for a time in the press room of a Portsmouth newspaper, the *Clay Banner and Naval Intelligencer*. By then he had learned to read, and he discovered that the stance of Henry Clay (the Whig presidential candidate in 1844) on slavery was somewhat different from that of the Democrats. The political education of this urban slave was proceeding apace.[4]

Well-disposed though she was, Jane Thomas nevertheless had not taught Teamoh to read. Living in a city, however, Teamoh heard that there was a school where a free black man taught free black children to read. As a slave, he was not eligible to attend, but his appetite to learn was whetted. When he was thirteen or fourteen, he was hired to work in a brickyard, and walking to and from work, he overheard white schoolchildren singing alphabet songs, which he memorized. Later (like Frederick Douglass in Baltimore) he was trained to the ship-caulking trade. Presumably, it was with earnings from this trade that Teamoh was able to buy, perhaps from a complaisant white shopkeeper, a copy of Walker's dictionary. Once able to read, an urban slave needed only to keep his eyes open in order to continue his political education. "I have learned much," Teamoh recalled, "from sign-boards, handbills, posters, &c. &c."[5]

In Norfolk the most popular religious establishment for slaves and free blacks was the First Baptist Church. Its white members had seceded in 1816, leaving it under its English-bred pastor, James Mitchell, who granted the blacks considerable autonomy in the administration of church affairs. Mitchell was a widower who dared in 1839 to challenge the mores of the local community by marrying the black woman who for years had been his housekeeper and had helped to raise the widower's white children. First Baptist, and Norfolk's two other black Baptist churches were, according to the historian Tommy Bogger, "run almost entirely by blacks. They had to have white preachers, but the individual congregations called the ministers to their churches and paid their salaries. The deacons, trustees, and clerks were usually free blacks who were responsible for carrying on the daily business of the churches and disciplining their fellow members."[6]

Teamoh, however, was not a Baptist. Jane Thomas was Methodist, and Teamoh was married in 1841 by the Methodist chaplain of the Gosport Navy Yard, where he was working as a ship caulker. Teamoh's record suggests that he had memorized passages from the Book of Common Prayer, read out perhaps in the local Methodist Episcopal church (which he may have supposed to be a branch of the episcopal Church of England). He even managed somehow to gain entry into the local theaters. Seeking information about slaves' place in the world, Teamoh claimed that he "took every opportunity to visit churches, political gatherings, theatres &c. with the hope that something might 'leak out.' I now regard the Theatre," he continued, ". . . as being one of the great educators of the nineteenth century. Next to this comes the Established Church of England. . . . Following the Episcopal form of worship, one who cannot read learns, verbatim . . . all that is laid down in the Book of Common Prayer, and can recite—after some years attention—any passages it may contain."[7] He thus gleaned much of his early education from institutions run wholly or primarily by white people, such as the Methodist church.

After learning the caulking trade, Teamoh was accorded the privileges, extended to many skilled urban slaves, of hiring himself out and finding his own housing, on condition that he pay his mistress a specified weekly sum from his wages. By these means he came into contact with a New England labor leader and journalist, Melzer Gardner, in the basement of whose Portsmouth boardinghouse Teamoh and his wife rented their lodgings. This association marked a significant step in Teamoh's political education.

Gardner's stance on slavery was shaped by the fact that black caulkers at the navy yard were paid 20 to 25 percent lower wages than were white caulkers for the same work. This naturally led to resentment. White workers complained that their wages were being undercut by blacks. Teamoh—unsure whether common ground could be found between the white workers and the black—soon discovered to what uses the term "abolitionist" might be turned. "I never did believe Gardner very favorably disposed to ward the colored race," Teamoh acknowledged; yet Gardner was attacked, by those hostile to the white workingmen's movement, as being antislavery. Gardner was killed in 1843 by a young lawyer who probably was part of this group: he "had been accused," Teamoh exclaimed, "and hunted down as an abolitionist by those from whose hands he received the fatal shot." Teamoh found himself laying out his acquaintance's corpse, and speculating whether Gardner's theories might "have resulted in the slaves' emancipation." He wondered whether black and white workers might ever have found common ground against the "ruling classes." Although Teamoh's report of these speculations was perhaps influenced by his later experiences of Reconstruction politics, they suggest the extent to which an urban slave could develop sophisticated political awareness even in the 1840s.[8]

It is possible, however, to exaggerate the extent of the privileges afforded to even the most favored bondman. After about 1845 Teamoh and other black caulkers were excluded from practicing their trade in the Navy Yard, because of pressure from white workers. The other government labor for which slaves could continue hiring themselves out was sometimes extremely dangerous, such as working on the fortifications of the artificial island named Fort Calhoun, only a few feet above the rushing ebb tide of the James River. An urban slave might be whipped "unmercifully for the merest fault, such as being late at work," and could even come into mortal danger from an arrogant white bully (as Teamoh did when working as an assistant fireman at the Navy dry dock). An enslaved laborer might also run afoul of a black overseer (as happened to Teamoh when a subservient black overseer discovered him with a hidden primer and terrified him for three years into not pursuing his study of that book).[9]

Above all else, family life, even of a privileged slave like Teamoh, could be torn asunder. Teamoh's wife was seized from him in 1853, a disaster that impelled him to flee from Virginia later that year. Yet even here his privileged position helped him, for Jane Thomas, his mistress, aided and abetted his escape to the free states, where he remained until he was able to return to Portsmouth after the Civil War.

Richmond was much the most important of Virginia's cities, and nearly half of the state's urban slaves lived there. In 1860 about 2,840 male slaves labored for Richmond manufacturers of chewing tobacco.[10] The largest tobacco factory employed 150 hands (all of them men, the great majority enslaved), and the next largest had 132 hands.[11] Nearly 500 of Richmond's tobacco-manufacturing slaves were owned by their employers. More than

2,300 of the others, however, were hired out to the tobacco-factory owners, nearly always on annual contracts (often by rural masters who had
more slaves than they could profitably use in agriculture). So common
was this hiring practice that numerous Richmond agents found a profit—
ranging from 5 percent to 7.5 percent of the annual hiring payment—by
serving as intermediaries, bringing rural masters into contact with factory owners who wished to hire slaves.[12]

A rural master could avoid paying the hiring agent's fee by permitting
his slaves—like free workers—to find their own factory jobs. And the factory owner could save trouble and expense by giving the enslaved worker
a bit of weekly cash, on condition that the worker find his own room and
board, instead of the factory owner's being obliged to provide these items.
The enslaved worker remained, of course, subject to factory discipline,
including whippings by white overseers. Factory owners discovered, however, that they could secure larger output by fixing a daily task and reward-
ing their enslaved workers with a cash bonus for any surplus production.
A quick worker might earn $1.00—or sometimes even up to as much as
about $4.00—in a week, for this extra output.[13] During the 1850s, because
of the cotton boom in the Deep South and the rapid increase in tobacco
growing in Virginia's Piedmont counties, there was a shortage of slave
laborers. Under these circumstances, a Richmond factory owner might
impel his overseers not to whip the hired hands too much, lest the factory
gain a bad reputation and find it difficult to secure enough hired labor the
following year. Although overseers did sometimes use their whips and pis-
tols,[14] labor practices in these factories began to look something like those
of a free-labor factory, and rather different from those on a plantation.[15]

Nearly 60 percent of Richmond's male slaves worked in its tobacco factories.[16] The others were scattered in a variety of occupations, including
factories in certain other industries. Best-known were the skilled workers
at the famous Tredegar Iron Works. Slaves had been used by the Tredegar
management to break a strike of white workers in 1847. Despite the racial
antagonisms inevitably produced by this crass management strategy—
analogous to similar tactics later employed by free-labor factory owners
both North and South—about 80 slaves were still working at Tredegar
beside some 720 white men by 1860. Tredegar slaves were paid cash if
they produced more than their quota, but the historian Ira Berlin reports
that they "usually received less than one dollar a month in 'over work' pay

and only rarely as much as three dollars." Two hundred fifty slaves were employed in two Richmond flour mills (which ranked as the second- and third-largest such mills in the whole United States). Others worked as artisans, laborers, or domestic servants. The black man and his wife who provided hotel room service—making up the fire, laying out his clothes— to the traveler Frederick Law Olmsted when he stayed in Richmond in December 1852 were slaves. Olmsted, a critical observer, declared the room service at this Richmond hotel the best he had ever enjoyed in the United States. Some of these Richmond slaves, like those in the city's to- bacco factories, were hired and shared the advantages of urban life expe- rienced by tobacco-factory slaves.

In some cases slaves embarked on self-hire, as in the case of the skilled carpenter and shoemaker Parke Johnston, whose lenient master let him self-hire in Richmond, Petersburg, and other towns where he could find well-paid work at his trades. Johnston "went back at intervals to stay with his wife and children on the [Charlotte County] plantation." Theoretically, self-hire of this sort was banned, but even after a reenactment of the prohibiting statute in about 1853, the ban was not strictly enforced. In Richmond there were no convictions at all for this offense in 1845, and only one in 1850; although there were more convictions during the follow- ing decade, the numbers were still smaller than in the 1830s. The historian Rodney Green concludes that "relatively light fines were levied against the masters. . . . [The] enforcement of the anti-self-hiring statutes was light." Some masters considered it convenient to allow a slave like Parke Johnston to find his own work. Self-hired slaves provided significant ser- vices to their employers, and the authorities felt little need to try to extir- pate what had proved to be a useful customary arrangement.[17]

Richmond's female slaves—as in other Southern cities—remained largely confined to domestic service; yet their association with hired male workers enabled them to share the somewhat less constricted lives of those bondmen. Some female domestics were hired out, just as in Norfolk, where Eliza Smith was rented out by her mistress, "but was not permitted to hire herself, as her mistress declared she should not do it, for 'it gave niggers such stuck up notions of freedom.'" In Richmond, however, a few female domestics no doubt *were* allowed to hire themselves, just as Susan Boggs did in Norfolk. "I paid my mistress a quarter of a dollar a day for my time, but I got more than that," Boggs recalled with satisfaction, "and had the rest for myself." Self-hire enabled Boggs to avoid both working for tyrannical employers and undertaking distasteful work, developing in her an independence that may have given her the self-confidence, sometime around 1850, to undertake a successful escape to Canada.[18]

Travelers remarked that some of Richmond's African Americans (many of whom, of course, were free blacks) had money to spend on colorful clothes, and that they seemed to walk the streets with a little more confidence than might have been expected. "There was no indication," Olmsted observed, "of their belonging to a subject race, except that they invariably gave the way to the white people they met. Once, when two of them, engaged in conversation and looking at each other, had not noticed his approach, I saw a Virginian gentleman lift his cane and push a woman aside with it." African Americans were expected to submit to insults of this sort, and the one man whom Olmsted saw defying bullies was probably a free black, not a slave. "In the evening," Olmsted reported,

> I saw three rowdies, arm-in-arm, taking the whole of the sidewalk, hustle a black man off it, giving him a blow, as they passed, that sent him staggering into the middle of the street. As he recovered himself he began to call out to, and threaten them. . . . "I'll teach you how to behave—knockin' people round!—don't care if I does hab to go to der watch-house." They passed on without noticing him further, only laughing jeeringly—and he continued: "You come back here, and I'll make you laugh; you is jus' three white nigger cowards, dat's what *you* be." . . .
>
> Except in this instance . . . I have seen not the slightest evidence of any independent manliness on the part of the Negroes towards the whites. . . . Their manner to white people is invariably either sullen, jocose, or fawning.[19]

Acts of public defiance might be rare, but they were less infrequent in the city of Richmond than in the more repressive atmosphere of rural Virginia. One reason for the difference was that contact with the city's 2,800 free blacks widened the perspective of Richmond slaves.[20] As early as 1830 some 2,000 free African Americans already resided in the city, and at that time they made up nearly one-eighth of Richmond's total population.[21] They established a substantial institutional life of their own, which enslaved blacks could to some degree share.

Their most important institutions were three black Baptist churches, claiming by 1860 a total membership of 4,433 (including children), a majority of whom may well have been slaves. The leading First African Church (established as a semiautonomous body in 1841) boasted a building so large—seating 1,500 people—that white Richmonders used it when they wanted a mammoth hall for big political meetings.[22] The church was legally obliged to have a white pastor, and it was ultimately governed by the nearby white "First Baptist Church" (of which the "First African Church" was an offshoot). But, as in Norfolk's black Baptist churches, Richmond's white Baptist pastor and the white governing committee accorded free blacks considerable autonomy, in both the religious and the administrative conduct of church affairs. Black assistant preachers—such as the famed John Jasper—preached to massive black congregations in the First African Church, and black deacons (nearly all of them free) ran the church administration much as they wished. These deacons were chosen by an electorate comprising *some* of the free blacks; the black assistant preachers seem to have been put forward by the deacons (subject to a veto by the white pastor). The pastor's salary was largely paid by voluntary contributions from black parishioners; and slaves (who made financial contributions toward the purchase of the church building, as well as toward the pastor's salary) seem gradually to have acquired customary rights within the church administration.[23]

The most notable instance of pressure from slaves to extend their privileges occurred as early as 1848. A petition was presented, praying that slaves—in addition to free blacks—be allowed to vote in electing the church's black deacons. True, this was not for a conventional "political" leader, only for a church administrator. But blacks were gaining, in the conduct of church affairs, the semipolitical experience that they later (during Reconstruction) used in conventional politics; these Richmond slaves, remarkably, proposed for themselves voting rights within the church. Not surprisingly, their appeal was at first ignored. But by 1852 the slaves had apparently acquired an unwritten right to participate in the recall of an unpopular free black deacon. (The white governing committee even appears to have backed the slaves in this dispute between two different factions within the black church.) That slaves could venture such an appeal, and could gain at least part of what they sought, demonstrates their relatively unconstricted life in Richmond.[24]

The privileges extended to black Baptists in Richmond were not, however, replicated in the tobacco-manufacturing town of Lynchburg. Black Baptists there were obliged to listen to a white pastor preaching the usual cant about obeying masters, very little relieved by exhortations from sympathetic black preachers. The administration of Lynchburg's black Baptist church remained firmly in the hands of white governors.[25] The problem may have arisen from a shortage of free blacks able to undertake administrative duties. Even by 1860 Lynchburg had only about 250 free adult blacks—only one-eighth the number in Richmond: scarcely enough to supply many church leaders. But Lynchburg, a much smaller city than Richmond, was also perhaps less likely to detach itself from the mores of the surrounding rural area than was the relatively cosmopolitan Richmond.

A benefit of urban life was that slaves in cities like Richmond and Petersburg were far more likely to be manumitted than were those in rural Virginia. This bias in favor of urban slaves only surfaced after 1830. Between 1782 and 1806 an appreciable number of planters had—for religious and moral reasons—freed thousands of Virginia's rural slaves. But in 1806 the state legislature placed a severe damper on this movement by requiring every slave freed after that year to leave the state (unless exempted by special legislative act). Thereafter the number of rural slaves who gained their freedom declined dramatically; and a substantial proportion of those few who were liberated were the mistresses or children of white men like Thomas Jefferson, hence light-skinned. A dark-skinned slave in rural Virginia no longer had much chance at all of being freed.[26]

After about 1830, however, economic conditions in Virginia's Piedmont cities improved to such an extent that an appreciable number of urban slaves—many of them not of mixed race—gained their freedom. Over 600 did so in Richmond and Petersburg between 1831 and 1860 (an average of 21 freedpeople per year), and more than 400 did so in other Virginia cities and towns. Only 10 percent of these freedpeople were probably liberated because they were the mistresses or children of white masters.[27] A few of the other freedpeople were liberated by the benevolence of their masters. But the vast majority of these African Americans became free because they (or their spouses or other relatives) had paid hard cash for their freedom. Such transactions required the consent of masters willing to grant freedom in exchange for cash (and many masters refused); nevertheless, these were not acts of benevolence, but commercial transactions.

Scores of heroic slaves labored, scrimped, saved, and finally succeeded in buying their own or their relatives' freedom.[28] Emanuel Quivers, for example, was hired to work at the Tredegar Iron Works (perhaps as one of the slaves against whose employment a famous strike of white workers was aimed in 1847). Quivers persuaded the Tredegar manager, Joseph Anderson, to purchase him—at the high price of $1,100—probably on the understanding that Quivers would then try to buy his freedom from Anderson. Quivers's skill was such that he was made a foreman, at a wage of $7.50 per week (over and above his room and board). By saving virtually this whole sum every week, Quivers was able by 1852 to buy, not only his own freedom, but that of his wife and their four or five children. The family then emigrated to the free states. Although Joseph Anderson had set a high price on Quivers, he helped the favored slave to purchase his freedom and that of his family by lending him money at a low interest rate, which Quivers repaid from his earnings. Doubtless Quivers was a strikebreaker in 1847, but he cannot be faulted for this, because the strike was aimed at excluding black workers at Tredegar. One can scarcely fail to be touched by the grit of this determined family.[29]

Unlike the Quiverses, most manumitted slaves stayed in Virginia, where they had friends and relatives. They were able to do so because after 1816 the legislature (to relieve itself of a time-consuming chore?) deputed to local courts decisions about whether a manumitted slave might be permitted to stay in Virginia.[30] If freed slaves supplied references from white people affirming their industry and high character, urban courts usually granted them permission to stay. Labor was scarce in the Piedmont cities, and a substantial number of whites could see that black people who had managed to earn their own purchase price were likely to be exemplary and useful members of the community. Self-interest inevitably governed the actions of some (though not all) well-disposed white people, but the story of slaves laboring for their freedom is an inspiring one.[31] Thus, Richard Hobson, an enslaved Richmond barber, bought his freedom in 1841, and later bought his wife and son, whom he then emancipated. By the 1850s, Hobson owned real estate.[32]

Another urban route to freedom was for a slave to "marry" a free black (this status was not legally binding), who might purchase the spouse and then—or later—free that person. For example, a free black woman in Richmond named Maria James managed to purchase her husband from

his white owner, and in 1854 she freed him. Probably more common, however, was the practice of free blacks buying their spouses but *not* then
freeing them—for fear that the local court might require the manumitted
slave to leave the state. Thus, in addition to those urban slaves who gained
freedom, others lived in a sort of quasi-freedom, because their legal owners were their spouses.[33]

All of this information, however, needs to be placed in perspective. The
average of just one dozen Richmond slaves (some of them children) manumitted each year, between 1831 and 1860, is minuscule compared with
Richmond's enslaved population, which in 1850 numbered about 10,000.
Manumission in Virginia's cities, for example, did not operate on the scale
it did in Cuba, where during the 1850s some 2,000 slaves annually gained
their freedom. (These were mainly skilled urban slaves who purchased
their own liberation.)[34]

Yet another route to freedom was taken by a few slaves from Richmond
and Petersburg. Although it was not impossible for a slave to escape to
the North from a city like Baltimore, as Frederick Douglass did, because
it was near the free states, it was much harder to flee most cities further
south. Surprisingly, however, Richmond and Petersburg were not quite
so difficult to escape as might at first appear. Oceangoing vessels still
made their way up the James River to Richmond (or to City Point near
Petersburg), and during the last antebellum decade at least twenty-six
slaves managed to escape by sea from those inland cities, apparently aided
by a black "underground railroad" system within Richmond, as well as by
black seamen on the vessels and sometimes by white captains willing to
risk aiding a fugitive in return for a large cash payment. During the same
decade at least forty other slaves escaped from Richmond and Petersburg
by overland travel. Although a handful of these may have been rural fugitives who had hidden in Richmond or Petersburg until they could make
arrangements to set off for the North, most appear to have been urban
slaves. Nevertheless, the number of slaves legally resident in Richmond or
Petersburg who successfully fled those cities was very small, compared to
the cities' total enslaved population.[35]

Richmond factory life, however, tells a different story about the benefits
a slave might gain from living in an urban setting. A rural slavemaster
in 1858 warned other rural masters to beware of being bamboozled by

Richmond factory owners, when the latter were hiring slaves for the coming year. According to this writer, work in tobacco factories undermined—
at least temporarily—the stamina of the slaves laboring there. "Servants
who have once worked in tobacco factories," he warned, "are in a measure
disqualified for other employments; at least it takes some time to make
them efficient laborers for other purposes, after they have been cooped
up in the unwholesome and destructive atmosphere of a tobacco factory.
. . . [If you hire out your servants to some other, rural employment,] in
one year your factory hands will become acclimated and seasoned to the
country."[36] During one stage of tobacco manufacture, according to the
historian Joseph Robert, "sweating Negroes constantly stirred [a murky
brew of licorice and sugar, in huge iron kettles] with wooden paddles to
prevent scorching or burning. The sticky black fluid, smoking hot, was
poured into troughs," into which tobacco leaves were immersed, ensuring
a product attractive to the palates of tobacco-chewing customers. Then
"dippers, stark-naked in their rooms near the drying roofs, applied sticky
flavorings." In the summer male slaves worked, steaming in these hot-
houses, for perhaps fourteen hours a day (including breaks for meals);
after months of this dreadful indoor labor, a slave might well have been
made temporarily unfit for the different outdoor demands of agricultural
work.[37]

Male slaves hired to factory owners, whether in Richmond or Lynchburg,
also endured the constant disruption of family life. Among slaves of marriageable age in both cities, there was a huge surplus of males to females.
From ages ten through thirty-five, Richmond counted some 4,450 male
slaves, but only about 2,690 females.[38] Some male slaves had wives back
on their home plantations; but this did little for a man miles away in
Richmond, who might not see his wife and children again until near the
New Year (when annual hiring contracts were made). Some male slaves
married free black women, of whom there was a surplus of about 150 in
Richmond.[39] But even allowing for these factors, prolonged separation inevitably undermined the solidity of the slaves' family institutions.[40]

Because urban slavemasters (especially factory owners) exercised less
supervision over the personal lives of their enslaved workers than did
plantation owners, municipal authorities devised regulations to control
the urban slave population, strengthening the municipal police system
in order to enforce them. Curfews kept slaves off the streets late at night,

unless a slave carried a pass signed by a master. "Disorderly conduct" was often punished by whippings. Assaults against white people were treated with severity. No doubt some of the most absurd attempts to regulate slaves' lives—such as bans on their selling goods in the public markets— were widely disregarded. Nor do bans against self-hiring or boarding out by slaves appear to have been much enforced.[41] But the historian Stephen Tripp has demonstrated that in Lynchburg municipal ordinances against assault, disorderly conduct, and public drunkenness were implemented much more rigorously against slaves and free blacks than against the white working classes. For example, in cases of assault or fighting brought before the mayor's court during a sample period, only 8 percent of the arraigned blacks were released without punishment, while 56 percent of the arraigned whites were either released or merely put on bond for good behavior.[42]

Despite these municipal efforts to impose discipline, urban slaves clearly were less subject to regimentation than on most plantations. Did this relative relaxation of slave discipline in Virginia's cities foster an increase in violent slave resistance? Was further urbanization thus incompatible with the long-term security of the slave system? The answers to these questions appear to be negative. It is true that, in a much-publicized 1852 case, a seventeen-year-old slave killed a nineteen-year-old white overseer in a Richmond tobacco factory, hitting him on the head with an iron tool when the overseer persisted in whipping him.[43] But there were always isolated instances of violent resistance against whippings, both on plantations and in the cities, and there is no convincing evidence that the number of such instances increased in Virginia cities during the 1850s. In Lynchburg (where slaves comprised 39 percent of the population) only one case of violence by a slave was serious enough to reach a state court (during a two-year sample period, 1858 and 1860), although during the same period there were twenty such cases involving white assailants (the violence always, so far as we know, directed against other whites), and one involving a free black.[44] In the whole state of Virginia, the number of slaves convicted of murdering white people, which averaged just over three annually during the 1850s, was *lower,* in proportion to the number of slaves, than in most previous decades. This suggests that lethal slave resistance was not on the increase in Virginia's cities (nor anywhere else in the state).[45]

One reason, in addition to the municipal police force, was that individual white people surely imposed their own private regulation of the
slaves' conduct. Olmsted supplied small illustrations of such private
enforcement: the "gentleman" pushing the black woman aside with his
walking stick, the rowdies knocking a black man into the street. More
seriously, in autumn 1852 overseers killed slaves in two separate tobacco-
factory incidents, one in Richmond and one in Lynchburg. In neither case
does the killer appear to have been prosecuted. Reporting the shooting
and killing of the Richmond slave (who was resisting a whipping), the
Lynchburg newspaper heartily condoned the overseer's action: "Nothing
short of the use of the deadly weapon will produce subordination in our
factories."[46] If not even killing a slave was likely to land a white assailant
in court, a mere assault was unlikely to do so. Thus, the fact that no white
person was ever arraigned (during Tripp's sample period) for assaulting a
slave suggests not that there were no such assaults, but that Lynchburg's
municipal authorities did not try to punish such attacks.[47] No slave could
testify against a white assailant, and white witnesses would seldom be
willing to testify. Why, except in the case of severe damage to enslaved
"property," should the authorities try to curb "minor" assaults by whites
against blacks? Slaves, even in urban areas, were still slaves.

Industrial slaves were used not only in cities but also in two rural set-
tings. Ironworks, principally in the central and southern portions of the
Valley of Virginia, employed during the 1850s perhaps 4,000 enslaved
workers; and bituminous coal mining in the "Richmond Basin" utilized
the labor of perhaps another 1,600 bondmen.[48] Although some of these
slaves were owned by the manufacturers, many were hired.[49] Some enslaved ironworkers gained privileges comparable to those of Richmond's
enslaved tobacco-factory workers; a few skilled ironworkers even reaped
benefits greater than those available to (relatively less skilled) tobacco-
factory hands. Work in the coal mines, by contrast, was so dangerous that
few slaves relished being hired away from agricultural tasks to labor underground.

A handful of enslaved ironworkers, if they were highly skilled, might,
by exceeding their quotas, earn from $90 to as much as $200 in a year; a
few other slaves, by Sunday work cutting firewood or hauling coal or iron
in a wagon, or by selling their own agricultural produce, might earn from

$60 to $140 annually. At least one enslaved ironworker is known to have deposited his savings in a local bank.[50] But an average ironworker appears likely to have earned less than $12 a year through overwork.[51]

Although most overwork payments were small, a slave hired on an annual basis to labor at an ironworks might nevertheless turn his situation to his own advantage. The fundamental explanation for this is that most iron manufacturers did *not* own their whole enslaved workforce. With limited amounts of capital to invest in their enterprises, manufacturers could not afford to spend too much money on buying slaves, because they needed considerable sums to invest in ore fields, woodlands (to supply timber for charcoal), blast furnaces, and forges; and to pay wages to certain skilled white workers and foremen. Furthermore, demand for iron fluctuated widely from year to year, and a Virginia ironmaker—who faced low-price competition from Northern and British manufacturers—needed to be able to reduce his labor force quickly, if the demand for his product should suddenly plummet. Consequently, most Virginia ironmakers hired many of their slaves on an annual basis.

All the jobs at these ironworks were hot and onerous, some were dangerous, and some required the exercise of considerable skilled judgment. If Virginia's economy was booming, as it was during much of the 1850s, there always seemed to be a shortage of suitable hands. If a slave proved to be a satisfactory worker, an iron manufacturer had a strong incentive to hire the slave again for the following year. The slave's owner, however, had a financial interest in the slave's being treated relatively well. Owners did not want their slaves injured by being exposed to unnecessary dangers, nor did they wish harsh treatment by the ironmaster to impel their slaves to flee to the woods (or to the North, which was not very far from the Shenandoah Valley). Many an owner talked with a slave at the end of the year to discover whether he was reasonably satisfied at the ironworks or whether it might be better to hire him to a different employer the following year. Alternative employment was available at other ironworks, or in the tobacco factories, or in the construction of the railways being built in the 1850s.

The owner of a slave hired to an iron manufacturer might listen to the slave's report of his experiences and instruct the hirer accordingly. "Davy Says that Working in the furnace is ruinous to his Eyes," wrote one slave owner to the ironmaker; "therefore I do not Wish him to work there against his will." Through the slaves' grapevine a slave could learn the reputation of an employer to whom his master purposed to hire him. "I have not been able to get you any hands," a hiring agent wrote to the iron manufacturer William Weaver; "some of the hands . . . have made somewhat an unfavourable impression on the negroes in the neighborhood as to the treatment at [your ironworks]." One owner, fearing that one of his slaves might permanently disappear, changed his mind about hiring this man out to a particular employer. "Recent declarations of his," the owner explained, "has left no doubt on my Mind, but he wou'd make an effort to reach the State of Ohio, and by being placed at your Works it wou'd greatly facilatate his Object. Was I to send him . . . , it might be the means of my loosing the fellow entierly." The owners' anxieties often impelled them to give their slaves a voice in determining to whom they would be hired. As one hiring agent explained to William Weaver, the owners "let their hands [who are to be hired] go pretty much where they please." That iron manufacturers competed against each other (or against the tobacco factories and the railways) for the next year's supply of suitable slave labor impelled them to treat their hired slaves more gingerly than they might have done, had they owned all of their enslaved workers.[52]

Against these substantial advantages of a slave's being hired out to an iron manufacturer must be set several disadvantages. Although workers *owned* by an ironmaker could often live with their families, many hired workers were separated from their own families by long distances, and they might be permitted to visit home only rarely, if at all, except during the Christmas hiring season. Furthermore, the danger of accidental injury at an ironworks was much greater than in agricultural labor. The cold January trek across the Blue Ridge from the Piedmont to the Valley of Virginia carried its own midwinter perils.[53] Nevertheless, a substantial number of slaves preferred being hired to an ironworks rather than the alternative—perhaps being sold into the Deep South and permanently separated from family, friends, and community.

The dangers of coal mining, on the other hand, were so great as to outweigh, for most slaves, any advantages that might have accrued to them from their situation as hired workers. Coal could be shipped cheaply from Richmond by water, down the James River and up the East Coast, to Baltimore, New York, Boston, and Philadelphia. Before about 1850 the Richmond Basin was the principal source of the bituminous coal already beginning to be used in those cities for domestic heating and to produce the gas burned there to illuminate city streets. Not until the extension of the Chesapeake and Ohio Canal to Cumberland, Maryland, in 1850, and the completion of northern trans-Allegheny railways at about the same time, did the coal mines near Richmond lose their geographical advantage in reaching the Northeastern market. The majority of the Richmond Basin coal miners were hired slaves, whose lives could be insured. Insurance substantially counterbalanced the reluctance owners might otherwise have felt about incurring the risk that an expensive slave could die in a mining accident. Slaves, unlikely to volunteer to work underground—uncompensated as they were except by small overwork payments—could be forced underground by masters insured against financial risks. Forty-five blacks—probably all or nearly all slaves—died in 1839 in a mine explosion twelve miles southwest of Richmond. Three years later an explosion at the Midlothian mine (the biggest firm in the Richmond Basin) killed over thirty-four workers; and about fifty-five more perished there in 1855. Workers not blown up in these explosions were afterward asphyxiated by carbolic acid gas, when trapped underground. Other injuries or deaths regularly occurred to enslaved miners from rock falls, or when a rush of water unexpectedly flooded a mine shaft. Charles Montague may not have been the only hard-nosed slaveholder to regard hiring out a man to work in the coal mines as a punishment that a refractory slave richly deserved. Thus, although being hired to an urban tobacco factory, or to a rural ironworks, might alleviate the hardships of a bondman's life, being hired to labor in a coal mine was a different matter.[54]

Although slavery seemed by 1860 to be withering away in the large border cities of Baltimore, St. Louis, and Washington, and although even in New Orleans the enslaved population had declined to scarcely more than half what it had been in 1840, urban slavery was thriving in Virginia's tobacco-manufacturing towns.[55] The presence in Virginia of cities like Richmond, Petersburg, and Lynchburg, where the regimentation of slaves was less strict than in rural areas, seemed to pose even as late as 1860 no threat to the stability of the slave system. The number of slaves in these cities greatly increased between 1820 and 1860, growing proportionately nearly as fast as the white population until 1850 (though less rapidly in the subsequent decade).[56] Richmond, which had some 4,400 slaves in 1820, had nearly tripled that count by 1860. Similarly, the number of slaves in Petersburg grew from 2,430 (in 1820) to nearly 5,700 (in 1860). In the latter year African Americans comprised 49 percent of Petersburg's total population.[57] Thus, Petersburg in 1860 was, proportionately, the most substantially black city in the whole United States; and this was largely the result of the employment of slaves in its tobacco factories.

The relative relaxation of slave discipline in Virginia's cities does not appear to have fostered an increase in violent slave resistance—indeed, slave violence may well have been decreasing, per capita, in these cities as it was elsewhere in the state. A few of Virginia's urban slaves managed to buy their own freedom (or that of family members), but not many. A handful of urban slaves escaped to the free states, but again, not many. If some white people in Virginia began, after the passage of the Kansas-Nebraska Act of 1854, to panic about the future of slavery, this was because Southern political leaders (mostly Southern Democrats) had provoked the growth of a substantial, if moderate, antislavery movement in the North, not because of an incompatibility between slavery and urbanization.

It is clear that urban slavery was flourishing in Virginia's interior cities. The annual rent a Richmond tobacco factory would pay to hire a rural slave more than doubled during the 1850s.[58] The number of slaves in Richmond and Petersburg continued to increase during that decade by nearly 20 percent despite the countervailing attraction to slavemasters of shipping bondpeople to the booming Cotton Kingdom (which led to a 30 percent decline in the enslaved population of Norfolk/Portsmouth during the same decade).[59] Industrial slavery in the tobacco-manufacturing cities was making Virginia slavemasters, both urban and rural, more prosperous than they otherwise would have been. Thus, the employment of slaves in tobacco factories, far from undermining slavery in Virginia, inoculated these inland Virginia cities from the "cotton fever" that reduced the slave populations of several other Southern cities.

Only a small minority of Virginia slaves, by residing in Richmond, Petersburg, and Lynchburg (and even in the old ports of Norfolk/Portsmouth and Alexandria), continued to gain wider experience of the world, and to lead somewhat less trammeled lives, than they would have done on rural plantations.[60]

Part II

OFFENSES

The publication in 1956 of Kenneth Stampp's *The Peculiar Institution* indicated that the offenses committed by slavemasters against bondpeople were finally being fully acknowledged by white historians. But although Stampp presented a powerful, accurate, and balanced picture of the conditions imposed upon slaves, he underestimated the slaves' capacity to defend themselves against their oppression. By the 1980s a series of path-breaking books argued that bondpeople had created a new Afro-Christian religion, had cherished their own strong family institutions, had nurtured a rich community life, and had developed their own "internal economy" (to supplement the food and clothing allowances allotted them by their masters). These books have vastly increased our understanding of the slaves' resilience, but they may sometimes have exaggerated how much space was left by slavemasters within which slaves could develop their own institutions. The Virginia interviews present a rich array of evidence, regarding both the conditions imposed on bondpeople and the slaves' responses to thralldom. Often a single piece of evidence throws light on both conditions and responses. It may nevertheless be useful to focus, for several chapters, mainly on the conditions imposed on slaves, reserving most discussion of the slaves' responses until later. This approach may help us assess where the balance lay between the slaves' oppression and their self-determination.

4

Family Disruption

Seventy years after Emancipation one Virginia interviewee after another boiled with indignation at how black people had been treated. I have already touched on the problem of family disruption for slaves working in urban factories. All slaves lived with the omnipresent threat that families would be disrupted when a master decided to sell some of his slaves, inevitably making black people feel they were being treated like animals. "They used to sell slaves . . . ," Robert Ellett reported angrily, "jes' like you sell sheep, cattle, or horses." The Reverend Ishrael Massie was equally enraged: "Dey put ya on dat block an' whosoever wanted ya, bid fer ya. De hig[h]est figger in de biddin' got ya," he exclaimed. "Ain't ya don seen auction sales of property like dat? . . . Sometimes de slaves be in pens like cattle." Patience Avery was too young to remember slave sales, but she had heard so much about the Richmond slave market that she knew what happened there. The traders, she explained, would "bring slaves in groups, tied an' chained together. Den dey would put 'em in pens lak cattle. You seen horses an' cows in a pen havencha? Well, dat's de way humans was treated" (*Interviews*, 85, 205, 15).

Black women were presented as breeding creatures like mares. "De ole masters didn't keer . . . ," Avery continued. "Firs' dey 'examine you a bit, den dey start off sellin' lak a auction sale o' property. You know how dey do. Say, '$50.00, $50.00, $50.00, etc., $100.00, $100.00, $100.00, Fine young wench! Who will buy? Who will buy? She got little niggers, good an' healthy.' De hig[h]es' bidder would get de slave. Um! Um! Um!" (*Interviews*, 15–16).

Of all the slaves who lived in Virginia at one time or another during the forty years before the Civil War, probably more than

one-fifth were sold away from the state (usually to the Deep South). At
least 183,000 slaves were sold away from Virginia during this period.[1] Of
these, some 42,000 were children under fifteen (a substantial number only
ten or eleven years old, and some even younger) sold separately from both
parents. Another 18,000 were young children taken away from their fathers (but sold with their mothers). Some 33,000 more were women taken
away from their husbands or men sold away from their wives.[2] These are
conservative estimates of interstate sales after 1820 and take no account
of the thousands of similar sales from 1790 to 1820. Nor do these figures
register the many thousands of other sales of slaves from one master to
another within the state's wide borders. Thus, in addition to all the bondpeople sold away from Virginia, there were probably (between 1820 and
1860) at least 366,000 other sales of slaves from one Virginia master to
another, many of which must have disrupted slave families.[3] These commercial transactions inflicted a body blow upon Virginia's enslaved population, which in 1860—after all of these sales—numbered about 500,000.
The threat of being sold away from one's family, or of some members of
one's family's being sold away—never to be seen again—was virtually
universal.

Young children growing up in rural southwestern Virginia learned early
that black people were moved in droves—like cattle—along the roads
toward the Deep South. Catherine Beale, age eleven, was sold to a Deep
South trader. Her master had died, and his sister felt bad about selling the
little girl away from her mother and her family, but conscientious scru-
ples did not deter the white woman from shattering the black family. This
woman, Beale recalled, "took me and my sister out on the back steps and
tol' us we would have to be sold. She said she hated it because she had to
sell us and take us away from our mother and family but there wasn't any
money an' they had to have some from some place and they had decided to
sell us. She took us to Richmond an' sold us to a slave buyer an' he brought
us to Macon [Georgia]."[4]

By the 1850s railway transport was available, but most of the Virginia
slaves sent into the overland interstate slave trade walked all the way to
their destinations.[5] "The only time I ever rode" in a wagon, Beale recalled,
"was when we come to the ferry. . . . We didn't travel on Sunday, we rested.
. . . One woman named Rosetta died. She had a little baby. . . . They buried
her side the road. . . . They brought the little baby on with 'em an' an-

other woman nursed it, but it died before we got to Macon."[6] Lorenzo Ivy lived, as a boy, a few miles north of Danville (bordering North Carolina), and witnessed shackled black people walking South. "I've seen droves of Negroes," he exclaimed, "brought in [to Danville] on foot goin' Souf to be sol'. Each one have an old tow sack on his back wif everythin' he's got in it. . . . Dey walk in double lines chained tergether in twos. Dey walk 'em heah to de railroad an' ship 'em Souf lak cattle." Robert Williams, who grew up on a plantation near Lynchburg, saw what happened when "de white folks would come up from de cotton country and buy slaves and carry dem back in droves." This was a sight that stamped upon a young boy a clear impression of his own animal-like status in the world. "I done seen groups of slaves," Williams testified, "women, men and children walking down the road, some of the women wid babies in dey arms and some on ox-carts wid babies all on dey way to de cotton country. Some of dem would hardly have on any clo'es. We lived near de road and dese groups of slaves would come ve'y often when cotton season was in. . . . I was a little boy wukin' 'round de house, and sometimes dese slaves would stop 'cause dey would git sick. Some of dem had on shoes and some didn't. Dey was just like cattle in a herd" (*Interviews*, 153, 323).[7]

When Robert Williams was older, he sometimes could obtain a pass on a Saturday to go to Lynchburg, where he made it his business to watch a slave auction. Lynchburg was a center of the tobacco trade, and slaves there were like tobacco, sellers hoping to reap a good price from their sale. "I seen dem sell slaves on de block down on Ninth Street in Lynchburg," Williams remembered:

De block was a big rock dat slaves would stand on so dey would be up over de crowd. De seller would cry bids just like dey sell tobacco: "$150, who will make it a $160," an' so on. Some of de bids would start as high as $400, 'cordin' to de condition of de person. De women would have just a piece around her waist (something like tights); her breast an' thighs would be bare. De seller would have her turn around and plump her to show how fat she was and her general condition. Dey would also take her by her breasts and pull dem to show how good she was built for raisin' chillun. Dey would have dem 'xamined to show dey was in good health. De young women would bring good money such as $1000 or more 'cause dey could have plenty chillun an' dat whar dey profit would come in. (*Interviews*, 325–26)

The sale of black people exerted fearsome fascination over the imaginations of young enslaved children. When Fannie Brown was a little girl in
Fredericksburg (north of Richmond), she pushed her way through a crowd
so that she could see what was going on. "I went up close among de white
folks gathered roun' de warehouse," she recalled, "peepin' in through de
windows to see de slaves. . . . Jim, a big six-foot, tall slave, come out smi-
lin', and his shirt was took off, and den dey start 'zaminin' him. Dey jerked
his mouth open an' look at his teeth an' den slapped him on his back,
an' den dey said, 'Dis is a prime nigger. Look at dese teeth.' . . . Jim was
knocked down to de highes' bidder [for $1000] an' was handcuffed an' put
in de coffle wid de other slaves dat had been sol'." The child never forgot
this experience (*Interviews*, 60).

These auctions tore families apart. Joe Dardin's master, for example,
sold him to a Richmond trader as punishment for making unauthorized
visits to his wife. Sargry Brown, who worked in Richmond, apparently
was sold to a trader and never saw her husband again. John Francis, a
fugitive slave interviewed in Canada in 1855, testified that "my mother
was sold away from me, when I was about eleven years old." In 1937 one
former slave after another poured years of accumulated bitterness into
accounts of how their families had been dismembered. Arthur Greene's
master sold Greene's brother to the Deep South at the age of about nine;
this was one reason, Greene surmised, that his master had gone to hell.
God, indeed, had punished the master's whole family. "Ole Dr. [George
Bland] never lived no time after de surrender [1865]. God took him away
from here—donno to which place. All his six chillun dead too," the old
black man reported.[8]

When a sibling was sold, the feelings of those left behind were of
bereavement, and the image of an angry God was again invoked. The
Reverend Ishrael Massie reported to a black interviewer things he would
never have told a white person: "I kin tell ya a mess 'bout reb times [i.e.,
before 1865], but I ain't tellin' white folks nuthin' 'cause I'm skeer'd to
make enemies. Lord chile," he continued, "dar wuz mo' grievin' an' mo'
crying over de family partin'—jes' like de grief when ya sister or brother
dies. . . . Speculatin' on us humans! God's gwine punish deir chillun's chillun . . . ! I had two brothers sold away an' ain't never seen 'em no mo' 'til dis
day." Similarly, Caroline Hunter's brothers were sold away from her and
her mother; Sister Harrison's two brothers were traded away (but had the

good fortune of being able to return home after Emancipation); and an older brother and an older sister of Minnie Folkes were sold down South. Matilda Carter's master, who otherwise was kindly, became enraged at the favoritism his wife displayed toward Carter's older sister, and out of spite he traded this older sister "down South. Mother never did git over dis ack of sellin' her baby to dem slave drivers down New Orleans" (*Interviews*, 205–6, 149, 135, 94, 68).

Carol Randall's saddest memory was of the sale of her older sister Marie. "I cried," Carol murmured. "Mother an' sister cried too, but dat didn't help. . . . Marie was pretty, dat's why [our master] took her to Richmond to sell her. . . . You could git a powerful lot of money in dose days for a pretty gal. Dey took her to de Carolinas. . . . I ain't never seen dat pretty sister of mine no more since de day she was sol'. . . . It nearly broke my heart" (*Interviews*, 236).

The most embittered curse among all the 1937 interviews was that of Anna Harris, born in 1846. "No white man ever been in my house," Harris intoned icily. "Don't 'low it. Dey sole my sister Kate. I saw it wid dese here eyes. Sole her in 1860, and I ain't seed nor heard of her since. Folks say white folks is all right dese days. Maybe dey is, maybe dey isn't. But I can't stand to see 'em. Not on my place" (*Interviews*, 128).

The threat of selling a slave South was a fearsome instrument for imposing discipline. Just as some masters circulated terrifying tales of life in the free states—in order to deter slaves from fleeing North—so they projected horrifying images of the Cotton Kingdom, to induce fear of sale to the South. "Child," Fannie Berry expostulated, "it makes me shudder when I hear talk of dat cotton country. I ain't never seen dar an' I don't wanta!" Charles Crawley—declaring that if long-term fugitives slaves were caught, they were sold South—continued, "Dey tell me dem marsters down Souf, was so mean to slaves dey would let 'em work dem cotton fields tel dey fall daid, wid hoes in dey han's." Caroline Hunter's three brothers (whose father was a free black man) were not docile, and when whippings failed to curb their spirits, their master converted them into cash: "If de massa couldn' rule you," Caroline phrased the maxim, "dey would sell you." James Taliaferro's father—who had been taught by his master's son—once supplied a mathematical drawing to support a slave woman's protest that her task had been measured unjustly. This challenge infuriated the master:

"Marsa came to my father," Taliaferro reported, "and said, 'Drat your picture, I'm going to sell you.' And he was going to, too, but Thomas, Marsa's son, persuaded his father not to sell my father. Father always kept his mouth shut after that 'cause he had heard the slaves talking about being sold to Georgia" (*Interviews*, 33, 78, 149–50, 282).

Another reason to sell slaves South—besides the wish to impose discipline—was to get rid of slave women who had incurred their mistresses' jealousy. Thus, Liza McCoy's aunt Charlotte "was sold to Georgia away from her baby when de chile won't no more 3 months. . . . Aunt Charlotte had white baby by her young master. Dats why de[y] sold her south." Similarly, after a slave woman named Fannie had had three children by her married master, his wife finally "rared and charged so [that] the next week they sold Fannie and the new marster carried her somewhere down South" (*Interviews*, 199, 201, 332).

By far the most important reason for sales, however, was neither to impose discipline nor to appease the jealousy of white women, but simply to make money. Such sales sometimes occurred when an estate was being settled. Virginia law—placing the interests of white "property" owners above those of the enslaved—authorized breaking up slave families in order to place the specified shares of a legacy into the hands of the various legatees. Painful though these sales might be, slaves regarded them as to some degree involuntary.

Slaves understood, however, that most sales were voluntary, consummated for financial reasons alone. Katie Johnson perceived that when she and her mother were auctioned, it was not an estate division. On the contrary, their bibulous master "was selling us because he had 'drank us up.'" George White expressed his contempt for the financial motives of many white sellers by making an exaggerated claim: "My mistress was a dressy woman an' when she wanted a dress, she would sell a slave." Susan Broaddus's master was prosperous enough to supply his wife with the luxury of having a little slave girl stand behind her at the dining table "an' reach her de salt an' syrup an' anything else she called fo'." Yet this master grumbled that, because he was not doing well enough, he intended to sell two of his men. "One day," Broaddus recalled, "Marsa was fit to be tied, he was in setch a bad mood. Was ravin' 'bout de crops, an' taxes, an' de triflin' niggers he got to feed. 'Gonna sell 'em, I swear fo' Christ, I gonna sell [two of] 'em,' he says" (*Interviews*, 161, 309, 55).[9]

Michael Tadman's book on the interstate slave trade focuses on the separation of husbands and wives from each other, and that of young children from one or both of their parents, yet it underemphasizes the place of family split-ups in the consciousness of Upper South slaves.[10] As we have seen, slaves were shaken by the sale of their siblings; and the interviewees' picture of their world was also shaped by family tragedies that had been experienced by their grandparents, aunts, uncles, and cousins. The marriage of Carol Randall's grandparents was broken when their Charlottesville master sold the grandmother and her two children to another Virginia master but retained the grandfather in his own service. Four or five of Louis Fitzgerald's grandmother's children were sold South when they were teenagers, and she never saw them again. Mary Wood's grandmother's brother was sold as punishment for resisting a whipping, and the grandmother's sister was also sold when her mistress discovered that her husband had been having sex with her. The Reverend C. W. B. Gordon's grandmother was sold to Louisiana, away from her daughter. (This is the only one of these stories with a happy ending: after Emancipation Gordon found his grandmother in Louisiana and brought her back to live with the family in Virginia) (*Interviews*, 236, 92, 331–32, 110).

When relatives were sold, the sellers' motives were usually mercenary. For example, one interviewee "had an aunt [who] took fever in war time— left her feeble minded. She wandered off sometimes." The masters therefore converted this otherwise relatively valueless slave woman into cash by selling her: "They knew at big house traders was coming—kept it from her. . . . We never saw her no more." When Ellis Bennett described an uncle's sale, he reported again the slaves' animal-like status in the eyes of their masters: "White folks sell colored folks lak cattle, sheep, pigs. Dey have whole pens of colored folks. . . . Sell 'em by carload. Sold mah uncle." Robert Williams's master—a lawyer in Lynchburg who also had a substantial nearby farm—was comparatively humane to Williams, and there is no reason to suppose him to have been a drunkard or improvident. Yet even in the prosperous 1850s he thought nothing of selling slaves in order to profit from the high prices then prevailing: "Dey sold my cousin an' sent her down in de cotton fields of de deep South, 'cause master got short of money. . . . Just fo' de War started, master had planned to sell 'bout four of us [but the war intervened]" (*Interviews*, 346, 29, 326). Beverly Jones had a "purty good" master, yet this man sold two of Jones's aunt's seven children. This was the Aunt Crissy who (as previously recounted), dared to express to her master's face the bitterness about his engagement in slave trading that most slaves felt obliged to dissimulate (*Interviews*, 183).[11]

The sale of her fifteen-year-old son outraged Susan Boggs—a privileged Norfolk slave—and impelled her to flee to Canada. Interviewed there in 1863, Boggs stated that she had been better off materially as a slave in Norfolk than as a free woman in Canada, because in Norfolk her rich mistress had allowed her to hire herself out and to keep for herself whatever she could earn over what she paid her mistress. "I was never distressed much in slavery myself," Boggs acknowledged. Her husband, by contrast, had been monstrously treated—"crippled in consequence of the overseer's kicking him so as to bring him down and make him humble." The offense that brought Susan Boggs to the breaking point was not, however, her husband's injury, but her son's sale: "A son of mine—the only son I had—was sold for a thousand dollars." He was sold, for purely mercenary reasons, by the young medical doctor for whom Susan Boggs had been the nanny when he was a child. She could not believe this young white man could do such a thing. "Although I had seen thousands of others sold," she said with some hyperbole, "I thought the selling of my son was the awfullest thing I ever saw." Boggs impelled her teenage son to escape (presumably on shipboard from Norfolk), and she was then jailed for three weeks as a suspected accomplice. Four months later she fled (presumably also on shipboard to a Northern port and then by the Underground Railroad to Canada) in order to rejoin her son. The sale of this youth had brought home to Boggs that, even though she herself was treated well, her strongest family tie could be arbitrarily sundered at the whim of a heartless white slavemaster.[12]

Young though most of the WPA interviewees were in 1865, a handful of them had already by then been sold or threatened with sale. Jane Pyatt, as her interviewer recorded, "was sold with her mother when she was only three months old." The sale was from a rural Tidewater county to Norfolk, and evidently it terminated her mother's marriage. When a woman in an "abroad marriage" was auctioned, the parcel could not include the husband (who was owned by a different master); white people took for granted that the marriage would be destroyed unless the buyer happened to live in the same neighborhood. Thus, when Katie Johnson's mother and the child Katie were sold, a discussion arose between seller and buyer about whether mother and child would be separated from each other, but there was no discussion of the mother's separation from her husband—which was assumed as a matter of course (*Interviews*, 234, 160–61).

Virginia Shepherd's mother (who, like Jane Pyatt's and Katie Johnson's mothers, had an abroad marriage) experienced two scares that she—with her two young children—would be sold. First, their rural "master began to get bad and threatened to sell mother and us children to a bad master. That was the worst punishment a slave could receive." The potential buyer, however, was not willing to pay the inflated price set by their master, and the negotiation fell through. Then during the Civil War—when Shepherd's mother was hired to cook at a Portsmouth hotel—Northern soldiers were nearby, and their master ordered Shepherd's family to be jailed, where "hundreds of other mothers and their children [were] sleeping on the floor at night just waiting their turn to be sold South. Each day some were sold off. Mother prayed we'd be spared. . . . My mother cried a lot." Although it turned out that their master had incarcerated them only to prevent his losing them to the Yankees, Shepherd's mother did not know this. In these instances, usually, the parcel sold—or putatively to be sold—was a mother with young children, separated from her husband; most such transactions, of course, destroyed nuclear families. Thousands of such sales occurred in Virginia, and mothers knew that if they were sold with their young children, they would probably never see the fathers of their children again (*Interviews*, 261, 256).[13]

Masters permitted slaves only such marriage vows as would incorporate these hard realities. To the slaves such ceremonies were obvious violations of Christian principle. Matthew Jarrett's voice burned with resentment as he contrasted slaves' ceremonies with Christian ones: "We slaves knowed that them words [in the slaves' ceremonies] wasn't bindin'. Don't mean nothin' lessen you say 'What God done jined, cain't no man pull asunder.' But dey never would say dat. Jus' say, 'Now you married.'" Fear of slave sales was built into Caroline Harris's wedding, over which her aunt presided. Aunt Sue, Harris explained, "called all de slaves arter tasks to pray fo' de union dat God was gonna make. Pray we stay together an' have lots of chillun an' none of 'em git sol' way from de parents" (*Interviews*, 158, 129).

This deeply rooted presumption among both white and black people—that if a woman had young children, the standard unit for sale did not include the children's father—surely had significant impact upon the slaves' understanding of family institutions. If Virginia's lawmakers had sought to strengthen slaves' nuclear families, they would have made it illegal to sell wives and husbands away from each other. But the legislature never considered doing so, because slavery in Virginia was, for the masters, primarily a business operation. Banning the separate sale of wives and husbands would have diminished the value of the masters' investment in their enslaved property. The feelings, and the marriages, of the wives and husbands remained legally unprotected, and slaves regarded those mistresses and masters who respected their feelings as "good."

The tentacles of the slave trade extended into every part of Virginia—and everywhere it aroused the same emotions. At an estate sale in Norfolk, a slave woman and her infant were auctioned because "each one of the young [white] folks wanted his share." The slave woman was sold, Virginia Shepherd recounted, "to one of those greedy Richmond nigger traders. She begged him to buy her baby, but he refused. So the poor woman just had fits right there. She couldn't stand the thought of being wrenched from her baby. But she was taken to Richmond just the same and sold down South. . . . Nothing worse could have happened to her." Although this woman was taken away from the father of her baby at the same time, this was standard practice; the separation of mother from infant was what struck Mrs. Shepherd's mind (*Interviews*, 258).

Inland from Norfolk similar events took place. "They used to sell slaves one mile below King William Court House [north of the York River] . . . ," Robert Ellett reported indignantly. "They would drive them up there in droves from [adjacent] counties and sell them. They would be handcuffed with chains and shackled with a long chain running down the middle of them, first two men and then two women, all in a long line waiting to be sold." William Johnson avowed that in his part of the country (west of Richmond), "White folks . . . didn't think anything of breaking up a family and selling the children in one section of the south and the parents in some other section." Johnson—born in 1840 and a credible witness—was cynical about the sellers' motives. "If they got short of cash, and wanted four or five hundred dollars," Johnson believed, "they would say, 'John, Mary, James, I want you to get ready and go to the courthouse with me this morning.' They would take you on down there and that's the last we'd see of them. When they put the women up on the auction block, bidders would come up and feel the women's legs, lift up their [g]arments and examine their hips, feel their breast, and examine them to see if they could bear children. If the women were in good condition they would bring anywhere from $150.00 to $500.00 a piece" (*Interviews*, 85, 166).

In Appomattox County, southwest of Richmond, Fannie Berry spoke of "an ol' white man who had one hundred head of slaves an' he sold 'em. . . . Dar was a great crying and carrying on mongst the slaves who had been sold. Two or three of dem gals had young babies taking with 'em. Poor little things." And miles south of Richmond, Sis Shackelford knew of "a slave-jail built at de cross roads wid iron bars 'cross de winders. Soon's de coffle git dere, dey bring all de slaves from de jail two at a time an' string 'em 'long de chain back of de other po' slaves. Ev'ybody in de village come out—'specially de wives an' sweethearts and mothers—to see dey solt-off chillun fo' de las' time. An' when dey start de chains a-clankin' an' step off down de line, dey [in de coffle] all jus' sing an' shout an' make all de noise dey can tryin' to hide de sorrer in dey hearts an' cover up de cries an' moanin's of dem dey's leavin' behin'. Oh, Lord!" (*Interviews*, 33, 253).[14]

No wonder, then, that in 1865, when freedpeople at one Virginia crossroads contemplated the meaning of freedom, an old woman's first thought was of freedom from the auction block. "Member de fust Sunday of freedom," Charlotte Brown testified:

We was all sittin' roun' restin' an' tryin' to think what freedom meant an' ev'ybody was quiet an' peaceful. All at once ole Sister Carrie who was near 'bout a hundred started in to talkin':

Tain't no mo' sellin' today,
Tain't no mo' hirin' today,
Tain't no pullin' off shirts today,
Its stomp down freedom today.
Stomp it down! . . .

Wasn't no mo' peace dat Sunday. Ev'ybody started in to sing an' shout. . . . Fust thing you know dey done made up music to Sister Carrie's stomp song an' sang an' shouted dat song all de res' de day. Chile, dat was one glorious time! (*Interviews*, 58–59)

When a slave (or a slave's child) was sold, the seller put that slave "into his pocket"; this understanding of the metaphor hovered in the mind of one former slave woman when, many years later, she zestfully told her granddaughter how she had reacted to the news of Emancipation. She had been hired out to do ordinary field labor on a farm seven miles from where her mistress lived. When she heard of freedom, "she dropped her hoe," her granddaughter explained, "an' run all de way to [her home plantation]— seben miles it was—an run to ole Missus an' looked at her real hard. Den she yelled, 'I'se free! Yes, I'se free! Ain't got to work fo' you no mo'. You can't put me in yo' pocket now!'" (*Interviews*, 180).

5

Physical Abuse

In Virginia physical brutality toward slaves was supposed to be less prevalent than in the Deep South, but the firsthand slave accounts make one question the meaning of such hopeful relativism. The old black people interviewed in 1937 found a kind of catharsis in talking about the physical violence they had experienced.

It was seldom feasible for a woman openly to resist a whipping, yet the spirit of resistance is often present in slave accounts. Thus, when Marrinda Singleton was very young, and hunger led her to steal vegetables from the plantation vegetable patch, she willingly undertook the risk. "Sometimes you'd be caught and git punished," she boasted. "We didn't keer 'cause us had gotten use to dem terrible beatings." With a (perhaps male) confederate Singleton successfully stole a pig and killed it. "Dis pig was now divided equally [with the confederate]," Singleton said,

> and I went on to my cabin wid equal share. All de chillun was warned not to say nothin' 'bout dis. If dey did, I tole 'em I would skin 'em alive, 'cause dis pig was stole to fill their bellies as well as mine. By some means de news got to Marster 'bout dis pig dat we had stolen.
>
> Ole Marster took me to de Big House right dar in de yard, stripped me stark naked and whipped me 'til de blood dripped to de ground.
>
> Now dis is de way dey whipped us slaves. Marster or a Colored overseer would stand on one side or so, so he could lash de whips on you in a row across your back, den he would turn on de t'other side and cross dem whips. They pickle you down wid salt, den re-

cross dem whips again. When dey got through wid you, you wouldn't want to steal no mo'. Yas sur, if you see a pig a mile off you'd, ha, ha, feel like runnin' from 'im.

The grim jest, after three-quarters of a century, nevertheless bespeaks a spirit of defiance, latent earlier but resurgent later (*Interviews*, 266–67).

Children could not protect their parents. Allen Wilson burned with hatred at how his mother had been treated. Although she—when a teenager—had been permanently injured from a fall, this disability won Wilson's mother no favor with the master or the overseer, and when Wilson was a boy he could scarcely bear what he witnessed. His master "use to whip mother awful. . . . I'se seen . . . dat dam [expletive] overseer," Wilson continued, "take my dear mother; strip her clothes off down to her waist; tie her to a ole peach tree . . . right behind the house whar we lived in and give her 9 and 30 [lashes] wid his cowhide. . . . I prayed Gawd dat someday he'd open a way fur me to protect mother. I use to tell my brother . . . , 'ef I [get to be] a big man, le's kill dat man [the overseer]!' Wid my bad temper I know ef de War hadn't ended I'd done hit" (*Interviews*, 327).

Nor could husbands protect their wives. "Husbands allays went to de woods when dey know [in advance] de wives was due fo' a whippin'," Jordan Johnson explained, "but in de fiel' dey dare not leave. Had to stay dere, not darin' even look like dey didn't like it. Charlie Jones was one slave dat had his wife workin' in de same fiel' wid him. Was plantin' tobacco—he was settin' out an' she was hillin'. Annie was big wid chile an' gittin' near her time, so one day she made a slip an' chopped a young shoot down. Ole man Diggs, de overseer, come runnin' up screamin' at her an' it made her mo' nervous, and she chopped off 'nother one. Ole overseer lif' up dat rawhide an' beat Annie 'cross de back an shoulders 'till she fell to de groun'. An' Charlie he jus' stood dere hearin' his wife scream an' astarin' at de sky, not darin' to look at her or even say a word." It is not hard to imagine the emasculating effect of such enforced passivity (*Interviews*, 160).

One of the rules was that a slave must never challenge a white man. If a slave met a white person, the slave must quickly cast his or her eyes to the ground, in order to avoid any appearance of contesting the white person's authority. "White folks was sho mean den," Horace Muse averred. "Better not look at 'em real hawd. Ef you did, you was sassin' 'em an' dey beat you to death. Yessuh!" The aim was to intimidate bondpeople so that they would be easier to govern. We would wish to believe that slaves were seldom intimidated, but we may fail to reckon how deeply the acid of enforced subordination ate into the self-confidence of appreciable numbers of bondpeople (*Interviews*, 215).

Like their husbands, enslaved women also had to keep their eyes to themselves when their spouses were flogged. "How did our Marster treat his slaves?" Marrinda Singleton asked, rhetorically. "Scandalous, dey treated us jes' like dogs. The Colored overseer would beat both men and women. If dey beat our husbands and we looked at dem dey would beat us too. Often dey stripped de women as well as men stark naked" (*Interviews*, 266).

White men had the power to try to flog women into submitting to sex. "Honey, I don't like to talk 'bout dem times," an old black woman said to her young female interviewer,

> 'cause my mother did suffer misery. . . . Dar was an overseer who use to tie mother up in de barn wid a rope aroun' her arms up over her head, while she stood on a block. Soon as dey got her tied, dis block was moved an' her feet dangled, you know, couldn' tech de flo'.
>
> Dis ole man, now, would start beatin' her nekked 'til the blood run down her back to her heels. I took an' seed de whelps an' scars fer my own self wid dese heah two eyes. (This whip she said, "was a whip like dey use to use on horses; it was a piece o' leather 'bout as wide as my han' f'om little finger to thumb.") After dey beat my mother all dey wanted, another overseer[—] Lord, Lord, I hate white people and de flood waters gwine drown some mo'. Well honey, dis man would bathe her in salt an' water. Don' you know dem places was a hurtin'. . . .
>
> I asked mother, "what she done fer 'em to beat and do her so?" She said, "Nothin' tother [than] 'fuse to be wife to dis man."
>
> An' mother say, "If he didn' treat her dis way a dozen times, it wasn' nary one."[1] (*Interviews*, 92–93)

White women could be as cruel as white men. "De ole 'oman was de devil," in Liza Brown's judgment. Brown was one of eight children. Her mother was the cook and fell under the dominion of her mistress. "When mother was in pregnant stage," Brown recalled, "if she happen to burn de bread or biscuits, Missus would order her to the granary, make her take off all her clothes . . . sometimes 'twon' but one piece. After she had stripped her stark naked she would beat mother wid a strap. You know it had so many prongs to hit you wid. She beat all de slaves cruelly, dat 'hell pigeon' did" (*Interviews*, 63).

The whipping of a pregnant slave woman led, occasionally, to disaster. Pregnancy offered less protection against whipping than one might expect, given the fact that a slave baby promised further income. Lucy, a pregnant young slave woman, was in the mornings "so sick she couldn't go tuh de field. Well," an interviewee continued, "dey thought dat huh time was way off an' dat she was jes' stallin' so as tuh git outa wukkin'. Fin'lly de overseer come tuh huh cabin . . . an' he dragged huh out. He laid huh 'cross uh big tebaccy barrell an' he tuk his rawhide an' whupt huh somepin terrible. Well suh, dat woman dragged huhse'f back tuh de cabin an' de nex day she give birth tuh uh baby girl. . . . De nex' day Lucy died" (*Interviews*, 190).[2]

Cases of apparent manslaughter like this one were seldom prosecuted, and rarely successfully. Even white people who murdered slaves were not often convicted—not even of manslaughter, and almost never of murder. The historian Thomas Morris, discussing the whole South, writes that "almost all homicides of slaves . . . ended in acquittals, or at most in verdicts of manslaughter. . . . There were also killings that never led to criminal actions."[3] The lives of slaves were in the hands of white people, and although various laws aimed to protect the lives of bondpeople, they were so ill-enforced that the enslaved normally had little genuine legal recourse.

Contempt for African Americans affected the way white people treated their slaves. Thus, even when a "switching" was not a severe one, the slaves resented it because of the callous inhumanity that lay behind it. Elizabeth Sparks recalled how her old mistress ("a mean ol' thin'") had treated Sparks's aunt. "She uster make my aunt Caroline knit all day," Sparks averred, "an' when she git so tired aftah dark that she'd git sleepy, she'd make her stan' up an' knit. She work her so hard that she'd go to sleep standin' up an' every time her haid nod an' her knees sag, the lady'd come down across her haid with a switch." Slavery provided Sparks's mistress the mildly sadistic pleasure of exercising dominion over a member of a despised race, its members believed to be powerless to defend themselves (*Interviews*, 274, 275).

Male slaves encountered their own forms of wretchedness. Indeed, the interviewee Clara Robinson seemed to imply that men had it even worse than women: "White folks beat everybody [i.e., both male and female] den. Yes dey beat me some too. Fasten you up an' whip you wif a switch. Beat men folks turrible." A credible witness reported that "one day in particular I remember the overseer on the Allen farm tied three slaves, Daniel Myers, Edmond Clarke, and Joe Prosser, up to a tree and lashed them with a big bull whip 'til they could hardly stand up; then he cut the ropes loose and made them go back to work." After a brutal beating, however, a slave might be unfit to return immediately to the field. William Lee recalled that an overseer, in order to inflict a whipping,

> lay you 'cross a barrel made for dis business. Your han' is fastened on one side, feet on t'other, strepped nacked. Can't move. . . . Start whipping you first wid cow hide; lays dat aside; take paddle. Dis paddle has holes in it with a piece of leather tacked on paddle and when ever he hit, dat leather sucks your meat up [and] makes blisters. After he makes blisters all over your behind, he takes up another an' strick down hard on dese blisters [until] dey bust. When dem dar blisters bust, he got a bucket of salt water settin' by an' he 'nints [anoints] you. You be jes' as raw as a piece of beef an' hit eats you up. He loose you an' you go to house; no work done dat day. Next day you got to work; if you don't, you is whipped again. (*Interviews*, 237, 166, 194)

When old black people elsewhere in the South talked to a white WPA interviewer, they often sought to avoid offending the interviewer by blaming severe whippings on enslaved black drivers. As has been seen, Virginia's interviewees (talking to black interviewers) also sometimes blamed black drivers, but more often they spoke plainly about the responsibility of their white masters and overseers. "White folks sho would whup you in dem days," Charles Grandy recalled bitterly. "Dey lay you flat on de groun' on yo' face. Den dey stake you [fasten wrists and ankles to stakes] so es you couldn' git thew de groun' much lessen git up an' fly. Take ev'y rag off'n you an' leave you plumb naked. Den dey whup you 'till de blood come. Dey whup you straight lak dis, see, straight up an' down. Den dey check you er, in other words dey beat you cross wise so's yo' flesh was cut up in squa'es. . . . Den a man would go over dere an' git a bucket o' pickle an' pickle you f'om haid to yo' foot jes lak you paint a house." The slaves' nakedness was what Arthur Greene particularly recalled. "Make you take off all yer clothes jes' lak you bo'n in de world," Greene exclaimed.

"Dey didn't call it whuppin' less'n you pull dem rags off. You know hit was hurtin' when we had to hole each other while de overseer did de' beatin'. . . . Blood run down lak water. Den dey wash you down in salt an' pepper." Even when a slave was not stripped, blood that had coagulated into clothing could torture long after a flogging ended. "I'se seen dem beat de slaves," Jeff Stanfield remembered, "until dere clothes would stick in dere flesh an' nearly kill dem" (*Interviews*, 116, 124, 280).

Although a slave's brief flight into the local woods was sometimes punished lightly, an attempt to flee permanently could unleash a master's unconstrained wrath. Her owner and his wife, according to Armaci Adams, "was bofe hell cats. . . . Marster daid now an' I ain' plannin' on meetin' him in heaven neither. He were too wicked." When Adams's uncle Toney had been caught fleeing, she recounted, "ole man Hunter an' his son beat 'im all de mornin'. Dey took turns. Atter a while dey got tired an' went in ter dinner an' lef' him hangin' dere. He was tied up in de air wid his han's crossed an' his toes jes touchin' de groun'. Dey had beat him somepin awful. I watched f'om de bushes. Blood was runnin' off him like rain. I heahed 'em in de big house a-laffin' an' goin' on. . . . Den dey wen' back ter beatin' Unc' Toney 'gain. 'Bout middle o' de afternoon dey stop an' pickle 'im an' let 'im down. He mos' nigh died."

Because Toney's flight occurred during the Civil War, when he probably was seeking to join the Union Army, his ordeal may have been particularly severe. But savage punishment of flight occurred during peacetime too, even when permanent flight was not the aim. One interviewee reported evidence still visible fifty years after the event. Virginia Shepherd was acquainted with a "smart strong and stubborn" black woman—a field laborer—who would work, but if driven too hard would

> git stubborn like a mule and quit. . . . One day she ran away and hid a long time. They found her by means of bloodhounds. . . . They took her back and chained her by her leg just as though she were a dog. The band was very tight, too tight, and the chain cut a round around her ankle. No one paid any attention to her and the sore became worse. Vermin got in the wound and ate the flesh from around the bone. Her back was a mass of scars the result of the terrible lashing she received [for] running away. They gave her especially cruel treatment in that they made an example of her for the other slaves. After several months they freed her from the chain. It was

quite a while before she could begin work again. After the war she came to Norfolk to live. The deep scars could be seen still on her back and her ankle bone was bare of flesh. The evidence of her punishment was so horrible that the sight of it 50 years afterwards sickened my daughters. (*Interviews, 1, 3, 259*)

Surprisingly, in view of these accounts, a master's brutality seldom led directly to a victim's death. But although a slave owner had an economic interest in keeping a slave alive, occasionally he acted contrary to that interest. One master of a house slave in Portsmouth went off the rails. "One day my cousin's marster didn' want to feed her chile," another reliable interviewee reported in clipped tones, "and when de chile kep' on asking for food, her marster beat her and tied her up in de attic and de chile died. 'Cause of dis awful thing my cousin went crazy" (*Interviews, 217*).

Even when a slaveholder acted strictly according to his own economic interest, this did not always limit the severity of punishment. A planter had a strong economic interest in imposing discipline on his workforce, and might feel that the (perhaps unintended) loss of the life of an excessively beaten slave was compensated by the subservience that such punishment might instill in the other bondpeople. Fannie Berry declared that on a neighboring plantation "old man Chelton's" overseer whipped a slave to death and that Chelton himself whipped another slave, named Nellie, so severely that she committed suicide (*Interviews, 43–44*).

Horace Muse told two stories of slaves killed by their masters for insolence. "One woman, ole Toots Smith," Muse alleged, "make ole marser Riles mad one day. She answer him back. He took her an' tied her to de thrashin' drum o' de wheat thrasher. Den he let de fan beat her 'till she fell, an' tol' her ole man ef he want her, to come an' git her. He took her to his cabin an' de po' thing died de nex' mornin'. He tol' de res' o' us, 'Dat's what you git effen you sass me'" (*Interviews, 216*).

Fugitive slaves interviewed in Canada in 1855 reported many cases of savage physical abuse of Virginia slaves. The whippings on the naked back of Henry Banks—a strong-willed, unservile bondman—often drew blood: afterward, Banks said, "I have frequently had to pull my shirt from my back with a good deal of misery, on account of its sticking in the blood where I had been lashed." Christopher Nichols's master whipped a slave woman, the mother of a small child, "until she fainted,—she was so bad that they sent for Dr. W——; but he was so angry at what my master had done, that he would not go." This woman recovered, unlike a young slave punished for carelessly giving a horse more ears of corn than he was supposed to. The overseer, as John Holmes reported, "seized a flail, and struck the young man breaking two of his ribs"; although a doctor was summoned, he could not save the bondman's life. Near Fredericksburg a captured fugitive was so severely whipped by his hirer (and the hirer's overseer) that he died under the lashing.[4]

Occasionally, the ritual of whipping was accompanied by the expectation that the victim would grovel, begging relief from the master. According to the WPA interviewee Alice Marshall, her master's cousin "whipped his niggers unmercifully. . . . For every lick he give 'em dey say, 'Pray Master.' Some time we stan' in de corn fiel' listen' to de whippin's. All we hear is 'Pow!' den, 'Pray Master!' 'Pow!' 'Pray Master!'" Similarly, Candis Goodwin, too young to have experienced whipping herself, heard that on other plantations slaves being whipped were not supposed to cry, but were made to "holler, 'Oh pray! Oh pray!'" (Interviews, 202, 107).

More often than a modern reader might wish to believe, the threat of whippings secured outward conformity to a master's wishes. His master's brutality had its desired effect upon Horace Muse, a field hand. "Marser Riles was a mean man," Muse testified. "He never knew when you had wuked a 'nough. I done jes' 'zackly ez he tol' me. Dat's why I never git any beatin'." Unsurprisingly, many slaves pursued a policy of survival even when this might seem to entail a loss of self-respect. Perhaps this was particularly true for favored slaves, who had privileges to lose. William Lee, for example—entrusted with light work, such as collecting his master's mail—made a point of doing as instructed. "I carried mail day after day walkin' two miles," Lee remembered. "You know if a white person saw you jes' lookin' at a letter, you'd get a beatin'. An' honey, I ain't looked at nair letter. I was feared of dem lashes. An' Marse might forget dat I was de pet" (Interviews, 215, 196).

If instead a slave responded to plantation discipline by fleeing, the severity of punishment was likely to be escalated. According to Fannie Berry, this happened to

a woman what had been beat so bad dat she run away one night—was gonna make uh try fo' freedom. Dey catched huh 'bout 5 miles off an' dey did huh dis way. Dey cut a fresh limb uh white oak an' den dey put uh notch in de end uh et. Den dey bent huh over an' catched uh big pinch in huh back, down roun' de buttops an' squeeze et tight in de notch uh dis limb. Dey tie de other end uh de limb round huh neck an' den roundst huh knees so dat she gotta walk stooped. An' dey tie huh hands round de stick so dat ef she pull on et she pull on huh meat dat is in de notch an' make et hurt worse. Den dey stick a corn-cob in huh mouth. Den dey "double-quick"— Huh? Dat is dey make huh tuk jump couple of quick steps an' den uh slow one, uh couple quick ones, den uh slow one, an' dey walk huh all de way back like dat. Ain't no body whut dats been done to ever run 'way no mo'.

But does Fannie Berry here appear to relish, just as the savage master perhaps relished, both the details of brutality and the way this brutality could break the spirit of its victim, destroying the captured fugitive's will to make another break for freedom? (*Interviews,* 45).

If ingenious or savage punishments failed to subdue a slave, a master could always call in the slave traders. This happened to Caroline Hunter's three older brothers. Caroline, her brothers, and their mother "all live[d] in one room back of my mastah's house." The children's father, a free black man who did not put up with being treated like a slave, perhaps inculcated unslavish ideas into his three boys. Their recalcitrance provoked their master. "I can' never forgit," Caroline grieved, "how my massa beat my brothers cause dey didn' wuk. He beat 'em so bad dey was sick a long time, an' soon as dey got a smatterin' better he sold 'em. . . . De oles' one I ain' never seen since" (*Interviews,* 149–50).

Nearly every master took for granted his right to flog recalcitrant slaves, and to sell those—like Caroline Hunter's brothers—who would not submit. Occasionally, however, an event occurred that the masters or mistresses could not easily forget. "See dis face?" the ninety-four-year-old Henrietta King asked her interviewer. "See dis mouf all twist over here so's I can't shet it? . . . Well, ole Missus made dis face dis way." King explained that when she was about eight years old, employed in the house (e.g., to empty the bedpan of her "stingy-mean" mistress), she stole a piece of candy and lied about it. Detecting the lie, the mistress—in King's vivid account—"got her rawhide down from de nail by de fire place, an' . . . she try to turn me 'cross her knees whilst she set in de rocker so's she could hol' me. I twisted an' turned till finally she called her daughter. De

gal come an' took dat strap like her mother tole her and commence to lay
it on real hard whilst Missus holt me. I twisted 'way so dere warn't no
chance o' her gittin' in no solid lick. Den ole Missus lif' me up by de legs,
an' she stuck my haid under de bottom of her rocker, an' she rock forward
so's to hol' my haid an' whup me some mo'." The whipping went on, with
the rocking chair pressing down on the side of the child's face, until the
girl lost consciousness:

> Nex' thing I knew de ole Doctor was dere, an' I was lyin' on my pallet in de
> hall, an' he was a-pushin' an' diggin' at my face, but he couldn't do nothin'
> at all wid it. Seem like dat rocker pressin' on my young bones had crushed
> 'em all into soft pulp. . . . [At first King could not open her mouth, but
> eventually the doctor got it so that the mouth would open (though not
> fully close again), and she could move her lips.] I ain't never growed no
> mo' teef on dat side. Ain't never been able to chaw nothin' good since. . . .
> Been eatin' liquid, stews, an' soup ever since dat day, an' dat was eighty-six
> years ago. . . . It was a debbil dat done it—a she-debbil what's burnin' an'
> twistin' in hell.

The white woman responsible for thus permanently injuring the little girl
apparently felt some silent pangs of guilt. King "used to see her sometime
lookin' at me whilst I was dustin' or sweepin'. Never did say nothin', jus'
set there lookin' widdout knowin' I knew it." As late as the 1930s descendants of King's old mistress still lived nearby. "Dey all know me," King affirmed, "an' know how come I look dis way. Met one of dem—Missus'
granddaughter, I reckon—not long ago. She crossed de street to de other
side an' made b'lieve she didn't see me" (*Interviews*, 190–92).

6

Regimentation

Eugene Genovese labeled the constant intrusion by resident antebellum slavemasters upon the lives of their thralls as "paternalism." The same word may also denote the paternalist ideology that was devised in order to justify holding human beings in bondage.[1] The term *regimentation* to describe masters' efforts to regulate almost every detail of their slaves' lives avoids confusion between the two meanings of *paternalism*.

The regimentation of a slave's life began early. "When I'se five years ole," recalled Caroline Hunter, "I had to wuk. I had a job cleanin' silver an' settin' de table. A few years after dat I was put out in de fiel's to wuk all day." Charles Grandy was five when he was made to weed the crops by hand. West Turner began later. "Guess I started workin' when I was 'bout six years old," he reported. "Had to go roun' stickin' slabs and branches in de fences where de hogs done pushed dey heads threw. After dat dey put me in de fiel'—guess I was 'bout seven or eight. Was big an' strong for my age, an' used to plow fo' I could reach up to de handles. Used to stick my head under de cross bar an' wrap my arms roun' de sides whilst another boy led de mule" (*Interviews*, 149, 111, 113, 115, 288).[2] Samuel Ballton's "good massa" nevertheless put him to work at age seven.[3] And by the time Robert Ellett was eight, he was already so reliable at his task—pulling worms off tobacco leaves—that a white man offered his master a high price for him. Georgina Gibbs was eight when she was put in the field with two paddles to scare off crows. The only reason Amelia Walker wasn't also set to work very young was that she seemed to be a sickly child. But when she was about ten, her master decided there was nothing wrong with her. "Put me in de fiel' de nex' day," Walker exclaimed, "—weedin' corn. Sho' foun' what fiel' work was about arter dat" (*Interviews*, 85, 105, 292).

Adult slaves normally had to be up before daylight so as to be in the field by sunrise (which might be at five or six in the morning). On some plantations there would be a pause for breakfast at about eight, and a half hour or longer for a midday dinner. Labor usually lasted until sundown, after which the bondpeople would eat supper in their cabins. This routine usually extended over the six working days each week, though some masters let the slaves—or at least the women—take off Saturday afternoons (*Interviews*, 228, 237, 105).[4]

The routine varied a little from one plantation to another and from one season to another. Some masters required their slaves to eat breakfast before daylight. "Had to git yo' breakfas' fo' day," West Turner pointed out, "'cause you got to be in de fiel' when de sun gits to showin' itself 'bove de trees." At the midday dinner a tug of war—concerning the length of their break—might take place between the overseer and the laborers. "De slaves lay down under a shade tree an' eat," Susan Jackson recalled. "Mos' times dey got half-hour, but nobody ain't gonna rush none. An' sometimes de ole overseer git impatient an' yell fo' de hands to come back to work fo' dey git done eatin'." At harvest time the bondpeople could expect their working hours to be extended. Normally, according to Elizabeth Sparks, "they worked six days fum sun to sun. [But] if they forcin' wheat or other crops, they start to work long 'fo day [i.e., during the dawn before sunrise]" (*Interviews*, 288, 154, 274).

The masters regimented not only working hours but the kinds of vocational skills a slave might be permitted to develop. Cornelia Carney's father—who liked woodwork (and who after Emancipation became a skilled cabinetmaker)—used his hobby to protest his being relegated to unskilled fieldwork. But his master refused to let him become an artisan. "Ole Marsa Littleton used to beat father all de time," Carney recalled. "His back was a sight. It was scarred up an' brittled fum shoulder to shoulder. Ole Marse didn't like father always whittlin' wid his jackknife. Wanted him to work in de fiel', same as de other slaves" (*Interviews*, 66).[5]

Masters also had the final say about whom a slave could marry. If a man wanted to enter an "abroad marriage" with a woman on another plantation, his master might ban the marriage for fear that his slave would visit his wife too often at night without permission, or for fear that his slave would become accustomed to the (perhaps less stringent) discipline at the wife's plantation on the weekends. A master might also ban a female slave who appeared likely to become a good "breeding" woman from marrying a puny husband, who might not produce with her big, strong, saleable children. Naturally, this regimentation of their lives was resented by slaves. Bird Walton's mother was permitted to enter an abroad marriage, and her master was in other respects extraordinarily generous to her. This woman nevertheless made a point of telling Walton that when two slaves wanted to marry, "You had de choice to pick, but de final decision was left to de marser" (*Interviews*, 297).

Regimentation extended to the slaves' leisure time. A slave owner, desiring to keep his bondpeople as tractable as possible, might be more tolerant of their holding a late-night dance than was an overseer, anxious to extract maximum production on workdays. Although Matilda Perry's master threatened to ban dancing, he never did so—probably because in this regard he sided with his slaves against the overseer. "Marse Fleming ain't cared how much we dance," Perry remembered, "but ole overseer would raise de debbil. Overseer always said a slave never would work arter he done dance all night. Used to complain to Marsa an' he threatened not to let us dance ef we didn't do our work, but he never did stop us. Had to dance or do somepin. Work in de field all day, an' got to have some fun on Sadday nights" (*Interviews*, 224).

A mean master, however, might ban his slaves from ever leaving the plantation, even for a Saturday-night dance at a neighboring plantation or on a Sunday. "We couldn' visit any slaves on other plantations," Horace Muse complained. "Marser say visitin' would take our minds offen our wuk." A cruel master might also wish to keep his bondpeople ignorant of less oppressive treatment of slaves at nearby plantations (*Interviews*, 216).

Liberty to travel thus became, for freedpeople, one of the most cherished aspects of Emancipation. Ellis Bennett escaped during the Civil War, served in the Union Army, and there met immigrant Irish and German ("Dutch") soldiers. He later boasted of what he had seen during his travels. "Da rebels dey fight," Bennett exclaimed, "but them Dutch an Irish was too much fer 'em. Ah know cause I'se traveled and ah'se seen" (*Interviews*, 29).

Masters tried to keep tabs on their slaves, in order to prevent their unauthorized departure from the plantation. Watchfulness increased during the war, when the slaves' chances of successful flight were greatly magnified. Susie Burns, for example, relished her master's discomfiture. "Ole Marse George," she chuckled, "used to drink somep'n terrible, especially in de war days when he thought de slaves was gonna leave him. Used to set in his big chair on de porch wid a jug of whiskey by his side drinkin' an' watchin' de quarters to see that didn't none of his slaves start slippin' away" (*Interviews*, 64).

But a master could not always keep an eye on his chattels. Slave patrols therefore became the principal instruments for regimenting slaves' off-plantation activities. The patrollers—the "meanest white men out," according to one vehement African American—were hated by slaves even more than overseers were (*Interviews*, 29). Sometimes too poor to own slaves themselves, patrollers savored the opportunity to exercise power over black people. They rode about at night on horseback, armed, usually in groups of three to six, and were authorized to challenge any African Americans, requiring them to show either free papers (if they said they were free) or a pass from the master legitimating the slave's being off the plantation. Patrols also entered slaves' cabins to discover whether unauthorized people were attending a meeting, or to find stolen goods. (This was done, of course, without a search warrant.) The patrollers' most important function was to catch fugitives seeking temporary or permanent flight, but they also tried to prevent slaves from making unauthorized visits to their spouses or friends and to deter slaves from stealing white people's chickens, hogs, and other property.[6]

Patrollers were loathed because of the savagery with which they beat slaves trying to evade the regimentation of their lives. Charles Crawley expressed succinctly the slaves' view of the matter. "Pattyrollers," he said, "is a gang o' white men gittin' together goin' thew de country catchin' slaves, an' whippin' an' beatin' 'em up if dey had no 'remit.'" Indeed, Liza McCoy thought "padyrollers" an inadequate term to characterize these fiendish agents of the slaveholders: "Padyrollers won't no name fur dem debils. . . . Come down de road on de horse back running men to de masters" (*Interviews*, 79, 201). To visit one's girlfriend without the master's permission, or to attend a dance illicitly, was one of a slave's dearest pleasures, and the patrols were cordially hated in direct proportion to the strength of the pleasures they attempted to frustrate. Dave Lowry told of a Saturday-night dance at a nearby plantation where the slaves attempted to keep down the noise, "because if de patrolers were to catch de slaves [off their plantation without a pass] . . . , de[y] would beat dem." To purloin a chicken was yet another substantial pleasure for an unpaid slave, and here again the patrols tried to bar the way. Charles Grandy explained that, after stealing a chicken, "we would cook de chicken at night, eat him an' bu'n de feathers. Dat's what dey had dem ole paddyrollers fer. Dey come roun' an' search de qua'ters fer to see what you bin stealin'. We always had a trap in de floor fo' de do' to hide dese chickens in" (*Interviews*, 198, 116).[7]

Among the slaves' most cherished memories were acts of successful defiance of the hated patrollers. Betty Jones alleged that "one night de patterollers come when we was havin' a big [presumably religious] mee- tin' in one o' de cabins. . . . Jes' as we heard 'em, ole man Jack Diggs an' Charlie Dowal shoveled fire an' coals right out de door on 'em debbils. Dey runned from de fire, an' we runned f'om dem. Ain't nobody git caught *dat* time" (*Interviews*, 180; emphasis added). Often slaves did, however, get caught, with memorable results. When patrollers surprised a religious meeting in a cabin, Hal Lewis (who had no pass) leaped out of the window: "Paterroler was outside de window an' dey shot Hal, right in his shoulder as he jumped." Hal's master, a medical doctor, "got de shot outa his shoul- der," but the injury was permanent—Hal "always had a . . . failure in dat shoulder even after he got well" (*Interviews*, 125).

Word of Hal Lewis's being shot no doubt circulated swiftly among the bondpeople, augmenting their hatred of the patrollers but also increasing their caution. Elizabeth Sparks believed that "if you went out at night, the paddyrols 'ud catch yer if yer was out aftah time without a pass. Mos' a the slaves was afeared to go out." Nevertheless, many slaves—especially males—did leave the plantation for a few hours at night, in defiance of the patrols. "Sometimes de men slaves would put logs in de beds," Georgina Gibbs testified, "and dey'd cover 'em up, den dey go out. Mastah would see de logs and think dey wuz de slaves" (*Interviews*, 276, 105).

Some masters won their slaves' regard by banning the patrollers' vis- its to their plantations. "We won't bothered by de paterrolers so much," Cornelius Garner averred, "'cause massa tol' dem 'twon't no need of watch- ing and peeping at us 'cause we was right good niggers and didn't have no reason to run away. They kinda kept one eye shut and one open at us jest de same in case we did start acting funny." The wry comment suggests the beginnings here of something like a contractual relation between this unusual master and his slaves, their outwardly submissive conduct winning for them the substantial concession of protection against intrusion by the hated patrollers (*Interviews,* 100).[8]

Enslaved children learned early that their lives were to be regimented. "You wasn't suffered to think or see or feel nothing in those days," one man complained. "If they caught you peeping through the cracks of the doors they would spit in your eyes and put [tobacco juice] in them. Sometimes they would twist your ears if they thought you had heard something that it wasn't proper for you to hear." This man, when he was a child, had devised a make-believe scheme that placed him in the position of overseer over the smaller slave children. He separated these children into a male gang and a female gang, to brush the yard outside the Big House, then sat on the doorsill giving orders, and "went on whipping the niggers" in order to enforce his orders. Observing that black people were bullied by white people, the bullied child transformed himself into a bully of other black people. This may have protected the little bully's self-esteem, but it was scarcely training in solidarity, and it did nothing for the other enslaved children. The white mistress would tolerate nothing that looked like role reversal. She "slipped up on me and smacked me across the face with the cowhide and burnt me something terrible for 3–4 days." Bullying was the prerogative of white people, and a black child must learn early his place in the world (*Interviews,* 300).

If slave children lived in quarters near the Big House, their games might disturb the master's peace and quiet. "Boys git to cuttin' up on Sundays an' 'sturbin' Marsa and Missus an' dey comp'ny," Cornelius Garner recalled. "Finally ole Marsa come clumpin' down to de quarters. Pick out de fam'ly dat got de mos' chillun an' say, 'Fo' God, nigger, I'm goin' to sell all dem chillun o' your'n lessen you keep 'em quiet.' Dat threat was worsen prospects of a lickin'. Ev'ybody sho' keep quiet arter dat" (*Interviews,* 104).[9]

Children's games might get out of hand. When Fannie Berry was small, her closest companion was a white boy named Tom—the master's son. Fannie once got a match from Tom and later, playing alone with it in a barn, started a fire that spread. She hid in the cornfield while the master organized the slaves into a bucket brigade to quench the flames. "Den ole Marse called all de nigger chillun together," Berry said, "an' tole em he gonna whup ev'y las' one of 'em cause he knows one of dem done made dat fire. An' he whupped 'em too till he got tired, whilst I lay dere in de corn fiel' not darin' to raise my head. Never did whup me." Even in retrospect Berry seemed to relish having avoided punishment herself, rather than feeling ashamed that other slave children had been whipped for what she had done. Enslavement could sometimes breed individualistic pursuit of self-interest rather than honorable solidarity (*Interviews*, 48).

A slave was normally expected to address his owners as "Master" and "Mistress," to remind everyone of their power relation. "In dem days . . . you had better say mistress and marster," Jennie Patterson recalled. A few slaves balked at doing so. "Mother's old mistress some how didn't like me," Margaret Terry (only eight years old when slavery ended) explained with pride, "because she just couldn't make me call her mistress. No, I never would; always called her Miss Kitty." This instance of a child's getting away with violating a rule of standard "etiquette" illustrates how town life might sometimes differ from that in the countryside. Terry was the child of an apparently privileged house servant, owned by a generally kindly master and mistress, who lived in the relatively cosmopolitan town of Charlottesville. Terry's mistress allowed the enslaved child, for a time, to read and study alongside her own children, but withdrew the privilege when the black girl outdid the white children at their lessons. After the war Terry was taught by a Northern teacher and then taken north by this teacher for further education. In 1877 she returned to teach school for the next sixty years in or near Charlottesville. The child's successful breaching of the rules of etiquette (and the fact that she was permitted to get away with it) helped breed in her the determination to make a real life for herself when Emancipation and Reconstruction opened the door to her developing her talents (*Interviews*, 218, 285).

Unlike Terry, the vast majority of slaves were of course barred from being taught to read. The ban was partly legal, partly customary. The law (passed by the 1830–31 Virginia legislature) forbade anyone to assemble with blacks—for example, in a school—to teach reading or writing. In about 1853 a white Norfolk seamstress was jailed for a month for violating this law. The law did not actually ban white people from teaching individual slaves, so long as no payment was involved, but local custom seems normally to have had the same effect on white people as if there had been a total legal ban. "If you pick up a piece of paper and look lak you gonna read," the interviewee Liza McCoy exclaimed, "dey act lak dey gonna beat you to death." Virtually the same words were used by Adeline Henderson

(who had been a house servant on a big plantation near Lynchburg) when
an Iowa journalist interviewed her in 1930. "If they caught us with a piece
of paper in our pockets, they'd whip us. They were afraid we'd learn to read
and write, but," Henderson mourned, "I never got a chance." Similarly,
Cornelius Garner lamented that during slavery "we won't 'lowed to read
and write. Dar won't no schools you know, in dem days like 'tis now and
no matter how we yearned fer knowing how to read and write we had no
way on earth of doing so."[10] Most masters feared that education (literally
a "leading out") might be a road to freedom.

But few slaves gained an education, and most white Virginians were
sanguine that their regimentation of bondpeople effactually quelled resistance. Occasionally, however, unfounded panic swept a white community,
as in 1856 and 1860, when the nomination of an antislavery presidential
candidate by the Republican Party seemed to lend greater plausibility to
the fear that an abolitionist conspiracy was about to engulf the South.
Fannie Berry reported that she could "remember my mistress, Miss Sara
Ann, coming to de window [probably in 1856 or 1860] an' hollering, 'De
niggers is arisin', De niggers is arisin', De niggers is killin' all de white
folks—killin' all de babies in de cradle!'" (*Interviews*, 35). Virginia slaves
had indeed once rebelled (in the famous Nat Turner Rebellion of 1831).[11]
They had also conspired to do so in 1800 and 1802, and individual slaves
did sometimes kill white people. But the draconian severity with which
any violence by slaves was normally suppressed gave white people good
reason to believe that slave dissidence would usually take a nonviolent
form (see chapter 10.)

Slaves sometimes directed their violent feelings against each other. The
Reverend Ishrael Massie recounted an incident in Greenville County—
south of Petersburg—when a slave named Thomas was suspected (mistakenly, in Massie's opinion) of killing another slave. The way white
people treated the alleged perpetrator of violence, even when the violence
was directed against another slave, helps to explain why slaves seldom
attacked white people. "White folks took Thomas . . . ," Massie reported
indignantly, "made him undress, smeared or dobbed tar all over his body
from heels up under his arms, strung him to a tree, an' set fur to him. . . .
He took an' blazed all up in a minute, seemed like, an' he swallowed de
blaze an' wuz dead in a little while" (*Interviews*, 207–8).

By seeking to regiment in every conceivable way the lives of bondpeople, slavemasters sought to control not only the behavior but also the mentality of their chattels. Perhaps they were partially successful. But masters could not take away the power of language. In telling sympathetic black interviewers the kinds of stories repeated here, old people found in 1937 a kind of revenge against those who had tried to regulate their lives. These stories bear witness to the capacity of the human spirit to resurrect itself, even under unlikely circumstances.

Contempt

In addition to family disruption, physical abuse, and regimentation, there were other means by which white people demonstrated contempt for slaves. Some of these, occurring alone, might have seemed relatively insignificant; cumulatively, however, their effects could be devastating.

Armaci Adams, after telling her interviewers her name and her place of birth, immediately pointed out that she did not know her date of birth. "Dey never give me my age," she lamented. "White folks kept hit an' never give it ter me." Similarly, Arthur Greene claimed that in "dem days . . . none us slaves knowed our 'zact age. Old white folks wouldn't tell niggers jes' how old dey was." This was one way by which slaves were made to feel they were "niggers"—a group undeserving the respect due to fully human beings. Lorenzo Ivy believed this form of disrespect arose from a crass financial motive. "I don' know jes' zackly how old I am . . . ," he explained. "De white folks was 'spose to keep de ages of de slaves in order to know when dey was 'spose to start payin' taxes on 'em. Guess you kin see now why dey warn' so anxious 'bout keepin' close tract of de ages of niggers" (*Interviews,* 1, 123, 151).

Disrespect began at almost the instant a child was born. During the Civil War Yankee soldiers in Virginia made an enslaved woman show them her three-day-old infant and asked what the baby's name was: "Ant Kiziah tole 'em dat Missus ain't got round to namin' it yet." Not even the naming of their own child was the parents' prerogative, if the mistress (or master) decreed otherwise (*Interviews,* 314).[1]

Little white children learned early that if they tormented a black child, they could probably get away with it. Fannie Berry recalled that "white boys . . . used to pester de life outa [her younger brother]. Had a dog named Bowser, dey used to sick on him [i.e., goad the dog to attack the child]. De dog would jump an' pull onto his shirt an' make him cry an' roll over. . . . 'Couse Miss Sarah Ann [Berry's mistress] didn't know it an' I tole her. She scolded dem boys but dat didn't stop 'em." Even a white child, so well-disposed that he would sometimes share his school lessons with a slave child, might later turn on that same child and whip him—to compensate for having himself been punished by his schoolmaster earlier in the day (*Interviews*, 46, 301).

Slave children were subject to the whims of their master, who might sometimes use them for his own obscure satisfactions, then terrify them with an act of unpredictable vehemence. Elizabeth Sparks's husband, for example, told her about how, when he was a "pickinnany," his bachelor master used to play with the little black children, egging them on to "run an' grab 'is laig so's he couldn't hardly walk." Having thus become entangled among the children, the master then thought the best way to free himself was to pull out his gun and shoot it over the children's heads. "He didn't shoot 'em; he jes' shoot in the air an' [the little boy] was so sceared he ran home an' got in his mammy's bed. . . . Ol' Massa," Elizabeth Sparks continued, "he, jes' come on up ter the cabin an' say, 'Mammy, whah dat boy?' She say, 'In dah undah the bed. Yer done scared 'im to deaf!' . . . Boy say, 'Yer shot me, master, yer shot me!' Master say, ' . . . I ain't shot yer. I jes' shot an' scared yer. Heh! Heh! Heh!' Yessir, my ol' husband sayed he sure was scared that day" (*Interviews*, 277).

Callous disregard of slaves' feelings extended into their adult lives. Heavy, unwieldy agricultural tools were supplied to field hands, with no heed for the fatigue that the superfluous weight of these instruments entailed upon the laborers. The "old slave-time hoes . . . [were] broad like a shovel," Allen Crawford remembered; "dey make 'em heavy." This was not sheer willfulness on the masters' part. A light hoe would have been easier for a slave to break if she or he wanted to sabotage the master's production, and a heavy hoe might more surely dig below the weeds' roots than a lighter one. "Dey make 'em heavy so dey fall hard," Crawford acknowledged, "but de bigges' trouble was liftin' dem up." Not only were these hoes much more tiring to use than they needed to be, but their handles were not even properly shaved. "Use a hick'ry limb fo' a handle," Crawford explained. "Slaves would always have special hoes. Had to shave de knots off smooth an' scrape 'em wid glass ef you want to keep any skin on yo' han's" (*Interviews*, 77). It had no effect on masters if slaves were left to cope as best they could with cheap, heavy, indestructible tools. After all, they were only "niggers."

This mode of thinking about slaves entered into the vocabulary of the bondpeople themselves. As has been seen, Elizabeth Sparks un-self-consciously used the demeaning term "pickinnany" to refer to her husband as a child. Repeatedly, interviewees called themselves "niggers" (as in the previously cited reports of Arthur Greene and Lorenzo Ivy). Some did so partly because they felt that calling themselves "niggers" was, at least, less humiliating than reminding themselves that they had been "slaves." This was nevertheless an acknowledgment that their place in the world was a lowly one. Whites' view of slaves as being like animals—for example, like cattle—also became incorporated into the language of some bondpeople. "My Marster an' Mistess . . . owned 'bout fifty head of Colored People," Charles Crawley testified. Fannie Berry said she "know'd an' ol' white man who had one hundred head of slaves an' he sold 'em"—as he might have sold cattle (*Interviews*, 78, 33).

Stories circulated among African Americans, long after slavery ended, about how enslaved children had been treated like animals and fed on cheap provender. "On some of de plantations," Mary Wood was told, "ole marsters had troughs made—you know, like hog troughs. Would pour buttermilk in dis trough and crumble bread—cornbread 'course—in dis ole sour milk 'cause sometimes hit was 2 or 3 days ole. What did dey keer? Oyster shells was used to git up wid like you use spoons." When Nannie Williams was a girl, she helped her aunt provide care for the young children of mothers working in the field. "Guess dey was 'bout fo'teen chillun she had to look arter . . . ," Williams remembered. "Ant Hannah had a trough in her back yard—jus' like you put in a pig pen. Well, Ant Hannah would just po' dat trough full of milk an' drag dem chillun up to it. Chillun slop up dat milk jus' like pigs" (*Interviews*, 332, 323).

That white people's ways of perceiving African Americans sometimes entered blacks' own vocabulary did not lessen the blacks' resentment at how they were treated. The offense was that they were dealt with, not like human beings, but like property (whether animate or inanimate). At the Lynchburg slave auctions, Robert Williams recalled, "de seller would cry bids just like dey sell tobacco: '$150, who will make it a $160,' an' so on."

One way of seeking protection from this callous view of one's own people was for a slave (unappealingly, but understandably) to turn this perspective against poverty-stricken white people. Robert Williams observed that poor whites were obliged to approach his rich master's house by the back door, where they were likely to be accosted crossly. "Po' whites," Williams said with satisfaction, "was just like stray goats" (*Interviews*, 325, 326).

Poor whites did not, however, make such good butts for masters' derisory jests as did slaves. Slaves presented their masters with an opportunity to laugh, together with poorer whites on the slave patrols, at the expense of the subordinate race (and particularly at the expense of black women). John Brice, a slave, had an abroad marriage with a woman named Sally, who lived six miles away. Brice's master—who bore the distinguished Virginia name of Carter—permitted Brice to visit Sally every Saturday night. Carter wrote a pass for John Brice that used such ribald language that the 1937 interviewer (or the typist) felt it would be prudent to leave the key words blank. "'Couse John couldn't read," Fannie Berry explained,

> an' marse would always laugh when he gave him de pass. An' whenever de patterollers stop John dey would always have themselves a good laugh too when dey read his pass. So John got to wonderin' what was on dis pass dat made 'em laugh so. So one night he went into Appomatox 'stead of goin' straight to Sally's place an' got a free nigger man to read it to him. An' de free nigger read to him:
>
> To my man John I give this pass,
> Pass an' repass to Sally's black ——,
> Ef don't nobody like dis pass,
> Dey can kiss —— ——.

Language is power, and this slave's enforced illiteracy had left him prey to the ridicule of the white men whose shared laughter bridged the class difference between rich master and poor patroller (*Interviews*, 46–47).

Another way of putting down African Americans was to circulate stories that they were credulous simpletons who could be made to believe any absurd yarn. Although some of the following events occurred long after Emancipation in 1865, they betray the persistence among white Virginians of a mode of thought conceived in the time of slavery. During a memorable snowstorm near Petersburg in 1857, a drunken white man named Dr. Cox froze to death because, returning from town, he was too intoxicated to stagger from his horse and buggy back to the Big House. So unusual was the snowstorm that a later generation referred to that storm as "Cox's snow" (although Cox's inebriation was not widely publicized). Many years later a white newspaper reporter asked Jennie Patterson—a former slave who had seen Dr. Cox's frozen corpse with her own eyes— what had happened; but the reporter falsified what she said, attributing to her a ghost story that would illustrate yet again the supposed credulity of black folk. "Chile, I'se bin feard to tell all I know 'bout dis here thing," Jennie Patterson later protested to her black WPA interviewer. "Dar's bin all kinds of tales de white folks bin all kiverin' hit over. Marse Cox liked his liquors so he was drunk an' couldn' make hit, not bein' of his self. I bet you ain' heard dat. Yes, yes, dar was a big botheration at de big house. Some of dat de man put on paper 'bout horse and buggy was right. Naw, I ain' said nothin' 'tall 'bout dem ghost; dar's whar another lie is tole. An' I got mad when my daughter read dat lie to me." Black people were to be laughed at, regarded as credulous, patronized (*Interviews*, 219).

Black people, the targets of a barrage of missiles—some small and apparently harmless, others deeply wounding—relished any indication that people (sometimes even white people) might respect them as human beings. Elizabeth Sparks was astonished and delighted when, during the Civil War, a Northern army officer who asked her for directions broke the Southern white taboo against giving a black woman her married title. He said, "'Goodbye, Mrs. Sparks.' Now what you think of dat? Dey call me 'Mrs. Sparks.'" A tiny civility made a lasting impression on a woman accustomed to the small indignities of Southern "etiquette" (*Interviews*, 277).

A male slave who successfully fled during the Civil War might gain the opportunity to earn even more respect for himself. In 1937 Candis Goodwin still proudly kept in her room the sword her husband had worn as a Union soldier. "Lemme tell you 'bout my Jake, how he did in de war," she said eagerly to her interviewer. "He big man in dey war. He drill soldiers e'vy day. . . . He wucked up to be Sergent-Major, in de Tenth Regiment. Jacob Goodwin his name was. He say dey all look up to him an' 'spect him too. See dat 'Sowd' [sword] over in dat corner? Dat's de ve'y sowd he used in de war, an' I kep' it all dese yeahs." To be looked up to and respected carried special meaning for a people normally regarded by whites with disdain (*Interviews*, 108).

If a good mistress or master accorded real respect to slaves during family religious devotions, bondpeople remembered this with strong feeling. On Annie Williams's plantation—southwest of Richmond—her master "prayed wid de family ev'y single night. An' he prayed fo' us slaves, too. All slaves had to come to de parlor same as de whites, an' any slave what wanted could jine in wid him or pray by deyselves when he done finished. Aunt Rebecca used to git up an' pray regular. Didn't let women do much prayin' in dem days but Marsa never sot Aunt Rebecca down. Pray sometimes fo' half-hour an' white folks would sit there jus as '*spectful* as if she was de white preacher" (*Interviews*, 313; emphasis added). Although "half-hour" may be an exaggeration, Annie Williams's emotion was genuine. Respect—balm to the soul—was in short supply for most slaves.

8

Deprivation

Famine did not stalk the antebellum South, as it did the Russian countryside in the mid-nineteenth century. Indeed (according to recent economic historians), the average antebellum Southern slave not only received food with a high calorific—and substantial protein—content, but often could supplement this basic ration with vegetables, sour milk, and a Sunday treat of wheaten biscuits.[1] *Did* slaves really feel deprived of proper food and clothing allowances? And if they did feel deprived, why?

A handful of former slaves actually expressed enthusiasm for the food that came their way. Levi Pollard grew up in a privileged family on a big plantation, owned by benevolent masters. Greasiness in food was, to him, a great virtue. "Us always have [salt pork] fer [noonday] dinner," he exclaimed. "Cuts it up in square pieces en let hit boil, den put in your salad, or cabbages, or beans, en dey was some kind er good. Det was good en greasy when der was much meat. . . . Us had all de milk us could drank. Dey was peach trees, en apple trees, dat us could have fo usself." Cornelius Garner, reared in Maryland just north of the Potomac River, also had a benevolent master. "A good eatin' meal," he declared, "consist o' fish or fried meat, 'lasses an' [corn]bread. You always got a plenty to eat" (*Interviews*, 227, 102–3).

Charles Crawley had a good master too, but remembered the food ration with less fervor. "We had plenty of food," he acknowledged, "sech as 'twas[:] corn brad, butter milk, sweet potatoes in week days. Ha! Ha! Ha! Honey, guess dat's why niggers don' lak cornbrad. On Sunday we had biscuits, and sometimes a little extra food, which ole Mistess would send out to Mother fer us." Similarly, Beverly Jones had a good master who, from motives of enlightened self-interest, gave his bondpeople plenty of food in comparison to the fare offered at many other plantations. Jones's mother, the plantation cook, "used to have to get up at sunrise to fix the food for the great house. First thing she did," Jones recalled, "was to feed the niggers. That didn' take no time. Jes' give them home-made meat an' hoe-cake, an' sometimes fish. Hoecake? Hoecake was [corn]meal mixed with water in a thick batter. Got its name from some of 'em slappin' it on a hoe an' holdin' it in de fire place tell its cooked. Mother ain' done that. She used to cook hoecakes in a big iron pan, two or three at a time. Simple fare, it was, but they was always plenty of it. Master believed in givin' his niggers a good meal. Niggers work better on a full stomach" (*Interviews*, 80, 181).

Most planters were little concerned about the quality of food supplied to their slaves. Elizabeth Sparks remarked that at her plantation the field hands "git some suet an' slice a [corn]bread fo' breakfas'. . . . Fo' dinner they'd eat ash cake baked on blade of a hoe." On a Piedmont plantation where tobacco was the cash crop—supplemented by corn and a bit of wheat for feeding the slaves—the master made it plain where his priorities lay. "Marse ain' raise nothin' but terbaccy," Matilda Perry recalled, "ceptin' a little wheat an' corn for eatin', an' us black people had to look arter dat 'baccy lak it was gold. . . . Git a lashin' . . . effen you cut a leaf fo' its ripe. Marse ain' cared what we do in de wheat an' corn fiel', cause dat warn't nothin' but food for us niggers, but you better not do nothin' to dem 'baccy leaves." Thus, "us niggers" were instructed about their subordinate position in a white man's world (*Interviews*, 274, 223–24).

Horace Muse's conception of a good midday dinner had been shaped by his experiences when (for most of his antebellum years) he was hired out to a mean master: "De only thing we got to eat [at midday] was a ash cake an' half a herrin' an water. Ole woman brung us our dinnar to de fiel. She brung [corn]bread an' fish in a big basket an' a boy brung us water in a gourd." By contrast, when Muse was at his owner's plantation, "dey feed us good." Instead of water and half a herring, "Dey give us a pint o' milk, a whole herrin' an' a ash cake too!" (*Interviews*, 216).

For every slave who received better-than-average food was one supplied with below-average fare. If there were a poor harvest, a financially strapped master might cut costs by scrimping on the quantity or quality of his slaves' weekly allowances. And a good many masters were simply mean. When Armaci Adams was a girl, her master and mistress "never give you 'nough ter eat. I mos' nigh starved all de time." A week's allowance didn't always last for a full week. May Satterfield's mother, for example, declared to her, "White fo'ks so mean didn't eben want nigger t'eat. . . . Done heard her say she been in de field 'long side de fence many day an' git [cress] an' poke sallet an' bile it 'dout a speck o' greese an' give it to us chillun 'cause de rashon de white fo'ks lounce out fo' de week done give out" (*Interviews*, 3, 244–45).

The interviewees blamed inadequate rations for widespread theft. If they were not supplied enough to eat, they would steal. May Satterfield's mother "tell me dat po' nigger had to steal back dar in slav'y eben to git 'nuf t'eat. . . . She say sometime de men would go at night an' steal hog and sheep, burry de hair in a hole way yonder in de swamp sommers whar dey knowed de white fo'ks cudden fine it and cook an' eat it after us chillun was sleep. Dey waited till us chillun was sleep so dat ef de white fo'ks axe us 'bout it we wouldn't know nothin'." Similarly, Beverly Jones (whose account of his master's enlightened self-interest is quoted earlier) declared that mean masters undermined the character of their slaves. Jones's own master (a "purty good ole codger") ensured "that his niggers git plenty to eat, see? Nobody on our place got to go steal food. But whar the ole master was mean an' ornery, den de niggers git to stealin' an' lyin' 'bout it. Yessir . . . , bad masters had lyin' thievin' slaves 'cause they made 'em that way" (*Interviews*, 244–45, 181).[2]

Behind the sense of deprivation of food lay a more fundamental awareness: slaves were deprived of justice. Because they didn't receive wages, they did not get a fair return for their labor; and they were deprived of a means of protesting, for if they stole food, this led to an inevitable cycle of whippings, flight, and even more terrible whippings. Former slaves told William Brooks—hyperbolically—that the weekly ration "ain' 'nough lasten a dog a day. So dem niggers steal," Brooks explained, "an' cose when dey steal dey git caught, an' when you git caught you git beat. . . . Some times dey beat 'em so bad dey run away an' hide in de woods. . . . Dey come back an' he beat 'em worse'n ever fer runnin' way." Brooks concluded bitterly, "White man's mean. Cullud man kain' git anything" (*Interviews*, 57).[3]

Without wages and a fair return for their labor, slaves took for granted that they were entitled to food and housing for their children, even when the children were too young to be economically productive. Many acquired a customary right to the use of a patch of their master's land, where they could grow vegetables for their own consumption. The joy of Emancipation was for some slaves tempered by bitterness that their mistresses or masters deprived them of even these small entitlements. By 1865 Clara Robinson's rich master had died, leaving his two plantations and his numerous slaves to his widow. Clara had four young children to provide for, but "when de surrender come, [Clara's mistress] jes' turned us loose wid out anything." Although George White's master "was a mean man," he did eventually, before 1865, "let mama raise a hog, an' have a garden, but after surrender," White exclaimed indignantly, "he didn' give us one thing." The freedpeople were robbed of just recompense for their previous labors (*Interviews*, 237, 309, 311).[4]

Masters distributed clothes to their slaves once or twice a year, in sufficient quantity. Yet the impression from the interviews is that masters—even good ones—provided inadequate clothing for their bondpeople.

Boys, for example, were not given trousers until they reached about the age of puberty. "I was a big boy," George White testified, "fo' I got any more clo'es than a long shirt." When Allen Wilson, as a boy, was stripped for a whipping, his only clothes "won't but one ole long shirt." In the last days of the Civil War, when Philip Ward was ten years old, Yankee soldiers billeted at his master's big house threw him more hardtack than he could eat, and in order to collect the surplus—Ward remembered with embarrassment—"I pult up my shirt what us slave boys used to wear an' held de cakes in dar. Dey kep' throwin' me de biscuits an' I kep' pullin' de shirt up higher an' higher. . . . An' dere was all dem white ladies [his mistress and her daughters] dere lookin' right at me, an' I had dat shirt up roun' my head wid not a thing else on. Soon's my grandfather saw me, he come over an' chased me away from dere" (*Interviews*, 309, 327, 302).[5]

Masters saved money on children's clothes, and on their footwear. "Father went barefooted the year round until he was seventeen," the Reverend W. P. Jacobs averred. Elizabeth Sparks explained that "if yer wuz workin', they'd give yer shoes. Children went barefooted, the yeah 'round." George White confirmed that "we children went bearfotted an' de ole folks did too" (*Interviews*, 155, 276, 309).

In warm weather slaves of working age often also went barefoot, but later in the year they were given shoes (frequently of primitive quality) to protect their feet against the cold. In winter the workers at George White's plantation "got wooden bottom shoes wid leather tacked on de top." At Georgina Gibbs's plantation "we had to wear wooden bottom shoes." And if the master supplied leather shoes, this did not guarantee their comfort. Horace Muse's mother had to grease the shoes every night with tallow grease. "Git stiff as a board in cold weather," Muse expostulated, "an' lessen you grease 'em dey burn [i.e., scrape] your feet an' freeze 'em too" (*Interviews*, 309, 105, 217).[6]

Mean or impecunious masters cut corners in other ways. If clothes were made of cotton, they might be reasonably comfortable, but there was not always enough cotton. "De women folks would spin de cotton, card it and weave it," according to Arthur Greene. "Den dey could cut it an' sew it. . . . Couldn't spin nuf clothes for ev'body. All dat didn't git homespun got guano bags [presumably burlap bags that had been used in transporting bird dung to fertilize depleted tobacco land]." Charles Crawley's master— very unusually—supplied his slaves annually with *two* pairs of shoes; yet the underclothes of even this master's slaves were "made [on the plantation] out of sacks an' bags." George White left to his interviewer's imagination the sensation of wearing the shirt his master supplied. "Our shirts was made from flax," White recalled, "an' we didn' have to scratch our backs; just wiggle an' our back was scratched" (*Interviews*, 126–27, 80, 309).[7]

In this atmosphere of steady deprivation, a master's acts of largesse were long remembered. The extent of liberality might depend on the size of the tobacco crop and the price the master received for it. At Gabe Hunt's Piedmont plantation "ev'ybody happy when de tobaccy curin' is done, 'cause den ole Marse gonna take it to market an' maybe bring back new clothes fo' de slaves." So drab were the slave women's standard clothes that they jumped at the opportunity to grab any colorful bit of secondhand clothing the mistress might provide. At Nancy Williams's plantation handouts were institutionalized into an annual springtime distribution of the mistress's used clothes. A house servant would spread out a big bundle of these castoffs, "an' all de niggers scramble fo' 'em. Never could git nothin' to fit you. Arter de scramble de slaves go round tradin' each other, tryin' to git fittin's." So strong was Mary Wyatt's sense of deprivation that she took a big gamble one Christmas, its success dependent on her master's inattention to the clothing worn by his own wife. Wyatt was a house servant with access to her mistress's wardrobe. "Ole Missus had one dress dat she wore only in de spring time," Wyatt remembered, with a shiver of satisfaction. "Lawdy, I used to take dat dress when she warn't nowhere roun' an' hole it up against me an' 'magine myself wearin' it. One Christmas de debbil got in me good. Got dat gown out de house 'neath my petticoat tied rounst me an' wore it to de dance. Was scared to death dat Misus gonna come in, but she didn't. Marsa come, but I knowed he warn't able to tell one dress from 'nother. Sho' was glad when I slipped dat dress back in place de nex' day. Never did dat no mo'" (*Interviews*, 148, 322, 333).

The cramped conditions of the slaves' living quarters are well-known. "Mastah give us huts to live in," said Georgina Gibbs. "De beds wuz made of long boards dat wuz nailed to de wall. De mattress wuz stuffed wif straw and pine tags. De only light we had wuz from de fire-place." If the family was lucky, the standard one-room hut had a loft, where the boys could sleep separated from the girls. "In the cabins, the good ones," according to one former slave, "the boys slept in the loft, the girls downstairs and the babies in a thing called a trundle bed." Although the baby would be wrapped in a piece of cloth like a diaper, by morning time, when the mother pulled out the trundle bed, the cabin's atmosphere was probably noisome. Cecilia Tyler's sister Prudence "was de baby an' whatever she got to do she got to do right in de [trundle] bed." If the slave family's room did not have a loft, the growing brothers and sisters slept in the same room, along with their parents. Thus, Caroline Hunter stated that "my mama, papa, me an' my three brothers all live in one room back of my mastah's house. We et, slep an' done ev'ything in jus' dat one room." The cabin might become stiflingly hot in the summer, when, to seek relief, everybody in the Reverend W. P. Jacobs's family "slept in the [airier] barn with the horses and cows" (*Interviews*, 105, 155, 291, 149, 155).

In addition to material deprivation, African Americans knew that slavery barred almost all bondpeople from book-learning. "During slavery there weren't any schools for slaves or free Negroes in this city [Portsmouth]," mourned Jane Pyatt. Her lament was principally on behalf of other slaves, for she herself—a privileged urban slave—had been taught to read by a kindly mistress. Pyatt wished that she had had a school education and that she had been taught to write. Peggy Burton had been less fortunate: "I never had privelege to go to school cause I come long during slavery days[,] where de white folks spit in de nigger chillun's faces and dey couldn't help dem selves. . . . I always wanted an education so dat

I could be somebody." By depriving her of an education, Burton felt, white people had stolen her birthright (*Interviews*, 234–35, 65).

Deprived of an education, many slaves turned more heartily to religion. Dave Lowry, for example, regretted that neither his grandparents, his parents, nor he himself had had any education, but he was proud that they had all been very religious. Black preachers (whom the slaves preferred to hear instead of white clergymen, if possible) pictured heaven as a place where slaves could finally enjoy those good things that had been denied them on earth. The preachers' heaven was tinged with material splendors that—to later readers—might seem inappropriate, but that dazzled a barefoot people normally clothed in dull colors (or at best in one of the mistress's castoff dresses) and accustomed to eating hoe cakes with—if they were lucky—a whole salt herring for dinner. "When Tom Knight [an African American preacher] git going good his sermon, he 'mence to sing," Alice Marshall fondly remembered:

> We gwan have a moughty bounty . . .
> Golden slippers all on my feet,
> De golden lace aroun' my waist . . .
> Golden crown all on my head . . .
> By king Jesus we'll be fed,
> We gwan have a moughty bounty.
>   (*Interviews*, 198, 203)

Why does the adjective "golden" appear so insistently in Tom Knight's song? The slaves' strong sense of material deprivation perhaps symbolized for them other things beyond their reach—for example, gold. They knew that, near the heart of bondage, lay their deprivation of wages. Archie Booker—who had been a slave near Richmond—scorned those backwoods slaves who, for a while even after 1865, continued to work for no pay (and distinguished the condition of most Virginia blacks in the 1930s from that of the terribly exploited contemporary sharecroppers of the Deep South): "Some white folks [in Virginia] kep' slaves wukin aftuh de war. Way back in de woods dey made ye wuk an' give ye nuffin fur it. Po' slaves! Dey didn' know no bettuh. Dey doin' it now down Souf. Dem sharecroppuhs is jes like slaves. Dey don' know slavery is ovuh." Booker—perceiving substantial continuities from slavery to post-Emancipation days—disliked white supremacy in general, not just slavery. Economics was at the root of the problem: "White folks is too greedy," Booker confided to his black interviewer. "Looks like de mo a man labors, de mo de othuhs try to git it fum im." To Charles Grandy, too, the essence of slavery was that you were "wukin' fer de white man fer nuttin'" (*Interviews*, 53, 54, 117).[8]

The whoops of joy with which slaves greeted Emancipation spoke volumes. Before 1865, by contrast, the lips of black people had nearly always been sealed, when white people were within hearing distance. On one remarkable occasion, however, a feeble old slave ("Uncle Silas was near 'bout a hundred"), with little to lose, dared publicly to challenge the white minister. The standard message from white preachers, at the separate religious services they held for slaves, was that bondpeople should obey their masters; then, if they were not sinners (or if they repented of their sins), they would find salvation in heaven—salvation, not freedom. Slaves perceived the masters' self-interest in hiring clergymen to intone this soporific message. Uncle Silas one day expressed the feelings that no other slave dared communicate to a white man. Reverend Johnson—according to Beverly Jones—

> was preachin' an' de slaves was sittin' dere sleepin' an' fannin' theyselves wid oak branches, an' Uncle Silas got up in de front row of de slaves' pew an' halted Reverend Johnson. "Is us slaves gonna be free in Heaven?" Uncle Silas asked. De preacher stopped an' looked at Uncle Silas like he wanta kill him 'cause no one ain't 'sposed to say nothin' 'ceptin' "Amen" whilst he was preachin'. Waited a minute he did, lookin' hard at Uncle Silas standin' there but didn't give no answer.
>
> "Is God gonna free us slaves when we git to Heaven?" Uncle Silas yelled. Old white preacher pult out his handkerchief an' wiped de sweat fum his face. "Jesus says come unto Me ye who are free fum sin an' I will give you salvation." "Gonna give us freedom 'long wid salvation?" ask Uncle Silas. "De Lawd gives an' de Lawd takes away, an' he dat is widdout sin is gonna have life everlastin'," preached de preacher. Den he went ahead preachin', fast-like, widdout payin' no 'tention to Uncle Silas.
>
> But Uncle Silas wouldn't sit down; stood dere de res' of de service, he did. (*Interviews*, 184)

Even if this story is apocryphal, it testifies to the fact that the slaves understood, and felt, their condition. Lack of *freedom:* that was their principal deprivation.

Part III

RESPONSES

9

Religion

The slaves' religion, as historians have convincingly demonstrated, moulded together African and Christian elements. African components were significant in this synthesis, both in early North America and—as late as the 1860s—in the Carolina Low Country.[1] But the Low Country was an atypical region, because African-born slaves were still being legally imported there until 1808 (much later than to the Upper South) and because Low Country slaves so heavily outnumbered local white people that influences from whites were weaker than elsewhere in the South. Consequently, several questions remain unsettled: How far (in other parts of the American South) did the slaves' religion actually differ from the orthodox evangelical Christianity of most Southern whites? Insofar as the slaves' religion *was* distinctive, did its distinctive features arise mainly from African influences or from the black people's experiences of bondage after they had been transported to America? Did Afro-Christianity really serve the interests of the slaves, or was its main effect to make life more comfortable for their white oppressors by subverting insurrectionary spirit among the bondpeople? Finally, have modern historians exaggerated the influence of religion in the slaves' lives?[2]

At first sight, it might appear that the Christianity offered to Virginia slaves held little to attract them. When white clergymen preached to bondpeople, they normally presented an expurgated version of Christianity, which affirmed that obedience to masters would be rewarded in the afterlife. Slaves saw through this use of religion to serve the interests of white people. "In de church," Charles Grandy recalled, "de white folks was on one side an' de colored on de other. De preacher was a white man. He preach in a way lak, 'Bey yo' marser an' missus' an' tell us don' steal f'om yo' marser an' missus." Beverly Jones characterized auditors' typical response to this sort of message, and specified the key biblical text upon which it was based. "Niggers had to set an' listen to the white man's sermon," he complained, "but they didn' want to 'cause they knowed it by heart. Always took his text from Ephesians, the white preacher did, the part what said, 'Obey your masters, be good servant.' Can' tell you how many times I done heard that text preached on. They always tell the slaves dat ef he be good, an' worked hard fo' his master, dat he would go to heaven, an' dere he gonna live a life of ease. They ain' never tell him he gonna be free in Heaven. You see, they didn' want slaves to start thinkin' 'bout freedom, even in Heaven" (*Interviews*, 116, 183).

Although slaves were sometimes authorized to listen to a black preacher, the presence of a white man was legally required in order to ensure the delivery of a properly obeisant message. "Couldn' no nigger preacher preach lessen a white man was present," Beverly Jones grumbled. This was a principal grievance for Ellis Bennett, who was indignant that "[black] preachuhs couldn't preach less white man say so." Consequently, slaves often organized unauthorized religious meetings at night, where they could express their real feelings without white supervision. One interviewee after another confirmed the ubiquity of such gatherings. "Nigguhs used to go way off . . . an' slip an' have meetin's," Elizabeth Sparks remembered. "They called it 'stealin' the meetin'." To attend such an assembly could be dangerous, because a principal function of the hated patrols was to break up such gatherings. The attachment slaves felt for these assemblies was proportionate to the dangers they incurred by attending. "Ol Harry Brown," one interviewee enthused, "he wuz a kinda preachuh. He ustuh preach to us rite sma't. Cose dey hada watch fe[r] de paddyrolluhs. . . . Dey come twixt eight an' twelve at night. Ef dey ketch ye havin meetins, dey'd [arrest] ye. Yessuh! Dey had bloodhounds wid em" (*Interviews*, 183, 29, 276, 52–53).

But this tale of white people's expurgation of the Bible, and of black people's stealing the meeting—while substantially true—does not tell the whole story. In Virginia the slaves' version of Afro-Christianity, though marked by distinct African influences, was by 1860 a thoroughly Christian faith. This would have been an unlikely outcome had white people's influence on slaves' beliefs been so slight as might at first seem to have been the case.[3]

Most of Virginia's black Christians were Baptists or Methodists. These denominations recruited blacks through conversion dependent on an emotional experience accessible to people often unable to read the written word of a Presbyterian catechism, and not attracted to what seemed the cold ritual of the Episcopal Church. In the early nineteenth century two-thirds of Virginia's Baptists were black, many of them members of autonomous urban black churches. For example, Norfolk's black First Baptist Church (autonomous between 1816—when its white members left to found their own church—and 1838, when whites reestablished control) had 477 members in 1830. The next year, when Richmond's First Baptist Church was still biracial, 80 percent of its members (i.e., about 1,470 of them) were black. Five of its preachers and seven of its "exhorters" (subpreachers) were black.[4]

This helps explain why large numbers of blacks were attracted to Christianity: they were often recruited—especially among Baptists—not by white preachers, but by black preachers and exhorters. During the eighteenth century, when evangelical Christianity first swept through Virginia, evangelicals preached a doctrine of spiritual equality; even when this message was watered down by white preachers, black converts retained their own understandings of it. The Baptists' decentralized system of church administration permitted considerable local autonomy to churches where blacks retained leadership positions (as in their Norfolk church from 1816 to 1838) or where they were granted increased powers (as in Richmond's First African Baptist Church after 1841). Thus, in these urban centers there was on offer not a white preacher's Christianity, but a message delivered (cautiously, of course, when a white auditor was present) by a black interpreter of the Word.

Even when a white preacher, in a biracial rural church, intoned the message of obedience, bondpeople could nevertheless enjoy attending church. The walk to church provided respite from field labor, offering slaves a chance to see the neighborhood and to meet blacks from other plantations, and providing the release of emotion through singing. "In slavery days Sundays was one day we glad to see come," Alice Marshall told her black interviewers. "Yes, we went to church. Had to walk four or five miles, but we went. We took our shoes in our hands an' walked barefooted. When we got near de church door, den we put on our shoes. In church we sat in de gallery. De white man preached all de sermons. But we could jine in de singin'. De white folks word off [i.e., started] de hymns an' we follow 'long." Marrinda Singleton's master, who "treated us jes' like dogs," nevertheless permitted his slaves to attend their own church after his own family set off to the white people's church. "After dey had gone and de house cleared up," Singleton recollected, "de slaves could go to their church, a little log cabin in edge of woods, whar a white preacher would be to overseer. Here we would pray and sing in our own feelings and expressions singin' in long and common meters soundin' high over de hills" (*Interviews*, 202, 266, 267).

Unlike Singleton's master, Mariah Hines's owner (probably John A. Persons) was an exceptionally kindly man whose conduct won the esteem of his bondpeople.[5] "Master had prayer with the whole family every night, prayed for us slaves too," Hines explained to her black interviewer. "Any of the slaves that wanted to jine him could. Or if they wanted to pray by dem selves they could." Hines observed that John Persons and the white preacher were both Sabbatarians, and that Persons did not require even his house servants to work on Sunday: "The master and the preacher both said dat was the Lord's day and you won't 'spose to work on that day. So we didn't." The idea that Sunday was the Lord's day provided Persons religious sanction to diminish his authority over his slaves on that day; and it fostered in the slaves a belief that God limited their master's authority over them. Hines remarked that some of Persons's neighbors called him a "'nigger lover.' He didn't pay dat no mind though. He was a true Christian man, and I mean he sho' lived up to it." Persons's religion augmented his determination to do what he thought right; together with his established position within the white social hierarchy, it reduced the likelihood that his neighbors would try to coerce him into conformity with local customs. He claimed the sanction of a religion to whose doctrines his neighbors felt impelled to pay at least lip service. This was a Christianity that might appeal to slaves (*Interviews*, 141, 140).

Levi Pollard reported an even more remarkable case, in which white people's religious doctrines promoted the granting of an unusual educational opportunity to slaves. Pollard's benevolent master had purchased a slave from Quakers who had taught the man to read. For a time Pollard's master permitted this slave, on Sunday evenings, to "open his house fer de nig-gers' chillun ter cum git education. [This slave] have Sunday School, where he read de Bible en pray, den he use de New York Primmer with great big letters in hit. He show us how ter make 'em en us wuz learnin' good." Then the mistress, however, confiscated their books, thus enforcing Virginia's ban on anyone's assembling with blacks to teach reading. The humani-tarian impulse behind the Sunday School was likely to have made this kind of white people's Christianity attractive to slaves (*Interviews*, 229).

A remarkable case of a slave sharing religious conviction with a Southern white person was reported in 1866 (to an antislavery Northern woman) by Richard Parker, a black Methodist minister. In the 1820s, when Parker was a youthful yard servant in Norfolk, the daughter of his master stealthily helped him learn to read. After Parker could read the Bible, he "became a christian [and] he was very anxious that his young mistress, who had so nobly braved her father's displeasure in teaching him, should also become a subject of renewing grace." Under Parker's influence, the young white woman became a convert too. When she joined her Presbyterian church, she told her pastor "that she wished Richard to be present and partake of the sacrament with her," and Richard was allowed to do so. This was an extraordinary breach of custom, illustrating how Christianity might at-tract an enslaved person.[6]

Even when a white preacher's message was unpalatable to bondpeople, a well-disposed mistress might permit them to attend an unsupervised meeting where they could enjoy their own form of Christian worship. Candis Goodwin, for example, described her enslaved mother as a rather "tender" woman who "couldn' stan' dat preachin'" [in the white people's church] no longer." In the slaves' kitchen (where she was the cook), how-ever, her mistress let "de ole folk . . . git togeder . . . to shout an' pray. Dat's where my mommer git 'ligion." These slaves were permitted to embrace a form of Christianity that was acceptable to their mistress but also to them (*Interviews*, 108).

Even when slaves "stole" the meeting, they sometimes did so with their masters' connivance. When their meeting place was near the mas-ter's house, they often reportedly "turned down the pots" (turned large kitchen utensils upside-down near the cabin door) in an effort to dampen the sound of their shouts and songs. Can this remedy have been wholly effectual? Perhaps a principal function of turning down the pots was to persuade the worshippers that their meeting remained secret from the masters, when in fact the masters, who sometimes authorized unsupervised meetings, and sometimes protected them from disturbance by local patrollers, realized that a meeting was taking place. Katie Johnson, as a young child, "always knew when they was goin' to have meetin' cause I would see the[m] 'turn down the pots' to keep the folks at the big-house from hearin' them singin' and prayin'." This master and mistress perhaps knew perfectly well what was going on, but felt that Christian songs and prayers posed no threat to the stability of the system (*Interviews*, 161).

Thus, black people found it relatively safe to express themselves in a Christian idiom, even in public, with both black and white auditors. Alice Marshall recalled a free black man, Tom Knight—a blacksmith in rural Virginia, southwest of Richmond—who loved to preach and sing: "Lord, ev'y time somebody pass Tom Knight blacksmith shop, he jump up on his block an' start a-preaching. . . . When Tom Knight git going good his sermon, he 'mence to sing:

> We gwan have a moughty bounty
>
> .   .   .   .
>
> By king Jesus we'll be fed,
> We gwan have a moughty bounty.

This black preacher reached auditors of both races (*Interviews*, 203).[7]

Innocuous though Christian ideas might sound to many white auditors, Christianity came to have strong and particular meanings for slaves. Bondpeople believed, for example, that God punished bad mistresses and masters by roasting them in hell. This was the consolation of the disfigured Henrietta King.[8] Nancy Williams was convinced that before 1865 God had allotted to mean slavemasters (like the neighboring planter Tom Covington) an especially severe punishment: "De white folks in hell," Williams passionately exclaimed, "heap wo'se den dese what's livin' now." Williams and other interviewees believed that God intervened directly in human affairs to see that justice was done. Thus, the memorable snowstorm of 1857 ("Cox's Snow") witnessed God's punishment to a cruel slavemaster. "Ole Phillip Cox . . . ," according to Sis Shackelford, "was a great drinkin' white man. . . . God knows he was so mean, God had to do suppin' to him; so He jes let him git drunk an' den frez him to def" (*Interviews*, 191–92, 320, 252).[9]

Indeed, God had intervened not only to punish wicked slavemasters, but to end slavery itself. "God done got angry 'bout dese sinful ways," Nancy Williams averred. "Said he's gonna unslave our bodies. He done set de word a-whisperin' thew God's country." At Horace Muse's plantation in 1861, "we heard it whispered 'roun' dat a war come fer to set de niggers free." This war was God's doing. During slavery, Muse explained, bondpeople were forced to work very long hours: "No res' fer niggers 'till God he step in an' put a stop to de white folks meanness." Charles Grandy, too, understood that God was responsible for Emancipation. At the indication that there would be a war, Grandy reported, "niggers got glad. All dem what could pray 'gin to pray more'n ever. So glad God sendin' de war" (*Interviews*, 320, 216, 115).[10] Ellis Bennett associated the wartime Emancipator with the biblical Abraham, and he identified the slaves with the Bible's chosen people: "Gawd tol Lincoln for ta free his people. He say to Abraham, 'Abraham, dey's got four million ob mah people down dah in bondage. Go down an set 'em free.' An he did" (*Interviews*, 29).

Many bondpeople believed not only that God intervened directly in human affairs, but that he set a standard against which the actions of slavemasters might be measured. Because masters were subject to God's higher authority, their authority over slaves was not absolute. Some slaves therefore were encouraged to acts of dissidence, in the assurance that God was on their side.

Masters often felt that their slaves' exuberant appeals to God challenged their own authority. Thus, although the master of Albert Jones (a privileged house servant) "wuz mighty good to me," he nevertheless prohibited his slaves from "prais[ing] God so he could hear yer." How God's authority might limit that of a slave owner was also illustrated by a previously mentioned incident that took place during the Civil War.[11] Here, Yankee soldiers visited a plantation west of Fredericksburg where a three-day-old slave infant had not yet been named. The baby's mother explained to the soldiers "dat Missus ain't got round to namin' it yet." The soldiers said they themselves would name the baby, and they wrote an absurdly long name into the white mistress's Bible. When the mistress returned, she "was furious, but de name was in de Bible an' she couldn't change it," thus acknowledging a religious limitation upon her authority over the slaves (*Interviews*, 178, 314).

In black folk-memory the Christian religion came to be associated with acts of dissidence. A woman called Aunt Crissy (whose master had sold two of her children) was an outspoken slave, and when a young child of hers died, she expressed her grief in religious language: "She went straight up to ole Master an' shouted in his face 'Praise gawd, praise gawd, my little chile is gone to Jesus. That's one chile of mine you never gonna sell'" (*Interviews*, 183).

Although Nancy Williams was a religious fanatic whose stories are not always believable, her implausible tale of Uncle Jimmy's death nevertheless illustrates how, in black folklore, religion fueled dissidence. According to Williams, Jimmy (a bondman on the adjacent plantation)

> usta sing an' pray all de time he wukin' in de fiel's. . . . Dat man was bawn o' God! . . . Overseer tol' Uncle Jimmy stop singin' cause he ain' wukin'. Jes' singin'. Uncle Jimmy ain' said nottin' jes' keep on plowin' dat cawn an' a-singin'. Dis mek de white man mad. Den de overseer went to de house an' tol' de marsa dat he got a nigger down in de fiel dat cain' be doin' no wuk cause he sing all de time. Den ole Tom Covington [the master] say, "Kill de nigger if he won't wuck!" . . .
>
> [The overseer] chained po' Uncle Jimmy an' th'owed him in de hole an' lit a match to him. . . . Uncle Jimmy say, "Ise fixin' to die to live agin' in Chris'." Den he commence to preach an' pray. . . . De las' thin' po' Uncle Jimmy did was sing:
>
> God is de spring of all my joy,
> De life of my delight.
>
> As de song fade away he died.

Slaves did indeed employ religious songs as a means of slowing down the pace of work, both in the fields and in Virginia's tobacco factories. Although Nancy Williams may not have been a credible witness to the details of Uncle Jimmy's alleged martyrdom, her story illustrates how Christian conviction might impel a slave to defy a cruel master (*Interviews*, 319–20).

Religion was sometimes associated with a guardedly egalitarian message. In Matilda Perry's interpretation of Trinitarian doctrine, for example, "Gawd made all mankind! Mankind is in de father! De Father is in de Son! And de Son is in de Holy Ghost! Derefo' you know dat all mankin' is in de Lawd." This was balm against Perry's succumbing to any allegation that black people were inferior to whites and might therefore be justly oppressed. A more explicitly egalitarian credo animated the life of Byrl Anderson, whose upbringing (as previously suggested) blended religious influences from his grandmother with a mainly secular doctrine from his master ("a Whig who owned slaves but was against slavery").[12] "Never call no white man master," Anderson's owner taught him as a young child. "For all are brothers and all are equal. Black is good as white. So always keep courage and never back off from a white man." Later this conviction did indeed give Anderson courage, during a remarkable career as a mine workers' trade unionist in Tennessee, and as a farmer in Virginia. The religious component of Anderson's self-belief came partly from his master, but largely from his grandmother. She early instilled in the child a fear of God and a conviction that if he led a good life he could keep the devil at bay. "Grandma knew all about the devil," Anderson boasted,

> and taught me all about him. . . . You see I can order him out when I get tired of him and he's got to go. . . .
>
> I feard God; God showed me many things in my life; I've always had visions. . . .
>
> God told me he wanted me to [be] a leader for my people like Moses. I complained that I was not prepared. And God said, "You go an' I'll go with you an' speak for you." From that day I became some sort of leader of my people. . . .
>
> Master used to tell many a fortune . . . by hanging the Bible on a key and saying certain words. . . . When the Bible would come to me, it would just spin. That meant that I was [a] lucky and righteous man. Too it said to me be afraid of no man.

Byrl Anderson (born in 1859) lived most of his life in a post-Emancipation era when, despite continued oppression of black people, his talents and religious self-belief could find greater scope for creative leadership than was available to any dissident slave (*Interviews*, 221, 9–11).

As is well-known, Christianity did not always foster nonviolence. Nat Turner, a Virginia bondman, found in the Book of Revelations messianic inspiration to lead the most famous North American slave insurrection, which in 1831 killed some sixty white people.[13] But rather than inspiring violence, Christianity much more often provided religious sanction for nonviolent dissidence. If fugitives were concealed near their home, clandestine supplies of food sent by family and friends might not suffice; they were likely then to try to steal enough to survive, with perfect confidence that God approved. When Cornelia Carney's father was hiding in the woods, "Mama used to send John, my oldes' brother, out to de woods wid food fo' father, an' what he didn't git fum us de Lawd provided. Never did ketch him" (*Interviews*, 67).

Religious conviction fostered defiance. Julia Frazier reports that at a white church near Fredericksburg, attended by slaves, an old man "would answer the preacher every Sunday meetin'. He made so much noise ole Marsa said, 'John, if you stop makin' dat noise in church, I'll give you a new pair of boots.' . . . De nex' meetin' he tried an' tried to be quiet so he could get his new boots, but de spirit got him an' he yelled out, 'Glory to God! Boots or no boots, glory to God!'" By claiming that he acted involuntarily—because seized by the spirit—the slave of an indulgent master might evade punishment for public disobedience of his master's wishes (*Interviews*, 99).

The most common link between the slaves' Christianity and their dissidence appeared in their attending unauthorized nighttime religious meetings. Although certain details narrated about these meetings are incredible, too many reliable interviewees described such gatherings for their existence to be doubted. Indeed, the Reverend Ishrael Massie spoke of these clandestine meetings as though they were the center of the slaves' religious lives. "In dese meetin's," Massie said, "de preacher didn't know a letter in a book but, ya know, he preached his kind of doctrine. Dar wasn't no Bible in dem days 'cept what de white folks had an' dey won't gwine let de nigger see hit—even ef he could read. . . . Ya see, paterrollers wuz mostly after de preacher 'cause he wuz de leader of de meetin' an' ef dey caught 'im, he knowd dar wuz a beatin' fer 'im. . . . Sometimes, yas, dey would ketch 'im but hit seldem." Here, and in numerous other cases, Christian faith proved a potent force fostering nonviolent dissidence among slaves (*Interviews*, 208).

A principal rival to Christianity in the slave quarters was belief in "conjure." This doctrine offered an explanation for the ills encountered in one's life, and protection against some of those ills; it also promised revenge against the machinations of one's enemies. Masters fought fiercely to extirpate "conjure," for fear that these ideas might embolden the slaves to challenge their authority. Belief in witchcraft was weaker among antebellum Virginia slaves than in the Carolina Low Country, and by 1937 few of the survivors said much about it.[14] Yet the occasional reference helps explain the masters' anxieties. A slave who believed he or she possessed the power to kill someone, undetected, simply by working a charm on them, might become dangerously insubordinate. Marrinda Singleton (a field hand born in 1840) explained to her skeptical black interviewer that "the practice of conjuration was carried on by quite a few" slaves. Singleton thought that conjuration had been imported from the West Indies, "although much of it," she said,

> was handed down from the wilds of Africa.
>
> The brewin' of certain concoctions composed of herbs, roots and scraps of cloth with certain fowl feathers was believed to wuk charms or spells on the persons desired. . . . They believed that medical science or skill would . . . [not] remove such spells. . . . Such superstitions and practices caused so much confusion among the slaves, along wid fear dat the Marsters took steps to drive it out by severe punishment. . . . This did not put an end to these practices. Many of us slaves feared de charm of witch craft more than de whippin' dat de Marster gave. Dey would keep their tiny bags of charms closely hidden under their clothes (*Interviews*, 267–68).[15]

Some of these charms were for good luck, others to wreak vengeance on putative enemies. If a mysterious malady afflicted you, it was believed advisable to consult a conjure doctor. Virginia Shepherd's stepfather, for example, had something like a boil on his buttocks, which burst: "He thought he was conjured. He said an enemy of his put something on the horse's back and he rode it and got it on his buttocks and broke him out." The stories Shepherd reported from her stepfather were entirely about enemies trying to get at you and how you could defend yourself from their conjuring. White doctors were thought incapable of preventing an enemy from doing his or her worst, such as inflicting on you a fatal malady; the only remedy was to consult a conjure doctor. This man "always brought a pack of cards [with instructions written on them] and a bottle with a live bug in it, string tied around the neck of the bottle." The doctor turned over the cards one by one, and the one he was holding at the moment the bug first moved "told how to fix the conjure. . . . [Furthermore,] the bug would tell the victim the direction of the enemy" (*Interviews*, 263).

This was a contest not only between conjure doctors and white doctors, but also between conjure and Christianity. Matilda Perry experienced a struggle between her Christian beliefs and her lingering attachment to conjuring. Although this battle took place some years after Emancipation, it illuminates the contest between the newer faith of forgiveness and the older one of vengeance, which caused "confusion" among antebellum slaves. Perry believed she had once been conjured, and she wished no repetition of that bad experience. Big bumps had appeared under both her arms, which she attributed to the unprovoked, malicious conjuring of the only woman who had recently had the opportunity to come into her home. When Perry (at her husband's urging) consulted a "root doctor," the doctor declared that she would soon have died had she not come to him for help. He said that if Perry wanted to save her own life, she should conjure the woman who had conjured her. But the root doctor's prescription conflicted with Perry's Christian belief that she should forgive her enemies. The root doctor—Perry explained—"sing out wid his eyes in a [trance?], 'Give it back to her what gived it to you an' I kin cure you.' . . . I say, 'I b'lieves in God. I aimin' to go to Heaben 'case he 'paring a place dere fo' me, an' I'se goin' to dat place 'case I ain't goin' give no spell like dis one what has done been given to me back to nobody.' . . . He say, '. . . dat de only quickes' way to git rid o' de spell. Jes' put it right back on her dat put it on you.' I say, 'No sir. Heaben is promised to me, an' I ain't goin' do nothin' ter break dat promise.'" The root doctor, despite this rebuff, gave Perry some medicine, and he predicted a reconciliation between Perry and the woman suspected of conjuring her. But when this woman next approached their house, Perry's husband—a firm believer in conjuration—seized an ax. "I swear 'fo God, Tilda," he cried, "ef anybody conjure you, I'se goin' to kill 'em." Perry begged her husband to calm down, and he did so just in time. Perry then effected a reconciliation with the suspected woman: "I give her my han' an' I been all right ever since." Thus, Christian forgiveness ended the feud and terminated the spell. But if, instead, Jake had killed the woman who he believed had conjured his wife, he would have been executed, leaving Matilda a widow and his children fatherless. Christianity, in Matilda Perry's narrative, served both her husband's interest and that of herself and their children, by keeping him alive (*Interviews*, 221–23).

No doubt the masters' attempts to extirpate conjuring from the slave quarters arose from fear that belief in conjuration would embolden bond-people to strike at their enemies—not just among the slaves, but in the white master class. Indoctrinating the slaves with a nonviolent version of Christian faith might prove an effectual antidote to an Africa-derived belief in conjuration. But in this instance what served the interests of the masters also served the interests of the slaves. Killing white people, for the slaves of Virginia, would have been a futile, self-destructive exercise. There were too many whites, and they were far too well organized, for any peacetime mass insurgency to succeed—as John Brown and his followers quickly discovered in 1859. A nonviolent version of Christianity encouraged the slaves to direct their massive discontent with slavery into more constructive channels than that of carnage.[16]

Christianity offered African Americans hope. The assurance of a woman like Matilda Perry that "heaben is promised to me" affected her conduct and inspirited her life. Even Aunt Nellie—a bondwoman so despairing (from repeated whippings) that she committed suicide—did so in the hope of finding a better world in the hereafter. "Fannie," Aunt Nellie confided to her friend before killing herself, "I don' had my las' whippin'. I'm gwine to God." As everyone knows, the slaves' religious songs were sorrow songs. "Look like right now I can hear some o' dem mournful voices; 'specially brother John," an eighty-two-year-old woman told the younger woman interviewing her. "He would always sing an' pray." Minnie Folkes's mother told her that at their secret nighttime meetings "de poor souls was prayin' to God to free 'em f'om dat awful bondage." If a house servant reported that the master was about to sell certain slaves, this would lead to a burst of prayer in the quarters. "Den sech prayin', honey," the Reverend Ishrael Massie exclaimed. "Dem what ain't named would pray to God ole Marsa ain't gonna sell dem, an' dem what been named would pray dey get a good Marsa" (*Interviews*, 222, 34, 186, 93, 211).

Sad or anxious though the slaves might be, their religion encouraged them to count whatever blessings they could—to thank God for every good thing in their lives. They prided themselves on understanding how to praise God better than white people did. Those caught by the patrol at an unauthorized meeting would pray with renewed vigor: they "would praise God in de way we knowd. Honey, we had answer from dem prayers." The favorite hymn of an old, paralyzed slave woman was:

Oh, Father of Mercy,
We give thanks to Thee,
We give thanks to Thee,
For thy great glory.

Jane Pyatt knew perfectly well that her mistress had taught her to read, yet such was her recognition of her good fortune (contrasted to that of most slaves) that her impulse was to thank God for teaching her—"Sometimes I believe my ability to read is a gift from God" (*Interviews*, 208, 127, 234).

Many slaves thought God was a being to whom they could talk personally about their lives. "Chile, God's a talkin' man," Nancy Williams assured her interviewer, "an' you gotta talk back to him." This conversation might take place in the fields: "We talk[ed] to God an' prayed by ourselves jes' wherever we was workin'," Louise Jones recalled. The conversation often occurred at a religious gathering. Charles Crawley's master gave his slaves passes to attend prayer meetings at various nearby plantations. "So marster's slaves met an' worshipped from house to house, an' honey," Crawley stated with satisfaction, "we talked to God all us wanted." Just as Matilda Perry's Christianity coexisted with a lingering belief in conjure, so George White's Christian intercourse with God strengthened his faith in the efficacy of herbal remedies. "Dere's a root for ev'y disease an' I can cure most anything," he boasted, "but you have got to talk wid God an' ask him to help out. . . . We is got to talk wid God an' ask Him to do His will, an' He will show us what to do" (*Interviews*, 320, 185, 79, 310).

One benefit of Christian deportment was that it might earn a slave better treatment, even if the master were not himself a religious person. The owner of Elizabeth Sparks's mother, for example, did not even turn to religion on his deathbed. "He was a tough one . . . ," Sparks exclaimed. "Is he in heaven! No, he ain't in heaven! Went past heaven." Yet even this man, a cruel master, moderated his rigor toward Sparks's mother: "She wuz a real Christian an' he respected her a little. Didn't beat her so much. Course he beat her once in a while." The Christian conduct of Sparks's mother won her not only less bad treatment, but even a modicum of esteem. "She wuz very religious," Sparks said proudly, "an' all white folks set store to 'er" (*Interviews*, 274, 276).

Christian faith might impel a black person to express forbearance toward even a cruel master. The slave's real feelings, however, might contradict Christian doctrine. In 1872 a Northern antislavery woman relished exposing this contradiction to Harry Jarvis, a former slave who had lost a leg fighting in the Union Army. Jarvis's Virginia master had been so cruel that the interviewer felt his conduct unpardonable, and she asked Jarvis whether religion had led him to forgive his master. Jarvis hesitated: "'De Lord *knows* I'se forgub him; but'—his eye kindled again as the human nature burst forth—'but I'd gib my oder leg to meet him in battle!'"[17]

Elizabeth Sparks, too, experienced a conflict between her feelings and her Christian beliefs. Sparks was terrified of her mother's owner; and that man's son, too, "was terrible. There was no end to the beatin'." The younger man "done so much wrongness I couldn't tell yer all of it." Yet Sparks was reluctant to narrate her masters' misdeeds to her black interviewer in 1937: "Tain't no sense fur yer ta know 'bout all those mean white folks. Dey all daid now. They mean good, I reckon. Leastways most of 'em got salvation on their death beds." Christian doctrine, as Sparks understood it, promised salvation even to lifelong sinners, so long as they sincerely confessed before they died. Thus, Sparks was able to conclude that "dey's good an' bad people everywhere. That's the way the white folks wuz. Some had hearts; some had gizzards 'stead o' hearts" (*Interviews*, 274, 277, 274, 276).

Lillian Clarke's aunt Cinda displayed Christian spirit not merely by a reluctant avowal that some white people had hearts, but by an act of extraordinary forbearance. When Cinda was a slave, her mistress had fed her badly and beaten her cruelly. Yet after the war, when the white woman was impoverished and hungry, Cinda bought some groceries for her. Cinda's justification for this act of forgiveness was that God had punished some white people so severely for their misconduct that justice had been done, and it now behooved black people to turn the other cheek. "De way white folks use to treat us niggers—," Lillian Clarke explained to her black interviewer, "God has whipped some of 'em worse dan dey beat us. Take Cinda's case. God suffered her mistress to come to Cinda fer food." When the white storekeeper (who knew how badly Cinda had been treated) remonstrated with her for being a fool to feed her old mistress, Cinda replied, "Yas, Mr. Jones, I know I is, but God is jes rod[d]ing her [i.e., beating her with a rod] fer some dem licks and starving she give me. 'Member, de good Bible say [and here the narrator made a Freudian slip] must turn evil fer evil." No doubt many African Americans felt the urge to return evil for evil, but in this case Christian precept had impelled Cinda to overcome that urge. Lillian Clarke proudly expressed to her black interviewer the belief that "some of us colored is got a tender heart." Perhaps the greatest gift of Christianity to the slaves was that it fostered in some of them, against all possible odds, a spirit of forgiveness (*Interviews,* 73).

Not only did religion help shape bondpeople's response to slavery, it also of course influenced the conduct of their personal lives. Most significantly, it fostered self-discipline, especially in regard to sexual morality and family responsibility. The slaves in a particular neighborhood were sometimes split into two parties: the "Christians" and (in the eyes of the Christians) the "sinners." Cornelius Garner recalled—a bit wistfully—that in his area "dey had frolics in dem days but I couldn' go. De Christians had dere 'fairs on one farm an' de sinners had dere frolics on 'nother farm. Mother was a Christian an' so was I." Garner nevertheless seemed to regret the subsequent decline of this sharp social division: "Nowadays [in 1937] you can' tell one from t'other. Christians an' sinners all go to de same things" (*Interviews,* 103).

When Nancy Williams was of courting age, she had exulted in being one of the sinners. She was a tireless, exuberant dancer, and dressed herself boldly so as to capture the attention of every beholder. Each dance became a competition between herself and a rival named Jennie, with young men betting substantial sums of money on which girl could outlast the other. Williams's later turn to Christianity enabled her to continue exulting in her youthful triumphs, while reassuring her that her earlier consorting with the devil would not jeopardize her subsequent desire to go to heaven. Conspicuously attired in a yellow dress with shoes painted yellow to match, Williams had rejoiced at being the cynosure of all eyes. "Whoops!" she cried. "Dem dances was somepin. Dem de day's when me'n de devil was runnin roun in de depths o' hell. . . . Woul'n do it now for nottin. . . . Guess I didn' know no better den. . . . Jes' danced ole Jennie down. Me'n de debil won dat night. One boy won five dollars off'n me [i.e., by betting on her to outlast Jennie]. . . . No, dem other gals didn dress lak me. Chile, den I won' nottin' but belong to de devil. Sech carryin's on!" In this instance Christianity did not regulate Williams's youthful conduct; instead it later assured her she would have no price to pay for her early satisfactions (*Interviews,* 316).

Many young slaves were not religious, and (like Nancy Williams) became so only later in their lives. Charles Grandy, for example, was twenty-eight before he was converted. "Ise a God fearin' man now," he confided to his interviewers, "[but] I didn' git to be a christian 'til March 8, 1870 . . . , when I felt de spirit." Among older slaves Christian allegiance helped promote marital fidelity. One slave verse, according to Virginia Shepherd's mother, instructed that

> To have peace at home,
> An' pleasure abroad,
> Love yo' wife,
> An' serve the Lord.

The deacons of Virginia's urban black Baptist and Methodist churches paid more attention to enforcing rules against adultery (by expelling convicted church members) than to any other single issue (*Interviews*, 118, 264).[18]

Christianity also directed slaves toward observing standards of honesty and veracity despite the pressures of slavery that conflicted with those standards. Thus, most slaves took for granted their right to steal from their masters (because their masters stole from them), and their right to deceive their masters in order to avoid whippings. Yet Christianity pointed in a different direction, instilling principles that might blossom later, under less oppressive circumstances. George White, for example, had a profound belief that on Judgment Day he would be called before God to account for his transgressions; this impelled him to tell the truth about his master. When White complained that, after Emancipation in 1865, his master "didn' give us one thing" to compensate his family for their previous years of unpaid labor, he assured the interviewer of his veracity: "I know what I'm talking about 'cause I got to answer for dis in de judgment" (*Interviews*, 311).

Religion of course served other functions besides helping to shape moral conduct. Attendance at religious gatherings gave slaves opportunities to socialize with black people from other plantations. Not only men, but women too might travel for miles at nighttime, without a pass, to reach such gatherings. The Reverend W. P. Jacobs's mother told him that "one night she and some other slaves walked eight miles out in the country to a camp meeting. They left the meeting late and ran almost all the way back. The fo' day horn was blowing just when they got in sight of the house. One of the women panted, 'Thank God!' Mother says she hushed her up 'cause some used to say that if you thanked God too soon, you'd be caught and whipped till your back was raw and bloody." These slaves conceived of God as a being who helped them defy the plantation rules (*Interviews*, 157–58).

Another function of Christianity was to give some slaves a sense of compensation for having been deprived of book learning. Dave Lowry mourned that his enslaved grandparents "didn't have any education. But de were very religious. My mother and father . . . didn't have any educa-tion. De believed in religion. . . . I don't have any education. But I know de Lord." Religion created self-esteem (*Interviews*, 198).

The role of religion in the slaves' lives should not be exaggerated. Christine Heyrman's revisionist statistical analysis suggests that, as of 1835, only about 28 percent of Southern African American adults were evangeli-cal Christians, as contrasted with about 66 percent of Southern white adults.[19] Even as late as 1861 many masters forbade their bondpeople to attend religious services, or discouraged them from doing so. When Sister Harrison was a slave, she worked seven days a week as nurse to the white children. "I was not allowed to go to Church, Sunday School, nor any kind of school," she said, "until after the war." Although Caroline Hunter and Horace Muse were not banned from attending church, they were discour-aged from doing so. "Church was something we seldom went to," Hunter reported. "We could sing an' shout 'round de house as much as we chose, but massa always said if we went to church we wouldn' keep our min's on our wuk durin' de week an' he would have to beat us." Horace Muse's master was somewhat less discouraging. "Onliest church we git to go to was de white folks church," Muse testified. "Marser didn' like dat. He say, 'Niggers learn too much.' When we went to church we had to walk; warn' 'lowed to ride" (*Interviews*, 135, 150, 216).

Even when masters made it easy for slaves to attend church, indiffer-ence often prevailed in the slave quarters. "Sundays we could go to church if we wanted to," Cornelius Garner recalled. "Some few went but de big-gest part of us jes stayed 'round de house and slept and talked." A principal reason for the slaves' staying at home was the distastefulness of the mes-sage served up by the clergyman. "Dat ole white preacher jest was telling us slaves to be good to our marsters," Garner grumbled. "We ain't keer'd

a bit 'bout dat stuff he was telling us." Lassitude on Sunday did not, however, signify indifference to Afro-Christianity. "We wanted to sing, pray,
and serve God in our own way," Garner explained. "You see, 'legion needs
a little motion—specially if you gwine feel de spirret" (*Interviews,* 100).

This Afro-Christianity differed substantially from the expurgated
version of Christianity intoned by most antebellum white preachers.
Although Christian slaves regarded many human beings as "sinners,"
the doctrines of Original Sin and Atonement did not interest them. They
viewed God and Jesus as beings who were readily approachable, who offered the faithful something like a warm, reassuring human friendship.
Afro-Christianity featured even greater congregational participation during religious services than occurred during white Baptist and Methodist
gatherings. Afro-Christianity fostered credulity about purported appear-
ances of the Spirit in human affairs. The role of spirits in Afro-Christianity
bore a noticeable resemblance to their role in West African religions.[20]

Despite all of these distinctive features, however, the Afro-Christianity
of antebellum Virginia was a profoundly Christian religion. Its promise of
salvation on Judgment Day offered hope to slaves who had all too little
to hope for in this world. Its doctrine of turning the other cheek helped
to impel some bondpeople to make the compromises that, though unpalatable, were usually necessary for survival. Christianity's injunction to
praise God for his works promoted healthy reverence for those aspects
of life that deserved reverence. Its doctrine that there was a higher law
than that of man encouraged slaves to believe that someday justice might
be done, and it set an ethical standard by which they might judge their
masters, as well as themselves. This Christian doctrine emboldened many
bondpeople to acts of dissidence—embarked upon with confidence that a
just God would approve, and that brave slaves would surely be rewarded
in heaven, whatever the outcome of their earthly enterprises.[21] The variant of Christianity devised and cherished in the slave quarters was one
of the slaves' best defenses against the dehumanization that slavery
might otherwise have bred in them. Unlike the Afro-Christianity of the
Carolina Low Country—where African influences still predominated into
the 1860s—Afro-Christianity in Virginia became a deeply Christian system that resembled orthodox Southern evangelical Christianity in many
of its features. Although substantially modified by African influences,
Afro-Christianity was fundamentally shaped by the slaves' experiences

of bondage and by their appropriation of some of the Christian beliefs to which they had been exposed in North America.[22]

This variant of Christianity served the interests of the slaves, but it also promoted the short-run interests of the slavemasters, insofar as it damped violent slave resistance. One might argue, however, that in the long run Afro-Christianity helped undermine the slave system. During the 1850s Northern white people (who eventually supplied most of the soldiers in the liberating Union Army) were more likely to sympathize with nonviolent dissident slaves—like the fugitive Anthony Burns, forcibly returned from Boston to his Virginia master in 1854—than with vengeful Nat Turners. Perhaps, by fostering nonviolent dissidence, Afro-Christianity best served both the short-run and the long-term interests of the slaves.

10

Dissidence

The slaves' strongest bulwark against dehumanization—stronger even than their Afro-Christianity—was their nearly universal spirit of dissidence. Although fostered by Afro-Christianity, this spirit of dissent would almost certainly have thrived even in the absence of that religion. Bondpeople stole from their masters, deceived them, disobeyed rules, protested ill treatment, went absent at nighttime without leave, fled the plantation for extended periods or sometimes permanently, and occasionally fought their masters. Stories of their own, or their ancestors', dissent were dearly cherished by former slaves. Dissidence was a tremendous morale booster, as bondpeople affirmed their active agency, denying that they were mere victims of oppression. Yet slaves paid a high price, perhaps, for being driven—by the scarcity of constructive alternatives—to direct so many of their talents and creative energies into the arts of dissidence.

Dissidence has for many years provided the central theme of slavery studies. Historians differ, however, about the aspects of dissidence most worthy of attention. Some have focused on violent resistance—insurrections, or assaults by individual slaves upon their masters. Other historians have stressed nonviolent dissidence—flight, deception, theft. Still others have focused on cultural resistance, or on the slaves' negotiations with their masters to improve the conditions of their servitude. Virginia's WPA interviews are particularly revealing about the balance between violent and nonviolent dissidence.

No form of dissent, it appears, was more important than unauthorized absence from the plantation. This often took place for just a few hours, under cover of darkness. Men would visit their women friends or their wives; young people would go off to parties; their elders would attend religious meetings. Georgina Gibbs complained that at her big plantation, during the weekend time off, "you won't 'lowed to visit [friends]"; but sometimes, she said, male slaves would go out at night anyway, deceiving their masters by putting logs in their beds (*Interviews*, 105).[1] Sis Shackelford reported that women as well as men defied the patrollers: "'Course if dey catch you, you got a sound lashin' comin', but us was young and spry an' could outrun 'em. Ole Huck Steps was de meanes' one of [the patrollers]. . . . We could keep still whilst he was near an' go on dancin' arter he was gone" (*Interviews*, 253).[2] Successful evasion of patrols crystallized into slave songs. Fleeing—far from being regarded as ignominious—was glorified. "We all use to sing dis," George White recalled:

> Run nigger run,
> Run nigger run,
> Don't let de paddlerollers catch you
> Run nigger run
> Run nigger run,
> Keep on runnin' 'till daylight come.
> (*Interviews*, 310)[3]

Nighttime religious meetings attracted bold souls from the slave quarters, and folklore grew up around the dissidents' successes in discommoding the patrollers. "Mother often told me how they used to slip away so they could pray together," the Reverend W. P. Jacobs testified. "If the patterollers got after them, they would run for the cornfield. . . . It was better still if they could get to a field with stumps in it. They would run around or jump over the stumps, an' if the patterollers come in they were like to break their horses' legs." Beverly Jones's uncle Jackson "was a favored nigger" who used his privileged position to protect the other slaves when they were attending unauthorized meetings. Apparently, Jackson's master ("a purty good ole codger") had warned the patrollers never to whip Jackson. This privileged slave then acted as "de 'raid fox' fo' de patterollers. . . . He use to stand out on de trail when de patterollers lookin' fo' the meetin' an' lead 'em off in the wrong direction. Effen they catched him, dey warn gonna do nothin' to Uncle Jackson." Garland Monroe told how, when patrollers chased his older brother from an unauthorized religious meeting, the brother (by putting a levering bar under one end of a log that served as a footbridge over a stream) "pried up dat log an' thowed 'em all in de water." West Turner boasted of having been the lookout boy for a nighttime meeting in the woods. The slaves made their preparations to discomfit the patrollers, then instructed Turner "to step out f'm de woods an' let [the patrol] see me. Well, I does, an' de paddyrollers dat was on horse back come a chasin' arter me, jus' a-gallopin' down de lane. . . . When they got almost up wid me I jus' ducked into de woods. Course de paddyrollers couldn't stop so quick an' kep' on 'roun' de ben[d], an' den dere came a-screamin' an' cryin'. . . . Dem ole paddyrollers done rid plumb into a great line of grape vines dat de slaves had stretched 'cross de path" (*Interviews*, 157, 181, 214–15, 290).

In addition to nighttime excursions, slaves sometimes briefly fled the plantation in broad daylight. A black man might fear he would be unable to control his rage at seeing his wife stripped and flogged by a white man; if the flogging were announced in advance, the husband might absent himself during the event. As described earlier, Jordan Johnson claimed, "Husbands allays went to de woods when dey know de wives was due fo' a whippin', but [if it came unexpectedly when they were] in de fiel' dey dare not leave."[4] Indeed, the physical pain of a whipping could be so intense that, if the victim were not bound, he or she might try to escape. Samuel Chilton reported that his mother's master sometimes "would whip his slaves so terrible dey would break loose an stay in de woods. Bout night time dey come out beggin'." But fugitives seldom returned quite so quickly as this. Liza McCoy's master, McCoy recalled angrily, was "mean—He whip me when he could ketch me, but I runned in de woods. Come back when I get hungry" (*Interviews*, 160, 71, 199).

The slaves' common experiences of roaming the neighborhood on Sundays (or at night, in defiance of patrollers) gave many bondpeople courage to flee from the plantation for periods longer than a single night. Hunger seldom impelled a prompt return to the plantation, because family or friends could be counted on to smuggle food out to the fugitive. "Sometimes they beat [female slaves] so bad," Elizabeth Sparks explained, "they jes' couldn't stand it an' they run away to the woods. If yer git in the woods, they couldn't git yer. Yer could hide an' people slip yer somepin' to eat." The length of time one remained absent was then sometimes negotiated between fugitive and master, much depending on whether the fugitive trusted the master's promise not to inflict condign punishment. Sparks declared that her mean master could not be believed. "After while," she said, "he tell one of colored foreman tell yer come on back. He ain'ta goin' beat yer anymore. . . . Foreman git yer to come back an' then he beat yer to death again" (*Interviews*, 274).

Lorenzo Ivy's grandmother fled under similar circumstances, but the negotiation led—at least for a time—to a less unsatisfactory outcome. Ivy's grandmother "stayed in de woods for three or four weeks. . . . Dey say dat her ole Marsa . . . treated her jus' like a dog. She was de cook, an' he would beat her ef he didn't like what she cooked. So she run 'way to de woods an' stayed in hidin' in de day time an' come out onlies' at night. My mama say she used to always put out food fo' her an' she would slip up nights an' git it. After gramma been out in de woods fo' couple of weeks, ole Marsa come down to my mama an' tell her to tell ole Sallie to come on back—he wasn't gonna hide her." The master suavely pretended to believe Ivy's mother's protestations that she knew nothing of the fugitive's doings. "Mama swore she ain't seed her," Ivy continued, "—didn't know where she was. 'Sho, I know, Mamie, but if you do see her you tell her if she gits back Monday I ain't gonna hide her, but if she don't I gonna give her 500 lashes.' Mama told gramma dat night, an' dey talked 'bout it tryin' to decide what to do. Finally gramma decided to come on back, so on Monday mornin' dar she was in de kitchen, an Marsa kept his word— didn't give her nary a lick." Ill treatment recurred, however, and Sallie fled repeatedly. It seemed as though "my grandmother lived in de woods . . . ," Ivy averred. "Dey treat her so bad she often come down to our place. After a while dey tell some one to tell her to come on home. Dey warn' goin' beat her anymore. She go on back fo' a while" (*Interviews*, 154, 153).

The most frequent goad to these temporary flights was a savage whipping, or the fear of one. Although most of the fugitives in the stories thus far considered have been women, men fled even more frequently. Old Arthur Greene was surprised that his interviewer seemed not to realize how often slaves absented themselves from their plantations. "Yes indeed," he replied to Mrs. Susie Byrd, "plenty of slaves uster run away. Why dem woods was full o' 'em chile." Virginia Shepherd's language was a bit less hyperbolic, but her point was the same. "If they were treated too cruelly," she said, "our folks would always run away and hide in the woods. They were seldom captured even with dogs" (*Interviews*, 125, 261).

Robert Williams graphically described his own flight. His master combined managing a farm with practicing law in Lynchburg. This part-time farmer did not employ an overseer. Evidently, he did not always have a whip to hand, and he failed to bind Williams before trying to flog him. The young bondman was a spirited lad, unwilling to be treated like a common slave, and he was proud of his speed and dexterity. He partially masked his pride, however, by pretending that his dislike of cold weather was a principal cause of his unwillingness to be whipped. One cold winter's day he realized his "master was goin' to whip me for somepin'. I turned and seen him gettin' some switches, den I broke an' ran, an' ran, 'cause I could travel. When I got to a fence, I just laid one han' on de fence an' over I went. . . . I had made up in my min' that I was'n goin' take dat beatin' dat day 'cause de col' weather was more'n I could stan' an' den to take my shirt off an' git a beatin' was more den I was goin' to take." When Williams's master yelled for the other slaves to "Catch him!" their response apparently was half-hearted, and Williams "got away an' slept in de woods 'hind logs at nights. Durin' de day I would hide an' at nights fo' I went to sleep, I would go 'round slave quarters an' git food. I got me all I wanted to eat an' plenty of rest. I stayed out in de woods about a year" (*Interviews*, 323–24).

Martha Showvely's uncle ran away for even longer, managing to make himself relatively comfortable at his hideout; and he did not return voluntarily (as Williams finally did). "De massa beat him," Showvely explained, "an' he ran away. He went up in de woods an' dug him a hole in de ground an' covered it with leaves. He stayed dere for two years. In de day he stayed up unda de ground an' at night he went about an' got food. When dey found him, he had plenty food an' a nice place back up under dere" (*Interviews*, 265).

Liza Brown (whose information about flights from her parents' plantation near Petersburg was secondhand) romanticized the diet available to the fugitives. "De slaves used to run away f'om our flock," she said, "an' stay in de woods. I reckon dey got plenty good somep'n to eat . . . , 'cause dey steal hogs an' kill 'em. . . . Den, too, you ketch a ole possum, ole hares, an' birds; all dem things is good eatin's. . . . When de runaway slaves git tired in de woods, dey come back home an' ole Marsa would beat 'em up again. Den sometimes dey take to de woods again an' stay." Mollie Booker was unsentimental about the appearance of these long-term fugitives. "Runaways useto come to our house all de time," she recalled, "to git

somepin to eat. Dey stayed in de woods a long time an' dere beards growed
so long dat no one could very well recerginize dem. Dey actually look like
wild men" (*Interviews*, 63, 54–55).

Booker's family were free blacks, and their regular practice of supplying
food to runaways illustrates how most Upper South blacks—whether free
or enslaved—showed solidarity with fugitives (*Interviews*, 54).[5] For example, Jennie Patterson (even though she was a slave treated exceptionally
well by her first mistress) did not hesitate to secrete a distressed fugitive
woman in her own bed, in order to save her from capture. Patterson was
proud that her first mistress had treated her "jes' as same as a white chile";
yet she identified with blacks in her hostility to the "white folks" pursuing
the fugitive woman. Patterson—awakened by a woman who rapped on
her door in the middle of the night and, "out a breath, wisper[ed], 'Can I
stay here all night?'"—let her sleep behind her in her bed. "I . . . heard de
horses an' talkin' in de woods. Dogs barkin'. Ha! Ha! Ha! I peeped out de
window an' saw dem white folks go by an' [they] ain' never dreamed of . . .
lookin' fer de 'oman whar was over 'hind me. . . . We never tole on each
other" (*Interviews*, 218, 220).

If a slave was likely to help an unknown fugitive, assistance from a
blood relative was even more certain. West Turner's aunt Sallie fled to the
woods, not because of a whipping, but because she was angry at having
been demoted (unjustly, she felt) from the position of children's mammy
to that of common field laborer. Sallie's master believed (correctly) that
Sallie's brother was supplying her with food. "Marse come down to de
quarters," Turner remembered clearly, "an' git my pa an' ast him whar was
Ant Sallie. Pa say he don' know nothin' 'bout her. Marsa didn' do nothin'
to pa, but he knowed pa was lyin' 'cause he done heard dat pa been feedin'
Ant Sallie in de night time. Well, pa used to put food in a pan 'neath de
wash bench 'side de cabin, an' it was so dark Ant Sallie come on inside to
eat it" (*Interviews*, 289).

Thus, fugitives could normally get food from the slave quarters, and
their whereabouts were unlikely to be betrayed by another black person.
"In dem days . . . ," the Reverend Ishrael Massie averred, "nigger didn't tell
on each other." Consequently, fugitives sometimes survived long periods
in the woods. Best known were the maroons in the vast Dismal Swamp of
Virginia and North Carolina, southwest of Norfolk. "When we was kids,"
Sis Shackelford (who grew up near the swamp) recalled, "we used to take

keer of cows 'bout four miles f'om home. De runaway slaves used to come out and beg us for food. At fust we was scared to deaf of 'em and jes' fly, but after while we used to steal bred an' fresh meat an' give to 'em. But dey never would let you foller 'em. Dey hide in Dismal swamp in holes in de groun' so hidden dey stay dere years an' white folks, dogs, or nothin' else could fine 'em." In other parts of the state, too, a surprising number of fugitives hid for months, or even years, at a time. "John Sally was a slave dat runned away," Charles Grandy reported admiringly. "He runned away an' didn' never come back. Didn' go no place neither. Stayed right roun' de plantation. Useto come in at night an' steal hawgs an' chickens fer food. Dat ole man died in de woods. Never did come out" (*Interviews*, 210, 252, 117).

A less extreme case was that of Cornelia Carney's father, who apparently returned voluntarily to the plantation, but only after a long absence. "Father got beat up so much," Carney explained, "dat arter while he run away an' lived in de woods." He was sustained by food sent by his wife (taken into the woods by their son), as well as by theft, his morale buoyed by the company of two other fugitives. Carney rejoiced at this evidence that black people could thus outwit the whites (*Interviews*, 67).

Lorenzo Ivy specified the most important distinction among fugitives: "Dere was two kin's of runaways—dem what hid in de woods an' dem what ran away to free lan'. Mos' slaves jes' runaway an' hide in de woods for a week or two an' den come on back" (*Interviews*, 153). But although the great majority of fugitives remained in the local woods, a substantial number sought total escape. A few of these tried to hide themselves permanently among the dark-skinned people of cities and towns like Washington, Alexandria, or Richmond; some others sought conveyance by oceangoing vessels sailing down the James River from Richmond or City Point (near Petersburg), or Norfolk; and many took overland routes toward Pennsylvania or Ohio. These attempts usually ended in failure, yet several dozen fugitives from Virginia reached the North, or Canada, annually during the antebellum years. In the peak year of 1856, about sixty-five Virginia fugitives got as far as Philadelphia (many of them crossing the Susquehanna River over its southernmost bridge at Columbia, Pennsylvania, sixty miles west of Philadelphia). From there they were forwarded northward along the well-organized Underground Railroad. Other

Virginia fugitives avoided Philadelphia and proceeded north through Harrisburg, Pittsburgh, or Ohio.[6]

One remarkable fugitive who sought permanent escape was Frank Bell's uncle Moses Bell, the enslaved "foreman" of 150 slaves on a big wheat plantation some miles west of Washington. There was no white overseer on this plantation, and Frank Bell thought his uncle—a towering figure—had a soft job. "Everybody skeered of him," Frank Bell remembered, "even ole Marser. Never whip him, don't believe he ever had a whippin' in his life. Had it easy, he did. All he had to do was see dat de other niggers did de work." But Moses Bell discovered that his privileges did not satisfy him; rather, they whetted his appetite for freedom. Often in the autumn, after he had supervised completion of the harvest, "Uncle Moses git hisself some food together an' de next day he be gone. Yessir, run away far as I can recollec' nine or ten times, but every time they caught him." Moses seems usually to have been apprehended in Alexandria or Washington: "Everytime Marser go an get him he come back mad as blazes, but he never whip him. If it been any other slave he give him a good whipping, but not Uncle Moses. . . . Ah guess he was little bit skeered to whip dat big man." Although Moses's master—"a pretty nice white man"—depended heavily on Moses to keep the plantation running smoothly, eventually his forbearance became exhausted: he threatened to sell Moses the next time he ran away. Undeterred, Moses joined a group of slaves seeking to reach Canada. Most of them, however—including Moses—were caught, and the intrepid slave was then sold to the Deep South (*Interviews*, 26–27, 25).[7]

Richard Slaughter, born near City Point on the James River, had heard of maritime escapes down that river. At any one time a dozen three-masted sailing ships might be anchored in the harbor. "Did slaves ever run away!" Slaughter exclaimed. "Lord yes. All the time. . . . In those days a good captain would hide a slave way up in the top sail and carry him out of Virginia to New York and Boston" (*Interviews*, 272). Although Slaughter exaggerated the number of these successful flights, there were enough maritime fugitives to cause the occasional furor. William Bayliss, a Delaware ship captain who during the 1850s carried a total of 27 slaves from Virginia to Philadelphia, was finally apprehended downriver from Petersburg with 5 more fugitives on board and was sentenced in 1858 to forty years imprisonment. During the 1850s a total of 115 fugitives escaped to Philadelphia on shipboard from Virginia cities, including 26 from Richmond or Petersburg and 89 from Norfolk or Portsmouth.[8]

More common than maritime escapes, however, were attempts to flee overland. A few advantaged escapees set off with a head start, so to speak. A light-skinned slave, for example, might hope—if he took enough money—to be able to ride part of the way on a stagecoach, passing for white. (This was true of a slave named Berkeley Bullock, although he was finally caught before he could cross the Ohio River.) James Smith, a slave who was three-quarters white and had often been taken for a white man, fled successfully from the Shenandoah Valley to Canada; Smith was so light-skinned that, once he was fifty miles from home, he dared to walk on the main road up the valley. The WPA interviewee William Johnson named four Virginia slaves who succeeded in reaching the North because they had a different sort of advantage: they possessed forged free papers sold to them by a literate slave, Joe Sutherland, who was a coachman on Johnson's own plantation. Just as white seamen took money from fugitives for aiding their escape (like the ship captain who transported Harriet Jacobs to freedom), so Joe Sutherland required payment for his dangerous enterprise of forging passes and free papers. "Joe was doing a big business," Johnson exclaimed, "—the slaves always paid him for the passes—but he was finally caught and sold way down south."[9]

Most fugitives set off without the advantage of either forged papers or a light complexion. Two slaves who successfully fled from a farm near Fredericksburg did, however, have the advantage of a forewarning that their master was about to sell them to the Deep South. They owed their warning to a quick-witted, illiterate young serving girl who—many years later—recounted her role in their escape. Fortunately, the girl's father knew how to spell, and he could pass on the warning to the threatened men. Susan Broaddus recalled that, when she was young, she

> was servin' gal fo' Missus. . . . Ole Marsa would spell out real fas' anything he don't want me to know 'bout. One day Marsa was . . . ravin' 'bout de crops, an' taxes, an' de triflin' niggers he got to feed. "Gonna sell 'em . . . ," he says. Den ole Missus ask which ones he gonna sell an' tell him quick to spell it. Den he spell out G-A-B-E, and R-U-F-U-S. 'Course I stood dere without battin' an eye, an' makin' believe I didn't even hear him, but I was packin' dem letters up in my haid all de time. An' soon's I finished dishes

I rushed down to my father an' say 'em to him jus' like Marsa say 'em.
Father say quiet-like: "Gabe and Rufus." . . . De next day Gabe and Rufus
was gone—dey had run away.

The narrator, exulting at her master's discomfiture, transformed his con-
temptuous phrase "triflin' niggers" into a banner of pride. So maddened
was the master at the discovery of Gabe and Rufus's absence that he
"nearly died, got to cussin' an' ravin' so he took sick. Missus went to town
an' tol' de sheriff, but dey never could fin' dose two slaves. Was gone to free
land. An' I spec' dey wondered many times how dem niggers knew dey was
goin' to be sol'" (*Interviews*, 55–56).

Frequently, however, flights were unsuccessful. Robert Williams named
two male slaves, Body and Ned Coleman, hired to help build a railway near
Lynchburg, who nearly succeeded in an attempt to reach Ohio but unluck-
ily were discovered and caught by two prowling Newfoundland dogs. So
determined was their employer to deter other hired slaves from fleeing
that he risked a lawsuit from Body's owner. When Body and Ned were
brought back to the construction site, "de boss beat dem until one of de
fellows was never no mo' good. De boss sent fo' de master to come an'
get dem. Dey tol' me," Williams recalled, "how near dey was to de [Ohio]
line when dem dogs caught dem. Body died soon after an' maybe from de
whippin'" (*Interviews*, 324–25).

The Reverend W. P. Jacobs's uncle Charlie had a similar experience, but
eventually there was a happier outcome. Uncle Charlie was cutting fence
rails on a plantation west of Roanoke and, unpaid for his labors, stubbornly
refused to work at the required pace. He was repeatedly flogged for failing to fulfill his quota. The enslaved driver who inflicted these whippings
happened to be Charlie's half-brother, and there probably was bad blood
between the two men. One day when the driver was laying on thirty-nine
lashes, "Charlie made up his mind he wouldn't stand it any longer, so he
jumped on the nigger-driver. They fought and Uncle Charlie won. Uncle
Charlie ran away," and got as far as the Ohio River but was caught swim-
ming it. Upon being returned, he was badly whipped and threatened with
sale; but he was neither disabled (as had happened to Body), nor was he
actually sold (as had finally happened to Moses Bell).

Uncle Charlie's master may have rued his "leniency," for Charlie later
successfully escaped to Canada. Fugitives, when still in the slave states,

were usually aided only by black people; even when they reached the North, they were mainly helped by other black people (though some Northern whites also substantially aided the Underground Railroad). But, unusually, Uncle Charlie owed his escape to the assistance of a white abolitionist who apparently met him in the woods west of Roanoke and conducted him all the way to Canada via Chicago. The abolitionist even returned to Virginia to bring Charlie's girlfriend to freedom too. "One night," Reverend Jacobs averred, "when [Uncle Charlie] came home from work to supper, he was shocked to see his Rachel at the table. Tears flooded his eyes, and he almost broke his neck by falling over a chair as he rushed to greet her. Uncle Charlie married that girl at once and later became a Methodist minister" (*Interviews*, 156–57).[10]

A slave represented a substantial capital investment, worth much more than the annual cost of hiring an experienced white overseer. The permanent loss of an Uncle Charlie, for most Virginia slavemasters, would have been a stinging financial blow. It was no wonder that the disappearance of Gabe and Rufus drove their master to distraction. To secure their investment, and to deter other slaves from trying to escape, masters sometimes sold captured fugitives to the Deep South; and they often threatened to do so. And a severe whipping was usually inflicted on fugitives who had sought permanent escape. Katie Johnson's mother told her that runaway slaves received the worst whippings. "They used to put them in stocks," Johnson said, "and whip their bare backs until they were as raw as a piece of beef. The moans and groans were sumptin' awful. When they finished with them they put them on the ground still in the stocks and would 'pint a slave to feed them. In about a week the slaves were whipped again until the scabs fell off the sores. Then their backs were rubbed with salt and pepper" (*Interviews*, 161–62).

A slave's flight to the local woods might be as nerve-wracking for the master as an attempt at permanent flight, because one could not always be sure that the absentee remained nearby. A brutal master might therefore punish a local flight as severely as—or more severely than—most masters would punish a bolt for the North. As previously indicated, Virginia Shepherd supplied a vivid account of the field worker Julia Wright's savage punishment. "This woman would work," Shepherd explained, "but if you drove her too hard, she'd git stubborn like a mule and quit. . . . When

they got rough on her, she got rough on them and ran away in the woods.
. . . They found her by means of bloodhounds. . . . [They] chained her by
her leg. . . . The chain cut a round around her ankle. . . . Vermin got in the
wound and ate the flesh. . . . Her back was a mass of scars. . . . The evidence
of her punishment was so horrible that the sight of it 50 years afterwards
sickened my daughters."[11]

Punishments this monstrous, for flight to the local woods, were rare.
Local flights, after all, were commonplace, and they seldom led to financial disaster. Sometimes a returning fugitive was even spared a whipping,
and occasionally a flight might be entirely overlooked by the slave's owner.
Thus, William Johnson described the remarkable stance of his uncles
Edmund and John, who worked satisfactorily for their owners but "were
always determined not to work for anyone else." Their masters owned
more slaves than could be profitably used on their home plantations
(west of Richmond), and for four or five years they hired out Edmund
and John on annual contracts. Johnson claimed that his uncles "would
go with the person who hired them, work about a month, then steal off
into the woods and stay until their [year's] time was out. Then they would
return to their original owners. . . . Of course, the master never punished
them for doing this—he didn't care cause he collected his contract just the
same" (Interviews, 166).

A local flight might not only be condoned, but even—in the long run—
rewarded. Fannie Berry's father, for example, protested against his sale to
a trader (which would have permanently destroyed his abroad marriage)
by fleeing to the woods for twelve months. His wife's owner, a kindly
woman, took pity on the enslaved black family and purchased the absent
father (probably at a substantial discount from the trader, who did not
know whether he would ever again see his absent property). Berry's father
learned of the purchase and promptly turned up for his new mistress.
Thus, his flight led, eventually, to his being united with his wife and their
three children (Interviews, 42).

The frequency of flights (especially temporary flights to the local
woods) exerted pressure on slavemasters to improve their treatment of
slaves. The nearer a plantation was to a route north, the greater was this
pressure—for a dissident slave accustomed to brief sojourns in the local woods might always decide that next time the flight would be a more
ambitious one. When Cornelius Garner's master told the patrollers that

they needn't bother *his* slaves because they "didn't have no reason to run away," he implied that the likelihood that an ill-treated slave would flee might make at least some masters think twice before skimping on rations or pressing their bondpeople too hard (*Interviews*, 100).

Another consequence of frequent flights, however, ran contrary to the slaves' own interests. This arose from the fact that the patrol system, designed to prevent slaves from moving about, was not very successful. White Southerners realized that slaves often took unauthorized leave. A sense of potential disorder was omnipresent, if usually latent. Occasionally, then, the rumor of a slave uprising would sweep through the white community, and draconian measures would be taken—the cabins of black people searched, suspected incendiaries mobbed, innocent people killed—in order to suppress what was usually a figment of the white people's vivid imaginations. There were so few genuine plots that one might easily regard these regular insurrection panics as irrational, or as merely the product of politicians' wish to win votes by stirring fears of abolitionism.[12] No doubt the insurrection panics of 1856 and 1860 were, indeed, substantially fueled by politicians' self-interested desire to fan paranoia. But although violence by slaves against white people was infrequent, running to the woods was so common that it fostered among white people a generalized anxiety about the slaves' disorderliness. Most white Virginians failed sufficiently to distinguish between the essentially nonviolent character of most flights to the woods and the images of unbridled violence that, with little justification, occasionally filled their imaginations.

Some twentieth-century historians, impelled by an admirable wish to destroy the old image of the "happy, contented slave," have carefully examined the evidence that slaves violently resisted their oppression. Every slave insurrection, or alleged conspiracy, has been scrupulously studied, attention drawn to the many cases of a slave violently resisting, or even killing, a member of the master race. This reaction against the image of the docile slave may, however, have in turn created a false picture of the usual course of slaves' lives. North American slavery was not, normally, a real "war" attended by frequent bursts of gunfire. On the contrary, slavery more closely resembled (if a military analogy is appropriate) a "cold war" where diplomatic skill was of the essence and where bursts of violence needed to be minimized because they usually proved contrary to the slaves' own interests.[13] The Virginia interviews throw light on these matters.

The most famous slave insurrection in North American history—the Nat Turner Revolt—took place in 1831 in Southside Virginia, some fifty miles southwest of Norfolk. The uncle of one of the Virginia interviewees participated in the insurrection, and was executed for doing so. The interviewee Allen Crawford later communicated not so much pride in his uncle's action as his grandmother's anger at Nat Turner for being responsible for her son's execution: "Grandma ran out and struck Nat in the mouth, knocking the blood out and asked him, 'Why did you take my son away?'"

This is not the whole story Crawford narrated. He reported that Nat Turner denied responsibility for his follower's death, telling the mother of the executed slave that her son had needed no persuasion, being "'as willing to go as I was'" (*Interviews*, 76). True as this may be, it nevertheless evades the question of responsibility. Nat Turner was responsible for this death: the insurrection would not have taken place—with the ensuing deaths of participants and innocent suspects—if Turner himself had not led the discontented slaves into translating their fantasies into action.

Events years later perhaps altered Allen Crawford's perception of the Turner insurrection. The Civil War, after all, *did* liberate the slaves, and the participation of former slaves in the Union Army proved a substantial factor in the North's winning that war. In retrospect Crawford seems to have seen Nat Turner's war as a heroic, if unsuccessful, predecessor of the later war that actually destroyed slavery. Thus, Crawford alleged that Nat Turner said that God had ordained him "to start the *fust* war with forty men" (*Interviews*, 75; emphasis added).

Crawford (who was born four years after the Turner insurrection and learned about it from his family and their neighbors) seemed to present an evenhanded account of Nat's enterprise, declaring, for example, that the insurrectionists were given a fair trial. This did not lessen his horror at how the captured insurrectionists were tortured. The white militiamen, he said, "had log fires made and every one dat was Nat's man was taken bodily by two men who catch you and hold yer bare feet to dis blazing fire 'til you tole all you know'd 'bout dis killing." Perhaps Crawford experienced a frisson of pleasure at the white people's come-uppance, when they learned how their slaves really felt about them. After Nat had killed a school mistress, another white woman named Venie Frances "ran in de house skeer'd ... and hid herself in a closet. ... Dar was two house gals [who thought their mistress, Venie Frances, had been killed]. ... So dem gals was standing dar 'viding her clothes and things—argueing who should have dis and dat. ... Miss Frances dar in closet couldn't say a word—fear'd to speak. Way in evening she—Miss Venie—came down out house—met her husband and she tole him what had happened. She left everything and went back to North Carolina with him." Allen Crawford reported not only Mrs. Frances's terror, but also Nat Turner's butchering of a white infant. "When he got to his mistress' house," Crawford had heard, "he commence to grab him missus' baby and he took hit up, slung hit back and fo'h three times. Said hit was so hard fer him to kill dis baby 'cause hit had bin so playful setting on his knee and dat chile sho did love him. So third sling he went quick 'bout hit—killing baby at dis rap." Slavery turned not only some masters but also some bondpeople into monsters (*Interviews,* 75–76).

Cornelia Carney, born in 1838, lived too far from Southampton County to have heard accurate details of the Nat Turner insurrection. Yet the story of Nat had worked its way into black folklore as proof that slaves could surprise and outwit their white oppressors. For a long time (probably during the 1850s) Carney's father and two other slaves had successfully hidden in the woods, and to Carney this illustrated that "niggers was too smart fo' white folks to git ketched. White folks was sharp too, but not sharp enough to git by ole Nat. Nat? I don't know who he was. Ole folks used to say it all de time. De meanin' I git is dat de niggers could always out-smart de white folks" (*Interviews,* 67). Thus, Nat Turner's example could inspirit some slaves, offering them the satisfaction of envisaging the discomfiture of their oppressors. But it also suggests that slavery could brutalize some of the oppressed, as well as some of the oppressors. It demonstrated to later generations (if this needed demonstration) that slaves were profoundly discontented. Yet it may remain an open question whether the benefits derived from the revolt counterbalanced the sorrow of the black families who lost their loved ones in an insurrection doomed to failure.

Because the military power of the thousands of nearby white people was overwhelming, slave insurrections in North America were rare. Apart from John Brown's futile raid, no insurrection or insurrectionary plot appears to have occurred in Virginia during the thirty years after 1831. The historian Philip Schwarz—the most thorough student of these matters—writes of "the virtual disappearance of insurrection prosecutions [in Virginia] between the end of 1831 and the beginning of the Civil War."[14] (During the Civil War itself, of course, the military balance of power completely changed, and thousands of Virginia slaves fled, joined the Union Army, and fought against their former masters.)

In contrast to the infrequency of insurrection prosecutions in antebellum Virginia, acts of violence by individual slaves took place much more often; and the Virginia interviewees reported a considerable number of such acts. These were usually directed against poorer whites (e.g., overseers) rather than against masters and mistresses, and they almost never resulted in the death of a white person. Sometimes a slave who lifted a hand against a white man might even escape severe retribution, if the master and the overseer disagreed with each other about how to govern bondpeople; but savage punishment was far more likely.

Among the most important provocations to slaves' violent resistance were the attempts of white men to rape enslaved women. Resistance sometimes came from the woman herself, occasionally from a black man on her behalf. One day a cook named Sukie—"a big strappin' nigger gal dat never had nothin' to say much"—was making several cauldrons of soap in the fireplace. "Ole Marsa," Fannie Berry declared, "was always tryin' to make Sukie his gal." He entered the kitchen and began to whip her for some offense. "He lay into her," Berry continued,

> but she ain't answer him a word. Den he tell Sukie to take off her dress. She tole him no. Den he grabbed her an' pull it down off'n her shoulders. When he done dat, he fo'got 'bout whuppin' her, I guess, 'cause he grab hold of her an' try to pull her down on de flo'. Den dat black gal got mad. She took an' punch ole Marsa an' made him break loose an' den she gave him a shove an' push his hindparts down in de hot pot o' soap. Soap was near to bilin', an' it burnt him near to death. He got up holdin' his hindparts an' ran from de kitchen, not darin' to yell, 'cause he didn't want Miss Sarah Ann [his wife] to know 'bout it.
>
> Well, few days later he took Sukie off an' sol' her to de nigger trader. . . . Marsa never did bother slave gals no mo'.

Violent resistance by a slave woman could sometimes, then, achieve its purpose. But the cost might be high: Sukie never saw her friends, relatives, and familiar neighborhood again (*Interviews*, 48–49).

A comparable event, with similar consequences, occurred in the town of Appomattox. One day Jeff Stanfield's grown sister was taken by their master into a room for a whipping, or perhaps for another purpose. "My sister Lizzie," Stanfield reported, "was a very mean woman and would fight de marster. One day de marster carried her in a room to whip her, but she beat him an' den broke out of de room an' ran away an' stayed all night an' came back de next day." Lizzie's resistance led to an unmerciful whipping (administered by town officers), after which she was sold (*Interviews*, 280).

The consequences of violent resistance might be even more severe if the resister were the woman's husband. "Dere was an' ole overseer . . . ," Charles Grandy recalled, "what wanted one o' de slaves wife. Started both-ern wid her right fo' de slave's face. De colored man made at him an' he shot 'im wid a gun. Den de colored man come at him wid a hoe. He kept shootin' 'till de man fell dead in his tracks" (*Interviews*, 117).

A slave violently resisting a rapist might sometimes, however, avoid punishment. Although Fannie Berry implied that most slave women would submit to coerced sex for fear of being terribly beaten, or even killed, she said that she herself had successfully resisted an attempted rape by a poor white man. "One tried to throw me," she proudly attested, "but he couldn't. We tusseled an' knocked over chairs an' when I got a grip I scratched his face all to pieces; an dar wuz no more bothering Fannie from him." Berry had a good mistress (who, e.g., banned patrollers from the plantation), and Berry's being owned by this woman probably protected her from being punished for fighting the poor white man.[15]

The interviewees loved to tell stories about slaves who had defied white people and had got away with it. A defiant slave, it becomes clear, had the best chance of avoiding punishment if he or she could find support from some other, well-disposed white person. Robert Ellett's father, for example, assaulted a white man who was trying to force sex on Ellett's older sister, and the resister avoided punishment—probably because he (like Fannie Berry) was protected by his mistress. Ellett's family members were "favored slaves," the interviewee declared; his parents were both of mixed-race origins, and they were the most valuable slaves on a large plantation.

"One day," Robert Ellett recounted, "a strange white man [presumably a house guest at the Big House] came down around our cabin and tried to get my sister out. Father jumped him and grabbed him in the chest. He pointed at the big house and said, 'If you don't git in that house right now, I'll kill you with my bare hands.' The white man flew." Although Ellett—a boastful man—may have sharpened his father's language, the story itself sounds authentic (*Interviews*, 84).

A few slaves made for themselves the reputation that they would not submit to a whipping. Ellett claimed that his father was one of these. "My master . . . ," Ellett averred, "was the meanest man out, but father wouldn't let him beat him. I've seen him time and again try to beat my father an' I always heard my father say, 'I'll die before I'll let you beat me!'" Although Ellett surely exaggerated here ("I've seen him time and again"), the story appears to be true in its essence. Ellett's mistress ("an angel") was devoted to Ellett's mother (the daughter of a white preacher whose will stipulated that she and her children were not to be sold out of her mistress's family). It was not in the interest of Ellett's master to lose the services of his most valuable slaves, nor to enrage his own wife, as surely would have happened if he had tried to break the spirit of Ellett's indomitable father; in this instance the master seems to have had the good sense to act in his own interest (*Interviews*, 84–85).

Just as a well-disposed mistress (like Ellett's) might protect a slave against being abused by her husband, so occasionally a well-disposed master might protect a slave who physically resisted being whipped by his mistress. This happened to William Lee (a "pet" body servant of the master of a large plantation) when he was a youth. One day his mistress, miscalculating William's strength and determination, tried to whip him and was thrown to the ground by the teenager. Her husband then pretended to flog the rebellious slave, as his wife demanded; but according to William Lee, he and his master conspired, with a charade of faked screams and tears, to deceive William's mistress into thinking that a severe whipping had been imposed when none had occurred at all (*Interviews*, 194–95).

In an analogous episode, a slave woman escaped retribution even though she had brandished a scythe when escaping to the woods. Once again, there was a division of opinion between the master and the mistress, and eventually the master seems to have taken the slave woman's side against the wishes of his wife. West Turner's aunt Sallie, as recounted earlier, was the nurse to the white children at his plantation, but she fled to the woods when her master, at his wife's instigation, demoted her from her relatively comfortable job to field labor. One night the fugitive Sallie returned to her brother's cabin for food and was trapped there by her master, who called on the other slaves to catch her. "She grabbed up a scythe knife f'om de corner," Turner recalled, "an' she [opened the door] . . . an' come out a-swingin'. An' dose niggers was glad cause dey didn't want to catch her. An' Marsa didn't dare tetch her. She cut her way out, den turned roun' and backed off into de woods, an' ole Marsa was just screamin' an' cussin' an' tellin' her one minute what he's gonna do when he ketch her an' de nex' minute sayin' he gonna take her back in de big house ef she stay. . . . De las' I saw was Ant Sallie goin' into de bushes still swingin' dat scythe. Didn't no one foller her neither." Probably Sallie eventually returned to the plantation in response to a promise that she would be restored to her position as a house servant, and probably she was not much punished for her act of violent resistance. After all, her threat was directed principally at the other slaves, only secondarily against the master (who apparently was behind the slaves nearest to the door). Further, such resistance from a female slave need not be crushed so harshly as a challenge from a male slave. Sallie did not in fact hurt anyone. And her master perhaps had acted reluctantly when, at his wife's behest, he demoted her in the first place: he probably felt that Sallie had some excuse for running away (*Interviews*, 288–89).

A well-disposed master might protect male slaves too—even if the slaves had assaulted an overseer—if the overseer had disobeyed the master's orders. "My master was a good man . . . ," Julia Frazier testified. "There wasn't any beatin' [by the overseer]. My master wouldn' 'low any. Ol' overseer tried to be mean. Slaves got hol' him once an' slung him real good an' they didn' have any mo' trouble out of him" (*Interviews*, 96–97).

A similar situation arose on the plantation of George Follkes, an extraordinarily benevolent master who nevertheless once hired a mean overseer to get more work out of his slaves. That autumn Follkes also hired a slave to help butcher pigs, and this hired bondman was determined not to be bullied by the overseer. The overseer's little boy, whip in hand, kept cracking it very close to the enslaved butcher, who told off the white boy. Both the overseer and George Follkes (who was sitting on the porch) could hear the altercation. The butcher complained, "'[Boy], stop dat whup crackin' so close to my back. De nex' thing you know, you'll be hittin' me.' De kid say, 'You got to take it. You got to take it.' [The butcher] said, 'Who's agoin' give it to me?' De boy said, 'Pa is. He done said so.' [The butcher] said, 'If yo' paw put his han' on me, I'll break his god dam neck. I jes' wish he would lay his han's on me.'" Evidently, the slave's threat deterred the overseer from trying to whip him for his defiant language.[16] But the reason this slave could openly challenge the overseer was that the overseer realized that his employer, George Follkes, was unlikely to back him in any unnecessary violence. As previously indicated, Follkes was so well-disposed toward his slaves that, after the war, he willed parcels of 100 acres, or even more, to some of the freedpeople.[17] A slave working for such a master might realistically hope to get away with defying an overseer.[18]

Even when the intercession of a well-disposed mistress or a benevolent master could not be counted on, a few slaves made it plain that they would not submit to a whipping. Doing so, they took their lives into their own hands. Colin Hodgins, for example, "just wouldn't be whipped after he was seventeen years old." But Hodgins "had scars on his arms, back and the other sides of his head from the lash," according to the testimony of Reverend W. P. Jacobs. Probably the young man refused to submit passively to being whipped, and most of the scars came from the savage beatings imposed on him as punishment when he resisted being flogged (*Interviews*, 155).

Virginia Shepherd's mother told of the even more terrible consequences that could befall a slave determined never to be whipped. "On a nearby plantation," Shepherd reported, "there was a certain overseer who was very mean. There was one slave on the plantation that was his match. He was afraid to beat him. One day the old overseer was walking through the field with his bull whip in his hand and he cursed this particular nigger because he wasn't working to suit him. The nigger jumped on the overseer to fight him. The overseer just pulled out his gun and shot the slave. He told the Master and nothing was ever done. But at the end of the year, the master just kept the overseer's year's salary in payment for the loss of property." If a master could secure adequate financial compensation for the killing of a slave, he was not likely to try to prosecute an overseer— particularly not when the overseer could truthfully claim that the dead slave had assaulted the white man.[19]

A slave ran into somewhat less danger if he fought an enslaved driver than if he battled a white overseer. For example, as recounted earlier, Reverend Jacobs's uncle Charlie dared to fight a driver who was whipping him. Charlie "jumped on the nigger-driver," defeated him, and fled, nearly reaching Ohio before being caught. Although Charlie was severely whipped, the punishment was at least as much for Charlie's flight as for his resistance to the driver; and although Charlie was threatened with sale, he was not in fact sold (and he survived to later flee successfully to Canada) (*Interviews,* 156).

Except for Allen Crawford's stories about the Nat Turner Revolt, the Virginia interviewees virtually never mentioned the killing of a white person by a slave. Nancy Williams's father, however, came close to knifing an overseer. "De overseers," she testified, "and my pappy, he a mean man, big strong half Injun, couldn' never git long. Pappy had plenty temper. Take nottin' off'm. . . . One day ole overseer tried to make him do somepin an' my father wouldn' do it. Overseer he got mad an cuss my pappy, den is de time dat ole po' white trash got jumped. My pappy reached down an' pull out his knife; was gonna cut dat debil's th'oat. All de niggers run an' shake de knife out'n my father's han'." Thus, instantaneous collective action was taken by the other slaves to disarm Williams's father. Their quick action saved the life of the assailant (who would probably have been executed if he had slit the overseer's throat); and it avoided the danger that some of them too might be executed as supposedly part of some imaginary plot. If the life of a mean overseer happened to be saved by the slaves' speedy action, this was a small price to pay for protecting the interests of the slave community and suppressing a foolhardy outburst against a white man (*Interviews,* 317).

To avoid a threatened flogging, however, a group of bondpeople might try to strike back at the hated patrollers. As mentioned earlier, Betty Jones preserved the happy recollection of a time when slaves at an unauthorized nighttime meeting violently resisted being apprehended by the patrol. A big log was burning in the cabin's fireplace, producing red-hot coals. When the patrollers approached, two slaves "shoveled fire an' coals right out de door on 'em debbils," Jones reported gleefully. "Dey runned from de fire, an' we runned f'om dem."[20]

On only one occasion did a Virginia interviewee report the actual killing of a white man, and he was an overseer, not a master. "Ole Saunders," the interviewee declared, "was de meanes' po' white debbil dat ever drawned a breath. Had beat an' beat us twell we made up our mind not to stan' it no longer." Forced to work clearing brush from a field on a bright, moonlit night, after working all day, the slaves—at a prearranged signal—pushed the overseer into the bonfire and got away with the murder. This event may well have occurred during the Civil War, when the masters' dominion over the slaves was suddenly becoming precarious; this may account for the interviewee's claim that the local white people overlooked this violent challenge to their authority (*Interviews*, 346–47).

Acts of violent resistance, then, did sometimes occur, and the memories of these acts were cherished by slaves. Such outbursts took place most often when people were provoked by some flagrant abuse, such as an attempted rape, or by a series of brutal whippings. For that reason (and because the masters regarded attacks on themselves or their families as an even greater threat to their dominion than attacks on poorer whites, and were likely to punish them even more severely), the slaves' aggressions were directed more commonly against poorer whites—overseers, patrollers, or abusive poor white neighbors—than against masters and mistresses. A slave was most likely to avoid condign punishment for physical resistance if the master and mistress were divided in their assessment of the situation, or if the master and the overseer were divided in their strategies for governing the slaves. Some slaves made it known that they would not passively submit to a whipping, and—especially if they were very valuable or particularly favored—they sometimes avoided ever being whipped. But the risks of fighting a white person—of being savagely flogged, sold, or even killed—were so great that violent resistance was relatively uncommon.[21] It was much safer for an angry slave to flee to the woods and stay there for a few weeks, until the anger had subsided.

To deceive white people, or to steal from them, were the most common expressions of slave dissidence. Deception might sometimes be achieved by a lie. Susan Broaddus's father, for example, instructed Susan (after she went to him from the master's house, in order to spell out the names "Gabe" and "Rufus") "to go on back to de house an' say I ain't been out." A blatant lie served the purposes of Sister Robinson's Uncle Jake, when a patrol descended upon his cabin. Jake's situation was eased by the fact that his master's son was among the patrollers. Three male slaves from other plantations, without passes authorizing their absence from home, had been visiting Jake, and they, for fear of a whipping, were hiding under his bed. Jake adopted a confidential tone with his young master, laid on his most subservient drawl, and assured him, "Hain't nobuddy heah 'ception me an' da ol' 'oman, marse." The master's son believed this lie, the patrol moved on, and eighty years later Sister Robinson was still chortling at her uncle's success in deceiving his young master (*Interviews*, 55, 241).

The Reverend W. P. Jacobs believed open resistance was so sure to be crushed that slaves were obliged to rely on deception. In doing so, they could play upon the credulity of many white people. "The slaves," Jacobs averred, "used superstition to fool the white man. No slave in those terrible days staked anything on [his] chance in the open." To support this view, Jacobs told a story, probably folklore rather than fact, that resembles a Brer Rabbit tale. A slave, Jacobs claimed, had succeeded in instilling fear into an overseer by his ability to make a red flannel jacket talk: "He would hang the jacket on a nail, say something, squeeze it and the jacket would groan, moan and carry on. If anyone else touched it, the jacket didn't move." The explanation was that the slave had sewn a bullfrog into the jacket. "When others touched it, the frog sat still; when the nigger touched it, he stuck a pin in the frog and the frog yelled and jumped. The ignorant overseer couldn't see through that and gave the slave very few orders." Although Jacobs here was probably passing on folklore, the story, like the Brer Rabbit tales, nevertheless illustrates how far slaves felt they must rely on deception in order to fool the slow-witted foxes (*Interviews*, 155).

Elizabeth Sparks told credible tales of deception. Sparks's mistress "wuz a mean ol' thin'. She'd beat yer with a broom or a leather strap or anythin' she'd git her hand on." But when Sparks was in her mid-teens, she had the good fortune to be transferred to the ownership of her mistress's good-natured daughter (as a gift when the daughter was married). It was incumbent on Sparks to pretend that she was distressed at being taken away from her old mistress: "I had to make 'er believe I 'uz cryin,' but I was glad to go with 'er [the young bride]. She didn't beat" (*Interviews*, 274).

The skills in deception bred by slavery could also serve a black man at his first encounter with the Union Army during the Civil War. By the time of the war, Elizabeth Sparks was married and had a small baby, and although her young husband, John Sparks, was keen to be free, he didn't wish to trust himself to Northern soldiers. When a recruiting party of these soldiers arrived at the plantation, John Sparks "played lame to keep fum goin'," Elizabeth Sparks cheerily recalled. "He was jes' a-limpin' 'round. It was all I could do to keep fum laffin'." Deception alone did not achieve John Sparks's purpose (he was also aided by the intercession of his young white mistress, and by the fact that he had a very young baby), but deception was his first reliance (*Interviews*, 275).

A common form of deception was to pretend that one was ill. Charles Grandy, for example, recalled that once when he was sowing peas in a cornfield, out of sight of his master, he lay down to rest. His master discovered him "an' say 'Boy whacha doin' lyin' down dar?' Scerred to death—had to think quick, den I say, 'Ise sick.' . . . Cose I was lyin' to keep de cowhide off [i.e., to avoid a whipping]." Although his master doubted the story, he could not be sure, and instead of whipping the young slave, he sent him off to be administered a strong emetic. Grandy vomited and was then really sick for several days. But although the experience was unpleasant, Grandy was satisfied with the result: "I got clear o' dat whuppin'" (*Interviews*, 115–16). Thus, malingering might benefit an individual slave, but it ran contrary to the interests of slaves as a group, because it created skepticism in a master's mind as to whether a complaining slave was really ill; malingering sometimes impelled skeptical masters to force slaves who really were ill to go to work.

So common was it for slaves to steal food that white preachers constantly inveighed against this practice. Slaves seem often to have accepted the general principle that stealing was wrong; but because of their circumstances, they felt easy about ignoring this precept. Charles Grandy reported that their white preacher would "tell us don' steal f'om yo' marser an' missus. 'Cose we knowed it was wrong to steal, but de niggers had to steal to git somepin' to eat. I know I did. . . . I got so hungry I stealed chickens off de roos'." Many interviewees told of stealing food because of being given inadequate rations. "Sometimes we'd get hungry," Marrinda Singleton recalled, "and go in the field whar dar was a plenty of good vegetables and steal us a mess or so. We knowd hit was de wrong thing to do but hunger will make you do a lot of things" (*Interviews*, 116, 266).[22]

Sheer hunger, however, was not the only goad to stealing food. The contrast between the masters' plenty and the slaves' scarcity impelled resentful slaves to try to even accounts. "Dey had plenty o' food dere," Charles Grandy complained. "Hawgs, cows, chickens an' ev'thing was plentiful.

Sometimes dey kill two an' three hundred hawgs but dey sell 'em." Similarly, Alice Marshall declared that "Mistess Sally had a plenty," yet she never gave Marshall and her mother enough to eat. The mistress probably skimped on the rations of these two slaves because she knew her husband had slept with Marshall's mother (a privileged, light-skinned housemaid and seamstress) and that Alice Marshall was their child. The mistress strewed sawdust on the floor of the meathouse in order that footprints might be detected, but Marshall's mother became adept at smoothing off the saw-dust evenly, after her many successful raids on the meat. Katie Johnson's uncle Lewis was another slave who stole food frequently, but in his case he seems partly to have done so just for the satisfaction of matching his wits against his master's. "We had plenty to eat," Katie Johnson testified, yet her uncle was a confirmed thief. Unlike Alice Marshall's mother (whose thefts remained undetected), Uncle Lewis "was caught stealin' hogs and chickens so often and whipped so much—I declare when he went to Gawd he didn't have the skin he was borned with." Uncle Lewis's life perhaps was so constricted that he thirsted for the excitement and adventure of successful thievery (*Interviews*, 116, 201–2, 162).

Stealing from or deceiving one's master were covert acts, but dissidence sometimes took the form of open verbal protest. Thus, Virginia Shepherd's mother told her that "one day she had worked and worked and worked un-til she just couldn't go any faster. The overseer told her to work faster or he'd beat her. She said she simply stopped and told them, 'Go a-head, kill me if you want. I'm working as fast as I can and I just can't do more.' They saw she was at the place where she didn't care whether she died or not; so they left her alone." A bondwoman was more likely than a male slave to speak her mind, because a white man was less likely to feel that his mas-culine pride was at stake and must be preserved by violent retaliation if the verbal challenge came from a female. Yet even female protesters were sometimes dealt with savagely, even by white women. "Mama never did anything mean," George White declared, "but she would say whatever she thought. Den de mistress would beat her." The slaves on White's planta-tion were banned from singing or praying when the whites could hear them, probably because the whites sensed the aspiration for freedom that lay behind these songs and prayers. White's mother was once sent to col-lect kindling wood. "While she was out dere," George White testified, "she kneeled down to pray an' Lucy Young [her mistress] came out an' kicked her over an' beat her awful" (*Interviews*, 259, 309–10).

Slaves accustomed to being governed mildly were more likely to speak frankly than those harshly treated. Margaret Terry grew up in Charlottesville, where her mother was a (probably privileged) house servant. For a time the little slave girl was accorded very special treatment.[23] She had never seen her mother beaten, and the one time this happened she sturdily protested. "I said to [the old white woman], 'Stop! Stop beating my mother! She is free!' I pulled her away and said, 'Let her alone; my mother is free!'" Margaret's mother was not free, but the beating occurred during the Civil War, and the little girl "had heard folks talking about being free" (*Interviews*, 285).

Julia Frazier told of a male slave whose master, Lewis Boggs, let the man get away with mocking him. Boggs, she said, was a "good man" who banned his overseer from whipping his slaves. He had a clever slave named Charlie who was adept at singing verses he had devised himself, and Boggs liked to display Charlie's talents to white visitors. Charlie trusted Boggs to keep a promise. Under all of these favorable circumstances, Charlie dared to commit lèse-majesté, if Frazier's story is to be believed. Her master, she said, was coming home one day, crossing a plowed field with a keg of whiskey on his mule, when the mule slipped and Boggs tumbled off. Unbeknownst to his master, Charlie witnessed this event. Soon thereafter—Frazier continued—

a visitor come an' Marsa called Charlie to de house to show off what he knew. Marsa say, "Come here, Charlie, an' sing some rhymes. . . ." So Charlie say, "All right, Marsa, I give you a new one effen you promise not to whup me." Marsa promised, an' den Charlie sung de rhyme he done made up in his haid 'bout Marsa:

Jackass rared,
Jackass pitch,
Throwed ole Marsa in de ditch.

Well, Marsa got mad as a hornet, but he didn't whup Charlie, not dat time anyway.

Charlie invented other verses on the same theme, which the slaves secretly sang among themselves. Lacking much opportunity for self-expression, the slaves derived what satisfaction they could from mocking this relatively lenient master behind his back (*Interviews*, 96, 98–99).

Even if a slave had a brutal master, the slave might nevertheless sometimes successfully defy that master's purposes by enlisting the support of a well-disposed white neighbor. This was what Diana Gaskins, a wretched housemaid, eventually did. Gaskins, according to Virginia Shepherd, was "dignity personified, the prettiest black woman I ever saw." This unfortunate woman was repeatedly raped by her master—a married man with children, whose wife sympathized with Diana but could not protect her because she was afraid of her husband. "Once when Diana was successful in fighting him off," Shepherd continued, her master "bundled her up, put her in a cart, and took her to Norfolk and put her on the auction block. But Diana was the sharpest black woman you ever saw. Before she was taken to town, she slipped around to one of the neighboring plantations and begged the master to buy her. He agreed. When she was put on the block the biggest bidder got her, and she went to live right back to the same neighborhood. Ole Gaskins was sore, but he couldn't do nothing about it." Here, as was not infrequently the case, successful defiance of one white person depended on a slave's having the good luck to be associated with— or (like Diana Gaskins) to enlist the aid of—another white person, well enough disposed to act as a sort of ally.[24] In the unequal battle against oppression, it often helped if one had a relatively lenient mistress or master, or if one could find a relatively trustworthy white ally to supplement the group of black relatives and friends who comprised for slaves by far their most significant circle of support.

A tragic consequence of slavery was that—because bondage offered most slaves little scope for the development of their talents, and few outlets for the positive use of their creative energies—those energies inevitably were channeled largely into the arts of dissidence. Dissidence was virtually omnipresent. To deceive white people, to steal from them, to flee (temporarily or permanently), even sometimes forcefully to resist them—these were splendid morale builders. The waste of human potential, however, was enormous, when most slaves were afforded so little opportunity to develop their own constructive skills.

11

Families

In the 1950s scholars—black and white alike—believed that slavery had weakened African American family institutions. A powerful reaction against this view surfaced during the 1970s, marked particularly by the publication of Herbert Gutman's *The Black Family in Slavery and Freedom*. Gutman observed that slave women often bore their first child before marrying, but he argued that once the woman married, long-lasting nuclear families were the norm. During recent years, however, Gutman's view has come under increasingly close examination. Perhaps the most explicit challenge has been made by the historian Brenda Stevenson, especially her article "Distress and Discord in Virginia Slave Families"—an article based partly on Virginia's WPA interviews.[1] These interviews suggest a less than roseate view of slaves' family lives.

Among the outstanding issues are these: How significant was the role of fathers in the slaves' families? How did the institution of "abroad marriages" function? What was the overall effect of slavery on the bondpeople's family lives?

Erotic excitement was for most slaves—as for most human beings—a profound interest. Perhaps it was even more important for slaves, because they were deprived of so many other satisfactions. Interviewers and interviewees shied off from discussing such matters in 1937, but the interviewees' remarks about dancing suggest the feelings of young slaves as Saturday night approached. Usually, dances were gladly accepted by the masters as safety valves that let bondpeople blow off steam.

Susie Melton's master, for example, "never cared how much his slaves danced an' carried on, jus' so long as dey didn't do it on Sundays. Danced mos' times on Sadday nights 'cause dey got Sunday to res'. Soon's dey git in fum de field Sadday arternoon dey would start gittin' ready." The dance, if taking place early in the year, would be in the barn; but "Marsa never would let 'em have de barn arter de crops was in—scared dey'd set it on fire." The bondpeople would therefore clean the biggest cabin for the dance; the women would iron their dresses, and everyone would get smartened up. The slaves knew that if they didn't attend this dance, there would be no other blowout for at least another week. An atmosphere of excitement prevailed: "While dey was gittin' ready," Melton reported, "dey would sing dis song":

All de ladies goin' to de ball?
Don't go Sadday night,
You can't go at all,
Hog-eye, hum um
Hog-eye, hum um.
All de gen'mens goin' to de ball? . . .

"Dey keep dat up, jus' laughin' an' jokin' each other an' ev'ybody know dey sho' gonna have a good time dat night. Hog-eye? Lawdy, chile," Melton replied evasively to her interviewer's query, "I don't know what dat mean. Some devilment, I reckon" (*Interviews*, 212).

If young people felt constrained under the eyes of their masters or their parents, they might leave the plantation surreptitiously. "Some time all de cou'tin' couples slip 'way an' go to de wood to a ole cabin to dance," Nancy Williams exulted. "Whoops! Dem dances was somepin. Dem de day's when me'n de devil was runnin roun in de depths o' hell." Similarly, Martha Showvely (a privileged house servant born in 1837) averred that "I was ve'y wicked when I was young. I'd rather dance den eat." And Sally Ashton, born about 1845, used exactly the same formulation about her priorities when she was a girl (*Interviews*, 316, 265, 14).

During their courtship days bondpeople's language sometimes subverted racial "etiquette" by awarding to slaves titles supposed to be reserved for white people. But this language was not uniformly decorous. "My father say when he went courting my mammy . . . ," Eliza Robinson testified, "he say, 'Miss Sally!' She say, 'Sir, Mr. Jones?' He say, 'Miss Sallie I got a terrible cold in my haid. What must I do 'bout hit?' She say, 'Mr. Jones, go home and burn a shoe sole and bind hit in your ass hole.' Dats de way dey courted in dem days. They talk like dat but don't put dat in your book" (*Interviews*, 238).

Dancing offered particular scope to female slaves. Women might organize the dance, they sometimes called out the steps, and they often led the dancers; and a young woman might star by outdancing her rivals. According to Dave Lowry, the girls from a nearby plantation would sometimes hold a dance that slaves from his plantation attended without a pass authorizing them to do so: "De head lady would say, 'Paunt your swing' [etc.]. . . . De head lady would dance around de ring to everybody. Den de next one, and so on. Den de[y] would have some love songs, while dancing." Although Martha Haskins never won a prize at a dance, she was proud of having been "a purty good stepper." What she remembered most vividly, however, was the brilliant dancing of a girl named Cora who came over from a neighboring plantation. "Slaves sho' would hoop an' holler when Cora git to steppin'," Haskins exclaimed. "Gal was graceful as a lily—bend her arms and elbows to de music jus' as purty as a picture. Long, tall, slim gal she was an' when she 'cut de corner,' tossin' her haid an' rollin' her eyes, ev'ybody knowed she was de bes'" (*Interviews*, 198, 135–37).

Many other interviewees attested to the importance of these dances as relief from the weekly routine. Georgina Gibbs claimed that on a Saturday the slaves at her plantation—even while they were still working in the field—"would sho' carry on 'cause dey was gonna celebrate dat night." The slaves, she said, would hoe the potatoes in time to the singing of the gang leader; and the overseer "couldn't stop all dem slaves from feelin' good, 'cause dey gonna 'set de flo' dat night." Robert Williams recounted how, at the Saturday dance, a banjo player sang, and "de niggers would be pattin' dey feet an' dancin' for life. Master an' dem would be settin' on de front porch listenin' to de music, 'cause you could hear it for a half mile. We would be in one of de big barns. We had a time of our life" (*Interviews*, 106, 326). Yet Williams did not suggest that slaves' lives were carefree. His interview presented a somber record of whippings, flight, and the sale of African Americans as though they were merchandise. The Romans knew that a slave culture was maintained by bread and circuses, and Saturday-night dances were the nearest African American slaves got to circuses.

When courtship led to marriage, diverse family structures were created. Although it was once held as axiomatic that slavery undermined a father's family position, there is in fact clear evidence that fathers frequently held honored places in their families. Thus, if a husband and wife lived on the same plantation, they often founded stable families, sons remembering their fathers with respect. West Turner recalled how—when his aunt fled temporarily to the woods—his father put food for her outside the cabin each night, and whispered with her when she crept into the cabin to eat. Frank Bell admired his father for working slowly enough during the wheat harvest that Frank's mother (who wasn't very strong) could keep up; and Bell's father taught all four of his sons to help their mother maintain her pace during the harvest time. The Reverend Ishrael Massie told how, after Emancipation, his father had promptly reunited a shattered family by discovering the whereabouts of Massie's sister (who had been sold away to another part of Virginia). Long after Emancipation, Byrl Anderson worked a farm successfully with his father on half-shares, and his father also encouraged Byrl in his ambition to be a writer. Archie Millner grew up in a single-parent family headed by his father; Millner was proud that after Emancipation his father took the family away from their old master and set them up near a long-established, prewar community of free blacks. William Johnson's full name—William I. Johnson Jr.—suggests the family pride of a former slave (born in 1840) who by the early twentieth century had become a well-to-do building contractor in Richmond. Although George White's parents had an abroad marriage, and White saw his father only on weekends, the father won the boy's esteem by handing on to him his knowledge of herbal medicine (*Interviews*, 289, 16, 211, 10, 213, 165, 310).

It was no less important for a girl to have fond memories of her father when she was growing up. Cornelia Carney's aesthetic ideal may not be what modern sensibilities would prefer, but this did not lessen her hostility to the way white people treated her father; nor did it diminish her pride in his achievements. His full name contributed, in her view, to his stature. "My father was de purties' black man you ever saw," Carney declared to her African American interviewer. "Name was John Jones Littleton. Had a long thin nose like a white man, an' had de lovelies' white teef, an' hones' chile, de purties' mouf. Father could make anything. Made dat ches' over dere in de corner. White folks been tryin' to buy it, but ain't gonna sell it to no white folks, 'cause dey treated my father so mean. . . . Father got beat up so much dat arter while he run away an' lived in de woods. Used to slip back to de house Saddy nights an' sometime Sunday when he knowed Marse and Missus done gone to meetin'. . . . Never did ketch him, though ole Marse search real sharp." The family's solidarity was demonstrated when, during the week, Carney's mother sent Carney's oldest brother out into the woods with food for their father (*Interviews*, 66–67).

Although Nancy Williams's mother imposed firm discipline on her, it was the extravagant punishment her father once administered that left the deepest impression, and that Williams seemed to feel had had the most salutary influence upon her character. Her father—the enslaved driver on the plantation—was entrusted with a money box, from which Williams once (when she was a little girl) stole a five-dollar bill. When her father asked whether she had seen the missing bill, Nancy Williams—as she recalled—"tole a black lie. He say fo' he beat me, 'Give up fo' God an' Christ an' be hones'." The whipping inflicted by her father terrified the little girl and distressed her mother. Yet "father said he'd rather die an' go to hell an' burn den to live agin in heaven . . . an' leave a passel o' tongue tied niggers here to steal. . . . I ain' never forgit dat," Williams remembered gratefully, "an' I ain never stole from nobody else" (*Interviews*, 317).

Another woman with strong positive feelings for her father was Caroline Hunter. Her father was a free African American permitted to live with his enslaved wife and their four children on the farm of his wife's master. Unbeknownst to Hunter's father, his dog had killed a sheep. "When massa found it out," Caroline Hunter recalled, "he beat my papa till he bled." But Hunter's father was unwilling to submit to being treated like a slave. "'Papa was free,'" she affirmed, "'an' he didn' think massa had no business beatin' him, so he left an' came to Norfolk an' [subsequently] jined de army.' All this time," Hunter's interviewer recorded, "the old lady's eyes were beginning to fill with water. Looking straight up she said, 'Lord I done been thew somepin'." Three-quarters of a century after the event, Caroline Hunter still grieved that her father, because he would not tolerate a slave's lot, had been obliged to abandon his family. Only as a consequence of Emancipation did this story have a partially happy ending. "When de war ended and we was free," Hunter concluded, "mama an' I came to Portsmouth, Virginia, to live. We foun' two of my brothers an' my papa here."[2]

Louise Rose was another woman who seems to have had warm feelings for her father, judging by her sympathetic account of his response when the news of Emancipation reached their plantation. Louise was about twelve in 1865. "Daddy was down to de creek," she recalled. "He jumped right in de water up to his neck. He was so happy he jus' kep' on scoopin' up han'fulls of water an dumpin' it on his haid an' yellin', 'I'se free, I'se free! I'se free!'" (*Interviews*, 242).

After Emancipation, previously enslaved fathers were able to assert over their children the full patriarchal authority earlier denied them. Their daughters often assented to this patriarchalism as a welcome change from their previous subjection to an owner's dominion. Julia Frazier declared with apparent satisfaction that, after the war, it was her father who took her and her sister away from the plantation where they had been enslaved; he put them instead into urban domestic service, where they could escape the narrowness of rural life. Susie Burns remembered with gratitude how, after Emancipation, her father obtained a piece of land that he bequeathed to her, and that she still owned in 1937. Thus, the patriarchal role assumed by some freedmen in 1865, though uncongenial to modern thinking, might be greeted by their daughters as liberation from an earlier subordination to the will of a patriarchal white man. Black women, as much as black men, needed fathers whom they could esteem (*Interviews*, 97, 64).

But it was their enslaved mothers who usually meant the most to children. Margaret Terry, for example, named her mother first—not her father—in identifying herself: "I am the daughter of Nancy and George Hailstock." In four of the seven paragraphs of Terry's interview, she mentioned her mother (including a detailed description of a whipping her mother endured), but she never said a word about her father beyond supplying his name. Similarly, although Samuel Chilton assumed his father's surname, he mentioned his mother first; he described the plantation where she was a cook, and where she raised her six children in an abroad marriage, but he said nothing about his father except to name the (different) master who owned him. In Beverly Jones's four-page interview he devoted a full paragraph to a description of his mother's work as cook (and he spoke with admiration and at length about certain enslaved adult males, such as his uncle Jackson), but he never said a word about his father (*Interviews*, 285–86, 71, 181–84).[3] Martha Showvely was another slave obviously closer to her mother than to her father, not even mentioning the latter once.

Showvely knew from her own experience how fragile an enslaved family might be, because when she was nine "dey took me from my mother an' sol' me . . . to a nigger trader" (not "took me from my mother and father"). Showvely never saw her mother again, but she recalled her mother's cautious, individualistic admonition: "I 'member one thing my mother use to tell me," Showvely concluded, "and dat was to mind my own business an' don' meddle in odder peoples' business."[4]

Occasionally, an interviewee explained why her mother was so much more important to her than her father. In Candis Goodwin's case, this was because her father was a white man—a planter on a neighboring estate—who never adopted a parental role in Goodwin's life (*Interviews,* 108, 107). In the far more common cases where the father was a slave, his emotional remoteness often arose from the fact that he lived, not with his children, but at another plantation. Katie Johnson, for example, was the child of a very unsatisfactory abroad marriage. "My father . . . ," Johnson said, "lived on another plantation. I only remember seeing him once. . . . My mother said that he was a great gambler and [that] he never come to see us without a jug of liquor." Katie Johnson believed that an abroad marriage was a slave marriage's standard form. "If a man saw a girl he liked," Johnson declared, "he would ask *his master's* permission to ask *the master of the girl* for her. If *his* master consented and *her* master consented then they came together. *She lived on her plantation and he on his*" (*Interviews,* 161; emphasis added).[5]

Some male slaves actively sought an abroad marriage partner because this would supply them a good reason for regular travel around the neighborhood, and would give them protection in doing so. "Slaves always wanted to marry a gal on 'nother plantation," Tom Epps alleged, "cause dey could git a pass to go visit 'em on Saddy nights. . . . Dey would live at de same place dey live befo' dey marry." In Epps's view slave marriages were likely to be contracted so quickly as to leave the young people little time for second thoughts: "When a man court a gal on 'nother plantation he would ax de gal's marsa could he marry her. If de marsa said, 'Yes' den dey would marry right away [at night time]. Marsa would hol' a light, read a lil' bit, an' den tell 'em dey was married." No doubt Epps's account was exaggerated, but it implies that a desire to be firmly embedded in the daily routines of family life did not rank high among the ambitions of a substantial number of male slaves (*Interviews,* 89),

The institution of abroad marriages nevertheless made it much more feasible for enslaved couples to marry for love than if a slave's choice of marriage partner had been confined to the (often very limited number of) suitable people resident on the home plantation. Consequently, many abroad marriages worked well.[6] Martha Robinson's grandparents lived twelve miles apart from each other, and her grandfather (because of the distance) could scarcely have slept with his wife more than one night in the week; yet the marriage seems to have stuck together. George White's father, who lived in a county adjacent to the one where White's mother resided, could visit his family only once a week, but he always brought food with him. Finally—after Emancipation—he was able to step in and protect his family from his wife's mean master. This unpleasant master "tried to hire us [after the war] but papa would not hire us to him 'cause he was so mean to mama an' de other slaves. We didn' take his name either, but we took my daddy's master's name, White." (White's presumption here was that *normally*, after Emancipation, children would be given their mother's surname, not their father's.) Allen Wilson's parents had an abroad marriage, and although Wilson seems not to have been very close to his father as a child, the marriage prospered. There were eleven children, and after the war the father returned from serving in the Union Army and moved his family to Petersburg, where they became homeowners (*Interviews*, 240, 311, 326, 328).

Thus, Emancipation permitted the partners in some abroad marriages—like the parents of Allen Wilson and of George White—to live together after the war. But for many slaves who had entered abroad marriages, freedom came too late. Liza McCoy's parents had an abroad marriage that was smashed when her father's master sold him to Georgia.[7] William Brown's master destroyed Brown's abroad marriage by trying to take him to Missouri in 1852, rejecting the offer by the master of Brown's wife to buy Brown at a reasonable price so that the bondman could stay in Virginia with his wife and children.[8] Among the slaves owned by a Virginia planter named Tunstall were seven adults who had abroad marriages. When Tunstall caught "cotton fever" in the 1850s and took his slaves with him to the Deep South, all seven of these marriages were permanently shattered (*Interviews*, 152). This suggests that the historian Michael Tadman—who has demonstrated the devastating impact of the interregional slave trade upon the family lives of Upper South bondpeople—may

have somewhat *under*estimated the number of Upper South slave marriages broken by the massive interregional movement of slaves during
antebellum years. Tadman vividly portrays the suffering of slave couples
whose abroad marriages were destroyed when one of their masters emigrated to the Deep South, declaring that "planter migrations would have
caused many families to be broken." But Tadman's conclusions are based
principally upon the *sales* of slaves: he convincingly argues that slaves'
family lives were disrupted considerably less often when an Upper South
master himself moved to the Cotton Kingdom, taking his slaves with him,
than when slaves were sold to traders. Very many Virginia slaves, however, had abroad marriages, and the majority of these would have been
destroyed—just like the marriage of a slave *sold* South—if one of the
slaves' masters emigrated to the Cotton Kingdom.[9]

Furthermore, the preceding discussion takes no account of the *intra*-
state slave trade. Historians have only recently recognized the massive
scale of this trade. Michael Tadman's estimates imply that the intrastate
trade was in fact more than double the size of the interstate trade.[10]
Subsequently, Steven Deyle has broadly assented to this estimate, plausibly arguing that at least twice as many slaves were sold in the intrastate
trade as to the Deep South. Thus, between 1820 and 1860 probably more
than 366,000 Virginia slaves were sold within the state.[11] Many of these
would have been to masters not resident in the slave's previous neighborhood; if a slave had an abroad marriage, it was likely shattered. Thousands
of abroad marriages were thus surely destroyed by the intrastate trade, in
addition to all those broken by the interregional trade.[12]

A few masters intervened to prevent the destruction of an abroad
marriage if one of the partners was sold. For example, the marriage of
Mary Jane Wilson's parents was threatened when her father's master took
him to the Norfolk jail, preparatory to selling him; the kindly mistress of
Wilson's mother, however, "bought my father so he could be with us." And
although Louis Fitzgerald's grandmother and her five-month-old infant
were auctioned for $500 (temporarily destroying her abroad marriage),
her former owner later bought her back again. Both of these marriages
were saved, but the threat that they could be broken reminded the slaves
of the fragility of their family institutions—subject as they were to the
whims, or calculations, of white masters. Louis Fitzgerald's grandmother,

for example, was able to breathe sighs of relief for only a limited period, because the owner who repurchased her appears to have been the same man who later sold four or five of her children to the Deep South. She never saw them again. Perhaps this master, reckoning that the slave woman was a good "breeder," had never intended to sell her permanently (selling her only because of some brief financial exigency). "If [a bondwoman] had five or six children she was rarely sold," according to Katie Johnson—because the owners of such women valued them for their breeding capacity. Thus, enslaved women had an incentive to produce children early and often, in order to diminish the chance of their being sold South and separated both from their husbands and from their relatives and community of friends (*Interviews*, 330, 92, 161).[13]

The strains upon the slaves' married lives were increased by the institution of hiring. If a bondman were hired on an annual contract to work in an urban tobacco factory, or in a Shenandoah Valley ironworks, or on a distant railway construction site—or even on a remote plantation—he might see his wife and children only once a year. Christmas would then, indeed, be a happy interlude. "Slaves lived jus' fo' Christmas to come round," claimed Fannie Berry. "General celebratin' time, you see, 'cause husbands is comin' home an' families is gittin' 'nunited agin. Husbands hurry on home to see dey new babies. Ev'ybody happy. Marse always send a keg of whiskey down to de quarters." The rejoicing was great, but an annual reunion and a big blowout scarcely compensated for the deprivation of family life during the rest of the year (*Interviews*, 49).[14]

The discontents of a bondperson's life took a further toll on family life when a married slave permanently fled a plantation (nearly always feeling obliged to leave spouse and children behind); or when an indomitable (i.e., "incorrigible") slave was sold South. "If de massa couldn' rule you," Caroline Hunter affirmed, "dey would sell you." Hunter knew whereof she spoke, for all three of her brothers were sold for this reason. A slave named Moses Bell furnished another illustration of the truth of this aphorism. As previously mentioned, Moses was a trusted "driver"—so privileged that "every Sunday Marser let Uncle Moses take a horse an' ride down to see his wife an' their two chillun [about twelve miles away], an' Sunday night he come riding back; sometimes early Monday morning just in time to start de slaves working in de field."[15] Yet Moses's privileges did not slake his thirst for freedom. He attempted to escape as many as ten times and eventually was sold South—his sale destroying the family life of yet another enslaved couple (*Interviews*, 149–50, 26–27).

Slavemasters exercised such extensive power to intrude upon the personal lives of bondpeople that their family bonds were shaped substantially differently from those of free people. May Satterfield's mother indicated the profound difference between a legally binding marriage and one that white people could terminate at any moment. Satterfield's mother explained to her that now, after 1865, "you can git *papers* an' a preacher an' git marr'd lack any white man kin, but den [in slavery times] it was diffunt. Ef you wanted to git marr'd, yo' had to axe de marster fo' de gal; den ef it was all right wid him, you an' de gal would go up to de Big House . . . , let de master say sumpin' f'om a book; den you would jump ovah de broomstick an' you was marr'd to go back to de cabin whar de gal come f'om and raise chillun." Because state legislatures never authorized "papers" to be issued to slaves, masters were legally free to sell marriage partners away from their spouses, and children away from their mothers. Both types of disruption occurred in Carol Randall's family. Her grandmother (and her grandmother's two young children) were sold away from Randall's grandfather; many years later, as previously recounted, Randall's beloved sister was sold away from the family.[16] Her master could sell her, at a very high price, for sex. "It was de saddes' thing dat ever happen to me," Randall mourned. "Ma's Marse . . . carry [my sister Marie] 'way f'om dere. Marie was pretty, dat's why he took her to Richmond to sell her. . . . You could git a powerful lot of money in dose days for a pretty gal. . . . I ain't never seen dat pretty sister of mine no more since de day she was sol'. . . . It nearly broke my heart too, 'cause I love dat sister mo'n any of de others." Similarly, Arthur Greene's older brother was sold away to South Carolina when he was only about nine years old; he would never have been seen again by his family if Emancipation had not intervened (*Interviews*, 245 [emphasis added], 236, 123).

The absence of legal papers consolidating slave marriages inevitably diminished the power of adult slaves to exercise authority within the family. If an enslaved mother should die, her husband could lose control over the upbringing of his own children, which might be taken over by white people. Thus, when Armaci Adams's mother died (when the little girl was about three), her owner removed her from North Carolina to Virginia, where Adams's father could never see her. Ten years later—after Emancipation—he came to reclaim his daughter; but white people contrived to frustrate his wishes, and they kept his child in semi-slavery until about 1872. Similarly, the slave Peter Plunkett lost authority over his daughter Daphne, who (after Daphne's mother died) was raised by white people. After the war Plunkett mounted a legal challenge, but he lost the case because by then his little girl recognized only these white people—in their adopted roles—as her mother and father (*Interviews*, 1, 3–4, 33).

If white people steadily intruded upon the personal lives of their bondpeople; if most wedding ceremonies were perfunctory affairs presided over, not by a preacher but by the master himself; if every marriage partner were dogged by the consciousness that the marriage might be abruptly terminated by sale, and that the children might well be sold away young; if a huge number of Virginia slaves had abroad marriages where the husband was likely to be absent at least six nights out of every seven; and if hundreds of discontented fugitive slaves left their families every year for at least brief sojourns in the woods—it would not seem realistic to suppose that nuclear-family institutions could acquire the strength they might have developed under more favorable circumstances. The depth of feeling many slaves had for each other, and the love of many children for their mothers, their fathers, and their siblings, testifies to the immense power of human endurance. But endurance had its limits, like the solidity of boulders in a mountainous riverbed—sometimes gradually, but tragically worn away by the rushing torrent of the masters' authority.[17]

12

The Black Community

Among slaves—as among any other people—tension existed between group solidarity and the pursuit of individual interest. Although the two did not always conflict, they sometimes did. Since 1970 historians of slavery—notably John Blassingame and Eugene Genovese—have stressed group solidarity. Genovese argues persuasively that enslaved preachers, mammies, artisans, and even drivers often used their privileged positions for the benefit of the slave community.[1] Insofar as historians have examined the slaves' pursuit of individual and family self-interest, attention has focused particularly on the slaves' "internal economy"—for example, on their raising chickens and growing vegetables (on small parcels of land allotted to them by their masters) for their own families' consumption and for marketing to white people.[2] Some slaves, however, pursued self-interest in different directions, and in doing so they sometimes became alienated from other members of the slave community.

One of the slaves' best defenses against the corrosive effects of their masters' power was to develop their own community life. As the historian Peter Kolchin has demonstrated, the communities developed by North American slaves were relatively weak compared to the communes of mid-nineteenth-century Russian serfs.[3] Nevertheless, the concept of "community" is indispensable to understanding the American bondpeople's responses to enslavement.[4]

Slaves often showed solidarity with each other. Sometimes this was restricted to members of their extended family. Thus, Moses Bell—the African American driver on a large wheat plantation—protected his sister (who was weak and unable to keep pace with the other harvesters) by allowing her husband and her sons to help her fulfill her quota. Uncle Moses (Frank Bell testified) "always looked out for his kinfolk." Reverend W. P. Jacobs's grandmother, a small woman, told Jacobs that although she too often failed to meet her quota, the other workers—not just her kinfolk—frequently helped her. She "was jolly and always ran to get water for the other slaves when they wanted it. At the end of the day one of the men would tell another, 'Give that little black gal five pounds of cotton. She's all right.' When they evened her up, she wouldn't get a beatin'." West Turner told of a black driver who—if he was directly under his master's eye—was obliged to whip slaves, but he often merely pretended to do so, allowing the supposed victim to scream loudly in order to make the master imagine that a severe flogging was taking place: "When ole Marsa warn't lookin', [this driver] never would beat dem slaves" (*Interviews*, 26, 157, 290).

Not only some drivers but also many house servants demonstrated solidarity with other members of the slave community.[5] The Reverend Ishrael Massie affirmed that "some nights house servants would come down to de quarters wid long faces an' tell de fiel' hands Marsa an' Missus been talkin' 'bout money. Dey know dat mean dey gonna sell some slaves to de nex' nigger-trader dat come 'roun'." When Bird Walton's mother was a young housemaid, she planned to leave her plantation without a pass one evening, to attend a dance at a neighboring estate. But the footman (who had accompanied their master that day to the county courthouse) had learned that the patrols would be out that night, and he managed to warn the young girl. He thus saved her the lashing the patrollers meted out to the other slaves without passes whom they caught at that dance the same evening (*Interviews*, 211, 299).[6]

The fact that field workers usually labored in gangs fostered community spirit; furthermore, leisure activities were often communal. In the evenings women came together, Mariah Hines recalled, to "spin on the old spinning wheel, quilt, make clothes, talk, tell jokes, and a few had learned to weave a little bit from Missus. We would have candy pulls, from cooked molasses, and sing in the moonlight by the tune of an old banjo picker." This account was from a plantation whose master was so exceptionally kindly that he was accused of being a "nigger lover"; but slaves with harsh masters also reported that slaves gathered, at least in small groups, whenever they could. "Evening after work slaves were allowed to visit each other," according to Marrinda Singleton. "Molasses candy pulls, quiltin' and maybe a little dancin' by de tune of an old banjo." On Sundays at Julia Frazier's plantation "de slaves would get together an' would sing an' have a big time" (*Interviews*, 141, 267, 97). Song-making was a communal activity. When in 1865 bondpeople learned they were free, at one plantation after another they devised the words for new songs of jubilation. At the news of Emancipation, Georgianna Preston averred, "Dar's one [song] dey sung purty nigh all night. Don't know who started it, but soon's dey stopped, 'nother one took it up an' made up some mo' verses." This spontaneous creation of songs drew on a prewar tradition of communal merrymaking (*Interviews*, 233–34).[7]

The considerable strength of community spirit is suggested by Mariah Hines, who claimed that if slave children talked disrespectfully in the presence of adult bondpeople (but in the absence of a parent), an adult who was *not* the child's parent would impose physical punishment. Mothers fully consented to this communal disciplining of their children. "Chillen dat did dat den," Hines averred, "would git de breath slapped out on 'em. Your mammies didn't have to do it either; any ole person would and send you home to git another lickin'." Jane Pyatt believed that slave children grew into adults who, on the whole, honored each other. In Pyatt's slightly rose-colored view, at Portsmouth (where she was raised) "the respect that the slaves had for their owners might have been from fear, but the real character of a slave was brought out by the respect they had for each other. Most of the time there was no force back of the respect the slaves had for each other, and yet, they were for the most part truthful, loving and respectful to one another" (*Interviews*, 141, 235).

Slave communities were nevertheless sometimes fractured. At a substantial number of Virginia plantations, male slaves were installed as drivers over other slaves, usually under the ultimate direction of a white overseer. Although some of these drivers to some extent tempered their authority, their special position furnished a rich source for division within the slave community. Katie Johnson spoke angrily about how "Uncle" Bob, the head hand in breaking oxen, abused his authority. As a child Katie walked in front of the oxen and was supposed to lead them in the correct direction at the driver's command, "Gee" or "Haw." But "if the oxen moved in the wrong direction 'Uncle' Bob took his long black snake whip and cracked me instead of the oxen and I never could understand why." Marrinda Singleton recalled that "the Colored overseer would beat both men and women"; while Elizabeth Sparks reported that at her plantation the black drivers let themselves be used by her master, Shep Miller, for his own deceitful purposes. If a bondwoman could no longer bear the whippings and fled to the woods, failing to return promptly, Miller after a few days would "tell one of colored foreman tell yer come on back. He ain'ta goin' beat yer anymore. . . . Foreman git yer to come back an' then he [the white overseer] beat yer to death again." In this case the whipping was administered by a white man, not the African American foreman, and the first time this happened, the foreman may have believed the master's promise. But the deception seems to have recurred, and the slave woman was likely to have been angered by the slave driver's complicity in the white man's breaking of his promise (*Interviews*, 161, 266, 274).

Drivers, because of their role in disciplining other slaves, may have been a particular focus of resentment, but there were other sources of division within the slave community as well. A bondperson, like any other individual, had quarrels that had nothing to do with anyone's being part of a plantation's disciplinary structure. When, at a dance, the boys called out the names of the girls, one by one, to display their dancing skills, the boys would sometimes "leave out one gal jus' fo' meanness. An any gal dat's left out feel mighty po'ly 'bout it too." Angry disputes sometimes flared up among enslaved adults. Those who believed in conjuring, for example, might sometimes try to place a deathly spell on their enemies (*Interviews*, 132, 267–68). One post-Emancipation illustration of such a feud—when Matilda Perry's husband nearly killed a black woman named Caroline Crip because he believed she was conjuring his wife—is already familiar, and similar feuds no doubt occurred among slaves.[8] Sexual rivalries sometimes divided slaves. Adultery seems to have been one of the most common offenses among black congregants considered by the deacons of antebellum Baptist churches, and rancorous explosions were inevitable.[9]

Furthermore, a major source for potential division between slaves lay in the masters' granting special privileges to certain bondpeople, especially house and yard servants, whose relatively close association with white people could arouse jealousy or contempt, and might alienate a privileged slave from the others. This topic is considered more fully in the next chapter, but the fragile relation in Virginia between free blacks and slaves suggests how the privileges granted to some house and yard slaves could give them a stake (just as legal rights gave a stake to some free blacks) in the status quo that might divide them from the rest of the slave community.

In principle, a sense of community might well have developed between slaves and nearby free blacks, who were often very poor and who, like the slaves, were subject to constant harassment by white people. Fellow feeling evidently grew in the heart of an illiterate slave named John Brice, who turned to a free black for help when he found himself ridiculed by his master and by the local patrollers.[10] Sarah Johnson—born free of two free parents—testified to the easy relations that sometimes existed between free and enslaved blacks. Johnson was raised in a rural area east of Petersburg, where she grew up in close contact with bondpeople, and when she told her interviewer what "cush" was, she identified with slave children. "Cush" was made by dunking cornbread into the greasy "pot liquor" left in the cauldron after the mistress's meat and vegetables had been boiled. In slavery days, Johnson explained, "some time an ole *slave mammy* had lots of chillun to feed. De days dat deir mistress had bile vituals fer dinner you could have dat liquer. . . . *Your mammy* would crumble dis [corn]bread in dat good and greasy liquer. . . . *We all chillun* was crazy 'bout cush." Johnson did not distinguish here between free and enslaved black children (*Interviews*, 164; emphasis added).

Most masters, however, took trouble to prevent community feeling from developing between their slaves and nearby free blacks. According to Archibald Milteer, born free in 1845, it was "bad [for free blacks] in slavery times. White folks shunned them. Wouldn't let them associate with slaves—wouldn't let slaves go to their houses." Mollie Booker, also freeborn, was so poor and so constantly hungry as a child that sometimes she went with her grandmother to visit slaves, who "always would give us somepin' to eat." But Booker confirmed that "mos' of de marsers wouldn' let free niggers visit dere slaves. . . . We couldn' go to any dances, 'cause dey wouldn' allow us on de plantations. . . . White folks watched you all de time" (*Interviews*, 214, 54–55). Elizabeth Sparks implied that only free blacks who had close relatives at a plantation were allowed to visit the slaves there.[11]

If free blacks were relatively prosperous, or at least not desperately poor, it benefited them to cultivate friendships with amenable white people, who might help them to maintain those legal rights that were likely to prove nugatory unless a free black person could enlist the support of white allies. Free blacks had a legal right to own slaves, and they sometimes purchased enslaved members of their own family and treated them as though they were free. Virginia Shepherd, for example, knew of a free black woman named Betsy, whose enslaved niece Caroline Deane had been born blind. Betsy bought Caroline from her white owner for $50, "and had the sale recorded in court. The receipt she put away for safe keeping." The blind slave woman later had five children, and her former owner now "demanded these five children to work for him as his slaves." But the children legally belonged to Betsy, who, according to Shepherd, "had sense enough to know it. So Aunt Betsy got the receipt, and took the case to court. *She had plenty of white friends to see that she got justice,* so [the former owner] never got a single one of them children." Legally, free blacks did have certain rights, but they needed white allies if those rights were to be enforced (*Interviews*, 256–57; emphasis added).

Shepherd went on to explain the difficulties faced by a prosperous free black man, James Bowser, who owned substantial amounts of farmland south of Portsmouth. "Free Negroes," Shepherd believed,

> had to be very careful of mixing with slaves or white folks in those days because both races were always watching them, especially the whites. Some white folks watched all the time, to keep them from mixing with the slaves. Consequently Bowser did his best to avoid trouble in any shape or form. He had five daughters who were in the courting stage. He wouldn't let them entertain any male slave company and allowed very few female slaves to come visiting. His policy was no slaves in his home any longer than possible. . . . Such attitude and action made Bowser very unpopular among the slaves. Bowser hated the fact that his own people despised him, but there was nothing else to do to protect himself from the white man's wrath. . . . He owned property which they desired and he knew association with slaves could be used as an excuse for attacking him by jealous white neighbors.

Yet Bowser "detested slavery because it kept him bound. . . . So whenever he could, he threw a monkey wrench in the machinery of slavery." During the Civil War, indeed, he acted as a spy for the Northern army, but word of this reached his white neighbors: "A band of white planters [*not* poor whites, in Shepherd's account] attacked the Bowser home," chopped off Bowser's head, severely beat his son, but left Bowser's son alive "to carry the news of this ghastly example back to the other Negroes." Stunned, the Bowser family "remained as meek as lambs." African American spies, Shepherd affirmed, were common during the Civil War, but very few of them were credited for their heroism in history books as they were written in 1937. Bowser, in Shepherd's opinion, "should be ranked with [Nathan] Hale." Yet, according to Shepherd, when news of Bowser's beheading circulated among blacks, "slaves chuckled gleefully in their quarters. Big hat Bowser had got what he deserved at last." Here the African American community was split, bondpeople embittered by a free black man's previous distancing of himself and his family from the slaves. The story suggests that bondpeople, inured to the violence surrounding them, might themselves become infected so as to relish the lynch mob's beheading of another human being (*Interviews*, 259–60).[12]

The dilemmas confronting James Bowser—a legally free African American living in a slave society—were faced, to some degree, by every black person, free or enslaved, who was granted a relatively privileged position in that society. Bowser's predicament may suggest caution when we assess the situation of slaves who received grants of privilege. Privileges tendered by white people could, as this last gruesome incident demonstrates, fracture the African American community.

13

Self-Development

This chapter first considers literacy. It then examines the privileges accorded to certain bondpeople. Finally, it discusses how far these privileges pulled favored individuals away from other slaves.

Some slaves learned to read, and even to write, despite the huge legal and customary obstacles placed in their way.[1] How did they acquire these skills? How many did so, and who were they?

One must first distinguish between reading and writing. "I can't write or spell," Jane Pyatt lamented, "but strange as it sounds I can read anything I wish." Similarly, although Candis Goodwin complained that in general "de white folks didn' want you to learn," she reported that at her plantation "de white chillun dey learn me to read . . . , but I can' write; never learn to write." Samuel Chilton declared, "Dar was a mighty few of us scarcely none 'tall could write deir names" (*Interviews*, 234, 107, 71).

In all of the Virginia interviews, there are only two clear references to slaves who knew how to write.[2] Both of them were males, and both of them were house or yard servants. Joe Sutherland, the slave who forged papers that enabled at least four other slaves to escape permanently, was a coachman who "always hung around the courthouse with [his] master. He went on business trips with him, and through this way, Joe learned to read and write unbeknown to master." The other slave who learned to write was Lorenzo Ivy's father. "When de slaves git married," Ivy explained, "de leadin' colored men dat had learned to read an' write could marry 'em. My father could marry folks an' he often did. Father's mistress learned him to read." Ivy's father "was a lackey boy 'roun de big house" (which explains how his mistress saw enough of him to take an interest in educating him). Her husband, Judge George Gilman, was an unusually kindly master who, unlike the overwhelming majority of masters, did not try to suppress the education of a talented slave. Indeed, Judge Gilman sent the young bondman to Lynchburg to learn the shoe-making trade, and eventually let him hire himself out. "Yessuh!" Ivy exclaimed to his black interviewer, in appreciation of his father's privileged position, "let him make his own barguns" (*Interviews*, 167, 151–53).

Although scarcely any slaves learned to write,[3] a perceptible number could read, and a few more began lessons that were later prohibited. Approximately equal numbers of male and female slaves could read. The majority were taught by white children, or by white youths under the age of about twenty. Most of the rest were taught by their white mistresses. Apparently, none recorded in the interviews was taught by an adult white man.[4] Further, there seems to have been little tradition of slaves being taught by other slaves, as Frederick Douglass famously (but of course secretly) taught other slaves.[5] Joe Sutherland, the forger of passes, did manage to make himself literate without known aid from white people; and Dr. Beale Bassette, a preacher educated by Quakers, taught a number of slave children until a white woman (perhaps the mistress's sister) impounded his New York primers (*Interviews*, 167, 229–30). But these were exceptions to what appears to have been the general rule: slaves learned to read mainly from well-disposed white people.

White children, imparting newly acquired school learning to those black children with whom they played around the Big House, were the slaves' most frequent teachers. Elizabeth Sparks stated simply that "the children used to teach me to read," and Mariah Hines confirmed that "what little learning you got [you got] it from the white chillen." These white children sometimes acted behind their parents' backs. Philip Ward offered a circumstantial account of the relation between a white child, named Russell, and his enslaved playmate Jerry. "Marse used to warn [his six children] about leaving their [school] books around where we could get to see them. But," Ward continued, "they didn't pay any attention to him. One day Marse came down to the barn and found [his son] Russell whipping a little slave boy his own age, named Jerry. Marsa grabbed Russell and took the whip away from him. 'Who tole you to whip that boy?' he asked. Russell started crying. 'Well, that's what the teacher did to me today 'cause I didn't know my lesson. And he doesn't know it no better'n I do.' All us slaves knew that Russell had been going over his lessons with Jerry a long time, but Marse didn't know it. He put a stop to it after that, though." This obviously was no interracial idyll. The little white boy, although fairly well disposed to the slave child, had already learned to use his power over that child to make himself feel better about a setback he had experienced in his own life (*Interviews*, 276, 142, 301).

A sort of comradeship might sometimes persist between a master's son and a young male slave even after they had passed the age of puberty. When the slave Allen Wilson was seventeen, he was deputed to live in Petersburg with his master's (younger) son, so that the white youth could attend a secondary school there. After working during the day in a tobacco factory, Wilson acted as a body servant to his young master during the evenings, sharing cramped quarters with him. Some camaraderie developed between the younger and the older youth, and Wilson later acknowledged in friendly fashion that, although he "never had a chance at schooling, [I] jest picked up a little learning from my ole young marster."[6]

A similar friendship may have subsisted between James Taliaferro's father (when he was a youthful slave) and his master's son. Taliaferro reported that his father "was taught to read and count by the young Marsa who was home from college." Book learning got this young slave into trouble—and this time it was much worse trouble than little Jerry had encountered. As noted earlier, Taliaferro's father used his new arithmetical skills to calculate that one particular slave woman's allotted task for weeding corn was unjustly large. Her complaints infuriated the plantation owner, and only the intervention of the master's son—the college student who had introduced the serpent of book learning into the slave quarters—persuaded the white man not to sell Taliaferro's father to the Deep South as punishment for instigating a protest at how the white people ran the plantation (*Interviews*, 282).[7]

While slaves' book learning usually came from their masters' children, an appreciable number of adult white women violated the customary bar against teaching slaves to read. It was the mistress of Lorenzo Ivy's father who taught that bondman his letters. And Jane Pyatt's mistress—an urban slaveholder in Portsmouth, Virginia—not only taught her to read but encouraged the eager slave woman to speak standard English. This appears to have been a case of genuine interracial cooperation. "When I was a slave," Pyatt testified, "I worked in the house with my mistress, and I was able to learn lots from her. By listening to my mistress talk, I learned how to use a lots of words correctly. Although it was against the law to teach a slave, my mistress taught me my alphabets" (*Interviews*, 153, 234).[8]

For one reason or another, however, reading lessons instituted by white women often ended abruptly. "De ole mistess [*sic*] started learnin' us slave chillun," the Reverend Ishrael Massie recalled. But "as soon as ole marster foun' hit tout, he stopped her from learnin' niggers anything." Margaret Terry's mistress, like Jane Pyatt's, was an urban slaveholder (in Charlottesville), willing to educate the child of a favored house servant. The little slave girl did her lessons with the white children. She got into trouble, however, because she learned the lessons better than her white peers did. Terry's mistress, she reported, "at times would whip her children about getting their lessons. We studied together, and the old lady would hear them. I would know mine. Now she would say, 'I can't see why Margaret always knows her lesson and you all do not.'" This invidious situation led Margaret Terry's mistress to stop letting her study with the white children. These children nevertheless—behind their mother's back—helped Terry to locate each day's lesson in the book. "I would find out where the lesson was and would get it just the same, but [my mistress] didn't know it." (Terry was the black woman who, after the war, was taken north by a Northern teacher and who later returned to teach for sixty years in segregated schools, in or near Charlottesville.) Terry owed her good education primarily to her own determination and intelligence, but also partly to a well-disposed Northern teacher after the war, and partly to opportunities offered her by her Southern white urban mistress and by that woman's children (*Interviews*, 208, 285).

We do not know how certain slaves learned to read. There is no clue, for example, how a slave called Aunt Lucky became literate. This woman performed the marriage ceremony for the parents of one interviewee: Aunt Lucky "read sumpin from de Bible, an' den she put de broomstick down." According to Mary Jones, slaves (or at least house servants) at the Thomas Nelson Page plantation attended the Episcopal church and were drilled to memorize the catechism and various passages of the Bible. This may explain Jones's bemused comment about her mother—a privileged mammy and wet nurse for the Pages. "It's so funny," Jones exclaimed, "mother could read the Bible but nothing else." Evidently, the Pages (presumably Mrs. Page) drilled Mary Jones's mother in biblical passages. Aunt Lucky may similarly have been drilled by a white woman, while Susan Broaddus's father may possibly have learned to spell from a literate slave (*Interviews*, 134, 187, 55). The evidence about other literate slaves points to the central roles of white children, and white mistresses, as teachers.[9]

It would be hard to overstate, however, the amount of steely determination as well as guile a slave normally needed in order to become literate. Thomas Johnson, an enslaved urban house servant, offers a case in point. Johnson started his journey toward literacy with advantages: his mother had taught him the alphabet, and then had surreptitiously paid a free black man in Washington to give her boy further instruction. But after a month Johnson's master discovered what was going on, and he banished Johnson from the city. Henceforth Johnson depended on guile. He flattered his master's son into spelling out certain words, the spelling of which Johnson then memorized. Later he inveigled the young white man into reading out loud, over and over, certain biblical passages that, again, Johnson virtually memorized, so that—on his own—he could recognize how to pronounce each printed word in a particular passage. It required formidable grit for Johnson to teach himself to read—and eventually to write—in this way.[10]

The Virginia interviewees probably underreported the extent to which urban slaves managed to learn to read. In Richmond, despite hostile public opinion, some slaves paid poor whites to give them secret reading lessons. And Thomas Johnson declared that by about 1862 he was secretly teaching a small class of other Richmond blacks to read.[11] The Virginia interviews, however, do suggest that those bondpeople who managed to become literate were disproportionately urban. Almost all of the literate slaves mentioned in the Virginia interviews were house or yard servants, or the children of slaves in those privileged positions. This conclusion is congruent with the way most slaves learned to read. White children would be most likely to play with the enslaved children of house and yard servants; and white mistresses would be most likely—if they favored any slave child at all—to favor the child of a trusted house servant. Jane Pyatt was raised in Portsmouth, Margaret Terry in Charlottesville, and Allen Wilson was domiciled with his young master in Petersburg. The mothers of both Pyatt and Terry were house servants who appear to have been treated relatively well. Once Allen Wilson was moved to Petersburg, he acted as a body servant to his young master (after working all day in a tobacco factory) (*Interviews*, 234, 285, 328). Candis Goodwin's mother cooked in the plantation kitchen (and the white mistress gave Goodwin clothes discarded by one of her own little girls). Lorenzo Ivy's father—as previously quoted—"was a lackey boy 'roun de big house." Elizabeth Sparks became a house servant, while Mary Jones's mother (who "could read the Bible but nothing else") was a wet nurse. Joe Sutherland—the forger of papers enabling slaves to escape—was a coachman (*Interviews*, 107, 152, 275, 187, 167). Thus, of all the slaves of known occupation who gained some access to book learning, only Mariah Hines was a field hand (and her master was so exceptionally lenient to his bondpeople that he was branded a "nigger lover").[12] Everything suggests that when white people favored individual slaves, offering them limited access to book learning, these favors were directed overwhelmingly toward certain house or yard slaves and some of their children. For most slaves book learning was strictly forbidden. As Ellis Bennett declared, with only a little exaggeration, in slavery times the white people "doan want you to know nuffin but masters tell you whut dey please. . . . White man let no nigguh read fore war. . . . [If a white man] see nigguh walking by wif buk [book] in 'is 'and . . . , wite man snatch buk. Say 'buk no fo' nigguh; buk fo' wite man.'"[13]

✸ A substantial number of Virginia slaves were granted by their masters privileged positions—intermediate between those of whites and field hands—within the plantation's occupational hierarchy. These positions often presented the favored slaves chances to develop substantial vocational skills, and to associate with the master or the mistress on terms that allowed a certain recognition of the slave's individuality. Usually, these positions also offered material rewards.

One such family was Levi Pollard's. His father was a wagon driver, his mother a seamstress. Unlike most slaves, who were obliged to live in one-room cabins, the Pollards were granted the extraordinary luxury of a two-story, three-room house within which to raise their fourteen children. Neither the mother's work nor the father's was terribly hard, and this family was treated differently from ordinary slaves—"'most like white folks," in Pollard's formulation. "What I means? I means Mars . . . ain't treat us like us wuz real slaves, like lots er niggers wuz treated."[14]

A perhaps comparable case was that of William Lee, a dining room servant and "pet" slave (the term is William Lee's) to John Lee, a nephew of General Robert E. Lee. At John Lee's death, after the Civil War, he bequeathed forty acres, $400, and a "big house" to this privileged servant. During the war William Lee was a body servant to John Lee's soldier-son Jerry, who was killed at Fort Fisher. "I was sent home wid Marse Jerry's corpse," William Lee recounted to his black interviewer. "I road right in de baggage care wid him. Poor Marse [John Lee], I did love him" (*Interviews*, 196). On the Lee plantation a fake whipping once allegedly arose from a male conspiracy that joined the master John Lee with his house servant William, in a plot to deceive John Lee's wife. The plantation was a vast one, apparently owned by Mrs. Lee, who disapproved of her husband's regard for William. Mrs. Lee once tried to whip William herself, and the slave resisted, whereupon she ordered her husband to "skin him, clean his hide." But instead of whipping him, John Lee took William to the whipping house, drank whiskey with him, and pretended to whip him, instructing the slave to cry out in order to deceive John Lee's angry wife, who—in William's exaggerated recollection—hollered, "Kill him! Kill him! a son of a bitch for dat nigger thinks he owens our plantation." John Lee told William to put water into his eyes to pretend he had been crying: "I put it all over my eyes jes' lak tears was comin'. He say, 'William my boy, you know I won't gwine whip you 'cause I loves you, but I jes' had to do dis thing 'cause your missus would make me leave home, an' dat you know I couldn't.'" Had this story been narrated to a white interviewer, its authenticity would be highly dubious; told even to a black interviewer, it sounds like the fanciful expression of the interviewee's (genuine) regard for his former master. It illustrates Michael Tadman's interpretation of antebellum "paternalism" and his concept of "key slaves": masters did in fact sometimes give benefits and favored treatment to a select group of "key slaves," and this allowed these masters to convince themselves that they were benevolent paternalists even when they treated most of their slaves unfeelingly. John Lee, for example, thought nothing of having the overseer inflict a savage whipping on a field hand who wasted time and lied about it.[15]

Another favored slave was William I. Johnson Jr., whose name alone bespoke his self-esteem. Trained from about age twelve to be a butler, Johnson, by the age of twenty-one, in 1861, was a house man. When his master with his four sons all went to war, Johnson said proudly, "they left me in complete charge of the plantation house . . . , because they knew

that I could be trusted to protect Mistress Nancy and her two daughters."
Yet Johnson's privileged position did not make him subservient. He knew
of, and wholly sympathized with, four slaves from a neighboring plantation who had permanently escaped with the help of documents forged by
his own master's coachman. He himself later escaped, during the war, and
he served in the Union Army until October 1865. That Christmas he returned to the old plantation to see his family. Surprisingly, a common religious culture, combined with the master's prewar regard for his privileged
butler, permitted the two men to reminisce easily about their wartime
experiences. Johnson's former master "laughed when I told him how we
escaped from the [Confederate] camp; he didn't show no anger at all but
instead said, 'Johnson, it was what the Lord intended to happen. . . . God
settled it all like he wanted it, so I suppose everything has happened for
the best.'" The story throws light on the origins of the African American
middle class of the early twentieth century; this privileged house servant,
assimilated to the culture of his white master—yet prepared to make a
break for freedom when the opportunity presented itself—learned the
bricklaying trade after the war, and from 1907 to 1932 (aged sixty-seven
to ninety-two) was reputed to be one of Richmond's leading building con-
tractors (*Interviews*, 166–70).

A parallel case was that of Albert Jones, a house and yard servant who
obeyed his master's rules so long as it served his interest to do so, but who
escaped to the Union Army when opportunity beckoned. "My work [as a
slave] won't hard . . . ," Jones reported. "I had to wait on my mastah, open
de gates fer him, drive de wagon and tend de horses." Jones may have appeared to be nothing but a self-interested conformist. "My mastah wuz
mighty good to me," he testified: "He won't ruff; dat is 'f yer done right.
. . . But you better never let mastah catch yer wif a book or paper, and yer
couldn't praise God so he could hear yer. If yer done dem things, he sho'
would beat yer. 'Course he wuz good to me, 'cause I never done none of
'em. . . . Fer twenty years I stayed wif mastah, and I didn't try to run away.
When I wuz twenty one, me and one of my brothers run away to fight
wif the Yankees." The greatest times of Jones's life were the three and a
half years (during and after the Civil War) he served as cavalryman in the
Union Army. Apparently, Jones had seized the opportunity, as a privileged slave, to learn to ride horseback, and he later used this skill to fight
for the liberation of his people.

"I was one of de first colored cavalry soljers," Jones glowingly recalled. He remembered proudly the uniform he wore and the fact that he had continued to fight after being wounded. Like the sharecropper Ned Cobb ("Nate Shaw") in 1910, parading his newly purchased mule in front of the house of his landlord so that the white man's family could take in Cobb's new status as the proud owner of his own work animal, Jones went back to see his former master after the war. "Attachment" to a master who had been "mighty good" to Jones no doubt played a part in Jones's return, but the cavalryman also wanted to flaunt his new status. "When de war ended, I goes back to my mastah," Jones exclaimed, "and he treated me like his brother. Guess he wuz scared of me 'cause I had so much ammunition on me."[16]

Cornelius Garner was another privileged slave, a hostler like Albert Jones, who played ball with the system when it paid him to do so, but whose proudest moments came later, when he served in the Union Army. "Did I fight in de war?" Garner asked his two African American interviewers indignantly. "Well if I hadn' you wouldn' be sittin' dere writin' today." Slaves weren't permitted to read and write, Garner explained to the two young people who were writing down his words. "No matter how we yearned fer knowing how to read and write we had no way on earth of doing so." A slave could, however, try to improve his situation by ingratiating himself with his master. "I was treated tolerably fair juring slavery times," Garner conceded. "Massa sorta took a liking to me. I guess it was 'cause I always hung 'round kinda handy and didn't mind wukin'. Massa always laked his ho'sses looking fine and kept looking good. Seeing dat massa laked dis, I made hit my business to keep dem ho'sses looking spic and span. Massa, seeing dat I was inrested in his ho'sses and stables, he kept me sorta close 'round de house—hitching up, feedin', curring, and holding his ho'sses fer him and missus. . . . Coase, I being 'round de house most ob de time, ole missus was always giving me some vituals." Garner came from a family of privileged slaves, and he had perhaps learned from his parents the advantages of working within the system. His father was a butcher permitted to pursue his own trade, in return for paying his master an annual fee. "Mother," he said, "was hired out as a nurse an' cook." Theirs was an abroad marriage, but when Garner was an infant, his father's master bought the butcher's wife and child, so that the family could be together. Owned by a "very good" master, Garner regarded it as

a status symbol that the master had paid for a white preacher to officiate
at his parents' marriage.

Yet this privileged slave joined the Union Army the first moment he
could, at age eighteen in 1864, and he later became copiously informed
about the role of black soldiers in the Civil War. He expatiated at length
(eleven paragraphs of the interview) on this topic. Every Northern general, Garner concluded, refused "de nigger troops but one. Dat general was
General [Benjamin] Butler. He say, 'I'll take dem.' After dey fight dere fust
battle, ev'y general wan' 'em. Dey won de war for de white man. Yessuh"
(*Interviews*, 102, 100, 99–100, 102 [two quotations], 104).

Male body servants, butlers, and yard servants tended to be the most
privileged class of slaves, but artisans (like Cornelius Garner's father, the
butcher allowed to hire his own time) made up another privileged class.
Lorenzo Ivy's father, for example, was trained as a skilled shoemaker.
When very young this slave had been employed by his master, Judge
George Gilman, in the big house. One day "he tuk a table fork an' made
a little [last (i.e., a frame around which a shoe might be built)] out of it.
An den he tuk de [last] an' made a little shoe. Old Judge Gilman saw him
make it an' was very pleased. He put him at shoe makin'. Sent him all de
way to Lynchburg to learn. . . . He studied hard an' became one of de bes'
shoemakers in de state. After he learned, he tuk him an' hire him out to
different shoe shops. Finally he let him hire himself out. . . . After de surrender, father had his own shop." Here, again, a privileged slave was in
a far better position to gain economic independence after Emancipation
than were less skilled slaves (*Interviews*, 152–53).

Similarly, Archie Booker's brother was the only slave on their plantation permitted by their master to hire himself out. The master trusted
this slave to pay the annual fee at Christmastime, thus saving himself
the trouble experienced by other masters (like President James Polk in
Mississippi) of dunning the annual fee from a reluctant white man. The
arrangement with Booker's brother probably also gave the favored slave
the privilege of hiring out his services to several different employers on
short-term contracts (or for weekly wages), instead of being bound to a
single employer for the whole year. Booker was intensely proud of the use
his brother had been able to make of Emancipation: "Bruthah . . . went to
school in Richmund aftuh de war. He tu[r]ned out to be a real smart school
teachuh. Yessuh!"[17]

Mary Wilson's was another family of privileged slaves who made a good life for themselves after Emancipation. Her mother was an urban slave—probably a cook—in Portsmouth, Virginia, while her father was apparently a teamster. Although this was an abroad marriage, Wilson's father's master permitted the man to live in town with his wife and child. And when this privilege was rescinded, and Wilson's father was put up for sale, his wife's Portsmouth mistress bought him in order to prevent the slave family from being shattered. After freedom Wilson's father, previously favored as a slave, "went to work in the Norfolk Navy Yard as a teamster. He began right away buying us a home," Mary Wilson continued. "We was one of the first Negro [residential] land owners in Portsmouth after emancipation. My father buil[d]ed his own house . . . , and it still stands [in 1937] with few improvements." This man's daughter Mary Wilson, born a slave in 1859, was able to go to school after the war. She went on to graduate from Hampton Institute (the college for Native Americans and freedpeople attended by Booker T. Washington), and "opened a school in my home. . . . After two years my class grew so fast and large that my father built a school for me in our back yard. I had as many as seventy-five pupils at one time. Many of them became teachers. I had my graduation exercises in the Emanuel A[frican] M[ethodist] E[piscopal] Church. Those were my happiest days." What a contrast to the constricted life Mary Wilson would have led as a slave! Yet her good fortune had derived, in part, from the privileges extended to her parents when they were bondpeople (*Interviews*, 330–31).

A few female slaves—as well as males—were also accorded extensive privileges. George Lewis testified that his mother, indeed, "was set free by her young mistress [in about 1857] two years before I was born." Lewis's father was a free African American who ran a business in Richmond, hiring out boats on the James River. Lewis himself married into another family of longtime free African Americans, his father-in-law having bought his freedom many years before 1861. Lewis, thus descended from members of a privileged elite group, graduated from Howard Law School, in Washington, D.C., in 1888, and was still practicing law in Richmond in 1937, at the age of seventy-eight. His two daughters both taught at black colleges in Virginia. "If you will excuse me," he briskly dismissed his young female WPA interlocutor after he had granted her a short interview in his law office, "I shall get to work" (*Interviews*, 196–97).

Jane Pyatt, unlike George Lewis's mother, remained a slave until freed by the Civil War, but her privileges as a slave had been considerable. "When I was growing up" in Portsmouth, Virginia, she declared to her black interviewer, "although I was a slave, I had everything a person could wish for except an education." Fannie Nicholson, another privileged house servant, apparently was also, like Jane Pyatt, an urban slave in Portsmouth. Nicholson was accorded the privilege of exercising a bit of authority over her young white mistress. "My mama was a seamstress," Nicholson reported, "and my chief duty was in de house. When my young missus had company and ef dey 'up[p]ed an' stayed too late, I had to hol' a candle over a large clock an' open de do'. Dis meant for de company to go" (*Interviews*, 234, 217).

But the privileges granted female house servants—except to a few women like Sally Hemings and Lucy Langston—were not normally so extensive as those granted to the most privileged male slaves. The favors offered most female house servants, indeed, were ladled out from a very small dipper. For example, Martha Showvely, a house girl and later a cook for the Tinsley family, never mentions having been whipped and probably never was. Yet her life was austere. At the age of nine she had been sold away from her mother, and even away from the two cousins whom the slave trader had bought at the same time. The little girl found herself a stranger in the Tinsley household, where at first she was put to work making beds and house cleaning. "After I finished my reg'ler work," she recalled, "I would go to de mistress' room, bow to her, an' stand dere 'till she noticed me. . . . We wasn't 'lowed to sit down. We had to be doing something all day. Whenebber we was in de presence of any of de white folks, we had to stand up." Showvely married a free African American (a fireman on the railway) and felt well-treated because, instead of being obliged to stay in the big house, she was allowed to live in a cabin where her husband could stay with her when he was not away at work (*Interviews*, 264–65).

Elizabeth Sparks was not so lucky. Evidently, even after she was married, Sparks was usually obliged to sleep in her mistress's room. "I ain't slep' in any bed" there, Sparks expostulated. "Nosir! I slep' on a carpet, an ol' rug, befo' the fiahplace"—presumably at the ready to leap up to answer any whim of her mistress.

Sparks reported that her mother—the laundrywoman in this household—"had to wash white folks clothes all day an' huh's after dark.

Sometimes she'd be washin' clothes way up 'round midnight. Nosir, couldn't wash any nigguh's clothes in daytime. My mother lived in a big one room log house wif an upstairs. Sometimes the white folks give yer 'bout ten cents to spend."

Although Sparks said that her mistress and master were both mean, their daughter Jennie was a much better mistress, partly, Sparks suggests, simply because she was younger. Genuine paternalist reciprocity operated between Sparks and this young mistress. When Northern soldiers arrived at the plantation during the war, they "took some of Miss Jennie's things [e.g., clothes] an' offered 'em to me. I didn't take 'em tho' 'cause she'd been purty nice to me." In return the young white mistress conferred a big favor on the slave woman. The Northern soldiers wanted to take Sparks's husband off to serve in the Northern army; but although the young black man wanted freedom, he did not want to leave his wife and their infant. Young Miss Jennie intervened on behalf of Sparks and her husband, and the Northern soldiers (no doubt influenced partly by the existence of this very young baby) relented and let Sparks's husband stay with her. This was a very substantial favor indeed, conferred by the young white mistress upon her female house servant, but one that she was not likely to have conferred on an ordinary field hand. Thus, for privileged female slaves, as well as for privileged males, it usually paid to cooperate with masters or mistresses, so long as power lay in the hands of the master class (*Interviews*, 275–76).

Such grants of privilege tended to divide the slave community. The evidence suggests that other slaves envied Joe Sutherland (the privileged coachman who traveled around with his master on business), who seemed to enrich himself by selling forged passes to enslaved blacks. Joe Sutherland was detected and sold South as punishment for his forgeries, and "it was always said [among the slaves] that . . . Ned Lee, who was a close friend of Joe's betrayed him." Similarly, a bondwoman at Jennie Patterson's plantation betrayed to her mistress a male slave who planned to escape. Presumably, this woman, like Ned Lee, sought to ingratiate herself with white people by stabbing a black person in the back. Children learned early this way of winning favor from their masters. When Allen Wilson was a boy, his cousin Jim Wilkins was assigned to climb apple trees, shake down the apples, and have Allen collect them. Allen, on the ground, selected the two best apples for himself and set about eating them. When their master came by, Jim ratted on Allen. "Marse Ben," said Jim, "Allen ain't helping none—jes eating all yer apples." Allen promptly retaliated by throwing a rock at his cousin, which knocked him out of the tree; their master then administered to Allen, as punishment, a memorable whipping, while Jim no doubt basked in the sunshine of his master's sympathy and approval (*Interviews*, 167, 220, 327).

Privileged slaves often were proud of their associations with well-disposed white people. Mildred Graves, for example, had been a house servant and nurse, but her sense of self-esteem derived most strikingly from her work as a midwife, and it was her service to white women in which she most exulted. "Whenever any o' de white folks 'roun Hanover was goin' to have babies dey always got word to [my master] dat dey want to hire me fer dat time. . . . Marser use to tell me I was a valuable slave." Graves's most vivid memory was of safely delivering Judge Leake's wife of a premature child, after the judge—and the two white doctors summoned from Richmond—had despaired of the woman's life. Mrs. Leake had more faith in the enslaved midwife than in the Richmond doctors, and Graves triumphantly recalled that, after both the mother and the five-pound infant were safe, "even de doctors dat had call me bad names said many praise fer me." The approbation of "respectable" white people continued to mean a great deal to Graves after Emancipation. She moved to Richmond, and after she was widowed she resumed her work as a midwife, in association with white doctors: "Many o' de important [white] people o' [Richmond] are 'my babies.' In dem days in Richmond when doctors was few I wuked wid a lot o' 'em" (*Interviews*, 120–21).

Privileged slaves were conscious of class divisions *between* white people (as well as of differences *among well-to-do* white people, in their attitudes to blacks). These slaves sometimes esteemed "respectable" white people—by which they meant those well-to-do whites who were reasonably well-disposed to blacks. Matilda Carter's mother—a cook whose mistress favored her and her children—was one such African American. Matilda was born in 1859 on a farm near Hampton, Virginia, just north of the mouth of the James River, in an area captured by Union troops early in the war. By about 1864 she was able to start school. Matilda's mother urged her to emulate her mistress's little white daughter. "My mother was always anxious to sen me to school," Matilda affirmed. "She uster tell me to try to be like Miss Mary Anne [Wynder], mistress' daughter, an' all de other *spectable* white folks' girls" (*Interviews*, 69; emphasis added). But the fact that Matilda's mother set before her eyes respectable little white girls as role models (for educational ambition and deportment) did not imply that Matilda should admire the white people's political ideas. Most former slavemasters welcomed the Reconstruction policies of President Andrew Johnson, after Lincoln's assassination made Johnson president; but Matilda Carter came to understand how Lincoln's assassination had been a disaster to African Americans: "After Lincoln, [Andrew] Johnson went in office. Things sho change den. Johnson give de rebels' lan' back to em an' give em all dey privileges what dey had fo' de war." Carter lamented in 1937 that black leaders had long since abandoned the Emancipation Day parades that had formerly been held on the first of January. Her complaint was that, in giving up these parades, "all de Negroes of today is tryin' to imitate de white folks." It might at first sight seem inconsistent for Carter to denounce the blacks who tried "to imitate de white folks" after she had herself sought, as a girl, to emulate little white girls. But there was no inconsistency: it was perfectly rational to reject the white people's political stance about Reconstruction policy and holding Emancipation Day parades, while seeking to emulate the educational ambition of "respectable" white people (*Interviews*, 69–70).

Bird Walton was from another enslaved family whose members esteemed certain white people. Among well-to-do whites Walton distinguished those who were well disposed to blacks from those who were not. "De riches' white people 'roun' heah was an' is de Wilsons," she told her black interviewer; "dey de meanes' white folks too." But Walton's mother, the housemaid Jane Follkes, was owned by the extraordinarily generous master George Follkes, who (as previously related) bequeathed after the Civil War most of his 1,700-acre plantation—in good-sized parcels—to his former slaves.[18] Although "de white folks tried to break de will," they failed to do so, because "de *bes'* white men in Chatham was fur it, an' de niggers wan' so dumb either." Walton's mother and father had good reason to esteem their remarkable master and those well-to-do whites who sided with them in the court case (*Interviews*, 297–98; emphasis added).

William Johnson (the young butler left in charge of the plantation house during the early years of the Civil War because he was trusted to protect the white women there) was another slave who cultivated good relations with his white masters.[19] In 1863 he was taken by his young master "as servant and horseman [to the Confederate cavalryman]. . . . Whenever there was fighting, all of us Negroes had the [Confederate] camp to look after. . . . In between battles we had to keep all our masters' boots polished, the horses and harness cleaned and the rifles and swords spic and span." Years later Johnson cherished the memory of the confidential talk he had with his young master at Christmas 1865, when they exchanged frank reminiscences about their wartime experiences. The tenor of this cordial encounter[20] can be explained by Johnson's much earlier experiences as a slave. When Johnson was very young, he had been selected for close association with his master's family and at least partial assimilation to their culture. At about age twelve "I was taken into the house and trained to be a butler." For two years, beginning when he was seventeen, he was hired to work for a man in Richmond, where he doubtless gained urban sophistication and probably was given advanced training for the butler's profession. He then returned to the plantation, and within about eighteen months he was left in charge of the plantation house when the white men all rushed off to war.

Yet this privileged (and "pampered"?) butler proved no Uncle Tom. In 1864, when acting as a body servant to his young soldier-master near Fredericksburg, he learned from captured Union soldiers that, if he could manage to cross the lines, he would be free. With four other slaves he started out one night toward Washington: "We carried along plenty of chewing tobacco, 'cause we knew the [Confederate] pickets would always like a chew and they didn't ask us no questions." Walking along the road as quickly as they could, and hiding in the woods each time they heard horses coming, the fugitives eventually reached Washington. Johnson's four companions were recruited into Union fighting regiments, but, presumably because Johnson let the Northerners know that he was a butler, "I was lucky enough to be . . . [assigned] to the Quartermasters Corps, in charge of food and rations."

After the war Johnson began working as a hod-carrier in Richmond, and he soon learned the bricklayer's trade. (Thus, a former butler easily crossed the permeable line between house service and manual labor.) Working for white men, Johnson by 1890 had become foreman of a brick construction works, a position he held for seventeen years. Then, beginning at age sixty-seven, he successfully ran his own building contracting firm for the next twenty-five years. He became an active member of half a dozen black fraternal organizations, as well as of Richmond's first Baptist church. Although Johnson never had a day of formal schooling, he appears to have seized every opportunity for self-development, both when he was a slave and afterward. He seems, at some time, to have become skilled at mental arithmetic, and (presumably after 1865) he had learned to "read a little."[21] He was proud to have been financially able to send to college those of his children "who wanted it. I've helped grandchildren and now I help to educate great grandchildren. The Lord is just blessing me that's all."

Here was a man who had grasped the opportunities presented to him by his privileged position when he was a slave, and who (starting as a hod carrier) had gone on to improve the vastly greater opportunities offered him by Emancipation. He did not fawn upon white people, although he conversed easily with them, and he spoke articulately and in detail about the wrongs of slavery. In those days, he said, "sometimes it would be raining hard, or storming and the ole poor white overseer [on the adjoining farm] would want some of the slaves to go out into the wood to get the cattle or other stock and if the slaves refused they would get a whipping." Johnson named three slaves on that farm whom the overseer tied to a tree and whipped "'til they could hardly stand up; then he cut the ropes loose and made them go back to work." Johnson preserved his sense of community with the other slaves while laying hold of every opportunity for self-development. He was, perhaps, one of the unsung heroes of slavery. His path to a sort of glory was not that of Nat Turner, but perhaps it was in its own way as deserving of esteem (*Interviews*, 165–70).

Some slaves embraced opportunities for self-development—learning to read, to ride a horse, to become a midwife, a seamstress, or an artisan—opportunities that were often opened to these bondpeople by previous grants of special privilege from white people. Such grants always brought with them the potential for alienating a privileged slave from the wider slave community. Indeed, some slaves succumbed to the temptation of ingratiating themselves with their masters by betraying fellow slaves. Nothing can be said in defense of the slave who betrayed Joe Sutherland (the forger of passes), or of the woman reported (by Jennie Patterson) to have betrayed the escape plan of a would-be fugitive. But the path of self-development did not necessarily conflict with that of loyalty to the wider slave community. The examples of the midwife Mildred Graves, and of the Union soldiers William Johnson, Cornelius Garner, and Albert Jones, suggest that the great majority of African Americans who took the path of self-development, while they were enslaved, deserve to be honored.

Part IV

RETROSPECT

14

Oppression and Self-Determination

Perhaps the strongest impression left by Virginia's WPA interviewees is the heartening sense that the morale of these old people had not been broken by their experiences of slavery. They felt pride in how they and their ancestors had responded to oppression. Stories abounded of the slaves' spirited dissidence. The slaves' religion sustained belief in the ultimate triumph of justice. Personal loyalties were deep, especially to mothers, but also to many fathers, siblings, and other members of extended families. A substantial number of interviewees had managed to develop skills, even when they were slaves, that helped them to make better lives for themselves after Emancipation.

The interviews and other sources demonstrate that escape from the constraints of plantation bondage was a principal goal for many slaves. Some Virginia bondpeople found a partial escape in urban life (or by working at an iron forge), which, especially for hired slaves in tobacco factories, allowed them to lead somewhat more autonomous lives than on the plantation. Urban slaves could associate with the hundreds of free blacks in small cities like Richmond, Petersburg, and Norfolk/Portsmouth. A handful of slaves, like Sally Hemings and her children, managed a partial escape from regimentation through their membership in Virginia's small third caste. A much larger number found temporary escape from physical abuse by flight to the local woods—the most significant outlet for the slaves' profound discontent with their lot. A small, yet appreciable number escaped permanently to the North or Canada.

Religion offered a spiritual escape from oppression. The slaves' Afro-Christianity was shaped mainly by their experiences in

North America—by their appropriation of many elements of white people's evangelical Christianity and by their encounter with slavery, which
dictated which aspects of Christianity resonated with their own experiences. In Virginia the legacy of African religions, by 1860, was much
attenuated though still perceptible (e.g., in funeral observances). Afro-
Christianity was a splendid morale booster, encouraging bondpeople to
see their masters as subject to a higher law, and fostering hope that one
day justice would prevail. The slaves' Christianity normally promoted
nonviolent forms of dissidence that, it may be argued, served the slaves'
interests better than violence would have done.

The disruption of families by sale (especially the sale of children away
from their mothers, or the sale of siblings away from each other) was the
focus of the most painful recollections of the elderly interviewees. Their
pain bespoke the strength of their family connections. In addition to the
attachments between children and their mothers, there were often also
strong attachments between children and their fathers. Yet it is unmistake-
able that the central family unit was a mother and her children, to which
the father was sometimes firmly—but often only weakly—attached. The
large number of abroad marriages, where the father only visited his wife
and children once a week, took a toll on the development of nuclear-family
traditions, as did the presumption of slavemasters and slave traders that
the normal unit of sale (if a family were sold together) was a mother and
her young children, sold separately from the children's father, and also
often separately from the mother's eldest children. Members of an extended family (especially the children's grandmother or aunts and uncles)
might help a mother raise her children, but the expectations and customs
of family life were substantially different from what they would have been
if Virginia's lawmakers had sought to strengthen nuclear-family institutions among the slaves.

A substantial number of slaves pursued paths of self-development as far
as they could. Some learned to read, or even to write; many became cooks,
and some learned to be midwives, seamstresses, or household managers;
some became drivers or preachers; some were trained as artisans, hostel-
ers, or butlers. Usually, access to these skills came with the assistance of
well-disposed white people (as when white children or a white mistress
taught a slave to read, or when a white master arranged the training of a
male slave as a cobbler or a butler). The term "self-determination" perhaps

suggests these slaves' goal more accurately than "autonomy," because their road to self-development often obliged them to depend on the assistance of some member of the ruling race, and they could not therefore be autonomous. This kind of dependence could fracture the slave community, but it did not inevitably do so. Usually, it took incredible grit for a slave to acquire literacy or to earn substantial amounts of money through a self-hire arrangement. Some of the most honorable slaves were those who followed these paths of self-development, even though they may have been forced to make difficult ethical compromises with white people in order to be allowed to develop their skills in the first place.

However, the interviews also make evident the obvious—that not all slaves were angels. Nat Turner acted like a monster when he smashed a baby's head; some brutalized slaves rejoiced at white people's beheading of James Bowser (the free black man discovered to be a Union spy); Fannie Berry, as a child, shamelessly let other children pay the price for the fire she had started; and the slave who betrayed Joe Sutherland (the forger of passes) deserves contempt. Although most slaves would help a distressed fugitive, the solidarity of the slave community was never complete. It cannot be expected to have been: some slaves were out for themselves, and many masters encouraged this kind of individualism.

The story is therefore a somber one. Oppression shaped the responses of slaves more than we might prefer. We might wish that there had been extensive slave rebellions in the American South, as there were in the Caribbean and in Brazil, but after 1831 violent slave resistance in Virginia was minimal. There were no insurrections and no support for John Brown's invitation to rebellion, and in most decades the proportion of slaves convicted of murdering white people continued on a downward trend. The slaves' massive discontent was expressed through nonviolent dissidence, especially through frequent flight to the local woods. Much of the slaves' creative energies were directed into the arts of dissent: deceiving masters, stealing from them, satirizing them behind their backs. Excellent though dissidence was as a morale booster, it is tragic that so few channels were open for the constructive expression of the slaves' creative energies. Oppression forced the slaves' family institutions into different shapes than they would have taken had white people cared to nourish strong nuclear-family life among the bondpeople. Afro-Christianity was an immense support to many slaves, but it may have been an inadequate substitute for the general education denied to bondpeople. Avenues of self-development were opened to a few slaves by well-disposed white people, but for a privileged slave to accept the favors of these people inevitably involved ethical compromises. Not every privileged slave could retain loyalty to the slave community, though many seem to have succeeded in doing so.

Thus, the legacy of bondage was mixed. Stories of valor and of strength were abundant. Yet, if the testimony of the Virginia interviewees is to be believed, the scars left by slavery were harsh.

Appendix

The counties included in each of the four Virginia regions discussed in the introduction, and in table 1, are as follows:

1. Eastern Virginia (and northern Piedmont counties):

Eastern Shore: Accomack, Northampton

Tidewater: Charles City, Elizabeth City, Essex, Gloucester, Henrico, James City, King George, King and Queen, King William, Lancaster, Matthews, Middlesex, New Kent, Northumberland, Richmond, Warwick, Westmoreland, York

Southside: Greeneville, Isle of Wight, Nansemond, Norfolk, Prince George, Princess Anne, Southampton, Surry, Sussex

Northern Piedmont: Alexandria, Culpeper, Fairfax, Fauquier, Loudon, Madison, Prince William, Rappahannock, Stafford

2. Tobacco Belt (central and southern Piedmont counties):

Albemarle, Amelia, Amherst, Appomattox, Bedford, Brunswick, Buckingham, Campbell, Caroline, Charlotte, Chesterfield, Cumberland, Dinwiddie, Fluvanna, Franklin, Goochland, Greene, Halifax, Hanover, Henry, Louisa, Lunenburg, Mecklenburg, Nelson, Nottoway, Orange, Patrick, Pittsylvania, Powhatan, Prince Edward, Spottsylvania

3. The Valley and the Southwest:

Valley: Allegheny, Augusta, Bath, Botetourt, Clarke, Frederick, Highland, Page, Roanoke, Rockbridge, Rockingham, Shenandoah, Warren

Southwest: Buchanan, Carroll, Craig, Floyd, Giles, Grayson, Lee, Montgomery, Pulaski, Russell, Scott, Smyth, Tazewell, Washington, Wise, Wythe

4. Counties That Became West Virginia

All of the counties within Virginia's 1860 borders not included in the three regions above.

Notes

Abbreviations

Interviews *Weevils in the Wheat: Interviews with Virginia Ex-Slaves,* eds. Charles L. Perdue, Jr., Thomas E. Barden, and Robert K. Phillips (Charlottesville: University Press of Virginia, 1976)

Refugee Benjamin Drew, *The Refugee: A North-side View of Slavery,* ed. Tilden G. Edelstein (Reading, Mass.: Addison-Wesley, [1855] 1969)

Slave Testimony John W. Blassingame, ed., *Slave Testimony: Two Centuries of Letters, Speeches, Interviews, and Autobiographies* (Baton Rouge: Louisiana State University Press, 1977)

Introduction

1. The "Middle South" comprised four slave states—North Carolina, Virginia, Tennessee, and Arkansas—all of which eventually joined the Confederacy in 1861. The "Deep South" comprised seven other slave states, stretching from South Carolina to Texas, which also joined the Confederacy.

2. Cf. William Dusinberre, "Commentary on Robert Olwell, 'The Long History of a Low Place: Slavery on the South Carolina Coast, 1670–1870,'" in *Slavery and the American South,* ed. Winthrop Jordan (Jackson: University Press of Mississippi, 2003), 139–46.

3. Kenneth M. Stampp, *The Peculiar Institution: Slavery in the Ante-Bellum South* (New York: Vintage, 1956).

4. John W. Blassingame, *The Slave Community: Plantation Life in the Antebellum South* (New York: Oxford University Press, 1972).

5. Eugene Genovese, *Roll, Jordan, Roll* (New York: Pantheon, 1974).

6. *Weevils in the Wheat: Interviews with Virginia Ex-Slaves,* ed. Charles L. Perdue Jr., Thomas E. Barden, and Robert K. Phillips (Charlottesville: University Press of Virginia, 1976) (hereafter cited here and in text as *Interviews*).

7. Of the 109 Virginia interviews conducted by workers whose race is known, 92 percent were conducted by black interviewers. The chief editor of the published

interviews convincingly argues that "internal evidence indicates that most if not all of [the remaining 50 interviews] were conducted by Negro workers" (*Interviews*, xxxviii).

8. Benjamin Drew, *The Refugee: A North-side View of Slavery*, ed. Tilden G. Edelstein (Reading, Mass.: Addison-Wesley, [1855] 1969) (hereafter cited here and in text as *Refugee*). In addition to the twelve Virginia fugitive slaves interviewed by Drew and listed in Charles Perdue's *Interviews* (392), six other fugitives to Canada spoke to Drew about slavery in Virginia. These were Charles Brown, Sam Davis, John Francis, George Johnson, James Smith, and William Thompson.

9. Michael Tadman, *Speculators and Slaves: Masters, Traders, and Slaves in the Old South* (Madison: University of Wisconsin Press, 1989), 12 (table 2.1).

10. Richard S. Dunn, "Black Society in the Chesapeake, 1776–1810," in *Slavery and Freedom in the Age of the American Revolution*, ed. Ira Berlin and Ronald Hoffman (Charlottesville: University Press of Virginia, 1983), 49, 51, 54–65. For wheat prices and production, see Lewis Cecil Gray, *History of Agriculture in the Southern United States to 1860*, 2 vols. (Washington, D.C.: Carnegie Institution of Washington, 1933), 2:1039–40. For tobacco prices and production, see Joseph Clarke Robert, *The Tobacco Kingdom: Plantation, Market, and Factory in Virginia and North Carolina, 1800–1860* (Durham, NC: Duke University Press, 1938), 134, 147, 152, 156.

11. Gray, *History of Agriculture*, 2:918–22; Lynda J. Morgan, *Emancipation in Virginia's Tobacco Belt, 1850–1870* (Athens: University of Georgia Press, 1992), 24. See also table 1, this volume.

12. See table 1.

13. See table 1.

14. William Kauffman Scarborough, *Masters of the Big House: Elite Slaveholders of the Mid-Nineteenth-Century South* (Baton Rouge: Louisiana State University Press, 2003), 483–84; also 138, 230 (Baylor), and 131 (William Tayloe). The Tayloe estate—in the early nineteenth century—is a principal focus of Richard S. Dunn's "A Tale of Two Plantations: Slave Life at Mesopotamia in Jamaica and Mount Airy in Virginia, 1799 to 1828," *William and Mary Quarterly*, 3rd ser., 34 (1977): 32–65.

15. Scarborough, *Masters of the Big House*, 138; and Virginia Auditor of Public Accounts, Record Group 48, Revenue & Assessment, Pay Ledgers, 1823–1885, Ledger Book 1847–1860, Box Barcode 1081739, Library of Virginia, Richmond. I am indebted to Mary S. Clark of the Library of Virginia for the governor's salary and for this citation, and to Professor William Link for guiding me to this source.

16. Scarborough, *Masters of the Big House*, 138–39; Gray, *History of Agriculture*, 2:921.

17. For example, in King George County (a Tidewater wheat-producing area) the median slave was owned by the owner of 25 slaves. In the Southside county of Southampton (Nat Turner's county, where—unusually for Virginia—a substan-

tial amount of cotton was raised) the median slave was owned by the owner of 22 slaves. These figures are my estimates from data in the 1860 Census of Agriculture, 243–45.

18. See table 1.

19. Tobacco prices during the 1850s were nearly 50 percent higher than during the two previous decades. Lynda Morgan depicts convincingly "slavery's continued vitality" in Virginia during the 1850s (Gray, *History of Agriculture*, 2:1038; Lynda Morgan, *Emancipation in Virginia's Tobacco Belt*, 19, 24; Robert, *Tobacco Kingdom*, 147, 152, 156; Scarborough, *Masters of the Big House*, 483–84, 26).

20. In Halifax County (which produced more tobacco than any other Virginia county) the median slave was owned by the owner of 26 slaves (computed from the 1860 Census of Agriculture, 243–45). See also Lynda Morgan, *Emancipation in Virginia's Tobacco Belt*, 8, 21; and William Link, *Roots of Secession: Slavery and Politics in Antebellum Virginia* (Chapel Hill: University of North Carolina Press, 2003), 40.

21. In Warren County (in the Shenandoah Valley) the median slave was owned by the owner of 12 slaves. In Tazewell County (in the southwest) the median slave was owned by the owner of 9 slaves (computed from the 1860 Census of Agriculture, 243–45).

22. See table 1. Because residents of West Virginia were not interviewed by Virginia's black interviewers in 1937, and because slavery was relatively insignificant in that area, I omit wherever possible in this book consideration of the counties that later formed West Virginia.

23. Allan Kulikoff, "Uprooted Peoples: Black Migrants in the Age of the American Revolution, 1790–1820," in Berlin and Hoffman, *Slavery and Freedom*, 147–49.

24. Kulikoff, "Uprooted Peoples," 151–52, 152n; Tadman, *Speculators and Slaves*, 12 (table 2.1), 30–31, 245–47. Tadman estimates that "about one in five of the first marriages of Upper South slaves would have been broken by the [interregional] trade" (169), and that about one-third of "Upper South [slave] children aged fourteen and under . . . were separated from one or both parents by the trade" (171).

25. *Interviews*, xxxviii–xxxix (and n. 81).

26. Virginia Writers' Project, *The Negro in Virginia* (1940; repr., New York: Arno Press, 1969). An additional one percent of Perdue's material comprises the transcription of a recording in the Library of Congress's Archive of Folk Song (*Interviews*, xxxvii).

27. *Interviews*, 128 (see chap. 4).

28. Paul D. Escott, *Slavery Remembered: A Record of Twentieth-Century Slave Narratives* (Chapel Hill: University of North Carolina Press, 1979), 11; James West Davidson and Mark Hamilton Lytle, *After the Fact: The Art of Historical Detection* (1982; repr., New York: Knopf, 1986), 191–201. The historian Stephen Crawford found significant differences between WPA interviews conducted by black inter-

viewers and those by white interviewers; see Stephen C. Crawford, "Quantified Memory: A Study of the WPA and Fisk University Slave Narrative Collections" (Ph.D. diss., University of Chicago, 1980), 40–42, 99n, 106, 118–19.

29. Elizabeth Tonkin, *Narrating Our Pasts: The Social Construction of Oral History* (Cambridge: Cambridge University Press, 1992).

30. Arthur Greene interview, *Interviews,* 125.

31. All but two of the Virginia interviewees had lived east of the Blue Ridge; but nearly 91 percent of the slaves in "residual Virginia" had also lived east of the Blue Ridge (calculated from the figures in table 1, this volume). See *Interviews,* 352–53.

32. Of thirty-seven interviewees whose occupations Perdue could identify, eleven were female house slaves and thirteen were male field slaves; there were ten female field slaves and three male house slaves (*Interviews,* xlii).

33. *Interviews,* 352–53.

34. *Interviews,* xxvi–xxviii, 377–82.

35. John W. Blassingame, ed., *Slave Testimony: Two Centuries of Letters, Speeches, Interviews, and Autobiographies* (Baton Rouge: Louisiana State University Press, 1977) (hereafter cited here and in text as *Slave Testimony*); *Refugee;* George Teamoh, *God Made Man, Man Made the Slave: The Autobiography of George Teamoh,* ed. F. N. Boney, Richard L. Hume, and Rafia Zafar (Macon, GA: Mercer University Press, 1990); Harriet A. Jacobs, *Incidents in the Life of a Slave Girl: Written by Herself,* ed. Jean Fagan Yellin (1861; repr., Cambridge, Mass.: Harvard University Press, 1987).

36. William Dusinberre, *Them Dark Days: Slavery in the American Rice Swamps* (New York: Oxford University Press, 1996); William Dusinberre, *Slavemaster President: The Double Career of James Polk* (New York: Oxford University Press, 2003).

37. Among many other such historians, see particularly Nell Painter, "Soul Murder and Slavery: Toward a Fully Loaded Cost Accounting," in *United States History as Women's History: New Feminist Essays,* ed. Linda Kerber et al. (Chapel Hill: University of North Carolina Press, 1995), 125–46; Brenda Stevenson, *Life in Black and White: Family and Community in the Slave South* (New York: Oxford University Press, 1996); Walter Johnson, *Soul by Soul: Life Inside the Antebellum Slave Market* (Cambridge, Mass.: Harvard University Press, 1999); Marie Jenkins Schwartz, *Born in Bondage: Growing Up Enslaved in the Antebellum South* (Cambridge, Mass.: Harvard University Press, 2000); Jonathan D. Martin, *Divided Mastery: Slave Hiring in the American South* (Cambridge, Mass.: Harvard University Press, 2004); and Richard Follett, *The Sugar Masters: Planters and Slaves in Louisiana's Cane World, 1820–1860* (Baton Rouge: Louisiana State University Press, 2005).

1. Good Mistresses and Masters

1. American Freedmen's Inquiry Commission interview, 1863, in *Slave Testimony,* 408–9.

2. *Pike County (Ohio) Republican,* 25 Dec. 1873, in *Slave Testimony,* 483–84.

3. According to the U.S. Census, 218 Virginia slaves were manumitted in 1850, and 277 in 1860 (*Historical Statistics of the United States,* ed. Susan Carter et al., 5 vols. [Cambridge: Cambridge University Press, 2006], 2:384). Self-purchase by slaves is discussed in chapter 3.

4. *Anti-Slavery Reporter,* 1 Feb. 1853, in *Slave Testimony,* 297. A similar case—of a well-disposed white mistress who facilitated the escape from Norfolk of her slave, George Teamoh—is mentioned in chapter 3.

5. Because sometimes a white person who gave or bequeathed large amounts of land to freedpeople after the Civil War was a blood relative of the beneficiaries, I infer that there may be some such explanation for Follkes's generosity. However, nothing supports this inference except the circumstantial evidence already presented in the text. Cf. Hortense Powdermaker, *After Freedom: A Cultural Study in the Deep South* (1939; repr., New York: Russell and Russell, 1968), 297–98.

6. Hines's probable master, John A. Persons, owned (in 1860) forty-eight slaves, and rented eight others (see Daniel W. Crofts, *Old Southampton: Politics and Society in a Virginia County, 1834–1869* [Charlottesville: University Press of Virginia, 1992], 21–22, and n. 19).

7. Interracial relationships, such as that between Hatcher's son and Patience Avery's mother, are discussed in chapter 2.

8. The interviewer was Mrs. Susie Byrd, who conducted thirty-five extant interviews, most of them very different in tone from this one with Mary Jones. Thomas Nelson Page (1853–1922) published *In Ole Virginia* (1887) and other much-read fiction and nonfiction that presented a romanticized view of antebellum plantation life (Theodore L. Gross, *Thomas Nelson Page* [New York: Twayne, 1967]).

9. This story was told to an unknown interviewer. But even if that interviewer may possibly have been white, the story, to my ears, has a ring of authenticity.

10. A slave child might play comfortably with the white children even if the white parents were *not* good masters. Thus, George White reports that he had a mean master and mistress, yet "when I was a little boy, I use to play wid de white chillun. Dey had one little boy about my age named Lawson an' mistress would nurse me when she nursed him, if mama was in de field. Mistress always would take a laking to me." As George White wouldn't have remembered nursing, he presumably got the story from his own mother, and it probably was true (*Interviews,* 309).

11. An extreme example of the supplanting of a slave's parental role by a white mistress appears in the case of Daphne, a slave child who—after her mother's death—was raised by white people. After the war Daphne's father and the woman he had married came to claim her, but the child chose the white people as parents, rather than her father and her stepmother (*Interviews,* 33).

12. *Providence (R.I.) Journal,* 25 May 1924, in *Slave Testimony,* 560.

13. *Refugee,* 184–85.

14. See chapter 5.

15. *Anti-Slavery Reporter,* 1 Mar. 1853, in *Slave Testimony,* 303.

16. Beverly Jones's reaction to the white preacher's sermon is quoted at the beginning of chapter 9.

2. Mixed-Race Ancestry and Long-Term Relationships

1. Harriet A. Jacobs, *Incidents in the Life of a Slave Girl: Written by Herself,* ed. Jean Fagan Yellin (1861; repr., Cambridge, Mass.: Harvard University Press 1987), 77, 262 n. 1. The authentication of Jacobs's memoir appears in Yellin's notes to her edition of *Incidents.* Harriet Jacobs's brother, John S. Jacobs, also published in 1861 an account of his life as a slave, which generally corroborates *Incidents* while differing from it in certain respects. See the essays by Jacqueline Goldsby and Jean Fagan Yellin in *Harriet Jacobs and "Incidents in the Life of a Slave Girl": New Critical Essays,* ed. Deborah M. Garfield and Rafia Zafar (Cambridge: Cambridge University Press, 1996), 11–43, 44–56.

2. Jacobs, *Incidents,* 35, 5 (quotation), 6, 56–57, 260 n. 1. Professor Stephanie Shaw has kindly drawn my attention to the major role of grandmothers in the upbringing of enslaved children.

3. Ibid., 6, 11–12, 262 n. 6, 263 n. 1 (to chap. 4), 264–65 n. 13.

4. Ibid., 12, 88 (quotation).

5. Ibid., 5 (quotation), 7 (quotation), 8.

6. Technically, Jacobs was bequeathed to the three-year-old daughter of Mrs. Norcom; but, so long as the legatee remained a minor, this placed the slave girl under the power of Dr. and Mrs. Norcom (ibid., 8, 261 n. 7, 261 n. 9, 261 n. 11, 262 n. 1.

7. Ibid., 215 (two quotations), 11 (quotation), 27, 32–34.

8. Ibid., 37–40 (quotations at 39).

9. Ibid., 54–55, 58, 60, 77–78, 80, 96, 105–7, 125–26, 137–41, 148, 166, 173, 188–89, 223–24, 242, 268 n. 1, 269 n. 2, 273 n. 3, 279 n. 1, 280 n. 1, 280 n. 3, 281 n. 2.

10. Ibid., 54–56.

11. No doubt many free women have also "consented" to sex with a well-to-do man for a mixture of reasons analogous to, if somewhat less exigent than those of Harriet Jacobs's. But Jacobs was pleading the cause of bondwomen; she cannot be expected to have made a plea for defenseless women in general.

12. Jacobs, *Incidents,* 67, 269.

13. Ibid., 64–65.

14. Ibid., 63–65.

15. Ibid., 63, 65–66.

16. Ibid., 94–95, 99 (quotation), 151–54, 156–60, 275.

17. The background to this remarkable act of defiance is sketched in chapter 10.

18. [Mary Chesnut,] *Mary Chesnut's Civil War,* ed. C. Vann Woodward (New Haven, Conn.: Yale University Press, 1981), 243, 29, 31.

19. Jacobs, *Incidents*, 55.

20. *Interviews*, 201, 199; *Refugee*, 96.

21. Cf. Elizabeth Fox-Genovese, *Within the Plantation Household: Black and White Women in the Old South* (Chapel Hill: University of North Carolina Press, 1988), 325–26, 338–71, and esp. 349–57.

22. The circumstantial account of Jefferson's connection to the Hemings family—which Madison Hemings (a son of Sally Hemings) published in an Ohio newspaper in 1873—is reprinted in *Slave Testimony*, 474–80. See also Joshua D. Rothman, *Notorious in the Neighborhood: Sex and Families across the Color Line in Virginia, 1787–1861* (Chapel Hill: University of North Carolina Press, 2003), 12–52, 247 n.4; Annette Gordon-Reed, "Logic and Experience: Thomas Jefferson's Life in the Law," in *Slavery and the American South*, ed. Winthrop D. Jordan (Jackson: University Press of Mississippi, 2003), 16–20; Annette Gordon-Reed, *Thomas Jefferson and Sally Hemings: An American Controversy* (Charlottesville: University Press of Virginia, 1997); Fraser D. Neiman, "Coincidence or Causal Connection? The Relationship between Thomas Jefferson's Visits to Monticello and Sally Hemings's Conceptions," *William and Mary Quarterly*, 3rd ser., 57 (2000): 198–210; Joseph J. Ellis, "Jefferson: Post DNA," *William and Mary Quarterly*, 3rd ser., 57 (2000): 125–38; Winthrop D. Jordan, "Hemings and Jefferson: Redux," in *Sally Hemings and Thomas Jefferson: History, Memory, and Civic Culture*, ed. Jan Lewis and Peter Onuf (Charlottesville: University Press of Virginia, 1999), 48–50.

23. Lucia Stanton and Dianne Swann-Wright, "Bonds of Memory: Identity and the Hemings Family," in Lewis and Onuf, *Hemings and Jefferson*, 178–80; Philip Morgan, "Interracial Sex in the Chesapeake and the British Atlantic World, c. 1700–1820," ibid, 52–84.

24. Rothman, *Notorious in the Neighborhood*, chap. 1, esp. 18, 45–49 (two quotations at 47, one at 45). Except for these six sentences, nearly the whole text—but not all of the endnotes—of my chapter was written before I could read Rothman's book. I believe his splendid analyses of the Jefferson-Hemings relationship, and of customs in Virginia regarding interracial sex, support the idea that something like a three-caste system existed in Virginia, and that it applied not only to free African Americans but also, sometimes, to slaves. Perhaps, however, my term "caste" is slightly inaccurate, since two of Hemings's children later passed as "white."

25. Madison Hemings, interviewed in *Pike County (Ohio) Republican*, 13 Mar. 1873, in *Slave Testimony*, 480.

26. Joel Williamson, *New People: Miscegenation and Mulattoes in the United States* (New York: Free Press, 1980), 49–50, 146.

27. Luther Jackson, *Free Negro Labor and Property Holding in Virginia, 1830–1860* (New York: Appleton-Century, 1942), 122, 126–28, 217, 222–25. On the rarity of rural manumissions after 1806, and on self-purchase by urban slaves, see chapter 3.

28. *The Papers of Frederick Law Olmsted*, vol. 2, *Slavery and the South, 1852–1857* (Baltimore: Johns Hopkins University Press, 1981), 91.

29. *National Anti-Slavery Standard,* 25 Mar. 1841, quoted in *Slave Testimony,* 211.

30. Loren Schweninger, "The Underside of Slavery: The Internal Economy, Self-Hire, and Quasi-Freedom in Virginia, 1780–1865," *Slavery and Abolition* 12 (1991): 13–16.

31. A different view of the ethics of slave women's liaisons with their masters may be implied in the pioneering article by the historian Brenda Stevenson, "Distress and Discord in Virginia Slave Families, 1830–1860," in *In Joy and in Sorrow: Women, Family, and Marriage in the Victorian South, 1830–1900,* ed. Carol Bleser (New York: Oxford University Press, 1991), 103–24, and esp. 115.

32. Although I cannot supply evidence to document this assertion (because the Virginia interviewers seldom specified the skin color of their interviewees), illustrations from all over the South indicate its validity. For example, the most privileged of South Carolina governor Robert Allston's slaves included "Mulatto Joe" (who was placed in a position of great authority on the farm that provisioned Allston's rice plantations) and the trusted mixed-race butler, Nelson (Dusinberre, *Them Dark Days,* 342–45, 330, 331).

33. On Stephen Gallant, see ibid., 331–32, 335–42.

3. Cities and Industry

1. The pioneering and valuable work on urban slavery was Richard C. Wade's *Slavery in the Cities: The South, 1820–1860* (New York: Oxford University Press, 1964). In this chapter, as elsewhere in this book, I discuss only those counties that comprise present-day Virginia, and exclude the areas that by 1863 had seceded from Virginia to form the state of West Virginia, including the urban area of Wheeling, [West] Virginia. The 26,420 slaves residing in the five urban areas discussed here comprised 5.6 percent of the slaves living in "residual Virginia" (excluding West Virginia).

2. In this calculation I count Richmond's adjacent cotton-mill suburb (Manchester) as part of the Richmond urban area.

3. George Teamoh, *God Made Man, Man Made the Slave: The Autobiography of George Teamoh,* ed. F. N. Boney, Richard L. Hume, and Rafia Zafar (Macon, Ga.: Mercer University Press, 1990), 63–65, 68 (quotations at 68, 63–64, 63).

4. Ibid., 72, 74 (quotation), 87, 182.

5. Ibid., 77, 71–72, 73 (quotation). Presumably, the school for free black children was closed sometime after the passage, in 1831, of a Virginia law banning free blacks from being taught to read and write. Jane Pyatt, a slave born in 1848 and raised in Portsmouth, recalled that in her experience, "there weren't any schools for slaves or free Negroes in this city" (Luther Jackson, *Free Negro Labor and Property Holding in Virginia, 1830–1860* [New York: Appleton-Century, 1942], 19–20; *Interviews,* 235).

6. Tommy L. Bogger, *Free Blacks in Norfolk, Virginia, 1790–1860: The Darker Side*

of Freedom (Charlottesville: University Press of Virginia, 1997), 145–52 (quotation at 152).

7. Teamoh, *God Made Man,* 70, 73 (quotations).

8. Ibid., 84–86, 181.

9. Ibid., 75–82 (quotation at 79).

10. Probably the most accurate count of male tobacco-factory slaves in Richmond's Henrico County, in 1860, is 2,723. In addition, 145 male hands worked in Manchester's two tobacco factories. If 80.5 percent of these were slaves (as in Henrico County), the total number of male tobacco-factory slaves in the urban area of Richmond/Manchester was 2,840. This implies that about 700 of the 3,529 male Richmond/Manchester tobacco-factory hands either were white, or were free blacks. Perhaps 150 of them were white men (principally overseers) and 550 were free black men. The figure 2,723 for Richmond's Henrico County is from Suzanne Schnittman, "Slavery in Virginia's Urban Tobacco Industry, 1840–1860" (Ph.D. diss., University of Rochester, 1987), 113. The total number of male tobacco hands in Henrico County was 3,384 (ibid., 113), from which the figure 80.5 percent is derived. The figure 145 (for Manchester's Chesterfield County) is from the 1860 Census of Manufacturing. Apparently, about 150 of Henrico County's tobacco hands worked in factories outside the Richmond city limits; but I have counted them as part of the Richmond/Manchester urban area (Midori Takagi, *"Rearing Wolves to Our Own Destruction": Slavery in Richmond, Virginia, 1782–1865* [Charlottesville: University Press of Virginia, 1999], 73). The figures I am using here are very close to those presented in Rodney Green, "Urban Industry, Black Resistance, and Racial Restriction in the Antebellum South: A General Model and Case Study in Urban Virginia" (Ph.D. diss., American University, 1980), 314. The Richmond/Manchester tobacco factories employed only 44 females. These seem to have been all—or nearly all—free black women, perhaps mainly working as cooks. Experiments at employing white women as tobacco-factory hands seem to have died out in Richmond by 1860, though about 48 white women, 160 free black women, and 592 slave women were employed in Petersburg's tobacco factories (Schnittman, "Slavery," 33, 163–64, 35, 64 n. 20).

11. Schnittman, "Slavery," 392–98.

12. Suzanne Schnittman, using the 1860 manuscript census of slave inhabitants, finds that of 2,685 adult male slaves (i.e., those over ten years old) in Henrico County's tobacco factories, 450 were owned by the factory owner and the other 2,235 (83 percent of the total) were hired. There were 155 other enslaved male tobacco hands (mainly at Manchester's two factories, plus a few boys under ten years old). If one assumes that 83 percent of these 155 males were hired, the total number of hired slaves would be 2,364, and the total number owned by the factory owners would be 476 (Schnittman, "Slavery," 149 n. 6). Rodney Green explains why Joseph Robert's earlier (much lower) estimate of the number of hired tobacco hands can no longer be accepted ("Urban Industry," 764–75). Cf. Joseph Robert,

The Tobacco Kingdom: Plantation, Market, and Factory in Virginia and North Carolina,
1800–1860 (Durham, N.C.: Duke University Press, 1938), 198–99n.

13. These weekly figures are for 1852, when Frederick Law Olmsted was told by
a manufacturer—a slavery enthusiast—that at his factory "nearly all [the slaves]
gained by overwork $5 a month, many $20, and some as much as $28." In 1853
another manufacturer spoke of "bonus money of $2 to $3 a week for 'overwork'"
(F. L. Olmsted, *A Journey in the Seaboard Slave States* [New York: Dix and Edwards,
1856], 103; Schnittman, "Slavery," 295–96). By 1860 the figure was somewhat
higher. Cf. Jackson, *Free Negro Labor,* 180.

14. For example, the case of a Richmond tobacco-factory overseer killing a
slave, and a similar case in a Lynchburg factory, are cited later in this chapter.

15. But cf. Takagi, *Rearing Wolves,* 37–49, esp. 89–92, which specifies some ways
in which the situation of Richmond's enslaved factory workers deteriorated during the 1850s (Claudia Dale Goldin, *Urban Slavery in the American South, 1820–*
1860: A Quantitative History [Chicago: University of Chicago Press, 1976], 35, 41).
Jonathan Martin's argument—that even relatively unskilled slaves often (if hired
to a third party) exploited this triangular relation to their own advantage—seems
particularly applicable, and convincing, for Virginia slaves hired to work in the tobacco factories of Richmond, Petersburg, and Lynchburg (see Jonathan D. Martin,
Divided Mastery: Slave Hiring in the American South [Cambridge, Mass.: Harvard
University Press, 2004], esp. 65–71, 128–60). On urban hiring, and its widening
the world of the hired slaves, see Lynda Morgan, *Emancipation in Virginia's Tobacco*
Belt, 57–75.

16. This statement refers to male slaves in Richmond itself (excluding
Manchester), aged fifteen to sixty, of whom there were 4,587 (i.e., 48 percent ×
9,557) (Takagi, *Rearing Wolves,* 75). The number over ten years old working in the
tobacco factories of Richmond itself was 2,685 (Schnittman, "Slavery," 149 n. 6)

17. Takagi, *Rearing Wolves,* 74–86, 115; 1860 U.S. Census of Manufacturing;
Charles Dew, *Ironmaker to the Confederacy: Joseph R. Anderson and the Tredegar Iron*
Works (New Haven, Conn.: Yale University Press, 1966), 26–28; Ira Berlin, *Slaves*
without Masters: The Free Negro in the Antebellum South (New York: Pantheon,
1974), 155n; Olmsted, *Journey,* 49; *Southern Workman,* Feb. 1881, in *Slave Testimony,*
489–90; Green, "Urban Industry," 691, 694.

18. Midori Takagi states that, of just over 5,000 enslaved workingwomen
in Richmond, 4,500 were domestics (*Rearing Wolves,* 88). See also *American*
Missionary, Sept. 1863, and American Freedmen's Inquiry Commission interview,
1863, both in *Slave Testimony,* 364, 420. Evidently, Boggs reached the North by
ship, helped to flee by others in Norfolk and farther north.

19. Olmsted, *Journey,* 28–29.

20. I include here the free black population of the adjoining suburb of
Manchester, Virginia.

21. Goldin, *Urban Slavery,* 52–53.

22. Takagi, *Rearing Wolves,* 104, 106–7; Schnittman, "Slavery," 281 n. 48; William

Link, *Roots of Secession: Slavery and Politics in Antebellum Virginia* (Chapel Hill: University of North Carolina Press, 2003), 146, 169, 170.

23. Takagi, *Rearing Wolves*, 103–11, 123; Mechal Sobel, *Trabelin' On: The Slave Journey to an Afro-Baptist Faith* (1979; repr., Princeton, N.J.: Princeton University Press, 1988), 207–10.

24. Takagi, *Rearing Wolves*, 109–11. The significant role of free blacks in ameliorating the conditions of life for Richmond's urban slaves suggests that the title of Ira Berlin's otherwise admirable book, *Slaves without Masters,* is somewhat misleading, because it tends to obscure the very real differences between being a slave and being a free black. Free blacks, of course, were subject to innumerable galling restrictions, as Berlin amply demonstrates. But the condition of free blacks differed substantially from that of the vast majority of slaves, as the history of Richmond's First African Baptist Church suggests, and as Berlin's own evidence indicates.

25. Steven Tripp, *Yankee Town, Southern City: Race and Class Relations in Civil War Lynchburg* (New York: New York University Press, 1997), 60–63.

26. Jackson, *Free Negro Labor,* 6, 12–13, 83, 194n, 172–76. On the emancipation of slave mistresses and their children, see chapter 2.

27. Jackson, *Free Negro Labor,* 174, 182n.

28. Ibid., 182–92.

29. Ibid., 198–99, 184; Berlin, *Slaves without Masters,* 157.

30. Philip J. Schwarz, *Slave Laws in Virginia* (Athens: University of Georgia Press, 1996), 57.

31. Jackson, *Free Negro Labor,* 192–98.

32. In this instance, however, Hobson was probably aided by the benevolence of his white owner, who set Hobson's purchase price at the low figure of $100 (ibid., 184, 197).

33. Ibid., 189, 201–4.

34. Hubert Aimes, "Coarticion: A Spanish Institution for the Advancement of Slaves into Freedom," *Yale Review* (1909): 428–29; Herbert Klein, *Slavery in the Americas: A Comparative Study of Virginia and Cuba* (London: Oxford University Press, 1967), 199. Cf. Franklin Knight, *Slave Society in Cuba during the Nineteenth Century* (Madison: University of Wisconsin Press, 1970), 62.

35. These figures are for the years 1850–60 inclusive, and refer only to fugitives who reached Philadelphia (which was by far the most important first destination for fugitives from "residual Virginia"). Compiled by Rodney Green ("Urban Industry," 511), they are based on William Still, *The Underground Rail Road* (Philadelphia: Porter & Coates, 1872); William Still rarely mentioned the case of a rural fugitive who had domiciled himself temporarily in Richmond. Still was the black man who, from 1852, headed the "Active Committee" of Philadelphia's "Vigilance Committee" (William Dusinberre, *Civil War Issues in Philadelphia, 1856–1865* [Philadelphia: University of Pennsylvania Press, 1965], 52–55; Takagi, *Rearing Wolves,* 121–22).

36. Evidently, the letter writer was referring to the physical "atmosphere" of the tobacco factory, not to its social atmosphere. "Seasoning" was the term used for the physical inuring of slaves to the hardships of plantation life—e.g., to their becoming hardened to the (malarial) atmosphere of the Deep South, after having been raised in an Upper South state like Virginia ("A Farmer," quoted in *The South* (Richmond), 7 Jan. 1858, cited in Robert, *Tobacco Kingdom*, 200).

37. Robert, *Tobacco Kingdom*, 216, 197; Takagi, *Rearing Wolves*, 90.

38. The surplus of male slaves in Richmond and Lynchburg contrasts with the situation in all other big Southern cities (except Mobile), where a majority of slaves were female. These tended to be domestic workers. Apparently, most other Southern cities failed to develop factories, like those of Richmond, Petersburg, and Lynchburg, dependent on employing male slaves. Cf. Wade, *Slavery in the Cities*, 330.

39. Among free blacks, Richmond/Manchester had 1,560 females and 1,238 males. One may therefore estimate a surplus of perhaps 150 women of marriageable age.

40. My conclusion on this point differs from that of the historian Midori Takagi, although we are using the same data. For Richmond slaves in 1860 (not including Manchester):

	Ages 10–23	Ages 24–35	Ages 36–54
Male	2,654	1,791	1,061
Female	1,620	1,067	1,017

Takagi observes that, among slaves aged 24–54, the surplus of males was only 768. But most of the hired slaves were between ages 10 and 35, and within these ages the male surplus was 1,758, as discussed in my text. (The data in this endnote are calculated from percentages printed in Goldin, *Urban Slavery*, 56, slightly adjusted to accord with Takagi's figures. Thus, my totals for slaves aged 24–54 are identical to those in Takagi, *Rearing Wolves*, 99—i.e., 2,852 males and 2,084 females.)

41. Takagi, *Rearing Wolves*, 61–70.

42. Of 36 arraigned blacks (25 of them slaves), 3 were released without punishment. Of 43 arraigned whites, 24 were either released or merely put on bond for good behavior (Tripp, *Yankee Town*, 263).

43. Link, *Roots of Secession*, 80–95.

44. Tripp, *Yankee Town*, 265.

45. The average annual number of Virginia slaves convicted of murdering white people is as follows: 1790–99: 2.9; 1800–1809: 2.9; 1810–19: 2.1; 1820–29: 5.3; 1830–39: 3.7; 1840–49: 1.5; 1850–59: 3.2. Because Virginia's population—both black and white—was substantially larger by 1850 than before 1840, the per capita rate of convictions was lower in the 1850s than in any decade (except the 1810s) before 1840. From 1790 to 1850 the average annual number of slaves, per 100,000 slaves, convicted in Virginia of murdering white people was 0.76. From 1850 to 1859 the average annual number was only 0.66. (The figures here are calculated from data

in Philip Schwarz, *Slave Laws in Virginia* [Athens: University of Georgia Press, 1996], 85, and from slave population statistics in Carter et al., *Historical Statistics of the United States*, 2:376.) It is true that after 1840 (and especially after 1850) the number of slaves convicted of attempted murder of whites exceeded, for the first time, the number convicted of actual murder (Schwarz, *Slave Laws in Virginia*, 85). But this change may reflect, not an increase in murderous assaults but an increase in the prosecution of slaves who previously would have been punished at the plantation without the case being taken to court. It may also reflect increased paranoia in Virginia after the rise of Northern antislavery sentiment. My suggestion that lethal slave resistance was not becoming more common—and therefore was not undermining urban slavery in Virginia—is consonant with the historian John Majewski's skepticism about attributing Richmond's relatively slow economic development to slave resistance. Majewski contrasts Richmond's slower development with the burgeoning growth of Philadelphia and, in a careful analysis, he attributes the difference substantially to the relative lack of consumer demand for manufactured goods by the heavily enslaved population of Richmond's rural hinterland (John Majewski, *A House Dividing: Economic Development in Pennsylvania and Virginia before the Civil War* [New York: Cambridge University Press, 2000], esp. 163 [his skepticism about slave resistance], and 158–61, 166–67, 171–72 [lack of consumer demand]).

46. Robert, *Tobacco Kingdom*, 207; *Lynchburg Virginian*, 16 Nov. 1852, in Tripp, *Yankee Town*, 24.

47. During a nineteen-month sample period, 1858–60, Tripp found that—in cases where the race of the assailant and that of the attacked person could be identified—31 assailants were arraigned before the Mayor's court. These included 18 instances of whites assaulting other whites, 7 cases of blacks assaulting other blacks, and 6 cases of blacks assaulting whites (apparently always black workers assaulting white overseers); but there were no arraignments of whites for assaulting blacks (Tripp, *Yankee Town*, 265, 24).

48. As this book concerns "residual Virginia" (excluding the area that by 1863 would form the Unionist state of West Virginia), I omit here the salt-mining, iron-working, and nascent coal-mining industries of the later West Virginia counties. Ronald Lewis estimates the number of slaves at Maryland and Virginia ironworks, 1800–1865, at 7,000. Eighty of the 115 ironworks were in Virginia (Ronald L. Lewis, *Coal, Iron, and Slaves: Industrial Slavery in Maryland and Virginia, 1715–1865* [Westport, Conn.: Greenwood Press, 1979], 7, 19). If the average number of employees at an ironworks was the same in Virginia as in Maryland, 4,870 of the workers would have been in Virginia. If about 870 of these were in the trans-Allegheny area that later became West Virginia, some 4,000 enslaved ironworkers would have been in "residual Virginia." Lewis estimates that from 1,600 to 1,900 slaves worked, in 1860, for coal companies in the Richmond Basin. I have adopted the lower figure (ibid., 7).

49. Ibid., 28–30, 82–83.

50. Ibid., 124, 126. A slave named Absalom was paid $97.16 in 1853, mainly for hauling iron and coal, and in addition was paid $120 for four head of cattle that he had raised. If it took him three years to raise these cattle (and if his costs in doing so were negligible), his $40 annual earnings from this sale would bring his total earnings, attributable to 1853, to $137.16 (ibid., 126).

51. This statement is based on overwork payments to thirty slaves at Cloverdale Furnace in 1854. I have assumed that "Total" in that record means "Total value of goods paid in kind," and that the actual total of the workers' overwork payments included not only the value of these goods but also the cash paid to them. Thus, the average overwork payment to each of these slaves was $11.20. Even the biggest earner among these thirty workers was paid much less than $1.00 per week for overwork (ibid., 125). (If my assumption is incorrect, the average annual overwork payment to each of these workers was a mere $6.44.)

52. Ibid., 100–101, 98, 97, 96, 86–88. This chapter was written before I was able to consult Jonathan Martin's splendid analysis of how hired slaves could exploit—to some degree—the triangular relationship between themselves, their owners, and their hirers. Martin also presents a powerful (though perhaps slightly overstated) argument criticizing the view that self-hired slaves were "quasi-free." I believe my discussion is generally consonant with Martin's, although I have stressed the advantages that might accrue to a slave hired to work in an urban tobacco factory or in a rural ironworks (see Martin, *Divided Mastery,* esp. 174–78, and 61 and 168 [on urban tobacco factories]).

53. Lewis, *Coal, Iron, and Slaves,* 83–84, 163.

54. Ibid., 84, 90–96; Martin, *Divided Mastery,* 79.

55. Goldin, *Urban Slavery,* 52.

56. Indeed, the enslaved population of Lynchburg declined by 21 percent during the 1850s (Goldin, *Urban Slavery,* 55). But this seems to have been caused, not by a decline of urban slavery in the tobacco-growing region, but by completion of new railways that enabled the Richmond and Petersburg factories to grow at the expense of those in Lynchburg (Tripp, *Yankee Town,* 9–10).

57. U.S. Census of Population, 1820, 1860.

58. The average annual rental for an unskilled male slave of working age— $53 in 1850—had increased to $126 by 1860 (these are averages for Richmond, Lynchburg, and Fredericksburg, Va.; see Goldin, *Urban Slavery,* 73). In Lynchburg by 1860 the rental for an experienced male tobacco factory worker might reach $200 (Tripp, *Yankee Town,* 23).

59. Goldin, *Urban Slavery,* 52–53, 55.

60. The (perhaps mistaken) view that "by 1860 the institution of slavery was in great disarray in every Southern city" is powerfully argued in Richard Wade's *Slavery in the Cities* (243). Wade does not attribute this supposed disarray to any putative incompatibility between slavery and the industrial employment of slaves. He also correctly points out that slaves, who made up about one-fifth of Southern urban dwellers in 1820, composed only about one-tenth by 1860. But he

exaggerates the decline of urban slavery, and oversimplifies the complex causes of the phenomenon. In his appendix—where he supplies population statistics for ten major Southern cities—Wade includes Norfolk (whose enslaved population declined during the 1850s), but he omits the larger city of Petersburg (whose enslaved population substantially increased, even during the 1850s). As Claudia Goldin points out (in her *Urban Slavery in the American South*), Wade fails to attribute sufficient weight to cotton booms as major causes for the exportation of slaves from some Southern cities during the 1830s and 1850s (and, probably, he fails to assign enough weight to the demands of Louisiana's sugar-cane production as an explanation for the export of New Orleans slaves after 1840). He does not sufficiently acknowledge the general decline of slavery in Maryland (and to some extent in Missouri—where slaves declined from 18 percent of the rapidly growing total population in 1830, to less than 10 percent by 1860) as partial explanations for the atypical declines in the absolute numbers of slaves in Baltimore, Washington, and St. Louis. He does not call attention to the fact that—even in the 1850s (when the cotton boom was at its height)—the absolute number of urban slaves nevertheless increased in five of the future Confederacy's eight largest cities—Richmond, Savannah, Mobile, Petersburg, and Memphis—declining only in New Orleans and in the old Atlantic seaports of Charleston and Norfolk/Portsmouth. Wade perhaps did not realize how far Southern white people's complaints during the 1850s, about the alleged ungovernability of urban slaves, reflected paranoia—induced by the growth of Northern antislavery sentiment—rather than a real increase in the system's instability. Thus, Wade mistakenly concludes that by 1860 urban slavery was in great disarray.

4. Family Disruption

1. About 366,000 slaves were moved from Virginia to other parts of the South (mainly to the Deep South) between 1820 and 1860 (Michael Tadman, *Speculators and Slaves* [Madison: University of Wisconsin Press, 1989], 12). Of these, at least 50 percent were sold (the others being moved when their masters emigrated—often taking nearly all of a plantation's slaves, young and old, with them). Sales often destroyed the slaves' family ties, because usually the people traded were young males or females, ages ten to thirty, sold individually or in a parcel comprising only a young woman with her youngest children. My conservative estimate (that "only" 50 percent were sold) is based on Tadman (*Speculators and Slaves,* 29–31, 246–47), as modified by Jonathan B. Pritchett ("Quantitative Estimates of the United States Interregional Slave Trade, 1820–1860," *Journal of Economic History* 61 [June 2001], esp. 468–73). The true figure (taking account of evidence in Tadman, *Speculators and Slaves,* 31–41) may actually be about 60 percent, in which case the number of slaves sold away from Virginia, in the forty-year period, would be even higher (a total of about 220,000). Tadman (*Speculators and Slaves,* 22–25), convincingly challenges an earlier estimate (Robert Fogel and Stanley Engerman,

Time on the Cross: The Economics of American Negro Slavery [1974; repr. London: Wildwood House, 1976], 49), that asserted that only 16 percent of the migrating slaves were sold.

2. Michael Tadman estimates that 51 percent of all slaves sold in the inter-regional trade experienced thereby a major family disruption: about 23 percent were children under fifteen, sold away from both parents; a further 10 percent were children sold away from their father (but sold with their mother); 10 percent were women sold away from their husbands; and 8 percent were men sold away from their wives. This makes a total of 51 percent. I have applied these percentages to the estimated total of 183,000 slaves sold from Virginia. (The figures above for children sold away from their parents omit orphans; thus they include only children with living parents.) See Tadman, *Speculators and Slaves,* 147, 150–51.

3. For example, the fugitive slave Dan Lockhart reported that he had been sold in Virginia at age five to a townsman shopkeeper and never saw his mother until years later (*Refugee,* 30). The historian Steven Deyle tentatively estimates that, in the whole South, at least twice as many slaves were sold in the intrastate slave trade as in the interstate trade (*Carry Me Back: The Domestic Slave Trade in American Life* [New York: Oxford University Press, 2005], 157–73, 282–96, and esp. 296). "At least 366,000" is my estimate, calculated by doubling the number of Virginia bondpeople sold into the interregional slave trade.

4. This interview was conducted in 1929, in Georgia, by a white interviewer (*Macon Telegraph,* 10 Feb. 1929, in *Slave Testimony,* 574–75).

5. Tadman, *Speculators and Slaves,* 77. In addition to the overland trade, many other Virginia slaves (e.g., Frank Bell's uncle Moses Bell) were sent to New Orleans by ship from ports like Washington, Alexandria, and Norfolk (*Interviews,* 27; Frederic Bancroft, *Slave-Trading in the Old South* [Baltimore: J.H. Furst, 1931], 275–79, and also 49, 58, 63, 91, 94).

6. *Slave Testimony,* 575.

7. The historian Mia Bay has called attention to, and carefully analyzed, bond-people's complaints that they were treated like domestic animals (*The White Image in the Black Mind: African-American Ideas about White People, 1830–1925* [New York: Oxford University Press, 2000], esp. 119, 127–33).

8. S. E. Foster, Nov. 1864, to *Freedmen's Record* (Jan. 1865), 4; Sargry Brown to Mores Brown, 27 Oct. 1840, printed in *National Anti-Slavery Standard,* 16 Sep. 1841, cited in *Slave Testimony,* 456, 46–47; *Refugee,* 138; *Interviews,* 123, 126.

9. In the case described by Broaddus, her master's intention to sell the two slaves was frustrated. The serving girl, overhearing him spelling out their names to his wife, ran to her literate father and spelled the names to him. The two men, thus informed, escaped and were not caught. See chapter 10 .

10. Tadman, *Speculators and Slaves,* 147, 150–51. Tadman does note the "geometric effect" of each sale: "siblings . . . and other relatives who were left behind all [felt] the impact of the separation" (153).

11. See chapters 1, 9.

12. American Freedmen's Inquiry Commission interview, 1863, in *Slave Testimony*, 418–20.

13. Michael Tadman states that, in the interregional slave trade, "virtually no child was traded with its father, nor wife sold with her husband" (*Speculators and Slaves*, 133). See also this chapter's note 2, above.

14. Shackelford refers to a slave jail not far from the North Carolina border, perhaps in Brunswick County or in adjacent Lunenburg County.

5. Physical Abuse

1. That is, he treated her this way a dozen times if he did so once.

2. A comparable case of an enslaved woman's dying, after being forced to work when she was ill, was reported to Bird Walton by her mother (*Interviews*, 297–98).

3. Thomas D. Morris, *Southern Slavery and the Law, 1619–1860* (Chapel Hill: University of North Carolina Press, 1996), 181.

4. In this last case, the hirer was arrested and heavily fined, probably in consequence of a civil suit brought by the dead slave's owner to recover the property value of the slave accidentally killed (*Refugee,* 50, 49, 114, 37–38).

6. Regimentation

1. Eugene Genovese, "On Paternalism," in *Roll, Jordan, Roll* (New York: Pantheon, 1974), 3–7.

2. Grandy was temporarily in Mississippi when he was first put to work.

3. *Brooklyn (N.Y.) Eagle,* 8 Sept. 1910, in *Slave Testimony,* 544–45.

4. I believe "Sunday" (105) is a 1937 mistranscription of "Saddy"—i.e., Saturday.

5. Carney's father was perhaps a prototype for the character named "Elias" in Edward Jones's novel about antebellum slavery in Virginia, *The Known World* (2003; repr., London: HarperCollins, 2004), 7–9).

6. Cf. Sally E. Hadden, *Slave Patrols: Law and Violence in Virginia and the Carolinas* (Cambridge, Mass.: Harvard University Press, 2001), 88, 99–103 (and n. 148), 105–36. In Virginia patrollers were supposed to bring captives before a justice of the peace before whipping them (ibid., 124). But it seems likely that this law, like so many of those regulating the treatment of slaves, was little enforced.

7. But not every patroller was a petty tyrant. Grandy reported that, when slaves were eating a stolen chicken, one patroller might sometimes come ahead of the others "ez a frien'." This man would warn the slaves that other patrollers were on their way. He would then falsely report to those patrollers that "Unc' John ain't got anything," and later (as his reward for protecting the slaves) would return to share with them in eating the chicken. This is evidence for the historian Timothy Lockley's observation that nonslaveholding whites "met and interacted

with African Americans" and sometimes cooperated with them (*Interviews*, 116; Timothy James Lockley, *Lines in the Sand: Race and Class in Lowcountry Georgia, 1750–1860* [Athens: University of Georgia Press, 2001], 163, 168, passim).

8. Garner may refer here to his time on a plantation in St. Marys County, Maryland (*Interviews*, 102), where slavery resembled that across the Potomac River in Tidewater Virginia.

9. Here again Garner may be referring to a plantation in St. Marys County; see n. 8 above.

10. Janet D. Cornelius, *"When I Can Read My Title Clear": Literacy, Slavery, and Religion in the Antebellum South* (Columbia: University of South Carolina Press, 1991), 32–34; *Interviews*, 201; *Des Moines (Iowa) Tribune-Capital*, 12[?] Feb. 1930, in *Slave Testimony*, 565; *Interviews*, 100. For an illustration of local pressure against teaching slaves to read, see Moncure Conway, *Autobiography, Memories, and Experiences of Moncure Daniel Conway*, 2 vols. (London: Cassell, 1904), 1:19. Slave literacy is discussed at the beginning of chapter 13.

11. See chapters 9 and 10.

7. Contempt

1. Cf. Dusinberre, *Them Dark Days: Slavery in the American Rice Swamps* (New York: Oxford University Press, 1996), 189.

8. Deprivation

1. Peter Kolchin, *Unfree Labor: American Slavery and Russian Serfdom* (Cambridge, Mass.: Harvard University Press, 1987), 152; Robert William Fogel, *Without Consent or Contract: The Rise and Fall of American Slavery* (New York: Norton, 1989), 132–46. But cf. Michael Tadman, "The Demographic Cost of Sugar: Debates on Slave Societies and Natural Increase in the Americas," *American Historical Review* 105 (Dec. 2000): 1558–60.

2. Like the WPA interviewees, fugitive slaves interviewed in Canada (in 1855) blamed stingy Virginia masters for obliging their slaves to steal food (*Refugee*, 38, 196).

3. Brooks was born free in 1860. His views on slavery were derived from older black people. He said he had fought in the Spanish-American War, and his bitterness arose partly from his belief that he had been cheated out of a veteran's bonus. He felt things were as bad, or worse, for black people in the 1930s as they had been during slavery.

4. Clara Robinson, born in 1837, mistakenly said that her four children were all in their teens by 1865 (*Interviews*, 236).

5. Similar evidence about girls' clothing can be found in *Interviews*, 238.

6. When George White states that "we got wooden bottom shoes," the anteced-

ent of "we" is ambiguous. By 1865 White was eighteen and had long since received trousers. In this context, I believe "we" refers to workers, not to young children.

7. The interviewees' reports of material deprivation may sometimes have been affected by the shortages of the Civil War years. But I believe most of these reports refer to peacetime conditions. For example, George White (born in 1847) and Arthur Greene (born in 1851) were old enough to remember prewar conditions, and they appear to have been describing the slaves' normal peacetime allowances. Charles Crawley (born about 1856) probably depended here on the memories of his mother, with whom he was still living when she died in 1925.

8. So strong was Archie Booker's sense of white people's continued exploitation of black labor that the ninety-year-old man (who had been the slave of a benevolent master—a Richmond medical doctor—and mistress) occasionally thought about the compensations that had been offered to slaves. In the 1930s pensionless old blacks (with no Medicaid) had no security; but in slavery, Booker said, "Ef you wuz sick, ye hadda doctuh. Den ye git food too. But now ef ye git sick an' ye hain' got no money, ye jis die" (*Interviews*, 54).

9. Religion

1. Eugene Genovese's formulations have shaped modern understanding of the slaves' religion. Mechal Sobel, Margaret Washington Creel, and Charles Joyner, among others, have demonstrated strong African influences in early North America and, as late as the 1860s, in the Carolina Low Country (see Eugene Genovese, *Roll, Jordan, Roll* [New York: Pantheon, 1974], 159–284; Mechal Sobel, *Trabelin' On: The Slave Journey to an Afro-Baptist Faith* [1979; repr., Princeton, N.J.: Princeton University Press, 1988]; Mechal Sobel, *The World They Made Together: Black and White Values in Eighteenth-Century Virginia* [Princeton, N.J.: Princeton University Press, 1987]; Margaret Washington Creel, *"A Peculiar People": Slave Religion and Community-Culture among the Gullahs* [New York: New York University Press, 1988]; Charles Joyner, "'Believer I Know': The Emergence of African-American Christianity," in *African-American Christianity: Essays in History*, ed. Paul E. Johnson [Berkeley: University of California Press, 1994], 18–46).

2. Albert Raboteau's pioneering *Slave Religion* suggests that the deviations of the slaves' religion from orthodox Southern evangelical Christianity were limited in number, and that those deviations arose principally from the slaves' experience of bondage, not from their African heritage. Raboteau believed Christianity had an almost entirely positive influence upon the slaves' lives (Albert J. Raboteau, *Slave Religion: The "Invisible Institution" in the Antebellum South* [New York: Oxford University Press, 1978], esp. chaps. 2, 5, and 6).

3. The historian John Boles lucidly specifies those elements of "African traditional religion" that resembled Christian belief and ritual, and that consequently prepared the ground for people of African heritage to accept central Christian

beliefs and practices. Boles also distinguishes those elements of Southern evangelical Christianity that might appeal to an enslaved people, even as they rejected
the "obey-your-master" motif. In biracial antebellum Southern churches, Boles
declares, blacks "participate[d] more nearly—not truly—as equals with whites
than anywhere else in the slave society. . . . [Church disciplinary procedures] were
probably the most important way that slave members were accorded a degree of
respect and equality, and slave testimony in church courts was unexampled elsewhere in southern society." Boles implies (though he does not explicitly assert)
that by 1860 the slaves' Afro-Christianity was a thoroughly Christian faith (John
Boles, *The Irony of Southern Religion* [New York: Peter Lang, 1994], 42–63 [quota-
tions at 57–58]).

4. Sobel, *Trabelin' On*, 85–91, 95–98; Sylvia R. Frey and Betty Wood, *Come
Shouting to Zion: African American Protestantism in the American South and British
Caribbean to 1830* (Chapel Hill: University of North Carolina Press, 1998), 153, 154,
239 n. 14, 156, 180, 166.

5. See Daniel W. Crofts, *Old Southampton: Politics and Society in a Virginia County,
1834–1869* (Charlottesville: University Press of Virginia, 1992), 21–22, and n. 19.

6. Miss S. F. Goodell, *American Missionary*, Apr. 1866, in *Slave Testimony*, 466.

7. This is quoted more fully in chapter 8.

8. See chapter 5.

9. Other examples of the belief that God punished bad masters appear at
Interviews, 80, 33, 94; and in *Refugee*, 196.

10. The idea that God sent the war in order to end slavery was also held by some
Northern white people, and was expressed most memorably in Lincoln's Second
Inaugural Address (see *The Collected Works of Abraham Lincoln*, ed. Roy Basler,
9 vols. [New Brunswick, N.J.: Rutgers University Press, 1953], 8:333; Richard J.
Carwardine, *Lincoln* [Harlow, U.K.: Pearson Longman, 2003], 222–31, 240–42).

11. See chapter 7.

12. See chapter 1.

13. See chapter 10.

14. Not only in the Carolina Low Country, but throughout the South, white
WPA interviewers often seem to have asked their elderly interviewees leading
questions about black people's "superstitions." Virginia's black WPA interviewers do not appear to have done so; consequently, their picture of the slaves'
Christianity may be more accurate than that elicited by white interviewers.

15. The historian Albert Raboteau argues that belief in conjure was compatible
with adherence to Christianity, because the two doctrines served different functions (*Slave Religion*, 275–88).

16. It must be acknowledged, however, that Christianity did not provide the
only set of beliefs that could foster nonviolence. Recourse to non-Christian good-
luck charms might also, sometimes, embolden a slave to risk nonviolent action.
When the fugitive slave Robert Williams had been absent from his plantation
for about a year, he considered whether he dared to return voluntarily. He feared

he would be punished with a severe whipping. Unsure what to do, Williams later recalled, "I wandered over to Dr. Ned Reed's quarters. He was a slave an' a hoo-doo doctor an' could help me out." Dr. Reed instructed Williams to sprinkle some powder under his master's doormat and in his master's hat. Williams succeeded in doing so, and these precautions gave him courage to turn himself in. Williams was prepared to seize a stick and hit his master if he tried to whip him, but the master refrained from any such attempt. Here, as with the civil rights movement of the 1960s, nonviolent conduct (backed by a latent, unspoken hint of potential violence) proved an effective strategy (*Interviews*, 324).

17. Mrs. M. F. Armstrong and Helen W. Ludlow, *Hampton and Its Students* (New York, 1874), in *Slave Testimony*, 611.

18. Frey and Wood, *Come Shouting to Zion*, 188.

19. Christine Leigh Heyrman estimates that 11 percent of Southern African Americans were members of evangelical churches, and that another 17 percent were "adherents" of an evangelical church without actually being members (*Southern Cross* [1997; repr., New York: Knopf, 1998], 264–65).

20. On the parallel to West African religions—as well as on the differences—see Sobel, *Trabelin' On*, 69–70, 101, 119.

21. For example, David West (a privileged, self-hiring carpenter who had been secretly taught to read) fled from Virginia to Canada in the perfect assurance that slavery was "breaking the laws of God." After West's good master died, the bond-man had escaped because he feared that his master's brother would take him to be sold in Alabama, as he had previously done to West's father, sister, and aunt. West's religious life had centered on a biracial Baptist church, where he took communion after the whites did so. He was convinced that God could not sanction a system where "the stronger takes the weaker by force, and binds them slaves." "These views," he declared to his interviewer in 1855, "I have not got since I left the South; they were in me all the time I was there" (*Refugee*, 60–63 [quotations at 61, 63]).

22. The classic statement of Afro-Christianity's role in preventing dehumanization is in Genovese, *Roll, Jordan, Roll*, 252–55, 281–82.

10. Dissidence

1. Quoted in chapter 6.

2. I infer that Sis Shackelford is likely to have been born in 1847, or earlier, in order for her to have been able to supply so many details about the great snow-storm of 1857.

3. Variants of this song, declared by the historian Sally Hadden to be "the most well-known song sung about patrollers," are printed in Sally E. Hadden, *Slave Patrols: Law and Violence in Virginia and the Carolinas* (Cambridge, Mass.: Harvard University Press, 2001), 119–20.

4. See chapter 5.

5. Booker's family actually lived in North Carolina; but most of Virginia's free blacks—who cooperated with slaves in black churches, seldom held secure economic positions, and were usually subject themselves to intense racial discrimination—are likely to have acted equally generously to fugitives.

6. From 1853 through 1860 the average annual number of Virginia escapees via Philadelphia was about 45. From 1839 through 1849 (before passage of the 1850 Fugitive Slave Law) the average annual number via Philadelphia may have been around 100. Virginia slavemasters reported to census-takers 83 fugitives (to all destinations out of the state) in 1850 and 117 in 1860. Relatively few of these were captured and returned to Virginia, despite considerable efforts by federal officials after 1850 to enforce the new law (William Dusinberre, *Civil War Issues in Philadelphia, 1856–1865* [Philadelphia: University of Pennsylvania Press, 1965]; *Historical Statistics of the United States,* ed. Susan Carter et al., 5 vols. [Cambridge: Cambridge University Press, 2006], 2:384; Stanley W. Campbell, *The Slave Catchers: Enforcement of the Fugitive Slave Law, 1850–1860* [1968; repr., Chapel Hill: University of North Carolina Press, 1970], 96–147, 207).

7. On Moses Bell and his master, also see chapter 1.

8. Bayliss was released from prison in January 1865 on the grounds of ill health (Philip J. Schwarz, *Slave Laws in Virginia* [Athens: University of Georgia Press, 1996], 144, and also 120–21, 143; Rodney D. Green, "Urban Industry, Black Resistance, and Racial Restriction in the Antebellum South: A General Model and a Case Study in Urban Virginia," Ph.D. diss., American University, 1980, 511). Green calculates the number of fugitives reaching Philadelphia from William Still, *The Underground Railroad.* (Philadelphia: Porter & Coates, 1872).

9. *Interviews,* 286–87; *Refugee,* 247–48; *Interviews,* 167; Harriet A. Jacobs, *Incidents in the Life of a Slave Girl: Written by Herself,* ed. Jean Fagan Yellin (1861; repr., Cambridge, Mass.: Harvard University Press, 1987), 153–54.

10. On fugitives' self-reliance, and on aid to them by other blacks, see Larry Gara, *The Liberty Line: The Legend of the Underground Railroad* (1961; repr., Lexington: University of Kentucky Press, 1967), esp. 42–55, 177–78.

11. See chapter 5; see also *Interviews,* 259. (Although Wright's first name is several times printed with an "n" ["Julian"], I surmise that this was a typographical error.)

12. David Grimsted, *American Mobbing, 1828–1861: Toward Civil War* (New York, Oxford University Press, 1998), 171.

13. I seek here to modify the military metaphor proposed before the Civil War by Richard Hildreth, and later developed powerfully by Norrece Jones (see Richard Hildreth, *Despotism in America* [Boston: J. Jewett, 1854], 49–50, 56; Norrece T. Jones Jr., *Born a Child of Freedom, Yet a Slave: Mechanisms of Control and Strategies of Resistance in Antebellum South Carolina* [Hanover, N.H.: University Press of New England, 1990], 10 and passim).

14. Philip J. Schwarz, *Migrants against Slavery: Virginians and the Nation* (Charlottesville: University Press of Virginia, 2001), 35–36. In 1841 a maritime

insurrection did take place on the *Creole,* a ship carrying 135 slaves from Hampton Roads, Virginia, for sale in New Orleans. Nineteen bondmen overpowered the crew, killing one person, and obliging a survivor to steer them to the Bahamas. The British authorities there—influenced by the mass action of local blacks—freed them (Howard Jones, "The Peculiar Institution and National Honor: The Case of the *Creole* Slave Revolt," *Civil War History* 21 [1975]: 28–50).

15. *Interviews,* 36; regarding the good mistress, see 44, and also 32, 40, 45.

16. I believe this report of a slave's unpunished defiance—if not the slave's exact language—is credible because the interviewee (the butcher's daughter) was an eyewitness to the altercation (*Interviews,* 298).

17. See chapter 1.

18. *Interviews,* 297. These cases suggest that the argument of the historian Jonathan Martin may be extended. Martin explores the adeptness of hired slaves at exploiting, for their own benefit, the contradictory interests of a hirer and of the slave's owner. Similarly, slaves were adept at exploiting differences of opinion between a master and a mistress, or between a master and an overseer (see Jonathan D. Martin, *Divided Mastery: Slave Hiring in the American South* [Cambridge, Mass.: Harvard University Press, 2004]).

19. *Interviews,* 255. In a perhaps comparable 1838 case, an overseer killed the slave Jack Long on a West Tennessee plantation. The overseer fled for fear of being prosecuted, but his family supplied overgenerous financial compensation to the slave's owners and the killer apparently was never brought to court (William Dusinberre, *Slavemaster President: The Double Career of James Polk* [New York: Oxford University Press, 2003], 38, 73, 218 n. 7).

20. *Interviews,* 180 (quoted in chapter 6, this volume).

21. A handful of slaves sold away from home did assault the person who had sold them, or the trader who was carrying them away. The historian Steven Deyle cites three such cases of homicide in Virginia (1834, 1836, and 1858) and one instance of assault and arson (1856). Deyle concludes, however, that "the overwhelming majority of black southerners did not respond to the domestic slave trade with violent resistance. Most perceived such behavior as futile. . . . A far more common form of resistance to sale was flight" (Steven Deyle, *Carry Me Back: The Domestic Slave Trade in American Life* [New York: Oxford University Press, 2005], 253–57 [quotation at 256–57]). Similarly, the historian of slave patrols, Sally Hadden, concludes that "on rare occasions, slaves physically threatened patrollers." The best-documented instance occurred near Alexandria, Virginia, in 1840, when five slaves assaulted patrollers with clubs, injuring some of them and releasing from custody two slaves accused of being out without a pass. For this assault, which resulted in no permanent injury to any patroller, one slave was hanged and another (originally condemned to be hanged, but the focus of a campaign by white petitioners for less draconian punishment) had his sentence commuted to deportation (Hadden, *Slave Patrols,* 132–35 [quotation at 132]). See also the discussion of violent resistance in chapter 3 of this volume; Schwarz, *Slave Laws in Virginia,*

85; and William Link, *Roots of Secession: Slavery and Politics in Antebellum Virginia* (Chapel Hill: University of North Carolina Press, 2003), 80–95. Link discusses violence by Virginia slaves (and white people's anxieties about a purported increase of such violence during the 1850s), but he does not conclude that violence was actually increasing.

22. See also *Interviews*, 237.

23. See chapter 6.

24. *Interviews*, 257. A similar mechanism still operated many years later in the Jim Crow South. Thus, in 1919 the cotton farmer "Nate Shaw" depended on being able to buy fertilizer from a well-disposed white man, "Mr. Harry Black," in order to break free from the control of the tyrannical "Mr. Lemuel Tucker" (see Theodore Rosengarten, ed., *All God's Dangers: The Life of Nate Shaw* [1974; repr., New York: Vintage, 1984], 148–61).

11. Families

1. Edward Franklin Frazier, *The Negro Family in the United States* (Chicago: University of Chicago Press, [1939]); Kenneth M. Stampp, *The Peculiar Institution* (New York: Vintage, 1956), 340–49; Herbert G. Gutman, *The Black Family in Slavery and Freedom, 1750–1925* (New York: Pantheon, 1976); Brenda Stevenson, "Distress and Discord in Virginia Slave Families, 1830–1860," in *In Joy and In Sorrow: Women, Family, and Marriage in the Victorian South, 1830–1900*, ed. Carol Bleser (New York: Oxford University Press, 1991), 103–24; Brenda Stevenson, *Life in Black and White: Family and Community in the Slave South* (New York: Oxford University Press, 1996).

2. Hunter's master had sold all three of her brothers because he believed them ungovernable. She never saw her eldest brother again (*Interviews*, 149–50).

3. The historian Brenda Stevenson calculates that 82 percent of Virginia's WPA interviewees "spoke of the physical presence of their mothers during most of their childhood years, while only 42 percent recalled continuous contact with their fathers. Moreover, fully one-third of those who did make mention of the presence of their fathers during their childhood indicated that these men did not live with them but only visited on their days off. . . . Many Virginia slave children born in the last decades before the Civil War . . . ," Stevenson concludes, "grew up without fathers or black male role models and nurturers, while women bore and reared children without the comfort and support of their husbands or other male kin" ("Distress and Discord," 108–9).

4. When Showvely once referred to "pa," it is clear that she was referring to her husband, with whom she had already had three children by 1865: "Mistress Tinsley wanted us [i.e., Martha Showvely, her husband, and their three children] to live with her after de War, but pa [i.e., the three children's pa] didn' want to stay. We moved to dis house [in Roanoke] an' raised all my [twelve] chillun hare" (*Interviews*, 264–65).

5. Here Katie Johnson—like other Virginia interviewees—presumes that male slaves (not females) were expected to take the initiative in courtship. The historian Rebecca Griffin suggests that the Uncle Remus folktales confirm slaves' presumption that males should take the lead in courtship ("Courtship Contests and the Meaning of Conflict in the Folklore of Slaves," *Journal of Southern History* 72 [2005], esp. 791–93, 801–2).

6. See Emily West, *Chains of Love: Slave Couples in Antebellum South Carolina* (Urbana: University of Illinois Press, 2004).

7. McCoy's mother's master later sold her to Georgia too; but it is most unlikely that they came together again at that time, and there is no assurance that husband and wife ever found each other again, even after Emancipation (*Interviews*, 199).

8. En route to Missouri, Brown succeeded in escaping to Canada, where in 1855 he recounted his misfortune: "It is three years ago that I left my family, and I don't know whether they are dead or alive" (*Refugee*, 196–97).

9. Michael Tadman, *Speculators and Slaves: Masters, Traders, and Slaves* (Madison: University of Wisconsin Press, 1996), 154–60 (quotation at 157). Tadman cites Paul Escott's calculation that, in the whole South, abroad marriages probably comprised only about 27.5 percent of all slave marriages. But the proportion of abroad marriages was surely significantly higher in the Upper South than in the Deep South, and the disruptive effects of planter migration may therefore have been substantially greater than Tadman implies (Paul D. Escott, *Slavery Remembered: A Record of Twentieth-Century Slave Narratives* [Chapel Hill: University of North Carolina Press, 1979], 50–51).

10. Tadman estimates that in South Carolina during the 1850s, "judicial sales to local private individuals were about 30 percent greater than purchases (from all sources) by [interregional] traders in that state." In addition, Tadman estimates that nonjudicial sales to local private individuals amounted to about two-thirds (i.e., 40%/60% percent) of judicial sales. These figures imply that total local sales amounted to 130% + 2/3(130%) = 217% of the number of purchases (i.e., more than twice as many) by interregional traders (Tadman, *Speculators and Slaves*, 120 [emphasis added], 121 n. 18).

11. Steven Deyle, *Carry Me Back: The Domestic Slave Trade in American Life* (New York: Oxford University Press, 2005), esp. 157–73, 191–96. "More than 366,000" is my calculation, based on the conservative estimate that at least 183,000 Virginia slaves were sold into the interregional trade between 1820 and 1860 (see chapter 4), and on Deyle's conclusion (296) that in the whole South the number of intrastate sales was more than double the number of sales into the interregional trade.

12. Based on Michael Tadman's estimates for the whole South, I have estimated that, between 1820 and 1860, some 33,000 Virginia slaves were sold to the Deep South away from their spouses (see chapter 4). This figure takes no account of the additional disruptive effects of the intrastate trade.

13. Brenda Stevenson calculates that the average age of Virginia slave women at the birth of their first child was 19.7 years ("Distress and Discord," 295).

14. The historian John J. Zaborney—suggesting that it was common for Virginia slaves to be hired to rural masters—argues that these hirings often exerted a severely disruptive effect upon slaves' family lives. "Slave hiring," he concludes, "rendered rural Virginia slaves' family and friendship ties even more fragile than previously assumed" ("Slave Hiring and Slave Family and Friendship Ties in Rural Nineteenth-Century Virginia," in *Afro-Virginian History and Culture,* ed. John Saillant [New York: Garland, 1999], 85–107 [quotation at 101]). For a somewhat contrary view, see Lynda J. Morgan, *Emancipation in Virginia's Tobacco Belt, 1850–1870* (Athens: University of Georgia Press, 1992), 71–75.

15. See chapters 1 and 10.

16. See chapter 4.

17. For a more optimistic view of slaves' family lives (with particular attention to the strength of abroad marriages), see Emily West, *Chains of Love: Slave Couples in Antebelllum South Carolina* (Urbana: University of Illinois Press, 2004), esp. chaps. 2 and 5. West's conclusions are based principally on analysis of testimony by 334 South Carolina WPA respondents, nearly all interviewed by white interviewers.

12. The Black Community

1. John W. Blassingame, *The Slave Community: Plantation Life in the Antebellum South* (New York: Oxford University Press, 1972); Eugene D. Genovese, *Roll, Jordan, Roll* (New York: Pantheon, 1974), 255–79, 327–98.

2. Larry E. Hudson Jr., *To Have and to Hold: Slave Work and Family Life in Antebellum South Carolina* (Athens: University of Georgia Press, 1997); Roderick A. McDonald, *The Economy and Material Culture of Slaves: Goods and Chattels on the Sugar Plantations of Jamaica and Louisiana* (Baton Rouge: University of Louisiana Press, 1993), 50–91. John Schlotterbeck's research seems to imply that the slaves' internal economy was less developed in Virginia than in the Deep South (see John T. Schlotterbeck, "The Internal Economy of Slavery in Rural Piedmont Virginia," in *The Slaves' Economy: Independent Production by Slaves in the Americas,* ed. Ira Berlin and Philip D. Morgan [London: Frank Cass, 1991], 170–81).

3. Peter Kolchin, *Unfree Labor: American Slavery and Russian Serfdom* (Cambridge, Mass.: Harvard University Press, 1987), 195–96, 199–207, 236.

4. Cf. Dylan C. Penningroth, *The Claims of Kinfolk: African American Property and Community in the Nineteenth-Century South* (Chapel Hill: University of North Carolina Press, 2003); Anthony E. Kaye, "Neighborhood and Solidarity in the Natchez District of Mississippi: Rethinking the Antebellum Slave Community," *Slavery and Abolition* 23 (2002): 1–24.

5. See chapter 10.

6. In Bird Walton's account, I follow the more circumstantial version of the story also narrated at *Interviews*, 297.

7. See also *Interviews*, 58–59 (quoted in chapter 4 of this volume), 128.

8. See chapter 9.

9. Cf. Sylvia R. Frey and Betty Wood, *Come Shouting to Zion: African American Protestantism in the American South and British Caribbean to 1830* (Chapel Hill: University of North Carolina Press, 1998), 188, which refers to the practices of biracial Baptist churches from 1775 to 1830 (three-quarters of which were Virginia churches, but whose deacons were mainly white males). See also Midori Takagi, *"Rearing Wolves to Our Own Destruction": Slavery in Richmond, Virginia, 1782–1865* (Charlottesville: University Press of Virginia, 1999), 107; and Mechal Sobel, *Trabelin' On: The Slave Journey to an Afro-Baptist Faith* (1979; repr., Princeton, N.J.: Princeton University Press, 1988), 175, 207, 231.

10. *Interviews*, 46–47. See also chapter 7 in this volume.

11. Sparks said that free blacks "could come see yer if yer was their folks" (*Interviews*, 276).

12. Bowser's strategy for surviving in a slave society resembled that of a substantial number of other free blacks (see Michael Johnson and James L. Roark, "Strategies of Survival: Free Negro Families and the Problem of Slavery," in *In Joy and in Sorrow: Women, Family, and Marriage in the Victorian South, 1830–1900*, ed. Carol Bleser [New York: Oxford University Press, 1991], 88–102). The historian Ira Berlin affirms "the close ties between free Negroes and slaves," yet he also depicts the depth of the divisions between these two groups. These divisions, Berlin argues convincingly, were particularly deep in the Lower South, where a three-caste system developed "whenever free Negroes were numerous." But even in the Upper South, Berlin acknowledges, status differences "continually . . . turned free Negroes and slaves against each other." The Virginia interviews suggest that, in the Upper South, racial unity between free and enslaved African Americans was broken even a little more than Berlin indicates (Ira Berlin, *Slaves without Masters: The Free Negro in the Antebellum South* [New York: Pantheon, 1974], esp. 269–73 [quotations at 269, 198, 271]).

13. Self-Development

1. These obstacles are defined in chapter 6. See Janet D. Cornelius, *"When I Can Read My Title Clear": Literacy, Slavery, and Religion in the Antebellum South* (Columbia: University of South Carolina Press, 1991).

2. Mildred Graves, a midwife, is a possible exception to this statement. She reported that a white boy (whom she had successfully brought through his mother's near-fatal delivery) later "use to teach me to write my name an' I learn lots o' things f'om dat boy." I infer (perhaps mistakenly) that the boy taught Graves only how to write her name, not how to write in general (*Interviews*, 121).

3. Slaves who sought permanent escape (and especially those who succeeded)

are an exception to this statement. Anthony Burns escaped from Richmond by forging his own pass. Among the eighteen Virginia fugitives interviewed in 1855 in Canada, five had learned to read when in slavery; but of these apparently only one had learned to write. This was Dan Lockhart, who had been taught by his master's white children (*Refugee*, 31, 34; 49, 61, 67, 247). Among 350 Kentucky slaves advertized to have fled, 10.6 percent were declared able to write (Cornelius, *When I Can Read*, 9, citing Ivan McDougle, "Slavery in Kentucky," *Journal of Negro History* 3 [1918]: 289). Thus, any historian depending substantially on fugitive slave memoirs might tend to exaggerate the incidence of writing skills among antebellum slaves.

4. A possible exception was Levi Pollard's cousin Paul, who "got his [learnin'] from his Mars when he drive him places." But although Paul was instructed how to count by ones, fives, and tens, he does not appear to have been taught to read. Another possible exception was Mary Jones's mother, who may have been taught to read by an adult male in the Thomas Nelson Page family, but is more likely to have acquired her limited reading skills from one of the Page women (*Interviews*, 230, 187). On Jones's mother, see below in this chapter.

5. *Narrative of the Life of Frederick Douglass, an American Slave: Written by Himself*, ed. Benjamin Quarles (1845; repr., Cambridge, Mass.: Harvard University Press, 1960), 113–15.

6. "After work, long in the evening, I went to our quarters which was his room and stayed dar to look after him—soughter companion like" (*Interviews*, 330, 328; quoted in chapter 1).

7. Cf. chapter 4 in this volume.

8. Virginia law did not actually forbid a white person to teach an individual slave, so long as no payment was involved. Cf. chapter 6.

9. I omit here the testimony of Eliza Brown (whose mother could read well) because the context suggests that Brown's mother—who lived in Charlottesville—was a free black woman who owned a house of her own (*Interviews*, 59). See chapter 10 for Susan Broaddus's father.

10. Apparently, it was when they were both house servants in Washington that Johnson's mother taught him the alphabet. He taught himself to read properly when he was a house servant in Richmond. Johnson's narrative indicates that essentially his status was that of a house servant, although he did also work for a time in a Richmond tobacco factory (see Thomas L. Johnson, *Twenty Eight Years a Slave* [Bournemouth, U.K.: W. Mate & Sons, 1909], 3, 5–6, 11–13, 18, 29; cf. Cornelius, *"When I Can Read*, 59–60).

11. Cornelius, *When I Can Read*, 60, 80; Thomas L. Johnson, *Twenty Eight Years*, 29.

12. *Interviews*, 140. I cannot determine the occupations of James Talliaferro's father, Susan Broaddus's father, the Reverend Ishrael Massie's family, or that of the parents of Jerry (the little slave boy with whom Russell—the master's son—"had been going over his lessons"). But I infer that Jerry was the child of a house servant (*Interviews*, 282, 55–56, 204–11, 301).

13. *Interviews,* 29. No one knows how many slaves could read, or how many could write. In the absence of hard evidence, historians have tended to accept the surmise (attributed to W. E. B. DuBois) that by 1860 perhaps 5 percent of antebellum slaves could read. DuBois actually suggested that fewer than 3.75 percent could read and write ("less than 150,000 of the four million slaves emancipated") (see W. E. B. DuBois, *Black Reconstruction* [1935; repr., New York: S. A. Russell, 1956], 638). Carter Woodson believed that "ten per cent of the adult Negroes had the rudiments of education in 1860"; but Woodson here combined free blacks with slaves (who were surely less literate than free blacks). I infer that, by "rudiments," Woodson was referring to reading skills but not to writing (Carter G. Woodson, *The Education of the Negro prior to 1861* [New York: Putnam's, 1915], 228). More recently, Janet Cornelius has suggested that 10 percent of slaves could read and write on a basic level (*When I Can Read,* 8–10). The Virginia interviews seem to suggest caution in accepting for that state any figure larger than 5 percent for reading skills, and substantially less for writing. After all, by 1860 only 12 percent of Virginia's white school-age children attended public schools (though of course others went to private schools) (see Timothy James Lockley, *Welfare and Charity in the Antebellum South* [Gainesville: University Press of Florida, 2007], 191). In all Southern states only about 5 percent of the WPA interviewees declared that they had learned to read during slavery, and the proportion who had learned to write was even smaller. Cornelius suggests (persuasively, I believe) that more female slaves could read than has previously been recognized (*When I Can Read,* 7–8, 77). She also argues convincingly that many literate slaves were taught by white children or by white women (61, 75–77). But I think she may not distinguish sufficiently between reading skills and the much less common skill of writing (though she discusses this distinction at 5, 72–73, and 109). See also Eugene Genovese, *Roll, Jordan, Roll* (New York: Pantheon, 1974), 561–66, and esp. 563.

14. *Interviews,* 228. Although Pollard's was one of the small minority of Virginia interviews conducted by a white interviewer, I think this report is credible.

15. *Interviews,* 194–95; Michael Tadman, "Introduction," *Speculators and Slaves: Masters, Traders, and Slaves,* 2nd ed. (Madison: University of Wisconsin Press, 1996), esp. xxxi–xxxvii.

16. *Interviews,* 178–79; Theodore Rosengarten, ed., *All God's Dangers: The Life of Nate Shaw* (1974; repr., New York: Vintage, 1984), 117.

17. *Interviews,* 53. On Polk, see William Dusinberre, *Slavemaster President: The Double Career of James Polk* (New York: Oxford University Press, 2003), 111–12.

18. See chapter 1.

19. See chapter 1 and discussion earlier in this chapter.

20. See discussion earlier in this chapter.

21. "When it comes to figures I don't ask nobody any question." Interviewed in May 1937, Johnson calculated easily that "I've been an active member of the first Baptist Church of 67 years—since, May, 1870" (*Interviews,* 170).

Index

CARTER G. WOODSON INSTITUTE SERIES

Michael Plunkett, *Afro-American Sources in Virginia: A Guide to Manuscripts* ·

Sally Belfrage, *Freedom Summer*

Armstead L. Robinson and Patricia Sullivan, eds., *New Directions in Civil Rights Studies*

Leroy Vail and Landeg White, *Power and the Praise Poem: Southern African Voices in History*

Robert A. Pratt, *The Color of Their Skin: Education and Race in Richmond, Virginia, 1954–89*

Ira Berlin and Philip D. Morgan, eds., *Cultivation and Culture: Labor and the Shaping of Slave Life in the Americas*

Gerald Horne, *Fire This Time: The Watts Uprising and the 1960s*

Sam C. Nolutshungu, *Limits of Anarchy: Intervention and State Formation in Chad*

Jeannie M. Whayne, *A New Plantation South: Land, Labor, and Federal Favor in Twentieth-Century Arkansas*

Patience Essah, *A House Divided: Slavery and Emancipation in Delaware, 1638–1865*

Tommy L. Bogger, *Free Blacks in Norfolk, Virginia, 1790–1860: The Darker Side of Freedom*

Robert C. Kenzer, *Enterprising Southerners: Black Economic Success in North Carolina, 1865–1915*

Midori Takagi, *"Rearing Wolves to Our Own Destruction": Slavery in Richmond, Virginia, 1782–1865*

Alessandra Lorini, *Rituals of Race: American Public Culture and the Search for Racial Democracy*

Mary Ellen Curtin, *Black Prisoners and Their World, Alabama, 1865–1900*

Philip J. Schwarz, *Migrants against Slavery: Virginians and the Nation*

Armstead L. Robinson, *Bitter Fruits of Bondage: The Demise of Slavery and the Collapse of the Confederacy, 1861–1865*

Francille Rusan Wilson, *The Segregated Scholars: Black Social Scientists and the Creation of Black Labor Studies, 1890–1950*

Gregory Michael Dorr, *Segregation's Science: Eugenics and Society in Virginia*

Glenn McNair, *Criminal Injustice: Slaves and Free Blacks in Georgia's Criminal Justice System*

William Dusinberre, *Strategies for Survival: Recollections of Bondage in Antebellum Virginia*